TEACH YOURSELF BOOKS

SANSKRIT

An Introduction to the Classical Language

Eric
552-3484

NTC Publishing Group

TEACH YOURSELF BOOKS

SANSKRIT

An Introduction to the Classical Language

Michael Coulson

Revised by

Richard Gombrich

and James Benson

NTC Publishing Group

ACKNOWLEDGEMENT

THE publishers wish to acknowledge the invaluable help of Dr. Richard Gombrich, Boden Professor of Sanskrit at Oxford University, in the preparation of the first edition of this book. They would also like to thank Dr. James Benson, Assistant Professor in Sanskrit at Harvard University, and Mrs Elizabeth Kelsall for their help with the second edition.

This edition was first published in 1992 by NTC Publishing Group, 4255 West Touhy Avenue, Lincolnwood (Chicago), Illinois 60646 – 1975 U.S.A. Originally published by Hodder and Stoughton Ltd.

Library of Congress Catalog Card Number: 92-80860

Printed and bound in Great Britain
by Cox & Wyman Ltd, Reading, Berkshire

Contents

Preface

THE plan, scope and length of this book have been determined primarily by the aim of enabling students to cope as rapidly as possible with straightforward Classical Sanskrit texts. The material has been drawn almost entirely from the Sanskrit (not Prakrit) prose dialogue of the major dramas, extracted onto cards and then graded according to the main morphological and syntactical features which required explanation. From Chapter 6 onwards all the sentences of the exercises and all the more elaborate examples given in the chapters themselves are taken without change from actual Sanskrit works. While the intention is to provide an introduction to the Classical language in general, because of the nature of the bulk of the material the book is, in the first place, a guide to Sanskrit dramatic prose; and it is probable that I have sometimes incautiously presented as generally valid points of usage which really hold good only of the Classical dramatists.

Existing Sanskrit primers tend to be admirably systematic in their presentation of the complicated morphology of Sanskrit (which includes a mass of verb forms little used by most writers) but rather cursory in their treatment of such basic facts of life as the prevalence of nominal constructions and compound formations. The student may get the misleading impression that Classical Sanskrit syntax is very similar to that of Latin and Greek, and emerge well drilled in the varieties of athematic inflexion and yet quite unprepared, for instance, for such simple discoveries as the fact that someone in a play, speaking from the heart, instead of saying 'Thank

God my children are alive' can and does say (literally) 'Thank God I am alive-childed'. In the present book thorough drilling in all the forms of declension and conjugation has been a secondary consideration, and the student will therefore benefit from a certain self-discipline in memorising accurately the paradigms introduced into each chapter. In part this shift of emphasis (though I think it desirable at any rate) has been dictated by the use of real Sanskrit material: second-person dual ātmanepada forms are not particularly thick on the ground whether in plays or in texts of any other kind. Serious inadequacy in this respect is, however, prevented by the fact that grammatical forms once introduced continue to be illustrated and required throughout the book: each exercise contains a natural element of revision of all previous exercises.

It is particularly students without a teacher who need a fuller explanation of Sanskrit syntax and idiom than existing primers give, and so I have been happy to model this book upon the Teach Yourself volumes which I myself in the past have found so helpful and stimulating. At the same time it seemed practical to assume a somewhat greater degree of sophistication in potential students of Sanskrit than in students proposing to teach themselves a language such as French. Someone who has never previously learnt a foreign language will probably find the early chapters rather heavy going unless he is fairly bright. A significant proportion of readers are likely to have some acquaintance with either Latin or Greek, and so I have cited parallels where these seemed illuminating, but knowledge of either language on the part of all readers is in no way assumed. In passing it is perhaps worth stating plainly that the present work is essentially intended to be an entirely 'synchronic' study of Classical Sanskrit: occasional references to the earlier history of the language, whether at the Vedic or Indo-European stage, have been introduced where it seemed that they might help to emphasise or clarify the point under discussion. Undoubtedly some readers would prefer more of such references, others less.

For reasons of both convenience and economy, the use of the nāgarī script is discontinued in the body of the text after the first five chapters. Ample practice in reading and writing the script continues to be provided in the exercises.

Many people have given help and advice during the long and laborious period of preparation of this book. A particularly deep debt of gratitude is due to the following: to Dr. Richard Gombrich, of Oxford, for detailed comment and unfailing sympathy and encouragement over many years; to Mr. C. A. Rylands, formerly of the School of Oriental and African Studies in London, for reading with a quite remarkably sharp eye much of the final draft, and for giving me in many acute observations the fruits of his years of experience as a teacher of Sanskrit; to my colleague at Edinburgh Mr. W. E. Jones, for much patient and careful discussion of the first two chapters; and to Mrs. Elizabeth Kelsall, without whose competent editorial assistance I should still be struggling to get the book finished. Much error has been eliminated with the help of these friends and of the students with whom I have used the work in draft form. I am keenly conscious that many imperfections remain.

Edinburgh, January 1973

Note. Dr. Coulson died before this book could be published. Dr. Gombrich has seen it through the press; he wishes to thank Miss Elizabeth Christie for her help with the proof-reading.

Introduction

SANSKRIT is a member of the Indo-European family of languages to which most of the languages of Europe (including, for instance, English, Welsh, Latin and Greek) also belong. These have all evolved from a single language (or, more immediately, a group of closely related dialects), namely 'Primitive Indo-European' or just 'Indo-European', spoken in about the third millennium BC, of which no direct record remains. The original Indo-European speakers seem to have been tribes inhabiting the plains of Eastern Europe, particularly the area north of the Black Sea (archaeological remains in the South Russian Steppes are in harmony with this supposition), from where migration subsequently occurred in many directions. With the discovery of Hittite, Sanskrit has ceased to be the oldest recorded Indo-European language: but for many reasons, including the fact that Hittite separated early from the main Indo-European stock, Sanskrit remains of central importance to the student of the history of the Indo-European languages.

Sanskrit belongs, more specifically, to the Indo-Iranian branch of Indo-European. The other most important member of this branch is Persian. The earliest Indo-Iranian speakers are conveniently known as Aryans, from the name which they gave themselves (Sanskrit **ārya**, Avestan *airya*—from the latter the modern name Iran is derived, while the name Éire, at the other end of the Indo-European spectrum, may also be cognate). Although it is reasonable to assume that the original homeland of the Aryan tribes was to the north of the Caucasus, our earliest record of them comes neither from this region nor from the Indo-Iranian area but from south of the Caucasus, from the Mitanni kingdom of Northern Mesopotamia, where a ruling dynasty bearing Aryan names and worshipping Aryan gods such as Indra had established itself in the first half of the second millennium BC. However, the main movement of Aryan migration was not south but east into Central Asia, and from there by separate penetrations into Iran and India. Thereafter the Aryans of Iran and the Aryans of India went their separate ways both culturally and linguistically. The oldest stage of Iranian is represented by Avestan, the sacred language of the Zoroastrians, and by Old Persian, the dialect used in the cuneiform inscriptions of the Achaemenian kings.

In India, a highly evolved and urbanised civilisation had existed long before the coming of the Aryans. This was the 'Indus Valley Civilisation', known to us in particular from excavations at Harappa and Mohenjo Daro, and dating from at least the middle of the third millennium. The culture was stable over a long period, and literate. It came to a sudden end, and it is tempting in the extreme to attribute its destruction to the coming of the Aryans. However, an awkward time gap exists, and has not yet been successfully explained, for the Indus civilisation seems to have perished in about 1700 BC and there is no evidence that the Aryans reached India before the latter half of the second millennium.

The survival in Baluchistan up to the present day of a Dravidian language, Brahui, so far from what is now the main Dravidian area in Southern India, makes it reasonable to conclude that before the arrival of the Aryans Dravidian was spoken over a much wider area, and the suggestion has naturally been made that the inhabitants of the Indus cities spoke a Dravidian language. At present this remains unproved, unless recent claims of successful decipherment of the Indus script are accepted, and other non-Aryan language families do exist in India, most notably the group of Muṇḍa languages. Although the language of the Aryans established itself over most of Northern India, it seems that in the long run the Aryans were affected both culturally and linguistically by the peoples they conquered, and Dravidian and Muṇḍa influences (particularly the former) can be traced in the development of Sanskrit itself.

The speech introduced by the Aryans into India developed and diversified, and the major modern languages of Northern India are descended from it. The generic term for such languages is Indo-Aryan. One may conveniently divide the development of Indo-Aryan into three stages: Old, Middle and Modern.

Old Indo-Aryan is equivalent to Sanskrit only in the widest sense of the latter term, and is divided principally between Vedic and the later Classical Sanskrit. Our record of Old Indo-Aryan begins with the hymns of the Ṛgveda, which date back to at least 1000 BC and are the product of a considerable literary skill. That they were composed a fair time after the arrival of the Aryans in India is shown both by the absence of any reference to a homeland outside India and by divergences, principally phonetic, in the language itself from what can be reconstructed as the common Indo-Iranian tongue. Intermediate between the language of the Ṛgveda and that of the Classical period is the language of the Brāhmaṇas, prose works which seek to interpret the mystical significance of the Vedic ritual, the earliest of them written well before the middle of the first millennium BC. The Upaniṣads are a part of the Brāhmaṇa literature.

With the passage of time the language of even the educated priestly class diverged more and more from that of the sacred hymns themselves, and it became increasingly a matter of concern that the hymns should be transmitted without corruption, in order to preserve their religious efficacy. Consequently, a study began to be made of the principles of linguistic, and more particularly of phonetic, analysis. From this developed a grammatical science which concerned itself not only with the sacred language but also with contemporary educated speech. The grammar of Pāṇini, the **Aṣṭādhyāyī**, usually attributed to the fourth century BC, is evidently the culmination of a long and sophisticated grammatical tradition, though the perfection of his own work caused that of his predecessors to vanish.

In less than 4000 sūtras, or brief aphorisms (supplemented on points of detail by the grammarian Kātyāyana), he analyses the whole phonology and morphology of Sanskrit. He anticipates much of the methodology of modern formal grammar: his grammar is generative and in some respects transformational. It cannot, however, be compared very directly with modern grammars, since its form is geared to the needs of oral transmission, and Pāṇini could not avail himself of the mathematical symbols and typographical conventions of the written page. The work was so brief that it could be recited from beginning to end in a couple of hours. It was so comprehensive and accurate that it quickly became the final authority on all questions of correct usage. By Classical Sanskrit is meant essentially the language codified by Pāṇini.

The formal differences between Vedic and Classical Sanskrit are not enormous. Phonologically, the most obvious is a difference of sandhi, whereby for instance a trisyllable such as **vīriam** (or **vīriyam**) becomes a disyllable **vīryam**. Morphologically, the wealth of inflected forms is somewhat reduced, for instance by the disappearance of the subjunctive. In vocabulary a fair number of ancient Aryan words are lost, but the loss is far outweighed by the acquisition of enormous numbers of words from non-Aryan sources. Classical Sanskrit is based on a more easterly dialect of Old Indo-Aryan than is the Ṛgveda, as is shown by the fact that it contributes a number of words which preserve an original Indo-European **l**, where the Ṛgvedic dialect (in common with Iranian) changes this sound to **r**: thus both Vedic **raghú** 'swift, light' and Classical Sanskrit **laghu** 'light, nimble' are cognate with Greek *elakhús*. Other Old Indo-Aryan dialects existed; we have no direct record of them, but from them various dialects of Middle Indo-Aryan evolved.

The beginnings of Middle Indo-Aryan antedate Pāṇini, for the speech of the ordinary people had been evolving faster than that of the educated classes. The term **saṃskṛta** means 'polished, (grammatically) correct', and is in contrast with **prākṛta** '(speech) of the common people'. Just as Sanskrit interpreted in a wide sense may conveniently stand for Old

Indo-Aryan, so Prākrit, interpreted equally widely, may stand for Middle Indo-Aryan. More narrowly, three stages of Middle Indo-Aryan may be distinguished. The first is represented by Pāli, the only Indian language in which the earliest Buddhist scriptures have been preserved on a large scale, and by the dialects used in the inscriptions of the emperor Aśoka (*c.* 250 BC). The process of morphological simplification which distinguishes Classical Sanskrit from Vedic here continues and is accompanied by drastic phonological simplification, including a reduction in the number of vowels and a simplification of consonant groups (thus Sanskrit **traividya** becomes Pali **tevijja**). These processes continue (for instance, with the loss of many intervocalic consonants) in the second stage, that of the Prakrits proper, including Māhārāṣṭrī, Śaurasenī and Māgadhī, and the various dialects of the Jain scriptures. The third stage is represented by Apabhraṃśa, a generic term for the further popular evolution of Middle Indo-Aryan up to the end of the first millennium AD, foreshadowing the final collapse of the old Indo-European inflexional system and the emergence of the Modern Indo-Aryan languages, Bengali, Hindi, Panjābi, Gujarāti, Marāthi, etc. Hindi in its wider sense denotes a group of dialects spoken from Rājasthān to Bihār: upon one particular dialect are based both the official language of Pākistān, Urdu, and the official language of India, (modern standard) Hindi. The term Hindustāni is sometimes used nowadays to denote the common substratum of these two languages, lacking both the extreme Persianisation of Urdu and the extreme Sanskritisation of Hindi.

The Sanskrit of Pāṇini's time had the *cachet* not simply of being the dialect of the educated classes but also of being much closer than was the popular speech to the language of the sacred scriptures themselves. Naturally the prestige of Sanskrit was resisted by those who questioned the authority of the Vedas, and for this reason the early writings of the Buddhists and the Jains are in varieties of Middle Indo-Aryan; the Buddha is reported to have said that his teachings should be given to the people in their own language. Nevertheless, Sanskrit continued to be cultivated, and not merely by the brahmins. Important evidence of this is provided by the two great Indian epics, the Mahābhārata and the Rāmāyaṇa. They were recited and handed down by non-brahmins (the Sūtas), and their audience was a popular one. Although their origins are no doubt more ancient, they evidently belong in something like their present form to about the beginning of the first millennium AD. Their language is Sanskrit, but of a later kind than Pāṇini's—Classical Sanskrit with an admixture of minor features of Middle Indo-Aryan morphology and syntax. It is Sanskrit composed instinctively rather than according to Pāṇini's rules by men for whom Sanskrit was not too remote from their own informal speech. The advantage of using Sanskrit, in addition to the dignity which it imparted to the verse, lay in its role as a *lingua franca* uniting the various regions of Aryan India. One may compare the way a Londoner and a Glaswegian often find the English of the BBC easier to understand than each other's.

As Middle Indo-Aryan developed and its various dialects drew further apart, this role as a *lingua franca* grew increasingly important, and at a time when brahminical influence was increasing. In the early centuries AD, first in the north and later in the south, Sanskrit became the only acceptable language both for administration and for learned communication. The Buddhist Aśvaghoṣa (second century AD) is a significant figure in the process. While early Buddhist literature had first eschewed Sanskrit completely, then compromised with a hybrid language or at least with a non-Pāṇinian Sanskrit, he himself not merely writes Classical Sanskrit but is a master of Sanskrit literary style, and is as important in the history of Sanskrit literature as in the history of Buddhism.

This is the beginning of the great period of Classical Sanskrit, and it lasted for something like a thousand years (possibly a little less for creative literature, but several centuries longer in various fields of speculative thought). For the early centuries AD our knowledge is sketchy, for much of what was written has perished. Part of the reason for Aśvaghoṣa's literary importance is that he is very nearly the only significant predecessor of the poet Kālidāsa whose work has survived.

Kālidāsa is commonly dated to the early fifth century, and on reading his poetry one cannot doubt that it represents the culmination of a great tradition; yet he is the earliest of the major classical poets. Perhaps, like Pāṇini, Kālidāsa eclipsed his predecessors and made their work seem not worth preserving.

By now Sanskrit was not a mother tongue but a language to be studied and consciously mastered. This transformation had come about through a gradual process, the beginnings of which are no doubt earlier than Pāṇini himself. Something of the true position must be reflected in the drama, where not merely the characters of low social status but also the women and young children speak some variety of Prakrit. Kālidāsa learnt his Sanskrit from the rules of a grammarian living some 700 years before his time. Such a situation may well strike the Western reader as paradoxical. Our nearest parallel is in the position of Latin in Medieval Europe. There is, however, an important difference. Few would deny Cicero or Vergil a greater importance in Latin literature than any Medieval author. Conversely, few Sanskritists would deny that the centre of gravity in Sanskrit literature lies somewhere in the first millennium AD, for all that its authors were writing in a so-called 'dead language'.

On this point it may be useful to make a twofold distinction—between a living and a dead language, and between a natural and a learned one. A language is natural when it is acquired and used instinctively; it is living when people choose to converse and formulate ideas in it in preference to any other. To the modern Western scholar Sanskrit is a dead as well as a learned language. To Kālidāsa or Śaṃkara it was a learned language but a living one. (The term 'learned' is not entirely satisfactory, but the term 'artificial', which is the obvious complementary of 'natural', is normally reserved for application to totally constructed languages such as Esperanto.)

The literary medium of any language contains elements of learned speech. Apart from any tendency to conform to conscious grammatical rules, one may observe a limitation or regularisation of sentence patterns, and a widening of vocabulary by the itemisation of more complex ideas. In the expression of a given idea, provided that in both cases it is contained in a single sentence, the syntax will therefore be *simpler* in formal than in conversational speech. Compare the subject–verb–object simplicity of 'an unexpected arrival will admittedly affect our numbers' with the relative syntactical complexity of 'it's true that how many we're going to be will depend on whether anyone turns up that we aren't expecting'. (A particular factor affecting the written style of English is the need to avoid sentences made seriously ambiguous by the lack of an appropriate voice inflection.)

Living languages, whether natural or learned, change and develop. But when a learned language such as literary English is closely tied to, and constantly revitalised by, a natural idiom, its opportunities for independent growth are limited. Sanskrit provides a fascinating example of a language developing in complete freedom from such constraints as an instrument of intellectual and artistic expression. To say that Classical Sanskrit was written in conformity with Pāṇini's rules is true, but in one sense entirely misleading. Pāṇini would have been astounded by the way in which Bāṇa or Bhavabhūti or Abhinavagupta handled the language. It is precisely the fact that Sanskrit writers insisted on using Sanskrit as a living and not as a dead language that has often troubled Western scholars. W. D. Whitney, a great but startlingly arrogant American Sanskritist of the nineteenth century, says of the Classical language, 'Of linguistic history there is next to nothing in it all; but only a history of style, and this for the most part showing a gradual depravation, an increase of artificiality and an intensification of certain more undesirable features of the language—such as the use of passive constructions and of participles instead of verbs, and the substitution of compounds for sentences.' Why such a use of passives, participles and compounds should be undesirable, let alone depraved, is left rather vague, and while there have been considerable advances in linguistic science in the past fifty years there seems to have been nothing which helps to clarify or justify these strictures. Indeed, Whitney's words would not be worth resurrecting if strong echoes of them did not still survive in some quarters.

Acceptance of Pāṇini's rules implied a final stabilisation of the phonology of Sanskrit, and also (at least in the negative sense that no form could be used which was not sanctioned by him) of its morphology. But Pāṇini did not fix syntax. To do so explicitly and incontrovertibly would be difficult in any language, given several ways of expressing the same idea and various other ways of expressing closely similar ideas. Certain major morphological simplifications typical of Middle Indo-Aryan were prevented by Pāṇini's codification: thus Sanskrit retains a middle voice and an obligatory dual number. On the other hand, the way Prakrit dealt with all past tenses, replacing them with a past participle and where necessary a passive construction, being a negative procedure could be imitated by Sanskrit (see Chapter 4), and as a result in certain styles of Classical Sanskrit a past finite tense is something of a rarity. Because it did not occur to Pāṇini to prohibit such a construction, or to limit its use to particular circumstances, supposedly 'Pāṇinian' Sanskrit could be written in a quite non-Pāṇinian way, eschewing a whole mass of difficult forms and conforming to the usage of the popular language.

But in other and more important respects the syntactical changes wrought in Sanskrit took it further from popular speech. Indeed, one such may be distinguished which actually depends upon the preservation of the full Old Indo-Aryan case system, namely the increasing exploitation of various cases to represent certain 'abstract' syntactical relationships: instrumental or ablative to express cause, dative purpose, locative circumstance and hypothesis, an abstract accusative with a verb of motion to express change of state, and so on. This development is inseparable from the most striking change of all, the exploitation of nominal composition. In Vedic, noun compounds are hardly more frequent than in Homeric Greek, but their frequency increases throughout the history of the language. More important still, the compounds which occur in the earlier language are seldom of more than two members, whereas in the later language the occurrence in a single short sentence of several compounds of four or five members is perfectly normal, and in certain styles compounds of twenty or more members are not thought excessive. Here again, advantage has been taken of a negative freedom. It is, in fact, an important feature of compounds that, coordinatives apart, they are binary in structure (i.e. can be analysed through repeated bisection—see particularly Chapter 7). Pāṇini gives rules for the construction of compounds. By applying these rules recursively, compounds of any length may be built up. At one and the same time Pāṇini is obeyed and bypassed. One may indeed wonder to what extent the style of the grammatical sūtras themselves encouraged this process; evolved to meet very specific scientific needs and utilising cases and compounds in a way quite foreign to the natural language, it may well have served as a partial model for other types of discourse.

The cumulative effect of such changes is certainly startling. The syntax of Classical Sanskrit in many major respects bears little resemblance to the syntax of any other Indo-European language (leaving aside similarities in certain kinds of Middle Indo-Aryan writing). Whitney is typical of many Western scholars who manage to convey contempt for the avoidance of the intricacies of the Old Indo-Aryan verbal system, with a simultaneous contempt for the pedantry of those who flex their grammatical muscles from time to time by using a number of *recherché* forms and irritation at the difficulty of understanding the ordinary language of the learned. The first two points are of little importance. As to the third, it is certainly true that modern scholars often meet with ambiguities and obscurities in reading Classical texts, and that some of the ambiguities arise out of the use of long compounds. But the texts were not written for us, and there is little to suggest that Sanskrit writers qualified to participate in academic discussion found any difficulty in following the language it was couched in: such a situation would indeed have been perverse. (The use of long compounds in creative literature (**kāvyaṃ**) is something of a separate issue: there, easy intelligibility might well be at odds with the desire to achieve some particular effect.) What is perhaps true is that such a style does not take kindly to textual corruption. A great burden of information may be carried by a single vowel or consonant, the alteration of which may give an entirely different twist to the meaning of a whole sentence. To this may be added the inadequacy of existing dictionaries for many kinds of Sanskrit texts, and the fact that modern scholarship has still a long way to go in reconstructing the cultural and intellectual presuppositions, the 'universe of discourse' implicit in Sanskrit literature.

Another striking feature of Classical Sanskrit is its wealth of synonyms. First (what is, of course, not quite the same thing), it has a huge vocabulary, a composite store of words from many sources, Aryan and non-Aryan. Secondly, there operates upon these words a tendency, no doubt normal to some extent in any learned language, to blur distinctions between words that to start with were close in meaning but not synonymous. One may compare the way writers of English will ring the changes on various series of words ('way, manner, fashion, mode', 'occupation, employment, pursuit') merely to avoid repeating the same word, not because some other is especially appropriate (the phenomenon of 'elegant variation'). Particularly significant is the way a hyponym (more specific term—'innovation, development, transformation') will alternate with its superordinate (less specific term—'change') for the same reason, and not because some particular level of precision is being aimed at. The usage of words that are more distinct 'emotively' than 'cognitively' ('hide', 'conceal') may also be assimilated, and this may come about because the literary context (e.g. committee report as opposed to advertising copy) neutralises possible differences of emotional effect.

Poetry written within such a literary idiom does not necessarily seek to reverse these trends. As the literary tradition develops, poets moving towards a classical style build up a useful stock of uncoloured synonyms (*amor*, *ardor*, *flamma*, *venus*; *amour*, *fers*, *feu*, *flamme*, *soupirs*, *vœux*) which they can draw on at will, confident that long use has made the words innocuous. Classical poets do not need these extra words because they are technically less competent than poets that stick ciosely to natural speech: they merely prefer to reserve their energies for other ends. The tendency to treat language in this way, perhaps only faintly observable in the Western tradition, is of central importance in the poetry of Classical Sanskrit. The poet has quite enormous reserves of cognitively and emotively synonymous words to draw upon. What most especially swells these reserves is the possibility of a sort of 'componential' compounding; thus the word **rājan** 'king' may be replaced by an indefinite number of compounds meaning 'lord of men', 'guardian of the people', 'enjoyer of the earth', etc. (the extent to which *any* word with the appropriate sense could be used in helping to form such compounds was partly a question of style; naturally, creative literature in general went further than academic prose, and thorough exploitation of the device was considered a particular characteristic of the Gauḍa (Eastern) poetic style). Because of these resources it was possible to write Sanskrit verse in metres of great complexity and beauty.

Furthermore, because of the long history of the language and the varied sources from which it drew its vocabulary, many Sanskrit words have a number of quite distinct meanings; and this feature, too, is much augmented by compounding (e.g. because it literally means 'twice-born', the word **dvijaḥ** can signify 'brahmin', 'bird' or 'tooth'). Thus punning is made possible on a scale inconceivable in a natural language—on far too large a scale, in fact, to be effective *per se* for any humorous purpose. Instead sustained paronomasia is used in certain literary styles for perfectly serious literary purposes—not (at least in good writers) for empty display or mere playfulness, but to achieve a density of expression that could be attained in no other way: the same words may convey simultaneously the imagery of an idea and the contrasting imagery of a metaphor or simile which comments upon that idea. In this as in other respects it is the peculiar merits of Sanskrit poetry which make it least translatable.

Using This Book

PROVIDED that the main features of Sanskrit phonology described in Chapter 1 are understood, it is not necessary to memorise the whole alphabet before proceeding to Chapter 2. The nāgarī script is complicated, and is best assimilated gradually; most learners need several weeks, even months, to read it with complete fluency. It would be possible to use this book without learning the nāgarī script at all (making use only of the transliterated versions of the exercises). This might suit some experienced linguists, anxious to gain a rapid impression of the langugage. But the ordinary student is advised against such a course. Transliteration has a distorting effect upon Sanskrit phonology, unless interpreted with a knowledge either of the nāgarī script or of phonetics. It is essential to have a sure grasp of the fact that letters distinguished from each other only by small diacritic marks represent totally independent items in the Sanskrit sound system and that **dh**, for instance, is no less a single phoneme than **d**.

Sanskrit is a language with a very different surface structure from that of English. Each chapter deals with a number of its more prominent morphological and syntactical features. The focus of attention should always be firmly upon the Sanskrit structure and not upon the English by which it is represented. Thus in Chapter 4 there should be no danger of an attempt to translate 'literally' into Sanskrit a sentence like 'it was he who made this garden', since neither the relative pronoun nor a verb 'to be' has been introduced at this stage. Such a sentence should be dealt with in the light of what is said in Chapter 4 on the use of the particle **eva**.

Those who do not find committing paradigms to memory an impossible burden would be well advised to learn the grammar for each chapter before tackling the exercises; time spent on this will be saved in doing the exercises themselves. Some may wish to go further, and to learn each special vocabulary by heart. If this is not done, it is at least worth reading slowly through the vocabulary (preferably aloud) before starting the exercises. As the vocabularies grow longer, it will become increasingly important to handle Sanskrit alphabetical order: a note on this is given at the beginning of the general Sanskrit–English vocabulary; the complications caused by the position of anusvāra should not give rise to much difficulty in the (comparatively short) special vocabularies.

It is assumed that the aim of anyone using this book is to acquire the ability to read original Sanskrit texts. The sentences contained in Exercise 6 onwards are all taken from Sanskrit authors. They should therefore be treated as interesting objects of study rather than as hurdles to be overcome. The test of your progress is not whether you have always achieved versions identical with those found in the keys (this is hardly possible) but whether you have fully understood how the key corresponds to the exercise.

A particular difficulty arises over the Sanskrit–English sentences. Deriving from real utterances, they will sometimes seem quirky or obscure when divorced from their literary context. The special vocabularies are designed to reduce this difficulty as much as possible. There is also the question of the more general context, i.e. the cultural background, of the material. In this connection all students of Sanskrit should be aware of the existence of Professor A. L. Basham's scholarly and yet highly readable account of ancient Indian civilisation, *The Wonder That Was India* (Sidgwick and Jackson, hardback; Fontana, paperback).

Those who do not learn languages easily may prefer to work through the book once using both parts of each exercise for translation out of Sanskrit only. Progress could then be consolidated by working through all the English–Sanskrit sentences a second time in the normal way.

Careful attention should be paid to the examples given in the text of each chapter, since these represent the types of sentence to be encountered in the exercises. Because each example is followed immediately by a translation, it has not seemed necessary to exclude an occasional form which anticipates the grammar of a later chapter (as well as grammatical forms dealt with later in the same chapter). These forms are explained in the general vocabulary, where there will also be found any words not listed in the special vocabulary of the exercises.

For clearness and convenience a topic is usually treated as a whole in a particular chapter, even if one or two aspects of it are not applicable until later in the book. Observations which may be passed over rapidly and returned to later are enclosed in square brackets.

Many Sanskrit words have a number of different meanings. The vocabularies in this book are not intended as a dictionary, and generally speaking therefore only meanings relevant to the material used in the book are given either in the special or in the general vocabulary.

Many Sanskrit words are synonymous with several others, at least in certain of their meanings. Such synonyms have often been differentiated by near-synonyms in English. The object of this is merely to guide towards a correct choice of Sanskrit word in a particular sentence (correct in the sense of corresponding to the original). There need be no head-scratching over the difference in meaning between a word translated as 'employ' and a word translated as 'engage': there is none of any consequence.

Conversely, when a Sanskrit word already met with occurs again in a related but slightly different sense, it is not put a second time into the special vocabulary but will be found listed with both meanings in the general vocabulary.

Certain typographical devices have been used in English versions of Sanskrit sentences. These should give no trouble if the following principle is borne in mind: rounded brackets (parentheses) enclose matter not directly represented in the Sanskrit; square brackets enclose what is not wanted in the

English version. A colon implies that what follows is a freer version of what precedes. Thus a sentence is often interrupted by a literally translated phrase in square brackets and with a colon, followed immediately by a more idiomatic or more intelligible rendering of the same phrase. Square brackets are also used in conjunction with an oblique stroke to provide an alternative interpretation of the Sanskrit: e.g. 'he [/she] is going'. Rounded brackets with an oblique stroke suggest an alternative phrasing: e.g. 'he said "that is so" (/that this was so)'.

Students with linguistic aptitude who are particularly impatient to grapple with a continuous text may like to experiment with something simple on their own at any point after Chapter 8. Advice on dictionaries, etc. is given on pp. 277–9. It would be advisable to glance ahead at the main features described in the later chapters, and in particular (if a narrative text is chosen) at the paradigms of the imperfect and perfect tenses.

Chapter 1

Before the introduction of printing into India in the eighteenth century, the script in which Sanskrit was written and taught varied from place to place in India, and was the same, or almost the same, as that used in writing the local vernacular language. Well-travelled paṇḍits might understand many forms of the alphabet, but the basis of Sanskrit tradition lay in recitation and oral communication. The widespread dissemination of printed Sanskrit texts, however, encouraged the predominance of one form of writing, the nāgarī (or devanāgarī) script of central India, in which the modern languages Hindī and Marāṭhī are also written. Today even the most traditionally minded paṇḍits are familiar with it, and Sanskrit publications of more than local interest are printed in no other script.

All the Indian scripts, however much elaborated in their forms, are developments over the course of centuries from a single source. This was the brāhmī script, written from left to right, first known to us from the inscriptions of the emperor Aśoka (third century BC). Its origin is unknown. Many suppose it to be an adaptation of the Semitic alphabet, but by the time of the Aśokan inscriptions the adaptation is already too thorough for positive identification. It reflects with considerable accuracy the phonetic structure of the Indo-Aryan languages. All later Indian scripts inherit its unusual graphic system; they differ from it and from each other solely as to the shapes into which the individual letters have evolved.

Your best way to learn the sounds of Sanskrit is therefore to learn to write the nāgarī script.[1] In this chapter the sounds and the letters are presented side by side. You may think it worth taking the trouble to learn to write Sanskrit well, even if your usual English handwriting is a scrawl: you will never need to cover page after page in a tearing hurry, and in what you do write you can take pleasure in forming the characters slowly and with control. You should use black ink and a pen with a nib capable of producing thick and thin strokes. The most convenient method is to acquire one of the inexpensive fountain-pens to which a variety of nibs can be fitted. For preliminary practice, an ordinary pencil can be sharpened to a broad, flat point.

Because of the way in which an Indian reed pen is cut, the thick and thin strokes lie in the reverse direction to our own Italic script: that is, the thick strokes run from bottom left to top right and the thin strokes from top left to bottom right: / \. Left-handed writers are thus at less of a disadvantage than in writing the Italic script; and right-handed writers will need to hold the pen at a different angle from usual in their hand and may find it helpful to use a nib with a moderately oblique

[1] It may be wondered why several references are made in this chapter to the values of the nāgarī letters as used for modern Hindī. The point is that basically the values are the same for both languages: spelling of the Indian vernaculars has never been allowed to ossify in the same way as that of Italian and Greek, in which words with a classical spelling (*voce*, *hugieia*) are given a quite unclassical pronunciation. Thus Sanskrit **karma** 'deed' changed to Prākrit **kamma** and Medieval Hindī **kāma**. These distinctions are reflected in the spelling. Only the latest change, to modern **kām** with final '**a** mute', remains unrecorded, and this can be justified both because final **a** still has a vestigial, 'latent' existence, like French '*e muet*', and because of the extreme inconvenience within the Indian system of writing of marking this particular change. That region which has most altered the traditional sound values of the alphabet, Bengal, shows an exactly parallel deviation in the way its paṇḍits (of the older school) actually pronounce Sanskrit itself. Another reason for mentioning certain features of modern pronunciation is that these may otherwise puzzle the learner when he hears Sanskrit spoken by an Indian.

cut of the sort normally intended for the left-handed. Right-handed and left-handed writers will make each stroke from opposite ends. (In this and what follows it should be emphasised that what is being taught is not traditional Indian calligraphy—for which see in particular H. M. Lambert's *Introduction to the Devanagari Script* (London, 1953)—but its adaptation in one of various possible ways to the modern fountain-pen.) The right-handed writer should hold the pen along the line of the thick stroke and pointing to the bottom left; the left-handed should also hold it along the line of the thick stroke but pointing to the top right. In as many of the strokes as possible the pen should be drawn towards you—up towards the right for the right-handed, down towards the left for the left-handed.

In addition to their distinctive element, most letters in the nāgarī script contain a vertical and a horizontal stroke. The right-handed writer will draw the vertical stroke upwards and the horizontal stroke to the right. The left-handed will draw the vertical stroke downwards and the horizontal stroke to the left. In each letter the distinctive element should be written first.

This is how a right-handed writer might form the sign **त ta**:

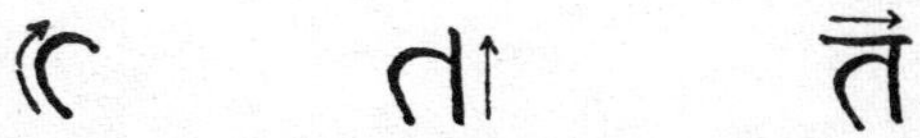

1 Distinctive element   2 Vertical stroke   3 Horizontal stroke

This is how a left-handed writer might form the same sign:

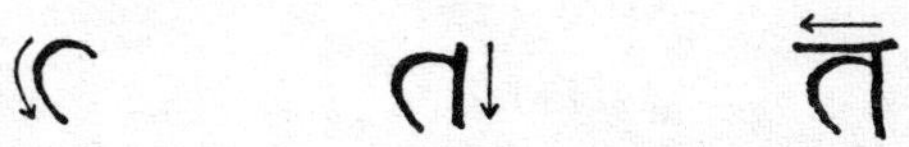

This sign is an illustration of the basic principle of the script, which is halfway in character between an alphabet and a very regular syllabary. The signs for the consonants such as **t** do not stand for themselves alone but possess an inherent

short **a** (which is by far the commonest of all Sanskrit vowel sounds). If you wish to represent the consonant **t** without a following **a**, you must add a special cancellation stroke (called a **virāma**) below the letter: **त्** **t**. Thus the word **tat** meaning 'it' or 'that' is written **तत्**.

Vowels

To represent vowel sounds other than **a** various marks are added above, below or on either side of the basic consonant sign. There are thirteen vowels in Sanskrit, of which one (**ḷ**) occurs only in one verb and another (**ṝ**) is not very frequent. They are given below as written after the consonant **t**. As additional guides to pronunciation, an appropriate IPA symbol is given in square brackets and the nearest equivalent sounds in French and English are added. The French sounds are seldom more inaccurate than the English, and often very much nearer the mark.

SIMPLE VOWELS (LONG AND SHORT)

	English 'equivalent'	French 'equivalent'
त ta [ə]	b*u*t	—
ता tā [a:]	f*a*ther	t*a*rd
ति ti [i]	f*i*t	*i*c*i*
ती tī [i:]	f*ee*	p*i*re
तु tu [u]	p*u*t	t*ou*t
तू tū [u:]	b*oo*	c*ou*rt

SYLLABIC LIQUIDS

तृ tṛ [r] American 'p*ur*dy' (but nowadays pronounced as in English 'p*re*tty')

तॄ	**tṝ**	[r:]	—(the preceding sound lengthened)—	
तॢ	**tḷ**	[l]	tab*le*	tab*le*

DIPHTHONGS

ते	**te** (i.e. **tē**)	[e:]	m*a*de (esp. Welsh)	*été* (but longer)
तै	**tai**	[ai]	b*i*te	trav*ai*l
तो	**to** (i.e. **tō**)	[o:]	r*o*pe (esp. Welsh)	f*au*sse
तौ	**tau**	[au]	f*ou*nd	c*aou*tchouc

Notes on the vowel sounds[1]

To the British in India, the short **a** sounded like the English vowel sound in the received pronunciation of 'but' and 'duck'—hence spellings such as 'pundit', 'suttee', 'Punjab' (**paṇḍit, satī, Pañjāb**). This English sound may be taken as a reasonable guide to the pronunciation, although the Indian sound is somewhat less open. The corresponding long vowel **ā** is completely open, and thus these two vowels are distinguished not merely in length but also in quality (for standard Western Hindi **a** is half-open, central, unrounded; **ā** is open, forward of central, unrounded). This distinction of quality held good over 2000 years ago and was known to Pāṇini.[2] On the other hand, the long vowels **ī, ū** and **ṝ** differ from the corresponding short vowels only in being held longer. This distinction of pure length has been almost lost in modern

[1] The sounds of Sanskrit are known to us with considerable accuracy. But difficulties in mastering the less familiar sounds need cause no great distress. Many western Sanskritists treat Sanskrit entirely as a written language, and when forced to pronounce a few words of it do so without distinguishing, for example, between retroflex and dental, or between aspirates and non-aspirates. How much trouble to take is thus a matter of personal choice, although the tendency nowadays is to pay more attention to such matters.

[2] The final aphorism of his whole grammar is the shortest grammatical rule in the world: simply **अ अ a a**—i.e. '/a/ → [ə]', 'The sound that (for convenience of grammatical statement) we have treated as differing from /ā/ only in length is, in fact, to be realised as [ə]'.

Hindi, and uneducated people regularly confuse **i** with **ī** and **u** with **ū** in their spelling. All three syllabic liquids, **ṛ**, **ṝ** and **ḷ**, vanished long ago from popular speech, and the memory of how to pronounce them correctly has faded. Syllabic **ḷ** occurs only in some forms of the verb **kḷp** and may be ignored. Paṇḍits nowadays tend to pronounce **ṛ** as if it were **ri** and **ṝ** even more improbably as **rī**. (Hence the anglicised spelling Rigveda for **ṛgveda**.) For convenience you may do the same. But it is by no means impossible to make [r] a syllable in its own right: American speakers do so in some pronunciations of 'pretty' ('pṛdy'), and upper- and middle-class Englishmen in some pronunciations of 'interesting' ('íntṛsting').[1]

Of the four diphthongs, **e** and **o** are known as 'short' diphthongs, and **ai** and **au** as corresponding 'long' diphthongs. Historically this is justified: while **e** and **o** are descended from normal Indo-European diphthongs, **ai** and **au** correspond to diphthongs of which the prior element was long (as in Greek *ēi*, *ōi*, *ēu*, etc.). But in Sanskrit at an early stage the long diphthongs shortened to ordinary diphthongs, and the ordinary diphthongs narrowed into simple vowel sounds. It is extremely important to remember, however, not only that **e** and **o** despite their pronunciation remain classified as diphthongs (for reasons that will be apparent when you learn the rules of sandhi) but also that phonetically and metrically **e** and **o** are not short but *long* vowels. The only reason they are not usually transliterated as **ē** and **ō** is that since short *ĕ* and *ŏ* do not occur at all in Sanskrit (because Indo-European *e*, *o* and *a* all converge into Sanskrit **a**) the distinction does not have to be marked. The process of diphthong narrowing has continued, and modern Indian speakers pronounce **ai** and **au** as

[1] This example is particularly close, in that ancient phoneticians analysed syllabic **ṛ** as consisting of the consonant **r** with a vocalic 'trace element' before and after it—like the two vestigial 'e's' in 'int'r'sting'. Phonemically, however, **ṛ** is a short vowel like any other: a word such as **kṛ-ta** 'done' is composed of two equally short (or 'light') syllables, e.g. for purposes of verse scansion.

very pinched, closer sounds (cf. the ultra-genteel pronunciation of English 'nice'), some even as monophthongs, so that it is often rather difficult to distinguish **ai** from **e** and **au** from **o**.

Notes on the vowel signs

Perhaps the most striking is the sign for short **i**—ि—which is written before the consonant sign, although the vowel sound itself follows the consonant. Originally, in fact, the sign consisted only of the curl at the top, but to distinguish it more clearly from other signs the tail was lengthened into a vertical line. If you are like most Sanskritists, you will often find at first that you have written a consonant sign without noticing that the next vowel is an **i**, for which a space should have been left.

Note that the four diphthong signs are constructed on a regular principle. The sign for **e** े is doubled to make ै **ai**; from these **o** and **au** respectively are distinguished by the addition of the vertical bar ा, which on its own is used to make **ā**. Usually the signs are placed above the bar, but very occasionally you may find them above the consonant sign itself, thus: तो **to** and तौ **tau**. This does have the advantage of distinguishing तो **to** more clearly from ती **tī**. Even so, it should normally be quite possible to tell them apart: you may occasionally come across bad printing in which it is difficult. In your own writing you should form the two differently: the **ī** is a single stroke, the vertical line being once again a prolonged tail. On the other hand, **o** is made up of two strokes, which should be written separately. First draw the vertical bar ा (upwards if right-handed, downwards if left-handed); then draw the hook ो (to the right if right-handed, to the left if left-handed).

Initial vowel signs

Whenever a vowel is preceded by a consonant, the vowel sign

is attached to the consonant, as described above. This applies not only within a single word but also when one word begins with a vowel and the preceding word ends in a consonant. For this reason, in printing Sanskrit in nāgarī (or in any other Indian script), it is not always possible to make a space between one word and the next, and it needs practice to spot where one word ends and the next begins. Even so, a vowel obviously cannot be combined with a consonant (a) when it begins a sentence, (b) when it is itself preceded by another vowel—in Sanskrit this is comparatively rare—and (c) when a word beginning with a vowel is written on its own, as in a dictionary entry.

For use in these circumstances there is a second set of vowel signs—initial (or more accurately 'free-standing') signs. They are:

अ or ॲ **a**, आ or ऑ **ā**; इ **i**, ई **ī**; उ **u**, ऊ **ū**; ऋ **ṛ**, ॠ **ṝ**, ऌ **ḷ**;
ए **e**; ऐ **ai**; ओ or ऒ **o**; औ or ऒॏ **au**

Examples for practice एति **eti** 'he goes'; अतीत **atīta** 'past'; तितउ **titaü** 'sieve'.

There are two signs in Sanskrit that have no 'free-standing' form because they represent modifications of vowel sounds, one by nasalisation, the other by adding aspiration.

Anusvāra

This is written as a dot at the top right of the syllable (represented in transliteration by **ṃ**). It signifies that the vowel sound is nasalised, probably rather in the way that some French vowel sounds are nasalised—although the ancient descriptions are not absolutely clear. Thus तों **toṃ** and तं **taṃ** are to be pronounced very roughly as the French *ton* and *teint* respectively.

Examples for practice तं **taṃ** 'him'; तां **tāṃ** 'her'; तितउं

titaüṃ 'sieve (*accusative case*)'; **अंत aṃta** less correct spelling of **anta** 'end'.[1]

Visarga

This is written as two dots after the syllable (represented in transliteration by **ḥ**). Its pronunciation presents more difficulty to a European than that of anusvāra. In theory it is a pure voiceless aspiration like an English 'h', but added after the vowel sound, whereas of course the English aspirate always precedes a vowel. To achieve this you might start by pronouncing it as the *ch* in German *ich*, or even Scottish *loch*, and then refine away the 'rasping' element until only a pure breathing is left. Alternatively, you may, like many paṇḍits, introduce a fainter echo of the preceding vowel sound: e.g. **तः taḥ** as 'tah[a]', **तीः tīḥ** as 'tīh[i]' (which is like English 'tee-hee' only if you put all the stress on the *first* syllable of the latter).

Examples for practice **ततः tataḥ** 'thereupon'; **ताः tāḥ** 'those women'; **तैः taiḥ** 'by them'; **आः āḥ** 'ah!'.

Consonants

All the vowel sounds of Sanskrit have now been mentioned. Their number is less than the number of vowel sounds in English. Of consonants, on the other hand, Sanskrit has a far greater number than English. This is principally due to the proliferation of plosive consonants (or 'stops'). These the grammarians grouped into five series according to their place of articulation, each series comprising four stops together with the related nasal consonant:

[1] When these less correct (or at any rate less precise) spellings are encountered, they should not affect pronunciation: **पंडित paṃḍita** is still to be pronounced **पण्डित paṇḍita.** For a fuller discussion of the ancient value of the anusvāra, see W. S. Allen's *Phonetics in Ancient India*, pp. 40–6.

STOPS AND NASALS

	Voiceless		*Voiced*		
	Unaspirated	*Aspirate*	*Unaspirated*	*Aspirate*	*Nasal*
Velar	क **ka**	ख **kha**	ग **ga**	घ **gha**	ङ **ṅa**
Palatal	च **ca**	छ **cha**	ज **ja**	झ **jha**	ञ **ña**
Retroflex	ट **ṭa**	ठ **ṭha**	ड **ḍa**	ढ **ḍha**	ण **ṇa**
Dental	त **ta**	थ **tha**	द **da**	ध **dha**	न **na**
Labial	प **pa**	फ **pha**	ब **ba**	भ **bha**	म **ma**

Unaspirated voiceless stops **k, c, ṭ, t, p**

These really are unaspirated, unlike their English equivalents. It is often not realised that one of the ways in which, for instance, the English word 'key' differs from the French *qui* is that the English *k* is followed by an aspirate, or '*h*-sound' (which, however, disappears when the *k* is preceded by an *s*, as in 'skill'). Unless you speak a language such as French in which the voiceless stops are never aspirated, you may have difficulty in eliminating this aspiration from your pronunciation.

क् **k** as *k* in 'kill'—better, as *c* in French *coup*
च् **c** as *ch* in 'chill'—better, as *c* in Italian *voce*
प् **p** as *p* in 'pill'—better, as *p* in French *pique*

Retroflex[1] *and dental*

Sanskrit distinguishes two types of *t*, *d*, etc. The dental series

[1] A frequent synonym of 'retroflex' is 'cerebral'. This is an unfortunate translation of the Sanskrit term **mūrdhanya** 'made in the head', itself unusually imprecise. The word 'cerebral' is still in common use among Sanskritists, but since retroflexion as a phonetic phenomenon is by no means confined to Sanskrit, I have thought it wiser to adopt the more accurate term preferred by phoneticians as being more likely to prevail in the end.

is the type found in European languages other than English. A French *t* or *d* is made by striking the edge of the teeth with the tip of the tongue. (In other words, the place of articulation is the same as for the English *th* in 'thin'.) An English *t* or *d* is made with the tongue drawn a little further back, so that the tip strikes against the front of the palate or the teeth-ridge, instead of against the teeth. This English *t* seems to Indians to be their retroflex **ṭ**, rather than a dental **t**—and when transcribing English words into the nāgarī script they employ retroflex consonants instead of dentals: e.g. the English word 'tip' would be written **टिप् ṭip.** However, the true Indian retroflex consonant is made rather by curling the tongue up and striking the palate (perhaps at a point further back) with the very tip or even the underside of the tongue.

ट ṭ as *t* in English 'try'
त t as the first *t* in French 'tout'

Examples for practice **तटः taṭaḥ** 'bank'; **पीत pīta** 'drunk'; **पचति pacati** 'he cooks'; **कूपः kūpaḥ** 'a well'.

Voiceless aspirates kh, ch, ṭh, th, ph

These are much *more* strongly aspirated than the English voiceless stops *k*, *t*, etc., which fall between the two stools. However, it is easier to add aspiration than to take it away: pronounce 'up-heaval' first in two distinct parts and then more rapidly, trying to run the *p* on to the following syllable. It should be plainly understood that all these sounds are merely aspirated forms of those in the preceding column: **ph** is NOT as in 'physic', **th** NOT as in 'thin', **kh** NOT as *ch* in Scottish 'loch'.

Examples for practice **अथ atha** 'hereupon'; **पीठं pīṭhaṃ** 'stool'; **फटा phaṭā** 'serpent's hood'; **खात khāta** 'dug up'; **छोटित choṭita** 'torn off'.

Unaspirated voiced stops **g, j, ḍ, d, b**

This is the simplest series. The corresponding English letters will serve as a guide. The only problem is in preserving the distinction described above between retroflex **ḍ** and dental **d**.

Examples for practice **गजः gajaḥ** 'elephant'; **जड jaḍa** 'numb'; **बीजं bījaṃ** 'seed'; **ददाति dadāti** 'he gives'.

Voiced aspirates **gh, jh, ḍh, dh, bh**

These are all equally troublesome. They are, of course, aspirated forms of the preceding series. The difficulty is that, since the letters are voiced, the aspiration must be a voiced aspiration. The last letter of the Sanskrit alphabet is **ह ha**, the Sanskrit *h*, which is also voiced. (The only voiceless *h* in Sanskrit is the rather special visarga, described above.) The key to the pronunciation of all these letters is learning to pronounce a voiced *h* instead of the voiceless English *h*[1] (it is true that some English speakers make voiced *h* a rather infrequent allophone of *h*—e.g. in the word 'in*h*erent').

Voiced sounds are those made with a vibration of the vocal cords. Some consonants are voiced, others voiceless. All vowels are voiced, unless you whisper them. An extremely easy way to tell whether a sound is voiced or not is to put your hands firmly over your ears: start by making a prolonged *sss* sound, which is voiceless; then make a *zzz* sound, which is voiced, and you will hear the vibration of the vocal cords very plainly as a droning in your ears. Lengthen the ordinary English *h* into a prolonged breathing and it will be quite

[1] I believe this to be so, from having taught myself in this way before I had ever heard a voiced aspirate pronounced correctly. On the other hand, in India **ह ha** itself is no longer a voiced sound, and consequently an Englishman I met there, who had lived in the country for several years, had difficulty when asked in producing a plain voiced *h* sound, even though he could pronounce the voiced aspirate stops perfectly.

obviously voiceless. The task now is to modify this breathing until you can hear that it is accompanied by the droning. The sound you are aiming at is similar to the sound children sometimes use when they want to make someone jump. The voiced **h**, once produced, can easily be combined with **g**, **j** etc., and practice will soon smooth the sound down until you do not seem to be trying to give your listeners a series of heart-attacks.

Examples for practice **आघातः āghātaḥ** 'blow'; **झटिति jhaṭiti** 'at once'; **बाढं bāḍhaṃ** 'certainly'; **धातु dhātu** 'element'; **बोधति bodhati** 'he awakes'; **भागः bhāgaḥ** 'portion'; **बिभेद bibheda** 'he split'.

Nasals **ṅ, ñ, ṇ, n, m**

Velar **ṅ** and palatal **ñ** are used almost entirely with stops of their own class, e.g. **अङ्गं aṅgaṃ** 'limb'; **पञ्च pañca** 'five'. **Aṅga** sounds rather like English 'anger'—or 'hunger' without the *h*; **pañca** is rather like 'puncher'. Between **ṇ** and **n** a distinction of retroflex and dental is regularly made by paṇḍits, although in Hindī this distinction—unlike that between retroflex and dental *stops*—has been lost, except as a (learned) spelling pronunciation.

Examples for practice **तृणं tṛṇaṃ** 'grass'; **जनः janaḥ** 'people'; **मति mati** 'thought'.

A note on handwriting

In practising the nāgarī letters, the most important general principle for the acquisition of good handwriting is to give the letters 'body' by keeping the distinctive portion of each full and uncramped. Too often, beginners produce a few tiny curls and loops in an acreage of white. The secret is to divide the vertical bar not into two parts but into three, so that the distinctive portion of letters such as **ज** and **त** occupy at least the lower two-thirds, and letters such as **प**, **भ** and **ध** at least the upper two-thirds:

Semi-vowels

Four sounds are classified as semi-vowels. They and the vowels associated with them are given places in four of the five series:

palatal	**य ya**	corresponding to the vowels	**i ī**
retroflex	**र ra**	,,	**ṛ ṝ**
dental	**ल la**	,,	**ḷ**
labial	**व va**	,,	**u ū**

y is often pronounced, nowadays at least, more lightly and unobtrusively than the English *y* in 'yes'. **r** is usually a tapped sound similar to an Italian *r*. It was described as being alveolar (against the arch of the gums) rather than fully retroflex. (However, for convenience of grammatical statement, all members of the 'retroflex' group are treated as truly retroflex.) Speakers of Southern or BBC English should be careful always to give **r** its full value, and should guard against letting it colour their pronunciation of a preceding vowel: distinguish **karma** 'deed', which approximately rhymes with an American's pronunciation of 'firmer', from **kāma** 'desire', which approximately rhymes with an Englishman's 'farmer'. **l** is dental, and so even more like a French than an English *l*. It does not have the 'dark' quality which in varying degrees an English *l* may have. In origin, **v** was a true labial, i.e. a bilabial like the English *w*, and it would be just as appropriate to transliterate it by **w** as by **v**. In most of India it is pronounced now as a labio-dental, that is to say with the upper teeth and the lower lips, and this seems to have been so from an early period. The best method is to try to produce a '*w* sound' but using the upper teeth instead of the upper lip. If you employ a full-blooded labio-dental fricative like the English *v*, it will sound odd when **v** is combined with another consonant, e.g. in the word **svastika**.

In combination with र **r**, the signs for **u** and **ū** are written in a rather different form, beside instead of below the consonant:

रु **ru** रू **rū**: e.g. रूपं **rūpaṃ** 'form'

The (rare) combination of consonant र **r** with vocalic ऋ **ṛ** is made with the aid of the conjunct form of र **r** described below:

र्ऋ **rṛ**: e.g. निर्ऋण **nir-ṛṇa** 'debtless'

Examples for practice छाया **chāyā** 'shade'; रीति **rīti** 'style'; लयः **layaḥ** 'dissolution'; वीरः **vīraḥ** 'hero'.

Sibilants

Three of the five series include voiceless sibilants:

palatal	श	**śa**
retroflex	ष	**ṣa**
dental	स	**sa**

Dental **s** is like an English *s*. The other two sibilants are confounded in modern popular pronunciation: they are similar to an English *sh* as in 'ship'. You may like to make your own distinction between the two on the basis that one is palatal and the other retroflex.

Note carefully that there is no voiced sibilant, i.e. no *z* of any kind, in Sanskrit: **s** is *always* to be pronounced as the *ss* in 'hiss' (so, for instance, in **tasya** 'of him'), *never* as the *s* in 'his'.

Examples for practice आशा **āśā** 'hope'; दोषः **doṣaḥ** 'fault'; रसः **rasaḥ** 'flavour'.

Voiced **h**

ह ha

As mentioned above, **h** was in classical times a voiced aspirate sound. Nowadays, however, it has lost its voicing and corresponds to an English *h*, although the other voiced aspirates (the five stops) are a fully preserved feature of most modern Indo-Aryan languages. The reason for the loss of voicing in this one case is no doubt connected with the fact that this sound, unlike the other five, is not in phonemic contrast with voiceless and other counterparts (**dh** has to be distinguished from **th** and also from **d**, and so on). The voiceless visarga appears only at the end of a syllable, exactly where **h** does not, and at any rate visarga disappeared completely from Middle Indo-Aryan onwards.

The vowels **ṛ** and **ṝ** are usually written within rather than below this consonant: **हृ hṛ**, **हॄ hṝ**.

Examples for practice **हत hata** 'killed'; **इह iha** 'here'; **बाहु bāhu** 'forearm'; **हृत hṛta** 'taken'.

Conjunct consonants

In the foregoing description of the alphabet, words in which one consonant immediately follows another have been avoided as far as possible. The only two printed in nāgarī were **अङ्गं aṅgaṃ** and **पञ्च pañca**. The use of the virāma stroke to cancel the inherent **a** of **ङ ṅa** and **ञ ña** is, however, a device contrary to the principles of the script, to be used only in the direst emergencies.[1]

[1] In the representation of the early Middle Indo-Aryan dialects for which the brāhmī script is often thought originally to have been designed, the problem of consonant clusters was not particularly acute. The phonology of the dialects limited these to doublings and combinations with class nasals, both of which might be dealt with by

The proper way to represent clusters of two or more consonants (even when the cluster is divided between two words) is to combine them into a single sign whose constituent elements are more or less easily discernible. In this way **aṅgaṃ** and **pañca** should have been represented by **अङ्गं** and **पञ्च**. The general principles for combining consonants are given below.

Those consonants from which a vertical bar can easily be separated lose this bar as the initial consonant of the group, and conjoin horizontally:

> **ग्घ = ग्घ ggha; घ्य = घ्य ghya; त्स्य = त्स्य tsya; न्म = न्म nma**

Where (*a*) the vertical bar does not exist or cannot easily be detached, or (*b*) the distinctive portion of the following consonant does not provide a convenient point of anchorage, the letters are conjoined vertically, the initial consonant being on top. In this case the letters are reduced in size to preserve symmetry:

> (*a*) **ङ्ग = ङ्ग ṅga; द्ग = द्ग dga; ट्ठ = ट्ठ ṭṭha; ह्ल = ह्ल hla; क्ल = क्ल kla**
>
> (*b*) **ञ्च = ञ्च ñca; घ्न = घ्न ghna; त्न = त्न tna; प्त = प्त pta; ष्ट = ष्ट ṣṭa**

Minor modifications

A straight line is substituted for the distinctive portion of **त ta** and the loop of **क ka** in some frequent combinations:

> **त्त = त्त tta; क्त = क्त kta**; (for **tra** and **kra** see below)

special means. The writing of Hindī, however, which has borrowed many words direct from Sanskrit as well as from foreign sources, demands an equally wide range of conjuncts—and this poses a considerable problem in the construction of Hindī typewriters, soluble only with some sacrifice of typographical elegance.

For convenience, श may be substituted for श śa in forming various combinations:

श्च = श्च śca; श्ल = श्ल śla; श्+उ = शु or शु śu

The letter य ya, although frequently the second member of a conjunct, is never written below another. Instead, an open form य or य is used:

क्य = क्य kya; ट्य = ट्य ṭya; ड्य = ड्य ḍya

(There is a similar open form for म ma: e.g. ङ्म ṅma ; द्म dma.)

Combinations with र **ra**

The forms रु **ru** and रू **rū** have been noted above. The isolate form र **ra** is never used in consonant combinations. As the initial member of a cluster, a semi-circle ᳚ is substituted and placed at the extreme top right of the syllable:

र्त = र्त **rta**; र्य = र्य **rya**; र्खीं = र्खीं **rkhīṃ**

At the middle or end of a cluster, a short diagonal ् is substituted:

प्र = प्र **pra**; त्र = त्र **tra**; क्र = क्र or क्र **kra**; श्र्य = श्र्य **śrya**

The combinations **kṣa** *and* **jña**

Two signs representing conjunct consonants cannot be resolved into constituent parts.

क्ष or क्ष **kṣa** is the equivalent of the roman *x*—e.g. लक्ष्मी **Lakṣmī**, the goddess of prosperity, occasionally transliterated as 'Laxmi'. In some parts of India क्ष **kṣa** is pronounced as **kkha** or **ccha**.

ज्ञ **jña**: the pronunciation of this varies widely. In some places, for instance, it is like **gya**, in others **dnya**. The palatal series is derived from original velar sounds (cf. **jan** 'to be born' with Greek *génos*). The point about **jñ** is that it is a palatalisation so to speak *en bloc* of an original *gn*. Thus

jñā 'to know' is connected with Latin *co*-gno-*scere* and English 'know'. Perhaps the most appropriate of the modern pronunciations to adopt is therefore **gnya**, which (by adding *y* to *gn*) does crudely represent a palatalisation.

A list of conjunct consonants is given at the end of this chapter.

Doubling of consonants

Where the same consonant is written twice, it should be held longer in pronunciation. This happens in English, but usually only between words (or at least morphemes)—cf. the *s*+*s* sound in 'less soap', the *t*+*t* in 'hat-trick' or the *n*+*n* in 'greenness'. Doubled *aspirates* are not written as such: rather, the first appears in unaspirated form. Thus, while **ग g** doubles to **ग्ग gg**, **घ gh** doubles to **ग्घ ggh**.

Miscellaneous

Other signs

Manuscripts were written continuously, and neither paragraphs nor chapters needed to begin on a fresh line. The only marks of sentence punctuation are a single bar **।** (called a **daṇḍa**) and a double bar **॥**. Their primary function is to mark respectively the halfway point and the end of a stanza of verse. In prose passages the single bar is used to mark off sentences and the double bar usually to mark off paragraphs.

A small circle above the line indicates an abbreviation. Thus **आघातः °तम् °तेन āghātaḥ -tam -tena** should be read as **āghātaḥ āghātam āghātena**. Similarly, **शकु°** stands, in context, for the name **Śakuntalā**.

The avagraha ('separation') **ऽ** is nowadays restricted to marking the disappearance of an initial short **a**. Thus **सो ऽवग्रहः so 'vagrahaḥ** 'that separation'.

Numerals

The numerical signs are very simple, since we owe our

modern zero-based system to India (by way of the Arabs). The shapes of the numerals vary with the shapes of the letters. For the nāgarī script they are:

१	२	३	४	५	६	७	८	९	०
1	**2**	**3**	**4**	**5**	**6**	**7**	**8**	**9**	**0**

१९८४ **1984** १०६६ **1066**

The figure 2 after a word (sometimes found in books printed in India) implies that the word is to be repeated:

अहो२ **aho aho** 'oh, oh!'

Names of the letters

Letters are designated either by their own sound alone or, more explicitly, with the addition of the suffix **kāra** ('making'). The inherent short **a** is added to the consonants:

ई or ईकार **ī** or **īkāra** 'long *i*'; ग or गकार **ga** or **gakāra** 'the letter *g*'.

The letter र् **r**, however, has a special name: रेफ **repha** 'tearing').

Transliteration

The letters and diacritic marks chosen to represent Sanskrit sounds in the roman alphabet are, of course, purely a matter of convention, but a convention by now so firmly established that it has not been deviated from here even to choose the one significant (but less common) variant, namely **ç** for **ś**, even though this would be less confusing than having three kinds of *s* and more immediately recognisable as a palatal letter.

This and the representation of anusvāra by **ṁ** instead of **ṃ** are probably the only two deviations still to be met with in specialist works. However, there are certain nineteenth-century devices still on occasion retained for the benefit of the general reader. They are:

ṛi, ṝī for **ऋ ṛ, ॠ ṝ**; **ch** for **च् c**, and **chh** for **छ् ch**; **sh** for **ष् ṣ** (or even for **श् ś**)

A further practice, now thoroughly discredited, whereby palatal letters are represented by italicised velars and retroflex by italicised dentals (e.g. ***k*a** for **च ca**, ***dh*a** for **ढ ḍha**), has unfortunately also to be mentioned, since it was followed in the *Sacred Books of the East* series and by Macdonell in his dictionary (though not in his grammar).

Prosody

Sanskrit verse is quantitative: it is based, that is to say, (as in Latin and Greek) on a regular arrangement of long and short syllables and not, as in English, of stressed and unstressed syllables. To distinguish long and short syllables more clearly from long and short *vowels* the former may be referred to as 'heavy' and 'light' (corresponding to the Sanskrit terms **गुरु guru** and **लघु laghu**).

A syllable is heavy if its vowel is long, or if its vowel, though short, is followed (even in another word) by two or more consonants. Thus **पश्यामि ग्रामौ paśyāmi grāmau** 'I see two villages' contains five heavy syllables (– – – – –).

A syllable is light if its vowel is short and not followed by more than one consonant. **अथ पचति atha pacati** 'next he cooks' contains five light syllables (⏑ ⏑ ⏑ ⏑ ⏑). (**थ् th** is, of course, only a single consonant.) Anusvāra and visarga are never followed by a vowel, and a syllable containing either of them is always heavy. **ततः कूपं गच्छति tataḥ kūpaṃ gacchati** 'then he goes to the well' scans ⏑ – – – – – ⏑ ⏑.

In ancient times Sanskrit was characterised by a tonic, or pitch, accent: one syllable in a word was pronounced with a higher musical pitch than the others. This is an Indo-European feature preserved also in ancient Greek, in which language parallel words usually have a corresponding accent (cf. **श्रुतस् śrutás** 'heard' with *klutós*). In Greek the accent, although retained, changed from one of musical pitch to one of stress. In Sanskrit the pitch accent, which was kept alive for some centuries after Pāṇini, finally disappeared and was replaced (as in Latin) by a regularly positioned stress accent bearing no relation at all to the original Indo-European accent. There are various graphical systems for representing the ancient accent in Vedic works, and it is only in certain methods of reciting the Vedas that any attempt is made nowadays to reproduce the pitch accent in pronunciation.

The position of the modern stress accent is much as in Latin, the principal difference being that it may go one syllable further back. Thus the stress falls on the penultimate syllable if that is heavy, failing which it falls on the antepenultimate if the latter is heavy. If both penultimate and antepenultimate are light, it falls on the fourth syllable from the end. Thus **आघातः āghā́taḥ, आघातेन āghāténa, शकुन्तला Śakúntalā, कामयते kā́mayate, गमयति gámayati.**

However, there is a tendency for all heavy syllables to receive a heavier stress than any of the light syllables. The key to reciting Sanskrit is to dwell exaggeratedly on every heavy syllable (and, in particular, to draw out long vowels to a great length) while passing lightly and rapidly over all light syllables.

List of conjunct consonants

(For reference only: most of the combinations listed are easily recognisable.)

क्क k-ka, **क्ख** k-kha, **क्च** k-ca, **क्ण** k-ṇa, **क्त k-ta**, **क्त्य** k-t-ya, **क्त्र** k-t-ra, **क्त्र्य** k-t-r-ya, **क्त्व k-t-va**, **क्न** k-na, **क्न्य** k-n-ya, **क्म** k-ma, **क्य** k-ya, **क्र** or **क्र k-ra**, **क्र्य** or **क्र्य** k-r-ya, **क्ल** k-la, **क्व** k-va,

क्व्य k-v-ya, क्ष or क्ष **k-ṣa**, क्ष्म k-ṣ-ma, क्ष्य k-ṣ-ya, क्ष्व k-ṣ-va.—ख्य kh-ya, ख्र kh-ra.—ग्य g-ya, ग्र g-ra, ग्र्य g-r-ya.—घ्न gh-na, घ्न्य gh-n-ya, घ्म gh-ma, घ्य gh-ya, घ्र gh-ra.—ङ्क ṅ-ka, ङ्क्त ṅ-k-ta, ङ्क्त्य ṅ-k-t-ya, ङ्क्य ṅ-k-ya, ङ्क्ष ṅ-k-ṣa, ङ्क्ष्व ṅ-k-ṣ-va, ङ्ख ṅ-kha, ङ्ख्य ṅ-kh-ya, ङ्ग ṅ-ga, ङ्ग्य ṅ-g-ya, ङ्घ ṅ-gha, ङ्घ्य ṅ-gh-ya, ङ्घ्र ṅ-gh-ra, ङ्ङ ṅ-ṅa, ङ्न ṅ-na, ङ्म ṅ-ma, ङ्य ṅ-ya.

च्च c-ca, च्छ c-cha, च्छ्र c-ch-ra, च्ञ c-ña, च्म c-ma, च्य c-ya.—छ्य ch-ya, छ्र ch-ra.—ज्ज j-ja, ज्झ j-jha, ज्ञ or ज्ञ **j-ña**, ज्ञ्य j-ñ-ya, ज्म j-ma, ज्य j-ya, ज्र j-ra, ज्व j-va.—ञ्च ñ-ca, ञ्च्म ñ-c-ma, ञ्च्य ñ-c-ya, ञ्छ ñ-cha, ञ्ज ñ-ja, ञ्ज्य ñ-j-ya.

ट्ट ṭ-ṭa, ट्य ṭ-ya.—ठ्य ṭh-ya, ठ्र ṭh-ra.—ड्ग ḍ-ga, ड्ग्य ḍ-g-ya, ड्घ ḍ-gha, ड्घ्र ḍ-gh-ra, ड्ढ ḍ-ḍha, ड्म ḍ-ma, ड्य ḍ-ya.—ढ्य ḍh-ya, ढ्र ḍh-ra.—ण्ट ṇ-ṭa, ण्ठ ṇ-ṭha, ण्ड ṇ-ḍa, ण्ड्य ṇ-ḍ-ya, ण्ड्र ṇ-ḍ-ra, ण्ड्र्य ṇ-ḍ-r-ya, ण्ढ ṇḍha, ण्ण or ण्ण **ṇ-ṇa**, ण्म ṇ-ma, ण्य ṇ-ya, ण्व ṇ-va.

त्क t-ka, त्क्र t-k-ra, त्त **t-ta**, त्त्य t-t-ya, त्त्र t-t-ra, त्त्व t-t-va, त्थ t-tha, त्न t-na, त्न्य t-n-ya, त्प t-pa, त्प्र t-p-ra, त्म t-ma, त्म्य t-m-ya, त्य t-ya, त्र or त्र **t-ra**, त्र्य t-r-ya, त्व t-va, त्स t-sa, त्स्न t-ṣ-na, त्स्न्य t-s-n-ya.—थ्य th-ya.—द्ग d-ga, द्ग्र d-g-ra, द्घ d-gha, द्घ्र d-gh-ra, द्द **d-da**, द्द्य d-d-ya, द्ध **d-dha**, द्ध्य d-dh-ya, द्न d-na, द्ब d-ba, द्भ **d-bha**, द्भ्य d-bh-ya, द्म d-ma, द्य d-ya, द्र d-ra, द्र्य d-r-ya, द्व d-va, द्व्य d-v-ya.—ध्न dh-na, ध्न्य dh-n-ya, ध्म dh-ma, ध्य dh-ya, ध्र dh-ra, ध्र्य dh-r-ya, ध्व dh-va.—न्त n-ta, न्त्य n-t-ya, न्त्र n-t-ra, न्द n-da, न्द्र n-d-ra, न्ध n-dha, न्ध्र n-dh-ra, न्न n-na, न्प n-pa, न्प्र n-p-ra, न्म n-ma, न्य n-ya, न्र n-ra, न्स n-sa.

प्त p-ta, प्त्य p-t-ya, प्न p-na, प्प p-pa, प्म p-ma, प्य p-ya, प्र p-ra, प्ल p-la, प्व p-va, प्स p-sa, प्स्व p-s-va,—ब्घ b-gha, ब्ज b-ja, ब्द b-da, ब्ध b-dha, ब्न b-na, ब्ब b-ba, ब्भ b-bha, ब्भ्य b-bh-ya, ब्य b-ya, ब्र b-ra, ब्व b-va.—भ्न bh-na, भ्य bh-ya, भ्र bh-ra, भ्व bh-va.—म्न m-na, म्प m-pa, म्प्र m-p-ra, म्ब m-ba, म्भ m-bha, म्म m-ma, म्य m-ya, म्र m-ra, म्ल m-la, म्व m-va.

य्य y-ya, य्व y-va.—ल्क l-ka, ल्प l-pa, ल्म l-ma, ल्य l-ya, ल्ल l-la, ल्व l-va, ल्ह l-ha.—व्न v-na, व्य v-ya, व्र v-ra, व्व v-va.

श्च ś-ca, श्च्य ś-c-ya, श्न ś-na, श्य ś-ya, श्र ś-ra, श्र्य ś-r-ya, श्ल ś-la, श्व ś-va, श्व्य ś-v-ya, श्श ś-śa.—ष्ट ṣ-ṭa, ष्ट्य ṣ-ṭ-ya, ष्ट्र ṣ-ṭ-ra, ष्ट्र्य ṣ-ṭ-r-ya, ष्ट्व ṣ-ṭ-va, ष्ठ ṣ-ṭha, ष्ण ṣ-ṇa, ष्ण्य ṣ-ṇ-ya, ष्प ṣ-pa, ष्प्र ṣ-p-ra, ष्म ṣ-ma, ष्य ṣ-ya, ष्व ṣ-va.—स्क s-ka, स्ख s-kha, स्त s-ta, स्त्य s-t-ya, स्त्र s-t-ra, स्त्व s-t-va, स्थ s-tha, स्न s-na, स्न्य s-n-ya, स्प s-pa, स्फ s-pha, स्म s-ma, स्म्य s-m-ya, स्य s-ya, स्र s-ra, स्व s-va, स्स s-sa.

ह्ण h-ṇa, ह्न h-na, ह्म h-ma, ह्य h-ya, ह्र h-ra, ह्ल h-la, ह्व h-va.

Exercise 1a

(Answers will be found at the beginning of the key in nāgarī to the English–Sanskrit exercises.)

Transcribe into the nāgarī script the following words, some of which may be familiar to you already:

mahārāja, Sītā, Rāvaṇa, maithuna, devanāgarī, himālaya, Śiva, Kālidāsa, guru, Aśoka, saṃsāra, upaniṣad, Śakuntalā, caitya, piṇḍa, manusmṛti, Viṣṇu, Kauṭilya, saṃskāra, anusvāra, śakti, Aśvaghoṣa, Vātsyāyana, vedānta, brahman, cakra, Candragupta, kāmasūtra, mantra, visargaḥ, nirvāṇa, dharmaśāstra, Bhāratavarṣa, yakṣa, vijñānavādin

Transcribe the following sentences, remembering that in the nāgarī script a word ending in a consonant (ḥ and ṃ apart) will be joined with the next word:

1 **ko niyogo ’nuṣṭhīyatām** 2 **evaṃ nv etat** 3 **anantarakaraṇīyam idānīm ājñāpayatv āryaḥ** 4 **atha kataraṃ punar ṛtuṃ samāśritya gāsyāmi** 5 **nanu prathamam evāryeṇājñaptam abhijñānaśakuntalaṃ nāmāpūrvaṃ nāṭakam abhinīyatām iti** 6 **ita itaḥ priyasakhyau**

7 sakhi Śakuntale tvatto 'pi tātakaṇvasyāśramavṛkṣakāḥ priyā iti tarkayāmi yena navamālikākusumaparipelavāpi tvam eteṣv ālavālapūraṇeṣu niyuktā

Exercise 1b

(Answers will be found at the beginning of the key in roman to the English–Sanskrit exercises.)

महायान। योग। महाभारत। रामायण। पुराण। जाति। भीम। पाणिनि। साधु। काशी। कैलास। विहार। मीमांसा। अग्नि। आत्मन्। पण्डित। क्षत्रिय। वैश्य। शूद्र। चण्डाल। ऋग्वेद। मुद्रा। कर्म। जगन्नाथ। गङ्गा। संस्कृत। प्राकृत। अर्धमागधी। सन्धि। अश्वमेध। बोधिसत्त्व। अवग्रह। इन्द्र। कृष्ण। अर्जुन। भगवद्गीता। पञ्चतन्त्र॥

सख्यनुसूये न केवलं तातस्य नियोगो ममापि सहोदरस्नेह एतेषु ।१।
उदकं लम्भिता एते ग्रीष्मकालकुसुमदायिन आश्रमवृक्षकाः ।२।
इदानीमतिक्रान्तकुसुमसमयानपि वृक्षकान्सिञ्चामः ।३।
अतिपिनद्धेनैतेन वल्कलेन प्रियंवदया दृढं पीडितास्मि ।४।
तच्छिथिलय तावदेनत ।५।
अत्र तावत्पयोधरविस्तारयितारमात्मनो यौवनारम्भमुपालभस्व ।६।
सख्यावेष वातेरितपल्लवाङ्गुलीभिः किमपि व्याहरतीव मां चूतवृक्षकः ॥७॥

Chapter 2

Roots and verb classes

Descriptions of Sanskrit verbs are based upon the verbal root (Sanskrit **धातु dhātu** 'element'). Just as in English we might analyse the forms 'bear, bearing, borne, burden' as having a common element 'b-r', so the Indian grammarians described the forms **भरति bharati, बभार babhāra, भ्रियते bhriyate, भृत bhṛta** as being derived from the verbal root **भृ bhṛ**. The verbal roots are not words in their own right but convenient grammatical fictions.

Roots are divided into ten classes according to the way in which their present tense is formed. These ten classes are analogous to the four conjugations of Latin or French, but it is essential to grasp that this classification refers solely to the method of forming the present tense and its derivatives: it has no relevance in forming, for example, the aorist or the past participle.

Verbs of classes I, IV, VI and X differ from each other only in the relationship that their present stem bears to the root; in all these classes the present stem, once formed, is thereupon conjugated according to the 'thematic paradigm' (see grammatical section, p. 290). The remaining classes are called 'athematic' because the personal endings are added without a connecting or 'thematic' vowel. Thus **भृ bhṛ**, which is exceptional in that it may be conjugated *either* in class I *or* in class III (reduplicated class), in the latter instance adds the third person singular ending ति **ti** directly to the reduplicated stem बिभर् **bibhar**: बिभर्ति **bibhar-ti** 'he bears'; but to the class I present stem भर् **bhar** thematic **a** is added before the personal ending: भरति **bhar-a-ti** 'he bears'.

Vowel gradation : guṇa and vṛddhi

The present stem भर् **bhar** is derived from the root भृ **bhṛ** by a regular process of 'vowel gradation'. The three forms भृ **bhṛ**, भर् **bhar** and भार् **bhār,** found in भृत **bhṛta** (past participle) 'borne', भरति **bharati** (present) 'he bears' and बभार **babhāra** (perfect) 'he bore', exemplify a characteristic pattern of vowel alternation in Sanskrit words. The Indian grammarians described this phenomenon by saying that अर् **ar** and आर् **ār** were two successively strengthened grades of the vowel ऋ **ṛ.** To the first of these, अर् **ar,** they gave the name गुण **guṇa** ; to the second, आर् **ār,** the name वृद्धि **vṛddhi.** The Sanskrit vowels are arranged in this analysis as follows:

basic grade	**a, ā**	**i, ī**	**u, ū**	**ṛ, ṝ**	**ḷ**
guṇa	**a**	**e**	**o**	**ar**	**al**
vṛddhi	**ā**	**ai**	**au**	**ār**	**āl**

From the point of view of the comparative philologist, the middle grade, guṇa, is the normal grade and the others result from weakening and strengthening. Failure to appreciate this landed Indian grammarians in some complications, since the regular pattern of strengthening from the basic to the guṇa grade presented above did not occur in all roots. If we compare the verbs स्रवति **sravati** 'flows', घोषति **ghoṣati** 'proclaims' and स्वपति **svapati** (or स्वपिति **svapiti**) 'sleeps' with their past participles स्रुत **sruta,** घुष्ट **ghuṣṭa** and सुप्त **supta,** we may detect the general principle that the formation of the past participle involves elimination of the element **a**–**srav/sru**, **ghoṣ/ghuṣ**, **svap/sup** (historically **e** and **o** may be taken to represent **ay** and **av**, and **y, r, l, v** to represent consonantal alternants of the vowels **i, ṛ, ḷ, u**). If, however, we take the reduced form as shown in the past participle as our starting-point (which in principle is what the Indian grammarians did), we shall on the analogy of **स्रवति sravati** and **घोषति ghoṣati** predict **sopati* instead of the correct **स्वपति svapati.** For this reason the root of verbs such as the last is formed according to the middle grade (thus root **स्वप् svap** 'sleep' as against **स्रु sru** and **घुष् ghuṣ**), and the appearance of reduced forms such as **सुप् sup** is accounted for by a special process called **संप्रसारण saṃprasāraṇa** ('vocalisation [of the semi-vowel]'). Other verbs such as **गम् gam** 'go' and **मन् man** 'think' are also quoted in what is essentially their middle grade: this is because the Indo-European vowels *m̥* and *n̥* (the sonant nasals) were replaced in Sanskrit by a short **a** (the past participles are **गत gata**, from **gm̥ta*, and **मत mata,** from **mn̥ta*), so that a reduced form of the root might be insufficiently distinctive.

The foregoing will help to explain why **a**, which is essentially a guṇa vowel, appears in the table also as a basic-grade vowel whose guṇa equivalent is identical.

Classes I, IV and VI

The present stems of these classes are formed according to the following basic principles:

Class I

The root is strengthened to the guṇa grade and is followed by the thematic vowel **a: शुच् śuc, शोचति śocati** 'he grieves'.

Roots containing **a** therefore remain unchanged: **वद् vad, वदति vadati** 'he says'.

If they immediately precede the thematic **a**, the vowels **e**, **o**, and **ai** appear as **ay**, **av** and **āy** respectively : **जि ji, जयति jayati** 'he wins'.

Roots containing a long vowel followed by a consonant, or a short vowel followed by two consonants, remain unchanged: **जीव् jīv, जीवति jīvati** 'he lives'. (*Note*: This is a general limitation upon the operation of guṇa, and it applies in other formations as well.)

Important irregular formations are **गम् gam, गच्छति gacchati** 'he goes' and **स्था sthā, तिष्ठति tiṣṭhati** 'he stands'.

Class IV

The suffix **ya** is added to the root, which usually remains unstrengthened: **नृत् nṛt, नृत्यति nṛtyati** 'he dances'.

Class VI

The root remains unstrengthened and is followed by the thematic vowel **a**. (Historically, it remains unstrengthened because the tonic accent fell not on the root, as in Class I, but on the thematic **a**.) **लिख likh, लिखति likháti** 'he writes'; **प्रछ् prach, पृच्छति pṛccháti** (by samprasāraṇa) 'he asks'.

Conjugation of the present indicative

The Sanskrit verb distinguishes, without the aid of pronouns, not only first, second and third persons but also three numbers: singular, dual and plural. Dual terminations are also found in Greek, but rarely, and applied only to things naturally paired together. In Sanskrit the use of the dual is obligatory, both in nouns and in verbs, wherever two people or things are in question. The plural is restricted in application to three or more.

The present indicative of the verb **नी nī** 'lead' is:

SINGULAR	DUAL	PLURAL
1st person		
नयामि nayāmi I lead	**नयावः nayāvaḥ** we two lead	**नयामः nayāmaḥ** we lead
2nd person		
नयसि nayasi you (*sg.*) lead	**नयथः nayathaḥ** you two lead	**नयथ nayatha** you (*pl.*) lead
3rd person		
नयति nayati he leads	**नयतः nayataḥ** the two of them lead	**नयन्ति nayanti** they lead

The order in which you learn this paradigm is a matter of taste. Traditionally in Sanskrit the third person (which is called the first) is taken as representative of the tense, and the order of recitation would be **nayati, nayataḥ, nayanti, nayasi**, etc. However, Westerners usually adopt the European order (as in Latin) **nayāmi, nayasi, nayati, nayāvaḥ**, etc.

The English distinction between simple present and continuous present does not exist in Sanskrit. **नयति nayati** means both 'he leads' and 'he is leading'. In addition, the present indicative may express an immediate intention or proposal: **पृच्छामि pṛcchāmi** 'I'll ask', **गच्छामः gacchāmaḥ** 'let's go'.

Prefixes

Verbs may undergo the addition of various prefixes, which may modify, sometimes considerably and sometimes not at all, the basic meaning:

विशति	**viśati**	he enters
प्रविशति	**praviśati**	he enters
उपविशति	**upaviśati**	he sits down

गच्छति	**gacchati**	he goes
आगच्छति	**āgacchati**	he comes
अवगच्छति	**avagacchati**	he understands

Negation is expressed by the word न **na**:

न वदति	**na vadati**	he does not say, he is not saying

Sandhi

In English a word that we spell only in one way may be pronounced differently according to its position in a sentence. Thus the definite article 'the' is pronounced with a neutral vowel (ðə) before consonants, 'the man, the hill', and with a short *i* vowel (ðĭ) before vowels, 'the owl, the end'. Moreover, in separating this word out in order to talk about it, we may use another, a lengthened vowel, and say 'the definite article ðī'. We have examples like the English non-standard 'doam be stupid'. Here the word 'don't', having lost its final *t*, changes its *n* to *m*, which is more like the following *b* (put more technically, the *alveolar* nasal *n* is replaced by the *bilabial* nasal *m* before the *bilabial* stop *b*). A different sort of example involves not a separate word but a 'morpheme', for example 'plural *s*': so, the plural of 'cat' is 'cats', but the plural of 'dog' is 'dogz', although in standard spelling of the latter the same letter, *s*, is used—the general rule is that voiceless *s* is added to voiceless consonants ('cats', 'pups') and voiced *z* to voiced consonants and vowels ('dogs', 'toes'), except that if the word itself ends in a sibilant the suffix takes the form '-iz' ('bases', 'phrases'). Similar sound changes occurred in Latin words, as the spelling of their English derivatives will indicate—compare for instance '*in*duce' and '*con*duce' with '*im*press' and '*com*press'.

The reason underlying such variations is one of euphony or ease of utterance, the fact that what is a convenient sound in one environment may not be at all convenient in another. The phenomenon is referred to (very often even in talking about languages other than Sanskrit) by the term sandhi, a Sanskrit word meaning 'juncture'. What we are concerned with at present, as in the first two examples above, is ***external*** sandhi, i.e. the changes in the appearance of complete words when they come together, or make a juncture, in a sentence. In Sanskrit these changes were particularly widespread and striking, which is why the word sandhi has become generally current among phoneticians. They were fully analysed by the ancient grammarians and are extensively reflected in the orthography. This is not necessarily a good thing. Writing 'thə' and 'thi' or 'cats' and 'dogz' in English would obscure the fact that a single word or morpheme is in question—though it would be marginally helpful to foreigners in learning to pronounce the language. Beginners in Sanskrit, being more concerned with reading and writing than with pronunciation, will find the operation of the rules of sandhi a considerable obstacle in the earliest stages of learning the language, but one that is fairly quickly surmounted because met with at every turn.

Use of the sandhi grids

The approach to the problem adopted in this book is primarily a practical one. Instead of attempting to master in one go all the phonetic principles involved in euphonic combination, you are encouraged to make use of the chart between pp. 33 and 34, where all the relevant combinations of final and initial sounds are set out in tabular form. In addition, certain preliminary remarks to aid you in using the tables are here offered.

When sandhi is made between two words, the first may end in a vowel or a consonant and the second may begin with a vowel or a consonant. Four main classes of sandhi are thus distinguished.

1 *Vowel+vowel*

When two vowels come together they coalesce, often into a single vowel. The body of the vowel grid represents the combination of the two vowels. Thus **तत्र tatra** followed by **इव iva** is written as **तत्रेव tatreva** 'as if there'. Most of the features of vowel sandhi will make sense if you remember that historically the Sanskrit diphthongs **e, o** represent **ay, av** (or **ăi, ău**) and the diphthongs **ai, au** represent **āy, āv** (or **āi, āu**). Hiatus is not permitted, in the sense that when the original vowels come together the appropriate rule of sandhi must be applied; but *secondary* hiatus is permitted, in that the resultant sandhi may contain two distinct vowels. So **वने vane+इव iva** results in **वन इव vana iva** 'as if in the forest' (by way of **vanayiva**, with elision of the **y**), and this remains and does *not* further combine into **vanèva.*

2 Vowel+consonant

The simplest of all possibilities. The words remain unchanged, with one very minor exception: if the vowel is short and the following consonant is **छ् ch**, this **ch** changes to **च्छ् cch**: so **न च्छिनत्ति na cchinatti** 'he does not cut'. If the vowel is long, the change is optional (except after the words **आ ā** and **मा mā**, when it is again obligatory): **सा छिनत्ति sā chinatti** or **सा च्छिनत्ति sā cchinatti** 'she cuts'.

3 Consonant+consonant

Here, the body of the consonant grid represents the form that the last letter of the first word assumes before the following consonant. In Sanskrit a word may end only in a vowel or in **k, ṭ, t, p, ṅ, n, m, r** or **ḥ** (on these last two, see below), which is why the grid is not even more complicated than it is. In the body of the grid a bracketed sound indicates a change in the form of the following initial: thus **तत् tat+शरीरम śarīram** becomes **तच्छरीरम tac charīram.**

4 Consonant+vowel

The possibilities of this are represented by the penultimate horizontal column in the consonant grid.

CONSONANTS

(*Bracketed letters indicate the form taken by a following initial*)

Permitted finals

k	ṭ	t	p	ṅ	n	m	(*Except* āḥ/aḥ) ḥ/r	āḥ	aḥ	*Initial letters:*
k	ṭ	t	p	ṅ	n	ṃ	ḥ	āḥ	aḥ	k/kh
g	ḍ	d	b	ṅ	n	ṃ	r	ā	o	g/gh
k	ṭ	c	p	ṅ	ṃś	ṃ	ś	āś	aś	c/ch
g	ḍ	j	b	ṅ	ñ	ṃ	r	ā	o	j/jh
k	ṭ	ṭ	p	ṅ	ṃṣ	ṃ	ṣ	āṣ	aṣ	ṭ/ṭh
g	ḍ	ḍ	b	ṅ	ṇ	ṃ	r	ā	o	ḍ/ḍh
k	ṭ	t	p	ṅ	ṃs	ṃ	s	ās	as	t/th
g	ḍ	d	b	ṅ	n	ṃ	r	ā	o	d/dh
k	ṭ	t	p	ṅ	n	ṃ	ḥ	āḥ	aḥ	p/ph
g	ḍ	d	b	ṅ	n	ṃ	r	ā	o	b/bh
ṅ	ṇ	n	m	ṅ	n	ṃ	r	ā	o	nasals (n/m)
g	ḍ	d	b	ṅ	n	ṃ	r	ā	o	y/v
g	ḍ	d	b	ṅ	n	ṃ	*zero*[1]	ā	o	r
g	ḍ	l	b	ṅ	l̐[2]	ṃ	r	ā	o	l
k	ṭ	c(ch)	p	ṅ	ñ(ś/ch)	ṃ	ḥ	āḥ	aḥ	ś
k	ṭ	t	p	ṅ	n	ṃ	ḥ	āḥ	aḥ	ṣ/s
g(gh)	ḍ(ḍh)	d(dh)	b(bh)	ṅ	n	ṃ	r	ā	o	h
g	ḍ	d	b	ṅ/ṅṅ[3]	n/nn[3]	m	r	ā	a[4]	vowels
k	ṭ	t	p	ṅ	n	m	ḥ	āḥ	aḥ	zero

[1] ḥ or **r** disappears, and if **a/i/u** precedes, this lengthens to **ā/ī/ū**.

[2] e.g. **tān+labhasva** = **ताल्लँभस्व tāl̃ labhasva.**

[3] The doubling occurs when the preceding vowel is short.

[4] Except that **aḥ+a** = **o ऽ**.

Note: Various alternative sandhis are permissible, but none has been noted, except in the case of **n+ś**.

VOWELS

(*A space is left between two elements where such a space would occur in the nāgarī script.*)

- - - - - - - - - - - - - - - - *Final vowels* - - - - - - - - - - - - - - -

ā̆	ī̆	ū̆	ṛ	e	ai	o	au	*Initial vowels:*
ā	ya	va	ra	e	ā a	o	āva	a
ā	yā	vā	rā	a ā	ā ā	a ā	āvā	ā
e	ī	vī̆	rī̆	a ī̆	ā ī̆	a ī̆	āvī̆	ī̆
o	yū̆	ū	rū̆	a ū̆	ā ū̆	a ū̆	āvū̆	ū̆
ar	yṛ	vṛ	ṝ	a ṛ	ā ṛ	a ṛ	āvṛ	ṛ
ai	ye	ve	re	a e	ā e	a e	āve	e
ai	yai	vai	rai	a ai	ā ai	a ai	āvai	ai
au	yo	vo	ro	a o	ā o	a o	āvo	o
au	yau	vau	rau	a au	ā au	a au	āvau	au

SANDHI GRIDS

5 Zero

There is one further possibility. One word instead of being followed by another may occur at the end of a phrase or sentence, i.e. 'before zero'. In this position the basic form of the word remains without change. To put the matter the other way round, the form that a word assumes by itself or at the end of a sentence has been selected as the basic form: so रमणीयं वनम् **ramaṇīyaṃ vanam** 'the forest is pleasant'. There is, unfortunately, one exception to this rule:

Sandhi of final r *or* ḥ

(If the following account seems discouragingly complicated, remember that it is only provided as background explanation; what is important at this stage is simply knowing how to use the sandhi grid.) Visarga (ḥ) is the last letter of many Sanskrit words as they appear at the end of a sentence. It may represent one of two original (Indo-European) sounds, *s* and *r*. Thus, from *s*, अश्वः **aśvaḥ** (cf. *equus*) 'horse'; अस्थाः **asthāḥ** (cf. *éstēs*) 'you stood'; गतिः **gatiḥ** (cf. *básis*) 'going'. But, from original *r*, मातः **mātaḥ** (cf. *māter*) 'O mother'; द्वाः **dvāḥ** (cf. the English cognate) 'door'; चतुः **catuḥ** (cf. *quattuor*) 'four'.

The sandhi of these words is complicated by two factors: first, by whether the visarga originates from *s* or from *r*; secondly, by the vowel that precedes the visarga. We can eliminate the first factor, and so reduce the confusion, by taking **r** as the basic letter in the comparatively few cases where **ḥ** derives from *r* and reserving **ḥ** for the cases where it represents original *s* (so **aśvaḥ, asthāḥ, gatiḥ**; but **mātar, dvār, catur**). (In practice, however, final **r** may be reserved for instances of **ar** or **ār** alone, since its sandhi when preceded by any other vowel is identical with the sandhi of final **ḥ**, and therefore a distinction in these cases could be made only after an etymological inquiry, and not always even then.)

After vowels other than **a** or **ā**, **ḥ** and **r** have the same sandhi (see grid). Broadly, **r** appears before a word beginning with a voiced sound, **s** or some other unvoiced sound before a word beginning with an unvoiced sound.

Furthermore, this is the sandhi of final **r** even after **a** and **ā** (**mātar**, **dvār**). But after **ā**, final **ḥ** is lost before voiced sounds, and words ending in **aḥ** change **aḥ** to **o** before voiced consonants. Before all vowels except short **a**, **aḥ** becomes **a**: thus अश्वः+इव **aśvaḥ+iva** becomes अश्व इव **aśva iva** 'like a horse'. In combination with an initial **a**, **aḥ** becomes **o**: thus अश्वः+अस्ति **aśvaḥ+asti** becomes अश्वोस्ति **aśvosti** 'there is a horse'. In modern printing this last sandhi is generally represented as अश्वो ऽस्ति **aśvo ऽsti**, with the avagraha (ऽ) representing the disappearance of an initial short **a**.

Here are some further examples of the operation of sandhi rules:

अपि **api**+अवगच्छसि **avagacchasi** = अप्यवगच्छसि **apy avagacchasi** do you understand?

ननु **nanu**+उपविशामः **upaviśāmaḥ** = ननूपविशामः **nanūpaviśāmaḥ** well, we are sitting down

उभौ **ubhau**+आगच्छतः **āgacchataḥ** = उभावागच्छतः **ubhāv āgacchataḥ** both are coming

कथम् **katham**+स्मरति **smarati** = कथं स्मरति **kathaṃ smarati** what, he remembers?

तत् **tat**+जयति **jayati** = तज्जयति **taj jayati** he is winning that

द्विट् **dviṭ**+हसति **hasati** = द्विड्ढसति **dviḍ ḍhasati** the enemy laughs

तान् **tān**+तु **tu** = तांस्तु **tāṃs tu** them however

नरः **naraḥ**+रक्षति **rakṣati** = नरो रक्षति **naro rakṣati** the man protects

पुनर् **punar**+रक्षति **rakṣati** = पुना रक्षति **punā rakṣati** again he protects

गायन् **gāyan**+आगच्छति **āgacchati** = गायन्नागच्छति **gāyann āgacchati** singing he comes

It will be observed in the above examples that frequently the nāgarī script cannot show where the first word ends and the second begins. Spellings such as **अप्य् अवगच्छसि apy avagacchasi** are never found, except in one or two texts intended for beginners. In transcription, on the other hand, the words can usually be separated out. But they still cannot be so where two vowels coalesce into a single vowel, and in such a case, furthermore, there may be considerable ambiguity as to the original vowels: **ā**, for instance, might represent **a+a**, **a+ā**, **ā+a** or **ā+ā**. In the system of transcription used in this book, these difficulties are overcome by the use of the signs **›** and **»**, which for convenience may be thought of as marks of elision. The former stands in the place of an original short vowel and the latter of an original long vowel. They always stand in place of the first of the two original vowels, except that **›** is used like the avagraha in the nāgarī script after **e** and **o** and also after **ā**. A circumflex over the sandhi vowel indicates that it is not the same as the original second vowel. The following table of possibilities should make things clear:

1st vowel	2nd vowel: a	ā	i	ī	u	ū	e	ai	o	au
a	› â	› ā	› ê	› ē	› ô	› ō	› aî	› ai	› aû	› au
ā	ā ›	» ā	» ê	» ē	» ô	» ō	» aî	» ai	» aû	» au
i			› î	› ī						
ī			» î	» ī						
u					› û	› ū				
ū					» û	» ū				

Instead of a circumflex, a macron is used over **e** and **o** to distinguish instances where the second original vowel was long. So **न na+इच्छति icchati = नेच्छति n› êcchati** 'he does not want', but **न na+ईक्षते īkṣate = नेक्षते n› ēkṣate** 'he does not see'.

Note that **›** always represents **a** and **»** **ā** except in the union of two like simple vowels (namely, **ĭ+ĭ**, **ŭ+ŭ**, **ṛ̆+ṛ̆**, the last being very rare).

In the early lessons, where Sanskrit is given both in nāgarī and in transliteration, the sandhis of the nāgarī text are usually resolved *completely* in the transliterated version. When this is done, the transliteration is put within brackets to show that it is an analysis and not an equivalent: e.g. **तन्नेच्छति** (**tat na icchati**) for **tan n› êcchati** 'he doesn't want that'. No account is taken, however, of a mere change of final **m** to anusvāra.

Notes on certain words

1 **च ca**. This is the Sanskrit for 'and'. It is the same word as Latin *-que* and Greek *te*, and like them it is *enclitic*, i.e. cannot stand as the first word in its sentence or clause. In fact, it always follows the word it connects: instead of 'eggs and bacon' one says 'eggs bacon **ca**'.

शोचति माद्यति च śocati mādyati ca he grieves and rejoices

When it connects a whole phrase it may (unlike *-que*) be placed at the very end of the phrase rather than after the first word:

जीवति पुत्रं पश्यति च jīvati putraṃ paśyati ca

alternatively:

जीवति पुत्रं च पश्यति jīvati putraṃ ca paśyati he is living and sees (his) son

When a whole series of items is listed **ca**, like 'and', may be used with the final item alone ('eggs, bacon, sausage tomato **ca**'). On the other hand, **ca** may be attached to the first item as well as to the subsequent item or items ('eggs **ca** bacon **ca**'). This is like the English 'both . . . and', but the usage is commoner in Vedic than in Classical Sanskrit.

2 **इव iva**. This enclitic word introduces comparisons. When

used with a verb it may be translated literally as 'as it were', and expresses the notion of 'to seem':

वदति **vadati** he is speaking
वदतीव (**vadati iva**) [he is speaking as it were:] he seems to be speaking

3 किम् **kim**, *and interrogative sentences.* Used as a pronoun, **kim** means 'what?':

किं वदति **kiṃ vadati?** what is he saying?

It may also mean 'why?':

किं शोचसि **kiṃ śocasi?** why do you grieve?

Finally, both **kim** and अपि **api** may be used at the beginning of a sentence to mark a question expecting a *yes* or *no* answer (note that, used in this sense, the word **api** is *not* enclitic):

किं तत्र गच्छति **kiṃ tatra gacchati?** is he going there? (*or* why is he going there?)

अपि जयति **api jayati?** is he winning?

Of the two particles **api** is the stronger and usually marks a definite request for information. As in English, questions may also lack any interrogative particle, context or tone of voice (**kāku**) indicating that the sentence is not a plain statement.

4 इति **iti**. Originally this word meant 'thus'. But in classical Sanskrit it is almost wholly confined to the special function of marking off a preceding word or phrase (or even paragraph) as being a quotation of some sort. It is the Sanskrit equivalent of inverted commas:

आगच्छाम इति वदन्ति (**āgacchāmaḥ iti vadanti**) 'we are coming', they say

There is no system of indirect speech in Sanskrit, and so the above might equally well be translated: 'they say that they are coming'.

The phrase isolated by **iti** need by no means consist of words actually spoken; it frequently expresses an attitude of mind, the grounds upon which something is done, and so in the right context may represent 'because', 'in order that', etc. Most frequently this '**iti** clause' stands at the beginning of its sentence:

> पुनर्वदतीति तिष्ठन्ति (**punar vadati iti tiṣṭhanti**) they stop to hear him speak further—*lit.* 'he is speaking again', *so-thinking* they halt

The uses of **iti** are discussed at greater length in Chapter 14.

Vocabulary

Verbs of class I

अवगम् ava+gam (अवगच्छति avagacchati) understand
आगम् ā+gam (आगच्छति āgacchati) come
आनी ā+nī (आनयति ānayati) bring
गम् gam (गच्छति gacchati) go
गै gai (गायति gāyati) sing
जि ji (जयति jayati) win, conquer
जीव् jīv (जीवति jīvati) live, be alive
दृश् dṛś (पश्यति paśyati[1]) see, look (at)
नी nī (नयति nayati) lead, take (with one)
भ्रम् bhram (भ्रमति bhramati) wander, be confused
वद् vad (वदति vadati) say, speak
वस् vas (वसति vasati) live (*i.e.* dwell)
शुच् śuc (शोचति śocati) grieve

[1] This form is *suppletive*, i.e. originally taken from another root, in the same way that in English 'went' is suppletive of the verb 'go'.

स्था **sthā (तिष्ठति tiṣṭhati)** stand, halt

स्मृ **smṛ (स्मरति smarati)** remember

Verbs of class IV

नृत् **nṛt (नृत्यति nṛtyati)** dance

मद् **mad (माद्यति mādyati)** rejoice

Verbs of class VI

इष् **iṣ (इच्छति icchati)** want, wish

उपविश् **upa+viś (उपविशति upaviśati)** sit down

प्रछ् **prach (पृच्छति pṛcchati)** ask

प्रविश् **pra+viś (प्रविशति praviśati)** enter, go in(to), come in(to)

लिख **likh (लिखति likhati)** write

Adverbs and particles

अत्र **atra** here; to here

अद्य **adya** today

अधुना **adhunā** now

अपि **api** also, too, even (*placed after word qualified*)

इतः **itaḥ** from here; in this direction, this way

एवम् **evam** thus, so

कथम् **katham** how?; (*also, introducing an exclamatory sentence*) 'what, . . .?'

क्व **kva** where?

तत्र **tatra** there; to there

न **na** not

पुनर् **punar** again; (*as an enclitic*) however, but

पुनरपि **punar api** yet again, again, once more

(For च **ca**, किम् **kim**, इव **iva**, इति **iti**, see text of Chapter 2.)

Exercise 2a

With the help of the sandhi grid, arrange the following sequences of separate words into continuous utterances. Two keys are provided: one in transliteration with punctuation of vowel sandhi (p. 345), the other as the sentences would appear in a normal nāgarī text (p. 356).

For those who like to know what they are writing, the words mean, in the order of sentence 1, 'stealthily; in the darkness; the master's; two horses; the villains; with knives; at last; release; from the reins; in fact'.

1 **svairam; tamasi; īśvarasya; aśvau; durjanāḥ; śastraiḥ; cirāt; muñcanti; raśmibhyaḥ; eva.** 2 **aśvau; īśvarasya; eva; svairam; śastraiḥ; raśmibhyaḥ; muñcanti; cirāt; durjanāḥ; tamasi.** 3 **svairam; eva; īśvarasya; muñcanti; aśvau; śastraiḥ; durjanāḥ; cirāt; tamasi; raśmibhyaḥ** 4 **muñcanti; eva; tamasi; aśvau; śastraiḥ; īśvarasya; cirāt; raśmibhyaḥ; durjanāḥ; svairam.** 5 **raśmibhyaḥ; tamasi; śastraiḥ; muñcanti; cirāt; eva; svairam; īśvarasya; aśvau; durjanāḥ.** 6 **śastraiḥ; tamasi; raśmibhyaḥ; svairam; durjanāḥ; īśvarasya; cirāt; aśvau; muñcanti; eva.** 7 **tamasi; durjanāḥ; raśmibhyaḥ; cirāt; īśvarasya; aśvau; svairam; muñcanti; śastraiḥ; eva.** 8 **muñcanti; durjanāḥ; eva; raśmibhyaḥ; aśvau; īśvarasya; cirāt; svairam; śastraiḥ; tamasi.**

Exercise 2b

Translate into English the following sentences. Comparison with the transliterated version (p. 314) will sometimes help to solve difficulties.

गच्छामि ।१। अत्र न प्रविशामः ।२। पुनरपि लिखति ।३। अधुना क्व वसथ ।४। एवमिच्छसि ।५। क्व पुनस्तिष्ठन्ति ।६।

कथमित आगच्छति । ७। अत्र किमानयतः । ८। पश्यामि लिखामि च । ९। भ्रमतीव । १०। नृत्यथो गायथश्च । ११। स्मरन्ति च शोचन्ति च । १२। अत्र प्रविशाव इति वदतः । १३। अधुनापि कथं नागच्छति । १४। जयामीति माद्यामि । १५। न जीवन्तीति शोचामः ॥ १६ ॥

Exercise 2c

Translate the following sentences into Sanskrit. Model word order on the Sanskrit–English sentences (adverbs are normally placed before verbs).

1 You are wandering. 2 Now we understand. 3 There too she dances. 4 The two of you live here? 5 What, are they winning? 6 Let us two sit down. 7 The two of them do not say so. 8 Are you asking yet again? 9 What shall I write here? 10 Do you not see? 11 You (*pl.*) seem to be singing. 12 They come and go. 13 Now she both lives and grieves. 14 He sees and seems to speak. 15 'What do you (*pl.*) want?' they ask. 16 We go because they are coming. 17 However we do not rejoice. 18 So also do the two of us remember—What do you remember?—That he is not coming today.

Chapter 3

Some nominal and pronominal paradigms

STEM FORM	SINGULAR *Nom.*	*Voc.*	*Acc.*	DUAL *Nom./ Voc./ Acc.*	PLURAL *Nom./Voc.*	*Acc.*
Nouns						
अश्व horse **aśva** *masc.*	अश्वः **aśvaḥ**	अश्व **aśva**	अश्वम् **aśvam**	अश्वौ **aśvau**	अश्वाः **aśvāḥ**	अश्वान् **aśvān**
फल fruit **phala** *neuter*	फलम् **phalam**	फल **phala**	फलम् **phalam**	फले **phale**	फलानि **phalāni**	
Pronouns[1]						
1st per.						
मत् अस्मत् **mat/asmat**	अहम् **aham** I	माम् **mām** me		आवाम् **āvām**	वयम् **vayam** we	अस्मान् **asmān** us
2nd per.						
त्वत् युष्मत् **tvat/yuṣmat**	त्वम् **tvam** you	त्वाम् **tvām**		युवाम् **yuvām**	यूयम् **yūyam**	युष्मान् **yuṣmān**
3rd per.						
तत् **tat** *masc.*	स सः **sa/saḥ** he	तम् **tam** him		तौ **tau**	ते **te** they	तान् **tān** them
तत् **tat** *neuter*	तत् **tat** it			ते **te**	तानि **tāni**	

[1] Though some do have productive stem forms (cf. Chapter 10), personal and demonstrative pronouns are referred to in this book by means of the nominative singular masculine: **aham, tvam, saḥ**, etc.

STEM FORM	SINGULAR *Nom.*	*Voc.*	*Acc.*	DUAL *Nom./Voc./Acc.*	PLURAL *Nom./Voc.*	*Acc.*
Interrog.						
—who? —*masc.*	कः **kaḥ** who?		कम् **kam** whom?	कौ **kau**	के **ke**	कान् **kān**
किम् what? **kim** *neuter*		किम् **kim**		के **ke**	कानि **kāni**	

(Vocative forms of the pronouns do not occur.)

The nominative and accusative cases are used to express the subject and object respectively of finite verbs.

आचार्यः शिष्यं पश्यति ācāryaḥ śiṣyaṃ paśyati teacher sees pupil

आचार्यं शिष्यः पश्यति ācāryaṃ śiṣyaḥ paśyati pupil sees teacher

There is no definite or indefinite article in Sanskrit: in one context **ācāryaḥ** is to be translated 'the teacher', in another 'a teacher'. (Where the difference of meaning is crucial, 'the' is sometimes represented by **saḥ** 'that': **चित्रमेतत् citram etat** 'this is a picture', **तदेतच्चित्रम् (tat etat citram)** 'this is the picture'.)

The accusative is also used to express the goal with verbs of motion: **नगरं गच्छति nagaraṃ gacchati** 'he goes to the city'. Verbs such as **nī** 'lead' may take this accusative in addition to that of the direct object: **नगरं त्वां नयामि nagaraṃ tvāṃ nayāmi** 'I'll take you to the city'.

The verb **vad** 'say, speak' may optionally take an accusative of the person addressed as well as an accusative of that which is said.

As was seen in Chapter 2, the finite verb forms in themselves distinguish person and number. The use of the nominative of the personal pronouns is therefore optional with finite verbs and is normally dispensed with unless at least a slight degree of emphasis is called for: **प्रविशामि praviśāmi** 'I'll go in' as opposed to **अहमपि प्रविशामि aham api praviśāmi** 'I too will go in'.

The vocative is the case of address. It is most frequently placed at the beginning of the sentence, and regularly precedes even connecting particles.

बाल किं वदसि bāla kiṃ vadasi what do you say, child?

वयस्य तत्किं शोचसि vayasya, tat kiṃ śocasi? then why, friend, do you grieve?

In a phrase such as 'the large cat' we often call 'large' an adjective and 'cat' a noun. More formally, both might be called nouns: 'large' a noun adjective and 'cat' a noun substantive. To preserve this wider sense of the word 'noun' in talking about Sanskrit is not mere pedantry, for many nouns may be used both adjectivally and substantivally, and the classification of nouns by inflexional type is independent of whether they are substantives or adjectives. In this book the terms 'noun' and 'nominal' are to be interpreted in their wider sense.

Adjectives ending in **a** inflect in the masculine like **aśvaḥ**, in the neuter like **phalaṃ**. An adjective accords in number, gender and case with the substantive it qualifies:

रमणीयानि वनानि शोभनं जलं च पश्यामि

ramaṇīyāni vanāni śobhanaṃ jalaṃ ca paśyāmi I see pleasant forests and shining water

Pronouns no less than nouns may be used both adjectivally and substantivally. Thus the pronoun **saḥ** means both 'that' and 'he/it' (i.e. 'that one'). Similarly, the interrogative pronoun may be used alone or qualifying a substantive:

तं शिष्यमिच्छन्ति taṃ śiṣyam icchanti they want that pupil

न तं पश्यामि **na taṃ paśyāmi** I don't see him
तदिच्छसि (**tat icchasi?**) do you want it/that?
को नगरं गच्छति (**kaḥ nagaram gacchati?**) who is going to the city?
कः शिष्य एवं वदति (**kaḥ śiṣyaḥ evam vadati?**) which pupil says so?

Irregularities of external sandhi

The vowels **ī**, **ū** and **e** when at the end of a *dual* inflexion (whether nominal, pronominal or verbal) are not subject to the operation of sandhi but remain unchanged before vowels:

ते फले इच्छामः **te phale icchāmaḥ** we want those two fruits

The nominative singular masculine of the pronoun **tat** has really two forms, **sa** and **saḥ** (cf. Greek *ho* with the *hós* in *ê d'hós*). **sa** is used before all consonants. **saḥ** is used in all other circumstances, namely at the end of a sentence and before vowels, but by the normal operation of sandhi it thereby becomes **sa** before all vowels except short **a**:

स गजः । स शिष्यः । स आचार्यः । सो ऽश्वः । अश्वः सः । **sa gajaḥ / sa śiṣyaḥ / sa ācāryaḥ / so ›śvaḥ / aśvaḥ saḥ**

Nominal sentences

There is an important type of sentence in Sanskrit which contains no verb. Such sentences, consisting of a juxtaposition of subject and non-verbal predicate, are a feature of many Indo-European languages. In English the type is almost lost, and when used it has a literary flavour, as in 'happy the man who. . .'. In Greek there are sentences like *sophòs ho philósophos* 'the philosopher is wise'; in a song of Edith Piaf occurs '*balayées les amours*' 'loves are swept away'. Regularly in such an English sentence the subject is *not* placed first. A twentieth-century poet, T. S. Eliot, can write 'dark the Sun and Moon, and the Almanach de Gotha', but 'the Sun and Moon dark' would hardly have been possible. This fact distinguishes such a sentence from one simply involving an ellipse of the verb 'to be': we *may* say 'John is intelligent, Peter stupid'.

In Sanskrit adjectives used predicatively agree in number, gender and case with their substantive, just as when used attributively. As a phrase, शीघ्रावश्वौ (**śīghrau aśvau**) means 'the two swift horses'; as a complete statement, it means 'the two horses are swift'.

रमणीयो बालः (**ramaṇīyaḥ bālaḥ**) the child is pleasant

The predicate may, however, be another substantive, and then agreement of number or gender is not necessary:

स्वल्पं सुखं क्रोधः **svalpaṃ sukhaṃ krodhaḥ** anger is a small pleasure

If the subject is a pronoun and the predicate a substantive, the pronoun usually reflects the number and gender of the predicate:

सूर्यः सः **sūryaḥ saḥ** that is the sun

The predicate may also be adverbial. Thus it may consist of an adverb, or of a substantive in some other case such as the locative.

एवं सर्वदा सुखानि **evaṃ sarvadā sukhāni** joys are ever thus

क्व देवदत्तः **kva Devadattaḥ?** where is Devadatta?

उद्याने देवदत्तः **udyāne Devadattaḥ** Devadatta is in the garden

Word order

Many of the relationships that English normally expresses by means of word order (subject–verb, verb–object, etc.) are expressed in Sanskrit by means of inflexions—e.g. **दुर्लभमभिलषति मनोरथः durlabhaṃ** (*object*) **abhilaṣati** (*verb*) **manorathaḥ** (*subject*) 'desire hankers-after the inaccessible'; to put these three words in some other order would make no difference to what is hankering after what. As a result, word order plays a less crucial role in Sanskrit than in English grammar, and more frequently than in English two or more different arrangements of the same words are possible without any strongly felt difference of effect. But this is not to say that if one were to shake up a sentence of even the most unpretentious Sanskrit prose and spill out the words in some random new order, that order would always have been equally acceptable to the writer. Word order is important to the rhythm and emphasis of a Sanskrit sentence. One might suggest that its role is sometimes analogous to that of stress and intonation in spoken English, but a detailed investigation of this would depend upon more adequate accounts both of Sanskrit word order and of the role of stress/intonation patterns in English than at present exist. The following generalisations (which anticipate some grammatical forms to be explained in later chapters) should be measured against sentences actually encountered, and particularly against the original sentences occurring in Chapter 6 onwards. Further remarks will be made later, for example in connection with imperatives and relative clauses.

Words that form a natural group are normally placed together. In particular, adjectives and dependent genitives are placed with (most often before) their substantives.

Small unemphatic words should not be placed last (unless they are actual enclitics forming one unit with what immediately precedes). Sentences usually end with a verb or a substantive.

The initial position is the position of greatest emphasis: **पश्यति त्वामाचार्यः paśyati tvām ācāryaḥ** 'the teacher sees

(/can see) you'; प्रलपत्येष वैधेयः (**pralapati eṣa(ḥ) vaidheyaḥ**) 'this fool is (just) babbling'. In lively discourse, and especially in nominal sentences or those whose predicate is an intransitive verb, the subject unless emphasised is enclitic; it does not occupy the initial position. It need not actually stand last. Especially if it is a pronoun, it may be inserted into the middle of a predicate of two or more words:

चित्रमेतत् **citram etat** this is a picture
तदेतच्चित्रम् (**tat etat citram**) this is the picture
विनय एष चन्द्रगुप्तस्य (**vinayaḥ eṣa(ḥ) Candraguptasya**) this is Candragupta's good breeding
द्वितीयमिदमाश्वासजननम् **dvitīyam idam āśvāsa-jananam** this is a further ground-for-optimism
बलवदत्रभवती परित्रस्ता (**balavat atrabhavatī pari-trastā** the lady is extremely frightened

Examples of emphatic subjects coming first are:

द्वयमपि प्रियं नः **dvayam api priyaṃ naḥ** both things alike are welcome to us
सौहार्दमेवं पश्यति **sauhārdam evaṃ paśyati** (it is) friendship (which) sees (things) so

There is another rhythm, found more particularly in longer sentences, which is more like the prevailing rhythm of English sentences, where a subject is first announced and then talked about. Where this happens, the subject is frequently marked either by the 'anaphoric' pronoun **saḥ** or by the addition of some particle: रामस्तावत् (**Rāmaḥ tāvat**) 'as for Rāma, he. . .', रामो ऽपि (**Rāmaḥ api**) 'and Rāma for his part'.

iva

The enclitic particle of comparison **iva** is employed much more commonly with nouns than (as in the previous chapter) with verbs. Where two substantives are compared, they will be in the same case. The word may be translated by English 'like', 'as if', etc.:

आचार्य इव शिष्यो मां पृच्छति (**ācāryaḥ iva śiṣyaḥ mām pṛcchati**) the pupil is questioning me like a teacher

आचार्यमिव मां शिष्यः पृच्छति **ācāryam iva māṃ śiṣyaḥ pṛcchati** the pupil is questioning me as if I were a teacher

When an adjective appears as the standard of comparison, the word 'as' may appear twice in English:

अहमिव शून्यमरण्यम् **aham iva śūnyam araṇyam** the forest is (as) desolate as I

An adjective may also be introduced with **iva** attached to it:

विस्मित इव पश्यति (**vismitaḥ iva paśyati**) he gazes as if astonished

Where **iva** is used with the predicate of a nominal sentence, either 'is like' or 'seems' may be appropriate:

विस्मित इव पण्डितः (**vismitaḥ iva paṇḍitaḥ**) the scholar seems astonished

जलमिव सुखम् **jalam iva sukham** happiness is like water

पण्डित इव स शिष्यः (**paṇḍitaḥ iva sa śiṣyaḥ**) that pupil seems a scholar (/is like a scholar)

Co-ordinative compounds (dvandva)

Sanskrit inherited from Indo-European a considerable facility in the formation of compound nouns, and subsequently extended the facility even further. English also forms compounds of two members fairly freely, but principally of the determinative type, particularly the dependent determinative ('hand-made', 'wife-beater', etc). In this chapter attention is confined to one class of compounds, co-ordinatives, which from the point of view of English are the most peculiar (we may find a faint echo of them in a word such as 'bitter-sweet' or the compound numerals such as 'sixty-seven').

In English we may wonder whether a phrase such as 'magazine stand' should be classified as a compound at all. In Sanskrit there is a simple criterion which is almost universally valid. All members of a compound except the last appear in their stem form. The stem form of a noun is the form lacking any case termination. **aśva, phala** and **ramaṇīya** are stem forms. Nouns are usually quoted in their stem forms in dictionaries: when quoted in this book, however, substantives in **a** usually have visarga or anusvāra added to them as an aid to remembering whether they are masculine or neuter.

To form a co-ordinative compound (called in Sanskrit द्वन्द्व **dvandva** 'couple') two or more stems are put together with a relationship between them such as would be expressed by the English word 'and': आचार्यशिष्य **ācāryaśiṣya** 'teacher and pupil'. The gender of the compound is that of its final member, and the number is that of the sum of the elements;[1] an appropriate inflexion is added:

आचार्यशिष्यावागच्छतः (**ācāryaśiṣyau āgacchataḥ**)
teacher and pupil are coming

The same notion may, of course, be expressed without the use of a compound, by means of the particle **ca**:

आचार्यश्च शिष्यश्चागच्छतः (**ācāryaḥ ca śiṣyaḥ ca āgacchataḥ**)

Stem forms are ambiguous as between singular, dual and plural. **ācāryaśiṣya** may therefore also mean 'teachers and

[1] A different type of dvandva (of restricted application) in which the termination is neuter singular has deliberately not been introduced here.

pupils', 'teacher and pupils' or 'teachers and pupil'. In all these instances the inflexions are inevitably plural (signifying three or more).

Any number of stems may be put together in a dvandva. Again, if more than two stems are involved, the final inflexion must necessarily be plural:

> अश्वगजबालनरा नृत्यन्ति (**aśva;gaja;bāla;narāḥ nṛtyanti**) horses, elephants, children and men are dancing

Because of the importance of correct analysis of compounds for the understanding of Sanskrit, a system of punctuating transliterated Sanskrit so as to make plain their grammatical structure is used throughout this book. In this system of punctuation, semicolons (as in the above example) indicate dvandva relationship between members.

Vocabulary

Substantives—masculine

अश्वः **aśvaḥ** horse
आचार्यः **ācāryaḥ** teacher
क्रोधः **krodhaḥ** anger
गजः **gajaḥ** elephant
चन्द्रः **candraḥ** moon
जनः **janaḥ** person, people
नरः **naraḥ** man
पण्डितः **paṇḍitaḥ** scholar, paṇḍit
पर्वतः **parvataḥ** mountain
बालः **bālaḥ** child, boy
ब्राह्मणः **brāhmaṇaḥ** brahmin
शिष्यः **śiṣyaḥ** pupil
सूर्यः **sūryaḥ** sun

Substantives—neuter[1]

क्षेत्रं **kṣetraṃ** field
जलं **jalaṃ** water
दुःखं **duḥkhaṃ** pain, unhappiness, sorrow

[1] *Note*: The anusvāra added to neuter **a** stems simply indicates gender: the basic form of the nominative/accusative singular ending should be thought of as **m**, which remains before vowels or zero and converts to anusvāra only before consonants.

फलं **phalaṃ** fruit, reward, advantage
भोजनं **bhojanaṃ** food
वचनं **vacanaṃ** word, speech
वनं **vanaṃ** forest
सुखं **sukhaṃ** pleasure, happiness

Adjectives

रमणीय **ramaṇīya** pleasant
विस्मित **vismita** astonished
शीघ्र **śīghra** swift, fast
शोभन **śobhana** shining, bright, beautiful
स्वल्प **svalpa** small, scant

(*Note*: अत्र **atra**, as well as meaning 'here', may be translated by 'in this (matter), on this (point)'.)

Exercise 3a

Translate into English:

आचार्यं शिष्या आनयन्ति । १ । अप्यश्वानिच्छसि । २ । अहं सूर्यचन्द्रौ पश्यामि । ३ । सुखं को नेच्छति । ४ । स्वल्पं भोजनम् । ५ । जलमश्वान्नरो नयति । ६ । कस्त्वमिति मां पृच्छतः । ७ । कं पर्वतं पण्डितो गच्छति । ८ । अत्र क्रोधो न वसतीति वनं प्रविशतः । ९ । शीघ्रं वचनं नावगच्छामः । १० । आचार्य पर्वत इव स गजः । ११ । कं पुनः पृच्छामि । १२ । किं शिष्या यूयम् । १३ । जलं नरबालाः प्रविशन्ति । १४ । रमणीयमधुना तत्फलमिति विस्मिता वदन्ति । १५ कथमत्रापि बालाः । १६ । दुःखान्यपि फलमानयन्ति । १७ । बाला अत्र किं सुखं पश्यथेति शिष्यानाचार्यो वदति ॥ १८ ॥

Exercise 3b

Translate into Sanskrit (using dvandva compounds where possible):

1 We want water and food. 2 The two of them see a swift horse. 3 Scholars, what do you want? 4 Anger conquers

you as if (you were) a child. 5 Which two teachers do you see? 6 The moon is as bright as the sun today. 7 Is he pleasant? 8 Teacher, what brahmin is coming this way? 9 What is the advantage in this? 10 Children, where is that teacher? 11 Do you (*pl.*) not remember even pleasant words? 12 We see scant advantage. 13 Are the teachers astonished? 14 The two boys see fields, mountains and forests. 15 Why do you (*pl.*) say that he does not want happiness? 16 They are taking the elephant to the field. 17 But where the food (is), you do not tell me. [*Use* **iti**.] 18 That man is speaking to the astonished people like a brahmin.

Chapter 4

The past participle

The past participle is the most important of the nominal formations from the verbal root (nominal forms of the verb being those which function not as finite verbs but as substantives or adjectives). Its sense corresponds to that of the English past participle in the latter's more adjectival use; it thus in general signifies completed action and, except in the case of necessarily intransitive verbs, passive voice. So **लिखित likhita** 'written', **स्मृत smṛta** 'remembered', **गत gata** 'gone', **मग्न magna** 'sunk', 'sunken'.

The past participle is formed by adding to the root one of three suffixes: (*a*) **-ta**, (*b*) **-ita**, (*c*) **-na**. Very few roots form their past participle in more than one of these three ways. In all cases the root remains unstrengthened (without guṇa or vṛddhi).

(*a*) **-ta**. Before this suffix, the root usually appears in its very weakest form (cf. the remarks on samprasāraṇa in Chapter 2) Thus **उप्त upta** (from **वप् vap**) 'sown' and **हत hata** (**हन् han**) 'killed'. The past participle of roots ending in **ā** or **ai** may end in **ita** or **īta** (and might therefore be mentioned under (*b*) below): **गीत gīta** (**गै gai**) 'sung', **स्थित sthita** (**स्था sthā**) 'standing' (in the sense of 'remaining standing'). Important irregular forms are **हित hita** (**धा dhā**) 'put' and **दत्त datta**

(**दा dā**) 'given'. The operation of internal sandhi often produces a considerable change of appearance: **दृष्ट dṛṣṭa** (**दृश् dṛś**) 'seen', **पृष्ट pṛṣṭa** (**प्रछ् prach**, with saṃprasāraṇa) 'asked', **लब्ध labdha** (**लभ् labh**) 'taken', **ऊढ ūḍha** (**वह् vah**, with saṃprasāraṇa and lengthening of the resulting **u**) 'carried'.

(*b*) **-ita**. Here the same suffix **-ta** is added to the root with insertion of the connecting vowel **i**. The root is not strengthened, neither in general is it reduced by saṃprasāraṇa or other processes; so **पतित patita** (**पत् pat**) 'fallen'. Among exceptional reduced forms are **उदित udita** (**वद् vad**) 'spoken' and, with long **ī**, **गृहीत gṛhīta** (**ग्रह् grah**) 'seized'.

(Class X verbs and other verbs with stems ending in **-aya** substitute **-ita** for this suffix: **कथयति kathayati** 'tells'; **कथित kathita** 'told'. Otherwise **-ita** is substituted only for the final **a** of a derivative stem: **कण्डूयति kaṇḍūyati** 'scratches'; **कण्डूयित kaṇḍūyita** 'scratched'.)

(*c*) **-na**. This suffix is taken by many roots ending in **ā/ai, ī, ū, ṝ, d** and **j**. **dn* becomes **nn** and **jn* becomes **gn**. **ṝn* generally becomes **īrṇ**, but after a labial consonant **ūrṇ**. **ā/ai** becomes sometimes **ā** and sometimes **ī**. So **भिन्न bhinna** (**भिद् bhid**) 'split', **तीर्ण tīrṇa** (**तॄ tṝ**) 'crossed', **पूर्ण pūrṇa** (**पॄ pṝ**) 'filled', **ग्लान glāna** (**ग्लै glai**) 'tired', **हीन hīna** (**हा hā**) 'left'.

No rule can predict the form that the past participle of a particular verb will take. To ascertain it you should therefore in future consult the list of verbs on pp. 298–310. But the following is a list in order of the past participles of verbs quoted in the vocabularies of Chapters 2 and 4: **अवगत avagata, आगत āgata, आनीत ānīta, गत, gata, गीत gīta, जित jita, जीवित jīvita, दृष्ट dṛṣṭa, नीत nīta, भ्रान्त bhrānta, उदित udita, उषित uṣita,** (past participle of **śuc** not found), **स्थित sthita, स्मृत smṛta, नृत्त nṛtta, मत्त matta,**

इष्ट iṣṭa, उपविष्ट upaviṣṭa, पृष्ट pṛṣṭa, प्रविष्ट praviṣṭa, लिखित likhita, कृत kṛta, त्यक्त tyakta, विस्मृत vismṛta.

The verb **कृ kṛ** 'do' forms a present stem of Class VIII, which inflects quite differently from the stems so far learnt (thus **करोति karoti** 'he does', **कुर्वन्ति kurvanti** 'they do'). Do not feel free therefore to use the *present* stem of any verb unless it is stated to belong to class I, IV, VI or X (the 'thematic' classes).

Use of the past participle

Past participles may be used in all the ways in which other adjectives are used (in fact, in the previous exercise **विस्मित vismita** 'astonished', like its English counterpart, is actually a participle).

इष्टं फलं न पश्यामि। iṣṭaṃ phalaṃ na paśyāmi I do not see the desired reward

जितो राक्षसः। (jitaḥ Rākṣasaḥ) Rākṣasa is beaten

शिष्यानुपविष्टः पृच्छति। śiṣyān upaviṣṭaḥ pṛcchati seated, he questions the pupils

In particular, the use of the enclitic particle **अपि api** 'even' with participles is noteworthy. It has a concessive force and may be translated by 'though' (with or without a finite verb):

इष्टा अपि पण्डिता नागच्छन्ति। (iṣṭāḥ api paṇḍitāḥ na āgacchanti) [even desired:] though wanted, the paṇḍits do not come: though we want the paṇḍits, they do not come

इष्टानपि पण्डितान्न पश्यामः। iṣṭān api paṇḍitān na paśyāmaḥ the paṇḍits, though wanted, we do not see: though we want the paṇḍits, we do not see them

Instrumental case

In addition to nominative, vocative and accusative, Sanskrit nouns distinguish instrumental, dative, ablative, genitive and locative cases. From now on, the paradigms in the grammatical section of the book should be consulted. However, the following are the instrumental forms of the words quoted in Chapter 3:

अश्वेन aśvena, अश्वाभ्याम् aśvābhyām, अश्वैः aśvaiḥ; फलेन phalena, फलाभ्याम् phalābhyām, फलैः phalaiḥ; मया mayā, आवाभ्याम् āvābhyām, अस्माभिः asmābhiḥ; त्वया tvayā, युवाभ्याम् yuvābhyām, युष्माभिः yuṣmābhiḥ; तेन tena, ताभ्याम् tābhyām, तैः taiḥ (*m.* and *n.*); **केन kena, काभ्याम् kābhyām, कैः kaiḥ** (*m.* and *n.*).

The instrumental case has both an instrumental and a comitative sense: it expresses both main senses of the English 'with'. It also denotes the agent in a passive construction. Among possible translations of its significance are therefore 'with', 'by means of', 'because of', 'through', 'together with', 'by'.

जलेनाश्वान्सिञ्चति। (jalena aśvān siñcati) he sprinkles the horses with water

सुखं योगेन गच्छति। sukhaṃ yogena gacchati he [goes to:] attains happiness by means of yoga

बालैरागच्छति। (bālaiḥ āgacchati) he is coming with the children

जितो राक्षसश्चाणक्येन। (jitaḥ Rākṣasaḥ Cāṇakyena) Rākṣasa is beaten by Cāṇakya

saha

The comitative sense of the instrumental is, however, usually reinforced by the addition of the preposition **सह saha** 'together with', which like most Sanskrit prepositions usually *follows* the substantive it governs:

बालैः सहागच्छति। (bālaiḥ saha āgacchati) he is coming with the children

Past passive sentences

The example given earlier, **jito Rākṣasaś Cāṇakyena** 'Rākṣasa is beaten by Cāṇakya', might with very little alteration of sense also be translated as 'Cāṇakya has beaten Rākṣasa'. But furthermore, since Sanskrit does not normally distinguish perfect from preterite, it might be translated as 'Cāṇakya beat Rākṣasa'. We thus have in Sanskrit a way of expressing past active statements in which the subject is represented by the instrumental case, the object by the nominative case and the verb by a past participle agreeing with the latter.[1]

In Sanskrit this is one among several ways of expressing past statements. Other possibilities include the use of a finite past tense (imperfect, aorist or perfect—often, in the later language, without distinction of meaning) and the use of the past active participle (see Chapter 9). In this and the immediately following exercises it is the past participle construction that is to be practised. In translating into Sanskrit you will find it convenient to recast the sentence mentally in English first:

though tired, the friends seized the very first opportunity
by the friends, though tired, the very first opportunity (was) seized

परिश्रान्तैरपि वयस्यैः प्रथम एवावसरो गृहीतः ।

(pariśrāntaiḥ api vayasyaiḥ prathamaḥ eva avasaraḥ gṛhītaḥ)

[1] This type of construction was so well favoured that it became the regular way of expressing such statements in some of the languages descended from Sanskrit. Thus the Hindi sentence रामने काम किया *Rāmne kām kiyā* 'Rām did the work' represents the Sanskrit रामेण कर्म कृतम् **Rāmeṇa karma kṛtam.** From this results the apparently curious phenomenon in Hindi that in the past tense the subject of a transitive verb takes a special suffix, and the verb agrees in number and gender with the object.

When a verb is intransitive, an impersonal passive construction might theoretically be used: thus **तेन गतम् tena gatam** 'by him (it was) gone'; 'he went'. But this is far less common than the use of such a participle in an intransitive sense, with the subject in the nominative case:

ते च वयस्यैः सह नगरं गताः। **te ca vayasyaiḥ saha nagaram gatāḥ** and they are gone/have gone/went with their friends to the city

There are, however, a number of past participles that may have both an active and a passive sense. Thus **पीत pīta**, like 'drunk' in English, can be applied both to the drink and to the drinker (though in Sanskrit there is no necessary implication of intoxication). Similarly, **प्रविष्ट praviṣṭa** 'entered' or 'having entered', **विस्मृत vismṛta** 'forgotten' or 'having forgotten'. Thus with an active construction:

रामोऽपि नगरं प्रविष्टः (Rāmaḥ api nagaram praviṣṭaḥ)

and with a passive construction:

रामेणापि नगरं प्रविष्टम् (Rāmeṇa api nagaram praviṣṭam)

the meaning of both versions being 'and Rāma entered the city'.

Omission of pronouns

It is not uncommon to find in Sanskrit sentences such as **हन्त न गतः hanta, na gataḥ** 'oh, he hasn't gone!'. Here, the pronominal subject 'he' is completely omitted and can only be inferred from the masculine singular form of the predicate **gataḥ**. This is parallel to the already mentioned omission of the personal pronouns with finite verbs (**न गच्छति na gacchati** 'he is not going' etc.) but is of more limited scope. First and second person subjects cannot normally be omitted (unless replaced by the appropriate form of the verb **as** 'be'—see Chapter 5), since they are not distinguished by any special form of the past participle.

The 'logical subject' of past passive sentences, in other words the agent expressed by the instrumental case, is also often omitted. But this omission is of a different order, since the Sanskrit sentence is grammatically complete without any expressed agent. While **jito Rākṣasaś Cāṇakyena** means 'Cāṇakya beat Rākṣasa', there is nothing lacking in the simple **jito Rākṣasaḥ** 'Rākṣasa got beaten'. Hence Sanskrit may not bother to express an agent whose presence is grammatically necessary in English: one person may ask किं दृष्टं तदुद्यानम् (**kiṃ dṛṣṭam tat udyānam?**), meaning 'have (you) seen that garden?', and another may reply दृष्टम् **dṛṣṭam**, meaning '(I) have seen it'. In the following exercises English pronouns are bracketed where they are not expressed or directly implied in the Sanskrit version.

(The term 'logical subject' points to the parallel between the nominative subject of present active sentences and the instrumental agent of past passive sentences. It is a blanket term useful in discussing sentences that attribute past or present behaviour to animate beings. But it cannot be pressed too far, for the term 'subject' is also used to cover the nominative subject of intransitive presents and nominal sentences, and the nominative of past passive sentences is itself often comparable to this latter type of 'subject'.)

eva

एव **eva** is an enclitic particle which serves to emphasise the immediately preceding word. It may thus correspond to the emphatic inflection of the voice which we represent in print, if at all, by the use of italics:

स्वल्पान्येवेच्छामः। (**svalpāni eva icchāmaḥ**) we want the *small* ones

(The degree of emphasis would often be better represented by the use of a stress mark such as ′ ('we want the smáll ones'), and such a mark is occasionally used in this book where the use of italics would be particularly distorting to the sense.)

This type of emphasis may also be represented in English by a relative clause construction (as regularly in French—'*c'est moi qui l'ai fait*', '*I* did it').

एतानेव गुणानिच्छामः। **etān eva guṇān icchāmaḥ** these are the qualities we want *or* it is these qualities we want

देवेनैवेतदिष्टम्। **(devena eva etat iṣṭam)** it was His Majesty who wanted this

eva may also be translated by a specific word such as 'really', 'actually', 'in fact', 'quite', 'very', 'just', 'only'. **अद्भुत एव (adbhutaḥ eva)** 'really extraordinary'; **बाल एवैष: (bālaḥ eva eṣaḥ)** 'he is just a child'; **स एव जन: (saḥ eva janaḥ)** 'that very person'. The use with the demonstrative **saḥ**, as in the last example, is particularly noteworthy and may be represented in English by the word 'same': **तदेव क्षेत्रम् (tat eva kṣetram)** 'that very field': 'the same field'.

eva is particularly used to mark the predicate of a nominal sentence:

एष एव स ब्राह्मण:। (eṣaḥ eva saḥ brāhmaṇaḥ) [that brahmin is *this* one] here is the brahmin

eṣaḥ

एष: eṣaḥ 'this' is a compounded form of the demonstrative pronoun **saḥ** 'that'. Its inflexion follows that of **saḥ** precisely, except that by internal sandhi the nominative singular masculine **saḥ/sa** and nominative singular feminine **sā** become **एष:/एष eṣaḥ/eṣa** and **एषा eṣā** respectively. The distribution of the forms **eṣaḥ/eṣa** is the same as that of **saḥ/sa**.

Whereas **saḥ** is an unemphatic pronoun used to qualify what is not immediately present to the speaker, **eṣaḥ** is a deictic pronoun normally referring to what is close at hand. When it qualifies an already defined substantive, it may be represented in English by 'here', 'here is/are', 'see', etc.

एष स ब्राह्मणः । (**eṣaḥ saḥ brāhmaṇaḥ**) here is the brahmin

एष रामो बालानानयति । (**eṣaḥ Rāmaḥ bālān ānayati**) see, Rāma is bringing the children *or* here is Rāma, bringing the children

The most striking example of this usage is in conjunction with a first or second person verb:

एष उद्यानं प्रविशामि । (**eṣaḥ udyānam praviśāmi**) see, I am going into the garden

vā

वा **vā** is yet another enclitic particle. It has the meaning 'or' and follows what it 'disjoins' as **ca** follows what it joins. 'Either . . . or . . .' is represented by . . . **vā** . . . **vā**.

आचार्येण वा शिष्यैर्वा गज एष आनीतः । (**ācāryeṇa vā śiṣyaiḥ vā gajaḥ eṣaḥ ānītaḥ**) either the teacher or the pupils brought this elephant here

kṛtam, *alam* and *kim*

कृतम् **kṛtam** 'done (with)' and अलम् **alam** 'enough (of)' are used with a substantive in the instrumental to express a negative exhortation, 'cease from' (the exhortation occasionally being addressed to oneself):

अलं शोकेन । (**alam śokena**) enough of sadness: do not be sad

कृतं कुतूहलेन। **(kṛtam kutūhalena)** have done with curiosity: I/you must not be curious

किम् **kim**? 'what (with)?' is used in a similar fashion:

किमुद्यानेन रमणीयेन। **kim udyānena ramaṇīyena?** what is the point of an attractive garden?

Adverbs of manner

Sanskrit adjectives do not have a termination exclusively reserved for adverbial usage. Instead, the accusative singular neuter (acting as an 'internal accusative') may do duty.

शीघ्रं चलति। **(śīghram calati)** [he moves a swift (moving):] he moves swiftly

Adverbs of manner are also frequently represented by substantives in the instrumental case. विषादेन **viṣādena** 'with dejection': 'dejectedly'. वचनैः **vacanaiḥ** 'by words': 'verbally'.

Internal sandhi

The rules of external sandhi, as covered by the sandhi grids, describe juncture phenomena between complete words within a sentence. Internal sandhi concerns the juncture of morphemes within a single word. External sandhi is the more regular and invariable because it is comparatively *ad hoc*: in principle, any Sanskrit word may find itself next to any other Sanskrit word. The rules of internal sandhi are both less invariable and, from the learner's point of view, less overwhelmingly important, because they describe a previously established set of forms, the forms which inflected words do in fact have, and which are due to other factors as well as to the operation of internal sandhi. (Similarly in English, while we may by rules of internal sandhi predict both 'cats' and 'dogz', that 'children' is the plural of 'child' is merely an historically determined fact about the language.)

The principles of internal sandhi are therefore best absorbed by observation of actual nominal and verbal formations. There are many features in common with external sandhi, but broadly speaking, instead of assimilation of the first sound to the second, the assimilation is two-way and a greater variety of combination is permitted. Instead of reducing to **k/ṭ/t/p**, stops preserve both aspiration and voicing, and the palatal series is also retained. Before vowels, semi-vowels and nasals, all these stops remain unchanged. The **t** of the past participle may assimilate the voicing and aspiration of a root final sound: so **बुध् budh** 'awake', **बुद्ध buddha** (for **budh-ta*) 'awakened'. Before vowels and **y**, the diphthongs revert to **ay/āy/av/āv**: so **ne+ati** = **nayati** (cf. Lesson 2).

Retroflexion of s and n

Included within the scope of internal sandhi are two important rules which are really about possible sequences of sound within a Sanskrit word. (Minor exceptions to both rules occur, but these are not important for the beginner.) The first rule is that **ṣ** is found instead of **s** immediately after **k**, **r** or any vowel except **a** or **ā**, provided that it is neither final nor followed by **r**. This happens even if there is an anusvāra or visarga between the preceding vowel and the **s**. The rule will appear plainer in tabular form:

k, r, **i, ī, u, ū,** **ṛ, ṝ,** **e, ai, o** *or* **au**	in spite of an intervening **ṃ** *or* **ḥ**	changes **s** to **ṣ**	unless final or followed by **r**

Thus **eṣa/eṣaḥ** in comparison with **sa/saḥ**. If the following sound is, in fact, **t**, **th** or **n**, this also becomes retroflex. Thus, in comparison with the root **sthā** 'stand', **tiṣṭhati** (for **tisthati*) 'he stands'.

The second rule is at once more important and more difficult to apply, for the reason that it is capable of operating over a much longer phonetic sequence (though only within a single word). First the rule in tabular form:

ṛ **ṝ** **r** *or* **ṣ**	in spite of any combination of velars (**k, kh, g, gh, ṅ**), labials (**p, ph, b, bh, m** and **v**) *or* **y, h, ṃ** (**ḥ** cannot occur) *or* vowels	changes **n** to **ṇ**	if followed by vowels, **m, y, v,** *or* **n** (which also becomes **ṇ**)

The point is this. The pronunciation of the retroflex sounds **ṛ, ṝ, r, ṣ** (but *not* of **ṭ, ṭh, ḍ, ḍh** or **ṇ**) is such that the tongue does not release the retroflex position even after the sound has been made. This retroflex position continues (within a single word) until there occurs either a retroflex sound of the releasing type (**ṭ, ṭh, ḍ, ḍh, ṇ**) or a sound that requires the use of the tongue in another position (**c, ch, j, jh, ñ, ś, t, th, d, dh, l, s**). But if **n**, an easily assimilable sound, occurs while the tongue is in the retroflex position, it is realised as a retroflex **ṇ** (thus causing release of the retroflex position)—unless, indeed, it is the last sound in the word or is followed by some less easily assimilable sound such as **t**, which guards the dental quality of both. Under the same circumstances **nn** becomes **ṇṇ**.

An illustration of both the above rules occurs in the past participle of **सद्** **sad** 'sit' when combined with the prefix **नि** **ni** 'down'. The past participle of **sad** is **सन्न** **sanna**. **nisanna* becomes by the first rule **niṣanna*, which in turn becomes by the second rule **निषण्ण** **niṣaṇṇa** 'seated'.

The rules do not apply between separate words or (with rare and unimportant exceptions) between the elements of a nominal compound: thus **नरनगराणि nara;nagarāṇi**, not **nara;ṇagarāṇi*. After a verbal prefix the rules do operate, but with many exceptions. Generally speaking, **n** and **s** are retroflected only if they are the first sound in the following stem (a restriction already naturally applicable to **s**), and not always even then. Thus, as quoted above, **निषण्ण niṣaṇṇa**, but as an exception **विसर्पति visarpati** (from **विसृप् vi+sṛp**) 'glides'. From **नम् nam**, **प्रणमति praṇamati** 'salutes'. But from **निन्द् nind**, either **परिणिन्दति pariṇindati** or **परिनिन्दति parinindati** 'censures'. The vocabularies will show whether or not retroflexion occurs after a prefix. As they will also show, particular lexical items do not always exhibit the expected retroflexion of **s**: e.g. **कुसुमं kusumaṃ** 'flower', not **kuṣumaṃ*. The most important sphere of application of both rules is in the addition of suffixes: e.g. **guru+su** = **गुरुषु guruṣu**, locative plural of **guru** 'heavy'. The terminations so far encountered containing an **n** liable to retroflexion are the neuter plural **-āni** and the instrumental singular **-ena**.

It is not easy at first always to remember to make **n** retroflex. If after several exercises you find this is still causing trouble, you should make a special check of each exercise to determine whether the rule has been fully applied.

Absence of external sandhi

When some pause of sense occurs within a sentence, the rules of sandhi are not necessarily observed (in prose). Thus, in particular, sandhi does not occur after interjections and is optional after initial vocatives. If you abstain from making sandhi in the latter circumstances, it is wiser to show that this is deliberate by inserting a dash or a comma.

Vocabulary

अवसरः avasaraḥ opportunity, occasion

उद्यानं udyānaṃ garden, park

कुतूहलं kutūhalaṃ curiosity, interest

गृहं gṛhaṃ house (*m. in pl.*)

जीवितं jīvitaṃ[1] life

दर्शनं darśanaṃ sight, spectacle

देवः devaḥ god; His Majesty; Your Majesty

नगरं nagaraṃ city, town

पुत्रः putraḥ son

प्रयत्नः prayatnaḥ effort, attempt

वयस्यः vayasyaḥ friend (*lit.* of same age)

विषादः viṣādaḥ despair, dejection

संदेहः saṃdehaḥ doubt

अद्भुत adbhuta extraordinary, marvellous

जीवित jīvita[1] alive

दूर dūra far off; *adv.* (**dūram**) a long way

परिश्रान्त pariśrānta[1] exhausted, tired

प्रथम prathama first, previous; *adv.* (**prathamam**) already

प्रिय priya dear, beloved

मदीय madīya my (*possessive adj.*)

कृ kṛ (VIII **करोति karoti**) do, make

त्यज् tyaj (I **त्यजति tyajati**) abandon, leave, give up

विस्मृ vi+smṛ (I **विस्मरति vismarati**) forget

अलम् alam enough; +*instr.* enough of, do not, *etc.*

एव eva in fact, actually, quite, only, (the) very

एष eṣaḥ *pron.* this

वा vā or

सह saha+*instr.* (together) with

हे he (*before vocatives*) O

[1] In origin a past participle.

Exercise 4a

Translate into English:

पुत्रैः सह गृहं त्यजति ।१। एतदुद्यानम्—प्रविशामः ।२। आचार्येण च शिष्यैश्चाद्भुतः प्रयत्नः कृतः ।३। प्रियो मदीयो वयस्य इति जीवितमेतेन त्यक्तम् ।४। क एष गृहमागच्छति ।५। रमणीयेन दर्शनेन किं न माद्यसि ।६। दृष्टमवगतं च ।७। अत्रैते नराः किमिच्छन्तीति कुतूहलेन गृहं प्रविशति ।८। दूरमेव नगरं वयं च परिश्रान्ता भ्रमामः ।९। इच्छथैवैतन्न वा ।१०। कृतं वचनैर्गतोऽवसर इति विषादेन वदतः ।११। पुत्राः स एवैषोऽवसरः ।१२। एते वयं नगरमागताः । १३। विस्मृतो वयस्याभ्यां प्रथमो विषादः ।१४। हे पण्डित त्वमश्वं क्व नयसीति पृष्टोऽपि वचनं न वदति ।१५। किं प्रयत्नेन—नैव त्वां पश्यति देवः ॥१६॥

Exercise 4b

Translate into Sanskrit:

1 Your Majesty is tired: let us sit down here. 2 The people did not forget these words. 3 This is quite beautiful. 4 He remembers (his) son although he has gone to the forest. [*Translate for both meanings of the second* 'he'.] 5 We came only today. 6 Your Majesty, these two children have even now not left the garden. 7 Here he stands with (his) friends. 8 What is extraordinary in this? I have *already* seen this man. 9 See, His Majesty Candragupta has actually arrived. 10 We have seen the garden with interest. 11 (He) has gone either to the forest or to the park. 12 Friends, we have been brought a long way by this horse. 13 An end of doubt: here come the two pupils alive. 14 Even today it is with pleasure that we remember that extraordinary sight. 15 Despair has conquered them. 16 Although astonished by this sight, they are not giving up the attempt.

Chapter 5

PARADIGMS: m. and n. of **kānta, aham, tvam, saḥ, eṣaḥ** and **ayam**; present indicative of **as** 'be'

Sanskrit grammarians discussed the cases of the noun in terms of inflexional morphemes modifying the nominal stem. In addition to the vocative (**saṃbuddhi**, not regarded as on a par with the other cases), those so far introduced have been the nominative (**prathamā** 'first (inflexion)'), the accusative (**dvitīyā** 'second') and the instrumental (**tṛtīyā** 'third'). The order of the cases in Sanskrit was principally determined by the wish to group like endings together. The following is a brief sketch (by no means a full account) of the chief uses of the remaining cases.

Dative (*caturthī* 'fourth'): 'to, for'

Of all the cases the dative has the smallest scope. In Middle Indo-Aryan dialects it was lost, merged into the genitive. Even in Sanskrit itself the tendency of the genitive to usurp the traditional functions of the dative is very noticeable. The dative may be used to denote the indirect object after verbs of giving, telling, etc.

> दत्तं मया ब्राह्मणेभ्यो द्रविणम्। (**dattam mayā brāhmaṇebhyaḥ draviṇam**) I have given the brahmins wealth

But in such a sentence the genitive **brāhmaṇānām** may be substituted for the dative.

However, the dative in Classical Sanskrit does have one function not shared by any other case, that of denoting purpose or result. The best translation in English is often by means of an infinitive:

लण्ड्रं गच्छामि नृपस्य दर्शनाय। **Laṇḍraṃ gacchāmi nṛpasya darśanāya** I'm going to London [for the seeing of:] to see the king

अङ्गानां भङ्गायारूढो बालैः प्राकारः। **aṅgānām bhaṅgāya ārūḍhaḥ bālaiḥ prākāraḥ** the children climbed the wall [for the breaking of:] only to break their limbs

Especially noteworthy is the use of such a dative as a predicate in itself:

सर्वमतिमात्रं दोषाय। **sarvam atimātraṃ doṣāya** all (that is) excessive [is for a fault:] becomes reprehensible

Ablative (*pañcamī* 'fifth'): 'from'

The ablative expresses the relationship 'from':

नगरात्क्षेत्राणि गच्छति। **nagarāt kṣetrāṇi gacchati** he goes from the city to the fields

When a causal relationship is implied, translations such as 'because of' may be used: क्रोधात् **krodhāt** 'from anger', 'out of anger', 'because of anger', 'through anger'.

The ablative of comparison will be mentioned later.

Genitive (*ṣaṣṭhī* 'sixth'): 'of, 's/s' '

The genitive is the case with the widest range of uses. It most often qualifies another substantive, and has a possessive sense of some kind:

नृपस्य क्रोधं नावगच्छामः। (**nṛpasya krodham na avagacchāmaḥ**) we do not understand the king's anger/the anger of the king

Where the substantive embodies a verbal notion, the relationship may be either subjective or objective, just as the word 'its' in English is subjective in the phrase 'its consumption of electricity' and objective in 'its consumption by the community'. **nṛpasya** in the preceding example is subjective (the king is angry); in नृपस्य दर्शनम् **nṛpasya darśanam** when this means 'sight of the king' it is objective (I see the king).

The use of the genitive as an alternative to the dative after verbs of giving, telling, etc. has been mentioned. Furthermore, it is the genitive and *not* the dative which should be used in relation to adjectives to express 'point of view', conveyed in English by 'to' or 'for'.

मित्राणामेव प्रियमेतद्दर्शनम् । (**mitrāṇām eva priyam etat darśanam**) to friends, this is a welcome sight

तत्स्थाने ऽस्य वृषलो देवश्चन्द्रगुप्तः। (**tat sthāne asya 'Vṛṣalaḥ' devaḥ Candraguptaḥ**) then appropriately is His Majesty Candragupta (just) 'Vṛṣala' to him

श्रुतम् — न पुनः पर्याप्तं हृदयस्य। (**śrutam — na punaḥ paryāptam hṛdayasya**) (I) have heard, yet (it is) not sufficient for (my) heart

Similarly, past participles formed from roots meaning 'to know', 'to desire' or 'to honour', such as विदित **vidita** 'known', take a genitive (instead of an instrumental of the agent) when used adjectivally:

अपि विदितमेतद्देवस्य। (**api viditam etat devasya?**) is this known to Your Majesty?

But:

अपि विदितो देवेन तेषामभिप्रायः । **(api viditaḥ devena teṣām abhiprāyaḥ?)** did Your Majesty (get to) know their intentions?

The possessive adjective **मदीय madīya** 'my, mine' was given in the previous chapter. There are various others—e.g. **मामक māmaka** (same meaning), **युष्मदीय yuṣmadīya** 'belonging to (all of) you', etc. More commonly, however, the genitive of the appropriate pronoun is used instead of the possessive adjective:

मम गृहम mama gṛham [the house of me:] my house
मम क्षेत्राणि mama kṣetrāṇi my fields
तव पुत्राः tava putrāḥ your sons (*addressing one person*)
युष्माकं पुत्राः (yuṣmākam putrāḥ) your sons (*addressing several persons*)
कस्य पुष्पाणि kasya puṣpāṇi? whose flowers?
तस्य हस्तौ tasya hastau his hands

The unemphatic forms of the first and second person pronouns (**मे me, नौ nau**, etc.) may also be used. Like the ordinary forms, they may either precede or follow their substantive, but as enclitics they may not stand first in the sentence.

इमे नो गृहाः । (ime naḥ gṛhāḥ) here is our house (*the plural of* **gṛha** *often has a singular sense*)

Generally speaking, neither possessive adjectives nor the genitives of pronouns may be used to refer to the subject or 'logical subject' of a sentence. If necessary, the reflexive adjective **स्व sva** 'my own, your own, his own, their own, *etc.*' or the genitive singular of the reflexive word **आत्मन् ātman** 'self' may be employed, but it is usually omitted unless exceptional emphasis is intended. [**sva** is often compounded with its substantive, while as a separate word **ātmanaḥ** is more normal.]

पुत्रान्रक्षति **putrān rakṣati** he protects his sons

तस्य पुत्रान्रक्षति **tasya putrān rakṣati** he protects his [*i.e.* the other's] sons

स्वानेव पुत्रान्रक्षसि **svān eva putrān rakṣasi** you protect your *own* sons

Because the omission of the reflexive possessive is standard, it is from now on *not* normally indicated in the exercises by any bracketing of the English word: 'he protects his sons', not 'he protects (his) sons'.

Locative (*saptamī* 'seventh'): 'at, in, on, among; into, onto'

The locative expresses such notions as station or circumstance:

चरति वने किं चित् **carati vane kiṃ cit** something is moving in the forest

फलके बाला उपविष्टाः **(phalake bālāḥ upaviṣṭāḥ)** the children are seated on the table

मित्राणां दर्शने न किं चिद्वदति **(mitrāṇām darśane na kiṃ cit vadati)** [at the sight of:] on seeing his friends he says nothing

It also expresses the end result of motion:

जले बालं क्षिपति **jale bālaṃ kṣipati** he throws the child into the water

It can bear the sense 'in the matter of':

अपापो ऽहं पर्वतेश्वरे **(apāpaḥ aham Parvateśvare)** I am guiltless [in the matter of:] towards Parvateśvara

In particular, it is used to denote the object of feelings (English 'towards', 'for'):

अवगच्छामि ते तस्मिन्सौहार्दम्। **avagacchāmi te tasmin sauhārdam** I understand your fondness for him

It thus occurs after a verb such as स्निह् **snih** 'feel affection (for)':

> किं नु खलु बाले ऽस्मिन्नौरस इव पुत्रे स्निह्यति मे हृदयम्।
> **(kim nu khalu bāle asmin aurase iva putre snihyati me hṛdayam?)** now why indeed does my heart feel affection for this child as for a son of my own loins?

The use of the locative in expressing circumstance leads to the 'locative absolute' construction (Lesson 11).

Expressions of time

Many of the cases are used in expressing statements of time. The following is an indication of the main usages:

(*a*) Accusative, 'time *during* which':

> त्रीन्दिवसान्भ्रमन्ति। **trīn divasān bhramanti** they wander for three days

(*b*) Instrumental, 'time *within* which':

> ते ऽपि त्रिभिर्दिवसैर्नगरं प्राप्ताः। **(te api tribhiḥ divasaiḥ nagaram prāptāḥ)** and they reached the city in three days

(*c*) Ablative (sometimes genitive), 'time *after* which':

> ते ऽपि त्रिभ्यो दिवसेभ्यः प्राप्ताः। **(te api tribhyaḥ divasebhyaḥ prāptāḥ)** and they arrived after three days
> चिरस्य कालस्य प्राप्तो ऽसि। **(cirasya kālasya prāptaḥ asi** you have arrived after a long time/at long last

(*d*) Locative, 'time *at* which':

> ते ऽपि तृतीये दिवसे नगरं प्राप्ताः। **(te api tṛtīye divase**

nagaram prāptāḥ) and they reached the city on the third day

ayam

The irregularity of the declension of the pronoun **ayam** is partly due to the fact that it derives from two stems: one **a** (cf. the adverbs **अत्र atra** and **अतः ataḥ**), the other **i** (cf. **इह iha** and **इतः itaḥ**).

Two pronouns are conventionally translated by the English 'that': **सः saḥ** and **असौ asau** (Lesson 13); and two by the English 'this': **अयम् ayam** and **एषः eṣaḥ**. Traditionally, the distinctions are that **saḥ** is used of what is not present to the speaker, **asau** of what is remote from him (though possibly visible), **ayam** of what is present and **eṣaḥ** of what is near at hand. Thus **asau** is the 'stronger' of the two which mean 'that', **eṣaḥ** the 'stronger' of the two which mean 'this'.

It is evident that even if these distinctions were adhered to there would be considerable overlap within each pair (and also that **ayam** in particular might represent 'that' as well as 'this'), In practice, the distinctions are somewhat blurred and, at any rate, not always easy to apply. A different distinction is that, used in reference to discourse, **eṣaḥ** means 'what precedes', **ayam** 'what follows'.

श्रुत्वैतदिदं वदति। (**śrutvā etat idam vadati**) hearing this, he says the following

This rule also is not universally observed, but it is true enough to be worth remembering.

In the oblique cases other than the accusative (and in practice to some extent in all cases), **ayam** may be used simply as an unemphatic third person pronoun. In this sense it is usually enclitic.

क्रोधमेषां नावगच्छामि। (**krodham eṣām na avagacchāmi**) I don't understand their anger

Pronominal adjectives

Certain common adjectives in **a** follow wholly or in part the pronominal rather than the nominal declension. **anya** 'other' does so wholly: its neuter singular nominative/accusative is **अन्यत् anyat** (cf. the *d* of Latin *aliud*). **सर्व sarva** 'all', **एक eka** 'one' and **स्व sva** 'own' are also wholly pronominal, except that their neuter singular nominative/accusative is **सर्वम् sarvam, एकम् ekam, स्वम् svam.**

सर्वेषां नृपाणामयं मार्गः। sarveṣām nṛpāṇām ayaṃ mārgaḥ this is the path for all kings .
एकस्मिन्नेव देशे सर्वे बालाः। (ekasmin eva deśe sarve bālāḥ) the children are all in a single place

In conjunction with an interrogative, **अन्य anya** may be translated by 'else':

अन्यः क आगच्छति। (anyaḥ kaḥ āgacchati?) who else is coming?

kaś cit and *ko ›pi*

The addition of an indefinite particle, usually either **चित् cit** or **अपि api,** turns the interrogative pronoun ('who?', 'what?') into an indefinite pronoun ('someone', 'anyone', 'some', 'any', 'a little', 'a few'). The addition of **न na** ('not anyone' etc.) gives the Sanskrit for 'no one', 'nothing', etc.

केन जलं पीतम्। kena jalaṃ pītam? who has drunk the water?
केनापि जलं पीतम्/केनचिज्जलं पीतम्। (kena api jalam pītam/kena cit jalam pītam) someone/somebody has drunk the water
केनापि जलं न पीतम्। (kena api jalam na pītam) no one/nobody has drunk the water

उद्याने न कश्चिच्चरति। **(udyāne na kaḥ cit carati)** no one is walking in the park

तव किंचिज्जलं भवति। न किंचिदेव। **(tava kim cit jalam bhavati?—na kim cit eva)** have you any/a little water?—none at all

Interrogative adverbs are used in the same way:

कलहंसकं न क्वचित्पश्यामि। **Kalahaṃsakaṃ na kva cit paśyāmi** I don't see Kalahaṃsaka anywhere

कृतः कथमपि घटः। **kṛtaḥ kathamapi ghaṭaḥ** somehow (he) made the pot

कथमपि kathamapi (or **कथंचित kathaṃcit**) has by extension the sense 'scarcely', 'with difficulty':

चन्द्रं कथमपि पश्यामि। **candram kathamapi paśyāmi** I can only just see the moon

as 'be'

The verb **as** 'be', a very common irregular verb, is an athematic of class II (Lesson 12). The six first and second person forms of the present indicative provide an alternative to (and are, in fact, much more frequent than) the use of pronominal subjects in nominal and past participial sentences. So **अतिकातरो ऽसि** **(atikātaraḥ asi)** as well as **अतिकातरस्त्वम्** **(atikātaraḥ tvam)** 'you are over-timid', and **गतो ऽस्मि** **(gataḥ asmi)** as well as **गतो ऽहम्** **(gataḥ aham)** 'I went'. Similarly, **धन्यौ स्वः dhanyau svaḥ** 'the two of us are lucky', **प्राप्तौ स्थः prāptau sthaḥ** 'the two of you have arrived', etc. These forms are normally enclitic.

The third person forms (**अस्ति asti**, **स्तः staḥ**, **सन्ति santi**), on the other hand, are seldom if ever used as a copula but have existential force ('there is', 'there are') and most frequently stand as the first word.

अस्ति पर्वतेषु नगरम्। **asti parvateṣu nagaram** there is in the mountains a city

अतः परमपि प्रियमस्ति। **ataḥ param api priyam asti?** is there (any) blessing beyond this?

अस्त्येतत्। **(asti etat)** this *is* —*i.e.* this is true, that is so

bhū 'be'

This verb, a regular verb of class I, may mean in its non-copulative uses either 'exist' (like **as**) or 'come into existence', 'arise':

भवन्ति चात्र श्लोकाः। **(bhavanti ca atra ślokāḥ)** and on this point there are stanzas

क्रोधाद्भवति संमोहः। **(krodhāt bhavati saṃmohaḥ)** from anger arises delusion

As a copulative verb it provides a less frequent alternative to a nominal sentence, more particularly in general statements.

दर्शनमेवास्य रमणीयं भवति परिश्रान्तानाम्। **(darśanam eva asya ramaṇīyam bhavati pariśrāntānām)** the very sight of it is delightful to the exhausted

'To have'

The notion of the English 'have' in the sense of 'possess' is generally expressed by means of the genitive case: i.e. instead of 'John has a hat', one says 'of John there is a hat'. However, even in this existential sense the verb **as** or **bhū** is sometimes omitted.

तव पुत्राणां धनं न भवति। **tava putrāṇām dhanaṃ na bhavati** your sons have no money

अस्ति चास्माकमन्यदपि मित्रम्। **(asti ca asmākam anyat api mitram)** and we have another friend too

श्रुतम् । असंतोषस्तु हृदयस्य । (**śrutam—asaṃtoṣaḥ tu hṛdayasya**) (I) have heard, but [(there is) dissatisfaction for my **heart**:] my heart has/feels no satisfaction (*Compare the use of* **vartate** [Lesson 9].)

'To feel'

As the above example suggests, there are various ways in which the notion 'to feel (an emotion *etc.*)' might be represented in Sanskrit. It may, however, be worth pointing out that the equivalent of **इव iva** in first person statements is often 'feel' ('seem' being inappropriate):

अशरण इवास्मि । (**aśaraṇaḥ iva asmi**) I feel helpless

The absolutive

Of an ancient verbal action noun in **-tu** (cf. the Latin supine) two cases survive in Classical Sanskrit: the accusative, supplying the Sanskrit infinitive (**नेतुम् netum** 'to lead', with strengthening of the root), and the instrumental, supplying the absolutive (or 'gerund', or 'indeclinable participle')—**नीत्वा nītvā** 'after leading, by leading', with weak grade of the root.

The absolutive in **-tvā** is not difficult to form. With very few exceptions it may be obtained by substituting **tvā** for the **-ta** or **-na** of the past participle (with internal sandhi as appropriate). So **उक्त्वा uktvā** 'after saying', **दृष्ट्वा dṛṣṭvā** 'after seeing', **लब्ध्वा labdhvā** 'after taking', **पतित्वा patitvā** 'after falling', **तीर्त्वा tīrtvā** 'after crossing'.

The absolutive in **-tvā** may *not* be used when a verb is compounded with a prefix or prefixes. In such a case the suffix **-ya** (probably itself the instrumental of an old action noun in **-i**) is added to the verb, which usually appears in its weaker form. In internal sandhi, fortunately, **y** is without effect on the preceding sound. Roots ending in a short vowel add **-tya** instead of **-ya**, and those roots ending in **-an/-am** which shorten to **-a** in the past participle may *optionally* do so (again shortening to **-a**). So **संदृश्य saṃdṛśya** 'after seeing', **प्रत्युच्य pratyucya** 'after replying', **विजित्य vijitya** 'after conquering', **आगम्य āgamya** or **आगत्य āgatya** 'after coming'.

(A minor exception to both the above formations is provided by derivative verbs in **-ayati**. They form their past participle in **-ita** but their simple absolutive in **-ayitvā**. In the compounded absolutive, they substitute **-ya** for **-ayati** in general but **-ayya** if the vowel of the stem is unstrengthened. So **गमयित्वा gamayitvā** 'after causing to go', **आगमय्य āgamayya** 'after causing to come', **प्रवेश्य praveśya** 'after causing to enter'. See pp. 102–5.)

The sense of the absolutive is generally that of action preceding the action of the main verb. Its closest equivalent is often therefore in primer English the perfect participle ('having led') and in ordinary English the present participle ('leading').

गृहं त्यक्त्वा वने परिभ्रमति gṛham tyaktvā vane paribhramati leaving his home, he wanders about in the forest

This might alternatively be translated as 'he leaves his home and wanders. . .'. In English both versions are possible. In Sanskrit a sequence of events is almost invariably represented by the use of absolutives rather than by clauses connected with **च ca**.

उद्यानं प्रविश्य कुमारं दृष्ट्वा प्रतिच्छन्दकमाच्छादयति udyānaṃ praviśya kumāram dṛṣṭvā praticchandakam ācchādayati he enters the garden, sees the young man, and hides the picture

पुत्रमाहूय पृच्छामि putram āhūya pṛcchāmi I'll call my son and ask him

The subject of the action expressed by the absolutive is not necessarily the grammatical subject of the sentence. Rather it is the logical subject, which in passive sentences will be in the instrumental case and in some other sentences in yet some other case:

तेनापि श्लोकमवगम्य प्रतिवचनमुक्तम् (**tena api ślokam avagamya prativacanam uktam**) and he understood the stanza and spoke a reply

नृपाणां तु कुमारं दृष्ट्वात्यन्तं कुतूहलं भवति (**nṛpāṇām tu kumāram dṛṣṭvā atyantam kutūhalam bhavati**) [but of the kings, having seen the young man, an intense curiosity arises:] but the kings, on seeing the young man, feel an intense curiosity

Sometimes the logical subject itself remains unexpressed:

कथमचिरेणैव निर्माय लिखितः श्लोकः (**katham acireṇa eva nirmāya likhitaḥ ślokaḥ**) [what, after composing within a very short while, a stanza has been written:] why, he has (/you/they have) rapidly composed and written out a stanza

हन्त भोः शकुन्तलां विसृज्य लब्धमिदानीं स्वास्थ्यम्। **hanta bhoḥ—Śakuntalāṃ visṛjya labdham idānīṃ svāsthyam** Oh, in bidding farewell to Śakuntalā (I) have now found ease

khalu

खलु **khalu**, like एव **eva**, is an enclitic particle of emphasis. But whereas **eva** is an affirmative particle stressing what is new, **khalu** is a confirmatory particle tending to stress what is already implicitly known. In consequence, whereas **eva** often marks out a predicate, **khalu** may equally well qualify the subject (or perhaps spread its emphasis more evenly over the whole statement). The subject is then usually placed first in the sentence. For convenience, **khalu** is represented in the exercises by 'indeed', 'assuredly', 'of course', 'after all', 'certainly'.

दारुणः खल्वसि । (**dāruṇaḥ khalu asi**) you are indeed cruel

कापालिकः खल्वेषः । (**kāpālikaḥ khalu eṣaḥ**) this man is assuredly a monster

अनुत्सेकः खलु विक्रमालंकारः । (**anutsekaḥ khalu vikrama-alaṃkāraḥ**) modesty, after all, is valour's ornament

External sandhi

Now that a wider range of forms is occurring in the exercises, attention is drawn to two disconcerting rules of external sandhi: (*a*) final **n** preceded by a short vowel is doubled when the next word begins with a vowel (thus when **n** closes a word, the final syllable can never be light) and (*b*) **t** combines with a following **ś** to make **cch**.

Vocabulary

आवेगः **āvegaḥ** alarm
उपायः **upāyaḥ** method, means, way
कुमारः **kumāraḥ** (well-born) young-man; prince; Your/His Highness
क्षणः **kṣaṇaḥ** instant of time, second, moment
देशः **deśaḥ** place; country
पादः **pādaḥ** foot
पुष्पं **puṣpaṃ** flower
पुस्तकं **pustakaṃ** book
प्रतिच्छन्दकं **praticchandakaṃ** portrait, picture
प्रतिवचनं **prativacanaṃ** answer, reply
मार्गः **mārgaḥ** road
मित्रं **mitraṃ** (*N.B. gender*) friend
मुहूर्त **muhūrta** *m./n.* short while, 'minute'
हृदयं **hṛdayaṃ** heart, mind

(**Kalahaṃsaka, Mādhava** and **Rāma** are proper names.)

अयम् **ayam** (*pron.*) this
अन्ध **andha** blind
अन्य **anya** (*pron.*) other
एक **eka** (*pron.*) one
कश्चित् कोऽपि **kaś cit/ko ›pi** (*see text of chapter*)

काण **kāṇa** one-eyed
पाप **pāpa** evil, bad; *m.* villain
सर्व **sarva** (*pron.*) all, every; *n. sg.* everything; *m. sg.* everyone

अभिलिख् **abhi+likh** (VI **अभिलिखति** **abhilikhati**) draw (picture)
अस् **as** (II **अस्ति** **asti**) be, exist
ग्रह् **grah** (IX **गृह्णाति** **gṛhṇāti**) seize, take
पत् **pat** (I **पतति** **patati**) fall
प्रभू **pra+bhū** (I **प्रभवति** **prabhavati**) arise; prevail, have power
भू **bhū** (I **भवति** **bhavati**) become, be
श्रु **śru** (V **शृणोति** **śṛṇoti**) hear, listen

अपि **api** and (*sentence connective, placed after subject*)
इदानीम् **idānīm** now
इह **iha** here; in this world

खलु **khalu** indeed *etc.*
तु **tu** (*enclitic*) but, however
हा **hā** ah! oh!

Exercise 5a

Translate into English:

इमौ स्वः ।१। प्रतिवचनं मे श्रुत्वा किमन्यदिच्छन्ति ।२। नास्त्येव ते पुस्तकम् ।३। वयस्य हृदयमिवासि मम ।४। अस्मिन्नुद्याने मुहूर्तमुपविशावः ।५। क्षेत्रेषु सर्वे भ्रमन्ति ।६। देव अन्यस्मान्नगराद्ब्राह्मणः कश्चिदागतः ।७। कमुपायं पश्यसि मम पुत्राणां दर्शनाय ।८। क्रोधमस्य दृष्ट्वावेग इव नो हृदये ।९। अयं कुमारस्तिष्ठति ।१०। कथं क्षणमेवोपविश्य दृष्टे मया पुनरपि मित्रे

। ११। अन्यः को ऽपि मार्गो न भवति । १२। दुःखायैव मित्रा-
णामिदानीं रामस्य दर्शनम् । १३। अन्येभ्यो ऽपि देवैर्नैतत्कृतम्
। १४। गृहं प्रविश्य क्व क्वेदानीं स पाप इति सर्वान्पृच्छति । १५।
अन्धानां देशे काण एव प्रभवति । १६। कलहंसक केनैतन्माधवस्य
प्रतिच्छन्दकमभिलिखितम् ॥ १७ ॥

Exercise 5b

Translate into Sanskrit:

1 You are blind indeed. 2 From this house he was led to the woods. 3 And they went to the park and seized the villains. 4 The anger of these two is extraordinary. 5 You have been seen, (my) sons. 6 But we have friends in Candanadāsa's house. 7 I ask because I'm tired. 8 We have seen this on all the country's roads. 9 Your Majesty, I am that same prince. 10 He falls at the blind (man)'s feet. 11 By some means I saw (them) all. 12 This reply of the prince (will make) for anger. 13 But hearing this they sit in the road. 14 Kalahaṃsaka, we have no interest in books. 15 In just one garden there are a few flowers. 16 Even after seeing everything Your Highness says nothing. 17 What, have you *doubt* about it [**atra**]? 18 Oh Makaranda, oh Kalahaṃsaka, your friend has gone. 19 But the prince stayed in another place and heard the villain's whole reply. 20 What advantage does this (man) see in anger?

Chapter 6

PARADIGMS: f. of **kānta**; f. of **saḥ, ayam** and other pronouns

Feminine gender

In addition to the masculine and neuter genders so far presented, Sanskrit has a feminine gender. Feminine substantives in **-ā** decline like the feminine of the adjective **kānta**. There are no masculine or neuter substantives that end in this **-ā**, and no feminine substantives in **-a**. The majority of adjectives (among them all past participles) that end in **-a** form their feminine in **-ā**. A substantial minority, however, form their feminine in **-ī** and inflect like **nadī** 'river' (among this group are most adjectives formed by vṛddhi derivation). A certain number of adjectives have the option of either formation: so **pāpā** or **pāpī** (the latter is the more archaic form), feminine of **pāpa** 'wicked'. Adjectives in **-a** with feminines in **-ī** are so indicated in the vocabulary, but the use of forms in **-ī** is not required in this chapter.

There is, of course, concord of adjectives, including pronominal adjectives, with feminine substantives:

vayasya, iyaṃ sā vārttā friend, this is that news

Determinative compounds

Present-day English shows a considerable fondness for forming determinatives. If the food we buy nowadays cannot be urged on us as either ‘home-[7]baked’ or ‘farm-[5]fresh’, it is at least quite likely to be ‘oven-[4]ready’. A determinative compound is one in which the final element, whether adjective or substantive, is merely further defined by what precedes it:

1	black:bird, girl:friend	new:found, ice:cold
2	door-stop	man-eating
3	sword-fight	hand-written
4	dining-room	accident-prone
5	book-learning	trouble-free
6	status-symbol	class-conscious
7	side-door	home-made

Each of the above examples is a limited exemplification of its final element. A blackbird is a bird, but of a particular kind; a dining-room is a room, but for a particular purpose. Similarly, the adjectives (including past participles) in the second column mean: cold to a particular degree, free from a particular thing, and so on.

If we compare determinative with other compounds, the point will become even clearer. Twenty;eight is not a particular kind of eight. Bare_foot is not a particular kind of foot (in fact, the compounded word is not even a substantive). Richard the Lion_heart was not a heart. And an over head railway is not a ‘head railway’ of a special sort. (Our use of the underscore is explained on p. 118.)

In analysing in English the meaning of determinatives, we can usually make use of a preposition, chosen according to the sense of the compound. ‘Home-made’ no doubt means made *in* the home or *at* home (cf. home-baked); but ‘hand-made’ must mean made *by* hand or *with* one’s hands. In Sanskrit it is broadly possible to express the relationship between the elements of any particular determinative (**tatpuruṣa**) compound in terms of one of the seven cases. The above English examples are set out according to this analysis. Compounds analysed as involving nominative relationship will be discussed below. Those involving relationship in any oblique case (accusative to locative) are known as *dependent* determinatives.

Dependent determinatives

In the punctuation of compounds in this book, dependent determinative relationship is represented by a hyphen. Occasionally, when a more precise analysis is desired, a number from 2 to 7 is superscribed, representing the particular case. So **pakṣa-^{7}dvāraṃ** 'side-^{7}door', with locative (**saptamī** 'seventh case') relationship.

Assignment to a particular oblique case may sometimes be arbitrary, and irrelevant to understanding of the compound. 'Book-learning' has been taken to be learning *from* books, but it might be thought of as learning *in* books (locative) or perhaps *by means of* books (instrumental). As an example of accusative case relationship, 'door-stop' may not be thought entirely convincing (it is here treated as 'a stop (which stops) a door', but perhaps it is simply 'a stop *for* a door' or 'the stop *of* a door'). The point is, of course, that the accusative case essentially relates nouns to verbs. The corresponding relationship between substantives is expressed by the objective genitive. In a sense **nṛpa-darśanaṃ** 'king-seeing' contains an accusative relationship, but expressed by separate words it would appear as **nṛpasya/nṛpayor/nṛpāṇāṃ darśanaṃ** 'sight of the king/kings'. (A subjective genitive relationship may also be expressed by a determinative compound: in the appropriate context **nṛpa-darśanaṃ** could also mean 'sight *by* the king' etc.)

The last example will serve to remind you of the principle that stem forms are indeterminate between singular, dual and plural. There is a similar indeterminacy in English, as the example 'book-learning' will have suggested. In the same way a 'garage-owner' may own one or many garages. A phrase such as 'child welfare' (the welfare of children) shows that determinative relationship in English may exist between words not joined by a hyphen.

Although such compounds are frequent in English, they are by no means substitutable in all circumstances for more analytical turns of phrase. In general they denote characteristic rather than *ad hoc* relationships. A 'hand-held' camera is such by virtue of its design or at least some deliberate policy of its user. We do not say 'He brandished the hand-held book' instead of 'He brandished the book held in his hand'. In Classical Sanskrit there is no such inhibition. Wherever nouns are connected among themselves by oblique case relationships, compounds are formed extensively. In fact, a long sentence composed entirely of short words each with its own case termination would have seemed unnecessarily clumsy.

saṃvadaty ubhayor Mālatī[3]-niveditaḥ śarīr›[6]-ākāraḥ [the appearance-of-body reported-by-Mālatī fits for both] they are both as Mālatī described them

kāla[2]-jñā devī—kāry›[6]-ôparodhaṃ me pariharati Her Majesty is ['occasion-knowing'] tactful—she avoids interruption-of-my-business

The compound **kāla-jña** illustrates the fact that a number of forms are found at the end of determinative compounds which would never be used as words by themselves. In particular, many verbal roots are so used, predominantly with an active participial sense. If the root ends in a consonant, it is inflected according to the consonant declension (to be described later). Furthermore, roots ending in **i**, **u** or **ṛ** add a euphonic **t**. But roots in **ā** and certain others are simplified so as to end in **a**, and are inflected like **kānta** (thus **kāla-jña**, from **jñā** know).

dṛś	see	**sarva[2]-dṛś**	all-seeing
kṛ	make	**vighna[2]-kṛt**	obstacle-making, interfering
ji	conquer	**satya[3]-jit**	conquering by truth
sthā	stand	**mārga[7]-stha**	standing (/being) in the road
jan	be born	**jala[7]-ja**	born in the water

Very frequent also in such compounds is the root extended

by the suffix **a**. So side by side exist **jala-[7]ruh** (consonant-stem) and **jala-[7]ruha** (inflected like **kānta**) growing in the water.

Occasionally compounds are found in which the first member appears in an inflected instead of a stem form, and this is not uncommon when the final member cannot be used as an independent word. So **agre-ga** 'going in front' from **agraṃ** 'front' and the root **gam**. From the same root **hṛdayaṃ-gama** 'going to the heart'. An example of a case termination (here dative singular) before a word which also occurs independently is the grammatical term **parasmai-padaṃ** 'word for another, active voice'. In such instances, one of the most important criteria for the existence of a compound rather than two separate words is lacking, but others remain: in Vedic, specialised meaning or unity of accent; in Classical Sanskrit, specialised meaning or the ability to occur as part of a longer compound.

The word **arthaḥ** 'purpose' is used adverbially at the end of compounds, usually in the accusative case, **artham**, to mean 'for the sake of': **udako-ârtham** 'for the sake of water', 'for water', 'to get water'; **kim-artham** 'for the sake of what', 'for what purpose', 'why?'.

The first member of a dependent determinative must be a nominal or pronominal substantive, or a substantivally used adjective (e.g. **priya** m. and **priyā** f. 'loved one'—or the first of these two forms, **priya**, used with neuter significance, 'benefit, service'). This does not apply to the other class of determinative compounds.

Descriptive determinatives

For this type of determinative there is a special name in Sanskrit, **karmadhāraya**. The notion that it expresses nominative relationship between the two members should not be pressed too far, for where the final member is an adjective it is not usually possible to achieve even an approximate representation of the sense of the compound merely by assigning the same case ending to the first member as to the second. The point is rather that in descriptives the first element stands in an attributive relationship (represented in the punctuation by a colon) to the second. Where the second element is a noun, the relationship is adjectival, the first element being either an adjective or a substantive used 'adjectivally', that is to say in apposition. Where the second element is an adjective, the relationship is adverbial, and the first element is either an adverbially used adjective (or sometimes an actual adverb) or an adverbially used substantive. Karmadhārayas may thus conveniently be discussed under four main headings.

1 *Adjective+substantive* (black:bird). What is true of such compounds in English originally applied in Sanskrit too. They were used principally where the compound had a conventional significance transcending the separate meanings of its parts. In the same way that 'blackbird' in English does not mean just any bird that is black, so the equivalent Sanskrit compound **kṛṣṇa:śakuni** meant, in fact, a crow. Even in the classical period it remains true that an adjective qualifying a substantive preserves its own inflexion in the vast majority of cases, in preference to being compounded in its stem form with the latter. However, there was a continuous whittling away at this principle. It was often violated in verse for reasons of metrical convenience. Common adjectives of unemphatic meaning such as **mahā** 'great' and **sva** '(my *etc.*) own' may be used fairly freely, and so may common collocations such as **priya:vayasyaḥ** 'dear friend'. In later Sanskrit prose words like **sarva** 'all' and **anya** 'other' are compounded in karmadhārayas with increasing frequency. In the exercises you should not yourself form karmadhārayas of adjective plus substantive unless directed to do so. (But this does *not* apply to karmadhārayas forming part of a longer compound: see Chapter 7.)

An adjective has only one stem form for all three genders, deriving from that of the masculine–neuter. So **priya:sakhī** 'dear [female] friend', not **priyāsakhī**, which could only be either two separate words or a dependent compound meaning 'friend of (my) sweetheart'.

2 *Substantive+substantive* (girl:friend). In these compounds the substantives are in appositional relationship: so **rāja:ṛṣi** 'king-seer'. In particular, titles are compounded: **amātya: Bhūrivasu** 'Minister Bhūrivasu', **bhaṭṭɔ:Ôdbhaṭaḥ** 'Dr Udbhaṭa'. Other types are **strī:janaḥ** 'womenfolk', **dhvani: śabdaḥ** 'the word "dhvani"'. Where proper names are involved, the expected order is sometimes reversed: thus **Rāma:bhadraḥ** 'dear Rāma', **Sītā:devī** 'Queen Sītā'.

One particular type of karmadhāraya made from two substantives is of great importance in literary style. It may be called the karmadhāraya of comparison. According to Sanskrit literary critics, it embodies the figure of speech called **rūpakaṃ** 'metaphor' (as opposed to **upamā** 'simile'), in which one makes a comparison by stating directly that something is something else. So if we take the word **padmaṃ** 'lotus' and qualify it by the word **pādaḥ** 'foot', we have the compound **pāda:padmaṃ** 'foot lotus, a lotus consisting of a foot'. This means, in effect, 'a lotus-like foot', and such compounds are often so translated, though strictly speaking such translations would exemplify **upamā** and not **rūpakaṃ**. The more literal way to translate these compounds is by means of the preposition 'of', also useful in translating other types of appositional karmadhāraya, e.g. **Kāñcī:puraṃ** 'the city of Kāñcī': so 'the lotus of (your) foot'; **smita:jyotsnā** 'the moonlight of (her) smile'; **nara:puṃgavaḥ** 'a bull of a man', etc.:

> **katham, idānīm unmādɔ:ôparāga eva Mādhavɔ:êndum āskandati** what, does the eclipse of insanity now attack the moon of Mādhava? (*i.e.* does insanity engulf him, like an eclipse engulfing the moon?)

3 *adjective/adverb+adjective* (new:found). So from **udagra** 'intense' and **ramaṇīya** 'lovely', **udagra:ramaṇīya** 'intensely lovely'. A past participle as a final member is particularly common: **nava:baddha** 'new-bound, newly bound'; **madhurɔ:ôkta** 'spoken sweetly'.

The first member may be an actual adverb: **punar:ukta** 'spoken again, repeated'; **anyathā:vādin** 'speaking otherwise'; **bahiḥ:śruta** 'heard outside'; **atra:stha** 'standing here'.

Certain past participles may be qualified adverbially by words which in a verbal sentence would stand in a predicative relationship. So corresponding to the sentence **sa śrānta āgacchati** 'he arrives tired' is the compound **śrānta:āgata** 'arriving tired'. In particular, substantives, adjectives or adverbs which would appear as the complement of the verb **bhū** 'be' may qualify its past participle **bhūta** 'having become, being': so **nimitta:bhūta** 'being the cause', **sukumāra:bhūta** 'being delicate', **evaṃ:bhūta** 'being so'. **bhūta** need not always be translated into English, serving merely to smooth or clarify the construction in Sanskrit, e.g.:

mad-anuja-maraṇa-nimitta:bhūtāyāḥ pāpāyā Bālacandrikāyāḥ of the wicked Bālacandrikā, cause of my brother's death . . .

(Occasionally an instance occurs of an adverb predicatively qualifying a *substantive*: **alam anyathā:saṃbhāvanayā** 'enough of supposing otherwise'.)

4 *substantive+adjective* (ice:cold). A substantive adverbially qualifying an adjective typically implies a comparison: **hima:śiśira** 'ice-cold, cold as ice'; **prāṇa:priya** 'dear as life'.

As karmadhārayas, these compounds have such a meaning. Ambiguity arises, however, because they may often be interpreted as dependent determinatives with, for instance, instrumental or ablative relationship: so **hima-śiśira** might mean 'cold because of the ice'. The same author may write in one place **priyaṅgu:śyāma** 'dark *as* the black vine', and in another **kādambinī-śyāmala** '(skies) dark *with* rainclouds'.

Prepositions

The relationships expressed by the Sanskrit case terminations are expressed in English by a number of prepositions: 'to', 'with', 'for', 'from', 'in', etc. The existence of six oblique cases, each used in a variety of circumstances, means that the use of prepositions is a comparatively unimportant feature of Sanskrit. In the Vedic language (as in other Indo-European languages) the particles used as verbal prefixes are also found functioning as prepositions, usually placed *after* the noun they govern. But in Classical Sanskrit only two of these remain really important, **ā** and **prati**. **ā** governs the ablative and usually means 'up to': **ā samudrāt** 'up to the ocean'. It is the only preposition regularly placed *before* its noun (the others would more appropriately be called *post*positions). **prati** means firstly 'towards, against' and, by extension, 'with regard to': **vanaṃ prati** 'towards the forest', **devasy› âsvāsthyaṃ prati** 'with respect to Your Majesty's illness'.

anu (with accusative) 'after' also occurs. Related to the verbal prefix **sam** is the preposition **saha** referred to in Lesson 4.

In addition, there are a number of prepositions of adverbial and nominal origin, for instance **vinā** (usually with instrumental) 'without', **paścāt** (with ablative or genitive) 'behind'. These shade into the use, with the genitive, of a number of nouns of somewhat blunted meaning, e.g. **madhye** 'in the middle of, among': **eka eva mama putrāṇāṃ madhye** 'one alone among my sons'. Instead of the genitive, a determinative compound may be formed:

tan-madhyāt kim idam ekam? is this one [from among:] of them?
jāla-mārgeṇa paśyāmaḥ let us watch [by way of:] through the window

Occasionally such compounding occurs even with actual prepositions: e.g. **rath›-ôpari** instead of **rathasy› ôpari** 'upon the chariot'.

Verbal action nouns in *a*

It is well worth noticing the more important types of nominal stem formation from the Sanskrit root, not in order to form such stems for oneself but in order to make sense of the relationship between various individual items of vocabulary. One of the most important is the addition of **a** to the root to form a masculine substantive. Normally the root appears in guṇa grade, and the predominant meaning is of an abstract 'action' noun: so from the root **krudh** 'be angry', **krodhaḥ** 'anger'. Similarly, but with some development of meaning, from **diś** 'point', **deśaḥ** 'point, place, country'.

The verbal root and the derived noun may have a prefix: **sam+dih** 'smear, confuse', **saṃdehaḥ** 'confusion, doubt'; **upa+i** 'approach', **upāyaḥ** 'approach, means'.

Vṛddhi instead of guṇa is quite often found, but only where the resulting vowel is **ā**: **vi+sad** 'be dejected', **viṣādaḥ** 'dejection'; **bhṛ** 'bear', **bhāraḥ** 'burden'. The longer grade is particularly found after a prefix: thus from **ru** 'roar', **ravaḥ** 'roar' but **saṃrāvaḥ** 'uproar'.

A point to be noted particularly is that (for historical reasons) roots ending in a palatal stop usually change that stop to the corresponding velar: **vij** 'start; tremble', **āvegaḥ/saṃvegaḥ** 'agitation'; **śuc** 'grieve', **śokaḥ** 'grief'.

Among examples of the formation in the vocabulary of Exercise 6 are:

anu+śī lie alongside, **anuśayaḥ** consequence, regret
abhi+laṣ crave, **abhilāṣaḥ** craving
ā+rabh begin, **ārambhaḥ** beginning
pari+has laugh, **parihāsaḥ** laughter
prati+sidh forbid, **pratiṣedhaḥ** prohibition
pra+viś enter, **praveśaḥ** entry
vi+ava+hṛ deal with, **vyavahāraḥ** dealings, usage

Ambiguities of external sandhi

Sometimes the operation of different sandhi rules can lead to a single result, so that the final form is ambiguous. The following are the ambiguities most likely to cause difficulty:

1 **nn** may represent **t+n** *or* **n+n.**

Example: **asmānna** ← **asmāt+na** *or* **asmān+na**

Furthermore, if the vowel preceding the **nn** is short, this may represent the sandhi of final **n** before a vowel.

Example: **paśyannāste** ← **paśyan+āste, paśyan+nāste** *or* **paśyat+nāste**

2 **a** before a vowel other than **a** may represent **aḥ** *or* **e.**

Example: **aśva eva** ← **aśvaḥ+eva** *or* **aśve eva**

(Theoretically the **a** might also represent a final **o**, but this is rare.)

3 **ā** before a voiced consonant may represent **āḥ** *or* simple **ā.**

Example: **kanyā nayati** ← **kanyāḥ nayati** *or* **kanyā nayati**

4 **cch** may represent **t+ś** *or* **t+ch.**

Example: **asmācchalāt** ← **asmāt+śalāt** *or* **asmāt+chalāt**

5 **ggh** etc. may represent a stop followed by **h** *or* by **gh** etc.

Example: **asmāddhṛtāt** ← **asmāt+hṛtāt** *or* **asmāt+dhṛtāt**

6 Long vowel followed by **r** may represent long/short vowel with **ḥ** *or* itself alone.

Example: **śucī rakṣati** ← **śuciḥ rakṣati, śucīḥ+rakṣati** *or* **śucī+rakṣati**

The sandhi of two vowels is also a source of ambiguity, but here a learner is less likely to assume one particular resolution of the sandhi. The possibilities implicit in the sandhi vowels **ā, ī, ū, e, ai, o, au** are set out in the table on p. 36.

Vocabulary

akṣaraṃ syllable, written character
anarthaḥ reverse, disaster
anuśayaḥ repentance, regret
abhijña conversant with (*gen.*)
abhilāṣaḥ craving, passion for (*loc.*)
amātyaḥ minister
ambā (*irreg. voc.* **amba**) mother (*either one's own or as a title of respect*)
avasthā state, condition
asphuṭa unclear, illegible
āgamanaṃ coming, arrival
ārambhaḥ beginning
ārya noble, honourable; *f.* noble lady
āśaṅkā apprehension
āśā hope
āśramaḥ hermitage
īdṛśa (*f.* **ī**) of this kind, such
uddeśaḥ region, part, place
uparāgaḥ eclipse
ubha both (*only dual*)
katama (*pr. adj.*) which?
kanyā girl, daughter
kaṣṭa grievous, harsh; **kaṣṭam** alas
kāryaṃ task
kālaḥ time
kulaṃ family
kuśalaṃ welfare
Kusumapuraṃ *name of city*
Kaumudī-mahotsavaḥ Full Moon Festival
caritaṃ conduct, deeds
cintā worry
tāpasaḥ ascetic
Duḥṣantaḥ *pr. n.*
dvayaṃ couple, pair (*one way of expressing* two)
niyata constrained; **niyatam** necessarily
niyojyaḥ servant
nirvāṇaṃ bliss
netraṃ eye
°pathaḥ (*usually ifc.*) path
parihāsaḥ joke
puraṃ city
pauraḥ citizen; **paura:janaḥ** citizens, townsfolk
Pauravaḥ descendant of Puru
prajā subject (of king)
pratiṣedhaḥ prohibition, cancellation
prathita widely known
pradeśaḥ place
prayojanaṃ purpose
pravātaṃ breeze
praveśaḥ entry, entering
priyā beloved (woman)
bhadra good; *f. voc.* madam
maṇḍapa *m./n.* pavilion, bower
mahā:rājaḥ great king
mah»:ôtsavaḥ [great] festival, holiday
Mādhavyaḥ *pr. n.*
Mārīcaḥ *pr. n.*
mudrā seal
mūḍha deluded, idiotic; *m.* idiot
mṛgaḥ deer
Lakṣmaṇaḥ *pr. n.*
latā creeper
lokaḥ world
vārttā news
Vāsavaḥ (*epithet of*) Indra
vistīrṇa extensive
vṛttāntaḥ news, happening
Vṛṣalaḥ *pr. n.*
vyavahāraḥ usage
vyasanaṃ vice, vicious failing
vrataṃ vow
Śakuntalā *pr. n.*
Śoṇottarā *pr. n.*
śravaṇaṃ hearing

śrotriyaḥ learned (brahmin), scholar
saṃvegaḥ agitation
satya true; **satyam** truly
subhaga delightful
sevā attendance (upon someone), servitude
sthānam place, occasion; **sthāne** in place, appropriate

ā+pat (I āpatati) befall, happen
upa+gam (I upagacchati) go to, reach
pari+grah (IX parigṛhṇāti) accept
pari+bhuj (VII paribhunakti; *p.p.* **paribhukta)** enjoy
pra+nam (I praṇamati) make obeisance to (*dat./gen./loc./ acc.*)
prati+sidh (I pratiṣedhati) restrain, forbid
labh (I *ātm.* **labhate**; *p.p.* **labdha)** take, gain, win
vi+pra+labh (vipralabhate) mislead, deceive

aho oh
ittham thus, so
iha here
kim-artham for what purpose, why?
kutaḥ? from where?
tat (*first word in sentence, frequent connecting particle*) so, then
tarhi (*usually enclitic*) in that case
nanu surely (*often in objection to a previous remark*)
prati (+*acc.*) to, towards; with regard to

Note: The abbreviations *ibc.* and *ifc.* signify respectively 'in the beginning (i.e. as first half) of a compound' and '*in fine compositi*, as second half of a compound'.

Exercise 6a

Translate into English:

शोणोत्तरे किमागमनप्रयोजनम् ।१। कष्टम्—अनर्थद्वयमापतितम् ।२। महाराज अपि कुशलं कुमारलक्ष्मणस्य ।३। कुतः पुनरियं वार्त्ता ।४। सत्यमित्थंभूत एवास्मि ।५। अमात्य विस्तीर्णः कुसुमपुरवृत्तान्तः ।६। त्वमार्याभिः पुत्र इव गृहीतः ।७। कतमस्मिन्प्रदेशे मारीचाश्रमः ।८। अम्ब कासि—किमर्थमहं त्वया प्रतिषिद्धः ।९। नन्वनुशयस्थानमेतत् ।१०। सैवेयम् ।११। उभा-

भ्यामपि वां वासवनियोज्यो दुःषन्तः प्रणमति ।१२। कष्टा खलु सेवा ।१३। न खलु वृषलस्य श्रवणपथमुपगतोऽयं मया कृतः कौमुदीमहोत्सवप्रतिषेधः ।१४। किं तवानया चिन्तया ।१५। माधव्य अप्यस्ति ते शकुन्तलादर्शनं प्रति कुतूहलम् ।१६। श्रोत्रिय-लिखितान्यक्षराणि प्रयत्नलिखितान्यपि नियतमस्फुटानि भवन्ति ॥१७॥

Exercise 6b

Words joined together by points (·) should be translated by a single compound.

1 This is a deer·of·the·hermitage. 2 A beginning·in·the·task has been made. 3 Here stands Minister·Rākṣasa. 4 Idiot, this is no time·for·jokes. 5 In that case whose is this seal? 6 You are indeed conversant with the usages·of·the·world. 7 Then did the townsfolk not accept [our·word:] what we said? 8 Oh, this part·of·the·wood is delightful·for·its·breeze. 9 Do not be apprehensive. 10 (I) have gained a bliss·for·the·eyes. 11 How (is it that) you do not see Rāma's condition? 12 Śārṅgarava, such agitation [of you:] on your part from·entering·the·city is indeed appropriate. 13 Descendants of Puru have this family·vow. 14 Madam, Duḥṣanta's·conduct is widely known among his subjects. 15 Then have done now with the vice·of·hope. 16 I do not of course *truly* have a passion for the ascetic's·daughter. 17 But with regard to the eclipse·of·the·moon, someone has misled you [*f.*]. 18 I'll stay for a while just here in the bower·of·creepers enjoyed·by·(my)·beloved.

Chapter 7

PARADIGMS: Unchangeable consonant stems (**suhṛd, manas,** *etc.*); **nadī**

Nominal stems ending in consonants

The largest class of nouns in Sanskrit is the 'thematic **a**' class, the members of which are inflected like **aśvaḥ** or **phalaṃ.** But historically speaking, thematic **a** is a formational suffix added either to a root or to an existing stem. Nominal stems ending in a consonant in general represent an earlier stage of Indo-European word formation. They may consist of a plain root used in a nominal sense (so from **yudh** 'fight', **yudh** f. 'battle'—and, more important in Classical Sanskrit, the use of a root form at the end of a determinative, as described in Chapter 6); or of the root extended by some consonantal suffix (so from **sad** 'sit', **sadas** n. and **sadman** n. 'seat'). There are two main reasons why the inflexion of consonant stems is more complicated than that of thematic **a** stems. One is that variations may occur in the basic form of the stem in inflexion, due ultimately to an ancient shift of accent. Stems exhibiting this variation are not introduced until Chapter 8. The other reason is that direct contact between the final consonant of the stem and the case terminations causes a number of internal sandhi changes. As opposed to a single stem in thematic **a**, we have in fact a series of related stems in **c, j, t, th, d, dh, p, bh, ś, ṣ, h, as, is, us**, etc.

The basic terminations of consonant stem nouns are exhibited in the declension of the stem **suhṛd** 'friend'. Before a *vowel* the stem final remains unchanged (except that **s** after **i** etc. becomes **ṣ** by internal sandhi—cf. Chapter 4); in the nominative singular or before a termination beginning with a *consonant*, it must be reduced to one of the 'permitted finals' and the rules of *external* sandhi thereafter applied (with consequent voicing before **bh**, lack of voice before **su**). This reduction is according to the following scheme (a number of sounds not actually occurring as nominal stem finals are included for completeness):

k, kh, g, gh ; c, *j, *ś, *h *become* **k**
ṭ, ṭh, ḍ, ḍh ; ch, *j, jh ; *ś, ṣ, *h *become* **ṭ**
t, th, d, dh ; *h *become* **t**
p, ph, b, bh *become* **p**
ṅ, ñ *become* **ṅ**
n, m *remain*
s *becomes* **ḥ**, **r** *remains*
ṇ, y, l, v *do not occur*

The asterisked sounds (**j ś h**) are those treated differently in different words: where ambiguity exists, the nominative singular form is added in brackets after the stem form in the vocabulary. In a number of words, for historical reasons, a final aspirate throws its aspiration back upon a preceding stop: **go-duh** 'cow-milking', nom. sg. **go-dhuk**.

Feminine consonant stems are inflected like the masculine (though changeable masculine stems may often form corresponding feminines in **ī**). Among the unchangeable stems, neuters are rare—except for stems in **s**, which are rarely masculine or feminine (unless at the end of an exocentric compound). Neuter stems have no termination in the nominative, vocative or accusative singular; add **ī** for **au** in the dual; and **i** for **aḥ** in the plural, with **n** infixed before a final stop or sibilant and assimilated as appropriate to the class nasal or to anusvāra. The nominative singular of masculine/feminine nouns in **as** is with lengthened **a**: **āḥ**.

In addition to learning the paradigm **suhṛd**, you should study carefully the examples listed after it of stems ending in other consonants.

Feminines in ī

The suffix **ī**, inflected as in **nadī**, is important as forming a large number of derivative feminine stems—in particular, as mentioned above and in Chapter 6, the feminine of changeable consonant stems and of many stems in **a**.

Causatives

In addition to a simple present tense formed according to one (occasionally more than one) of the ten classes, and to perfect and aorist tenses, to be described later, a verbal root may form some five other finite tense systems, all inflected as if they were thematic presents like **nayati/nayate**. They are: future (**neṣyati** 'will lead'), passive (**nīyate** 'is led'), causative (**nāyayati** 'causes to lead, makes (someone) lead, has (someone) lead/led'), desiderative (**ninīṣati** 'wants to lead') and intensive (**nenīyate** 'leads forcibly'). From the point of view of their formation, all these five are on a more or less equal footing; but since the last three are felt to involve a more fundamental modification of the meaning of the verb and may make formations from their stems (e.g. a past participle) outside the thematic **a** paradigm, they are usually classed together as derivative or secondary conjugations.

Of these three the causative is by far the most important. It may be regarded as having evolved out of the tenth verb class through specialisation of form and meaning. The principal features of its formation are the suffix **aya** and a strengthening of the root. The syllable before **aya** should usually be heavy. Therefore guṇa of the root is almost always employed where this produces a heavy syllable: so from **dṛś, darśayati** 'causes to see, shows'. If the root when strengthened to guṇa grade is still light, vṛddhi is usually employed: **kṛ, kārayati** 'causes to do'; **bhū, bhāvayati** 'causes to be'. But a few causatives with light first syllable are found: **gam, gamayati** 'causes to go'; **tvar, tvarayati** 'causes to hurry'. Among exceptional forms with neither guṇa nor vṛddhi (but still with heavy first syllable) are **duṣ, dūṣayati** 'spoils' and **pṝ, pūrayati** 'fills'.

Most verbs ending in **ā** and some others, including **ṛ** 'go', **adhi+i** 'study' and optionally **ruh** 'rise', take the suffix **p**: **sthā, sthāpayati** 'establishes'; **ṛ, arpayati** 'transfers'; **ruh, rohayati** or **ropayati** 'raises'. An important anomalous form (evidently denominative in origin) is **ghātayati** 'has killed, puts to death' functioning as the causative of **han** 'kill'.

Causatives exist in English, though they are not a morphologically prominent feature of the language. 'Fell' is the causative of 'fall'—'he fells the tree': so 'lay' of 'lie', 'raise' of 'rise'. More frequently, what is expressed by the Sanskrit causative we express by transitive use of otherwise intransitive verbs:

vṛkṣo rohati a tree grows **artho vardhate** wealth grows, increases
vṛkṣaṃ ropayati he grows a tree **arthaṃ vardhayati** he increases his wealth

The frequency of causative forms in Sanskrit means that often what we express by pairs of unrelated words in English is directly expressed in Sanskrit by a causative formation: **jan** 'be born', **janayati** 'begets'; **vi+dru** 'run away', **vidrāvayati** 'puts to flight, chases away'. In the same way the French causative *faire voir* 'make to see' or the Sanskrit equivalent **darśayati** may be translated by the English 'show'.

Where, as in the earlier examples, a causative is formed from an intransitive verb, the original subject becomes the object. Where a causative is formed from an already transitive verb, the displaced subject may either join the existing object as a further object in the accusative case or be treated as an agent in the instrumental case:

dāso harati bhāram a servant carries the luggage
hārayati bhāraṃ dāsam he has a servant carry the luggage
hārayati bhāraṃ dāsena he has the luggage carried by a servant

Choice of one or the other is a matter of usage. Construction with the instrumental may be taken as the general rule. But some verbs, notably **kṛ** 'do' and **hṛ** 'carry', are found with either construction. A number of others are regularly found with a double accusative: among these are **smārayati** (**smṛ** 'remember') 'reminds', **āśayati** (**aś** 'eat') 'feeds', **pāyayati** 'makes to drink', **adhyāpayati** 'teaches', **bodhayati** (**budh** 'learn') 'informs', **lambhayati** (irreg. from **labh**) 'causes to take'; and some other verbs with similar meanings.

The formation of absolutives and past participles from the causative stem has already been mentioned (Chapters 4 and 5). In the past participle **ita** is simply substituted for **aya.** A point to note in connection with the past participle is that causatives construed with two accusatives often make the 'secondary' object into the subject of the passive voice, leaving a 'retained accusative' as in English:

udakaṃ lambhitā ete vṛkṣāḥ these trees have been [caused to take:] given water

samanantaraṃ garbh›-aîkādaśe varṣe kṣātreṇa kalpen› ôpanīya trayī-vidyām adhyāpitau thereafter in the eleventh year from [the womb:] conception, after being initiated according to the kṣatriya rite, (the two of them) were [caused to study:] taught the Science of the Three (Vedas)

Some roots form causatives without causative meaning: so from **dhṛ** 'hold', **dhārayati** 'he holds'. This might be considered a class X verb if the forms **dharati** etc. were not also theoretically possible. Outside the present, formations are often made from the simple root: past participle **dhṛta** is commoner than **dhārita**. Much the same is true of **pṝ**, **pūrayati** 'fills', p.p. **pūrṇa.** With some other verbs, although the simple present is not uncommon, causative forms often seem to occur without any obvious distinction of sense: e.g. **yunakti** or **yojayati** (**yuj**) 'joins'; **muñcati** or **mocayati** (**muc**) 'releases'; **niṣedhati** or **niṣedhayati** (**ni+sidh**) 'prevents'.

Some causatives with well-established meanings behave like simple verbs in their constructions. So **darśayati** 'shows', in addition to the construction with two accusatives, often takes a genitive of reference: **indrāyudhaṃ na kasya cid darśayati** 'he does not show the rainbow to anyone'. Similarly, **nivedayati** '[causes to know:] informs', like other verbs meaning 'tell', may take a dative (or genitive) of the indirect object, while **arpayati** 'transfers, hands over' may behave like any verb of giving: **ābharaṇaṃ sūtasy› ârpayati** 'he hands over his insignia to his driver'.

Class X verbs

The present stem of verbs belonging to class X is formed with the addition of the suffix **aya**: so from the root **spṛh** 'desire', **spṛhayati** 'he desires'. But, as has just been described, the suffix **aya** in conjunction with a strengthening of the root is used to form causatives, while another suffix, **ya**, frequently preceded by a short **a**, is used in the formation of denominative verbs (see Lesson 9). And, in fact, all but a handful of the verbs classified by the grammarians under class X may be looked on either as causatives (but lacking obvious causative significance) or as denominatives (but receiving the old tonic accent upon the first **á**, instead of upon the **yá** as do regular denominatives):

chad, chādayati covers
varṇ, varṇayati depicts, describes (*really from* **varṇaḥ** colour, appearance: *the root* **varṇ** *is artificially contrived*)
kath, kathayati relates, tells (*really from* **katham** how?—*i.e.* says how, relates circumstances)

Karmadhārayas with inseparable prefixes

Just as the second member of a *dependent* determinative may be a form that cannot occur in isolation, so the first member of a *descriptive* may be a prefix incapable of independent use. Under this heading might logically be included all verbal nouns beginning with prefixes. Thus, as a compound of **gamanaṃ** 'going', **nirgamanaṃ** 'outgoing'. But where corresponding verbal forms occur or are possible (thus **nirgacchati** 'goes out'), this analysis is unnecessary.

Occasionally, however, verbal prefixes are compounded with nouns where no corresponding verbal form exists: so **adhi:pati** 'over:lord', **ati:dūra** 'extremely far', **prati:nayanaṃ** 'encountering eye', **prati:śabdaḥ** '[responding sound:] echo', **ā:śyāmala** 'darkish'.

More frequent are a number of prefixes never compounded with finite verbs:

su (laudatory particle) 'well, very'—**su:kṛta** 'done well', **su:pakva** 'well cooked, very ripe', **su:bhadra** 'very good', **su:janaḥ** 'nice person', **su:vicāraḥ** 'proper thought'.

dus (pejorative particle) 'ill, badly'—**dur:ukta** 'ill spoken', **duś:ceṣṭā** 'misconduct', **dur:gandhaḥ** 'bad smell, stench'. Like other prefixes ending in s and a few other initial forms in compounds (e.g., **namas** 'obeisance' in **namaskāra** 'making obeisance'), **dus** retains a final sibilant before **k/kh** and **p/ph** (except when these in turn are followed by a sibilant). In conformity with external sandhi it appears as **duṣ** : **duṣ:kṛta** 'ill done'. (Sandhi before other sounds follows the usual pattern.)

Corresponding to the verbal prefix **saṃ**, occurs occasionally **sa** or **saha** 'together': **saha:maraṇaṃ** 'dying together', **sa:brahmacārin** 'fellow-student'.

The most important karmadhāraya prefix is the negative particle **a** (before consonants) or **an** (before vowels). Unlike other 'non-verbal' prefixes, it may be compounded freely not only with ordinary adjectives and substantives and with past participles but also with other participles and with absolutives and gerundives: **a:kṛta** 'unmade, undone', **an:ukta** 'unspoken', **a:dharmaḥ** 'unrighteousness', **an:ati⁝dūra** 'not particularly far', **an:āgacchant** 'not coming'. The negation not infrequently qualifies a whole compound: **a:guṇa˘jña** 'not recognising merit', **a:loka˘sāmānya** 'not common in the world', **a:kāla˘kṣep›˘ârha** 'not brooking delay'.

Especially noteworthy is the use with the absolutive. The best translation is usually 'without': **a:dṛṣṭvā** 'not having seen, without seeing'. Note that the addition of **a/an,** unlike that of a verbal prefix, does not in itself entail the use of the compounded (ya) form of the absolutive.

uttaram a:dattv» aîva prasthitā she set off without giving any reply

pūrva

A curious anomaly in the formation of karmadhāraya compounds is that the word **pūrva** 'previous' used adverbially may be placed after the word it qualifies; so **pūrva:kṛta** or **kṛta:pūrva** 'previously done, already done'.

kim atrabhavatī mayā pariṇīta:pūrvā? Did I previously marry this lady?

Compounds of more than two members

Determinative compounds are based upon a relationship between a prior element and a final element. In a sense therefore a determinative, considered in itself, cannot possibly consist of more than two parts. However, either of these parts may in turn on closer analysis be found to consist of a compound expression, itself resolvable into its constituent parts. In English 'waste paper basket' is a dependent: a basket not 'for paper' but 'for waste paper'. But the prior element is itself a compound, a descriptive determinative 'paper which is waste', subordinated to a larger whole. We may represent the subordination by brackets: (waste:paper)-basket. Thus in Sanskrit:

Mālatī-mukhaṃ Mālatī's face
(Mālatī-mukh›)-âvalokanaṃ gazing on Mālatī's face

From a different starting-point, **mukh›-âvalokanaṃ** 'gazing on a face', we may arrive at a compound with the same form but a different meaning:

Mālatī-(mukh›-âvalokanaṃ) Mālatī's gazing on a face

The fact that this latter is a far less natural interpretation illustrates an important point about Sanskrit compounds: they build up as they go along. As each element is added to the compound, it should form by itself a complete final element, to which all that precedes will stand in the relation of prior element:

Mālatī-mukha

(Mālatī-mukh›)-âvalokana

[(Mālatī-mukh›)-âvalokana]-vihasta clumsy from gazing on Mālatī's face

This is not an absolute rule. But it represents the first interpretation that will occur to the reader's mind. If therefore two or more elements are to be added *en bloc*, i.e. 'bracketed', they must form a natural group: in other words, the first of the added elements must group itself more naturally with what follows than with what precedes, as in the following:

(sāyaṃtana:snāna)-(saviśeṣa:śītala) completely cool from the evening bathe

Since it merely represents the normal rhythm of a Sanskrit compound, it is not necessary to indicate by successive bracketings the progressive expansion of the prior element of a compound. Where, on the other hand, a subordinated group is added as the *final* element (for the moment) of the compound, this may be most simply indicated by some sign for subordination, such as ˇ, above the relationship sign within the group. The above thus becomes:

sāyaṃtana:snāna-saviśeṣa:̌śītala

Slightly more complex is the following:

pratyagra:sāyaṃtana:̌snāna-saviśeṣa:̌śītala completely cool from the recent evening bathe

This is a compound built up in three stages:

pratyagra recent
pratyagra:sāyaṃtana:̌snāna recent evening-bathe
pratyagra:sāyaṃtana:̌snāna-saviśeṣa:̌śītala

The first three words in this compound illustrate two points. First, as remarked in Chapter 6, there is no restriction on the use of karmadhāraya compounds as part of a longer compound, provided that the finally completed compound is not in itself a karmadhāraya (the rule boils down to this: in general, if you can avoid a karmadhāraya simply by putting an inflexion on an adjective, or on a compound functioning as an adjective, do so). Secondly, where two adjectives qualify the same substantive within a compound, it is more likely that the second is in a closer relationship with the substantive and thus forms a subordinate unit with it than that the two adjectives are linked in a co-ordinative relationship. So in English 'startled: oldˇ:woman' means an old woman who is startled, not a woman who is startled and old.

Like karmadhārayas, dvandva compounds occur very frequently as a subordinate part of a longer compound:

Pārā;Sindhu-saṃbhedam avagāhya nagarīm eva praviśāvaḥ let us bathe at the confluence of the (rivers) Pārā and Sindhu, and go into the city

aho samāna:vayoˇ;rūpa-ramaṇīyaṃ sauhārdam atrabhavatīnām how delightful [for the similar age-and-looks:] for its equality in youth and looks is the friendship of you (young) ladies

Within a subordinate group a further subordinate (or 'double-bracketed') group may sometimes be detected. This is even less frequent than one-degree subordination. Subordination in general is more frequent in bahuvrīhi compounds (see Chapter 8) than in determinatives. Here is an example of such a compound, one that can actually be analysed as including *three* degrees of subordination. The point is that such compounds are possible because the way the elements group together is natural and immediately evident to anyone who knows Sanskrit.

virājat:katipayaˇ:komalaˇˇ:dantaˇˇˇ:kuṭmalˇˇˇ:âgra with (a few (tender (tips of budlike teeth))) gleaming out

If you find any difficulty in grasping the logic of subordinate groupings, remember the analogy with algebra, and 'first solve what is within brackets'—i.e. determine the meaning of words linked by the sign ˇ before relating them to the rest of the compound.

In theory, any word standing outside a compound may form a grammatical relationship only with the compound as a whole, not simply with some prior portion of it. In practice, in Classical Sanskrit this rule is sometimes violated if the alternative of incorporating the extra word into the compound is inconvenient or not sufficiently clear. Typically one may find that a word or phrase in the genitive qualifies the first element or elements of a following compound:

tasya kām›-ônmattasya citra:vadha-vārttā-preṣaṇena (please me) by sending news of the [variegated death:] death by torture of that love-crazed (one)

Here the genitive **-unmattasya** qualifies **citra:vadha** not **-preṣaṇena.**

The use of long compounds

A single compound inserted into a Sanskrit sentence may serve the purpose of a whole clause or even of a separate sentence in English. The following sentence:

itaḥ pradeśād apakramya Mādhav›-âpakāraṃ praty abhiniviṣṭā bhavāmi I'll withdraw from this place and become intent upon the ruin of Mādhava

may be augmented by a compound qualifying **pradeśāt**:

ito Mālatī-vivāha-parikarma-satvara:pratīhāra-śata-saṃkulāt pradeśād apakramya *etc.* I'll withdraw from this place, (which is) crowded with hundreds of porters busy on preparations for Mālatī's wedding, and work for Mādhava's ruin

But the announcement of withdrawal in the word **apa-kramya** occurs late in the sentence. We would therefore be more faithful to one aspect of the original, the order of ideas, by translating:

This place is crowded with porters busy on preparations for Mālatī's wedding: I'll withdraw and *etc.*

or even

Preparations for Mālatī's wedding have brought hundreds of porters flooding into here *etc.*

On the other hand, if we always adhere religiously to the order of the original, this may involve us in destroying its structure, and the latter may sometimes be the more important. This is the dilemma of all translators faced with the more elaborate styles of Sanskrit, and there is no general solution: each case must be judged on its merits.

The construction of long compounds is exploited to good effect in both literary and academic prose, making possible the handling of a vast mass of detail without any obscuring of the main thread of narrative or argument. Beginners in writing Sanskrit prose, however, often misguidedly attempt large numbers of exceptionally long compounds. These are difficult to handle successfully, and the translation of ordinary English prose offers little scope for them. A practical limit to aim at is the compound of three, four or, very occasionally, five members. Page after page of elegant, perspicuous Sanskrit may be read containing no compound longer than this.

gata

The past participle **gata** 'gone to' is often used at the end of a compound to mean '[being] in', without any sense of prior motion. Thus **citra-gatā nārī** 'the woman in the picture'; **kara-tala-gatā ›kṣamālā** 'the rosary in (his) hand'.

Sugāṅga:prāsāda-gatena deven› âham āryasya pāda-mūlaṃ preṣitaḥ His Majesty was in the Sugāṅga Palace when he sent me to Your Honour['s feet]

(It would be wrong to translate this as 'having gone to the palace, His Majesty *etc.*' For the latter sense one should rather use the absolutive **gatvā**.)

gata may also be translated by 'referring to, about', or it may represent the locative used with verbs of feeling: **putra-gataḥ snehaḥ** 'affection towards a son, love of a son'.

Vocabulary

atyanta excessive, extreme
atyāhitaṃ calamity
a:darśanaṃ lack of sight, not seeing
Avalokitā *pr. n.*
a:vinayaḥ lack of breeding, discourtesy
astraṃ missile, weapon
a:sthāne not in place, inappropriate
ābharaṇaṃ ornament
āryaḥ Your Honour; *voc.* sir
āharaṇaṃ (act of) fetching
udvigna distressed
Urvaśī *pr. n.*
ṛtvij (ṛtvik) m. priest
auṣadhaṃ medicine
kathā story; talk, speaking
kṣīra-vṛkṣaḥ fig-tree
kṣudra mean, common, low
gātraṃ limb
ghātakaḥ executioner
Candraguptaḥ *pr. n.*
cira long (*of time*); **ciram** for a long time
cūrṇaṃ powder
chāyā shade
tātaḥ (one's own) father
tīraṃ bank
darbhaḥ (*and pl.*) a type of (sacrificial) grass
dūre far away
devī goddess; (the) Queen, Her (/Your) Majesty
nirvṛta content, happy
puruṣaḥ man
pūrva previous; *in karmadhāraya* previously, before, once, already
prakāraḥ manner, way
pratīkāraḥ remedy
prabhāvaḥ power
bhagavatī Her Reverence
bhayaṃ fear, danger
bhavatī you (*polite form of address to woman*)
madanaḥ (sexual) love
madana‿ôdyānaṃ park of (temple to the god of) Love
miśra mixed
yatnaḥ effort
yoga-cūrṇaṃ magic powder
Rākṣasaḥ *pr. n.*
Rāmāyaṇaṃ *name of an epic poem*
vaṇij (vaṇik) m. businessman, trader
vatsala affectionate, loving
vadhya condemned to death
vibhāgaḥ part, portion
vivādaḥ disagreement, dispute
vṛkṣaḥ tree
vedanā ache, pain
vedī (sacrificial) altar
vaidyaḥ doctor
vyakta evident, clear; **vyaktam** clearly
śarīraṃ body
śiras *n.* head
saṃstaraṇaṃ (act of) strewing
sakhī [female] friend
samidh *f.* firewood
sarasī lake
sahya bearable
Sītā *pr. n.*
suhṛd *m.* friend
saujanyaṃ kindness
snehaḥ affection, love
sparśaḥ touch
sva *pron. adj.* (one's) own
svāgatam (*lit.* 'well come') welcome to (*dat.*)

anu+grah (IX anugṛhṇāti) favour

apa+hṛ (**I apaharati**) carry off
ava+tṝ (**I avatarati**) descend; *caus.* (**avatārayati**) remove
ā+śri (**I āśrayati/āśrayate**) resort to (*acc.*)
upa+ram (**I uparamate**) cease, die
upa+hṛ (**I upaharati**) offer
kath (**X kathayati**) say, tell, relate
kḷp (**I kalpate**) be suitable; *caus.* (**kalpayati**) arrange, prepare
kṣud (**I kṣodati** *p.p.* **kṣuṇṇa**) trample, tread
dṛś *caus.* (**darśayati**) show
dhṛ *caus.* (**dhārayati**) hold, carry, wear
ni+yuj (**VII niyuṅkte**) engage (someone) upon (*loc.*)
pā (**I pibati**) drink; *caus.* (**pāyayati**) make to drink
prati+pāl (**X pratipālayati**) wait for
prati+budh *caus.* (**pratibodhayati**) wake (someone)
prati+i *caus.* (**pratyāyayati**) make confident
pra+yuj (**VII prayuṅkte**) employ
pra+sthā (**I pratiṣṭhate**) set out
pra+iṣ *caus.* (**preṣayati**) despatch, send
lajj (**VI lajjate**) be embarrassed; *caus.* (**lajjayati**) embarrass
vi+krī (**IX vikrīṇīte**) sell to (*loc.*)
vi+cint (**X vicintayati**) consider, think of
vi+dru (**I vidravati**) run away; *caus.* (**vidrāvayati**) disperse, chase away
vi+dhā (**III vidadhāti**) arrange, manage
vi+yuj (**VII viyuṅkte**) disjoin, deprive of (*instr.*)
vṛdh (**I vardhate**) grow; *caus.* (**vardhayati**) increase

aye ah!
tena hi therefore
tāvat (*enclitic, lit.* meanwhile) *and* **yāvat** (*usually first word, lit.* during which time) *are used to express a present intention, and may be represented by* just *in English* (*as in* I'll just buy a newspaper)

Exercise 7a

अये इयं देवी ।१। प्रतिबोधित एवास्मि केनापि ।२। इदममात्यराक्षसगृहम् ।३। अहो वत्सलेन सुहृदा वियुक्ताः स्मः ।४। सुविचिन्तितं भगवत्या ।५। आर्य अपि सह्या शिरोवेदना ।६। लज्जयति मामत्यन्तसौजन्यमेषाम् ।७। तेन हीमां क्षीरवृक्षच्छायामाश्रयामः ।८। चिरमदर्शनेनार्यस्य वयमुद्विग्नाः ।९। स्वागतं देव्यै ।१०। अलमस्मदविनयाशङ्कया ।११। अमात्य कल्पितमनेन

योगचूर्णमिश्रमौषधं चन्द्रगुप्ताय ।१२। अये उर्वशीगात्रस्पर्शादिव निर्वृतं मे शरीरम् ।१३। आर्ये किमत्याहितं सीतादेव्याः ।१४। यावदिमान्वेदीसंस्तरणार्थं दर्भान्नृत्विग्भ्य उपहरामि ।१५। कथितमवलोकितया मदनोद्यानं गतो माधव इति ।१६। कष्टम् उभयोरप्यस्थाने यत्नः ।१७। नायं कथाविभागो ऽस्माभिरन्येन वा श्रुतपूर्वः ।१८। वयमपि तावद्भवत्यौ सखीगतं किंचित्पृच्छामः ।१९। अमात्य इदमाभरणं कुमारेण स्वशरीरादवतार्य प्रेषितम् ॥ २० ॥

Exercise 7b

1 I am Ātreyī. 2 You increase my curiosity. 3 This is the bank·of·the·lake. 4 I will just wait for these (girls) [having resorted to:] in the shade. 5 This is a road trodden·by·common·people. 6 Clearly these [*n.*] too were sold to us by a trader employed·by·Cāṇakya. 7 Oh, (you) have shown love·for·(your)·friend. 8 The danger is at (your) head, the remedy·for·it far away. 9 Dear [*use* **sakhī**] Madayantikā, welcome. You [**bhavatī**] have favoured our·house. 10 It is this dispute which makes me confident. 11 The two of us set out [for·the·fetching·of:] to·fetch·firewood. 12 Why did you two ladies check me? 13 That is well·managed on the occasion·of·the·entry·of·Kalahaṃsaka·and·Makaranda. 14 What, (was) this ornament once·worn by (my) father? 15 I have in fact engaged her·dear·friend Buddharakṣitā on the matter [**tatra**]. 16 Are *these* the two·men·in·the·Rāmāyaṇa·story? 17 This dear·friend Siddhārthaka chased the executioners away and carried me off from the [place·of·the·condemned:] execution ground. 18 Quite different [**anya**] is this [un·trodden:] unhackneyed way·of·speaking by [*use gen.*] Her Reverence. 19 This must be [*use* **khalu**] the power·of·the·Vāruṇa·weapons·employed·by·Prince·Lava. 20 That doctor indeed was made to drink the same medicine, and at once died. [*Express* at once *by linking the two verbs with* **ca . . . ca**.]

Chapter 8

PARADIGMS: Consonant stems in **an** (**rājan**, **ātman**, **nāman**)

Changeable consonant stems

Indo-European vowel gradation was based on the position of the accent: guṇa or vṛddhi occurred in an accented syllable, zero grade in an unaccented syllable. From Vedic texts, in which the ancient accentuation is preserved, we know that this distinction is broadly true of Sanskrit itself. It applies to gradations of the root not only in derivative formations (from **i** 'go', **éti** 'he goes', **itá** 'gone', **áyanaṃ** 'path') but also within the inflexion of a single tense: e.g. **émi** 'I go', **imáḥ** 'we go'. In nominal inflexion we should expect the root to undergo similar changes, but only the traces of such a system remain, even in Vedic. An interesting example, mentioned in Chapter 5, is the infinitive (**nétum** 'to lead') in comparison with the absolutive (**nītvā́** 'after leading'): in origin these are the accusative and instrumental singular respectively of an obsolete verbal action noun. Similarly, in Vedic, from **kṣam** 'earth' occur nominative plural **kṣā́maḥ** and ablative singular **kṣmáḥ**. But most nouns have standardised one grade of the root throughout their inflexion. For instance, from **vac** (or **uc**) 'speak' the noun **vāc** 'speech' has standardised vṛddhi grade throughout (cf. Latin *vōx*, *vōcis*). So the nominative plural is **vā́caḥ** and the ablative singular **vācáḥ**, with no distinction of grade despite the fact that the shift of accent is preserved. And since the ancient system of accents was lost early in the

Classical period and is not marked in Classical texts, it is reasonable to say that in Classical Sanskrit the ablative and genitive singular, and the nominative, vocative and accusative plural of **vāc** are identical in form.

Nevertheless vowel gradation remains an important feature of nominal inflexion, for although gradation of the root is almost entirely lost, gradation of the *suffix* is preserved in many types of declension. In this chapter attention is confined to the declension of stems ending in the suffix **an.** [Latin has a corresponding declension, but has standardised the strong grade in one type (*sermō*, *sermōnis*) and a weaker grade in another (*nōmen*, *nōminis*).]

Strong cases of the noun (those in which the accent stood originally not on the termination but on the stem) are nominative, vocative and accusative singular, nominative, vocative and accusative dual, and nominative and vocative (not accusative) plural for the masculine; and nominative, vocative and accusative plural only for the neuter. Feminines hardly occur, the feminine of changeable stems being formed by the addition of the suffix **ī.** The other cases are the weak cases. Of these, however, there is a subdivision in many types of declension between 'weakest' and 'middle' cases. The weakest cases are those whose termination begins with a vowel (**-aḥ**, **-i**, etc.); the middle cases are those whose termination begins with a consonant (**-bhiḥ**, **-su**, etc.) and also the nominative, vocative and accusative neuter singular, which has no termination.

Stems in **an**, such as **rājan** 'king' **nāman** 'name', are in fact among those which distinguish these three grades, strong, middle and weakest. Here the difference between middle and weakest is straightforward, and historically easily explained. The suffix **an** reduces to **n** in the weak grade, and this **n** remains before a vowel but appears as **a** (representing **n̥* 'syllabic *n*') in the middle cases: so **nāmnā** instrumental singular of **nāman**, but **nāmabhiḥ** (for **nāmn̥bhiḥ*) instrumental plural. The **n** is assimilated where appropriate to the class of the preceding consonant: so **rājñā** 'by the king'.

Except in the vocative singular the strong stem appears not in the guṇa grade **an** but in the vṛddhi grade **ān**: **rājānau** 'the two kings'. In the nominative singular masculine the final **n** is lost: **rājā** (cf. Latin *sermō*).

In the locative singular and in the nominative, vocative and accusative dual neuter, **an** may optionally replace **n**: **rājñi** or **rājani** 'in the king', **nāmnī** or **nāmanī** 'the two names'. In stems ending in **-man** or **-van** preceded by a consonant, **man/van** necessarily replaces *mn/vn* (for ease of pronunciation) in all the weakest cases: so **ātmanā, karmaṇā.**

An important practical point about nouns with changeable stems (and some consolation for the greater difficulties of inflexion) is that in the masculine plural they distinguish the nominative from the accuative. **suhṛdaḥ** (as well as being ablative and genitive singular) may be either nominative or accusative plural; **rājānaḥ** can only be nominative (or vocative)—and **rājñaḥ**, if plural, can only be accusative.

Exocentric compounds: bahuvrīhi

If a nominal compound functions neither as an aggregate in some sense of its parts (co-ordinative) nor as a hyponym, 'special instance', of one of its parts (determinative—in Classical Sanskrit that part is, in fact, always the *final* element, if we except rarities like **dṛṣṭa:pūrva**), then it must function as the qualifier of some substantival notion outside itself, whether the latter is expressed or left unexpressed. For this reason the term 'exocentric' is used to describe the third main class of nominal compounds. The class is extremely various: in principle, any meaningful collocation of words may be isolated and used as a descriptive tag. This is, in fact, our practice in English: we talk of a *ne'er-do-well* husband, *ban-the-bomb* marchers, the *two-car* family. The English practice helps to explain the way in which such compounds may have arisen in the Indo-European period, namely as survivals of an earlier stage of the language in which nouns had lacked inflexion, and relationships could be expressed by simple juxtaposition, much as in English: to give an example based on Sanskrit, **aśva mukha** 'horse's face'. When a system of inflexions arose, such collocations, where used with their primary value, could easily be superseded: so **aśvasya mukham**. Therefore compounds with determinative sense survived only if well established or of specialised meaning. Used, on the other hand, with exocentric value, **aśvamukha** 'horse face' could not be replaced by two inflected words and would thus survive as an adjective: **aśvamukhaḥ** 'the horse-faced (man)'.

There are very few instances of exocentric compounds in Sanskrit simply based on some random phrase (one example would be **ahaṃpūrva** 'wanting to be first' based on the phrase **ahaṃ pūrvaḥ** 'I'm first!'). The commonest type is that exemplified in the preceding paragraph, the compound based on two nouns standing in determinative relationship. This is termed in Sanskrit a **bahuvrīhi** compound (literally 'much-riced', an example of the class). In the system of punctuation here adopted, exocentric value is denoted by an underscore, and this is placed beneath the mark of the relationship between the elements. So based on the *dependent* determinative **aśva-mukhaṃ** 'horse's face' is the exocentric compound **aśva_̲-mukha** 'horse-faced'. In fact, however, the vast majority of bahuvrīhis are based on *descriptive* (karmadhāraya) relationship. Examples are **ugra:̲mukha** 'grim-faced', **tri:̲śīrṣa** 'three-headed', **kṛṣṇa:̲varṇa** 'black-coloured'.

In general, as these examples indicate, the type of compound in English which represents the bahuvrīhi most closely is that formed with the possessive suffix '-ed'. Truly parallel English bahuvrīhis are few, but a useful one to remember is 'bare:̲foot'. Like the determinative 'tooth-brush', it illustrates the fact that stem forms do not distinguish singular from plural: a bare-foot man is one whose *feet* are bare.

All bahuvrīhis are essentially adjectival. The compound on which a bahuvrīhi is based is reduced to a stem form, and then inflected to agree with a substantive expressed or understood. The stem form must in the first place be a masculine stem form. Thus a feminine substantive in **ā** at the end of a bahuvrīhi has its final vowel reduced to short **a**: e.g. from **svalp›:êcchā** 'small desire', **svalp›:̲êccha** 'having small desire'. But although in theory almost any noun might be used at the end of a bahuvrīhi, in practice restraint is observed so as to avoid awkward terminations. For instance, a polysyllabic feminine in **ī** is hardly to be found at the end of a bahuvrīhi (cf. Chapter 10). Among bahuvrīhis ending in consonants, a notable type (paralleled in Greek) is that formed from neuters in **-as**: e.g. from **su:manas** 'good mind', **su:̱manas** 'well-disposed', nom. sg. m. or f. **su:̱manāḥ** (cf. Gk. *eumenḗs*).

The adjective **mahānt** 'great' (Chapter 10) when used as the first member of a karmadhāraya or bahuvrīhi compound takes the form **mahā**: **mahā:puruṣaḥ** 'great man', **mahā:̱bala** 'of great strength'.

The term bahuvrīhi is often translated 'possessive compound', and this certainly reflects the prevailing sense of these compounds in Sanskrit. In perhaps nine cases out of ten the sense can be represented by putting the word 'having' before the determinative meaning of the compound: 'having three heads' and so forth. However, the sophisticated exploitation of bahuvrīhis is a striking feature of Classical Sanskrit, and the simple notion of 'possession' can be unhelpful or positively misleading in their interpretation, particularly in the many instances where a past participle forms the first element in the compound. Sanskrit commentators have standardised a more adequate analysis by means of a relative clause, the full neatness and usefulness of which will be more obvious later when the construction of Sanskrit relative clauses is explained (cf. Chapter 11, p. 175). For the present, the analysis is introduced in a translated version. Let us begin by labelling the first element in the compound A and the second element B. The compound then means

of/by/in *etc.*	whom/which	B (*sg.*/*du.*/*pl.*)	is/are	A (*or* of *etc.* A)
or simply whose				

By this analysis the compounds already encountered might become 'whose face is grim', 'whose heads are three', 'of which the colour is black', 'whose feet are bare', 'whose desires are few', 'whose disposition is good'. Where there is dependent determinative relationship, a preposition or 'apostrophe *s*' needs to be attached to A: 'whose face is a horse's', 'of whom there is the face of a horse'. As in the last example, the formula may be varied by substituting 'there is/there are'. This works very well for the normal possessive bahuvrīhis—'of whom there are three heads' etc.—but is not always appropriate elsewhere: the Sanskrit version of the formula usefully blurs this distinction.

Bahuvrīhis based on various special types of karmadhārayas occur. The prefixes **su** and **dus** are perhaps even commoner in bahuvrīhis than in simple karmadhārayas. **su:manas** has been mentioned; similarly, **dur:ātman** 'evil-natured'. The negative prefix **a** is probably rather less common in bahuvrīhi than in karmadhāraya sense (the alternative being the use of the prefix **nis**—see Chapter 9): examples are **a:nimitta** 'for which there is no cause' and **a:viśrāma** 'from which there is no respite, ceaseless'. An example of **sa** converted from karmadhāraya to bahuvrīhi sense is found in **sa:piṇḍa** 'having the ancestral offering in common', but **sa** usually has a different sense in exocentric compounds (see Chapter 9).

The prefixes **su** ('easily') and **dus** ('with difficulty') are used with verbal action nouns to give a 'gerundive' sense: e.g. **dur:jaya** 'difficult to conquer', **su:bodha** 'easy to understand'. The noun is normally in guṇa grade, even in the case of a medial **a**: thus **su:labha** 'easily got', **dur:labha** 'hard to get', even though **labhaḥ** does not occur as an independent word, the form being **lābhaḥ** 'acquisition'.

Corresponding to the karmadhāraya of comparison is a bahuvrīhi in which the same elements appear in reverse order: **vadana:paṅkajaṃ** 'the lotus of (her) face', but **paṅkaja:vadanā** 'the lotus-faced (girl)'. (This latter was classed by critics as simile rather than as metaphor.)

The first element of the bahuvrīhi may be an adverb instead of an adjective. Examples are **sarvato:mukha** '[whose face is in all directions:] facing all ways', and **tathā:vidha** or **evaṃ:vidha** (from **vidhā** 'form, sort') '[whose sort is thus:] of such a kind'.

When the first element of the bahuvrīhi is a past participle, an ambiguity exists which makes correct analysis important.

dṛṣṭ›:ârtha 'whose purpose is seen, having a visible purpose' is easily understood. **dṛṣṭa:kaṣṭa**, however, is used to mean not 'whose calamity is seen' but '*by whom* calamity has been seen', i.e. '(one) who has experienced calamity'. Similarly, **kṛta:śrama** means 'by whom exertions have been made', **vidita:vārtta** 'by whom news has been learnt'. A past participle like **datta** 'given' introduces a further ambiguity: **datt›:ādara** may mean either '*by whom* respect is given' or '*to whom* respect is given'.

Besides the mainly literal translations mentioned above, the use of bahuvrīhis may correspond to various kinds of idiom in English.

The 'having' of the 'possessive' translation may be replaced by a preposition such as 'of' or 'with', as in:

ramaṇīya:darśanaḥ (a man) *of* attractive appearance
bahu:svara (a word) *of* many syllables
ālakṣya:danta˸mukulāḥ a:nimitta:hāsaiḥ (children) *with* their buds of teeth just visible through causeless chuckles
ek›:ânvayo ›yam asmākam he is *of* one family with us

In apposition to the subject, a bahuvrīhi may often be translated by an absolute phrase in English:

ubhe vismayād urasi nihita:haste parasparam ālokayataḥ the two (girls) look at each other in astonishment, *their hands placed on their breasts*

The addition of **api** results in a concessive clause:

avasita:pratijñā˸bhāro ›pi Vṛṣal›-âpekṣayā śastraṃ dhārayāmi [though one by whom the burden of the promise has been fulfilled, through regard for Vṛṣala I bear the sword:] though I have discharged the burden of my promise, I bear the sword (of office) out of regard for Vṛṣala
van›:aûkaso ›pi vayaṃ loka-jñā eva though our home is the forest, we do know the world

The difference between Sanskrit and English idiom is most

strikingly illustrated in the many sentences in which a bahuvrīhi forms the predicate to a nominal sentence. The way of translating these will vary, but as a general rule the most naturally corresponding English sentence will make the final element of the bahuvrīhi into the subject, and the subject of the Sanskrit into a word dependent on it:

diṣṭyā jīvita꞉vatsā ›smi thank God *my* children are alive

mṛga-pracāra-sūcita꞉śvāpadam araṇyam the forest is one·in·which·the·beasts·are·indicated·by·the·movements ·of·the·deer:] the game in the forest has been tracked by the movements of the deer

nanv iyam saṃnihita꞉vetr›-āsan» aîva dvāra-prakoṣṭha-śālā [why, this hall of the entrance-court is in fact one·in·which·a·seat·of·cane·is·present:] why, there is already a canework couch here in the hall of the forecourt

In questions the neuter singular interrogative **kim** may be used as a stem form:

kiṃ꞉vyāpāro bhagavān Mārīcaḥ? [the revered son of Marīci is one whose occupation is what?:] how is the revered son of Marīci occupied?

teṣāṃ Daśarath›-ātmajānāṃ kiṃ꞉nāmadheyāny apatyāni? what are the names of the offspring of those sons of Daśaratha?

Where a past participle is used, a simple English perfect may be the obvious translation:

pratyāpanna꞉cetano vayasyaḥ [(my) friend is one·by·whom·consciousness·is·regained:] my friend has regained consciousness

labdh›꞉âvakāśā me manorathāḥ [my desires are ones·for·which·scope·has·been·obtained:] I have won the scope for my desires

It has already been pointed out that karmadhārayas are not freely formed as complete compounds. One reason for this will now be clear, namely the ambiguities of interpretation which would arise: **hataputraḥ** is not used in the sense of 'a slain son' because it is needed in the sense of '(he) whose son is slain' or '(he) who has slain a son'. Conversely, although bahuvrīhis as the earlier part of some longer compound are not impossible, they are not particularly common in simple prose style. The rule of thumb in translating from Sanskrit is therefore: expect **hataputra** as a complete word to be a bahuvrīhi, but as a stem form to be a karmadhāraya—thus **hata:putra-darśanam** 'the sight of (his) slain son [/sons]'.

'Called'

To express the idiom 'a man called Devadatta' the word **nāman** may be used in either of two ways: adverbially in the accusative, e.g. **nāma** 'by name':

Devadatto nāma puruṣaḥ a man, Devadatta by name

or else at the end of a bahuvrīhi compound (feminine in **ī**):

Devadatta:nāmā puruṣaḥ a man whose name is Devadatta

Madayantikā:nāmnī kanyakā a girl called Madayantikā

ātman

This is a masculine substantive meaning 'self'. It is also used, in the masculine *singular*, as a reflexive pronoun for all three numbers, genders and persons:

ātmānaṃ praśaṃsatha you are praising [the self:] yourselves

ātmany eṣā doṣaṃ na paśyati she sees no fault in herself

In the genitive, **ātmanaḥ**, it is thus a frequent alternative to the reflexive adjective **sva**:

ātmano gṛham idānīṃ praviśāmi I'll now enter my own house

Often a phrase qualifies **ātman** which in English would qualify the subject:

> **purā kila . . . Sītā:devī prāpta:prasava-vedanam ātmānam ati:duḥkha-saṃvegād Gaṅgā-pravāhe nikṣiptavatī** Once, it seems, Queen Sītā, when the pangs of childbirth were upon her, cast herself in the extremity of her suffering into the Ganges' stream

Neither **ātman** nor **sva** is restricted to referring to the nominative subject: they may refer to any appropriate substantive or pronoun in the vicinity: hence a phrase such as **asya sva:bhṛtyaḥ** 'this man's own servant'. In the following example, the first **sva** refers to **amuṣya,** the second to **mahī-patiḥ**:

> **sva:bhavan›-ôpanayanam apy amuṣya sva:māhātmya-prakāśanāya mahī-patir anvamaṃsta** and [for the displaying of:] to display his generosity, the king permitted [the carrying to his own home of that one:] him to be carried to his own home

svayam

The stem **sva** provides an indeclinable form **svayam.** This represents the notions 'personally' or 'of one's own accord' (the instrumental **ātmanā** is sometimes used in the same way) It may therefore correspond to the emphatic use of the English reflexive: **svayam āgacchati** 'he is coming himself (/in person)'. In combination with a past participle an agentive sense is uppermost: **svayam adhigata** 'acquired by oneself'.

Predicative accusatives

In sentences such as 'he likes his curry hot', 'they drink their martinis dry' much of the burden of statement is carried by an adjective ('hot', 'dry') syntactically dependent upon a subordinate element ('curry', 'martinis') in a sentence that might already appear to be structurally complete. Such an adjective is 'predicative' in rather the same way as is the adjectival complement of a nominal sentence: the sentences are, in fact, closely similar in meaning to 'the curry he likes *is hot*', 'the martinis they drink *are dry*'. In Sanskrit, too, the object of a verb may be qualified by such a predicate. The verb **avagam** 'understand, perceive, *etc.*' may be used to illustrate possible equivalents of the construction in English:

mūrkhaṃ tvām avagacchāmi
(*a*) I think you a fool
(*b*) I perceive you *to be* a fool
(*c*) I recognise you *as* a fool (/*for* a fool)
(*d*) I realise *that* you are a fool

There is no 'accusative and infinitive' construction of the Latin kind in Sanskrit, but an 'accusative and accusative' construction as illustrated by the above is not uncommon and may be an alternative to the use of an '**iti** clause'. Thus the above might also have been expressed by **mūrkhas tvam ity avagacchāmi.**

tat kiṃ khalv idānīṃ pūrṇam ātmano manorathaṃ n› âbhinandāmi? [so do I not now rejoice in my own desire (as) fulfilled:] may I not now rejoice that my desire is fulfilled?

Here again, **pūrṇam ātmano manoratham** might conceivably be replaced by **pūrṇo me manoratha iti.**

Particularly noteworthy is the predicative use with a verb such as **iṣ** 'want' of a present participle (Chapter 10):

bhadra Bhāsvaraka, na māṃ dūrī˜bhavantam[1] icchati kumāraḥ good Bhāsvaraka, His Highness does not want me [being far away:] to be far away

Verbal action nouns in *ana*

The suffix **ana** added to the verbal root (normally strengthened to guṇa grade) is sometimes used to form nouns with adjectival or agentive force: thus from **śubh** 'shine', **śobhana**

[1] For the tilde ˜ in compounds of **kṛ** and **bhū** see Chapter 12.

'brilliant'; from **nand** 'rejoice', **nandana** 'gladdening'. But its far more frequent function is to provide neuter action nouns. So from **dṛś** 'see', **darśanaṃ** '(act of) seeing'; from **ā+gam** 'come', **āgamanaṃ** '(act of) coming, arrival'. There is thus an overlap of meaning with the masculine action nouns in **a** already described, and sometimes both formations are found from the same root in much the same sense, e.g. **uparodhaḥ** or **uparodhanaṃ** '(act of) blocking'. A more concrete meaning is also not uncommon with this formation: **bhojanaṃ**, from **bhuj** 'enjoy, eat', means 'thing eaten, food' more often than it means 'act of eating'; **vacanaṃ** usually means 'thing spoken, word' rather than 'act of speaking' (cf. in English the two senses of the word 'utterance' and the frequent ambiguity of words ending in '-ation', so that, for instance, 'formation' can equally well mean 'act of forming' and 'thing formed').

The first **a** of the suffix coalesces with the vowel of roots ending in **ā**: **sthānaṃ** 'place', **jñānaṃ** 'knowledge', etc. The roots **labh** and **rabh** insert a nasal: **vipralambhanaṃ** 'deception'. Lengthening of a medial **a** is little found, except to some extent in distinguishing a causative significance: **maraṇaṃ** 'dying', **māraṇaṃ** 'killing'. More generally, however (and especially in later Sanskrit), derivative stems both causative and denominative make use of a related feminine suffix **anā**: **gaṇanā** 'counting', **prārthanā** 'solicitation', **vijñāpanā** 'requesting'.

saṃvṛtta

The past participle of **saṃvṛt** 'happen' is frequently used to express the 'change of state' equivalent (in past time) of a nominal sentence. It thus represents English 'became' or 'has become'.

eṣo ›smi kārya-vaśād Āyodhyakas tadānīṃ˜tanaś ca saṃvṛttaḥ behold, through (theatrical) need I have become (/turned into) an inhabitant of Ayodhyā and a man of the period

Often **jāta**, the past participle of **jan** 'be born, arise', is used in the same way:

niḥsahā ›si jātā you [*f.*] have become exhausted

'Palace', 'temple'

Sanskrit usually designates types of buildings more analytically than English. There is no single word that exclusively denotes either the residence of a king or the place where a god is worshipped. Therefore the notion 'palace' may be represented by an indefinite number of phrases meaning 'king's house', e.g. **nṛpa-bhavanaṃ**. (The word **prāsādaḥ** normally denotes a fine building and may therefore be used by itself to mean 'palace' if the context makes it plain who the owner is.) Similarly, 'temple' is expressed by the phrase 'house of god', e.g. **deva-kulaṃ**. Where a specific deity is named, the inclusion of a word such as **devaḥ** or **devatā** is, of course, not necessary: **Śiv›-āyatanaṃ** 'temple of Śiva'.

Vocabulary

aṅgurīyaka *m./n.* ring (for finger)
ati:bībhatsa extremely repulsive, foul
atrabhavatī this lady
anukūla favourable
anvayaḥ succession, lineage, family
aparādhaḥ offence
apavārita hidden
abhiyukta diligent
araṇyaṃ forest
arthaḥ meaning, matter; purpose, object
avasānaṃ termination, end, conclusion
avasita terminated, over
ātman *m.* self
āmodaḥ scent
āyatanaṃ abode
āsakta fastened, fixed, occupied
autsukyaṃ eagerness
kaṭaka *m./n.* (royal) camp
karman *n.* deed, work
kaṣāya astringent, sharp (of scent)
Kāma:devaḥ the god of Love
kusumaṃ flower
kesaraṃ hair, filament
kautukaṃ curiosity
krauryaṃ cruelty
gamanaṃ going
guṇaḥ merit, quality, worth
caryā movement, riding (in vehicle)
cittaṃ thought, mind
jāpyaṃ (muttered) prayer

tādṛśa (*f.* **ī**) (of) such (a kind)
dakṣiṇāpathaḥ southern region (of India), the Deccan
Dāruvarman *m.*, *pr. n.*
divasaḥ day
dur:bodha difficult to understand
dur:vipākaḥ cruel turn (of fortune)
daivaṃ fate, chance, fortune
doṣaḥ fault, inconvenience
dharmaḥ religious law, duty, piety
nāmadheyaṃ appellation, name
nāman *n.* name
nṛśaṃsa injurious; *m.* monster
Padmapuraṃ *name of a city*
pariṇāmaḥ evolution, outcome
parinirvāṇaṃ complete extinction
parivṛta surrounded, having a retinue
pariṣad *f.* assembly, audience
parīta encompassed, overcome
pādapaḥ tree
puṇḍarīkaṃ lotus
pratigrahaḥ present (*to a brahmin from a king*)
prabandhaḥ (literary) work
bahumānaḥ respect for (*loc.*)
manas *n.* mind
manda sluggish, slack
mahānt (*stem form in compound* **mahā**) great
mukhaṃ face
mudrā authorising seal/stamp, 'pass'
rathaḥ chariot
rājan *m.* king
vatsaḥ dear child
vṛttāntaḥ news; event, scene (of activity)
veśman *n.* residence
vaikhānasaḥ hermit, anchorite
vaitālikaḥ royal bard
vaimanasyaṃ despondency
vairaṃ hostility
vyañjanaṃ sign, insignia, disguise
śaṅkā suspicion, fear
śāpaḥ curse
śītala cool
°sad *ifc.* dweller (in)
sadṛśa (*f.* **ī**) similar, suitable, worthy
saṃdhyā twilight, evening
siddha achieved
sundara (*f.* **ī**) beautiful
stambhaḥ pillar

aṅk (X aṅkayati) brand, stamp
adhi+gam (I adhigacchati) find; realise, perceive
anu+kamp (I anukampate) sympathise with, take pity on
abhi+as (IV abhyasyati) practise; *p.p.* **abhyasta** familiar (to one through practice)
ava+nam (I avanamati, *p.p.* **avanata)** bow down, bend down
ut+śvas (II ucchvasiti) bloom, blossom
upa+śru (V upaśṛṇoti) hear of, learn of
jan *caus.* **(janayati)** beget, produce, arouse
nis+diś (VI nirdiśati) designate, specify
nis+kram (I niṣkrāmati) go out of (*abl.*)
pari+īkṣ (I parīkṣate) examine, scrutinise
pari+aṭ (I paryaṭati) wander about

prati + vas (I **prativasati**) dwell, live (in)
prati + abhi + jñā (IX **pratyabhijānāti**) recognise
bandh (IX **badhnāti**, *p.p.* **baddha**) bind, fix; enter into (friendship *or* hate)
vās (X **vāsayati**) perfume
vid (II **vetti**, *p.p.* **vidita**) know, learn, discover
sam + vṛt (I **saṃvartate**) happen, become (*see chapter*)

adhastāt + *gen.* beneath
itaḥ from here; over here
kiṃ tu (*first in sentence*) but
tadā then, at that time
nanu why! well!
bho bhoḥ ho there!
svayam (*emphatic pron.*) myself *etc.*, personally
hanta ah! alas!
hi (*enclitic*) for (*as conj.*)

Exercise 8a

हन्त सिद्धार्थौ स्वः ।१। कृतं रामसदृशं कर्म ।२। अस्ति दक्षि-
णापथे पद्मपुरं नाम नगरम् ।३। वयस्य इतः स्तम्भापवारित-
शरीरौ तिष्ठावः ।४। रमणीयः खलु दिवसावसानवृत्तान्तो
राजवेश्मनि ।५। किमर्थमगृहीतमुद्रः कटकान्निष्क्रामसि ।६।
वत्स अलमात्मापराधशङ्कया ।७। भो भोः किंप्रयोजनो ऽयमश्वः
परिवृतः पर्यटति ।८। कां पुनरत्रभवतीमवगच्छामि ।९। कुमार
नायमत्यन्तदुर्बोधो ऽर्थः ।१०। किंत्वमात्यराक्षसश्चाणक्ये बद्धवैरो
न चन्द्रगुप्ते ।११। तदेष स्वयं परीक्षितगुणान्ब्राह्मणान्प्रेषयामि
।१२। हा कष्टम् अतिबीभत्सकर्मा नृशंसो ऽस्मि संवृत्तः ।१३।
कथम् कृतमहापराधो ऽपि भगवतीभ्यामनुकम्पितो रामः ।१४।
यावदिदानीमवसितसंध्याजाप्यं महाराजं पश्यामि ।१५। स तदैव
देव्याः सीतायास्तादृशं दैवदुर्विपाकमुपश्रुत्य वैखानसः संवृत्तः
।१६। अफलमनिष्टफलं वा दारुवर्मणः प्रयत्नमधिगच्छामि ।१७।
सुन्दरि अपरिनिर्वाणो दिवसः ।१८। शकुन्तलादर्शनादेव
मन्दोत्सुको ऽस्मि नगरगमनं प्रति ॥ १९ ॥

Exercise 8b

1 This is a present from the king. 2 I went, my·curiosity·aroused·by·Avalokitā, to the temple·of·Kāmadeva. 3 This

signet ring is stamped·with·the·minister's·name. 4 We do not find a work with·the·qualities·specified·by·the·audience. 5 Why, you [*pl.*] too are exhausted by this work·of·piety. 6 'See, I [*m.*] have become Kāmandakī.' 'And I Avalokitā.' 7 Vṛṣala, these inconveniences happen to [**bhū**+*gen.*] kings (who are) themselves not·diligent. 8 Then why are you standing [**sthita**] with·the·lotus·of·your·face·bent·down? 9 For there lives a dear·friend [of me:] of mine, [having·the·disguise·of:] disguised·as·a·royal·bard, called Stanakalaśa. 10 Did (my) friend [*m.*] learn her·family·and·name? 11 Dearest, even the cruelty practised [**prayukta**] by me upon you has come [*use* **saṃvṛt**] to·have·a·favourable·outcome. So now I want [myself recognised:] to be recognised by you. 12 Though my mind·is·concerned·with·[**gata**]·Urvaśī, I have the same respect for Her Majesty. 13 But we are forest·dwellers, to·whom·riding·in·a·chariot·is·un·familiar. 14 So let us (both) just sit beneath this very kāñcanāra·tree, [by·which·is·perfumed:] which·perfumes·the·garden·with·a·sharp·cool·scent·from·the·filaments·of·blossomed·flowers.

Translate the following as nominal sentences with bahuvrīhis for predicate:

15 She has learnt·the·news·of·Sītā. 16 Oh, His Majesty's mind·is·occupied·with·other·(things). 17 What·is·the·name·of this vow of Her Majesty's? 18 And that curse [has·as·its·conclusion:] is ended·by·the·sight·of·the·ring. 19 Though (he is) overcome·with·despondency, the·sight·of His Majesty is·pleasant [**priya**].

Chapter 9

PARADIGMS: **śuci, mṛdu**; **dhanavant**; present ātmanepada of **nī**

Stems in short i and short u

Substantives in **i** and **u** occur in all three genders, corresponding in inflexion to the adjectives **śuci** and **mṛdu.** In these stems, however, a fair number of alternative forms are possible.

1 For clarity, the distinctively feminine endings **yai/yāḥ/yām, vai/vāḥ/vām** of the singular have been listed in the paradigms. These endings have really spread by analogy from the **ī** declension, and it is not uncommon for feminines in the dative, ablative, genitive and locative singular, whether adjective or substantive, to decline like the masculine (reverting, in other words, to their original inflexion): so **tan-matau** or **tan-matyām** 'in his opinion'.

2 The special neuter forms with infix **n** (sg. **ne/naḥ/ni**; du. **noḥ**) are optional in adjectives but *not* in substantives. Therefore neuter adjectives may be declined like the masculine in all cases but the nominative, vocative and accusative: **śucino vāriṇaḥ** or **śucer vāriṇaḥ** (but *not *vāreḥ*) 'from the clean water'.

3 The vocative singular of neuters may take guṇa like the masculine–feminine: **vāri** or **vāre, madhu** or **madho.**

4 Adjectives in **u** may also form their feminine by adding the

suffix **ī**: **laghu** f. or **laghvī** f. 'light'. (Feminines in lengthened **ū** are also occasionally found.)

Substantives in **i** occur freely at the end of bahuvrīhi compounds: so from **buddhi** f. 'intelligence', **mugdha꞉buddheḥ** '(this is the argument) of a simple-minded (person)'—a terse comment on another scholar's views.

Stems in *vant* and *mant*

Corresponding in sense to English compounds such as 'white-winged', formed with the possessive suffix '-ed', are bahuvrīhis such as **sita꞉pakṣa** 'of whom there are white wings', formed without any suffix. The English suffix may also be added to a single word: so 'winged', in the sense of 'possessing wings'. In these latter circumstances Sanskrit, like English, must make use of a suffix. One of the most widely used is the suffix **vant**: so **pakṣavant** 'of whom there are wings, winged'. It combines very freely with stems which either end in a stop, **m, a** or **ā** or have **m, a** or **ā** as their penultimate sound. Care should be exercised in attaching it to a consonant stem, since it normally but not always follows the rules of *internal* sandhi (e.g. **payasvant** 'juicy' but **sragvant** 'garlanded').

The suffix **mant** (also with internal sandhi) normally replaces **vant** after stems ending in **i, ī, u, ū, ṛ, o** and **iṣ, uṣ,** and sometimes after stops: **dhīmant** 'having wit, wise'; **Garutmant** '[the Winged One:] the divine bird Garuḍa'.

The inflexion of these stems is straightforward: the strong stem ends in **ant,** the weak in **at**; the feminine ends in **atī**; and the nominative singular masculine in **ān.** In forming compounds the stem form is **at.**

Ātmanepada

The forms of the present indicative so far learnt are those of the active voice or **parasmaipada** ('word for another'). But in Sanskrit, finite tenses (and the participles attached to them) show a second set of forms, those of the **ātmanepada** ('word for oneself'). The distinction is not made in such nominal formations as the past participle, absolutive, etc. The ātmanepada corresponds to the middle voice of Greek, and its underlying implication is that the action or state expressed by the verb affects the subject. Thus **yajati** 'sacrifices' is used of the officiating priest (or in earlier times of the Fire God who carries the oblation), while **yajate** 'sacrifices' is used of the one for whose benefit the sacrifice is being made. But except in a few instances like this, the underlying implication is so blurred that it is not worth pursuing. It must rather be taken as a fact of the language that some verbs are found only in the parasmaipada, a few only in the ātmanepada, and some show both sets of forms with little evident distinction of meaning. (Sometimes there are differences within a single verb, for example between ātmanepada in the present system and parasmaipada in the perfect.) The form of the present indicative quoted in the vocabulary will show whether a verb is to be inflected in the parasmaipada (termination **ti**) or the ātmanepada (termination **te**).

vartate

It is, however, worth noting that verbs regularly conjugated in the ātmanepada are more usually intransitive in sense. One important such verb is **vṛt** (I **vartate**), literally 'turn, revolve' ('turn' in transitive sense is expressed by the causative **vartayati**). It is common in such meanings as 'proceed, be current' and thus often translates 'be, exist' in an 'active' as opposed to a stative sense, particularly where the subject is an abstract noun.

hanta, bībhatsam agrato vartate [Oh, repulsiveness is going on in front:] What ghastliness is before me!
atīva me kautukaṃ vartate [there is curiosity in me excessively:] I am feeling intensely curious
kā velā vartate? what time is it?

Past active participle

The possessive suffix **vant**, in addition to its regular use with substantives, may be added to past participles. Its effect is to convert a passive sense into an active: so **likhita** 'written', **likhitavant** 'having written'. In itself, however, such a description gives a misleading impression of the scope of the formation, for in practice (apart from its occurrence in locative absolutes) it is usually confined to a particular function–that of providing an active alternative to past passive sentences by standing in the nominative as a predicate to a nominative subject. The object, if there is one, stands in the accusative case. So instead of **tena likhito lekhaḥ** '[by him (is) written the letter:] he has written the letter', we may have **sa lekhaṃ likhitavān** '[he (is) having written the letter:] he has written the letter'. When the subject is first or second person, it is usually expressed by the appropriate form of **as** 'be' (occasionally by the pronoun):

> **Menakā kila sakhyās te janma-pratiṣṭh» êti sakhī: janād asmi śrutavān** I heard from (her) friends that Menakā was the mother of your friend's wife (*the first* **sakhī** = wife of a friend, **janma-pratiṣṭhā** *lit.* birth-foundation)

The participle naturally agrees with the subject in number and gender as well as case:

> **atha tāḥ . . . mām aṅgulī-vilāsen› ākhyātavatyaḥ** then they (*f.*) announced me with a playful movement of their fingers

The chief effect of this construction is to enable the subject of past statements to be put into the nominative rather than the instrumental case. The formation is unnecessary with past participles which do not bear a passive sense, and is not usually found in such cases. Occasionally, however, a form such as **(sā) āgatavatī** 'she came' for **(sā) āgatā** does occur. The subject of a past active participle is normally personal, and masculine or feminine in gender.

Exocentric compounds : prepositional compounds

In addition to the ubiquitous determinative-based bahuvrīhis, there exists a rather smaller class of exocentric compounds in Sanskrit in which the first member stands in the relationship of a governing preposition to the second member. These compounds are exceptional in that the relationship between the elements is neither co-ordinative nor determinative: in punctuating them, this relationship has therefore been left unmarked, and only the underscore, denoting exocentric value, is employed.

Typical examples are: **ati_mātra** 'exceeding the proper measure', from **ati** 'beyond' and **mātrā** f. 'measure'; **prati_loma** 'against the nap, *à rebours*'; **upari_martya** 'above mortals, superhuman'. An English example would be 'over_head' as in 'over_head railway'.

The prepositions thus have a different value from when they are used with determinative relationship. This may be illustrated by examples of the prefixes **ati** 'beyond' and **ut** 'up, high', which in prepositional compounds carries the significance 'eschewing':

(*a*) karmadhāraya (substantive or adjective):

ati:bhāraḥ excessive load **ut:svanaḥ** high sound **ati:bībhatsa** excessively repulsive **uc:caṇḍa** highly violent

(*b*) determinative-based bahuvrīhi:

ati:̲bala having excessive strength **ut:̲karṇa** having the ears (pricked) up

(*c*) prepositional compound:

ati_bodhisattva surpassing the bodhisattvas **un_nidra** renouncing sleep, wakeful

sa and *nis*

Particularly common is a pair of prefixes of opposed meaning, **sa** 'with, having' and **nis** 'without, lacking'. [Since these prefixes do not occur as independent prepositions, it would be possible to treat them as contracting a karmadhāraya relationship like **su**, **dus** and **a**: the present treatment is adopted because it is convenient to distinguish, for example, **sa_rūpa** 'having form' from the more indisputably karmadhāraya value of **sa:rūpa** 'having the same form', and because **nis** is not normally an alternative to **a** in forming simple karmadhārayas.] So **nir_āśa** 'without hope, hopeless'; **sa_viṣa** 'with poison, having poison' (e.g. **sa_viṣam auṣadham** 'poisoned medicine').

sa is so common a prefix that it is worth distinguishing various shades of meaning and possible translations:

1 'Accompanied by':

sa_putra āgataḥ 'he has come with his son' (This is a common alternative to saying **putreṇa saha**.)

2 'And':

This is the previous usage extended to cases where we would probably use co-ordination in English: **sa_śaraś cāpaḥ** '[bow with arrow:] bow and arrow'.

ataḥ khalu me sa_bāhya꞉karaṇo ›ntar:ātmā prasīdati [from this of course:] so that is why my soul within and my external senses are at peace

3 'Possessing, containing, having':

Here the sense is close to that of the suffix **vant**. Both **balavant** and **sa_bala** may be translated 'possessing strength, strong'. When a distinction can be drawn, it is that **sa** marks a temporary, **vant** a more permanent characteristic: so **sa_putra** means 'having a son with one' as opposed to 'alone'; **putravant** means 'having a son' as opposed to 'childless'. Compounds with **sa** are particularly common in the neuter singular as adverbs of manner: e.g. **sa_kopam** 'with anger, angrily'.

Compounds with *yathā*

Conveniently classed with prepositional compounds, although strictly distinguishable from them, are compounds whose first member is a relative adverb, most often **yathā** 'as': so **yathā_›rtha** 'as (is) the meaning, corresponding to the meaning'; **yathā_›rha** 'as deserved'; **yath»_ôkta** 'as stated', **yathā_nirdiṣṭa** 'as specified'.

The term *avyayībhāva*

These latter particularly, and prepositional compounds in general, are most frequently employed in the neuter singular as adverbs. (The same usage is found in English, as in 'the aeroplane passed overhead', in contrast with the non-compound form 'the aeroplane passed over our heads'.) When so used, the class has a special name in Sanskrit, **avyayībhāva** 'conversion to indeclinable'. Thus **ā_mūlam** 'down to the root, radically', **anu_Mālinī˘tīram** 'along the bank of the Mālinī'. Particularly noteworthy is the distributive use of the preposition **prati**: from **kriyā** 'action', **prati_kriyam** 'action for action'; from **dinaṃ** 'day', **prati_dinam** 'day by day, daily'.

Polite forms of address

In Sanskrit it is not positively impolite to address someone in the second person singular, but more specifically polite forms of address are also common. These usually involve a substantive construed with a third person verb form and having a literal meaning something like 'Your Honour' (cf. Spanish *usted*). Much the commonest, so common that its force is very little different from that of the second person pronoun, is **bhavant** 'you'. (The various translations here attached are merely matters of convenience.) This is usually considered to have originated from a contraction of **bhagavant** 'Your Reverence' and is inflected like any other stem ending in the suffix **vant**: it is thus to be distinguished from **bhavant** 'being', present participle of **bhū** 'be', of which the nominative singular masculine is **bhavan** with short **a**.

sulabh» aîva Buddharakṣitā-priyasakhī bhavataḥ Buddharakṣitā's dear friend [is really easily-won by Your Honour:] is easy enough for you to win (*one young man talking to another*)

In talking of someone in his absence, the compound form **tatrabhavant** 'His Honour [there]' may be used; similarly, **atrabhavant** 'His Honour [here]', usually of someone actually present, whether addressed directly or not.

The feminine forms of these pronouns are **bhavatī, tatrabhavatī, atrabhavatī.**

Sometimes as a mark of respect the plural of the second person or of **bhavant (yūyam, bhavantaḥ)** is used in addressing one person. Among other possible forms of polite address are:

āryaḥ [the noble one:] Your/His Excellency; *f.* **āryā**

āyuṣmant [the long-lived one:] Sire *etc.—used particularly but not exclusively of kings and monks*

bhagavant [the blessed one:] Your/His Reverence—*used of religious people and gods*: *thus* **bhagavad-gītā** Song of the Blessed One (*i.e.* Krishna); *f.* **bhagavatī.**

mahābhāgaḥ [the fortunate one:] noble sir, the noble gentleman *used especially by women in addressing or referring to men of good birth*

These forms (from **āryaḥ** onwards) are also used freely in the vocative. In addition, the vocative form **bhadra** 'my good fellow, my dear man' is often used in addressing men of comparatively low social status.

janaḥ

The word **janaḥ** 'person, people' is used at the end of a determinative compound to imply indefiniteness or plurality: **kāmi:janaḥ** 'a lover, some lovers, lovers in general'. As part of a longer compound it thus helps to suggest a plural: **suhṛd-vacana-saṃmūḍha** 'bewildered by the word of his friend', **suhṛj:jana-vacana-saṃmūḍha** 'bewildered by the words of his (various) friends'. A respectful vagueness rather than plurality may be implied: **guru:janaḥ** 'elders, tutor, guardian'; **mātṛ:janaḥ** '(my) mother'.

diṣṭyā

The form **diṣṭyā**, literally 'by good luck', is used to express strong pleasure:

> **sakhe Śakaṭadāsa, diṣṭyā dṛṣṭo ›si** Śakaṭadāsa my friend, thank heaven I see you

In particular, it is used with the verb **vṛdh** 'grow, prosper' to express congratulations, the reason for the congratulations being expressed in the instrumental:

> **bhadre Madayantike, diṣṭyā vardhase bhrātur Mālatī-lābhena** dear Madayantikā, you are congratulated (I congratulate you) on your brother's winning of Mālatī

[The causative of **vṛdh** thus has the same construction as the English 'congratulate' and is used where the simple verb cannot be (as it can in the previous example): **tāṃ diṣṭyā vardhitavān asi** 'you congratulated her'.]

Denominative verbs

Denominative verbs are verbs formed from nouns: thus in English 'bowdlerise' from the proper name 'Bowdler'; 'hand' ('he hands') from the substantive 'hand'; 'blacken' from the adjective 'black'. Where verbs and nouns exist side by side, we may hesitate (unless we have historical information) as to which has priority—what, for instance, of 'a brush' and 'he brushes'? A practical distinction exists in Sanskrit, in that the grammarians assigned *roots* to all verbs which they did not regard as denominative.

The most usual type of denominative in Sanskrit is made by the addition of the suffix **ya** to the noun stem (the third person singular present thus ends in **yati**). The significance of the formation varies with the noun. From **tapas** 'religious austerity' is formed **tapasyati** 'he practises austerities'; from **namas** 'homage', **namasyati** 'he pays homage'. It may be noted that the roots **tap** 'be hot' and **nam** 'bend' (both class I verbs), from which the above nouns in turn derive, have 'suffer pain, practise austerities' and 'bow, pay homage' among their meanings. Thus **tapati** and **namati** are more 'primitive' non-denominative alternatives to the specialised denominatives **tapasyati** and **namasyati**. Stems in **a** do not lose the vowel before the suffix: so from **deva, devayati** 'he cultivates the gods, is pious'.

Stems in **a** also form denominatives with lengthened **ā**. These latter are usually intransitive and conjugated in the ātmanepada, and may correspond to a transitive form in **ayati**: so from **śithila** 'slack', **śithilayati** 'slackens (*trans.*), makes loose' and **śithilāyate** 'slackens (*intrans.*), becomes loose'.

More rarely, another type of denominative is found which lacks the **ya** suffix: thus from **ut:kaṇṭha** '[having the neck raised:] eager', **utkaṇṭhate** 'longs for, is in love with'.

Examples of denominative verbs which, because of their accent, are classed as class X verbs have been given in Chapter 7. Another such example is **mantr** (X **mantráyate**) 'takes counsel', which is really based on **mantraḥ** 'counsel', the latter deriving in turn from the root **man** 'think'. The absolutives of **mantr** are **mantrayitvā** and **-mantrya**.

Vṛddhi derivatives

Secondary nominal formations from existing nominal stems are made in a wide variety of ways in Sanskrit: thus from **rūpaṃ** 'beauty', **rūpavant** (or **rūpin**—see Chapter 10) 'beautiful', **rūpavattara** 'more beautiful', etc. One of the most characteristic types of formation involves a strengthening to vṛddhi grade of the first syllable of the stem and the addition of a suffix, most usually **a** or **ya**. Stems ending in **a** or **ā** lose their final vowel before either suffix (so that one **a** may merely be exchanged for another). The general sense of the formation is something like 'belonging or appertaining to, deriving from', etc. From **puraṃ** 'city', **paura** 'urban'; as a masculine substantive, **pauraḥ** 'citizen'. From **puruṣaḥ** 'man', **pauruṣa** 'manly'; as a neuter substantive, **pauruṣaṃ** 'manliness'. From a consonant stem, **tapas** 'religious austerity', **tāpasaḥ** 'one who practises austerities, an ascetic'. From a feminine substantive **Yamunā** 'the river Yamunā (Jumna)', **Yāmuna** (*f.* **Yāmunī**) 'relating to the Yamunā'. Similarly, from **vidyā** 'learning', **vaidya** 'learned', **vaidyaḥ** 'physician'. Where sandhi has reduced the prefix **vi** to **vy** in the original noun, it is expanded by vṛddhi to **vaiy**: thus **vyākaraṇaṃ** 'analysis, grammar', **vaiyākaraṇaḥ** 'grammarian'.

Two types of formation are especially noteworthy:

1 Many patronymics ('son or descendant of') are formed with vṛddhi and the suffix **a**: **Saubhadraḥ** 'son of Subhadrā'; **Mārīcaḥ** '(Kaśyapa) son of Marīci'; **Daivodāsa** 'descended from Divodāsa'. Stems ending in **u** usually make guṇa of this vowel as well as vṛddhi of the initial syllable: **Pauravaḥ** 'descendant of Puru'. The feminine of these forms is always in **ī**: **Draupadī** 'daughter of Drupada'. Instead of patronymic value, the forms may sometimes bear the sense of 'king' or 'leader': **Śaibyaḥ** 'king of the Śibis'; **Vāsavaḥ** '(the god Indra) chief of the Vasus'. And there are yet other kinds of relationship which may be similarly expressed—thus **Śaivaḥ** 'follower of the god Śiva'.

2 From adjectives and substantives, neuter abstract substantives are often formed by vṛddhi and the suffix **ya**. So **adhika** 'superior', **ādhikyaṃ** 'superiority'; **sadṛśa** 'like, similar', **sādṛśyaṃ** 'likeness, similarity'; **vi**:**manas** 'despondent', **vaimanasyaṃ** 'despondency'; **sujanaḥ** 'good person', **saujanyaṃ** 'benevolence, kindness'; **paṇḍitaḥ** 'scholar', **pāṇḍityaṃ** 'learning, scholarship'.

Although both types of formation (and especially the latter) are fairly productive, the above remarks are intended merely to be explanatory: vṛddhi derivatives are listed in the vocabulary as required.

Vocabulary

agni *m.* fire
aṅguli *f. or* **aṅgulī** finger
añjali *m.* the hands joined together (*in salutation or for alms*)
atikrānta [gone beyond:] past, bygone
atidāruṇa dreadful
atyudāra proud, noble
anu_rūpa conformable, suitable, proper
anvita accompanied by, full of
aparāgaḥ disaffection
a:pūrva unprecedented, strange
arthaḥ meaning
avagrahaḥ obstacle, restraint
a:viṣayaḥ [non-sphere:] matter beyond the scope (of)
ākhyā appellation, name
ātapaḥ heat (*esp.* of sun)
ātma-jā [born of oneself:] daughter
āyuṣmant long-lived (*see chapter*)
āśrama-padaṃ site of hermitage, hermitage
āsanna near; *ifc.* beside
ugra fierce
utsuka eager; **utsukaṃ** eagerness
upakāraḥ help, aiding (of)
upajāpaḥ instigation to rebellion, 'overtures'
upapanna suitable, possible
ṛṣi *m.* seer
Kaṇvaḥ *pr. n.*
gāthā verse (*esp. in the āryā metre*)
guru heavy; *m.* teacher, elder, senior, guardian
cetas *n.* mind, heart
-jña *ifc.* knowing, aware of, recognising
tatrabhavant His Honour *etc.* (*see chapter*)
tatrabhavatī that lady *etc.* (*see chapter*)
tapas *n.* (religious) austerity
dāruṇa cruel
dhī˜mant wise
nir_utsuka without eagerness
patnī wife; **dharma-patnī** lawful wife
para˜vant [having another:] under another's control; beside oneself, overwhelmed
paryāpta sufficient
pārthivaḥ king, ruler
Puṇḍarīkaḥ *pr. n.*
prakṛti *f.* nature, disposition; *pl.* subjects (of king)
praṇidhi *m.* (secret) agent
pratijñā promise
prahṛṣṭa delighted
bakulaṃ bakula-tree blossom
bahumānaḥ respect
brahman *n.* (religious) chastity
bhagavant reverend (sir) (*see chapter*)
bhadra good; *m. voc.* my good fellow
bhavanaṃ house, residence
bhavant you (*see chapter*)
Bhūrivasu *m., pr. n.*

mandārah, mandāra:vṛkṣakaḥ coral-tree
mahiman *m.* greatness
Mah»:êndraḥ [the great] Indra
mālā garland
mṛgayā hunting, the chase
yath»_ôkta as stated, as described
rathyā [carriage-]road, street
ramaṇīya attractive
lajjā shame, embarrassment
lekhaḥ letter, epistle
valaya *m. n.* bracelet; circle, enclosure
vikramaḥ valour
vighnaḥ obstacle, hindrance
vibhūti *f.* splendour, wealth; *pl.* riches
vivasvant *m.* [the Shining One:] the sun
viṣaṃ poison; **viṣa-kanyā** poison-girl
Viṣṇuśarman *m., pr. n.*
vismayaḥ astonishment
velā time (of day)
Vaideha belonging to (the country of) Videha
vyasanaṃ weak spot, weakness
vyāpāraḥ occupation
śatru *m.* enemy
śāśvata (*f.* ī) perpetual
sakhe *voc. of* **sakhi** *m.* friend
sacivaḥ counsellor, minister
saṃdarśanaṃ sight, beholding (of)
saṃnihita present (*as opp.* absent)
samāgamaḥ meeting with, union
saṃbhāvya credible
saṃmardaḥ crush, encounter, throng
sādhu good; *n.* **sādhu** bravo!
sutā daughter
Saudhātaki *m., pr. n.*
hetu *m.* motive, ground for (*loc.*)
homaḥ oblation, sacrifice

anu+sthā (I anutiṣṭhati, *p.p.* **anuṣṭhita)** carry out, perform, act
anu+smṛ (I anusmarati) remember
abhi+dhā (III abhidadhāti, *p.p.* **abhihita)** say, speak
abhi+vad *caus.* **(abhivādayate)** greet
ā+diś (VI ādiśati) order, proclaim
ā+śaṅk (I āśaṅkate) fear, doubt, be afraid
utkaṇṭhate *denom.* long for, be in love with (*gen.*)
upa+labh (I upalabhate) acquire, ascertain, discover
upa+sthā (I upatiṣṭhate) stand near, be at hand
kṣam (I kṣamate) be patient, endure
gam *caus.* **(gamayati)** spend (time)
tarj *caus.* **(tarjayati)** threaten, scold
dah (I dahati) burn
ni+kṣip (VI nikṣipati) throw, cast into (*loc.*); place, deposit
ni+vid *caus.* **(nivedayati)** report, inform someone (*dat./gen.*) of something (*acc.*)
ni+vṛt (I nivartate) go back, return
pari+vṛdh *caus.* **(parivardhayati)** cause to grow, tend (plants)
prati+budh (IV pratibudhyate) wake up (*intrans.*)

pra + sthā *caus.* **(prasthāpayati)** despatch
man (IV manyate) think, suppose
vac (II vakti, *p.p.* **ukta)** tell, say
vṛt (I vartate) exist *etc.* (*see chapter*)
vṛdh (I vardhate) increase, prosper; **+ diṣṭyā**: *see chapter*
sam + car (I saṃcarate) walk, stroll
sam + diś (VI saṃdiśati) command
sam + ṛ *caus.* **(samarpayati)** hand over to (*dat.*/*gen.*)
sam + mantr (X saṃmantrayati) take counsel, consult
smṛ *caus.* **(smārayati)** cause to remember, remind
han *caus.* **(ghātayati)** cause to be killed, have killed

atha now (*as unemphatic introductory particle*)
kaccid (*interrogative particle introducing tentative enquiry*) perhaps?
kim iti with what in mind? why?
tataḥ thereupon, then
nāma (*often used as an emphatic particle*) indeed *etc.*
nis *ibc.* without, lacking (*see chapter*)
prāk previously, before
prāyeṇa generally
bahuśaḥ often
yathā *ibc., see chapter*
sa *ibc., see chapter*
saṃprati now
hi assuredly

Exercise 9a

किमुक्तवानसि । १ । संप्रति निवर्तामहे वयम् । २ । कृताञ्जलिः प्रणमति । ३ । सर्वानभिवादये वः । ४ । सखे पुण्डरीक नैतदनुरूपं भवतः । ५ । यावदुपस्थितां होमवेलां गुरवे निवेदयामि । ६ । कच्चिदहमिव विस्मृतवांस्त्वमपि । ७ । परवन्तो वयं विस्मयेन । ८ । आर्य अपि शत्रोर्व्यसनमुपलब्धम् । ९ । तत्किमित्याशङ्कसे । १० । अहमधुना यथादिष्टमनुतिष्ठामि । ११ । भगवन् न खलु कश्चिदविषयो नाम धीमताम् । १२ । शकुन्तला सखीमङ्गुल्या तर्जयति । १३ । साधु सखे भूरिवसो साधु । १४ । किमयं प्रतिबुद्धो ऽभिहितवान् । १५ । अथ सा तत्रभवती किमाख्यस्य राजर्षेः पत्नी । १६ । भद्र अथाग्निप्रवेशे सुहृदस्ते को हेतुः । १७ ।

परवती खलु तत्रभवती न च संनिहितगुरुजना । १८ । दिष्ट्या धर्मपत्नीसमागमेन पुत्रमुखसंदर्शनेन चायुष्मान्वर्धते । १९ । तत्किमयमार्येण सलेखः पुरुषः कुसुमपुरं प्रस्थापितः । २० । तत्रभवान्कण्वः शाश्वते ब्रह्मणि वर्तते इयं च वः सखी तस्यात्मजेति कथमेतत् । २१ । ममापि कण्वसुतामनुस्मृत्य मृगयां प्रति निरुत्सुकं चेतः । २२ । अपि चन्द्रगुप्तदोषा अतिक्रान्तपार्थिवगुणान्स्मारयन्ति प्रकृतीः । २३ । एतामसंभाव्यां ब्राह्मणस्य प्रतिज्ञां श्रुत्वा ससचिवो राजा प्रहृष्टमना विस्मयान्वितः सबहुमानं तस्मै विष्णुशर्मणे कुमारान्समर्पितवान् ॥ २४ ॥

Exercise 9b

Use the past active participle where appropriate. 'You' when preceded by an asterisk is to be translated by **bhavant.**

1 Is (your) austerity without·hindrance? 2 Friend Makaranda, are *you in love with Madayantikā? 3 But where did Mālatī see Mādhava before? 4 Lady, a shame·less Lakṣmaṇa herewith [**eṣaḥ**] salutes (you). 5 What do *you [*pl.*] say? 6 Mālatī has·a·noble·nature. 7 The riches of Minister·Bhūrivasu are indeed attractive. 8 There is a dreadful throng·of·people. 9 I told *you the story·[**vṛttāntaḥ**]·of·(my)·first·sight of Śakuntalā. 10 Reverend Arundhatī, I Sīradhvaja (King) of Videha greet (you). 11 Are Candragupta's·subjects responding to [**kṣam**] our·overtures? 12 He thinks me actually not·present. 13 A rather [**ko ›pi**] strange ground·for·respect towards [*loc.*] (one's) elders, Saudhātaki! 14 This (man), employed·by·Rākṣasa, had Parvateśvara killed by a poison·girl. 15 (She) casts the garland·of·bakulas into Mādhava's joined hands. 16 (I) congratulate *you on your greatness·in·valour, sufficient·for·the·aiding·of·Mahendra. 17 Thereupon there enters, her·occupation·as·described, together with two [female] friends, Śakuntalā. 18 Truly [**nanu**] friend, we [two] often walk along [*instr.*] the very street·beside·

the·minister's·residence—so this is possible. 19 To Candra-gupta's·subjects assuredly it is Cāṇakya's·faults which are grounds·for·disaffection. 20 Friend, the sun burns without·restraint, as cruel as fate. 21 Bravo, Vṛṣala, bravo! You have commanded (this) after consulting with my own [**eva**] heart. 22 Ah! the meaning·of·the·verse is 'I am one·who·has·[**jña**]·news·of·Kusumapura, and *your·agent'. 23 See, we two have entered Prajāpati's hermitage, its·coral·trees·tended·by·Aditi. 24 This time when·the·heat·is·fierce that lady generally spends with·her·friends on the banks·of·the·Mālinī with·[**vant**]·(their)·enclosures·of·creepers.

Chapter 10

PARADIGMS: Stems in **ī** and **ū**, **strī**; stems in **in**; present participles in **ant**, **mahānt**; imperative (para. and ātm.) of **nī**

Stems in *ī* and *ū*

Polysyllabic stems in **ī** such as **nadī** were introduced in Chapter 7. The declension of the few polysyllables in **ū** is exactly parallel, with the important exception that they add **ḥ** in the nominative singular. Quite different from these, and parallel to each other, are the monosyllabic stems in **ī** and **ū**: these in effect are like consonant stems, with **ī/ū** changing to **iy/uv** before vowels (though they have the option of the special feminine endings **ai**, **āḥ** and **ām**).

It will be noted that the word **strī** 'woman' behaves more like a polysyllabic than a monosyllabic stem: it is to be treated as one, and probably was one in origin.

It has already been mentioned that nouns like **nadī** are rare at the end of an exocentric compound. Sometimes the difficulty is surmounted by the addition of the adjectival suffix **ka**: so **sa_patnī˜ka** 'with one's wife', **pravṛtta꞉bībhatsa꞉kiṃvadantī˜ka** '(citizens) among whom foul rumours are current'. Exocentric compounds based on **ī/ū** monosyllables and determinatives formed with verbal roots in **ī** and **ū** do occur, and are most usually inflected like the plain monosyllables (alternative forms being possible, but neuter forms of any kind being little found). Examples are **su꞉dhī** 'of good intelligence', **padma-bhū** 'sprung from a lotus'.

Stems in *in*

The inflexion of stems in **in** presents little difficulty. They are essentially single-stem, but the final **n** drops before consonants and in the nominative (vocative) and accusative neuter singular. The nominative singular masculine ends in **ī**, and the nominative, vocative and accusative neuter plural in **īni**; the feminine adds **ī**—thus **dhaninī**.

The suffix **in** is a common alternative to the suffix **vant** after stems in **a** or **ā**, the final vowel being dropped. Thus **balavant** or **balin** 'possessing strength, strong'; **śikhāvant** or **śikhin** 'crested'. With the same meaning, but rare, are the suffixes **vin** (in particular, after a number of nouns in **as**) and **min**. Two common examples of the former are **tapasvin** 'practising austerities, ascetic' (also 'pitiable') and **manasvin** 'possessed of intelligence'. The substantive **svāmin** 'owner, master' derives from **sva** 'own' and the suffix **min**.

in as a verbal suffix

The same suffix may also be added, with strengthening of the root, to verbs: so from the root **pat**, **pātin** 'flying, falling'. [In this instance at least, it might seem that the suffix can be regarded as added to the verbal action noun **pātaḥ** 'flight, fall', and certainly the distinction between the 'primary' formation described here and the 'secondary' formation described above is not absolute. But there are limiting cases of difference of form: thus from **bhuj** 'enjoy', the velar consonant of **bhogaḥ** 'enjoyment' contrasts with the palatal of **bhojin** 'enjoying'.] In this formation the root syllable is almost invariably heavy, medial **a** being lengthened where necessary to **ā**. Roots ending in **ā** take a connecting **y**: thus **sthāyin** 'remaining, stable'.

The formation has an active verbal meaning, close to that of the present participle. Where it differs from this latter is in tending towards a more general, characterising sense: e.g. **nagara-gāmī mārgaḥ** 'the road going to the city'. The difference is conveniently illustrated by the phrase **Candra-gupt›-ânuyāyinā rāja-loken› ânugamyamānaḥ** 'being attended (on this occasion—*present participle*) by the princes that (would normally—*adjective in* **in**) attend Candragupta'.

Here are examples from the verbs **chid** 'cut out', **anu+kṛ** 'imitate', **hṛ** 'carry', **śaṃs** 'proclaim':

vimarśa-cchedi vacanam [the speech is doubt-removing:] (her) words are such as to remove all doubt

sakhe, kv› êdānīm upaviṣṭaḥ priyāyāḥ kiṃ cid anukāriṇīṣu latāsu dṛṣṭiṃ vinodayāmi? Friend, where shall I now [being seated, distract:] sit and distract my gaze among vines that somewhat imitate my beloved?

kiṃ Kaṇva-saṃdeśa-hāriṇaḥ sa_strī˜kās tapasvinaḥ? ascetics with women, bringing a message from Kaṇva (you say)?

aye, dakṣiṇena priyā-caraṇa˘nikṣepa-śaṃsī nūpura-śabdaḥ ah, a sound of anklets to the right, proclaiming my beloved's tread

While it may not always be easy to distinguish the meaning of this formation from that of the present participle, certain clear-cut distinctions of a formal nature do exist. The present participle may govern an accusative and may not normally stand at the end of a compound (in these respects it resembles a finite verb form). The verbal noun in **in**, on the other hand, with rare exceptions cannot govern an accusative and (as the above examples illustrate) is commoner at the end of a compound than as an isolated form.

Present participle

Two participles are attached to the present stem (and other thematic **a** paradigms), one in **ant** (parasmaipada) and one in **amāna** (ātmanepada): so **nayant** 'leading', **vartamāna** 'going on, current, contemporary'.

The declension of participles in **ant** differs from that of stems in **vant/mant** in only two particulars: the nominative singular masculine ends in **an** (not **ān*), and the feminine (and the neuter dual form) is **antī** (not **atī*). (Remember that by sandhi a final **an** becomes **ann** before vowels.)

[On the formation of athematic participles (Chapter 12 onwards) the following points should be noted. The feminine (and neuter dual) is in **atī** (this is also an option for class VI verbs and futures). The strong stem is like the third person plural parasmaipada without the final **i**, and in reduplicated verbs is therefore simply **at**: note that as a further consequence the nominative singular *masculine* (as well as neuter) in these verbs ends in **t** not **n**, e.g. **dadat** '(he) giving'. For athematics, the ātmanepada termination is **āna** not **amāna**.]

It was pointed out in Chapter 5 that where the English participle in '-ing' represents an action prior to that of the main verb its usual Sanskrit equivalent is the absolutive. The Sanskrit present participle is therefore normally reserved for actions or states which can be seen as contemporaneous with those of the main verb:

purā kila Karāl»-āyatane Mālatīm upaharann Aghoraghaṇṭaḥ kṛpāṇa:pāṇir Mādhavena vyāpāditaḥ some time ago, it seems, while (engaged in) sacrificing Mālatī in the temple of Karālā, Aghoraghaṇṭa knife in hand was slain by Mādhava

ati:kṛpaṇāḥ khalv amī prāṇāḥ, yad upakāriṇam api tātaṃ kv> āpi gacchantam ady> āpi n> ānugacchanti that life (of mine) is indeed extremely niggardly, in that even today it does not follow (my) father, although he was my benefactor, as he goes somewhere *(the father has died)*

vanaṃ gatena mayā kā cid a:śaraṇyā vyakta:kārpaṇyā> śru muñcantī vanitā vilokitā having gone to the forest I saw a woman without refuge and of obvious wretchedness shedding tears

Beyond simple contemporaneity, a casual or (with the addition of **api**) a concessive force may be implied. One particular implication, that of responsibility, 'doing B by virtue of doing A', deserves special mention. It may usually be turned in English by the translation 'in/by (doing *etc.*)':

ātmanā kṛto ›yaṃ doṣaḥ Saṃjīvakaṃ Piṅgalakasakāśam ānayatā it is (I) myself, in bringing Saṃjīvaka to Piṅgalaka, who have done this mischief

evam atidurmanāyamānaḥ pīḍayati māṃ vatsaḥ

the dear child tortures me by being so miserable

The verb **as** 'be' forms a present participle **sant**, feminine **satī**, which may function as an adjective meaning 'real, true, good, virtuous' (hence 'suttee'). As a participle it is sometimes added pleonastically to predicative adjectives, particularly compounds: e.g. **prasanna:manasā satā Mādhavena** 'by Mādhava, being of tranquil mind'.

mahānt

The adjective **mahānt** 'great' is irregular in having a strong stem in **ānt** (the middle and weak stem is **mahat**). The feminine is **mahatī**, the nominative singular masculine **mahān**. The stem form for karmadhāraya and bahuvrīhi compounds is **mahā**.

enam

enam is an enclitic pronoun, occurring only in the accusative (**enam, enām, enat; enau, ene; enān, enāḥ, enāni**), the instrumental singular (**enena, enayā**) and the genitive/locative dual (**enayoḥ**). (Of these the commonest forms are **enam** and **enām**.) It is used as an unemphatic third person pronoun ('him, her'), not usually adjectival, and normally referring to persons. Oblique cases other than the accusative may be supplied by the pronoun **ayam** (see Chapter 5).

Stem forms in composition

It may be useful to summarise here the ways in which the form of a stem as it appears in a compound may differ from the form in which the word is quoted in a dictionary (apart from the normal operation of the rules of external sandhi). Of nouns in general it need only be pointed out that consonant stems show their middle form: so **ātman** becomes **ātma**;

dhanin, dhani; and **bhagavant, bhagavat** (this last being at any rate the form in which such stems are often quoted). The use of pronouns in composition is somewhat restricted. The first person forms **mat** and **asmat**, second person **tvat** and **yuṣmat** (dual forms are hardly found), and the demonstrative **tat** are used freely, except as the final member of the compound. The relative **yat** is also used freely, but only as the first member. Of the interrogative pronoun **kaḥ**, the (primarily neuter) form **kim** occurs quite often: not, of course, in the animate sense of 'who(m)', but capable of qualifying a substantive of any gender—as in **kim:vyāpāra** 'of whom the occupation (**vyāpāraḥ** *m.*) is what?' The pronouns **ayam, enam** and **asau** do not have productive stem forms.

Certain words change to forms from different, though related, stems when used in composition. So, at the end of a compound, **ahan** 'day', **rājan** 'king', **rātri** 'night' and **sakhi** 'friend' become **a** stems: **aha, rāja, rātra** and **sakha. mahānt** 'great' when forming the prior member of a karmadhāraya or, in consequence, a bahuvrīhi compound regularly changes to **mahā**: the stem form **mahat**, even in the substantival sense of 'great man', is not very much used. Two of the changes mentioned are illustrated in the karmadhāraya **mahā:rājaḥ** 'great king'.

The imperative

One way of expressing a command or wish in Sanskrit is by means of the imperative mood, which is a part of the present stem: so **gaccha** 'go!', **paritrāyasva naḥ** 'save us!'. The imperative is in effect confined to the second and third persons. The first person forms given in grammars to complete the paradigms are really survivals of the old subjunctive mood, and at any rate are not particularly common; first person expressions like 'let's go' are usually put in the indicative—thus **gacchāvaḥ.**

In moderately urgent second person commands, the verb, as is natural, tends to stand first (after any vocative), unless special emphasis is put on some other item in the sentence:

sūta, prerayʾ âśvān driver, start the horses
masī-bhājanaṃ pattraṃ cʾ ôpanaya bring inkpot and paper

But if an absolutive is also used, chronological sequence should be preserved:

vayasya, upasṛtya Lavaṅgikā-sthāne tiṣṭha go up and stand in Lavaṅgikā's place, friend

If less urgent instructions or a wish are in question, the verb may stand elsewhere, often (and particularly in the latter case) at the end:

sakhe Virādhagupta, tvam anenʾ aîvʾ āhituṇḍika-cchadmanā punaḥ Kusumapuram eva gaccha Virāḍhagupta my friend, you are to go back again to Kusumapura in this same disguise of a snake-charmer
vatsa, ciraṃ pṛthivīṃ pālaya my child, long may you protect the earth

When an imperative is genuinely 'third person', the same various principles apply:

ārye, tiṣṭhatu tāvad ājñā-niyogaḥ good (wife), for the moment [let the entrusting of orders stand:] never mind what orders I have for you
atrabhavatī tāvad ā prasavād asmad-gṛhe tiṣṭhatu this lady, then, should remain in our house till her confinement

But where the third person is used as a polite form of address, it is particularly common for the imperative to stand as penultimate word followed by the quasi-pronoun:

bho bhos tapasvinaḥ, tapo-vana-saṃnihita:sattva-rakṣaṇāya sajjībhavantu bhavantaḥ ho there ascetics, prepare [for the defending of:] to defend the creatures about the ascetic grove

The second person imperative of **bhū** does not usually stand first word. So **sthiro bhava** 'be firm'. The second person forms of **as** are rare, but the third person forms are freely used and, of course, are necessary as copula where indicative forms could be dispensed with:

viditam astu deva-pādānām be it known to Your Majesty['s feet] . . .

The use of the imperative in an **iti** clause is a device allowing the representation of 'indirect command' in the widest sense. Translation by means of the English infinitive is usually appropriate:

nanv idānīm eva mayā tatra Kalahaṃsakaḥ preṣitaḥ 'pracchannam upagamya Nandana-āvāsa-pravṛttim upalabhasva' êti why, I have just now sent Kalahaṃsaka there, [(saying) 'after approaching stealthily find out events in Nandana's house':] to find out discreetly what has been happening in Nandana's house

To express a prohibition the negative particle to be used with the imperative is **mā**, e.g. **mā gaccha** 'don't go'. This, however, is rare, the more elegant alternative (as mentioned in Chapter 15) being the use of **mā** with the unaugmented form of the aorist or occasionally of the imperfect. Even this is not especially frequent. The usual way of expressing a prohibition if it implies 'cease to' is simply **alam** or some other particle with the instrumental: **alaṃ śokena** 'do not grieve (any more)'. But in other circumstances, probably commonest is the use of the gerundive (Chapter 12):

Vṛṣala, sa_viṣam auṣadham—na pātavyam Vṛṣala, the medicine's poisoned—don't drink it

Abstract nouns

Mention was made in the previous chapter of the formation of neuter abstract nouns (i.e. substantives) by means of vṛddhi, e.g. **pāṇḍityaṃ** 'learning'. Another device to achieve the same effect, and a simpler one to apply, is the use of the suffixes **tvaṃ** (neuter) and **tā** (feminine, this latter normally restricted to occurrence after a stem ending in a short vowel, usually **a**): so **paṇḍitatvaṃ** and **paṇḍitatā** 'learning', or more explicitly 'being a paṇḍit'. These suffixes may be added not merely to simple words but also to whole compounds: e.g. **ramaṇīya:darśana˜tā** 'the state of having an attractive appearance'. [The use of the sign ˜ indicates that the suffix is to be added to the compound as a whole. The following example will illustrate the potential difference of meaning: **niṣ_pāṇḍitya** means '(who is) without scholarship'; **niṣ_paṇḍitatva** would be a very improbable formation with the same meaning; but **niṣ_paṇḍita˜tva** means 'the state of being without a paṇḍit', as in the sentence **lajjayati grāma-nivāsino niṣ_paṇḍita˜tvam** 'being without a paṇḍit embarrasses those living in the village'.]

Most of the uses of abstract nouns possible in English are possible also in Sanskrit. In particular (and in contrast to Latin and Greek), their use as the subject of an active verb does not imply any vivid personification of the abstract concept:

ata eva māṃ prayojana-śuśrūṣā mukharayati that is why the desire to learn [**śuśrūṣā**] of (your) motives is making me [talkative:] so persistent

Often an abstract noun is the subject of a nominal sentence:

rājñāṃ tu carit›:ârtha˜tā ›pi duḥkh›:ôttar» aîva but for kings, [even the state of being one whose aims are effected has as a consequence unhappiness:] even success is attended with unhappiness

The difference between Sanskrit and English idiom lies in the thoroughness with which Sanskrit exploits the various possible uses of abstract nouns, and particularly in the potential length of abstract compounds. The following sentence easily permits of literal translation:

sa c› Auśanasyāṃ daṇḍa-nītau catuḥṣaṣṭy:aṅge jyotiḥ-śāstre ca paraṃ prāvīṇyam upagataḥ and he has attained a high proficiency in the political science of Uśanas and the [sixty-four-limbed:] sixty-four branches of astronomy

But what in this particular sentence is unremarkable represents a regular Sanskrit idiom whereby almost any verb of motion (and some others implying acquisition etc.) may be construed with the accusative of almost any abstract noun to express what we most usually represent in English by 'become': so, in the above, 'he has become highly proficient'. Another example, showing better the scope of the idiom, is:

tad idānīṃ rāj›-ârtha˘tām āpadyate that now [arrives at king-property-ness:] becomes the property of the king

Hence the common idiom for 'he dies', **pañcatvaṃ gacchati** 'he becomes five', i.e. 'is resolved into the five elements'. Furthermore, the causative of these verbs, and any other verb of appropriate sense such as **nī** 'lead', can be used in the sense of producing a certain condition in someone or something, i.e. 'making A [into] B':

loke gurutvaṃ viparītatāṃ ca
sva:ceṣṭitāny eva naraṃ nayanti

in (this) world it is his own actions which [lead a man to important-ness and opposite-ness:] make a man important or the reverse

In English we know without thinking about it that the phrase 'the greenness of the grass' is related to the phrase 'green grass'. In Sanskrit it is often advisable to keep the point more explicitly in mind. To take an example of extreme simplicity, a commentary discussing an author's use of the term **vyavahāra** 'litigation' in the plural says **tasy› âneka:vidha˘tvaṃ darśayati bahuvacanena** 'he shows by the plural the several-sortedness of it'. We may, if we wish, translate this as 'he indicates by the plural its manifoldness'. But we shall remind ourselves more plainly what we are talking about, besides being fairer to the simplicity of the original, if we say 'he indicates by the plural that it is of several sorts'. Often at any rate literal translation is impossible:

> **n› âsty eva dhvaniḥ, prasiddha:prasthāna-vyatirekiṇaḥ kāvya-prakārasya kāvyatva-hāneḥ** [*dhvani* (*a technical term of literary criticism*) just does not exist, from the abandonment of [/deficiency in] poetry-ness of a type of poetry distinct from established ways:] there is no such thing as *dhvani*, for a kind of poetry which transgressed the recognised norms would cease to be poetry

It would be quite mistaken to suppose, on the basis of such usages, that the 'thought' of Sanskrit writers is somehow more 'abstract' than our own. It would be truer to say that their style is nominal rather than verbal. In coming to grips with academic prose, students tend to be vague and ill at ease about the meaning of sentences until the purely syntactical nature of this difference sinks in. And, as was implied above, even in translating quite simple nominal phrases the possibility of 'denominalisation' in English should always be kept in mind.

In brief, the difference between English and Sanskrit usage is that English noun clauses ('that the grass is green') and noun phrases with a verbal component such as an infinitive ('for the grass to be green') tend to be replaced in Sanskrit by a straight abstract noun ('the greenness of the grass'). Normally, when both subjective and objective genitives are involved, only the objective genitive is compounded with the abstract—e.g. **bālānāṃ kusum›-âvacayaḥ** 'children's flower-picking': 'for children to pick flowers'.

Furthermore, the use of the abstract noun in various oblique cases corresponds to English adverbial clauses and phrases of various kinds. Commonest is the ablative of cause:

> **suhṛt-saṃpādita˜tvāt sādhutara:phalo me manorathaḥ** [from being brought about by (my) friend:] because (you my) friend brought it about, my desire (has been) better rewarded

No doubt because its ablative is not distinct in form from

its genitive, the suffix **tā** is less usual here than **tvaṃ** or a vṛddhi derivative. But it is common enough in the instrumental, another case which is used to express cause ('by (reason of)'):

> **asau punar abhiniviṣṭayā dṛśā Mālatī-mukh›-âvalokana-vihasta˜tayā viṣama:viracit›:aîka:bhāgāṃ tām eva bahu manyamānā 'mahān ayaṃ prasāda' iti gṛhītavatī** but she with an intent glance, highly esteeming that same (garland) of·which·one·portion·was·worked·unevenly [by clumsiness through gazing:] because·(I)·had·been·clumsy·through·gazing·on·Mālatī's·face, accepted it (with the words) ['this is a great favour':] 'thank you very much indeed'

The dative is normally used with another type of abstract noun, the verbal action noun, to express purpose. Examples of this, such as **nṛpa-darśanāya** 'in order to see the king', have already been encountered. The locative expresses circumstance of one kind or another: **kula-kṣaye** 'on the destruction of the family: when/if the family is destroyed', **prayojan›-ôtpattau** 'if/when/as the need arises'. The addition of **api** gives concessive force: **kula-kṣaye ›pi** '[even on destruction of the family:] despite destruction of the family: though the family is/were to be destroyed'.

Exclamations

The English 'what (a) . . .', though it has direct Sanskrit equivalents such as **kīdṛśa**, is more usually represented by the particle **aho** 'oh!' followed by a substantive in the nominative case:

> **aho saṃvaraṇam** what duplícity!
> **aho rāga-parivāhiṇī gītiḥ** [oh the song overflowing with passion/'musical mood':] what an impassioned sóng!

Where the whole emphasis would be put on an adjective qualifying the substantive, the phrase is often turned round and the adjective becomes an abstract noun: in other words, 'oh the blúe sky!' becomes 'oh the sky's blúeness!' Similarly in English, according to the particular emphasis intended, we may say either 'what a blue ský!' or 'how blúe the sky is!' The normal suffix here is **tā**, or a vṛddhi derivative, rather than **tvam**:

aho vaidagdhyam [oh the cleverness:] how cléver (she is)!

aho sukha-pratyarthi˜tā daivasya [oh the·being·hostile·to·happiness of fate:] how hóstile fate is to happiness!

Sentences containing 'how' are slightly ambiguous in English because they can be stressed more than one way. For this reason, an acute accent has been added to mark the main sentence stress: this falls somewhere on the word or phrase which appears as a nominative substantive in the Sanskrit:

aho vyabhrā diśaḥ what a cloudless ský! *or* how cloudless the ský is!

aho diśāṃ vyabhratā how cloúdless the sky is!

aho ceṣṭā-pratirūpikā kāmi:jana-manovṛttiḥ how like to the deed (itself) is a lover's imaginátion!

'Containing'

The word **garbhaḥ** 'womb, foetus' occurs at the end of a bahuvrīhi compound with the sense 'having inside, containing': e.g. **dhana:garbhaṃ bhāṇḍam** 'box containing money'; or, as a sentence, 'the box has money in it'.

Verbal nouns in *ti*

The suffix **ti** may be added to the weak grade of a root to form a feminine substantive. Thus **gati** (cf. Greek *básis*) 'going, procedure, course'. The formation is less productive than those in **a** and **ana**, and less 'action-oriented', tending towards a more general sense. The **ti** is normally treated exactly like the **ta** of the past participle (and is seldom found with verbs that form their past participles in **ita** or **na**). Other examples are **bhakti** 'devotion', **dṛṣṭi** 'sight, faculty of sight', **mati** 'thought', **siddhi** 'achievement', **vṛddhi** 'growth'. A number of roots ending in **d**, although forming a past participle in **na**, do take this suffix: thus **utpatti**, from **ut+pad**, 'arising'.

Vocabulary

añcalaḥ border (of dress)
atiśaya surpassing
apathya-kārin [doing what is unwholesome (to king):] traitor
apavādin decrying
a:pramādin [not negligent:] vigilant
abhiyogaḥ intentness, pre-occupation
avayavaḥ portion, particle
asuraḥ demon
ādeśaḥ command
āyudham weapon
āveśaḥ attack (of emotion)
utsarpin high-soaring
utsāhaḥ enthusiasm
upagrahaḥ conciliation, winning over
uparodhanaṃ besieging (of)
upādhyāyaḥ teacher
eka *pron. adj.* one, alone
enam *see chapter*
kalakalaḥ disturbance, noise
kārin doing
kāryaṃ affair, business
kīdṛśa (*f.* **ī**) of what kind? of what kind! what (a)!
kṣitipati *m.* king
kṣipra:kārin [swift-acting:] precipitate
:garbha *see chapter*
gṛhaṃ quarters, chamber
gṛha-janaḥ family (*more particularly* wife)
cakravartin *m.* emperor
an:adhyayanaṃ [non-studying:] holiday from lessons
daṇḍaḥ stick; punishment
darśanīya attractive
darśin seeing, that see
diś (**dik**) *f.* cardinal point, region (of sky); *pl.* sky, skies
duḥ:śīla irritable
dur:ātman vile
dṛḍha firm
Nandanaḥ *pr. n.*
nir_daya pitiless
nṛpaḥ king
nyāyya regular, right
pakṣa-pātin on the side of, partial to
paṅkti *f.* row, line
Pañcavaṭī *name of a place*
paṭaḥ cloth, robe
pati *m.* lord (of)
parijanaḥ attendant, servant
pipīlikā ant
pauraḥ citizen
pratijñā promise, assertion
pratividhānaṃ precaution, countermeasure against (*gen.*)
pratyavāyaḥ reverse, annoyance
pratyāsanna near, at hand, about
pratyutpanna prompt, ready
pratyutpanna:mati ready-witted
prabhūta numerous
prārthanā longing

Candanadāsaḥ *pr. n.*
chidraṃ hole, chink
tapasvin *m.* ascetic
tīkṣṇa sharp, severe
tīkṣṇa:rasaḥ [sharp liquid:] poison
tīkṣṇa:rasa-dāyin [poison-giving:] poisoner
tīrthaṃ ford, sacred bathing place
taikṣṇyaṃ sharpness
trikālaṃ [the three times:] past, present and future
mati *f.* thought, wit
Madayantikā *pr. n.*
Manmathaḥ (name of the god of) Love
mahārghya valuable
Mādhavyaḥ *pr. n.*
muni *m.* sage
mlecchaḥ barbarian
rakṣas *n.* devil
vayas *n.* youth, age
Vasiṣṭhaḥ *pr. n.*
vidhā kind, sort; **-vidha** such as
vimardaḥ conflict
vivekaḥ discrimination
vihārin roaming
vyagra engrossed, intent
śayanaṃ repose, sleeping; **śayana-gṛhaṃ** bed-chamber
śarad *f.* autumn
śiṣṭa learned; **śiṣṭ›-ânadhyayanaṃ** holiday in honour of learned (guests)
śūnya empty, devoid (of)
śokaḥ grief
baṭu *m.* young brahmin (student); fellow (*used contemptuously*)
balaṃ force, strength; *sg. or pl.* (military) forces
balāt forcibly
bahu many
bhaktaṃ food
bhakti *f.* devotion, loyalty
bhāvin future, imminent
bhitti *f.* wall
bhīru fearful
madhura sweet
śobhā brilliance, beauty
śreṣṭhin *m.* eminent businessman, merchant
sakhī [female] friend; wife of one's friend
samayaḥ occasion, season
samādhi *m.* concentration [religious] meditation
saṃbandhaḥ union
saṃbhṛta assembled, prepared; augmented
sarpaḥ snake
salilaṃ water
sahabhū inherent, natural
sāṃnidhyaṃ presence
s›_âvadhāna careful
siddhi *f.* accomplishment, success
suraḥ god
suhṛttamaḥ close friend
strī woman
svāmin *m.* master
svīkaraṇaṃ marrying
svairaṃ gently

anu+gam (I anugacchati) follow, attend
anu+bhū (I anubhavati) experience, undergo
anu+rudh (IV anurudhyate) adhere to, comply with (*acc.*)
ava+lok (X avalokayati) see
ākulayati *denom.* confuse, disturb
ā+kṛṣ (I ākarṣati) drag, draw

ā + pad (IV **āpadyate**, *p.p.* **āpanna**) attain, come to
ut + pad *caus.* (**utpādayati**) cause to arise, cause
ut + veṣṭ *caus.* (**udveṣṭayati**) unwrap, open (letter)
khel (I **khelati**) play
cint (X **cintayati**) reflect, think things over
tvar (I **tvarate**) hurry; *caus.* **tvarayati**
dah *caus.* (**dāhayati**) make burn, cause to be fired
dṛś *caus.* (**darśayati**) cause to see, show
ni + grah (IX **nigṛhṇāti**) repress, restrain
nis + gam (I **nirgacchati**) go away, retire from (*abl.*)
pari + tuṣ *caus.* (**paritoṣayati**) make satisfied, tip, reward
pari + trai (I **paritrāyate**) rescue, save
pari + pāl (X **paripālayati**) guard, preserve, keep intact
pari + bhraṃś (IV **paribhraśyate**, *p.p.* **paribhraṣṭa**) fall, drip, slip
pari + hṛ (I **pariharati**) avoid, shun, resist
prati + as (IV **pratyasyati**) cast aside
pra + sthā (I **pratiṣṭhate**) set forth
bhañj (VII **bhanakti**, *p.p.* **bhagna**) break, shatter
mudrayati *denom.* stamp, seal
vand (I **vandate**) venerate, worship
vi + jñā *caus.* (**vijñāpayati**) say politely, request, entreat, beg
vi + sṛj *caus.* (**visarjayati**) release, dismiss
vīj (X **vījayate**) fan
sam + stambh (IX **saṃstabhnāti**, *absol.* **saṃstabhya**) make firm, sustain, compose

ataḥ from this
aho bata oh alas!
kila apparently, it seems that
˜tā, ˜tvaṃ *abstract noun suffixes; see chapter*
bhoḥ (*in calling*) oh! ho! (*irreg. sandhi* **bho** *before vowels and voiced consonants*)
sāṃpratam now, at once

Exercise 10a

पश्य माधवस्यावस्थाम् । १ । महति विषादे वर्तते ते सखीजनः
। २ । इदं तत्प्रत्युत्पन्नमतित्वं स्त्रीणाम् । ३ । अहो दर्शनीयान्य-
क्षराणि । ४ । मुहूर्तमुपविशत । ५ । भोः श्रेष्ठिन् चन्दनदास
एवमपथ्यकारिषु तीक्ष्णदण्डो राजा । ६ । अनुभवतु राजापथ्य-
कारित्वस्य फलम् । ७ । प्रत्यासन्नः किल मृगयाविहारी पार्थिवो

दुःषन्तः । ८ । गच्छतां भवन्तौ । ९ । भोस्तपस्विन् चिन्तयन्नपि न खलु स्वीकरणमत्रभवत्याः स्मरामि । १० । सखे माधव्य दृढप्रतिज्ञो भव । ११ । अहो निर्दयता दुरात्मनां पौराणाम्— अहो रामस्य राज्ञः क्षिप्रकारिता । १२ । भगवन्मन्मथ कुतस्ते कुसुमायुधस्य सतस्तैक्ष्ण्यमेतत् । १३ । ननु भवत्यः पटाञ्चलैर्वत्सौ वीजयध्वम् । १४ । भग्नोत्साहः कृतो ऽस्मि मृगयापवादिना माधव्येन । १५ । अहो बत कीदृशीं वयोऽवस्थामापन्नो ऽस्मि । १६ । अद्य शिष्टानध्ययनमिति खेलतां बटूनामयं कलकलः । १७ । स्वैरं स्वैरं गच्छन्तु भवत्यः । १८ । परित्रायतां सुहृदं महाराजः । १९ । तत्रभवतः कुलपतेरसांनिध्याद्रक्षांसि नस्तपोविघ्नमुत्पादयन्ति । २० । भद्र अनया मुद्रया मुद्रयैनम् । २१ । शत्रुप्रयुक्तानां च तीक्ष्णरसदायिनां प्रतिविधानं प्रत्यप्रमादिनः परीक्षितभक्तयः क्षितिपतिप्रत्यासन्ना नियुक्ताः पुरुषाः । २२ । संप्रति मदयन्तिकासंबन्धेन नन्दनोपग्रहात्प्रत्यस्तशङ्काः खलु वयम् । २३ । भाविनमेनं चक्रवर्तिनमवगच्छतु भवान् । २४ । मया तावत्सुहृत्तमस्य चन्दनदासस्य गृहे गृहजनं निक्षिप्य नगरान्निर्गच्छता न्याय्यमनुष्ठितम् । २५ । देवि संस्तभ्यात्मानमनुरुध्यस्व भगवतो वसिष्ठस्यादेशमिति विज्ञापयामि ॥ २६ ॥

Exercise 10b

1 Look, Your Excellencies. 2 What valuable jéwels! 3 She stands gazing. 4 This lady must hurry. 5 Sages that·see·past·present·and·future have proclaimed [ā+**diś**] a conflict·(between)·gods·and·demons (to be) imminent. 6 Being a king has·many·annoyances. 7 [It is from this:] That is why (men) such·as·*you are great. 8 May you have success·in·your·affairs. 9 Keeping the seal intact, open (it) and show (me). 10 How devoid·of·discriminátion is the barbarian! 11 Restrain [*dual*] your attack·of·grief and follow me. 12 It is preoccupation·with·affairs, dear child, that is disturbing us,

and not [**na punar**] the irritability towards pupils natural·in·a·teacher. 13 Though I am resisting [**pari+hṛ**], love·of·Pañcavaṭī seems to draw me forcibly. 14 How sweet is the sight of these (girls)! 15 Citralekhā, get Urvaśī to hurry. 16 The gods (do) have this fearfulness·of·the·meditations·of·others. 17 The longing of great (men) is of course [high-soaring:] for higher things. 18 At once let our·forces set forth to·besiege·Kusumapura. 19 (Being) partial·to·*your·merits, I have forgotten the merits·of·(my)·master. 20 Priyaṃvadaka, we have no interest in snakes. So tip him and dismiss him. 21 (It) slipped from your friend's wife at the ford·of·Śacī as she was worshipping the water. 22 Be careful, dear child. 23 Because (my) mind is engrossed·in·affairs and (my) agents numerous, (I had) forgotten. 24 Noble Jājali, you too go back with·the·servants: Bhāgurāyaṇa alone shall attend me. 25 How surpassingly·lóvely the skies are, their·wealth·of·beauty·augmented·by·the·autumn·season. 26 Then, seeing a line of ants emerging from a [**eka**] hole·in·the·wall carrying·[*use* **gṛhīta**]·particles·of·food, (he) grasping·the·fact [**gṛhīta:ârtha**] that [**iti**] the chamber had·men·in·it, caused that same bed·chamber to be fired.

Chapter 11

PARADIGMS: **kartṛ, pitṛ, svasṛ, mātṛ**

Stems in *ṛ*

In origin the inflexion of stems in **ṛ** is parallel with that of consonant stems in **an**. They exhibit a strong stem with vṛddhi or guṇa grade (**kartāram, pitaram**: cf. **rājānam**); a weakest grade with the stem in consonant form (**kartrā**: cf. **rājñā**); and a middle grade with the stem in vocalic form (**kartṛbhiḥ**: cf. **rājabhiḥ** <**rājn̥bhiḥ*).

These stems are nevertheless classified as vowel stems rather than consonant stems, for two reasons: **r** has a distinctive vocalic alternant (**ṛ**), whereas **n** does not (since **n̥* became **a**); and some terminations have been acquired through the analogy of other vowel stems. Thus by analogy with **kāntān, śucīn,** etc., an accusative plural in **ṝn** (f. **-ṝḥ**); and by analogy with **kāntānām** etc. a genitive plural in **-ṝṇām.** (These formations create the long alternant of syllabic **ṛ**, which is not part of inherited Indo-European phonology.)

As with **an** stems, the nominative singular takes vṛddhi and loses its final consonant: **kartā, pitā.** An unusual feature is the genitive singular in **uḥ** (or **ur**). Guṇa grade of the locative singular, an alternative form for stems in **an**, is here obligatory: **kartari.**

Stems in **ṛ** fall into two main classes, agent nouns and nouns of relationship. Agent nouns end in **tṛ** (though the **t** is sometimes changed by internal sandhi) and are added to a guṇa grade of the root, often with connecting **i**. [The description of the infinitive in Chapter 13 may be taken as a guide to the formation of this stem, with substitution of **tṛ** for **tum**.] The suffix of agent nouns is always inflected with vṛddhi in the strong grade: **netāram** 'leader' acc. (cf. Latin *amātōrem*). A derived feminine is made with the suffix **ī**: **netrī** 'she who leads'. Neuter forms on the analogy of the neuter of **śuci** etc. are theoretically possible but not very common.

Nouns of relationship normally take guṇa in the strong grade, and may be feminine as well as masculine (in which case the accusative plural ends in **ṝḥ**); **naptṛ** 'grandson', **bhartṛ** 'husband' and **svasṛ** 'sister' are exceptional in taking vṛddhi. Thus **pitaram, mātaram,** but **svasāram** (cf. Latin *patrem, mātrem*, but *sorōrem*). The dual form **pitarau** means 'parents'. The suffix **ka** may be employed when one of these nouns occurs at the end of a bahuvrīhi compound: **mṛta:bhartṛ˜kā** 'she whose husband is dead'.

Like the present participle active, the agent noun does not normally stand at the end of a determinative compound. But, as might be expected, whereas the present participle construes with an accusative, the agent noun construes with an objective genitive: **varṇ›;āśramāṇāṃ rakṣitā** 'protector of (all) classes and conditions (of men)'.

The agent noun in **tṛ** is not so prominent a feature of Sanskrit as are nouns in '-er' of English. Other suffixes also denote the agent. For instance, 'leader' may be expressed by **nāyakaḥ** as well as by **netṛ**. 'Potter' ('pot-maker') may be translated by **kumbha-kāraḥ** or possibly **kumbha-kṛt,** but not by **kumbha-kartṛ**. Noun phrases will often be represented by a compound ending in the suffix **in,** e.g. **upatyakā›raṇya-vāsinaḥ** 'dwellers in the forests of the foot hills'. There is, however, one distinctive usage of the agent noun which is worth noting. It may have potential force—'someone to do something'. Thus **netā jana upaiṣyati** 'a person will come [as guide:] to guide (you)', or the following:

tvādṛśaṃ punaḥ pratipakṣ›-ôddharaṇe saṃbhāvya: śaktim abhiyoktāram āsādya kṣipram enaṃ pari-

tyajya tvām ev› āśrayante However, having found (someone) like yourself, with enough power to destroy the enemy, [such as to attack:] to be their champion, they (will) quickly abandon him and flock to you

[*Periphrastic future.* Allied to this potential sense is the use of the agent noun to form a comparatively rare tense known as the periphrastic future. Mention of it is included briefly here, since it will not be introduced into any of the exercises. The agent noun is used predicatively to refer to future time, with the verb **as** in the first and second persons, without in the third person: **kartāsmi** 'I am to do', **kartā** 'he/she is to do'. Three features distinguish the tense formally from a straightforward deployment of the agent noun. Feminine and (in so far as they occur) neuter subjects do not affect the masculine form of the verb; the ending **-tā** remains unchanged in the first and second persons, even in the dual and plural (**kartā smaḥ** 'we are to do'; and a direct object appears in the accusative, not in the genitive (**kumbhaṃ bāle kartārau** 'the two girls are to make a pot').

The tense is used especially for events fixed for a particular future time: often, in fact, the verb is accompanied by an adverb of time. Thus **śva āgantā** 'he is to come tomorrow'.]

The suffix *tra*

Allied to the agent suffix **tṛ** is the neuter suffix **tra** denoting the instrument used by the agent. Thus **pātṛ** 'drinker', **pātraṃ** '[that which is a drinker's (when he drinks):] drinking-vessel'. Similarly, **astraṃ** '[instrument of throwing:] missile', **gātraṃ** '[instrument of movement:] limb', **śastraṃ** '[instrument of cutting:] knife'—this last to be carefully distinguished from **śāstraṃ** '[instrument of instruction:] treatise'.

The suffix occurs in other Indo-European languages. Thus Greek *árotron*, Latin *arātrum* 'plough', beside *arotḗr*, *arātor* 'ploughman'.

The passive

In origin the passive may be regarded as a specialisation of the ātmanepada of class IV verbs. It is formed with weak grade of the root, the suffix **ya** and the thematic ātmanepada endings. [Secondary differentiation occurred, in that passives retained the accent on the suffix, while class IV verbs shifted the accent to the root. But this distinction being inoperative in Classical Sanskrit, forms such as **manyate** may be interpreted according to context either as ātmanepada ('thinks') or as passive ('is thought').] The passive is a present system, comprising a present indicative, imperfect, imperative and optative, and a participle in **māna**. [In the future, the perfect, and to some extent the aorist, ātmanepada forms may be used with passive significance.]

With the following exceptions, the root generally remains unchanged before the suffix **ya**:

Final **i** and **u** lengthen: **ci, cīyate** 'is heaped'; **śru, śrūyate** 'is heard'.

Final **ṛ** becomes **ri** after a single consonant, **ar** after two: **kṛ, kriyate** 'is done', but **smṛ, smaryate** 'is remembered'.

Final **ṝ** becomes **īr** generally, but **ūr** after a labial: **kṝ, kīryate** 'is scattered'; **pṝ, pūryate** 'is filled'.

Roots liable to saṃprasāraṇa display it here: **vac, ucyate** 'is told'; **grah, gṛhyate** 'is taken'.

Roots liable to lose an 'infixed' nasal do so: **bhañj, bhajyate** 'is broken', but **nand, nandyate** 'is rejoiced in'.

Roots ending in **ā** or **ai** most often convert to **ī**: **sthā, sthīyate** 'it is stood'. But among several exceptions is **jñā, jñāyate** 'is known'.

When a passive is formed not directly from a root but from a derived stem, the derived stem loses any suffix it may have before adding the suffix **ya**. Thus class X verbs and causatives change **ayati** to **yate**: **coryate** 'is stolen'; **nāyyate** 'is made to lead'; **sthāpyate** 'is made to stand'.

The passive is used, as one would expect, when the agent of action is unknown or indefinite:

tat ko nu khalv evaṃ niṣidhyate then who can it be (whom I hear) being thus checked?

vatse, uparudhyate me tapovan›-ânuṣṭhānam dear child, my duties in the ascetic grove are being hindered (*to specify* by you *would strike a jarring note*)

But the fondness for passive constructions so prominent in past statements may be observed to a lesser extent in the present also, so that the natural English translation is often by means of the active voice:

niyatam anayā saṃkalpa-nirmitaḥ priya-samāgamo ›nubhūyate assuredly she is experiencing an imagined union with her beloved

Priyaṃvade, kasy› êdam uśīr›-ânulepanaṃ mṛṇāla-vanti ca nalinī-dalāni nīyante? Priyaṃvadā, to whom are (you) taking the uśīra ointment and the lotus leaves complete with fibres?

The notion of 'logical subject' (to which, for instance, an absolutive refers) is, of course, applicable here as in past statements:

kim ity avijñāya, vayasya, vaiklavyam avalambyate? why without knowing (for certain), friend, [is despondency adopted:] do you grow despondent?

Even commoner than the passive indicative is the passive imperative (usually third person forms only):

anubhūyatāṃ tarhi narapati-kopaḥ experience, then, the king's anger

Raivataka, senāpatis tāvad āhūyatām Raivataka, summon the general, will you?

The imperative, and more particularly the passive imperative, is often best represented in English by 'must', 'should', etc., and may be used in ways the English imperative is not, for instance in a question:

tat kim anyad anuṣṭhīyatām then what else [must be performed:] do you wish done?

The Sanskrit passive may be used impersonally in the third person singular:

purastād avagamyata eva [from there on, it is quite understood:] I can imagine the rest

datta:pūrv» êty āśaṅkyate that she has already been given (in marriage) [it is worried:] is what worries (us)

The neuter demonstrative **idam** is often added with deictic force to an impersonal passive: **idam gamyate** [this is being gone:] 'see, (we) are going'.

In the imperative this impersonal passive is extremely common. Probably the most frequent Sanskrit for 'listen!' is **śrūyatām** ['let it be heard']. Similarly, **āsyatām** *or* **upaviśyatām** 'be seated'.

ayi bhinn›:ârtham abhidhīyatām ah, speak plainly

sukhaṃ sthīyatām remain at your ease

Śārṅgarava, jñāyatāṃ punaḥ kim etad iti Śārṅgarava, find out again what it is

Locative absolute

Analogous to the ablative absolute of Latin (or nominative absolute of English), there is in Sanskrit a locative absolute. So **kāle śubhe prāpte** 'an auspicious time having arrived'. The phrase consists of a small nominal sentence put into the locative, the natural case to express an attendant circumstance. The predicate may be a participle (present or past), an adjective or a predicatively used substantive, and in any of these cases the present participle **sant** of the verb **as** 'be' is sometimes added pleonastically. The force of the construction may usually be represented in English by a temporal clause introduced by 'when' or, where a present participle marks contemporaneous action, by 'as' or 'while': **tasmin dahyamāne** 'as it was burning'. An impersonal passive is not uncommon: **tathā ›nuṣṭhite** '[it having been performed thus:] this done'. According to context there may be a causal or conditional implication as well as the temporal, while the addition of **api** adds a concessive force· **aparādhe kṛte ›pi** 'though an offence be committed'; **evam ukte ›pi** 'despite this being said'. The past active participle may be used in the locative absolute construction: **evam abhihitavati pārthive** 'the king having spoken thus'.

The locative absolute is not as prominent a construction in Sanskrit as its counterpart in Latin. As has already been pointed out, English absolutes are often to be represented by bahuvrīhis—e.g. **śoka-saṃvigna:mānasaḥ** 'his mind overwhelmed with grief'. The locative absolute is better avoided when either of its elements is easily relatable grammatically to the rest of the sentence: one says **vayasyaṃ dṛṣṭvā** 'after seeing (his) friend' rather than **dṛṣṭe vayasye**, if the subject of 'see' is also the subject of the main sentence. We are left with instances like:

bhoḥ śreṣṭhin, Candragupte rājany a:parigrahaś chalānām oh merchant, now that Candragupta is king, there is no welcome for errors

a:gṛhīte Rākṣase, kim utkhātaṃ Nanda-vaṃśasya? with Rākṣasa not taken, what [has been uprooted:] uprooting has there been of the Nanda dynasty?

Another factor which militates against the frequency of locative absolutes as such is the possibility of using an abstract noun of circumstance in the locative. Thus the previous example might be rewritten as **Rākṣasasy› âgrahaṇe,** or even **Rākṣasasy› âgṛhītatve.**

[There also occurs occasionally a genitive absolute. It is used mostly with a present participle, sometimes with a verbal adjective in **-in**. A typical example would be **paśyatas tasya** 'while he looked on', the implication usually being 'looked on powerless and disregarded'. And there are borderline examples which might be classified as genitive absolutes but where the genitive can equally be seen as having some other function.]

The relative pronoun

The relative clause in Sanskrit is less frequent than its English counterpart. The reason is evident enough. In English an adjectival relative clause provides a more substantial qualification of a noun than a single adjective can. In Sanskrit the possibility of compound adjectives, whether determinative or bahuvrīhi, enables very lengthy and elaborate qualification without resort to a relative clause. The use of the Sanskrit relative clause, therefore, tends to be confined to the expression of restrictive clauses (the kind written without commas in English) or, rather less commonly, of 'afterthoughts'.

As in other languages, the relative pronoun agrees with its antecedent in number, gender and (in so far as the fact is manifested) person but appears in the case appropriate to its own clause. Two features more special to Sanskrit are striking: the relative clause almost never appears within the main clause but either before it or after it; and the relative pronoun may be placed anywhere within its own clause, occasionally even as last word.

When the relative clause is placed before the main clause, its sense is prevailingly restrictive and the relative pronoun is normally picked up in the main clause by a demonstrative pronoun (most often **saḥ**) as correlative, usually standing at or near the beginning of the main clause. Often, as is natural, the antecedent (if expressed at all other than by the demonstrative pronoun) appears *within* the relative clause, usually immediately after the relative pronoun, and therefore in the same case as the latter.

Putting these points together, one would rearrange an English sentence such as 'I have asked the upholsterer who came to look at the sofa yesterday for his estimate' rather on the following lines: 'to look at the sofa which upholsterer came yesterday, him I have asked for his estimate'.

yeṣāṃ prasādād idam āsīt, ta eva na santi those by whose grace this was (so), are no (more)

sarvathā Cāṇakya;Candraguptayoḥ puṣkalāt kāraṇād yo viśleṣa utpadyate, sa ātyantiko bhavati at all events, that estrangement between Cāṇakya and Candragupta which arises from a strong cause, will be lasting

tad atra yat sāmpratam, tatra bhavān eva pramāṇam so what is proper in this matter, in that *you* are the judge

In the following example a relative clause has been used purely to add restrictive force to a word:

'etad āryam pṛcchāmi'—'kumāra ya āryas tam pṛccha. vayam idānīm an:āryāḥ saṃvṛttāḥ' 'I ask (your) honourable (self) this—' 'Your Highness, ask one who *is* honourable. [We:] I am now become without honour'

The addition of **kaś cit** to the relative gives an indefinite sense—'whoever, whatever':

yaḥ kaś cid garbha-dohado ›syā bhavati, so ›vaśyam acirān mānayitavyaḥ any [longing of the womb:] pregnant fancy that she gets, [necessarily after not long must be honoured:] (you) must be sure to satisfy at once

When the relative clause follows the main clause, this may be a mere reversal of the above pattern (but with the antecedent remaining within the main clause):

tayā gavā kiṃ kriyate, yā na dogdhrī, na garbhiṇī? what is (to be) done with a cow which is neither a yielder of milk nor productive of calves?

(Note that in general statements in English the antecedent of a restrictive clause may be qualified equally well by 'the'/ 'that' or by 'a', the last having the sense of 'any'.)
When the main clause stands first, the correlative pronoun is often **eṣaḥ** or **ayam** instead of **saḥ**. And if the main clause consists of no more than a word or two, the correlative is sometimes omitted:

kriyate yad eṣā kathayati (we) are doing what she says

If the antecedent is indefinite or negative, it is naturally not qualified by a demonstrative pronoun:

Vijayasena, apy asti Vindhyaketor apatyaṃ yatr› âsya paritoṣasya phalaṃ darśayāmi? Vijayasena, has Vindhyaketu (any) offspring towards whom [**yatra** =

yasmin] I (may) show [fruit:] a token of [this:] my satisfaction?

In this following position, on the other hand, the relative clause may also be added to an already complete sentence as an additional statement. Here especially there is no need for a preceding demonstrative, and the force of the relative is roughly that of 'and' plus a demonstrative pronoun, r of 'one who/which'.

athı êdam ārabhyate mitrabhedaṃ nāma prathamaṃ tantraṃ, yasyı âyam ādyaḥ ślokaḥ now here begins the first chapter, called Separation of Friends, of which [= and of it] the following is the initial stanza

asty atra nagaryāṃ mahā:śmaśāna-pradeśe Karālā nāma Cāmuṇḍā . . . yā kila vividha:jīvı-ôpahāra:priy» êti sāhasikānāṃ pravādaḥ there is in the city in the area of the great burning-ground (an image of) the Fierce Goddess, named Karālā—one who, it seems, is fond of the sacrifice of living creatures of various kinds: so (runs) the report of adventurous (people)

Another very common variety of following relative clause also deserves mention. It is one which gives the reason for the preceding statement. It may be paraphrased by 'for' or 'in that' with a pronoun, and its natural equivalent in English is often an infinitive:

aho a:sādhu:darśī tatrabhavān Kaṇvo, ya imāṃ valkala-dhāraṇe niyuṅkte oh, His Honour Kaṇva is not right-seeing [who puts her:] to put her to wearing a bark-dress

kṛta:puṇya eva Nandano, yaḥ priyām īdṛśīṃ kāmayiṣyate Nandana's really lucky [who will love:] to be going to love such a sweetheart

vayam evı âtra nanu śocyā, ye Nanda-kula-vināśe ıpi jīvitum icchāmaḥ *we* rather are the ones to be pitied, who even on the destruction of the house of Nanda seek to live (on) (*Note the abstract noun as an alternative to a locative absolute such as* **vinaṣṭe ıpi Nanda-kule.**)

Analysis of bahuvrīhis

An example may now be given of the way analysis of bahuvrīhis can be made in Sanskrit glosses, taking advantage of the fact that relative clauses may precede their antecedent and that the relative pronoun may stand at the end of its clause. The two parts of the compound are resolved into a nominal sentence or phrase; the relative pronoun indicates the case-relationship with the substantive that is being qualified; and finally the demonstrative recalls the inflexional termination of the original compound. So **vidita-vārttebhyaḥ paurebhyaḥ** 'from the citizens who had learnt the news' becomes

viditā vārttā yais tebhyaḥ paurebhyaḥ by whom the news was learnt, from those citizens

Pronouns and pronominal adverbs

Now that a fair number of adverbial and other pronominal forms have been encountered in the exercises, it is worth drawing attention to relationships between them.

The list overleaf, and particularly the fourth column, is intended to be illustrative, not exhaustive. It could be extended either vertically or horizontally. Most pronominal adjectives have at least some adverbial forms—thus **anyatra** 'elsewhere', **ekadā** 'at one time', **sarvathā** 'in every way'.

Attributively used adverbs

The adverbs of 'place where and place from where' listed in the second and third lines of the above table have an obvious affinity of meaning with the locative and ablative cases of the corresponding pronouns—'where?' means 'at, in *or* on what (place)?'; 'from where?' means 'from what (place)?' In fact, to talk of adverbs of *place* in Sanskrit is somewhat misleading, since their reference may be as wide as that of the corresponding pronominal cases, extending to people and things as well as places. Thus a common meaning of **tatra** at the beginning of a sentence is 'among those (people or things just

INTERROGATIVE	RELATIVE	DEMONSTRATIVE	
		Normal correlative	*Other demonstratives*
kaḥ? who?	**yaḥ** who	**saḥ** he, that	**ayam** this, **asau** that
kva? } where?	**yatra** where	**tatra** there	**atra, iha** here
kutra? } [to] where?			
kutaḥ? from where?	**yataḥ** from where	**tataḥ** from there	**itaḥ** from here; in this direction
,, for what reason?	,, because	,, therefore	**ataḥ** hence, for this reason
kadā? when?	**yadā** when	**tadā** then	**idānīm, adhunā** now
katham? how?	**yathā** as	**tathā** } **evam** } so, thus	**ittham, evam** in this way
kīdṛśa? of what kind?	**yādṛśa** of which kind	**tādṛśa** of that kind, such (a)	**īdṛśa** of this kind, such (a)
kiyant? how much?	**yāvant** as much as	**tāvant** so much	**iyant** this much
kiyacciram? } **kiyantaṃ kālam?** } for how long?	**yāvat** as long as, while	**tāvat** for so long	**iyacciram** } **iyantaṃ kālam** } for this long
	yadi } **cet** } if	**tat** *etc.* then	
	yady api } **kāmam** } even if, granted that	**tathā 'pi** } **punar** } even so, nevertheless	

mentioned)': e.g. **tatra kenʾ âpy uktam** '[among them someone:] one of them said'.

Similarly, by a common idiom these adverbs may be used as attributive adjectives qualifying substantives in the locative or (apparently rather less frequently) the ablative case. So **atra vane** does not mean 'here in the forest' but is synonymous with **asmin vane** 'in this forest'. Other examples of the usage are:

tatra kāle at that time
atrʾ ântare at this juncture
kutaś cid vyañjanāt from some indication
atra *or* **atra vastuni** in this matter
iha *or* **iha loke** in this world

The suffix *taḥ*

It will be noticed that this suffix is used to form all the adverbs with ablative sense. In fact, it may also be added to the first and second person pronouns as a commoner alternative to the theoretical ablative forms: one usually says **mattaḥ** rather than **mat** for 'from me' and so on.

The sense of the suffix is not always strictly ablative: **itaḥ** as well as meaning 'from here' is common in the sense of 'over here' or 'in this direction'. Unlike other adverbial suffixes, **taḥ** is combined with a wide range of nouns as well as pronouns and converts them to adverbs with some such sense as well as pronouns and converts them to adverbs with some such sense as 'in accordance with' or 'in respect of'. The suffix often alternates not only with the ablative case but also with other cases, particularly the instrumental:

saṃkṣepaḥ abridgement **saṃkṣepeṇa, saṃkṣepāt** *or* **saṃkṣepataḥ** in brief
vistaraḥ expansion **vistareṇa, vistarāt** *or* **vistarataḥ** in detail
prasaṅgaḥ occasion **prasaṅgena, prasaṅgāt** *or* **prasaṅgataḥ** incidentally, in passing
api jñāyante nāma˜taḥ? do (you) know them by name?

tau ca bhagavatā Vālmīkinā dhātrī-karma vastu˜taḥ parigṛhya poṣitau parirakṣitau ca and the revered Vālmīki, adopting [as to substance:] in effect the role of a foster-mother, reared and looked after the two of them

Numerals

Complicated numerals are too infrequent in ordinary texts to justify the devoting of much space to them in an elementary primer. It is, however, worth committing to memory the list of numerals at the back of the book. From 1 to 4 the cardinal numerals agree with the substantive they qualify in number, gender and case; from 5 to 19, in number and case, but with only one form for all genders; from 20 onwards, in case only. Thus **tisṛbhir nadībhiḥ** 'with three rivers', **ṣoḍaśabhir nadībhiḥ** 'with sixteen rivers', **śatena nadībhiḥ** 'with a hundred rivers'. From 20 onwards the numbers are, in fact, collective nouns, and alternatively therefore the qualified substantive may be put in the genitive plural: **śatena nadīnām** 'with a hundred [of] rivers'. Or, again, a determinative compound may be made: **nadī-śatena** 'with [a river-century:] a hundred rivers'.

Compounds with collective nouns ('pair', 'triad', etc.) may also be used to express the smallest numbers. A dual form is very often avoided by using one of the many words for 'pair': **go-dvayaṃ, go-yugaṃ, go-mithunaṃ**, etc. '[cow-pair:] two cows'.

All the numerals may be compounded attributively in their stem form: **dvi:pāda** 'two-footed', **śata:mukha** 'having a hundred mouths', **daśa:kumāra-caritam** 'the story of the ten princes'.

Concord

The principle that a predicate should agree with its subject is modified in Sanskrit when the subject consists of a number of co-ordinated items. In such cases there is a tendency for the predicate to agree with the nearest item. This happens regularly when the verb precedes the subject.

tataḥ praviśaty Arundhatī Kausalyā kañcukī ca then enter Arundhatī, Kausalyā and the chamberlain (*not* **praviśanti**)

tad idaṃ tāvad gṛhyatām ābharaṇaṃ dhanuś ca so just take this decoration and (this) bow (*not* **gṛhyetām**)

prabhavati prāyaśaḥ kumārīṇāṃ janayitā daivaṃ ca (what) generally governs girls (is) their father and their fate (*not* **prabhavataḥ**)

Nominative with *iti*

Where in English we would quote a word such as a proper name and isolate it between inverted commas, a Sanskrit word may be isolated by **iti** and it is then normally put in the nominative case: so **'Rāma' iti viśrutaḥ** 'known as "Rāma" '.

'aśva' iti paśu-samāmnāye sāṃgrāmike ca paṭhyate 'horse' is mentioned in the list of sacrifical animals, and in the military (list)

mātra

The word **mātrā** 'measure' is used at the end of a bahuvrīhi compound in the sense of 'sharing the size of' both literally (**aṅguṣṭha-mātra** 'thumb-sized', **khadyota-mātra** 'no bigger than a firefly') and in the sense of 'fully measured by, being nothing more than', and so 'mere' or 'merely', 'only'. In this sense it may form a neuter substantive: **jala-mātraṃ** 'only water', **pravāda-mātraṃ** 'mere talk'.

Especially striking is the combination of this **mātra** with a past participle to express 'as soon as': thus **dṛṣta-mātra** 'no more than seen, as soon as seen'.

praviṣṭa-mātreṇ› aîva śayana-gṛhaṃ durātmanā Cāṇakya:hatakeṇ› âvalokitam the very moment he entered, the evil and accursed Cāṇakya examined the sleeping quarters

Vocabulary

aṅgaṃ limb (*the four 'limbs' of an army are elephants, chariots, cavalry and infantry*)
adhikāraḥ authority, office
adhiṣṭhātṛ *m.* superintending, at the head of
antevāsin [resident] disciple
apanodanaṃ driving away
abhidhānaṃ statement; appellation, name
abhiprāyaḥ intention, inclination
abhivyakta manifest, visible
abhīśu *m.* rein, bridle
arth›-ôtsargaḥ expenditure [of money]
ardhaḥ half (portion)
alaṃkaraṇaṃ ornament
ātmajaḥ son
ānuyātrikaḥ escort to (*gen.*)
iṣṭa:janaḥ the loved one
ucita suitable, appropriate
utsavaḥ festival
kalatraṃ (*NB gender*) wife
kalikā bud
Kuśaḥ *pr. n.*
garbhaḥ womb
catur (*stem form*) four
Candraketu *m., pr. n.*
candrikā moonlight
cāpa *m.n.* bow
citta-vṛtti *f.* [activity of mind:] mental process, thought
cūtaḥ mango tree
Jānakī *pr. n.*
tarkaḥ conjecture
trayaṃ triad (of) (*at end of cpd. expresses 'three'*)
dārāḥ *m. pl.* (*NB number and gender*) wife
divya celestial
dīpikā lamp
duṣkara difficult [to do]
duhitṛ *f.* daughter
dvitīya second, another
dhūrtaḥ rogue
dhairyaṃ firmness
nibandhanaṃ bond
paṇāyitṛ *m.* hawker
para *pron. adj.* other, another
Parvateśvaraḥ *pr. n.*
pāṇi *m.* hand
paunaruktaṃ redundancy
pracalita in motion
prabhu *m.* master
pramādaḥ mishap
pravṛtti *f.* news
prasādaḥ favour
prāṇāḥ *m. pl.* [breaths:] life
prārthayitṛ *m.* suitor
Priyaṃvadakaḥ *pr. n.*
bhaṅgaḥ breaking; plucking (of buds); dispersal (of crowd)
bhāgaḥ division, portion, tithe
bhrātṛ *m.* brother
madhu *m.* (season or first month of) spring
Mandārikā *pr. n.*
mahānt great, vast, numerous
mahā:māṃsaṃ human flesh
mātṛ *f.* mother
-mātra mere, only (*see chapter*)
mānuṣaḥ human being, mortal
māmakīna my
Mālatī *pr. n.*
mūrkha foolish; *m.* fool
medhya fit for sacrifice, sacrificial
yamaja twin[-born]
yātrā procession
yādṛśa (*f.* ī) *relative adj.* of which kind, such as, just as
rakṣitṛ *m.* guard
ratnaṃ jewel
rājyaṃ kingdom
rāśi *m.* heap
lajjā-kara (*f.* ī) embarrassing

Lavaḥ *pr. n.*
lābhaḥ profit
vane-caraḥ forest dweller
vallabhaḥ sweetheart
Vasuṃdharā *pr. n.*
vastu *n.* thing, matter, subject-matter
Vāmadevaḥ *pr. n.*
Vālmīki *m. pr. n.*
vikretṛ *m.* vendor
vicitra variegated, various
viśeṣaṇa:padaṃ [distinguishing word:] epithet
Vairodhakaḥ *pr. n.*
Vaihīnari *m., pr. n.*
śataṃ a hundred
śāstraṃ treatise, law-book
ślāghya laudable, virtuous
saṃvyavahāraḥ transaction
saṃkulaṃ throng
saṃpradāyaḥ tradition
-saṃbhava *ifc.* arising from, offspring of
sahasraṃ a thousand
sādhanaṃ army
suvarṇaḥ gold; gold piece
snigdha affectionate
hastaḥ hand

ati+sṛj (VI atisṛjati) bestow
anu+pra+hi (V anuprahiṇoti) send (someone after something), despatch
anu+mantr (X anumantrayate) consecrate with mantras, bless
anu+i (II anveti) follow, attend
anu+iṣ (I anveṣate) look for, search
abhi+nand (I abhinandati) rejoice in, prize; greet with enthusiasm
ava+āp (V avāpnoti) obtain, acquire
ava+īkṣ (avekṣate) watch, watch over
ā+rabh (I ārabhate) undertake, begin
ās (II āste) sit, stay, remain; **joṣam ās** remain silent
ā+hve (I āhvayati *pass.* **āhūyate)** summon, call
īh (I īhate) long, for, desire
upa+kḷp *caus.* **(upakalpayati)** equip; assign
upa+nī (I upanayati) bring
krī (IX krīṇāti) buy
jñā (IX jānāti) know, learn, find out
dā (III dadāti) give
nis+vap (I nirvapati) sprinkle, offer, donate
ni+vṛ *caus.* **(nivārayati)** ward off, drive off
ni+sidh (I niṣedhati) prohibit, cancel
pari+tyaj (I parityajati) leave, abandon
pari+rakṣ (I parirakṣati) protect, save, spare
pra+ci (V pracinoti) accumulate (*the pass. corresponds to the English intrans.*)
prati+śru (V pratiśṛṇoti) promise
rakṣ (I rakṣati) protect
vi+ghaṭ (I vighaṭate, *p.p.* **vighaṭita)** become separated
vi+muc (VI vimuñcati) release, loose
vi+śram (IV viśrāmyati) rest, cease, take a rest

vi+sṛj (VI **visṛjati**) discharge, release
vi+īkṣ (I **vīkṣate**) discern, spy
vi+ava+hṛ (I **vyavaharati**) act, behave towards (*loc.*)
sam+ṛ *caus.* (**samarpayati**) hand over
sam+bhū *caus.* (**saṃbhāvayati**) conceive, imagine
stu (II **stauti**) praise

an-antaram [without interval:] immediately
ayi ha!
ekadā at one time, once
kiṃ ca moreover
cirasya after a long time
tathā in that way, thus, so
prasaṅgataḥ in passing
madhyāt from the middle of, from among
mṛṣā vainly
vihāya ['having left behind':] beyond (*acc.*)
sarvathā in every way, altogether, totally

Exercise 11a

कथम् इयं सा कण्वदुहिता शकुन्तला ।१। वत्से यदहमीहे तदस्तु ते ।२। हे धूर्त लेखो नीयते न च ज्ञायते कस्येति ।३। प्रिये मालति इयं वीक्ष्यसे ।४। विश्रम्यतां परिजनेन ।५। मन्दारिके यदत्र वस्तुन्येष ते वल्लभः कथयति अपि तथा तत् ।६। देवेनैवं निषिद्धे ऽपि मधूत्सवे चूतकलिकाभङ्गमारभसे ।७। परिरक्ष्यन्तामस्य प्राणाः ।८। भो राजन् किमिदं जोषमास्यते ।९। तदनुष्ठीयतामात्मनो ऽभिप्रायः ।१०। किं चातिसृष्टः पर्वतेश्वरभ्रात्रे वैरोधकाय पूर्वप्रतिश्रुतो राज्यार्धः ।११। कथं शकुन्तलेत्यस्य मातुराख्या ।१२। कः स महापुरुषो येनैतन्मानुषमात्रदुष्करं महत्कर्मानुष्ठितम् ।१३। प्रियंवदक ज्ञायतां का वेला वर्तत इति ।१४। आर्य वैहीनरे दीयतामाभ्यां वैतालिकाभ्यां सुवर्णशतसहस्रम् ।१५। वृषल किमयमस्थान एव महानर्थोत्सर्गः क्रियते ।१६। भोः श्रेष्ठिन् अपि प्रचीयन्ते संव्यवहाराणां लाभाः ।१७। भगवति वसुंधरे श्लाघ्यां दुहितरमवेक्षस्व जानकीम् ।१८। कथं निवार्यमाणो ऽपि स्थित एव ।१९। भगवन्वाल्मीके उपनीयेतामिमौ सीतागर्भसंभवौ रामभद्रस्य कुशलवौ ।२०।

यादृशो ऽयं तादृशौ तावपि । २१ । विसृष्टश्च वामदेवानुमन्त्रितो मेध्यो ऽश्वः । उपकल्पिताश्च यथाशास्त्रं तस्य रक्षितारः । तेषामधिष्ठाता लक्ष्मणात्मजश्चन्द्रकेतुरवाप्तदिव्यास्त्रसंप्रदायश्चतुरङ्गसाधनान्वितो ऽनुप्रहितः । २२ । हन्त हन्त सर्वथा नृशंसो ऽस्मि यश्चिरस्य दृष्टान्प्रियसुहृदः प्रियान्दारान्न स्निग्धं पश्यामि । २३ । अथ तस्मादरण्यात्परित्यज्य निवृत्ते लक्ष्मणे सीतायाः किं वृत्तमिति काचिदस्ति प्रवृत्तिः । २४ । अस्ति तावदेकदा प्रसङ्गतः कथित एव मया माधवाभिधानः कुमारो यस्त्वमिव मामकीनस्य मनसो द्वितीयं निबन्धनम ॥ २५ ॥

Exercise 11b

Translate all present actives (except in 14, 18 and 24) and all imperatives by means of the passive.

1 Give him an answer. 2 We are twin brothers. 3 Masters do not summon (those) holding·[**vant**]·office without·a·purpose. 4 Stop right here. 5 Give (me) one [from among:] of those three·ornaments which (I) bought. 6 Loose the reins. 7 Why speak of 'firmness'? 8 Hurry, my good fellows, hurry. 9 The moonlight (being) visible, what point in a redundancy·of·lamps? 10 Lātavya, call Urvaśī. 11 Oh, this is the decoration which I removed from my·own·person and sent to Rākṣasa. 12 Ha, dear child [*f.*]! (You) are thus praising yourself. 13 Reward the vendor and accept it. 14 Your Excellency, have (you) anyone who is going to Kusumapura or coming from there? 15 Have him come in. 16 Why vainly [search with conjecture:] speculate? 17 'Minister' is now an embarrassing epithet. 18 Alas, I am quite deluded to behave towards this forest-dweller (in a way [*n. sg.*]) appropriate·to·my·friend·Makaranda. 19 Hand over Rākṣasa's family—enjoy for a long time (to come) the·king's·favour with·its·various·advantages. 20 Protect, at the cost of [*simply use instr.*] another's·wife, your own wife and your life. 21 This is the son·of·Kāmandakī's·friend, Mādhava, (here) to hawk

human flesh. 22 (As) escort to the disciples by whose hand (he) has sent that book to Bharata's·hermitage, (he) has sent our·brother bow·in·hand [**cāpa:pāṇi**] to·drive·away·mishap. 23 And she having immediately become separated (from me) by the throng of numerous [**mahānt**] townsfolk in·motion·upon·the·dispersal·of·the·procession, I came (here). 24 Fool, these ascetics donate a quite different tithe, one which is prized beyond even heaps·of·jewels. 25 Thus, imagining· [*use* *p.p.*]·by·his·own·inclinations·the·thoughts·of·the·loved·one, the suitor is deceived.

Chapter 12

PARADIGMS: Present of classes II, V and VIII

Athematic presents

The four present classes so far dealt with (I, IV, VI and X) are the thematic classes: they differ from each other only in the way in which the stem is formed from the root, for the stem thus formed always ends in (or: is linked to the endings by) the thematic vowel **a**. The other six classes are comparable with the nominal consonant stems, and their inflexion is of far greater difficulty and variety mainly because the stem is in direct contact (collision may sometimes seem a better word) with the personal endings. One may distinguish practically between the lesser complications of those classes where the stem ends in a suffix (V, VIII, IX) and the greater complications of those where the final letter of the stem is also the final letter of the actual root (II, III, VII).

In class II, the root class, the stem consists simply of the root itself. This generally strengthens to guṇa in the strong grade and remains unchanged in the weak grade. In this and all other athematic classes, the strong grade appears in the whole of the singular parasmaipada both present and imperfect, in the third person singular parasmaipada of the imperative, and in all first person forms of the imperative, while two noteworthy features of the personal terminations of athematic verbs are the absence of **n** in the third person plural ātmanepada present, imperfect and imperative, and the addition of the suffix **dhi** (after consonants) or **hi** (after vowels) in the second person singular imperative parasmaipada.

The conjugation of the commonest class II root, **as** 'be', has already been introduced. The inflexion of **i** 'go' is typical of a root ending in a vowel: among sandhi changes one may note retroflexion of **s** (**eṣi** 'you go') and consonantalisation of **i** (**yanti** 'they go'). The inflexion of **dviṣ** 'hate' illustrates some of the sandhis of final **ṣ**: thus **ṣ+s = kṣ, ṣ+dh = ḍḍh.**

The strong grade of **han** 'kill' is **han**: so **hanti** 'he kills', which looks misleadingly like a plural form. The weak grade is also stated as **han**, but it appears as **ha** before **t/th** and as **ghn** before **a**: **hatha** 'you kill'; **ghnanti** 'they kill'. The second person singular imperative is **jahi.**

Some roots retain strong grade throughout: **śī, śete** 'he lies'. Some, though classed as root verbs, add the suffix **i** before some terminations: **rud, roditi** 'he weeps'. **brū** 'speak' adds **ī** in the strong forms before a consonant: **bravītu** 'let him speak'.

Class V verbs add the suffix **nu** before the terminations, and this strengthens to **no** in the strong grade. The root **śru** 'hear' forms a present stem **śṛṇu/śṛṇo** (on the basis of a more primitive form of the root, **śṛ**): **śṛṇoṣi** 'you hear'. Roots ending in a *vowel* (*a*) do not take the suffix **hi** in the second person singular imperative, (*b*) may optionally reduce **nu** to **n** before **v** and **m**: **śṛṇu** 'listen'; **śṛṇumaḥ** or **śṛṇmaḥ** 'we hear'. Roots ending in a *consonant* (*a*) must add **hi** in the imperative, (*b*) must change **nu** to **nuv** before vowels: **āpnuhi** 'obtain'; **āpnuvanti** 'they obtain'.

Class VIII verbs add the suffix **u**, strengthening to **o.** Of the eight verbs in this class, seven have roots ending in **n** and behave in the same way as class V roots ending in vowels, as described above: **tan, tanoti** 'he extends'; **tanuvaḥ** or **tanvaḥ** 'we two extend'. The eighth verb is the common **kṛ** 'do'. The strong stem is **karo,** the weak **kuru,** but this latter *must* appear as **kur** before **v, m** and **y.** The second person singular imperative parasmaipada is **kuru.**

The formation of the present participles of athematics is mentioned in Chapter 10. Remember that the ātmanepada participle is in **-āna**, not **-amāna**. The present participle of **ās** 'stay' is anomalous, **āsīna.**

Gerundives

The gerundive (sometimes called the future passive participle) is a verbal adjective with passive sense expressing such notions as obligation or necessity—'(requiring) to be done' etc. It may be formed in a number of alternative ways, by the addition to the root of any of three suffixes: **ya, anīya, tavya.**

The gerundive in **ya** is the most ancient of the three and shows the greatest variety of formation. In general, the following are the changes undergone by the root before this suffix. Final ā becomes **e**: **dā, deya** 'to be given'. Final **i/ī** strengthens to **e**: **nī, neya** 'to be led'. Final **u/ū** strengthens to **av** or to **āv**: **śru, śravya** or **śrāvya** 'to be heard'. Final **ṛ/ṝ** strengthens to **ār**: **kṛ, kārya** 'to be done'. Followed by a single consonant, medial **i/u** becomes **e/o**, medial **ṛ** is unchanged, medial **a** sometimes remains and sometimes strengthens to **ā**: **śuc, śocya** 'to be mourned for'; **bhid, bhedya** 'to be split'; **dṛś, dṛśya** 'to be seen'; **gam, gamya** 'to be gone to'; but **vac, vācya** 'to be spoken'.

As well as exceptions to the above, there are a number of alternative forms: most notably, final **i/u/ṛ** may remain unstrengthened and add a connecting **t**: so **śrutya** besides **śravya** and **śrāvya, kṛtya** besides **kārya.**

Derivative stems drop **aya** before adding **ya**: **varṇya** 'to be described'. Gerundives in **ya** from causatives are, however, little found, since they would not usually be distinguishable from the gerundive of the simple verb.

The suffix **anīya** is an adjectival extension of the suffix **ana,** which is most commonly used to form neuter action nouns (see Chapter 8). The root almost always appears in the guṇa grade, being strengthened to the same extent as in forming class I presents: **kṛ, karaṇīya** 'to be done'; **nind, nindanīya** 'blameworthy'. Derivative stems again drop **aya.** A number of causative forms are found, e.g. **bhāvanīya** 'to be caused to be'.

The suffix **tavya** is an adjectival extension of another suffix, this time of the obsolete verbal noun in **tu** on which the infinitive and the absolutive are based. This type of gerundive may in fact be formed by substituting **tavya** for the **tum** of the infinitive, and so the remarks in Chapter 13 (p. 203) on the formation of the infinitive should now be studied and the list of principal parts of verbs consulted. A point to note particularly is that, as in the infinitive, derivative stems retain the suffix **ay**: from **vid** 'know', **veditavya** 'to be known' but **vedayitavya** 'to be made known'. Causatives form gerundives of this type freely.

As was mentioned in Chapter 8, the prefixes **su** and **dus** (as also **īṣat** 'slightly') combine not with a gerundive but with a verbal noun in **a**: **dur:jaya** 'difficult to conquer' etc.

Gerundives may be used predicatively in sentences expressing obligation or necessity: **ahaṃ bhavadbhir draṣṭavyaḥ** 'I am to be seen by you'. As with past participles, a passive is often best translated by an active, and so the above may be represented by 'you must see me'. In English, in fact, it is often appropriate to translate a gerundive as an imperative, and so we may also say '(come and) see me'.

While there is a considerable overlap between the three types of gerundive, certain differences of usage can be distinguished. The types in **ya** and **anīya**, and particularly the former, tend to have a wider, more characterising sense: thus **a:nirvarṇyaṃ khalu para-kalatram** 'one ought not of course to gaze upon the wife of a stranger'—whereas 'don't look at her' would probably be expressed by **na draṣṭavyā**. These forms are thus far more likely than the **tavya** form to be used as simple adjectives—e.g. **ślāghya** 'praiseworthy', **śocanīya** 'lamentable'. They are particularly used after verbs with prefixes; they may also combine with the negative prefix **a**, and even appear to a limited extent at the end of determinative compounds: e.g. **anantara:karaṇīya** 'to be done immediately'. The implication of necessity may be entirely lost in the more general notion of potentiality: 'such as to be', and therefore 'capable of being'. The meaning then comes close to that of the past participle but is normally to be distinguished by the absence of any factual implication: **dṛṣṭa** '(actually) seen', but **dṛśya** 'visible' and **prayatna-prekṣaṇīya** 'to be discerned with difficulty'.

> **ari-balaṃ ca vihata;vidhvastaṃ strī;bāla-hārya: śastraṃ vartate** and the enemy's forces, broken and shattered, are in a state where their weapons [are takeable:] could be taken by women or children

The gerundive in **tavya**, on the other hand, while it can be used in both general and particular statements and with prefixed and unprefixed verbs, seldom loses the notion of necessity and is normally used as the predicate of a sentence rather than as an attributive adjective. (It may appear as the predicate of a locative absolute: thus **durga-saṃskāra ārabdhavye** '(at a time) when fortifications ought to be undertaken'.) It should not be used at the end of a nominal compound or in combination with the prefix **a**.

A strictly passive sense is more universally prevalent in gerundives than in past participles, even for verbs normally intransitive. Thus **gamya, gamanīya** and **gantavya** may all mean '(requiring) to be gone *to*'. However, a gerundive construction can be given to an essentially intransitive verb by means of the impersonal passive:

> **nanu Lavaṅgike, Kāmandakyā ›pi na khalv ataḥ param . . . jīvitavyam** why Lavaṅgikā, Kāmandakī too shall certainly not live any longer (*lit.* it is not to be lived by Kāmandakī *etc.*)

Particularly noteworthy, as defying literal translation into English, is the frequent impersonal use of the gerundive of **bhū** 'be'. The complement of the verb like the logical subject itself must be put in the instrumental case:

> **tad bhagavati Godāvari, tvayā tatra s›_āvadhānayā bhavitavyam** So venerable Godāvarī, you must be watchful in the matter
>
> **viśrāntena bhavatā mam› ânyasminn an:āyāse karmaṇi sahāyena bhavitavyam** when rested, you

must be my companion in another task, which is not a strenuous one

This particular gerundive is often used to mark an inference:

vyaktam āhituṇḍika-cchadmanā Virādhaguptena anena bhavitavyam this (person) must obviously be Virādhagupta disguised as a snake-charmer
aye dhīra-praśāntaḥ svaraḥ—tat tapasvibhir bhavitavyam such strong, calm tones! It must then be ascetics (I can hear)

Similarly, in an inference about a past event, **evam anayā praṣṭavyam** '[thus:] this is what she must have asked'.

kṛ and compounds of *kṛ* and *bhū*

The verb **kṛ** may be translated by 'do' or 'make' in English: **kiṃ kurmaḥ?** 'what shall we do?'; **kumbhaṃ karoti** 'he is making a pot'. With an abstract noun in the accusative it has the effect of creating a more complex verb: **vandanāṃ karoti** 'makes salutation, salutes'; **āśvāsana-mātraṃ karoti** 'makes mere consolation, merely consoles'. Like 'make' in English, it may also be used with an accusative and a predicative adjective to give causative sense: **tvām a-kāmaṃ karomi** 'I'll [make you one·whose·desires·are·not:] frustrate you'.

tat kim atra vipine priyā-vārttā-hāraṃ karomi? what then in this forest shall I make a carrier of news to my beloved?

In this sense of 'turn into', however, there is an alternative construction. One may compound the predicative adjective with the verb by changing the **a** of the adjective's stem to **ī** and adding it directly to the front of **kṛ**: so **tvām a-kāmaṃ karomi** might appear instead as **tvām akāmīkaromi** (if we wish to preserve the punctuation we may write **a-kāmī-karomi**). The rule is that nouns change final **a**, **ā**, **i** or **in** to **ī** and final **u** to **ū** (as in **laghu** 'light', **laghūkṛ** 'lighten'), while most other stems would appear without change; but the formation is far commoner with nouns in **a** than with any others. Substantives are as freely used as adjectives in this construction, e.g. **aṅgī˜karoti** 'turns into a limb, subordinates'.

The same construction is found with the verb **bhū** in the sense of 'become', e.g. **aṅgī˜bhūta** 'become a limb, subordinated'. This is distinct in meaning from the karmadhāraya **aṅga:bhūta** 'being a limb, subordinate'.

In this way we have pairs of transitive and intransitive denominative verbs. Mention was made in Chapter 9 of the denominative pair **śithilayati** 'slackens (*trans.*)' and **śithilāyate** 'slackens (*intrans.*)'. With the same meanings we may form **śithilī˜karoti** and **śithilī˜bhavati.**

This construction forms a small exception to the general principle in Sanskrit that nouns may compound with each other but not with finite verbs (and even this construction occurs most commonly of all in non-finite forms, in particular in the past participle).

In a similar way there are a number of adverbs and other non-verbal forms which may be combined with **kṛ** and **bhū** (and to a limited extent also with **dhā** 'put' and **as** 'be'). So from the Vedic adverb **āvis** 'openly', **āviṣ˜kṛ** 'reveal', **āvir˜bhū** 'become apparent'. Similarly, from **tiras** 'secretly', **tiras˜kṛ** 'conceal', **tiro˜bhū** 'vanish'. It is **kṛ** which combines with the widest variety of such forms. Among other examples one might mention **alaṃkaroti** 'ornaments', **namaskaroti** 'pays homage to', **satkaroti** 'does honour to'.

In all such compounds the absolutive used should be the compound form in **ya.**

Relative adverbs

The tendency of pronominal adverbs to act as extensions of the case system was mentioned in the previous chapter—e.g. **atra vane** = **asmin vane** 'in this forest'. Relative adverbs used in this way are simple extensions therefore of the relative pronoun. This is often true of **yatra** 'where, in which' and **yataḥ** 'from where, from which'. Thus **tad etat**

Prācetas›-âdhyuṣitam araṇyaṃ, yatra kila devī parityaktā 'this is the forest inhabited by Prācetasa, in which [*or* where], I believe, Her Majesty was abandoned'. One may substitute **yasmin** for **yatra** in the above sentence without affecting the meaning.

In their characteristic use, however, relative adverbs have simply a more limited scope than the relative pronoun, in that the correlative adverb plays the same role in the main clause as the relative adverb in the relative clause (as when relative and correlative pronoun are in the same case): so **yadā . . . tadā** 'at which time, . . . at that time', **yathā . . . tathā** 'in which way . . . in that way', etc. Thus the relative clause and the main clause share a common feature: in 'where the rain falls, there the plants grow', the falling of the rain and the growing of plants are given a common location; if one substituted 'when . . . then', they would be given a common time.

The general feature of adverbial relative clauses are those already described for other relative clauses. The correlative adverb will correspond in function to its relative, but there may be a choice of forms. For instance, the correlative of **yathā** 'as' may equally well be either **tathā** or **evam** 'so, thus':

kim nu khalu yathā vayam asyām, evam iyam apy asmān prati syāt? could she for her part possibly [be:] feel towards us as we (do) towards her?

'kim tu katham asmābhir upagantavya iti sampradhārayāmi'—'yath» aîva gurus tath» ôpasadanena' 'but I am wondering in what way we ought to approach him'—'with the same respectful salutation as (one would) one's preceptor'

A particular use of **yathā** is in inferences—'from the way that':

yath» ôn_mukham ālokayati, tathā vyaktaṃ 'pravās›-ôtsuka:manasā mayā na dṛṣṭ»' êty āha from the way he gazes up, he is obviously saying, 'with my mind eager for the journey, I didn't see her'

The most usual correlative of **yadā** 'when' is **tadā** 'then', but others such as **tataḥ** 'thereupon' and **atha** 'hereat' are also found. Even if **tadā** itself is used, the relation of the two clauses is often one of sequence rather than of strict contemporaneity. Temporal clauses in narrative tend to be rather long, and for the usual reason that short clauses may be expressed in other ways in Sanskrit. Because it is not necessary for a relative pronoun or adverb to stand at the beginning of its clause, it is quite possible for the writer or speaker to be well launched on his sentence before deciding to subordinate it as a relative clause:

tataḥ 'kutas tav› âyaṃ mahān dhan›-āgama?' iti pṛcchyamāno yadā vākya-bhedam ākulam akathayat, tadā Cāṇakya:hatak›-ādeśād vicitreṇa vadhena vyāpāditaḥ then, when on being asked 'where did your great accession of wealth (come) from?' he told a confused variety of stories, he was by order of the accursed Cāṇakya [killed by a variegated death:] put to death by torture

The word **yāvat** 'while' deserves comment. It is in origin the adverbially used neuter singular of the relative pronoun **yāvant** 'as much . . . as', whose use is illustrated by

yāvān artha udapāne sarvataḥ saṃplut›:ôdake,
tāvān sarveṣu vedeṣu brāhmaṇasya vijānataḥ

As much point as (there is) in a water-tank when it has water flooding all round it, so much (is there) in all the Vedas for a brahmin who discerns [*gen. sg. pres. part. of* **vijñā**]

yāvat thus means in origin 'for all the time that, for as long as', and this is the meaning which it has in forming 'prepositional' compounds similar to those made with **yathā** described in Chapter 9, where it may represent the same notion as the English 'throughout': e.g. **yāvad_rājyam** 'throughout the reign', **yāvad_adhyayanam** 'throughout the (period of) study'. As a conjunction **yāvat** may mean 'during all or some of the time that' and thus correspond to 'while':

yāvat prāṇimi, tāvad asya . . . madana-saṃtāpasya pratikriyāṃ kriyamāṇām icchāmi I want a remedy to be contrived for this love-torment while I am (still) breathing

Vijaye, muhūrtaṃ nibhṛta:pada-saṃcārā bhava, yāvad asya parāṅ:mukhasy› aîva pāṇibhyām nayane niruṇadhmi Vijayā, keep your footsteps quiet for a moment, while I cover his eyes with my hands as he is looking the other way

upaśleṣaya rathaṃ yāvad ārohāmi bring up the chariot while I get in

In the last two examples the idea of purpose is present, and the notion of 'while' shades into that of 'until', which is another meaning of **yāvat**. In this latter sense it is often but not necessarily construed with the future tense:

pratīkṣasva kāni cid dināni, yāvad iyam . . . prakṛtāv eva sthāsyati wait a few days, until she [shall abide in her actual nature:] comes to her senses

tat sarvathā ›smāt sthānād anyat sthānam āśrayāmi yāvad asya mayā vijñātaṃ cikīrṣitam so at all events I'll go from this place to another, until I have found out his intentions [*p.p. in the sense of a* (*future*) *perfect*]

'Until, up to' is also the usual meaning of **yāvat** when it is a preposition governing (and following) a noun in the accusative: e.g. **sūry›-ôdayaṃ yāvat** 'until sunrise'. This contrasts with the meaning 'throughout' which it usually has in prepositional compounds. (However, the difference will normally also be conveyed by the presence, on the one hand, of a word more naturally implying duration, such as 'life', or, on the other, of one more naturally implying an event, such as 'arrival'.)

Finally, **yāvat** with a negative may be translated 'before' (although there are other ways of expressing this notion, such as the use of **prāk** or **pūrvam** with the ablative of an abstract noun):

> **. . . na yāvad āyāti, tāvat tvaritam anena taru-gahanen› âpasarpata** [while he is not coming:] before he comes, escape quickly through this wood

The following example combines **yāvat** 'while' and **yāvat + na** 'before':

> **yāvad eva sa_cetanā ›smi, yāvad eva ca na parisphuṭam anena vibhāvyate me madana-duśceṣṭita-lāghavam etat, tāvad ev› âsmāt pradeśād apasarpaṇaṃ śreyaḥ** it is better to escape from this place while I am still conscious, and [while by him is not clearly detected:] before he clearly detects in me this disrespect (arising) from the mischievous workings of passion

The adverbial suffix *vat*

The possessive suffix **vant** is used adverbially in the neuter singular with the special sense of expressing a comparison: thus **brāhmaṇa˜vat** 'like a brahmin'. There is nothing in the form to indicate the grammatical role played by the subject of the comparison in the rest of the sentence, and so according to context **brāhmaṇa˜vat** may be the equivalent of **brāhmaṇa iva, brāhmaṇam iva**, etc. In the following example the context shows that **pitṛ˜vat** is the equivalent of **pitṝn iva**:

> **Kāśī-pati;Maithil›;Âṅga-˜rājāṃś ca suhṛn-niveditān pitṛ˜vad apaśyat** and he (the prince) looked on the kings of Kāśī, Mithilā and the Aṅgas, presented by his friends, as his fathers

viśeṣaḥ

viśeṣaḥ literally means 'distinction, difference, particularity', and is is often used in this literal sense. At the end of a determinative compound (analysable as either dependent or descriptive) it may also be used idiomatically to express the notion 'a particular . . ., a special . . .'. Thus **brāhmaṇa-viśeṣaḥ** '[a particularity of brahmin, a specialty that is a brahmin:] a particular brahmin'; **strī-viśeṣaḥ** 'a particular woman'; **ratna-viśeṣaḥ** 'a special jewel, a particularly excellent jewel'. Less frequently, **viśeṣa** may be used with this same meaning as the prior member of the compound.

Vocabulary

Agastyaḥ *pr. n.*
apadeśaḥ pretence, pretext
a:parikleśaḥ lack of vexation
apsaras *f.* nymph (of heaven)
a:vighna unhindered
aśokaḥ aśoka-tree
ākula confused; **ākulī˜bhū** grow confused; *p.p.* in confusion
āyus *n.* life
ārta oppressed
āsanaṃ sitting, seat
udghātin having elevations, bumpy
kathitaṃ thing spoken, talk, conversation
kaṣṭa˜tara more grievous
kāla-haraṇaṃ delay; **kāla-haraṇaṃ kṛ** (to) delay
kiyant how much?
kṣudh *f.* hunger
tantraṃ administration
tapasvin ascetic; poor, wretched
tapo-vanaṃ ascetics' grove
devatā divinity, god
dhanaṃ wealth
dhyānaṃ meditation, meditating
nayanaṃ eye
patatrin bird
panthan *m., irreg. noun* (p. 283) road, path, way
para other; *m.* enemy, (hostile) stranger
parikleśaḥ vexation
parigrahaḥ occupation, occupying
parityāgaḥ giving up, sacrificing; liberality
paścāt:tāpaḥ [after-pain:] remorse
piṇḍapātin *m.* mendicant
pracchāyaṃ shade
pratyākhyānaṃ rejection
prayogaḥ performance (of play)
prasādaḥ graciousness, favour; free gift; **prasādī˜kṛ** bestow [as free gift]
prārabdhaṃ thing undertaken, enterprise
prāvīṇyaṃ proficiency
bharataḥ actor, player
bhūmi *f.* ground; fit object (for); **parityāga-bhūmi** object of liberality, suitable recipient (of)
maṅgalaṃ welfare, auspicious omen, good luck
manda slow, slack; **mandī˜bhū** slacken
manyu *m.* passion, anger
maraṇaṃ death
maru *m.* desert
Mānasaṃ *name of a lake*
mohaḥ delusion

raśmi *m.* rein, bridle
rahas *n.* solitude, secrecy; **rahasi** in secret
ripu *m.* enemy
lavaḥ fragment; **lavaśo lavaśaḥ** piece by piece
lobhaḥ greed
viklava bewildered, distressed
vinīta disciplined, modest
viśeṣaḥ distinction; *ifc. see chapter*; **viśeṣa˜taḥ** in particular
viśrambhaḥ confidence; **viśrambha-kathā/kathitam** confidential *or* intimate conversation
vṛṣṭi *f.* rain
vegaḥ haste, speed
vetasaḥ cane, reed
veṣaḥ dress, attire
vyasanam vice; weakness; misfortune, misery
śālaḥ sal tree
Śrīparvataḥ *name of a mountain*
saṃyamanam restraint, tightening
saṃjñā signal
saṃbandhin *m.* relative [by marriage]
sahadharmacārin *m.* lawful husband
sahadharmacāriṇī lawful wife
sāmājikaḥ spectator
sāra *m. n.* substance; property
su:caritam good deed
su:nayana fair-eyed
sthalī [dry] land
sthira firm; **sthirī˜kṛ** make firm, sustain; **sthirī˜bhū** be-[come] firm
svī˜kṛ make one's own, appropriate

ati+kram (**I atikrāmati**) transgress, go against
apa+nī (**I apanayati**) remove, take away
ava+gam *caus.* (**avagamayati**) procure
ākarṇayati *denom.* (ger. **ākarṇanīya**) give ear, listen to
ā+dā (**III ādatte**) take, take hold of, bring
āp (**V āpnoti**) obtain, get
ut+pat (**I utpatati**) fly up
ut+ās (**II udāste**) sit idle
upa+ā+labh (**I upālabhate**) reproach, blame
upa+ās (**II upāste**) sit by, wait upon, honour
ceṣṭ (**I ceṣṭati**) move, act, behave (towards), treat (*loc.*)
taḍ (**X tāḍayati**, *pass.* **tāḍyate**) strike, beat
ni+kṛt (**VI nikṛntati**) cut up, shred
parā+pat (**I parāpatati**) approach, arrive
prati+ā+diś (**VI pratyādiśati**) reject; put to shame (by example)
pra+dru (**I pradravati**) run (*p.p. intrans.*)
pra+āp *caus.* (**prāpayati**) cause to reach, convey
brū (**II bravīti**) say, tell
vah (**I vahati**, *p.p.* **ūḍha**) carry, take, marry
sam+yam (**I saṃyacchati**) restrain, arrest
sam+ā+sad *caus.* (**samāsādayati**) approach, attain, meet
sam+upa+diś (**VI samupadiśati**) point out, show

a:samyak wrongly
āvir~bhū become manifest, reveal oneself
āviṣ~kṛ make manifest, reveal
itas tataḥ hither and thither
tiro~bhū become hidden, vanish
tūṣṇīm ās stay silent
tūṣṇīṃ bhū be[come] silent
nanu *may be translated as* 'rather' *in rejoinders*
bahiḥ outside
bhavatu [let it be:] right!
yatra, yathā, yadā, yāvat *see chapter*
~vat like (*see chapter*)

Exercise 12a

भद्र भद्र न प्रवेष्टव्यम् ।१। भवतु शृणोमि तावदासां विश्रम्भकथितानि ।२। तूष्णीं भव यावदाकर्णयामि ।३। अमात्य तथापि प्रारब्धमपरित्याज्यमेव ।४। तदत्र शालप्रच्छाये मुहूर्तमासनपरिग्रहं करोतु तातः ।५। समुपदिश तमुद्देशं यत्रास्ते स पिण्डपाती ।६। हृदय स्थिरीभव । किमपि ते कष्टतरमाकर्णनीयम् ।७। किमन्यद्ब्रवीतु ।८। इयं चोर्वशी यावदायुस्तव सहधर्मचारिणी भवतु ।९। तद्यावच्छ्रीपर्वतमुपनीय लवशो लवश एनां निकृत्य दुःखमरणां करोमि ।१०। अस्ति नः सुचरितश्रवणलोभादन्यदपि प्रष्टव्यम् ।११। तत्किमित्युदासते भरताः ।१२। तत्र चैवमनुष्ठेयं यथा वदामि ।१३। ननु भवतीभ्यामेव शकुन्तला स्थिरीकर्तव्या ।१४। गृहीतगृहसारमेनं सपुत्रकलत्रं संयम्य रक्ष तावद्यावन्मया वृषलाय कथ्यते ।१५। संप्रत्यगस्त्याश्रमस्य पन्थानं ब्रूहि ।१६। विनीतवेषप्रवेश्यानि तपोवनानि ।१७। मरुस्थल्यां यथा वृष्टिः क्षुधार्ते भोजनं तथा ।१८। उद्घातिनी भूमिरिति रश्मिसंयमनाद्रथस्य मन्दीभूतो वेगः ।१९। चक्रवर्तिनं पुत्रमाप्नुहि ।२०। तत्कियन्तं कालमस्माभिरेवं संभृतबलैरपि शत्रुव्यसनमवेक्षमाणैरुदासितव्यम् ।२१। यदैवाङ्गुरीयकदर्शनादनुस्मृतं देवेन सत्यमूढपूर्वा रहसि मया तत्रभवती शकुन्तला मोहात्प्रत्यादिष्टेति तदैव पश्चात्तापमुपगतो देवः ।२२। महाधनत्वाद्बहुपत्नीकेनानेन भवितव्यम् ।२३। अमात्य

ईदृशस्याभरणविशेषस्य विशेषतः कुमारेण स्वगात्रादवतार्य प्रसादीकृतस्य किमयं परित्यागभूमिः ।२४। यावच्च संबन्धिनो न परापतन्ति तावद्वत्सया मालत्या नगरदेवतागृहमविघ्नमङ्गलाय गन्तव्यम् ॥ २५ ॥

Exercise 12b

For convenience, gerundives in **tavya** are represented by 'must' and those in **ya** and **anīya** by 'should'.

1 What do you say? 2 With this letter (I) must defeat Rākṣasa. 3 (You) must remain right there until the arrival·of·Makaranda·and·Madayantikā. 4 Let the two of us just listen. 5 Alas, (my) enemies have made even my heart their own. 6 Stay, Your Majesty [**āyuṣmant**], in this aśoka-tree's·shade, while I announce you to Indra's·sire. 7 His·Excellency's·instructions are that I should safeguard Rākṣasa's life. 8 So let it be as it must [be]. 9 The *whole* administration is in confusion. 10 Why do *you stay silent? 11 So one should·not·blame Rākṣasa in this matter. 12 Good Bhāsvaraka, take him outside and beat him till he talks. 13 Listen to this wonderful (thing). 14 Śakuntalā must be in this very bower·of·reed·and·creeper. 15 So now you should not [make:] feel anger towards your lawful husband. 16 I'll go to the very spot where that fair·eyed (girl) vanished before [*loc.*] my eyes. 17 The dear child has revealed proficiency·in·speaking. 18 In that case let us wait upon their honours here the spectators by [*abl.*] an actual [**eva**] performance·of·it. 19 *You too, like His Highness, are one·whose·words·(I)·should·not·go·against. 20 I behaved wrongly in delaying after I had met my beloved. 21 Alas! See how [*use* **eṣaḥ**], sitting idle like·a·stranger in our friend's·misfortunes, we are put to shame by this (man). 22 Oh merchant! You must rather [**nanu**] ask *us* 'and how does that lack·of·vexation reveal itself?' 23 Before these birds fly up from the lake, eager·for·Mānasa, (I) must procure news·of·(my)·beloved from them. 24 Then, they having run hither and thither in [*abl.*] a pretence·of·fear

on·receiving·the·signal [*use* **gṛhīta** *in bahuvrīhi*], you must take Śakaṭadāsa away from the execution-ground and convey him to Rākṣasa. 25 As soon as [**yad» aîva . . . tad» aîva**] Menakā came to Dākṣāyaṇī from the nymphs'·pool [**tīrthaṃ**] bringing Śakuntalā distressed·by·(her)·rejection, I learnt·what·had·happened [**vṛttānta** *in bahuvrīhi*] from meditating—that, as a result of [*abl.*] Durvāsas' curse, this poor (girl) had been rejected by her lawful husband.

Chapter 13

PARADIGMS: Presents of classes III, VII and IX; **asau**

Reduplication

Reduplication (as a grammatical phenomenon in Sanskrit) is the prefixing to the root of some initial part of that root in either identical or altered form. Thus from the roots **tud** 'strike' and **kṛ** 'do', the first person plural parasmaipada perfect forms **tutudima** 'we struck' and **cakṛma** 'we did'. Reduplication is a feature of class III presents, of the perfect tense, of some aorists, and of desiderative and intensive formations. The principles of reduplication differ somewhat in each of these formations, but for convenience the following rules may be taken as a norm on the basis of which any variations will be described:

Only the first syllable of the root, i.e. the vowel and what precedes it, is reduplicated: **yuj, yuyuj; dih, didih.**

Of an initial consonant group only the first consonant is repeated: **kruś, cukruś.** But when the group consists of **s** followed by a stop (or by an unvoiced sound—the rule may be stated either way, since **s** is never followed by either a sibilant or a voiced stop), it is the stop which is reduplicated. Thus **stu, tuṣṭu** (with retroflexion by internal sandhi); whereas **sru, susru** follows the general rule.

Long vowels are shortened, and diphthongs represented by **i** or **u** as appropriate: **nī, ninī; dā, dadā; jīv, jijīv; sev,**

siṣev. However, roots ending in **e/ai/o** (often given as ending in **ā** in Western grammars) reduplicate with **a**: **mlai, mamlai.**

Aspirated consonants reduplicate in unaspirated form: **bhid, bibhid.**

Velars are represented by corresponding palatals, and **h** by **j**: **kram, cakram; khan, cakhan; gup, jugup; hu, juhu.**

Roots beginning with a vowel follow the same general pattern of reduplication, but internal sandhi produces considerable changes of appearance. For instance, in the weak reduplicated form of **iṣ, iiṣ** becomes **īṣ**; but in the strong reduplicated form, **ieṣ** becomes **iyeṣ.**

The most important variation of the above principles is that the vowel of the reduplicated syllable is in some circumstances strengthened and in others replaced by **a** or by **i**. The vowels **ṛ/ṝ** never reduplicate without change.

Presents of classes III, VII and IX

The present stem of class III verbs is formed by reduplication of the root: **hu** 'offer (sacrifice)', **juhoti** 'he sacrifices', **juhumaḥ** 'we sacrifice'. The rules of reduplication are in general those described above. **ṛ/ṝ** reduplicates as **i**: **bhṛ** 'carry', **bibharti.**

The chief peculiarity of these reduplicated stems is that in the indicative and imperative parasmaipada the third person plural termination is **ati atu**, not ******anti* ******antu*: **juhvati** 'they sacrifice'. [In the imperfect there is a special third person plural termination **uḥ**.]

Among the more important stems of this class are **dhā** 'put' and **dā** 'give'. Their weak stems reduce to **dadh** and **dat**, and **dadh** becomes **dhat** before **t/th**: **dadhāti** 'he puts', **dadhati** 'they put', **dadhmaḥ** 'we put', **dhattha** 'you put'. The imperative second person singular parasmaipada is **dhehi/dehi.** A noteworthy compound of **dhā** is **śrad-dhā** 'put trust in, believe' (cf. Latin *credo*): **śraddhatte** 'he believes', etc.

The roots **mā** 'measure' and **hā** 'go forth' have weak stems **mimī/jihī** which reduce to **mim/jih** before vowels.

The distinguishing 'suffix' of class VII verbs is the nasal **n** infixed after the vowel of the root and strengthening to **na** in the strong forms. Thus from **yuj** 'join', **yuñj** and **yunaj**: **yunakti** 'he joins', **yuñjanti** 'they join'. One or two roots, such as **bhañj** 'break', are quoted in a form already incorporating the nasal: this is because the nasal remains in various forms outside the present stem—e.g. **bhañjanaṃ** 'a breaking'.

Class IX verbs add a suffix which has the strong form **nā** and the weak forms **nī** before consonants and **n** before vowels: **krī** 'buy', **krīṇāti** 'he buys', **krīṇīmaḥ** 'we buy', **krīṇanti** 'they buy'. Roots in **ū** shorten to **u**: **pū, punāti** 'purifies'. The infix nasal found in various forms of roots such as **bandh** 'tie' is dropped: **badhnāti** 'he ties'. Two of the commonest roots of this class are **jñā** 'know' and **grah** 'seize, take': they shorten to **jā** and **gṛh** respectively—**jānāti** 'knows', **gṛhṇāti** 'takes'.

A peculiar termination **āna** for the second person singular parasmaipada imperative is found in verbs of this class whose roots end in a consonant: so **gṛhāṇa** 'take (it)'.

The infinitive

The infinitive is formed by adding the suffix **tum** to the root strengthened to guṇa grade: **nī, netum** 'to lead'; **budh, boddhum** 'to learn'; **jīv, jīvitum** 'to live'; **gam, gantum** 'to go'. In a fair number of verbs, most of them ending in a consonant, the suffix is added with connecting **i**: **car, caritum** 'to move'; **bhū, bhavitum** 'to be'. Generally, but by no means invariably, it is verbs which add **ita** in the past participle which add **itum** in the infinitive. Quite frequently, infinitives of both forms are found: thus **nayitum** beside **netum.** Derivative stems retain the suffix **ay**: **cārayitum** 'to cause to move'.

Strengthening to guṇa is not invariable: thus **likh, likhitum** (as well as **lekhitum**) 'to write'. Several verbs containing **ṛ** strengthen this to **ra**: the commonest of them is **dṛś, draṣṭum** 'to see'. The infinitive of **grah** 'take' is **grahītum.**

The Sanskrit infinitive has a more limited range of uses than the English infinitive: various ways of representing the English infinitive have, in fact, been encountered in previous chapters. The nominalisation of verbal notions may be accomplished in Sanskrit by means of various nominal suffixes, or (though much less frequently) by means of relative clauses. Apart from being employed like the English infinitive to express purpose, the infinitive is generally restricted to 'prolative' use after a number of verbs and adjectives with meanings like 'want to, (be) able to, begin to, (be) ready to', etc.: thus **śrotum icchāmi** 'I want to hear'. (However, in implying a request, such a turn of phrase does not have the abruptness of the English expression, and so 'I should like to' would usually be a more appropriate translation.) Similarly, **śrotuṃ śaknoti** 'he can hear'; **śrotuṃ samarthaḥ** '(he is) capable of hearing'. **jñā** with an infinitive means 'have enough knowledge to, know how to'.

alam with an infinitive usually means 'has the capacity to':

bhuvam adhipatir bāl-âvastho py alaṃ pari-rakṣitum
a ruler, though a child in years, is capable of guarding the earth

The verb **arh,** literally 'be worthy to', may express the notion 'should, ought'. It is frequently used in particular as a polite way of conveying a request or instruction:

śanaiḥ śanair ārodhum arhati devaḥ Your Majesty should ascend very gently: be careful as you ascend, Your Majesty

The second main use of the infinitive is to express purpose ('in order to'). It has the same sense as a verbal noun in the dative or in composition with **artham** but is especially used with verbs of motion or where a verbal noun is not readily available.

tad eṣa Vṛṣalas tvāṃ draṣṭum āgacchati here then is Vṛṣala coming to see you
paścāt kopayitum āyuṣmantaṃ tathā kṛtavān asmi thereafter to make you angry, sire, I acted thus

An infinitive may be used with words such as **avasaraḥ** and **samayaḥ** 'opportunity to, (right) time to':

avasaraḥ khalv ayam ātmānaṃ darśayitum this is certainly the moment to reveal myself

Sometimes an infinitive comes near to functioning as the subject of a sentence, when it is an extension of an impersonal passive—e.g. **ālikhituṃ vismṛtam asmābhiḥ** 'we forgot to draw'. Similar and quite frequent is the use with **yukta** 'right, proper', **ayukta** 'wrong', etc. (The finite verb form **yujyate** 'is proper' may be used in the same way.) The construction may be with a genitive of reference, or with a predicative instrumental, as in the impersonal gerundive:

na yuktam anayos tatra gantum it is not right for the two of them to go there
nir_udyogair asmābhir avasthātum ayuktam it is wrong for us to remain without exertion

There is no special passive form of the infinitive. It may, however, bear a passive sense when used in a passive context, e.g. **hantuṃ nīyate** 'is taken to be killed'. In particular, the passives of **ārabh** 'begin' and **śak** 'be able' are used where we use a passive infinitive in English: **kartum ārabhyate** 'is beginning to be done'; **kartuṃ śakyate** 'can be done'. The adjective **śakya** 'possible, able to be' is frequent in this passive sense, used either personally or impersonally:

śakyaḥ khalv eṣa . . . prajñayā nivārayitum he can of course be checked by guile
adhunā śakyam anena maraṇam apy anubhavitum it is now possible for him to suffer even death

The infinitive suffix appears exceptionally in its stem form **tu** with the nouns **kāmaḥ** 'desire' and (less often) **manas** 'mind' to form bahuvrīhi compounds: **apahnotu-kāma** 'having a desire to conceal, anxious to conceal'; **kartu-manas** 'having a mind to do, intending to do'; **kim asi vaktu-kāmaḥ?** 'what are you wanting to say?'

Future tense

The future tense is formed by adding the suffix **sya**, or **iṣya** (which is the preceding suffix with connecting **i**), to the root strengthened to guṇa grade, the resulting stem being inflected in the thematic **a** class. Thus **nī, neṣyati** 'will lead'; **bhū, bhaviṣyati** 'will be'. There is a general correspondence as to the strengthening of the root and the addition of the connecting vowel between this formation and that of the infinitive: so **drakṣyati** 'will see', **grahīṣyati** 'will take', **likhiṣyati** 'will write'. The most important difference is that all roots ending in **ṛ** must add the connecting vowel: so **kartum** 'to do', but **kariṣyati** 'will do'.

The sense of the future corresponds to that of English 'shall' and 'will', more particularly in the 'uncoloured' usages of these words. If the distinction between 'shall' and 'will' is crucial, it must be represented in some other way in Sanskrit; but a sentence such as **acirād asya pariśramasya phalam anurūpam adhigamiṣyasi** may be translated equally well as 'you shall soon receive' or 'you will soon receive, a suitable recompense for this exertion'.

ardharātra-samaye Candraguptasya Nanda-bhavana-praveśo bhaviṣyati Candragupta's entry into the Nanda palace will happen at midnight
n› êdam vismariṣyāmi I shan't/won't forget this
ramaṇīyaṃ hi vatsa:Makarandam avalokayiṣyati Madayantikā Madayantikā will see dear Makaranda (looking) most attractive

Many instances have already been given of the present tense used to announce an immediate intention. If the future tense used in the same way has any difference of force, it is perhaps in making the statement of intention a shade more deliberate: **pṛcchāmi** 'I'll ask (him)', **prakṣyāmi** 'what I'll do is ask (him)'.

evaṃ rājā ›ham iti parijñānaṃ bhavet. bhavatu, atithi-samācāram avalambiṣye (if I act) like that, there might be the realisation that I am the king. Well then, I will adopt the behaviour of a (normal) guest

The future may express a prediction about an already existing state of affairs ('it will turn out to be the case that'), as also in English—'that will be the postman'.

jñāsyati Candanadāsasya vṛttāntam (this man) will (be sure to) know what has happened to Candanadāsa

The prediction may also be about a past event, and here, as in the English use of the future perfect, a generalisation may be implied: 'he won't have done anything foolish' implies '—because in general he would not do anything foolish'. Thus 'would' or 'would have' are sometimes possible English translations of the Sanskrit future.

eṣa . . . ratho dṛśyate—na khalu so ›kṛt›:ârtho nivartiṣyate look, I can see the chariot! He won't have/wouldn't have returned [/wouldn't return] unsuccessful

na hy an:ātma˘sadṛśeṣu Rākṣasaḥ kalatraṃ nyāsī˜ kariṣyati Rākṣasa certainly won't have/wouldn't have entrusted [/wouldn't entrust] his wife to those [not worthy of:] less worthy than himself

Relative adverbs continued

Examples have been given in Chapters 11 and 12 of subordinate clauses having a nominal or adverbial feature in common with a main clause. In any language there also arises the need to make the whole notion of one clause a subordinate part of the notion of another. One might alternatively talk of subordinating the *verbal* notion of one clause. These two concepts are not in fact equivalent, but languages have some tendency to treat them as such. For instance, in the English 'his acquiescence has been unhappy', 'unhappy' may qualify the verbal notion of acquiescense ('acquiescence in an unhappy spirit') or the implicit total notion ('that he should have acquiesced is to be regretted'). We may use devices such as intonation and pause to distinguish the two: 'he has acquiesced unhappily' as against 'he has acquiesced, unhappily'.

As should already be clear (e.g. from the discussion of the use of abstract nouns in Chapter 10), Sanskrit deals with such relationships principally by means of nominal constructions. But where finite constructions are used, they are achieved by extending the sense of the relative pronouns and adverbs. (Certain subordinating conjunctions exist, notably **cet** 'if', which are not formally related to the relative base **ya-**, but they may usually be treated as the equivalent of some relative adverb—the major exception being, of course, **iti**.) As a result of this extension of usage, certain ambiguities arise. This is not surprising, for even in English, where subordinate clauses are far more important, there is a similar situation—cf. the two possible interpretations of the phrase 'the fact that we must not forget', or the mere comma (or slight change of intonation) which distinguishes 'he said nothing which annoyed me' from 'he said nothing, which annoyed me'.

In what follows, a number of the more important extensions of usage will be described. The translations of the examples given should usually make the usage plain. The (perhaps rather elaborate) theoretical framework has been introduced to help account for some ambiguities.

First, there is the simple case in which a following ('connecting') relative has as its antecedent the whole of the preceding statement:

. . . ācakranda rāja-kanyā, yena tat sakalam eva kanyā-'ntaḥpuram . . . ākulībabhūva the princess screamed—[by which (screaming) that whole girls' quarters was thrown into confusion:] which threw the whole of the girls' quarters into confusion

bakula-māle upakāriṇy asi, yataḥ svāgataṃ bhavatyāḥ bakula garland, you are my ally—[as a result of which:] and therefore, welcome to you

katham iyaṃ bhagavatyāḥ . . . ādyā śiṣyā Saudāmanī?—yataḥ sarvam adhunā saṃgacchate what, is this Her Reverence's earliest pupil Saudāmanī? [as a result of which:] in that case everything now fits

This use of **yataḥ** to mean 'therefore' (introducing an effect) contrasts sharply with its use to mean 'for' (introducing a cause) as described below.

Where the total notion of the clause is subordinate to another statement, it is introduced most neutrally by the neuter singular form **yat**. (In traditional terms, **yat** may be said to represent the 'internal accusative' of the subordinate verb.)

yan mithaḥ:samavāyād imāṃ madīyāṃ duhitaraṃ bhavān upayeme, tan mayā prītimatā yuvayor anujñātam that you, sir, married this my daughter by mutual union, I gladly assent to for you both

eken› âbhisaṃdhinā pratyarpayāmi . . . yad idam aham eva yathā_sthānaṃ niveśayāmi I'll hand (it) over on one condition—that I should be the one to put it in place

When a noun clause is the object of a verb meaning 'say', 'know', etc., the regular construction is, of course, with **iti**. But where the noun clause follows the main clause, a frequent alternative is to introduce it with **yathā**. (One might compare the use of 'how' for 'that' in sentences like 'he told me how a man had come to see him'.) In fact, in such cases **iti** is frequently added pleonastically at the end of the clause (in the second of the following examples it is not pleonastic, being needed for the sub-subordinate clause):

vatsa, ucyatāṃ Bhāgurāyaṇo yathā 'tvaritaṃ saṃbhāvay› aînam' iti child, let Bhāgurāyaṇa be told to find him at once

idaṃ tāvat prasiddham eva, yathā Nandanāya Mālatīṃ prārthayamānaṃ Bhūrivasur nṛpam uktavān 'prabhavati nija:kanyakā:janasya Mahā:rāja' iti Now it is entirely established that Bhūrivasu told the king when the latter was seeking Mālatī for Nandana, 'Your Majesty has power over his own daughter'

The subordinate clause may be related as reason to the main clause. The implied correlative of **yat** is then **tat** in its sense of 'then, so', and its force may be represented literally in English by 'inasmuch as':

kim atyāhitaṃ Mādhavasya, yad aniṣṭaṃ vyavasito ›si? is there (some) disaster to Mādhava, that you have (this) dreadful resolve?

This has the same force as the use of the personal relative pronoun described in Chapter 11 (p. 174), but the latter is, of course, more restricted in its scope, since it can be used only when there is some identifiable common element in the two clauses. In the three examples given in Chapter 11, on the other, hand, **yat** might be substituted without change of meaning.

As well as **yat**, other forms of the relative are used. These forms are somewhat illogical and represent the attraction of the relative into the case of the antecedent. Thus **yena** really means **tena yat** 'in view of the (fact) that'.

aho mahā:prabhāvo rājā Duḥṣantaḥ, yena praviṣṭa: mātra ev› âtrabhavati nir_upaplavāni naḥ kāryāṇi saṃvṛttāni how great is the power of King Duḥṣanta, in that from the moment His Honour entered, our rites have become unmolested

[Note that, without the locative absolute phrase, **yena** might have been interpreted personally—'he by whose agency'.]

na yathāvad dṛṣṭam, yat kāraṇam bhavān a:pradhānaḥ (you) did not see it properly, for the reason that you are not one in authority

abhimatā vā bhavanam atithayaḥ saṃprāptāḥ, yata eṣa pāka-viśeṣ›-ārambhaḥ? or have honoured guests come to the house, that there is this embarking upon special cooking?

na khalv anyathā vastu-vṛttam, yataḥ śrāvak›-âvasthāyām asmat;Saudāmanī-samakṣam anayor vṛtt» êyaṃ pratijñā the facts are not really [otherwise:] at variance (with what has been said), for when they were students the two of them made this promise before Saudāmanī and myself

The meaning of 'inasmuch as' shades into that of 'for' (in which sense the emphatic particle **hi** is common) and finally into that of 'because':

yato ›yaṃ cirān nirvṛto mam› ôpayogaṃ na jānāti, ten› âdhunā mam› āhāra-dāne ›pi mand›:ādaraḥ because this man, satisfied for (so) long, does not recognise my utility, he is now careless even in providing fodder for me

When the subordinate clause is related as a result to the main clause, it may be introduced by **yathā**. This again is a case of attraction into the form of the correlative: **tathā . . . yathā** means 'in such a way that (as a result)':

bhos tathā ›ham utpatitā yathā sakala eṣa giri;-nagara;grāma;sarid;araṇya-vyatikaraś cakṣuṣā parikṣipyate oh, I have flown up so (high) that this whole expanse of mountains, cities, villages, rivers and forests is encompassed by my eye

upoḍha:rāgeṇa vilola:tārakaṃ
tathā gṛhītaṃ śaśinā niśā-mukham
yathā samastaṃ timir›:âṃśukaṃ tayā
puro ›pi rāgād galitaṃ na lakṣitam

The moon, with passion [/redness] increased, has seized the tremulous-eyed [/winking-starred] face [/forepart] of the night in such a way that she has not noticed all the garment of her darkness slip away even in front [/in the east] because of (her answering) passion [/redness]

Other relatives and correlatives are possible in result clauses. Thus:

īdṛśas te nirmāṇa-bhāgaḥ pariṇato, yena lajjayā svacchandam ākranditum api na śakyate your [allotment of creation:] destiny in life has turned out to be such that for very shame one cannot even weep as one would wish

However, Sanskrit usually expresses consequence by subordinating the reason rather than the result: 'he was so miserly he never spent a shilling' would become 'by him being miserly not a shilling was spent'.

aho, Rākṣasaṃ prati me vitarka-bāhulyād ākulā buddhir na niścayam adhigacchati [oh, confused from the multitude of doubts about Rākṣasa, my mind attains no certainty:] I am in such a storm of doubt about Rākṣasa, I cannot make up my mind

evaṃ nirbhinna꞉hṛday›˘āvegaḥ śiśu:janen› âpy anukampito ›smi [thus with the agitation of my heart betrayed, I am pitied even by children:] I betrayed my distress so clearly that even a child takes pity on me

atibhūmim ayaṃ gato na śakyate nivartayitum [having gone to excess, this one cannot be turned back:] he has gone too far to be turned back

The use of **yathā** in expressing result is commonest in a particular idiom with verbs like **kṛ** 'act' and **vidhā** 'arrange', to express 'act in such a way that', 'see to it that':

yathā svāmī jāgarti tathā mayā kartavyam I must see to it that my master wakes up

yathā ›haṃ bhavadbhyāṃ sah› ākāśa-vartmanā yāmi, sa upāyo vidhīyatām [so that I go with you two by the way of air, let that expedient be arranged:] find a way for me to accompany the two of you in your flight

Similarly with **niṣidh** 'forbid' (note how the common subject is placed with the first verb rather than with the main verb):

yathā ca sainikās tapo-vanaṃ n› ôparundhanti dūrāt pariharanti ca, tathā niṣeddhavyāḥ [and so that the soldiers do not molest the ascetic grove and avoid it from afar, thus (they) are to be checked:] and you must restrain the soldiers from molesting the ascetic grove and have them keep well clear of it

The notion expressed by a noun clause may be a possibility rather than a fact (and even so—as in the example **eken› âbhisaṃdhinā . . .** above—the verb may remain in the present indicative):

yac ca 'śṛgālo ›yam' iti matvā mam› ôpary avajñā kriyate, tad apy ayuktam and that (he) should feel (/for him to feel) contempt for me thinking 'he is (just) a jackal', that also (would be) wrong

Here we might most naturally say 'if he should feel'. And the usual word for 'if', **yadi**, is in fact in origin merely **yat** with a strengthening particle. A correlative is often lacking (regularly so when the conditional follows the main clause). When expressed, it is probably most usually **tat**, but other correlatives are often found, such as **tataḥ, tadā, tarhi.**

ārye, yadi nepathya-vidhānam adhyavasitam, tad ih› āgamyatām lady, if arrangements backstage are completed, come here

iha devam upatiṣṭhatu, yadi na doṣaḥ let him attend Your Majesty here, if there is no [fault:] objection

The alternative word for 'if', **cet**, must not stand as the first word in its clause:

na ced anya:kāry›-âtipātaḥ, praviśy› âtra gṛhyatām atithi-satkāraḥ if (it means) no neglect of other duties, enter here and accept (our) hospitality

Other words, such as **atha**, are also found:

atha kautukam, āvedayāmi if (you feel) curiosity, I'll tell you

With **api** added, we have **yadi api** 'even if, though'. Similar in sense is **kāmam** 'granted that, though'. The correlative may be **tathā ›pi, punar, tu** 'even so, yet'.

kāmaṃ khalu sarvasy› âpi kula-vidyā bahumatā, na punar asmākaṃ nāṭyaṃ prati mithyā gauravam though of course everyone thinks highly of his own hereditary learning, our regard for the drama is not misplaced

yady apy ete na paśyanti, lobh›-ôpahata:̱cetasaḥ,
kula-kṣaya-kṛtaṃ doṣaṃ mitra-drohe ca pātakam—
kathaṃ na jñeyam asmābhiḥ pāpād asmān nivartitum,
kula-kṣaya-kṛtaṃ doṣaṃ prapaśyadbhir, Janārdana?

Even if these men, their understanding killed by greed, do not see
The sin caused by the ruin of a family and the crime in the injuring of a friend,
How should we not know (enough) to turn back from this wickedness,
We, Krishna, who can see such sin?

asau

The pronoun **asau** 'that, he' is less common than the other demonstrative pronouns. It is used specifically of what is not near at hand, but anything to which it refers may also be referred to, if absent by the pronoun **saḥ** and if present by the pronoun **ayam.** To give stronger deictic force ('thére is, look at that') the combination **ayam asau** may be used:

ayam asau mahā:nadyor vyatikaraḥ thére is the confluence of the two great rivers

Used of what is absent, **asau** offers a perhaps slightly more emphatic alternative to **saḥ**:

Vṛṣala Rākṣasaḥ khalv asau Vṛṣala, he (/the man you are talking about) is Rākṣasa, don't forget
hṛt›:̱âdhikāraḥ kva sāṃpratam asau baṭuḥ? where is that fellow, now that he has lost his job?

ādi = 'etc.'

ādi m. and less frequently some other word such as **prabhṛti** f., literally meaning 'beginning', may be used at the end of a bahuvrīhi compound with the sense 'of which the beginning is X', and therefore 'beginning with X/[consisting of] X, *etc.*/ such as X'

Indr›:ādayaḥ surāḥ the gods Indra, *etc.*, Indra and the other gods
śrotr›:ādīn› îndriyāṇi the senses such as hearing
Viśvāvasu:prabhṛtayas trayo bhrātaraḥ Viśvāvasu and his two (younger) brothers

Note the possibility of the translation 'X *and*', particularly in the last of the above examples.

Such compounds are often used without the substantive they qualify being expressed. If the omitted substantive has a rather general reference, there is a tendency for the compound itself to be put into the singular:

mṛto ›sau Saṃjīvako, ›smābhiś c› âgny:ādinā satkṛtaḥ that Saṃjīvaka is dead, and we have [honoured him with fire etc.:] given him a cremation ceremony and so forth
na hy etābhyām atidīpta:prajñā;medhābhyām asmad:ādeḥ sah›:âdhyayana-yogo ›sti for (anyone) like us, there is no managing common lessons with those two, whose understanding and intellect are exceptionally brilliant

The neuter singular form **prabhṛti** comes to be used adverbially with the ablative or with a form ending in the suffix **taḥ** in the sense of 'from X onwards, since': **cirāt prabhṛti** 'since a long time', **tataḥ prabhṛti** 'from that (point) on'.

ājñāpayati and *vijñāpayati*

The causatives of **ājñā** and **vijñā** (of which the past participles have the anomalous alternative forms **ājñapta** and **vijñapta**) may often be translated 'order' and 'request' respectively. More widely, they may both mean 'say', the first with the implication that the speaker is someone (such as a king or guru) whose word is not to be questioned, the second with the reverse implication that the speaker is someone (such as a counsellor or pupil) who should show deference to the person addressed. A form such as **vijñāpayāmi** 'I beg to state' may, of course, simply indicate politeness between equals.

Vocabulary

atithi *m.* guest
anucaraḥ companion, attendant
anutāpaḥ remorse
antaraṃ interval
anveṣin searching, in search of
apatyaṃ offspring
aparāddha (*p.p.*) *and* **aparādhin** offending, guilty
abhiyogaḥ attack
amṛtaṃ nectar, ambrosia
ājñā command, order
ādi *m.* beginning; **:ādi** *see chapter*
āpta trustworthy
iṣu *m.* arrow
upapanna equipped with, possessed of
upasaṃgrahaḥ embracing; collecting; looking after
etāvant this much
kanyakā girl
kāmaḥ wish, desire, love; **°tu:kāma** wanting to, anxious to (*see chapter*)
kāyasthaḥ scribe, letter-writer
kāraṇaṃ reason
kāvyaṃ [that which derives from a **kavi** 'poet, creative writer':] literature
kumārakaḥ young man, son
kṛta-vedin conscious of [things done for one:] debt: grateful, obliged
koṣaḥ treasury, resources, wealth
kriyā doing; rite
kṣatriyaḥ [member of] warrior [caste]
guhya [to be concealed:] secret
Gautamī *pr. n.*
gauravaṃ high esteem, duty of respect [towards an elder]
ghaṭaḥ pot
cakṣus *n.* eye
jāta *p.p.* born; **jāta-karman** *n.* birth-ceremony
jñātṛ knower, person to know/understand
tīkṣṇa:rasa-daḥ poisoner
tuccha trifling
dāsī slave girl, servant girl
Devarātaḥ *pr. n.*
dauhitraḥ daughter's son, grandson
dhurā pole, yoke, burden
Nandaḥ *pr. n.*
nṛpati *m.* king
payas *n.* water
para far, ultimate, supreme
parigrahaḥ acquisition, possession
paritoṣaḥ satisfaction
puṇya auspicious, holy
purātana (*f.* **ī**) former
pṛthvī, pṛthivī earth
pracchādanaṃ concealment
pratikūla contrary, hostile

pramāṇaṃ measure, size
prākṛta (*f.* ā/ī) of the people, vulgar, common
priyaṃ benefit, service
bādhā molestation, damage
brahmacārin *m.* student; **sa:-brahmacārin** *m.* fellow-student
bhārika burdensome
bhūṣaṇaṃ ornament
bhraṃśaḥ fall, decline; **sthā-na-bhraṃśaḥ** fall from position, loss of place
mati˜mant possessing wit, sensible
madhya-stha [mid-standing:] neutral
manorathaḥ desire
mantrin *m.* minister
yukta proper, right
rahasya secret
rāja-kāryaṃ, rājya-kāryaṃ [business of king/kingdom:] state affairs, state administration
rāmaṇīyakaṃ loveliness, delightful aspect
lakṣaṇaṃ characteristic, (auspicious) mark
Lopāmudrā *pr. n.*
-vacanāt [from the speech of:] in the name of
varāka (*f.* ī) wretched, poor
varṇaḥ colour, appearance
vāc *f.* speech, words
vādin speaking, talking
vāsin living in, dweller
vijñāpanā request
vidhi *m.* injunction [*esp. for performance of religious rite*]; **vidhi˜vat** according to [the injunction of] ritual
vivakṣita (*desiderative p.p.*) wished to be said, meant
vihāraḥ (Buddhist) monastery/convent
vedin knowing, conscious of, appreciative of
vyapadeśaḥ designation, name
vyayaḥ loss; expense, extravagance
vyāghraḥ tiger
Śakaṭadāsaḥ *pr. n.*
śaṭha cunning
Śatakratu *m.* (*name of*) Indra
Śākuntaleya born of Śakuntalā
śāsanaṃ command
śuddhāntaḥ women's apartments, household
śūla *m. n.* stake; **śūlam ā+ruh** *caus.* [cause to mount the stake:] impale
śṛgālaḥ jackal
śrotṛ *m.* listener, someone to listen
śrauta derived from scripture, scriptural
śvapākaḥ outcast
saṃcayaḥ collection, quantity
satkāraḥ hospitality
samartha capable, able
sācivyaṃ being minister, post of minister
Siddhārthakaḥ *pr. n.*
secanaṃ (act of) sprinkling, watering
Somarātaḥ *pr. n.*
sainikaḥ soldier

ati+śī (II atiśete) surpass, triumph over
anu+jñā (IX anujānāti) allow, give someone leave to (*dat. of verbal noun*)
abhi+druh (IV abhidruhyati) do violence to
abhi+vṛt (I abhivartate) approach, go towards, make for
arh (I arhati) be worthy; 'should' (*see chapter*)

ava+jñā (IX **avajānāti**) despise
ā+khyā (II **ākhyāti**) declare, tell
ā+dṛ (IV **ādriyate**) heed, respect, defer to, refer to
ā+ruh *caus.* (**āropayati**) cause to mount, raise onto
ut+ghuṣ (I **udghoṣati**) cry out
ut+hā (III **ujjihīte**) start up; depart
upa+bhuj (VII **upabhuṅkte**) enjoy, consume, spend
upa+rudh (VII **uparuṇaddhi**) besiege, invade
ut+laṅgh *caus.* (**ullaṅghayati**) transgress, violate
kam *caus.* **kāmayate** desire, be in love with
kup *caus.* **kopayati** anger
duṣ *caus.* (**dūṣayati**) spoil, defile
pari+ci (V **paricinoti**) become acquainted with, recognise
pīḍ (X **pīḍayati**) squeeze
pū (IX **punāti, punīte**) purify
pṝ (*caus.* **pūrayati**, *p.p.* **pūrṇa**) fill, fulfil
pra+khyā *caus.* (**prakhyāpayati**) publish, proclaim
prati+nand (I **pratinandati**) receive gladly, welcome
prati+vi+dhā (III **pratividadhāti**) prepare against, take precautions
pra+bhā (II **prabhāti**) shine forth, dawn
pra+yat (I **prayatate**) strive, exert oneself
pra+yuj (VII **prayuṅkte**) employ; perform (on stage)
man *caus.* (**mānayati**) esteem, honour
mṛṣ *caus.* (**marṣayati**) overlook, excuse
vi+ā+pṝ *caus.* (**vyāpārayati**) set to work, employ
śak (V **śaknoti**) be able, can
śam *caus.* (**śamayati**) quieten, appease
śrad+dhā (III **śraddhatte**) trust, believe
sat+kṛ (VIII **satkaroti**) receive with hospitality, entertain
sam+dhā (III **saṃdhatte**) bring together; aim (arrow)
sam+ā+sañj (I **samāsajati**) attach something to (*loc.*), impose upon
spṛś (VI **spṛśati**) touch

ati: (*karmadhāraya prefix*) too, over-, extremely, very
aticirāt after very long
anyatra elsewhere
asau that, he
itaretara (*stem form*) mutual, of/to *etc.* each other
kaccit? I hope that . . .?
kāmam admittedly; granted that
cirāt at long last
cet (*enclitic*) if
prabhṛti+*abl.* starting with, from . . . onward, ever since
prādur+bhū become manifest, arise
yat satyam [what is true:] truth to tell, in truth
yady evam [if so:] in that case
yataḥ, yadi, *etc.*: *see chapter*

Exercise 13a

देहि मे प्रतिवचनम् ।१। त्वया सह गौतमी गमिष्यति ।२। कथं शून्या इवामी प्रदेशाः ।३। एष तमिषुं संदधे ।४। यदि रहस्यं तदा तिष्ठतु । यदि न रहस्यं तर्हि कथ्यताम् ।५। अहमप्यमुं वृत्तान्तं भगवत्यै लोपामुद्रायै निवेदयामि ।६। स खलु मूर्खस्तं युष्माभिरतिसृष्टं प्रभूतमर्थराशिमवाप्य महता व्ययेनोपभोक्तुमारब्धवान् ।७। दिष्ट्या सुप्रभातमद्य यदयं देवो दृष्टः ।८। किं चिदाख्यातुकामास्मि ।९। उपालप्स्ये तावदेनम् ।१०। भद्र सिद्धार्थक काममपर्याप्तमिदमस्य प्रियस्य तथापि गृह्यताम् ।११। अयमसौ राजाज्ञया राजापथ्यकारी कायस्थः शकटदासः शूलमारोपयितुं नीयते ।१२। ज्ञास्यथः खल्वेतत् ।१३। पुण्याश्रमदर्शनेनात्मानं पुनीमहे तावत् ।१४। भद्रे न तत्परिहार्यं—यतो विवक्षितमनुक्तमनुतापं जनयति ।१५। नायमवसरो मम शतक्रतुं द्रष्टुम् ।१६। सखे न तावदेनां पश्यसि येन त्वमेवंवादी ।१७। अये एतास्तपस्विकन्यकाः स्वप्रमाणानुरूपैः सेचनघटैर्बालपादपेभ्यः पयो दातुमित एवाभिवर्तन्ते ।१८। न चेन्मुनिकुमारको ऽयं तत्को ऽस्य व्यपदेशः ।१९। मतिमांश्चाणक्यस्तुच्छे प्रयोजने किमिति चन्द्रगुप्तं कोपयिष्यति । न च कृतवेदी चन्द्रगुप्त एतावता गौरवमुल्लङ्घयिष्यति ।२०। तेन हि विज्ञाप्यतां मद्वचनादुपाध्यायः सोमरातः - अमूनाश्रमवासिनः श्रौतेन विधिना सत्कृत्य स्वयमेव प्रवेशयितुमर्हसीति ।२१। स्मर्तव्यं तु सौजन्यमस्य नृपतेर्यदपराधिनोरप्यनपराद्धयोरिव नौ कृतप्रसादं चेष्टितवान् ।२२। हे व्यसनसब्रह्मचारिन् यदि न गुह्यं नातिभारिकं वा ततः श्रोतुमिच्छामि ते प्राणपरित्यागकारणम् ।२३। आर्य वैहीनरे अद्य प्रभृत्यनादृत्य चाणक्यं चन्द्रगुप्तः स्वयमेव राजकार्याणि करिष्यतीति गृहीतार्थाः क्रियन्तां प्रकृतयः ।२४। वयमप्याश्रमबाधा यथा न भवति तथा प्रयतिष्यामहे

। २५ । किमिदानीं चन्द्रगुप्तः स्वराज्यकार्यधुरामन्यत्र मन्त्रिण्यात्मनि वा समासज्य स्वयं प्रतिविधातुमसमर्थः । २६ । यत्सत्यं काव्यविशेषवेदिन्यां परिषदि प्रयुञ्जानस्य ममापि सुमहान्परितोषः प्रादुर्भवति । २७ । चन्द्रगुप्तशरीरमभिद्रोग्धुमनेन व्यापारिता दारुवर्मादय इति नगरे प्रख्याप्य शकटदासः शूलमारोपितः । २८ । स खलु कस्मिंश्चिदपि जीवति नन्दान्वयावयवे वृषलस्य साचिव्यं ग्राहयितुं न शक्यते । २९ । इदमत्र रामणीयकं यदमात्यभूरिवसुदेवरातयोश्चिरात्पूर्णो ऽयमितरेतरापत्यसंबन्धामृतमनोरथः ॥ ३० ॥

Exercise 13b

(In this exercise translate 'should' where appropriate by **arh**.)

1 Vijayā, do *you recognise this ornament? 2 That fellow is certainly cunning. 3 Lavaṅgikā has managed·well, since Mādhava's·attendant Kalahaṃsaka is in love with that servant·girl·of·the·convent, Mandārikā. 4 But where will *you (ladies) wait for me? 5 Why, quite without·giving an answer he has started to dance. 6 What, are soldiers in·search·of·me invading the ascetic grove? 7 Granted that this is to be prized, yet we are neutral about it [**atra**]. 8 After not very long the minister will restore [*use* **ā+ruh** *caus.*] us to (our) former state. 9 It is not right to despise even a common man. 10 King Candragupta, it is already known to you that we lived for a certain interval·of·time with [*loc.*] Malayaketu. 11 Oh Viṣṇugupta, you should not touch me (who am) defiled·by·the·touch·of·an·outcaste. 12 My dear child, I hope you have greeted [**abhi+nand**] this son born of Śakuntalā whose·birth·ceremony·and·other·rites·were·performed by us according to ritual? 13 Then give me leave to go. 14 *We* are not able to triumph with words over Your Excellency's words. 15 If Your Excellency thus sees the time·for·attack, why delay? 16 Come in, my dear fellow: you will get someone to listen and to understand. 17 'Just now (he) has directed his

daughter to (show) hospitality·to·guests and gone to Somatīrtha to appease a fate hostile to her'—'In that case she is the one I will see.' 18 Why do you ask, friend, un·believing(ly)? 19 Is the earth without·warriors, that (you) cry out in this way? 20 I should like to employ you, my dear fellow, on a certain task that·must·be·performed·by·a·trustworthy·person. 21 If the grandson·of·the·sage proves to be [**bhū**] possessed·of·those·marks, you will welcome her and introduce her into your household. 22 Do you then not pity the poor (girl) whose·life·is·departing? 23 Loss·of·place will not oppress one·without·possessions. 24 (We) have established Śakaṭadāsa with a great quantity·of·wealth to·look·after the poisoners·and·so·forth employed·by·us to do violence to Candragupta's·person, and to·instigate·(his)·subjects·to·rebellion. 25 Mādhavya my friend, you have·not·obtained·the·reward·of·your·eyes, since you have not seen the ultimate of things to see [**draṣṭavya**]. 26 Oh merchant Candanadāsa, a king so severe·in·punishment towards traitors will not overlook *your concealment·of·Rākṣasa's·wife. 27 Since those tigers·and·others, deceived·by·mere·appearance, without·knowing (him to be) a jackal regard that one (as) king—see [*pl.*] to it that he is recognised. 28 Your Majesty, who else anxious·to·live would have violated Your Majesty's command? 29 Though (your) master's·merits cannot be forgotten, Your Excellency should honour my·request.

Chapter 14

PARADIGMS: Imperfect and optative of present stems; **śreyāṃs**

Imperfect tense

Like the imperative, the imperfect is part of the present stem of the verb. It shares its two most prominent characteristics with the aorist tense (Chapter 15): the stem is prefixed by an augment, and the terminations are the 'secondary terminations'.

The augment consists of the vowel **a**: **nayati** 'he leads', **anayat** 'he led'; **karoti** 'he does', **akarot** 'he did'. When the stem begins with a vowel, the combination with **a** always results in vṛddhi, even in the case of **i/ī/u/ū/ṛ**: thus **icchati** 'he wants', **aicchat** 'he wanted'. When a verb is compounded with a prefix, the augment is always placed *after* any such prefix, immediately before the verb: **samudatiṣṭhat** 'he rose up', from **sam+ut+sthā.**

The personal endings of the present tense (e.g. **-ti**) are called 'primary', and those of the imperfect and aorist (e.g. **-t**) are called 'secondary'. The terminology is in fact misguided, since from an historical point of view the 'primary' endings are derived from the 'secondary'. Thus on the basis of a primitive **nayat** (surviving in Vedic as a form of the 'injunctive' mood), the imperfect **anayat** is differentiated by the addition of the augment and the present **nayati** by the addition of a suffix **i** (while the imperative **nayatu** is differentiated by the addition of another suffix, **u**). The relationship of primary and secondary endings is not always so transparent, and there is no alternative to committing the paradigms to memory, but it is perhaps also worth pointing out that the third person plural form **anayan** is reduced (because Sanskrit words cannot normally end in more than one consonant) from an original **anayant*.

In the imperfect, as in the present, of athematic verbs, the three parasmaipada singular forms are strong, the rest weak. Those verbs which take **-ati** not **-anti** in the third person plural parasmaipada present (class III verbs and some other reduplicated stems) take **-uḥ** not **-an** in the corresponding imperfect form. Final **ā** disappears before this suffix, but **i/ī/u/ū/ṛ** take guṇa: **ajuhavuḥ** 'they sacrificed'. In a few further verbs of class II this ending is an optional alternative.

The imperfect is used as a simple past narrative tense—'he did', 'he went', etc. It is frequent in certain styles of Sanskrit, but since its sense may also be represented by the past participle and the past active participle (and to some extent by the aorist or perfect) there are other kinds of Sanskrit in which it occurs rarely. The examples of the imperfect in Exercise 14 are taken mainly from Classical prose romances. The imperfect tense is so named because it is parallel in *formation* with the imperfect of various other Indo-European languages, notably Greek. But it is important to realise that in sense it normally has no progressive or durative implication ('he was doing', 'he used to do', etc.). Such implications tend, even in past time, to be expressed in Sanskrit by the present tense (sometimes with the addition of the particle **sma**):

> **atha sā yadā vāyu-preritair vṛkṣa-śākhā-›graiḥ spṛśyate, tadā śabdaṃ karoti, anyathā tūṣṇīm āste** now when the tips of the tree-branches, stirred by the wind, touched that (drum), it would make a noise, (while) otherwise it would remain silent

(Conversely, it should be mentioned, the use of the present as an ordinary past narrative tense—'historic present'—is not characteristic of good Classical writers.)

An exception to the general significance of the imperfect is provided by the imperfect of **as** 'be', which normally has a stative sense (except in a phrase such as **tūṣṇīm āsīt** 'fell silent'):

Ṛṣyaśṛṅg›-āśrame guru:janas tad» āsīt (his) elders were at that time in Ṛṣyaśṛṅga's hermitage

priy›:ārāmā hi sarvathā Vaidehy āsīt the Princess of Videha was always fond of the woodland

Sometimes, by combining with a past participle, this verb can convey a pluperfect sense:

atha tāmbūla-karaṅka-vāhinī madīyā Taralikā nāma may» aîva saha gatā snātum āsīt now my betel-box carrier, called Taralikā [was having gone:] had gone to bathe with me

Imperfect forms may be made from the future stem, giving a tense known as the conditional: thus from **kariṣyati** 'he will do', **akariṣyat** (lit. 'he was going to do') 'he would have done'. The use of this tense is mentioned below.

The optative

From the paradigms it will be seen that the optative links the secondary endings to the present stem by means of a suffix **ī** or **yā**, which in the case of thematic verbs becomes **e** (from **a**+**ī**). Before either form of the suffix the stem of athematic verbs appears in its weak form.

While a prescriptive usage ('he shall do') is common in law-books and similar texts, the prevalent sense of the optative in Classical literary texts is potential, to express what 'may' or 'might' be the case now or in the future (or even occasionally in the past). In plain statements **kadācit** 'perhaps' is often added:

atha vā mayi gate nṛśaṃso hanyād enām but no, with me gone the monster may kill her

kumāra, anyeṣāṃ bhūmipālānāṃ kadācid amātya-vyasanam a:vyasanaṃ syāt, na punaś Candragup-

tasya Your Highness, for other rulers a deficiency in ministers might perhaps be no deficiency, but not for Candragupta

ārāma-prāsāda-vedikāyāṃ krīḍadbhiḥ pārāvataiḥ pātitaṃ bhavet it [may be having been dropped:] may have been dropped by the pigeons while playing in the balcony of the pleasure-pavilion

kv› êdānīm ātmānaṃ vinodayeyam where can I now distract myself?

api khalu svapna eṣa syāt? could this indeed be a dream?

The combination **api nāma** is frequent with the optative, and may express anything from speculation or anxious hope to a wish, even an impossible wish ('if only'):

tad api nāma Rāma:bhadraḥ punar idaṃ vanam alaṃkuryāt? might dear Rāma, then, (be going to) grace this forest again?

api nām› âhaṃ Purūravā bhaveyam if only I (a woman) could become Purūravas!

Remote conditions

The optative is used to express remote hypotheses in relation to the future ('if he were to do') or the present '(if he were doing'). The construction does not in itself distinguish clearly between 'if this were to happen, this would be so' and 'if this were to happen, this *might* be so'.

tad yadi kadācic Candraguptaś Cāṇakyam ati:jita-kāśinam a:sahamānaḥ sācivyād avaropayet, tataḥ . . . amātya:Rākṣasaś Candraguptena saha saṃda-dhīta so if by any chance Candragupta, not enduring Cāṇakya('s being so) extremely arrogant, were to dismiss him from his ministerial post, Minister Rākṣasa might come to terms with Candragupta

One of the optatives may be replaced by a present indicative, as in the following beautiful verse of Kālidāsa:

anadhigata:manorathasya pūrvaṃ
śataguṇit» êva gatā mama triyāmā
yadi tu tava samāgame tath» aîva
prasarati subhru, tataḥ kṛtī bhaveyam

[Earlier with my desire unobtained:] before I won my desire,
The night passed for me as if multiplied by a hundred:
But if it could stretch like that [upon your union:] when I am with you,
I should be satisfied, my fair one

As in any language the conditional clause may be implied (or conveyed by an adverbial word or phrase) rather than directly expressed:

vyaktaṃ n» âsti—katham anyathā Vāsanty api tāṃ na paśyet? obviously she does not (really) exist. Otherwise how would Vāsantī not [be seeing:] be able to see her too?

sādhu, sādhu! anena ratha-vegena pūrva:prasthitaṃ Vainateyam apy āsādayeyam, kiṃ punas tam apakāriṇaṃ Maghonaḥ bravo, bravo! With this speed of the chariot I could even overtake [Vinatā's son:] Garuḍa [previously set out:] after giving him a start, let alone that offender against Indra

Conversely, there is an idiom whereby the main clause is suppressed and a tentative supposition is expressed by **yadi** with the optative:

. . . **pārāśarī Divākaramitra:nāmā giri-nadīm āśritya prativasati—sa yadi vinded vārttām** a wandering mendicant called Divākaramitra is living (in those parts) by a mountain stream—it is possible that he might possess some information

The conditional tense may be used (in both the subordinate and the main clause) to express a past unfulfilled condition. To quote Kālidāsa again:

yadi surabhim avāpsyas tan-mukhɔ-ôcchvāsa-gandhaṃ,
tava ratir abhaviṣyat puṇḍarīke kim asmin?

If (O bee) you had discovered the sweet fragrance of her breath,
Would you (after that) have found pleasure in this lotus?

But for various reasons the conditional is not a very common tense. Despite its origin, it is not needed in reported statements to express a non-conditional, 'future in the past' sense ('he said he would do it') since a direct construction with **iti** is available in such circumstances. Secondly, sentences of the type 'he wouldn't have done it without asking' are expressed by the future (Chapter 13). Thirdly, even in its special function of expressing past unfulfilled conditions it may be replaced by the optative:

Vṛṣala, Rākṣasaḥ khalv asau—vikramya gṛhya-māṇaḥ svayaṃ vā vinaśyed yuṣmad-balāni vā vināśayet Vṛṣala, the person (you are speaking of) is Rākṣasa after all: [being seized:] if we had seized him by force either he would have died himself or else he would have destroyed your forces

Comparatives and superlatives

The normal comparative suffix is **tara**, and the normal superlative suffix is **tama**: **mṛdu** 'soft', **mṛdutara** 'softer', **mṛdutama** 'softest'. These suffixes are freely attached to adjectives, and are also found with past participles (**utpīḍita-tara** 'particularly squeezed') and occasionally substantives (**suhṛttama** 'very close friend').

Stems in **-yāṃs** (usually **-īyāṃs**) also in principle have comparative force and are paired with superlative forms in **-iṣṭha**. They are primary derivatives of ancient formation, added always to monosyllabic stems, and do not necessarily correspond directly to any adjective in the positive degree. What correspondence there is will be in meaning and/or in ultimate derivation from the same root rather than in form. Thus **kṣodīyāṃs** 'meaner, inferior' and **kṣodiṣṭha** 'meanest' are derived directly from the root **kṣud** 'trample'; and the simple adjective **kṣudra** 'mean' is a separate formation from the same root; while **kanīyāṃs** 'smaller' and **kaniṣṭha** 'smallest' are related only in meaning to **alpa** 'small'. Some other examples of these stems are:

guru heavy, important	**garīyāṃs**	**gariṣṭha**
vṛddha old	**jyāyāṃs** elder	**jyeṣṭha**
antika near	**nedīyāṃs**	**nediṣṭha**
paṭu sharp	**paṭīyāṃs**	**paṭiṣṭha**
priya dear	**preyāṃs**	**preṣṭha**
balin strong	**balīyāṃs**	**baliṣṭha**
bahu much	**bhūyāṃs**	**bhūyiṣṭha**
mahānt great	**mahīyāṃs**	**mahiṣṭha**
(*cf.* **śrī** splendour)	**śreyāṃs** better	**śreṣṭha**

It should be noted that while some of the forms listed above are frequent, they do not exclude the use of the suffixes **tara** and **tama**: thus 'dearer' may be represented by **priyatara** as well as by **preyāṃs**.

The other term of the comparison is represented by the ablative (or by a form in **-taḥ**):

sv›:ârthāt satāṃ gurutarā praṇayi-kriy» aîva more important to the virtuous than their own interests is carrying out the request of a petitioner

It is not, in fact, necessary for the adjective to be in the comparative degree for the use of this ablative of comparison. 'Dearer even than life' may be represented simply by **prāṇebhyo ›pi priyaḥ**. Similarly:

vajrād api kaṭhorāṇi, mṛdūni kusumād api
lok›-ôttarāṇāṃ cetāṃsi ko hi vijñātum arhati?

harder even than adamant, softer even than a flower—
who can aspire to understand the minds of those who
are above the world?

On the other hand, in Sanskrit (unlike English) the comparative adjective by itself need not have overtly comparative force but may be simply a more emphatic equivalent of the positive: **balīyāṃs**, rather than meaning 'stronger', often just means 'notably strong, particularly strong'. As a result, the comparative force is expressed much more by the ablative of comparison than by the adjective, with the exception of a few adjectives of almost invariably comparative significance such as **jyāyāṃs** 'elder' and **bhūyāṃs** 'more'. One should, in fact, beware of translating **balīyāṃs** as 'stronger' unless the context makes it quite plain that a comparison is intended.

Similar to the ablative of comparison is the ablative after an adjective such as **anya** 'other (than)' or after a verb such as **pari+hā** (*passive*) 'be inferior to':

na tarhi prāg:avasthāyāḥ parihīyase in that case you are [not inferior to your previous state:] no worse off than you were before

Occasionally, an analytical construction with a negative is found replacing the ablative of comparison. This is the regular construction with the word **varam** 'a preferable thing, the lesser of evils'.

varaṃ vandhyā bhāryā na c› âvidvān putraḥ [a barren wife is the preferable thing and not:] better a barren wife than an ignorant son

'sarvathā ›mātya:Rākṣasa eva praśasyataraḥ'—' "na bhavān" iti vākyaśeṣaḥ' 'at all events it is Minister Rākṣasa who is more to be admired—'["not you" is the rest of the sentence:] than I am, you mean?'

Just as comparatives do not always have comparative force, so superlatives need not imply literal supremacy: **mṛdutama** may mean simply 'pre-eminently soft', 'very soft', rather than '(the) softest (of all)'. The field of comparison may be expressed either by the genitive (**sodaryāṇāṃ ṣaṇṇāṃ jyeṣṭhaḥ** 'eldest of the six [co-uterine] brothers') or by the locative (**buddhimatsu narāḥ śreṣṭhāḥ** 'men are supreme among sentient beings').

Once again, a superlative form is not necessary to express superlative force:

vihageṣu paṇḍit» aîṣā jātiḥ [among birds this is the clever species:] this is the cleverest species of bird

Constructions with *iti*

The uses of the particle **iti** may now be considered in greater detail than was practicable when the word was first introduced into the exercises.

iti is in origin an adverb meaning 'thus, in this way'. But its use in this wider sense is almost entirely lost in Classical Sanskrit. Instead, its function is to indicate that the preceding utterance is a quotation or is in some sense being treated as a quotation. (Unfortunately, there is no corresponding formal indication of where the quotation begins: more often than not it begins with the beginning of the sentence, but ambiguities can occur.) Although in principle (with rare exceptions in verse) **iti** is placed immediately after the quotation, it is not necessarily enclitic. After a long quotation, **iti** may be the first word in a new paragraph or a new stanza of verse. Or it may even refer to the words of another speaker.

iti śrutvā devaḥ pramāṇam having heard (what I have told you), Your Majesty is the judge (of what to do)

vatsa, ity ev› âhaṃ pariplavamāna-hṛdayaḥ pramugdho ›smi my dear (brother), from just such (thoughts as you have voiced) my heart is trembling and I am faint

The construction with **iti** may represent both direct and indirect discourse in English. In the latter case various appropriate changes must be made: according to circumstance, 'I' and 'you' may be represented by 'he' etc., 'is' by 'was', 'here' by 'there', 'now' by 'then', and so forth.

For greater clarity, the words of the **iti** clause in all the Sanskrit examples which follow have been isolated by inverted commas.

aye 'Candraguptād aparaktān puruṣān jānām›' îty upakṣiptam anena oh, he has hinted ['I know men disloyal to Candragupta':] that he knows men disloyal to Candragupta

tato bhagavaty Arundhatī 'n› âhaṃ vadhū-virahitām Ayodhyāṃ gamiṣyām›' îty āha thereupon the revered Arundhatī said ['I will not go . . .':] that she would not go to an Ayodhyā bereft of its bride

abhūc ca ghoṣanā 'śvaḥ kām›-ôtsava' iti and there was a proclamation ['tomorrow (there will be) a Love Festival':] that the next day was to be a Love Festival

However, the principle that the words of the **iti** clause should represent the original form of the quotation is not invariable. Occasionally in practice a first or second person form belonging in the main sentence intrudes into the **iti** clause to avoid a clumsy third person periphrasis. Theoretically, this can lead to ambuiguity, but context or common sense will normally make the meaning plain.

bhartṛdārike, 'tvam asvastha:śarīr»' êti parijanād upalabhya mahādevī prāptā mistress, the Queen has arrived, having heard from her attendants [' "*you*" are unwell':] that you are unwell (*The words actually addressed to the Queen would have been* 'the Princess is unwell'.)

A verb of telling, being told, etc. need not be expressed after **iti**. From its original meaning of 'in this way' it can naturally imply 'with these words'—becoming in effect the equivalent of **ity uktvā**. Thus a speech may conclude with **iti pādayoḥ papāta** 'with these words (she) fell at (the other's) feet', or **iti kiṃ cid asmayata** 'so (saying) she smiled slightly', '—she said, with a slight smile'. This use is especially common in the stage-directions of plays. A line of dialogue will be followed, for example, by **iti Mādhavam āliṅgati** '[so saying] she embraces Mādhava'.

The usage permits great flexibility of construction, since the **iti** clause may represent not actual dialogue but the substance of what is said:

'eṣā ku:matir na kalyāṇ»' îti nivārayantyāṃ mayi

vana-vāsāya kopāt prasthitā [upon my restraining (her) by saying 'this ill notion is not beneficial':] when I remonstrated that no good would come of such wrong-headedness, she went off in a temper to live in the forest

'mahān ayaṃ prasāda' iti gṛhītavatī she accepted (it) [with the words 'this is a great favour':] with grateful thanks

'pitā te Cāṇakyena ghātita' iti rahasi trāsayitvā Bhāgurāyaṇen› âpavāhitaḥ Parvataka-putro Malayaketuḥ after secretly frightening him by claiming that Cāṇakya had had his father murdered, Bhāgurāyaṇa helped Parvataka's son Malayaketu to escape (*Note here how the second person in the Sanskrit avoids the ambiguities of the English third person forms.*)

That **iti** clauses, as well as combining with verbs meaning 'tell' or 'hear' ('be told'), may be used with verbs of knowing, thinking, supposing, etc. needs little illustration:

'tat-sahacāriṇībhiḥ sakhī te hṛt»' êti me hṛdayam āśaṅkate my heart suspects that your friend's wife was carried off by the companions of that (goddess)

But just as **iti** can be used without a verb of saying actually expressed to mean 'with these words', so it can be used without a verb of thinking actually expressed to mean 'with these thoughts, with this in mind'. **iti** thus becomes the equivalent of **iti matvā**, and represents English 'because' or 'since' where these have the sense of 'on the grounds that'.

'prāṇa-parityāgen› âpi rakṣaṇīyāḥ suhṛd-asava' iti kathayāmi I speak out because a friend's life must be saved even at the cost of sacrificing (one's own) life

'kaṭhora-garbh»' êti n› ānītā ›si (we) did not bring you (with us) because (you were) late in pregnancy

ahaṃ tvayā tasminn avasare nir_dayaṃ nighnaty api 'str»' îty avajñātā on that occasion though I struck (you) fiercely, you despised me [thinking '(she is) a woman':] as a woman

As well as expressing statements and suppositions, **iti** clauses are used to some extent to represent situations—'the possibility that', 'the fact that'. The first of the following examples, where a finite verb occurs and where a relative construction with **yat** might perhaps have been used, is less typical than the others:

'tatrabhavān Kaṇvaḥ śāśvate brahmaṇi vartate, iyaṃ ca vaḥ sakhī tasy› ātmaj»' êti katham etat? how is it that His Honour Kaṇva lives in perpetual chastity and (yet) this friend of yours is his daughter?

bhagavan, 'prāg abhipreta-siddhiḥ, paścād darśanam' ity apūrvaḥ khalu vo ›nugrahaḥ revered one, for the fulfilment of (our) wishes to be first and the audience (with you) to come afterwards (constitutes) a quite unprecedented kindness on your part

athavā 'kāmam a:satyasandha' iti param ayaśo, na punaḥ śatru-vañcanā-paribhūtiḥ but in fact to be wilfully false to one's word is a greater disgrace than to be beaten by an enemy's tricks

iti clauses have so far been considered from the point of view of their relation to the main sentence. The examples quoted have been of clauses of statement. But **iti** clauses may also take the form of commands or questions. Where these may best be represented by direct speech in English, they require no special mention. Elsewhere they correspond broadly to the syntactical categories of indirect command and indirect question, and may be treated from that point of view.

Clauses of command

Indirect command in English is generally expressed by an accusative and infinitive construction—'I told him to do it'.

tatrabhavatā Kaṇvena vayam ājñāpitāḥ 'Śakuntalā-hetor vanaspatibhyaḥ kusumāny āharat›' êti His Honour Kaṇva has ordered us ['bring blossoms . . .':] to bring blossoms from the trees for Śakuntalā

As well as by an imperative, the command may be expressed in Sanskrit by other means such as a gerundive:

'rakṣaṇīyā Rākṣasasya prāṇā' ity ārya-ādeśaḥ His Excellency's orders are ['Rākṣasa's life should be protected':] to protect Rākṣasa's life'

By the use of **iti** in its **ity uktvā** or **iti matvā** sense, the equivalent of a clause of purpose may be obtained.

nanv idānīm eva mayā tatra Kalahaṃsakaḥ preṣitaḥ 'pracchannam upagamya Nandana-āvāsa-pravṛttim upalabhasva' êti why, I have just now sent Kalahaṃsaka there [with the words 'approaching stealthily find out . . .':] to find out discreetly what has been happening in Nandana's house

'mā bhūd āśrama-pīḍā' êti parimeya-puraḥsarau (the two of them travelled) with a limited entourage [with the thought 'let there not be affliction of the hermitage':] lest they should trouble the hermitage

Interrogative clauses

These, of course, often occur with verbs meaning 'enquire' or 'speculate':

tad yāvad gṛhiṇīm āhūya pṛcchāmi 'asti kim api prātarāśo na vā' êti so I'll just call my wife and ask ['is there breakfast at all or not?':] whether she has any breakfast for me or not

kiṃ tu 'katham asmābhir upagantavya' iti saṃpradhārayāmi but I am wondering how we should approach him

Indirect questions also occur with verbs of knowing or stating, and here it is interesting to note another modification of the principle that the words of an **iti** clause represent a direct quotation: what is known or stated is the *answer* to the question. There is, in fact, no direct speech equivalent of the indirect interrogative in 'he said who had come', unless it is a statement of the form 'such-and-such a person has come'.

ārye, yady evaṃ tat kathaya sarvataḥ 'ka eṣa vṛttānta' iti Lady, if so then tell (us) exactly what this is that has been happening

na tv evaṃ vidmaḥ 'kataro ›yam āyuṣmatoḥ Kuśa; Lavayor' iti but we do not know [the following,] which of the two princes Kuśa and Lava he is

Not infrequently, the **iti** is omitted, so that the interrogative pronoun has the function in itself of introducing an indirect question:

paśyasi kā vārttā you see what the news is

na jāne kim idam valkalānāṃ sadṛśam, utāho jaṭānāṃ samucitam I do not know if this is in keeping with the bark garment (of an ascetic), or in accord with his matted locks

jñāyatāṃ bhoḥ kim etat ho there, find out what that is

Sometimes a relative pronoun serves to introduce the same kind of clause:

brūhi yad upalabdham tell me what (you) have discovered

tad etat kārtsnyena yo ›yaṃ, yā c› êyaṃ, yathā c› âsya śravaṇa-śikharaṃ samārūḍhā, tat sarvam āveditam so (I) have told it all completely—who he is, what that (spray of blossoms) is, and how it [attained:] came to be placed at the tip of his ear

Once again, **iti** may be used in its **ity uktvā** and **iti matvā** senses: thus **'kiṃ kim' iti sahas» ôpasṛtya** 'rushing up [with the words "what (is it), what (is it)?":] to find out what was happening'; **'kuto ›yam' ity uparūḍha:kutūhalā** 'with her curiosity mounting as to where it came from'.

Word repetition

Word repetition in Sanskrit may be employed for emphasis (intensive or iterative use). Thus **sādhu sādhu** 'bravo, bravo!'; **hato hataś Caṇḍavarmā** 'Candravarman is murdered,

murdered!'; **pacati pacati** 'he cooks and cooks, he's always cooking' (an example given by Sanskrit grammarians); **mandaṃ mandam** 'very slowly'; **punaḥ punaḥ** 'again and again'.

Repetition may also have a distributive sense ('each various one'). This is typical of pronouns. Thus **svān svān bālān ānayanti** 'they bring their various children'; **tat tat kāraṇam utpādya** 'producing [this and that reason:] various reasons'. Similarly with relatives: **yo yaḥ** (alternative to **yaḥ kaś cit**) 'whichever person, whosoever'; **yathā yathā . . . tathā tathā** 'in proportion as, the more that'.

Vocabulary

adhyavasāyaḥ resolution
an:adhyavasāyaḥ irresolution, hesitation
anilaḥ wind, breeze
an:iṣṭa undesired, unpleasant
anurāgaḥ passion, love
antaḥ end
antaḥpuraṃ women's quarters (of palace), harem
antarita hidden, concealed
apadeśaḥ pretext
apara other, different
apasarpaṇaṃ getting away, escape
abhilāṣin desirous, anxious
arthin having an object, wanting, petitioning
a:̱śeṣa [without remainder:] complete, whole, all
a:śobhana unpleasant, awful
ahamahamikā rivalry
ādaraḥ care, trouble; **ādaraṃ kṛ** take care (to)
ādhoraṇaḥ elephant-driver
āpanna:̱sattva [to whom a living creature has occurred:] pregnant
ārti *f.* affliction, distress
ārdra moist, tender
ārya-putraḥ [son of] nobleman; *voc.* noble sir
indriyaṃ (organ or faculty of) sense
uttama uppermost, supreme, top
unmāthaḥ shaking, disturbance; **manmatha-ônmāthaḥ** pangs of love
upakāraḥ help, service
upanyāsaḥ mention, allusion
upasthānaṃ (religious) attendance
ekākin alone
Aikṣvāka descended from King Ikṣvāku
kātara timid, nervous
kānanaṃ forest
kārmukaṃ bow
kiṃvadantī rumour
kusuma:̱āyudhaḥ [the flower-weaponed:] god of love
kūlaṃ bank, shore
kṛpālu compassionate
kolāhalaḥ clamour
khedaḥ exhaustion
gaṇikā courtesan

gandhaḥ smell, scent
garīyāṃs important, considerable; worthy/worthier of respect
gahanaṃ dense place
gir *f.* speech, voice, tone
guṇaḥ merit; strand, string
ghrāṇaṃ smelling, (sense of) smell
candana *m. n.* sandal, sandalwood tree
cūtaḥ mango tree
jaraṭha old, decrepit
jālapādaḥ goose
jyāyāṃs older, elder
taru *m.* tree; **taru-gahanaṃ** thicket of trees, wood
tāmbūlaṃ betel
dakṣiṇa right, on the right hand
dur:nimittaṃ ill omen
dṛṣṭi *f.* gaze
drohaḥ injury, hostility
dvandvaṃ pair; **dvandva-saṃprahāraḥ** single combat, duel
dvār *f.* door
dharma-vit learned in the sacred law
nava:yauvanaṃ [fresh] youth
nikhila entire
nipuṇa clever, sharp
nirbhara excessive, full
nivedaka announcing, indicating
pañca five
paṭu sharp; **paṭīyāṃs** sharper
pati *m.* lord; husband
padaṃ step
paravaśa in another's power, helpless
parimalaḥ perfume
pāṭhaḥ recitation, reading; part (in play)
pātraṃ vessel, receptacle; worthy recipient; actor; **pātra-vargaḥ** cast (of play)
potakaḥ young animal/plant; **cūta-potakaḥ** young mango tree
pratikriyā remedy, remedying
pradhāna principal, important
prastāvaḥ prelude
prāsādaḥ mansion; terrace; [upstairs] room
bāṇaḥ arrow
bisaṃ lotus fibre
Bharataḥ *pr. n.*
bhājanaṃ receptacle, box
bhāryā wife
bhūyāms more, further
matta in rut, rutting
madaḥ intoxication
madhukaraḥ, madhukarī bee, honey-bee
mūrchā faint, swoon; **madana-mūrchā** amorous swoon
mūlaṃ root, basis, foundation
mṛgatṛṣṇikā mirage
raṃhas *n.* speed
rūpaṃ form; beauty
laghu light; brief
locanaṃ eye
vargaḥ group
vigrahaḥ separation; body
viṭapa *m. n.* branch, bush, thicket
vitarkaḥ conjecture, doubt
vipinaṃ forest
vilakṣa disconcerted, ashamed
vihvala tottering, unsteady
vīthikā row, grove
śastraṃ knife, sword
saṃskāraḥ preparation, adornment
sa-phala [having fruit:] fulfilled
saṃprahāraḥ fighting, combat
saṃmūḍha confused
saras *n.* lake
sārathi *m.* driver of chariot

su:rataṃ love-making
surabhi fragrant
su:labha easily got, natural
skhalanaṃ failure, lapse
svapnaḥ dream
svāminī mistress
svedaḥ sweat
Hari *m.*, *pr. n.*
harṣaḥ joy, delight
hastin *m.* elephant
hita beneficial; well-disposed, good (friend)

ati+vah *caus.* **(ativāhayati)** spend (time)
adhi+ruh (I adhirohati) ascend, mount
anu+bandh (IX anubadhnāti) pursue, importune
anu+lip (VI anulimpati) anoint
anu+vṛt (I anuvartate) go after, attend upon
apa+yā (II apayāti) go away, depart
abhi+ghrā (I abhijighrati) smell
abhi+bhū (I abhibhavati) overpower
abhi+syand (I abhiṣyandate) flow
ava+gam (I avagacchati) understand; suppose, consider
ava+dhṛ *caus.* **(avadhārayati)** determine, resolve
ava+lamb (I avalambate) cling to, hold on to
ā+gam *caus.* **(āgamayati)** acquire
ā+ghrā (I ājighrati) smell
ā+car (I ācarati) conduct oneself, act, do
ā+śvas *caus.* **(āśvāsayati)** cause to breathe freely, comfort
ut+cal (I uccalati) move away; rise
ut+sthā (I uttiṣṭhati) stand up, get up
ut+as (IV udasyati) throw up, throw out, push out
upa+kṛ (VIII upakaroti) furnish, provide
upa+kṣip (VI upakṣipati) hint at
upa+jan (IV upajāyate, *p.p.* **upajāta)** come into being, be roused
upa+sthā *caus.* **(upasthāpayati)** cause to be near, fetch, bring up
upa+i (II upaiti) approach, come to
kḷp (I kalpate) be suitable, conduce to, turn to (*dat.*)
tṛp *caus.* **(tarpayati)** satisfy
nigaḍayati (*denom.*) fetter, bind
ni+śam *caus.* **(niśāmayati)** perceive, observe
pari+trai (II paritrāti) rescue, protect
prati+dṛś (I pratipaśyati) see
prati+ni+vṛt (I pratinivartate) return
prati+pad (IV pratipadyate) assent, admit
pra+budh *caus.* **(prabodhayati)** inform, admonish
pra+svap (II prasvapiti) fall asleep
pra+hi (V prahiṇoti) despatch, send
bhid (VII bhinatti) split, separate
vi+kas (I vikasati) burst, blossom, bloom
vi+car (I vicarati) move about, roam
vi+car *caus.* **(vicārayati)** deliberate, ponder

vi+lok *caus.* **(vilokayati)** look at, watch
vi+sṛp (I visarpati) be diffused, spread
sam+jan (IV saṃjāyate, *p.p.* **saṃjāta)** come into being, be aroused
sam+ā+car (I samācarati) conduct oneself, act, do
spand (I spandate) quiver
syand (I syandate) flow, move rapidly

agrataḥ in front of (*gen.*)
ati: (*karmadhāraya prefix*) extreme(ly)
api nāma if only
kadācit perhaps
jhaṭiti suddenly
nu khalu (*enclitic stressing interrogative* now (who *etc.*) I wonder?
sakāśam to [the presence of]
yathā yathā . . . tathā tathā in proportion as, the more that

Exercise 14a

प्रियंवदक ज्ञायतां को ऽस्मद्दर्शनार्थी द्वारि तिष्ठति ।१। क्व नु
खलु गता स्यात् ।२। आसीत्तादृशो मुनिरस्मिन्नाश्रमे ।३।
आयुष्मन् श्रूयतां यदर्थमस्मि हरिणा त्वत्सकाशं प्रेषितः ।४।
एवमुक्तो ऽप्यहमेनं प्राबोधयं पुनः पुनः ।५। चिरात्प्रभृत्यार्यः
परित्यक्तोचितशरीरसंस्कार इति पीड्यते मे हृदयम् ।६। विस्मय-
हर्षमूलस्य कोलाहलो लोकस्योदजिहीत ।७। तदुच्यतां पात्रवर्गः
स्वेषु स्वेषु पाठेष्वसंमूढैर्भवितव्यमिति ।८। सखे चिन्तय तावत्के-
नापदेशेन पुनराश्रमपदं गच्छामः ।९। अपि नाम दुरात्मनश्चा-
णक्याच्चन्द्रगुप्तो भिद्येत ।१०। अयमसौ मम ज्यायानार्यः कुशो
नाम भरताश्रमात्प्रतिनिवृत्तः ।११। सुरतखेदप्रसुप्तयोस्तु तयोः
स्वप्ने बिसगुणनिगडितपादो जरठः कश्चिज्जालपादः प्रत्यदृश्यत।
प्रत्यबुध्येतां चोभौ ।१२। तदन्विष्यतां यदि काचिदापन्नसत्त्वा
तस्य भार्या स्यात् ।१३। आर्यपुत्र नायं विश्रम्भकथाया अवस-
रस्ततो लघुतरमेवाभिधीयसे ।१४। कथमीदृशेन सह वत्सस्य
चन्द्रकेतोर्द्वन्द्वसंप्रहारमनुजानीयाम् ।१५। इत्यवधार्यापसर्पणाभि-
लाषिण्यहमभवम् ।१६। कस्मिन्प्रयोजने ममायं प्रणिधिः प्रहित
इति प्रभूतत्वात्प्रयोजनानां न खल्ववधारयामि ।१७। यदि

कश्चिदस्तूपायः पतिद्रोहप्रतिक्रियायै दर्शयामुम् । मतिर्हि ते पटीयसी । १८ । अनयैव च कथया तया सह तस्मिन्नेव प्रासादे तथैव प्रतिषिद्धाशेषपरिजनप्रवेशा दिवसमत्यवाहयम् । १९ । तदुपायश्चिन्त्यतां यथा सफलप्रार्थनो भवेयम् । २० । श्रुत्वा चैतत्तमेव मत्तहस्तिनमुदस्ताधोरणो राजपुत्रो ऽधिरुह्य रंहसोत्तमेन राजभवनमभ्यवर्तत । २१ । उपलब्धवानस्मि प्रणिधिभ्यो यथा तस्य म्लेच्छराजबलस्य मध्यात्प्रधानतमाः पञ्च राजानः परया सुहृत्तया राक्षसमनुवर्तन्त इति । २२ । यदि पुनरियं किंवदन्ती महाराजं प्रति स्यन्देत तत्कष्टं स्यात् । २३ । इत्यवधार्यान्वेष्टुमादरमकरवम् । अन्वेषमाणश्च यथा यथा नापश्यं तं तथा तथा सुहृत्स्नेहकातरेण मनसा तत्तदशोभनमाशङ्कमानस्तरुगहनानि चन्दनवीथिकालतामण्डपान्सरःकूलानि च वीक्षमाणो निपुणमितस्ततो दत्तदृष्टिः सुचिरं व्यचरम् । २४ । एकस्मिंश्च प्रदेशे झटिति वनानिलेनोपनीतं निर्भरविकसिते ऽपि कानने ऽभिभूतान्यकुसुमपरिमलं विसर्पन्तमतिसुरभितयानुलिम्पन्तमिव तर्पयन्तमिव पूरयन्तमिव घ्राणेन्द्रियमहमहमिकया मधुकरकुलैरनुबध्यमानमनाघ्रातपूर्वममानुषलोकोचितं कुसुमगन्धमभ्यजिघ्रम् ॥ २५ ॥

Exercise 14b

Translate past tenses by the imperfect except in sentence 23.

1 Lātavya, do *you know whose arrow this is? 2 Ah you fool! Are *you more·learned·in·the·sacred·law than our preceptor? 3 And I observed in that hermitage in the shade of a young·mango-tree an ascetic of·melancholy·appearance. 4 The writing might be spoiled, friend, by the sweat·from·(my)·fingers. 5 What then is this great hesitation at every step? 6 And so saying she drew it (**pattrikā** the letter) from the betel-box and showed it (to me). 7 The allusion to (such) considerable love·and·service is indeed opportune [**avasare**]. 8 Raivataka, tell our·driver to bring up the chariot complete·

with·[sa_]·bow·and·arrows. 9 He may even, perhaps, ashamed·of·his·lapse·from·self-control, do something dreadful [aniṣṭa]. 10 Now [yāvat] I heard that it was Mālatī who was the cause·of^ his ^pangs·of·love. 11 And she became mistress·of^ his ^entire·harem. 12 Tell (me) what further benefit I (can) provide for you. 13 After speaking thus he fell silent, his·gaze·fixed·on·my·face (to see) what I [*f.*] would say. 14 Whereabouts then in this forest may I acquire news·of·my·beloved? 15 He forsooth [kila], (feeling) compassionate, comforted those people in a tender tone and asked the courtesan the reason·for·her·distress. 16 Your Highness, Śakaṭadāsa will never ever [na kadācid api] admit in front of minister·Rākṣasa that he wrote it. 17 Why my dear Bhāgurāyaṇa, minister·Rākṣasa is the dearest and best (of friends) to us. 18 *You [*f.*] having departed, I stayed alone for a little while [muhūrtam iva], and my·doubts·aroused as to what he was now doing I returned and with·my·body·concealed·in·the·thickets watched the place. 19 If only this prelude does not, like a mirage, turn in the end to disappointment. 20 Come to me (who am) Purūravas, returned from attendance·upon·the·Sun, and tell me what (I) must protect *you [*f. pl.*] from. 21 While speaking thus I [*f.*] managed, with limbs unsteady·from·the·exhaustion·of·my·amorous·swoon to get up by holding on to hér. And (when I had) risen, my right eye quivered, indicating·an·ill-omen. And my·anxieties·roused, I thought, 'here is something untoward [apara] hinted at by fate'. 22 If (you) consider Rākṣasa worthier of respect than we are, then give him this sword of ours. 23 To start with [tāvat] friend, I should like to hear what the poisoners·and·others employed·by·me have done since Candragúpta's entry·into·the·city. 24 Yet if the descendant of Ikṣvāku King Rāma were to see you such (as you are), then his heart would flow with tenderness. 25 Just as I [*f.*] was pondering in this way, the love natural·to·youth, by·which·distinctions·of·merit·and·demerit·are·not·pondered (but which is) solely·partial·to·beauty made me as helpless as the intoxication·of·the·season·of·blossoms does the honey-bee.

Chapter 15

PARADIGMS Perfect and aorist tenses; **ahan**

Perfect tense

The perfect tense is formed by reduplication of the root and the addition of a special set of personal endings. As in athematic present stems, the three parasmaipada singular forms are strong, involving guṇa or sometimes vṛddhi of the root, while the other forms are weak. Thus from **dṛś** 'see', **dadarśa** 'he saw', **dadṛśuḥ** 'they saw'.

The vowel of the reduplication is **i/u** for roots containing **ĭ/ŭ**, **a** for other roots. Initial **a** reduplicates to **ā**: **as** 'be', **āsa, āsuḥ**. Initial **i** reduplicates to **ī** (from **i+i**) in the weak forms, **iye** (**i+e**) in the strong: **iṣ** 'want', **iyeṣa, īṣuḥ. yaj** 'sacrifice', **vac** 'speak', and a number of other roots liable to samprasāraṇa, reduplicate with samprasāraṇa of the semi-vowel: **iyāja, ījuḥ** (**i+ij-**); **uvāca, ūcuḥ** (**u+uc-**); similarly, from **svap** 'sleep', **suṣvāpa, suṣupuḥ**.

The strong grade is normally guṇa. In the third person singular it is vṛddhi in the case of roots ending in a vowel or in **a** followed by a single consonant—in other words, where guṇa would produce a prosodically light syllable. Thus **dṛś, dadarśa**, but **kṛ, cakāra**; **nī, nināya**; **pat, papāta**. This vṛddhi is optional in the first person singular, and such verbs may therefore distinguish the first from the third person singular, whereas these forms are necessarily identical in other verbs. Thus **cakara** 'I did,' **cakāra** 'I did/he did'; **ninaya** 'I led', **ninaya** 'I led/ he led'; **papata** 'I fell', **papāta** 'I fell/he fell'. Roots ending in **-ā** make a first and third person form in **-au**: **sthā** 'stand', **tasthau** 'I stood/he stood'.

The terminations **-itha, -iva, -ima, -iṣe, -ivahe, -imahe** contain a connecting **i** which is omitted in a few verbs ending in **ṛ** or **u**, including **kṛ** 'do' and **śru** 'hear': thus **śuśruma** 'we heard'. In the second person singular form **-itha**, the **i** is omitted in a number of other verbs as well, and is optional in yet others, including those ending in **-ā**.

The form of weak stem which requires most comment is that of roots with medial **a**. Sometimes this **a** is eliminated: **gam** 'go', **jagāma, jagmuḥ**; **han** 'kill', **jaghāna, jaghnuḥ**. Similarly, by a process of internal sandhi the root **sad** 'sit' gives **sasāda, seduḥ** (from **sasduḥ*). But the analogy of this last form is followed by other roots with medial **a** if the initial consonant reduplicates unchanged: **pat** 'fall, fly', **papāta, petuḥ** (the expected form **paptuḥ** does occur in Vedic); **tan** 'stretch', **tatāna, tenuḥ**.

The root **bhū** 'be' is irregular in reduplicating with **a** and in failing to strengthen to guṇa or vṛddhi: **babhūva, babhūvuḥ**.

The root **vid** 'know' forms a perfect without reduplication which has a present sense: **veda** 'he knows', **viduḥ** 'they know'.

The root **ah** 'say' is very defective. It occurs only in the perfect and only in the third person forms **āha, āhatuḥ, āhuḥ**, and the second person forms **āttha** and **āhathuḥ**. It may have a present as well as a past sense—'he says/he said'.

The ātmanepada forms of the perfect may have a passive as well as a middle sense—**ninye** 'was led', **jagṛhe** 'was seized', etc.

The ātmanepada participle in **-āna** attached to the perfect stem scarcely occurs at all in Classical Sanskrit; and the parasmaipada participle in **-vāṃs** is rare, with the exception of **vidvāṃs**, which is formed from the non-reduplicated perfect of **vid** referred to above and is used as an adjective meaning 'wise, learned'.

Perfect forms may be made from causative and other derivative verbs by means of the periphrastic perfect. This arose from the combination of the accusative of an abstract noun (not otherwise used) with the perfect of the verb **kṛ**: **darśayāṃ cakāra** '[he did a showing:] he showed'. In the parasmaipada, however, **kṛ** is normally replaced in Classical Sanskrit by the perfect of **as** (very occasionally of **bhū**): **darśayām āsa** 'he showed', **darśayām āsuḥ** 'they showed'. This formation is also utilised by one or two simple verbs which do not form an ordinary perfect: e.g. **īkṣ** 'look', **īkṣāṃ cakre** 'he looked'.

Despite its name (and its Indo-European origins) the perfect is not used in Classical Sanskrit to express any stative or perfective sense. It is a tense of historical narrative, which according to the grammarians should not be used to describe events within the personal experience of the speaker. In consequence the first and second person forms are not at all common and the tense as a whole is not much used in dialogue. Its frequent use is a characteristic of narrative poetry, both epic and Classical, as in the extract given in Exercise 15a from the *Kumārasaṃbhava* of Kālidāsa.

Aorist tense

The aorist and imperfect tenses are specialisations of a single past tense characterised by the augment and the 'secondary' endings. From the point of view of its formation, the imperfect might be looked on as an 'aorist of the present stem'. An aorist is an aorist, and not an imperfect, if no corresponding present forms exist. Thus **ayāt** 'he went', from **yā** 'go', and **atudat** 'he struck', from **tud** 'strike', are imperfect forms because they correspond to the presents **yāti** 'he goes' (class II) and **tudati** 'he strikes' (class VI). But **adhāt** 'he put' and **agamat** 'he went' are aorist forms derived directly from the root, since **dhā** 'put' and **gam** 'go' form presents of a different kind, **dadhāti** (class III) and **gacchati** (class I), with corresponding imperfect forms **adadhāt** and **agacchat**. These remarks concern formation: in *meaning* an imperfect form (such as **ayāt**) should differ from an aorist form (such as

adhāt), although the distinction becomes of little importance in Classical Sanskrit.

Some forms of aorist, the sigmatic aorists, are characterised by the addition of some variety of suffixal **s**. These aorists are more sharply differentiated from an imperfect, since no present stem employs such a suffix. There are seven main varieties of aorist, three non-sigmatic and four sigmatic. The endings of two of the non-sigmatic and one of the sigmatic aorists are thematic, i.e. precisely similar to those of the imperfect of **nī**. The other types of aorist have athematic endings comparable with the imperfect of athematic verbs but without the same pattern of strong and weak forms. In all athematic types the third person plural parasmaipada ending is **-uḥ** (as in the imperfect of class III and some class II verbs). In all athematic types of the sigmatic aorist, the second and third person singular parasmaipada forms end in **īḥ** and **īt** respectively.

Non-sigmatic aorists

1 *root aorist* (small class: athematic endings; parasmaipada only). This type of aorist is confined in the Classical period to a number of roots ending in **ā** and to **bhū**. [The class was originally much larger, and other isolated forms of it survive—notably to supply the second and third person singular ātmanepada in the sigmatic aorist of some verbs: thus from **kṛ** 'do', **akārṣīḥ, akārṣīt** parasmaipada, but **akṛthāḥ, akṛta** ātmanepada.] The third person plural ending **an** in **abhūvan** is anomalous.

2 **a** *-aorist* (thematic endings; weak grade of root). The class is not particularly large, and ātmanepada forms are uncommon. The class includes two reduplicated forms: **pat** 'fall', **apaptat**; and **vac** 'speak', **avocat** (*a-va-uc-at*).

3 *Reduplicated aorist* (thematic endings; root syllable light, reduplicated syllable heavy; sense normally causative). This form is analogous to the periphrastic perfect. It provides the ordinary aorist of one or two verbs: thus **dru** 'run', **adudruvat**

'he ran'. But, while formed directly from the root, it normally supplies the aorist of causative and class X verbs: **nī, nāyayati** 'he causes to lead', **anīnayat** 'he caused to lead'; **cur, corayati** 'he steals', **acūcurat** 'he stole'. Vowels other than **u** reduplicate as **i**. The reduplicated **i** or **u** lengthens to **ī/ū** if the reduplicated syllable would otherwise be light. The root syllable does not appear in guṇa grade unless it can continue to be prosodically light (and not invariably even then—cf. **adudruvat**).

grah	seize	**ajigrahat**	he caused to be seized
jan	be born	**ajījanat**	he begat
dṛś	see	**adīdṛśat**	he showed
muc	free	**amūmucat**	he caused to be freed
ji	conquer	**ajījayat**	he caused to be conquered
mṛ	die	**amīmarat**	he put to death

If the root syllable even in its reduced grade remains heavy, the reduplicated syllable is light. But even in such verbs a special shortening of the root often occurs, to preserve the normal rhythm of 'heavy-light'. Thus from **dīp** 'shine', either **adidīpat** or **adīdipat** 'caused to shine, kindled'.

Sigmatic aorists

4 **s**-*aorist* (suffix **s**; athematic endings; vṛddhi in parasmaipada, guṇa or weak grade in ātmanepada). All roots take vṛddhi throughout the parasmaipada; in the ātmanepada, roots ending in **ĭ** or **ŭ** take guṇa, others remain unstrengthened. The paradigm of **dah** illustrates complications caused by internal sandhi.

5 **iṣ**-*aorist* (suffix **iṣ**; athematic endings; vṛddhi or guṇa in parasmaipada, guṇa in ātmanepada). This is the suffix **s** added with connecting **i**. The basic grade is guṇa, but in the parasmaipada final **ĭ/ŭ/ṝ** is strengthened to vṛddhi (thus ensuring a heavy syllable before the suffix), and medial **a** is sometimes strengthened to **ā** and sometimes remains unchanged.

6 **siṣ**-*aorist* (small class: suffix **siṣ**; athematic endings; parasmaipada only). This aorist (inflected like the **iṣ** aorist) is formed only from a number of roots ending in **-ā** and from **nam** 'bow', **yam** 'hold' and **ram** 'take pleasure'.

7 **sa**-*aorist* (small class: suffix **s** with thematic endings; weak grade). This aorist is confined to a number of roots containing **i**/**u**/**ṛ** and ending in some consonant which by internal sandhi combines with the **s** of the suffix to make **kṣ**. In the ātmanepada, three of the terminations are athematic—**i**, **āthām** and **ātām**.

8 *Aorist passive*. There is a formation, independent of the types of aorist listed above, which conveys the sense of a third person singular aorist passive: e.g. **akāri** 'was done', **adarśi** 'was seen', etc. The augment is prefixed to the root, and a suffix, **i**, is added. Medial **i**/**u**/**ṛ** take guṇa; otherwise vṛddhi is normal. A **y** is inserted after roots ending in **ā**: thus **ajñāyi** 'was known'.

The aorist tense, like the imperfect, expresses simple past statements. In particular, it is supposedly the most appropriate tense where the speaker is describing a recent event. But this function was usurped at an early stage by participial constructions, and the aorist became a learned formation little used in simple Sanskrit. In the Classical literature it takes its place beside the imperfect and the perfect as a narrative tense. Despite its complicated variety of forms, the aorist is easy to spot because of the augment and the secondary terminations; the best way to acquire familiarity with it is to read extensively in a work which makes use of it (e.g. the *Daśakumāracarita* of Daṇḍin).

Injunctive

In the Vedic language unaugmented forms of the aorist or imperfect are often used with imperative or subjunctive force and are then described as 'injunctive' forms. This usage has disappeared in Classical Sanskrit, with the following exception. The particle **mā** may be used with the unaugmented forms of the aorist, or very occasionally the imperfect, to express prohibition. Thus **mā bhaiṣṭa** 'do not fear', **m» aîvaṃ maṃsthāḥ** 'do not suppose so', **mā bhūt** 'let it not be', **mā ›dhyavasyaḥ sāhasam** 'do not resolve (anything) rash'.

Precative

The precative, or benedictive, is a kind of aorist optative. In Classical Sanskrit it is used only in the parasmaipada. It is formed by the addition of the suffix **yās** to the unstrengthened root, which appears as before the passive suffix **ya**. It is used to express wishes and prayers:

a:virahitau dampatī bhūyāstām may husband and wife be unseparated
kriyād aghānāṃ Maghavā vighātam may Indra cause elimination of evils

ahan 'day'

The neuter substantive **ahan** 'day' has **ahar** as its middle stem. The form **ahar** is thus nominative, vocative and accusative singular, and also the normal stem form as the prior member of a compound; it has, however, the further irregularity of appearing before the voiced middle case endings as **aho** (as if it were from *ahas*)—thus instrumental, dative and ablative dual **ahobhyām** etc. As the last member of a compound it appears as a (masculine) short **a** stem in one of two forms, **aha** or **ahna**.

antaram

Among the meanings of the word **antaram** is 'interval, difference'. At the end of a determinative compound, as well as meaning literally 'a difference of', it can signify 'a different —, another —': thus **varṇ-ântaram** 'a difference of colour' or 'a different colour'.

likhit-ântaram asy āṇīyatām bring another [thing written of him:] example of his writing

śastrapāṇi, aśrumukha

There are a few bahuvrīhis in which the second member expresses the location of the first. Thus **śastra-pāṇi** 'sword-handed', i.e. '[having a hand in which there is a sword:] whose hand holds a sword'; **aśru-mukha** 'tear-faced', i.e. '[having tears on the face:] tearful-faced'. Grammarians analysed such compounds by putting the second member in the locative case: e.g. **gaḍu-kaṇṭha** 'goitre-necked', **gaḍuḥ kaṇṭhe yasya** 'on whose neck there is a goitre'. Similarly, 'in whose hand there is a sword' etc.

Sanskrit metre

Mention was made in Chapter 1 of the quantitative nature of Sanskrit verse and of the rules for distinguishing light and heavy syllables. A general description of Classical Sanskrit metre is given here, and individual details of the commoner metres will be found in the grammatical section at the back of the book. The subject is often omitted from standard Sanskrit grammars, which is a pity, since Sanskrit poetry cannot be fully appreciated by those who are metrically deaf. Much of a poet's creative effort is obviously lost upon the reader for whom a poem might just as well have been written in prose. The need, of course, is not simply to understand metrical structure analytically but to be able to feel the rhythm of the verse without conscious effort as it is read or recited. (A practical advantage of this ability, and a test of it, is that one may, through simply noticing that a line does not scan, be alerted to some of the small misprints which plague many editions of Sanskrit texts.) While learning to master the rhythms of Sanskrit verse, there is no harm in exaggerating to any degree that is helpful the natural tendency in Sanskrit recitation to prolong and stress the heavy syllables.

The anuṣṭubh metre

This is the bread-and-butter metre of Sanskrit verse, comparable in function and importance with the Latin hexameter or the English iambic pentameter. As well as being frequently used in Classical poetry, it is the staple metre of Saṁskrit epic and of the many didactic works composed in verse. It is a simple, easily handled metre, since the pattern of light and heavy syllables is not fixed throughout the line.

As with other Sanskrit metres, a normal anuṣṭubh stanza is divisible into four quarters, called pādas. The word **pāda** literally means 'foot', and the latter word is therefore better avoided where possible in discussing Sanskrit versification, although in the case of the anuṣṭubh each pāda falls naturally for purposes of analysis into two groups of four syllables which might well be termed 'feet' in the English sense. The last group in each half-verse, i.e. the last group in the second and fourth pādas, consists of a double iambus: ⏑ – ⏑ –. Any of the preceding four syllables may in principle be either light or heavy. If we represent such a syllable of indeterminate quantity by o, the pattern of the second or fourth pāda is therefore o o o o ⏑ – ⏑ –. In the first and third pādas the pattern of the last two syllables is reversed, which gives o o o o ⏑ – – ⏑.

An anuṣṭubh stanza thus consists of two half-verses of sixteen syllables each and has the following basic rhythm (with the sign ´ indicating a rhythmically prominent syllable):

o o o o ⏑ –́ –́ ⏑ / o o o o ⏑ –́ ⏑ –́ |
o o o o ⏑ –́ –́ ⏑ / o o o o ⏑ –́ ⏑ –́ ||

The syncopation at the end of the first and third pādas gives a feeling of suspense which is resolved at the end of each half-verse.

There should be a caesura (a break between words—or sometimes a break between two members of a long compound) at the end of each pāda. But the break between the second and third pādas, i.e. at the half-verse, is stronger than that between first and second or third and fourth. Thus the break at the half-verse is treated for purposes of sandhi as the end of a sentence, whereas sandhi is obligatory at all points within the half-verse.

The scheme given above is subject to the following qualifications:

1 The final syllable of the second and fourth pādas (as in other metres) and also of the first and third pādas may, in fact, be either heavy or light. (It was given as above merely to emphasise the underlying rhythm.)

2 No pāda may begin o ⏑ ⏑ o (i.e. either the second or the third syllable must always be heavy).

3 The second or fourth pāda must not end ⏑ – ⏑ – ⏑ o (i.e. in three iambi).

4 The above pattern for the first or third pāda is the **pathyā** (regular) form. The less common **vipulā** (permitted) forms are given at the back of the book.

The first stanza of Exercise 15 scans as follows:

– – – ⏑ ⏑ – – – – – ⏑ ⏑ ⏑ – ⏑ –
e vaṃ vā di ni de var ṣau / pār śve pi tu ra dho mu khī|

– – ⏑ ⏑ ⏑ – – ⏑ ⏑ ⏑ – – ⏑ – ⏑ –
lī lā ka ma la pat trā ṇi / ga ṇa yā mā sa pār va tī||

Even (samacatuṣpadī) metres

In addition to the anuṣṭubh, Classical literature employs a wide range of more elaborate metres, some of the commoner of which are listed at the back of the book (pp. 310 ff.). In most of these, each pāda is identical and consists of a fixed pattern of light and heavy syllables normally between eleven and twenty-one in number. Thus the fourteen-syllabled Vasantatilakā metre, which has the pattern – – ⏑ – ⏑ ⏑ ⏑ – ⏑ ⏑ – ⏑ – – (if such a long 'unstructured' string seems daunting at first sight, it may be helpful, purely as an aid to learning, to think of it as made up of – –́ ⏑ –́ ⏑ ⏑ ⏑ –́ ⏑ ⏑ –́ ⏑ –́ –):

preyān manoratha-sahasra-vṛtaḥ sa eṣa,
supta ;pramatta:janam etad amātya-veśma |
prauḍhaṃ tamaḥ—kuru kṛtajñatay» aîva bhadram,
utkṣipta ;mūka:maṇi-nūpuram ehi yāmaḥ ||

(*A girl is persuaded to elope:*) Here is that lover wooed in a thousand dreams. Here is the minister's house where the people are asleep or inattentive. The darkness is thick. Simply from gratitude [do good:] treat your lover well. With jewelled anklets raised and muffled, come, let us be off.

Similarly, the nineteen-syllabled Śārdūlavikrīḍita, – – – ⏑ ⏑ – ⏑ – ⏑ ⏑ ⏑ – / – – ⏑ – – ⏑ – (or –́ – –́ ⏑ ⏑ –́ ⏑ –́ ⏑ ⏑ ⏑ –́ / – –́ ⏑ –́ –́ ⏑ –):

manda:kvāṇita:veṇur ahni śithile vyāvartayan go-kulaṃ
barh›-āpīḍakam uttamāṅga-racitaṃ go-dhūli-dhūm-raṃ dadhat |
mlāyantyā vana-mālayā parigataḥ śrānto ›pi ramy›: ākṛtir
gopa-strī-nayan›-ôtsavo vitaratu śreyāṃsi vaḥ Keśa-vaḥ ||

(*A benediction:*) Sounding his flute gently, driving the cattle back [the day being slack:] as the day declines, wearing [placed] on his head a crest of peacock feathers grey with the dust from the cows, encircled with a fading garland of wild flowers, though tired attractive to look at, a feast for the eyes of the cowherd girls, may Kṛṣṇa bestow blessings upon you

Many metres, particularly the longer ones, contain one or more fixed caesuras within the pāda. Thus in the Śārdūlavi-krīḍita there is always a break after the twelfth syllable, so that the final seven syllables form a separate rhythmical unit. The final syllable of the pāda in any of these metres is supposed to be heavy. A light syllable may, however, be substituted at the end of the half-verse or verse, since it is compensated for by the following pause. A light syllable at the end of the first or third pāda is not normal, but it is permissible in some metres, notably the Vasantatilakā.

The way to master any of these metres is simply to fix its rhythm in one's head. This may be achieved pleasantly enough by committing stanzas of Sanskrit poetry to memory. But for those who do not find it too arid, another possibility with practical advantages, which, of course, does not preclude the other method, is to memorise a Sanskrit definition of each metre. Such definitions can embody in a single pāda of the appropriate metre a statement of its metrical pattern, including any caesuras, and its name. The last is especially useful since it is all too easy to recognise a particular metre without remembering what it is called. (The name of a metre always fits somewhere into its metrical pattern, and may perhaps sometimes have been a phrase taken from an early example of the type.)

Sanskrit prosodists refer to a heavy syllable as **guru** 'heavy', or simply **g** or **ga**; and to a light syllable as **laghu** 'light', or simply **l** or **la**. They proceed to an economical analysis by similarly assigning a letter to each possible group of three syllables:

y ⏑ – –	**bh** – ⏑ ⏑	**m** – – –	**g** –
r – ⏑ –	**j** ⏑ – ⏑	**n** ⏑ ⏑ ⏑	**l** ⏑
t – – ⏑	**s** ⏑ ⏑ –		

(The value of these letters can be learnt by memorising them in the following pattern:

yamātārājabhānasalagāḥ

where each letter initiates its own pattern—**yamātā, mātārā, tārāja, rājabhā**, etc.)

Thus the definition of the Vasantatilakā, as given by Kedāra in his *Vṛttaratnākara*, is:

uktā Vasantatilakā ta ;bha ;jā ja ;gau gaḥ the Vasantatilakā is described as **t, bh** and **j**, (then) **j** and **g**, (then) **g** —i.e. – – ⏑, – ⏑ ⏑, ⏑ – ⏑, ⏑ – ⏑, –, –

The group of three syllables is, of course, in no sense a rhythmical unit, and the pāda is analysed continuously without reference to any caesura (**yati**). Caesuras are mentioned separately by a numerical grouping—e.g. the Śārdūlavikrīḍita is said to consist of twelve syllables plus seven. Symbolic numbers rather than the ordinary numerals are mostly used for this purpose (these symbolic numbers are found in other contexts in Sanskrit, for instance in verses giving dates). For the ordinary numeral there is substituted some noun frequently associated with that particular number (as if we were to say 'sin' for 'seven' in English because there are seven deadly sins). Thus **yuga** 'age of the world' means 'four'; **sūrya** 'sun' means 'twelve' (with reference to the signs of the zodiac); **aśva** 'horse' means 'seven' (because there were seven horses of the sun). Kedāra's definition of the Śārdūlavikrīḍita is:

> **sūry›;âśvair yadi māt sa;jau sa;ta;ta;gāḥ, Śārdūlavikrīḍitam** if, with twelve (syllables) plus seven, (there is) after **m** both **s** and **j**, (and then) **s**, **t**, **t** and **g**, (we have) the Śārdūlavikrīḍita

(The ablative to express 'after' is a grammarian's usage mentioned below.)

Semi-even (ardhasamacatuṣpadī) metres

There exists a number of metres which are not absolutely identical in each pāda, although each half-verse corresponds exactly. The commonest of these comprise a small family group in which the second or fourth pāda differs from the first or third simply by the insertion of an extra heavy syllable. Of these metres the Puṣpitāgrā is the most frequently occurring.

The Āryā metre

This metre, which was adopted into Sanskrit from more popular sources, differs fundamentally in structure from all the preceding. It is divided into feet (here the English term is appropriate and difficult to avoid), each of four **mātrās** in length. A **mātrā** 'mora' is a unit of prosodic length equivalent to a light syllable. Each foot (except the sixth) may therefore consist of ⏑ ⏑ ⏑ ⏑, – –, – ⏑ ⏑ or ⏑ ⏑ –; and the second, fourth and sixth may further take the form ⏑ – ⏑. A stanza is normally made up of two lines of seven and a half feet each, with the sixth foot of the second line consisting of a single light syllable. In its Classical Sanskrit use, the metre usually contains a caesura after the third foot in each line.

In this metre the rhythmical ictus often falls upon a light syllable, and it can be difficult when reading some Āryā stanzas to keep a proper grip on the rhythm and at the same time avoid an unnatural manner of recitation. The following example, however, flows smoothly.

gacchati puraḥ śarīraṃ, dhāvati paścād a:saṃsthitaṃ cetaḥ |
cīnāṃśukam iva ketoḥ prati_vātaṃ nīyamānasya ||

(as I think of the girl I have just parted from) my body moves forward, but my unsteady mind runs back, like the silk of a banner being carried into the wind

The Kumāra-saṃbhava of Kālidāsa

Kālidāsa, in almost every estimation the greatest of Sanskrit poets, wrote both plays and poems. Among the latter are two examples of the **mahā:kāvya** or major narrative poem, **Raghu-vaṃśa** 'The race of Raghu' and **Kumāra-saṃbhava** 'The birth of Kumāra'. Kumāra (lit. 'the Prince') is another name of Skanda or Kārttikeya, god of war and son of the mighty god Śiva. Cantos I to VIII of the poem (all that are regarded as genuinely the work of Kālidāsa) describe the events leading up to his birth, but stop short of the birth itself. The gods need a powerful general to defeat the demon Tāraka, and such a general will be born only from the union of Śiva with Pārvatī, the daughter of the mountain-god Himālaya. However, Śiva is a practising ascetic and has no thought of marriage. Kāma, the god of love, attempts to inflame Śiva's feelings and is reduced to ashes for his pains; but Pārvatī finally wins Śiva's love by becoming an ascetic herself and practising the severest austerities. Canto VI describes how Śiva sends the Seven Sages (accompanied by Arundhatī, wife of one of them) to ask Himālaya for his daughter's hand in marriage. The extract given in Exercise 15 begins just after the Sage Aṅgiras has conveyed this request.

Each canto of a mahākāvya is normally written in a single metre, with the exception of one or more closing verses. The metre used is either the anuṣṭubh or one of the shorter of the other metres, Indravajrā, Vaṃśastha, Viyoginī, etc. (but never the Āryā). The longer metres such as the Śārdūlavikrīḍita do not lend themselves to use in continuous narrative; and even with the shorter metres actually employed, the stanzaic structure, with each stanza a polished and self-contained unit, is one of the more striking features of such poetry. The concluding stanza or stanzas of each canto are written in a different and normally somewhat more elaborate metre: this is illustrated by the present extract, which extends to the end of the canto and closes with a Puṣpitāgrā stanza.

The extract has been chosen because it is a simple passage which illustrates both the anuṣṭubh metre and the perfect tense, but in its slight way it does also suggest some of the qualities of Kālidāsa's genius: his luminous and unerringly exact use of language, the mark of the great poet everywhere, and his ability to view human life and activity (here, the giving of a daughter in marriage) under a transfiguring sense of divine order—an ability sometimes superficially seen as a tendency to treat the gods in secular and sensual terms.

Here, as a preliminary guide to the general sense of the passage, is a comparatively free translation of it:

84 When the divine sage had spoken,
Pārvatī, at her father's side,
Keeping her face bent down began to count
The petals of the lotus she was playing with.

85 The Mountain, though he had all he could wish for,
Looked enquiringly at Menā.
For where his daughter is concerned
A man's eyes are his wife.

86 And Menā gave her assent
To all that her husband longed for.
The wishes of a devoted wife
Are never at odds with those of her husband.

87 Determining inwardly
The way he should reply,
When the speech was over
He took hold of his daughter, adorned for the happy occasion.

88 'Come, dearest child,
You are destined as alms for the Most High.
The Sages themselves are here to sue for you.
My life as a householder has found its fulfilment.'

89 Having said this much to his child
The Mountain spoke to the Sages:
'The bride of the Three-eyed God
Herewith salutes you all.'

90 Joyfully the sages acknowledged
The noble generosity of these words,
And bestowed upon Ambā
Blessings that would immediately be fulfilled.

91 She, in her anxiety to do them homage,
Displaced the golden ornaments at her ears,
And as she showed her confusion
Arundhatī took her upon her lap,

92 And the mother, whose face was full of tears,
Made anxious by love for her daughter,
She reassured about the merits of that bridegroom,
Who had no other to make prior claims on him.

93 When Śiva's father-in-law
Had consulted them upon the wedding-date,
And they had answered it should be three davs hence,
The sages departed.

94 After taking their leave of Himālaya
They returned to the Trident-holder,
Announced the success of their mission,
And, dismissed by him, flew up to heaven.

95 And the Lord of Creatures passed those days with difficulty,
Longing for union with the Mountain's daughter.
When even our Lord is not immune from such feelings,
What ordinary, helpless man can escape the torments?

In stanza 87 'adorned for the happy occasion' refers to the occasion of the Sages' visit; but by a literary resonance it hints also at the coming occasion of the wedding. In stanza 92 the compound **ananyapūrva**, as well as meaning (as Mallinātha takes it) 'not having another more senior wife', is a pun meaning 'having none other than Pārvatī herself as a previous wife'—a reference to the fact that Śiva's earlier wife Satī was a previous incarnation of Pārvatī. (I am indebted to Dr. Wendy O'Flaherty for both these observations.)

Mallinātha's commentary

The extract from the Kumāra-saṃbhava is accompanied by a commentary upon it by the medieval scholar Mallinātha, the author of standard commentaries on Kālidāsa's two other main non-dramatic works, as well as on the mahākāvyas of other Sanskrit poets. His work is an excellent example of the more literal type of Sanskrit commentary, which expounds the original text by means of a continuous close verbal paraphrase. It is an interesting reflection of the structure of the Classical language and the difficulties of Classical literary style that such a word-for-word paraphrase should be worth making. The style of such commentaries should be mastered, since when they are by good scholars they are an extremely important aid in the interpretation of Classical texts. It should also be noted that many major works by writers on philosophical and other subjects are, formally speaking, commentaries upon earlier texts (or even upon some more succinctly expressed version of the writer's own views) and exhibit certain peculiarities of style deriving from this fact. The following remarks, although concerned primarily with the present extract from Mallinātha, should be of some help in the interpretation of commentaries in general.

The basis of the commentatorial style is oral exposition, and the simplest starting-point in understanding Mallinātha is to imagine him as a teacher sitting with a manuscript of the original text in front of him. He reads out or recites from memory—inevitably the latter, had he been expounding Pāṇini or the Vedas—the portion of the original, normally one stanza, which he is about to explain. (This is indicated in the written text of the commentary by the first word of the original followed by **iti**: thus in Exercise 15 **evam iti** means 'the portion beginning with the word **evam**', i.e. stanza 84.) He then goes back and takes the words one at a time or in small phrases, selecting them in the order most convenient for exposition and resolving sandhi as necessary.

As he takes up each word or phrase, he follows it with a literal equivalent, unless he considers it too obvious for helpful paraphrase. This habit of making paraphrase (or 'gloss') the rule rather than the exception is a useful one. It may seem pointless at times: on stanza 92 it is hardly likely to help anyone to be told that **duhitṛ-snehena** means **putrikā-premṇā.** But this is a small price to pay for the advantage of having a check on the interpretation of passages which are not so obvious as they seem at first sight.

The commentary is often unobtrusively helpful in analysing compounds by resolving them into separate words. When this is done the compound is frequently not quoted in its original form in the commentary. Thus in 88 **gṛhamedhi-phalam** 'reward of a householder' occurs only as **gṛhamedhinaḥ phalam** (with **gṛhamedhinaḥ** glossed as **gṛhasthasya**). When the original form of the compound *is* quoted, it tends to appear after the analysis: e.g. 92 **tasyāḥ . . . mātaram tan-mātaram.** This forms an exception to the general principle that the paraphrase is placed after the original. (In the transliterated version of Exercise 15 any direct gloss is placed in parentheses, and a colon is placed between the gloss and the original—i.e. normally immediately before the gloss, sometimes immediately after.) The practice serves to 're-establish' an original form after analysis and is commoner with less straightforward compounds such as bahuvrīhis: e.g. 92 (**aśrūṇi mukhe yasyās tām:**) **aśrumukhīm.** Even in such cases the original compound may be replaced by a phrase like **tath» ôktaḥ** '(being one) so described': thus in 85 **gṛhiṇī:netrāḥ** 'having a wife as one's eye' appears as **gṛhiṇy eva netram . . . yeṣāṃ te tath» ôktāḥ** 'of whom the eye is in fact the wife—those such' (the particle **eva** serving, as frequently, to distinguish the predicate).

The formula **yathā tathā** is used to indicate adverbial value. Thus if **śīghram** has the meaning 'swiftly', this may be made clear by the gloss **śīghraṃ yathā tathā** 'in such a way as to be swift'.

While bahuvrīhi compounds are regularly analysed by means of relative clauses, the analysis of other formations is generally by means of an **iti** clause, with the relative pronoun replaced by **ayam** (or, in the nominative case, omitted): e.g. **balam asy› âst› îti balī** 'the word **balin** means ["this has strength":] "that which has strength" '; **pacyata iti pākaḥ** 'the word **pāka** means ["it is cooked":] "that which is cooked" '.

As in the above examples (**balī, pākaḥ**), a formation to be analysed is normally mentioned in the nominative case. The formation is thereafter 'picked up', and if necessary returned to the appropriate oblique case, by means of the pronoun **saḥ**. The discussion of **an:anya:pūrvasya** in stanza 92 illustrates the use of **saḥ** and also of the relative clause and the **iti** clause:

1 **anyā pūrvaṃ yasy› âsti so ›nya:pūrvaḥ** '**anya:pūrva** means "one who has another (woman) as a prior (claim)" '.

2 **sa na bhavat› îty an:anya:pūrvaḥ** '**an:anya:pūrva** means "one who is not **anya:pūrva**" '.

3 **tasya an:anya:pūrvasya** 'this latter formation when placed in the genitive singular provides (the word contained in the text, namely) **an:anya:pūrvasya**'.

The present participle of **as**, **sant**, is often inserted in the course of exegesis and serves to distinguish attributive words from the substantive they qualify: so in stanza 84 **adhomukhī satī** '(Pārvatī counted the petals) being downward-gazing (as she did so)'. The phrase **tathā hi** 'for thus' indicates that the following portion of the text is an explanation or amplification of the preceding.

The syntactical structure of the original text provides a framework for the commentary, but syntactical continuity is frequently interrupted by the insertion of explanatory remarks (such asides being natural in a spoken exposition.) One type of insertion, that occasioned by detailed grammatical analysis, has already been touched upon. In the same way the word-for-word gloss may be interrupted by a freer paraphrase of the preceding words, followed by **ity arthaḥ** 'such is the meaning', 'in other words . . .', or **iti bhāvaḥ** 'such is the essence or implication', 'i.e. . . ., that is . . .'. **iti yāvat** 'which is as much as to say', 'in fact' is especially used where something is glossed in terms of a simpler or more precise concept which might not have occurred to the reader. Where something is to be supplied in the original, this is indicated by **iti śeṣaḥ** 'such is the remainder', 'understand . . .'.

Quotations and opinions from other authors are indicated by **iti** plus the name of the writer or the work. The use made of Pāṇini's rules in explaining grammatical forms is discussed below. Lexicons are also appealed to. The oldest and most reliable of these is the Amarakoṣa by Amara or Amarasiṃha (written in verse, for ease of memorisation). Lexicons make continual use of the locative case in a technical meaning of 'in the sense of'. Thus **udāro dātṛ;mahatoḥ**, quoted under stanza 90, means '(the word) **udāra** (occurs) in (the sense of) **dātṛ** or **mahānt**'.

The use of punctuation and sandhi in commentary style is naturally different from their use in a normal text. The daṇḍa may be used at any 'pause for breath' and separates the asides from the mainstream of the commentary. The following policy on sandhi has been adopted in editing the present extract: no sandhi has been made between the words of the text quoted directly in the commentary and the surrounding words of Mallinātha himself, and similarly none before **iti** where this marks a quotation by Mallinātha from any other author.

Pāṇinian grammar

When Mallinātha considers a form worthy of grammatical analysis, he explains it by quoting the relevant rules of Pāṇini's grammar. For the non-specialist, in fact, the operation of the Pāṇinian system can be studied more enjoyably in a literary commentator such as Mallinātha, where its application to the normal forms of the language can be observed, than in the commentaries upon Pāṇini himself, which are frequently concerned with *recherché* forms and complex theoretical considerations. A brief explanation of the references to Pāṇini in Exercise 15 may help to give a first faint inkling of how his grammar works.

Pāṇini's sūtras, or aphoristic rules, are formed with the greatest possible succinctness. They are arranged in such a way that they frequently depend for their understanding upon the statements made in the sūtras immediately preceding, and have indeed in principle to be interpreted in the light of all the other sūtras in the grammar. The suffixes which combine with word bases to form actual words are abstractions just as the verbal roots are. Thus the causative–denominative suffix is treated as having the basic form **i**, which by the operation of various sūtras changes to **ay** and combines with the inflexional endings. Systematic use is made of anubandhas, 'indicatory letters' attached to these suffixes. Thus the past participle suffix is known as **kta**, the **k** indicating that the preceding stem appears in its weak form. The causative–denominative is similarly known as **ṇi**: the **ṇ** permits the vṛddhi of a root such as **kṛ** in **kārayati**, while other sūtras ensure other grades of the root where necessary. The **ṇ** also serves to distinguish **ṇi** from other **i** suffixes, such as **śi** the neuter plural ending (**kāntāni, manāṃsi**, etc.) or the Vedic **ki** as in **papi** 'drinking'. The compound-final suffix **ṭac** referred to in sūtra 5.4.91 is one of a host of **a** suffixes: the **ṭ** indicates that the feminine is in **ī**, and the **c** that the accent is on the final. These artificial words are inflected like ordinary stems of the language, so that **ṇi** is a substantive in short **i** (gen. **neḥ**, loc. **ṇau**) and **ṭac** is a consonant stem. But **ṭac** illustrates the fact that certain sounds may occur in final position in made-up words that are not so found in the natural words of the language.

The cases are used in technical senses: the ablative to signify 'after', the locative 'before', the genitive 'for, in place of', while the substitute which is put 'in place' is expressed in the nominative. It is as if one were to say 'after *child* for *s* (there is) *ren*' to express the irregular plural of *child*; or 'for *soft* (there is) *sof* before *en*' to indicate that the *t* of *soften* is not pronounced. To describe the sandhi of *the* mentioned in Chapter 2, we may (if we select *ði* as the basic form) say 'for *ði* (there is) *ə* before consonants'. It is not necessary to say in full '(there is) *ðə*', since (with certain qualifications) it is a principle of interpreting Pāṇinian rules that a single-letter substitute is to be treated as replacing only the final letter of the original.

The first sūtra which Mallinātha quotes, Pāṇini 7.3.43, illustrates this last point. It concerns the fact that the causative of **ruh** 'ascend' may take the form **ropayati** as well as the regular **rohayati**. It runs **ruhaḥ po ›nyatarasyām**. From an earlier sūtra (7.3.36) the word **ṇau** 'before **ṇi**' is to be supplied. **ruhaḥ** is the genitive of **ruh**. **anyatarasyām** means 'optionally'. The sūtra therefore means 'before the causative suffix, for (the final **h** of) **ruh**, **p** is substituted optionally'.

The discussion of the word **try:ahaḥ** 'period of three days' in stanza 93 is more complex. It may be observed in passing that such compounds, which correspond to the English 'a fortnight', 'a twelvemonth', are best looked on as having exocentric value—'that (period) in which there are fourteen nights/twelve months'. But Sanskrit grammarians include them in a special class called **dvigu** 'numerical compound', which is treated as a sub-variety of tatpuruṣa.

Mallinātha begins by quoting 2.1.51 **taddhit›:ârth›; ôttarapada;samāhāre ca. samān›:âdhikaraṇena** must be supplied from 2.1.49, which states that certain words may combine 'with (another word) having the same case relationship' to form a compound. This is a way of saying that they may be prefixed with adjectival or appositional value to another word so as to form a descriptive determinative. **dik;saṃkhye** must be supplied from 2.1.50, which deals with the fact that '(words denoting) either region or number' combine in the same type of compound to express various proper names. The present sūtra thus says that words expressing region or number may compound with a word having the same case relationship 'in the following further circumstances (**ca**): to express the sense of a **taddhita** (secondary suffix), or when there is a further member (added to the compound), or to express collective sense'. The first two possibilities will not be discussed since they are not relevant here. In **tryahaḥ** we have the numeral **tri** 'three' combining with **ahan** 'day' to express the sense 'collection consisting of three days'. The locative **samāhâre** does not here have its sense of 'before' but its other technical sense of 'in the sense of' as used in lexicons.

The following sūtra, 2.1.52, not quoted by Mallinātha, says **saṃkhyā:pūrvo dviguḥ**, i.e. 'the name **dvigu** is given to a compound (of one of these three kinds) when the first member is a numeral'. (This explains why Pāṇini did not make 2.1.50 and 2.1.51 a single sūtra: the name dvigu does *not* apply to a compound like **sapta:rṣayaḥ** (nom. pl.) 'the Seven Sages', the Sanskrit name for the Great Bear.)

Although the word **ahan** 'day' is a consonant stem, **tryahaḥ** is an **a**-stem. Mallinātha quotes 5.4.91 **rāj›;âhaḥ;sakhi-bhyaṣ ṭac**. This is governed by 5.4.68 **samās›-ântāḥ** 'the following suffixes (down to the end of Book 5, in fact) are compound-final'. The sūtra thus means 'after the words **rājan**, **ahan** and **sakhi** there occurs as a compound-final suffix **ṭac**'.

Mallinātha does not bother to quote 6.4.145 **ahnaṣ ṭa;khor eva**, which shows how to apply this last rule. The words **lopaḥ** 'elision', i.e. 'zero-substitution', and **ṭeḥ** 'in place of **ṭi**' are to be supplied. **ṭi** is a technical term meaning 'the final vowel of a word plus the following consonant if any'. The sūtra therefore means 'zero is substituted for the final vowel and consonant of **ahan**, but only before a suffix with indicatory ṭ or **kha**'. Thus **ahan+ṭac** becomes **ah+ṭac**, i.e. **aha.**

Mallinātha refers to, without actually quoting, 2.4.1 **dvigur ekavacanam** 'dvigu compounds are singular'; and finally justifies the masculine gender of **tryahaḥ** (though Kālidāsa only uses the ambiguous ablative form **tryahāt**) by 2.4.29 **rātr›;âhn›;âhāḥ puṃsi.** From 2.4.26 **dvandva;tatpuruṣayoḥ** is supplied: 'the words **rātra, ahna** and **aha** (used at the end of a co-ordinative or determinative compound) occur in the masculine'.

To summarise the above:

tri+ahan means 'group of three days' by 2.1.51
the compound takes the suffix **ṭac** by 5.4.91
ahan+ṭac becomes **aha** by 6.4.145
the compound is a dvigu by 2.1.52
and therefore singular by 2.4.1
and masculine by 2.4.29.

Sūtra 5.2.80 **utka unmanāḥ** is interesting as an example of **nipātaḥ**, a formation listed ready-made by Pāṇini without justification in terms of its components. **utka** 'eager' is listed among formations made with the suffix **kan**, but is anomalous both because **kan** is added not to a nominal stem but to the prefix **ut** and because its meaning, which refers to a mental state, it is not fully explicable from its elements. Pāṇini thus lists it as a special form and gives its meaning. The word **nipātaḥ** is better known in the sense of 'particle', a meaning it acquires because particles exist ready-made without undergoing grammatical formation.

Lastly, in his comment on stanza 87 Mallinātha shows his knowledge of Pāṇini's analysis of the word **nyāyya** 'proper'. Sūtra 4.4.92, **dharmapathyarthanyāyād anapete,** teaches that the **taddhita** suffix **yat,** whose real form is **ya,** is added to the forms **dharma, pathin** (the stem form of **panthan** as analysed by the Sanskrit grammarians), **artha** and **nyāya** in order to form words which mean 'not departed from **dharma**', etc.

Although Mallinātha does not quote Pāṇini exactly, his gloss of the word **nyāyyam** as **nyāyād anapetam** echoes the relevant sūtra.

Quotations from literary critics

Besides citing grammarians and lexicographers, Mallinātha quotes from many other sources, including popular sayings and works on right conduct (dharma-śāstra) or political science (nīti-śāstra), and in particular from many literary critics. He seldom gives the name of the work he is quoting from, and sometimes when he does so the attribution is wrong. It may be assumed that his quotations are normally made from memory.

Sanskrit literary criticism as it is known from about the ninth century onward is the development of an earlier alaṃkāra-śāstra 'Science of Embellishment' in combination with certain elements of nāṭya-śāstra 'Theatrical Science'. The term alaṃkāra 'ornament, embellishment' is wider than the English 'figure of speech' and somewhat different in scope. It includes almost all the usages by means of which a poet's language departs from the most colourless possible presentation of facts and ideas, and covers devices of sound such as assonance and rhyme as well as devices of sense such as simile and metaphor. In addition to the alaṃkāras proper, various possible 'Qualities' (guṇas) are enumerated. Mallinātha observes that stanza 94 illustrates the Quality known as Conciseness (saṃkṣepa) and quotes a rather tautologous definition of this Quality from a work called the Pratāparudrīya. An examination of the stanza will indeed show that Kālidāsa's telescoping of the narrative at this point is sufficiently marked and deliberate to be considered a literary device.

Although Mallinātha does not bother to point the fact out, the second half of stanza 85 (like the second half of 86, which is parallel) illustrates a common rhetorical figure known as arthāntaranyāsa 'Substantiation' or 'Corroboration'. In its most typical form, as here, it consists of a general reflection provoked by the particular facts of the situation that is being described, and is frequently signalled by the presence of a word such as **prāyeṇa** 'generally'. The figure thus has the flavour of 'moral-drawing', There is a similar flavour to the second half of stanza 95, but here, as Mallinātha points out, the precise figure involved is arthāpatti 'Strong Presumption', i.e. reasoning *a fortiori*.

From nāṭya-śāstra literary critics adopted the theory of rasa (lit. 'flavour, taste'), which in its most developed form is a subtle theory of the nature of aesthetic experience. Its basis is the division of the spectator's experience of a play into a number of 'flavours' (at first eight, later usually nine)—comic, horrific, etc. To each of these rasas corresponds a basic human emotion (**sthāyi:bhāva** 'Stable or Dominant State'), which will normally be represented in one or more of the characters of the drama. Around the basic emotion various minor emotions come fleetingly into play—the thirty-three Transitory or Subordinate States, called either **vyabhicāri:bhāva** or **saṃcāri:bhāva.** Thus in the Amorous or Romantic rasa (**śṛṅgāra**) the hero and heroine feel the sthāyibhāva of Love (**rati**) and the vyabhicāribhāvas of Impatience, Disappointment, Contentedness and so on. Mallinātha points out that stanza 84 illustrates the vyabhicāribhāva of Dissimulation (**avahittha** or **avahitthā**). In fact, this stanza is the one most quoted in textbooks as an example of this particular State.

Vocabulary

aṅkaḥ hook; curve of the body, lap
Aṅgiras *m., pr. n.*
aṅgī˘kṛ make a part, subordinate; adopt, accept, promise
adri *m.* rock, mountain
adho:mukha (*f.* **ī**) downfaced, with face bent down
antaraṃ interval, difference; **-antaraṃ** *ifc.* a different, another
anyatarasyām (*gram.*) optionally
apara *pron. adj.* other
apūpaḥ cake: *see* **daṇḍāpūpikā**
apeta departed; free from (*abl.*)

abhīpsita desired; **abhīpsitaṃ** thing desired, desire
Amaraḥ, Amarasiṃhaḥ *pr. n., author of the lexicon* **Amara-kośaḥ**
Ambā, Ambikā *pr. n., the wife of Śiva*
arth›-ântara-nyāsaḥ (*lit. crit.*) Substantiation
arth›-āpatti *f.* (*lit. crit.*) Strong Presumption
alaṃkāraḥ ornament; (*lit. crit.*) embellishment, literary figure
a:vaśa powerless, helpless
avahitthaṃ, avahitthā dissimulation
aśru *n.* tear; **aśru:mukha** 'tear-faced', tearful-faced
ahan *n. irreg.* day
-ahaḥ, -ahnaḥ (*ifc. for* **ahan**) day
ākāraḥ form, appearance, (facial) expression
ākāśaṃ ether, sky
āpatanaṃ occurrence, (sudden) appearance, arising
āpatti *f.* happening, occurrence
āśis *f. irreg.* prayer, benediction
āśīrvādaḥ blessing, benison
āsakti *f.* adherence, intentness (on)
itara *pron. adj.* other
iṣṭaṃ thing wished, wish
īpsita desired, wished for
utka eager, longing for
uttara following, subsequent, further; **uttaraṃ** answer
udāra noble, generous
un:manas eager, longing
eka-vacanaṃ (*gram.*) singular (number)
kanakaṃ gold
kamala *m. n.* lotus
karaṇaṃ doing, performing
kavi *m.* poet, creative writer
kāraṇaṃ instrument, means
kuṭumbaṃ household, family
kuṭumbin *m.* householder, family man
kuṇḍalaṃ earring, ear-ornament
kṛcchraṃ hardship; **kṛcchrāt** with difficulty
kaimutika deriving from the notion **kim uta** 'let alone'; **kaimutika:nyāyāt** [from the principle of 'let alone':] *a fortiori*
khaṃ hole; vacuum; sky, heaven
gaḥ the letter **g**; (*in prosody*) heavy syllable
gaṇanā counting
gārhasthyaṃ being a householder
giri *m.* mountain
gṛhamedhin [performer of domestic sacrifices:] householder
gṛha-sthaḥ one who is in a house, householder
gṛhiṇī housewife, wife
gopanaṃ concealment, hiding
caturtha (*f.* **ī**) fourth
cīraṃ strip of bark (worn by ascetic)
jaḥ the letter **j**; (*in prosody*) the syllables ⏑ – ⏑
jāmbūnada (*f.* **ī**) golden
jijñāsā desire to know, wish to determine
jñānaṃ knowledge, perceiving
ṭac (*gram.*) the suffix **a**
tat:kṣaṇam at that moment, thereupon
taddhitaḥ [*i.e.* **tat-hitaḥ** 'suitable for that'] (*gram.*) secondary suffix
tanayā daughter

tāraka causing to cross over, rescuing, liberating
tithi *m.f.* lunar day (*esp. as auspicious* date *for ceremony*)
tri three
tri:locanaḥ the Three-eyed (god), Śiva
Tryambakaḥ *name of Śiva*
try:ahaḥ [period of] three days
daṇḍāpūpikā the stick-and-cake principle ('if a mouse eats a stick he'll certainly eat a cake'), reasoning *a fortiori*
dalaṃ petal
dātṛ giver, granting
dānaṃ gift, bestowal
dvigu *m.* [from **dvi:gu** 'worth two cows'] (*gram.*) numerical compound
naḥ the letter **n**; (*in prosody*) the syllables ᴗ ᴗ ᴗ
namas-kāraḥ making obeisance
nipātaḥ (*gram.*) ready-made form (laid down without grammatical analysis)
niścayaḥ determination, resolve
nyāyaḥ rule, principle; propriety
paḥ, pa-kāraḥ the letter **p**
pattraṃ feather; leaf, petal
padaṃ word, member of a compound
para:tantra under another's control, not in control (of)
pariṇayaḥ marriage
:paryanta [having as an end:] ending with, up to
Paśupati *m. name of Śiva*
pākaḥ cooking; ripeness, fulfilment
Pārvatī *pr. n. wife of Śiva*
pārśvaṃ flank, side
pitṛ *m.* father
puṃ:liṅga having masculine gender
puṃvant (*gram.*) masculine
puṃs *m.* (*irreg.*) man, male, masculine
putrī, putrikā daughter
puraskṛta placed in front, before the eyes
puṣpitāgrā (*in prosody*) *name of a metre*
pṛthag:janaḥ separate person, ordinary person
praṇāmaḥ salutation
pratyayaḥ (*gram.*) suffix
:pradhāna having as one's authority
preman *m. n.* affection
bandhu *m.* kinsman
buddhi *f.* intelligence, mind
bhartṛ *m.* husband
bhāvaḥ state of being; essence, meaning; emotional state, emotion
bhikṣā alms
bhīta afraid
mahīdharaḥ mountain
mṛtyuṃ-jayaḥ Conqueror of Death
Menā *pr. n. Pārvatī's mother*
ya-kāraḥ the letter **y**; (*in prosody*) the syllables ᴗ – –
yācitṛ *m.* suer, petitioner
yukti *f.* argument
yugaṃ pair; *ifc.* two
yuj joined, even (in number); **a:yuj** uneven, odd
yogya suitable
raḥ the letter **r**; (*in prosody*) the syllables – ᴗ –
rātraḥ *at the end of compound for* **rātri** *f.* night
ruh the root **ruh**
rephaḥ = **raḥ**
lakṣaṇaṃ mark, characteristic; definition

liṅgaṃ mark, sign; phallus; (*gram.*) gender
līlā play, sport
vacas *n.* word, words, speech
vataṃsaḥ/vataṃsakaḥ ornament, *esp.* earring
vadhū *f.* woman, bride
varaḥ suitor
valkala *m. n.* bark (of tree)
vaśaḥ power; **-vaśāt** from the power of, because of
vasanaṃ dress
vākyaṃ utterance
vikāraḥ transformation; mental disturbance; *ifc.* made out of
vipratipanna perplexed, uncertain; **a:vipratipanna** not uncertain, entirely fixed
vibhu powerful, *esp. as an epithet of Śiva*
vilambaḥ delay
vivāhaḥ wedding
vi꞉śoka free from sorrow, at ease
viśvɔ-ātman *m.* Soul of the Universe, Supreme Godhead
viṣayaḥ dominion, sphere, field of action
vistaraḥ expansion, prolixity
vṛttaṃ metre
vṛtti *f.* behaviour, conduct; (*gram.*) synthetic expression (*by compounding, as opp. analytic expression by separate words*)
vaivāhika (*f.* **ī**) (suitable) for a wedding
voḍhṛ bridegroom
vyabhicāraḥ deviation, swerving
vyabhicārin liable to deviate, swerving; **a:vyabhicārin** unswerving
vyājaḥ fraud, pretence
Śivaḥ *pr. n.*
śūlin Trident-bearer, *epithet of Śiva*
śeṣaḥ remainder, portion to be supplied
śailaḥ mountain
ślokaḥ stanza
saṃketaḥ agreement, assignation; **saṃketa-sthānaṃ** place of assignation
saṃkṣipta abbreviated, in concise form
saṃkṣepaḥ conciseness
saṃcārin going together, transitory; **saṃcārī bhāvaḥ** (*lit. crit.*) Subsidiary Emotional State
samarthanaṃ establishment, confirmation
samāsaḥ (*gram.*) compound
samāhāraḥ group, collection
saṃpūrṇa fulfilled
sarva-nāman *n.*(*gram.*) [name for anything:] pronoun
sāpatnyaṃ the state of being the sharer of a husband (**sapatnī**)
siddha accomplished
sūtraṃ aphorism, aphoristic rule
stambaḥ clump of grass
-stha standing, being at/in *etc.*
Smara-haraḥ the Destroyer of Love, *epithet of Śiva*
Haraḥ *name of Śiva*
Himavant *m.*, **Himālayaḥ** the mountain (range) Himālaya

anu+yuj (VII **anuyuṅkte**) question, examine

alam+kṛ (VIII **alaṃkaroti**) adorn, embellish

ah (*defective verb, perf.* **āha**) say, speak

ā+pat (I **āpatati**) occur, befall, appear suddenly, present oneself

ā+prach (VI **āpṛcchati**) take leave of, say goodbye

ā+mantr (X **āmantrayate**) salute; take leave of

ā+ruh *caus.* (**āropayati**) cause to mount, raise onto

ut+īkṣ (I **udīkṣate**) look at

ut+yā (II **udyāti**) rise up

upa+īkṣ (I **upekṣate**) overlook, disregard

edh *caus.* (**edhayati**) cause to prosper, bless

gaṇ (X **gaṇayati**) count

gup (*denom. pres.* **gopāyati**) guard; hide

car (I **carati**) move, go, depart

cal (I **calati**) stir, move, go away

jñā *caus.* (**jñāpayati**) inform, announce

nam (I **namati**) bow, salute

nis+ci (V **niścinoti**) ascertain, settle, fix upon

nis+pad (IV **niṣpadyate**) come forth, be brought about; *p.p.* **niṣpanna** completed

pac (I **pacati**) cook, ripen; *pass.* **pacyate** be cooked, ripen

pari+kīrt (X **parikīrtayati**) proclaim, declare

pari+kḷp *caus.* (**parikalpayati**) fix, destine for (*dat.*)

pra+āp (V **prāpnoti**) reach, go to; obtain, win

bhī (III **bibheti**) fear; *p.p.* **bhīta** afraid

yā (II **yāti**) go

yā *caus.* (**yāpayati**) spend (time)

lajj (VI **lajjate**) be shy, blush, show confusion

vi+kṛ (VIII **vikaroti**) alter, change, distort, cause mental disturbance (**vikāraḥ**) to

vid (VI **vindati**) find; *pass.* **vidyate** is found, exists

vi+pra+kṛ (VIII **viprakaroti**) injure, torment

vi+mṛś (VI **vimṛśati**) perceive, reflect, deliberate

sam+vṛdh *caus.* (**saṃvardhayati**) congratulate

sam+stu (II **saṃstauti**) praise

sam+khyā (II **saṃkhyāti**) count, reckon up

sah (I **sahate**; *irreg. inf.* **soḍhum**) withstand, endure, bear

sūc (X **sūcayati**) point out, indicate

sraṃs (I **sraṃsate**; *p.p.* **srasta**) drop, slip

upari after (*abl.*)

ūrdhvam after (*abl.*)

ehi (*imperv. of* **ā+i**) come

paratra elsewhere, in the next world

puraḥ in front, immediate

yasmāt inasmuch as, since

Exercise 15

Note: The transliterated version of this exercise should be of particular help in solving difficulties.

एवंवादिनि देवर्षौ पार्श्वे पितुरधोमुखी ।
लीलाकमलपत्त्राणि गणयामास पार्वती ॥ ८४ ॥

एवमिति ॥ देवर्षौ अङ्गिरसि एवंवादिनि सति पार्वती पितुः पार्श्वे अधोमुखी सती । लज्जयेति शेषः । लीलाकमलपत्त्राणि गणयामास संचख्यौ । लज्जावशात्कमलदलगणनाव्याजेन हर्षं जुगोपेत्यर्थः । अनेनावहित्याख्यः संचारी भाव उक्तः । तदुक्तम्— अवहित्या तु लज्जादेर्हर्षाद्याकारगोपनमिति ॥

शैलः संपूर्णकामो ऽपि मेनामुखमुदैक्षत ।
प्रायेण गृहिणीनेत्राः कन्यार्थेषु कुटुम्बिनः ॥ ८५ ॥

शैल इति ॥ शैलः हिमवान् संपूर्णकामो ऽपि । दातुं कृतनिश्चयो ऽपीत्यर्थः । मेनामुखमुदैक्षत । उचितोत्तरजिज्ञासयेति भावः । तथा हि । प्रायेण कुटुम्बिनः गृहस्थाः कन्यार्थेषु कन्याप्रयोजनेषु गृहिण्येव नेत्रं कार्यज्ञानकारणं येषां ते तथोक्ताः । कलत्र-प्रधानवृत्तय इत्यर्थः ॥

मेने मेनापि तत्सर्वं पत्युः कार्यमभीप्सितम् ।
भवन्त्यव्यभिचारिण्यो भर्तुरिष्टे पतिव्रताः ॥ ८६ ॥

मेन इति ॥ मेनापि पत्युः हिमालयस्य तत्सर्वमभीप्सितं कार्यं मेने अङ्गीचकार । तथा हि । पतिरिव व्रतं यासां ताः भर्तुरिष्टे अभीप्सिते न विद्यते व्यभिचारो यासां ताः अव्यभिचारिण्यो भवन्ति । भर्तृचित्ताभिप्रायज्ञा भवन्तीति भावः ॥

इदमत्रोत्तरं न्याय्यमिति बुद्ध्या विमृश्य सः ।
आददे वचसामन्ते मङ्गलालंकृतां सुताम् ॥ ८७ ।

इदमिति ॥ सः हिमवान् वचसामन्ते मुनिवाक्यावसाने अत्र

मुनिवाक्ये इदम् उत्तरश्लोके वक्ष्यमाणं दानमेव न्याय्यम् न्यायादनपेतम् उत्तरमिति बुद्ध्या चित्तेन विमृश्य विचिन्त्य मङ्गलं यथा तथालंकृतां मङ्गलालंकृतां सुतामाददे हस्ताभ्यां जग्राह ॥

एहि विश्वात्मने वत्से भिक्षासि परिकल्पिता ।
अर्थिनो मुनयः प्राप्तं गृहमेधिफलं मया ॥ ८८ ॥

एहीति ॥ हे वत्से पुत्रि एहि आगच्छ । त्वं विश्वात्मने शिवाय भिक्षा परिकल्पितासि निश्चितासि । रत्नादि स्तम्बपर्यन्तं सर्वं भिक्षा तपस्विनः इति वचनादिति भावः । अर्थिनः याचितारः मुनयः । मया गृहमेधिनः गृहस्थस्य फलं प्राप्तम् । इह परत्र च तारकत्वात्पात्रे कन्यादानं गार्हस्थ्यस्य फलमित्यर्थः ॥

एतावदुक्त्वा तनयामृषीनाह महीधरः ।
इयं नमति वः सर्वांस्त्रिलोचनवधूरिति ॥ ८९ ॥

एतावदिति ॥ महीधरः हिमवान् तनयाम् एतावत् पूर्वोक्तम् उक्त्वा ऋषीन् आह । किमिति । इयं त्रिलोचनवधूः त्र्यम्बकपत्नी वः सर्वान् नमति इति । त्रिलोचनवधूरिति सिद्धवदभिधानेनाविप्रतिपन्नं दानमिति सूचयति ॥

ईप्सितार्थक्रियोदारं ते ऽभिनन्द्य गिरेर्वचः ।
आशीर्भिरेधयामासुः पुरःपाकाभिरम्बिकाम् ॥ ९० ॥

ईप्सितार्थेति ॥ ते मुनयः ईप्सितार्थक्रियया इष्टार्थकरणेन उदारं महत् । उदारो दातृमहतोः इत्यमरः । गिरेः हिमवतः वचः वचनम् अभिनन्द्य साध्विति संस्तुत्य । अम्बिकाम् अम्बाम् । पच्यत इति पाकः फलम् । पुरःपाकाभिः पुरस्कृतफलाभिः आशीर्भिः आशीर्वादैः एधयामासुः संवर्धयामासुः ॥

तां प्रणामादरस्रस्तजाम्बूनदवतंसकाम् ।
अङ्कमारोपयामास लज्जमानामरुन्धती ॥ ९१ ॥

तामिति ॥ प्रणामादरेण नमस्कारासक्त्या स्रस्ते जाम्बूनदे सुवर्ण-

विकारे वतंसके कनककुण्डले यस्यास्तां लज्जमानां ताम् अम्बिकाम् अरुन्धती अङ्कमारोपयामास। रुहः पो ऽन्यतरस्याम् इति पकारः॥

तन्मातरं चाश्रुमुखीं दुहितृस्नेहविक्लवाम्।
वरस्यानन्यपूर्वस्य विशोकामकरोद्गुणैः॥ ९२॥

तदिति॥ दुहितृस्नेहेन पुत्रिकाप्रेम्णा विक्लवां वियोक्ष्यत इति भीताम्। अत एवाश्रूणि मुखे यस्यास्ताम् अश्रुमुखीं तस्याः अम्बिकायाः मातरं तन्मातरं मेनां च। अन्या पूर्वं यस्यास्ति सो ऽन्यपूर्वः। सर्वनाम्नो वृत्तिविषये पुंवद्भावः इति पूर्वपदस्य पुंवद्भावः। स न भवतीत्यनन्यपूर्वस्तस्य अनन्यपूर्वस्य। सापत्न्यदुःखमकुर्वत इत्यर्थः। वरस्य वोढुः गुणैः मृत्युंजयत्वादिभिः विशोकां निर्दुःखाम् अकरोत्॥

वैवाहिकीं तिथिं पृष्टास्तत्क्षणं हरबन्धुना।
ते त्र्यहादूर्ध्वमाख्याय चेरुश्चीरपरिग्रहाः॥ ९३॥

वैवाहिकीमिति॥ चीरपरिग्रहाः वल्कलमात्रवसनाः ते तपस्विनः तत्क्षणम् तस्मिन्नेव क्षणे हरबन्धुना हिमवता वैवाहिकीं विवाहयोग्यां तिथिं पृष्टाः केत्यनुयुक्ताः सन्तः। त्रयाणामह्नां समाहारस्त्र्यहः। तद्धितार्थोत्तरपदसमाहारे च इति समासः। राजाहःसखिभ्यष्टच् इति टच्प्रत्ययः। द्विगुत्वादेकवचनम्। रात्राह्नाहाः पुंसि इति पुंलिङ्गता। तस्मात् त्र्यहात् ऊर्ध्वम् उपरि आख्याय चतुर्थे ऽहनि विवाहः इत्युक्त्वा चेरुः चलिताः॥

ते हिमालयमामन्त्र्य पुनः प्राप्य च शूलिनम्।
सिद्धं चास्मै निवेद्यार्थं तद्विसृष्टाः खमुद्ययुः॥ ९४॥

त इति॥ ते मुनयः हिमालयमामन्त्र्य साधु याम इत्यापृच्छ्य पुनः शूलिनम् हरं संकेतस्थानस्थं प्राप्य च। सिद्धम् निष्पन्नम् अर्थम् प्रयोजनम् अस्मै निवेद्य ज्ञापयित्वा च। तद्विसृष्टाः तेन

शूलिना विसृष्टाः खम् आकाशं प्रति उच्चयुः उत्पेतुः । अत्र संक्षिप्तार्थाभिधानात्संक्षेपो नाम गुण उक्तः । तदुक्तम्—संक्षिप्तार्थाभिधानं यत्संक्षेपः परिकीर्तितः इति ॥

भगवान्पशुपतिस्त्र्यहमात्रविलम्बमपि सोढुं न शशाक तदौत्सुक्यादित्याह

पशुपतिरपि तान्यहानि कृच्छ्राद्
अगमयदद्रिसुतासमागमोत्कः ।
कमपरमवशं न विप्रकुर्युर्
विभुमपि तं यदमी स्पृशन्ति भावाः ॥ ९५ ॥

पशुपतिरिति ॥ उत्कं मनो यस्य सः उत्कः । उत्क उन्मनाः इति निपातः । अद्रिसुतासमागमोत्कः पार्वतीपरिणयोत्सुकः पशुपतिरपि तानि । त्रीणीति शेषः । अहानि कृच्छ्रादगमयत् अयापयत् । कविराह — अमी भावाः औत्सुक्यादयः संचारिणः अवशम् इन्द्रियपरतन्त्रम् अपरम् पृथग्जनं कं न विप्रकुर्युः न विकारं नयेयुः । यत् यस्मात् विभुम् समर्थम् । जितेन्द्रियमिति यावत् । तम् स्मरहरम् अपि स्पृशन्ति । विकुर्वन्तीत्यर्थः । अत्र विभुविकारसमर्थनादर्थादितरजनविकारः कैमुतिकन्यायादापततीत्यर्थापत्तिरलंकारः । तथा च सूत्रम् — दण्डापूपिकयार्थान्तरापतनमर्थापत्तिः इति । अर्थान्तरन्यास इति के चित् तदुपेक्षणीयम् । युक्तिस्तु विस्तरभयान्नोच्यते । पुष्पिताग्रा वृत्तम — अयुजि नयुगरेफतो यकारो युजि च नजौ जरगाश्च पुष्पिताग्रा इति लक्षणात् ॥

Appendix 1

Further Sanskrit Study

ANYONE who has mastered the present volume is adequately equipped to read simple Classical Sanskrit. Those whose interest lies particularly in Indian religious thought may well wish to begin with the best loved of all Hindu religious texts, the *Bhagavad Gītā*, written in eighteen short cantos of easy, straightforward verse. Innumerable texts and translations of this work exist. For the student, the most scrupulously faithful translation is probably that by F. Edgerton (Harper Torchbooks). Other distinguished scholars who have translated the work include R. C. Zaehner (*Hindu Scriptures*, Everyman; also *The Bhagavad Gītā* with commentary and text in transcription, Oxford University Press) and S. Radhakrishnan (Allen & Unwin, including text in transcription). The pocket edition with a text in nāgarī by Annie Besant (Theosophical Publishing House) is cheap and convenient, though the accompanying translation is unreliable.

In secular literature a good starting-point is the *Pañcatantra*, a witty and sophisticated collection of animal fables (the ultimate source of La Fontaine), written in fluent, racy Sanskrit. Many versions of this work have survived, and these were collated by Edgerton, who produced a recension as near as he thought it was possible to get to the original. His translation of this has been reprinted recently (Allen & Unwin), but not unfortunately the Sanskrit text (American Oriental Series, Volume 2, New Haven, 1924), which should, however, be obtainable from specialist libraries.

An especially attractive and accessible branch of Classical Sanskrit literature is the drama. The prose dialogue is straightforward (many sentences are likely to seem familiar to the student of this book!). Certain characters speak in Prakrit, but almost all editions include a Sanskrit translation (**chāyā**) of these passages. The stanzas of verse interspersed among the prose are more elaborate in style but should not prove too difficult with the help of a translation and notes such as have been provided for most standard Sanskrit plays by M. R. Kale: Kale's student editions are very useful and workmanlike, and are usually in print in India—though regrettably these reprints often bristle with grotesque printing errors. The best known of all Sanskrit plays is the *Śakuntalā* of Kālidāsa. Other masterpieces include the *Mṛcchakaṭikā* ('Toy Cart') of Śūdraka, the *Mudrārākṣasa* '(The Signet Ring and Rākṣasa') of Viśākhadatta and the *Uttararāmacarita* ('The Later Story of Rāma') of Bhavabhūti—the last, although a moving and beautiful work, being of the four perhaps the least immediately attractive to Western taste in its style and feeling.

Sanskrit dictionaries

A. A. Macdonell's *A Sanskrit Dictionary for Students* (Oxford University Press, 382 pp.) is much the most convenient in the early stages of study. The author lists in the preface the Sanskrit works for which the dictionary is specifically a vocabulary. In reading other works or for more scholarly use, M. Monier-Williams' *A Sanskṛit-English Dictionary* (Oxford University Press, 1333 pp.), effectively a translation and condensation of the great *Sanskrit-Wörterbuch* of Böhtlingk and Roth, is indispensable. Unfortunately, it suffers the irritating drawback of being arranged not in strict alphabetical order but according to verbal roots. All present dictionaries are grossly out of date: Sanskrit studies will be revolutionised when the vast work at present under preparation in Poona finally sees the light of day.

Sanskrit grammars

A. A. Macdonell's *A Sanskrit Grammar for Students* (Oxford University Press) is again the most convenient work available and, despite some inaccuracies and omissions, is a model of clarity and conciseness. The standard Sanskrit grammar in English is still that of W. D. Whitney (2nd edition 1889, reprinted by Oxford University Press), but this is now very out of date, the presentation of Vedic and Classical material is confusingly intertwined and the treatment of syntax is sketchy in the extreme. The really standard work is in German, the monumental *Altindische Grammatik* of Wackernagel and Debrunner (Göttingen, 1896–1957); but special mention should be made of a French work, the *Grammaire sanscrite* of Louis Renou (Paris, 2nd edition 1961), which, while of a more manageable size than Wackernagel, treats of Classical Sanskrit in considerable detail and is full of valuable observations on syntax.

Vedic studies

Students primarily interested in comparative Indo-European philology may like to turn to the Vedic language at an early stage in their studies, and here yet again the path is smoothed by A. A. Macdonell. His *Vedic Reader for Students* (Oxford University Press) contains a selection of Vedic hymns transliterated, analysed and translated, with very full notes on points of linguistic interest and a complete vocabulary at the back of the book. The Vedic hymns, which are not without their attraction from the literary point of view, are thus made easily accessible to the non-specialist. Macdonell's *Vedic Grammar for Students* is arranged to correspond paragraph for paragraph with his Sanskrit Grammar mentioned above, so facilitating the comparison of Vedic grammar with Classical.

Appendix 2

Grammatical Paradigms

(For use in conjunction with the foregoing chapters, where further irregularities and alternative forms may be mentioned.)

NOUNS

It will be noticed that in all nouns each of the following groups has a single form:

(i) Nominative, vocative and accusative dual
(ii) Instrumental, dative and ablative dual
(iii) Genitive and locative dual
(iv) Dative and ablative plural
(v) Nominative and vocative dual or plural
(vi) Nominative and accusative *neuter*, any number

1 Vowel stems

Stems in a/ā: **kānta** 'beloved'

		Masculine	*Neuter*	*Feminine*
Nominative singular		**kāntaḥ**	**kāntam**	**kāntā**
Accusative	,,	**kāntam**	**kāntam**	**kāntām**
Instrumental	,,	**kāntena**	**kāntena**	**kāntayā**
Dative	,,	**kāntāya**	**kāntāya**	**kāntāyai**
Ablative	,,	**kāntāt**	**kāntāt**	**kāntāyāḥ**
Genitive	,,	**kāntasya**	**kāntasya**	**kāntāyāḥ**
Locative	,,	**kānte**	**kānte**	**kāntāyām**
Vocative	,,	**kānta**	**kānta**	**kānte**

	Masculine	Neuter	Feminine
N. V. A. dual	**kāntau**	**kānte**	**kānte**
I. D. Ab. ,,	**kāntābhyām**	**kāntābhyām**	**kāntābhyām**
G. L. ,,	**kāntayoḥ**	**kāntayoḥ**	**kāntayoḥ**
N. V. plural	**kāntāḥ**	**kāntāni**	**kāntāḥ**
A. ,,	**kāntān**	**kāntāni**	**kāntāḥ**
I. ,,	**kāntaiḥ**	**kāntaiḥ**	**kāntābhiḥ**
D. Ab. ,,	**kāntebhyaḥ**	**kāntebhyaḥ**	**kāntābhyaḥ**
G. ,,	**kāntānām**	**kāntānām**	**kāntānām**
L. ,,	**kānteṣu**	**kānteṣu**	**kāntāsu**

Stems in **ī** *and* **ū**: **nadī** f. 'river', **vadhū** f. 'woman', **strī** f. 'woman', **dhī** f. 'thought', **bhū** f. 'earth'

	Polysyllabic		Irregular	Monosyllabic	
N. sg.	**nadī**	**vadhūḥ**	**strī**	**dhīḥ**	**bhūḥ**
A.	**nadīm**	**vadhūm**	**strīm/ striyam**	**dhiyam**	**bhuvam**
I.	**nadyā**	**vadhvā**	**striyā**	**dhiyā**	**bhuvā**
D.	**nadyai**	**vadhvai**	**striyai**	**dhiye**	**bhuve**
Ab. G.	**nadyāḥ**	**vadhvāḥ**	**striyāḥ**	**dhiyaḥ**	**bhuvaḥ**
L.	**nadyām**	**vadhvām**	**striyām**	**dhiyi**	**bhuvi**
V.	**nadi**	**vadhu**	**stri**	**dhīḥ**	**bhūḥ**
N. V. A. du.	**nadyau**	**vadhvau**	**striyau**	**dhiyau**	**bhuvau**
I. D. Ab.	**nadībhyām**	**vadhūbhyām**	**strībhyām**	**dhībhyām**	**bhūbhyām**
G. L.	**nadyoḥ**	**vadhvoḥ**	**striyoḥ**	**dhiyoḥ**	**bhuvoḥ**
N. V. pl.	**nadyaḥ**	**vadhvaḥ**	**striyaḥ**	**dhiyaḥ**	**bhuvaḥ**
A.	**nadīḥ**	**vadhūḥ**	**strīḥ/ striyaḥ**	**dhiyaḥ**	**bhuvaḥ**
I.	**nadībhiḥ**	**vadhūbhiḥ**	**strībhiḥ**	**dhībhiḥ**	**bhūbhiḥ**
D. Ab.	**nadībhyaḥ**	**vadhūbhyaḥ**	**strībhyaḥ**	**dhībhyaḥ**	**bhūbhyaḥ**
G.	**nadīnām**	**vadhūnām**	**strīṇām**	**dhiyām**	**bhuvām**
L.	**nadīṣu**	**vadhūṣu**	**strīṣu**	**dhīṣu**	**bhūṣu**

Stems in **i** *and* **u**: **śuci** 'clean', **mṛdu** 'soft'

	m.	n.	f.	m.	n.	f.
N. sg.	**śuciḥ**	**śuci**	**śuciḥ**	**mṛduḥ**	**mṛdu**	**mṛduḥ**
A.	**śucim**	**śuci**	**śucim**	**mṛdum**	**mṛdu**	**mṛdum**
I.	**śucinā**	**śucinā**	**śucyā**	**mṛdunā**	**mṛdunā**	**mṛdvā**
D.	**śucaye**	**śucine**	**śucyai**	**mṛdave**	**mṛdune**	**mṛdvai**
Ab. G.	**śuceḥ**	**śucinaḥ**	**śucyāḥ**	**mṛdoḥ**	**mṛdunaḥ**	**mṛdvāḥ**
L.	**śucau**	**śucini**	**śucyām**	**mṛdau**	**mṛduni**	**mṛdvām**
V.	**śuce**	**śuci**	**śuce**	**mṛdo**	**mṛdu**	**mṛdo**

	m.	n.	f.	m.	n.	f.
N. V. A. du.	**śucī**	**śucinī**	**śucī**	**mṛdū**	**mṛdunī**	**mṛdū**
I. A. Ab.	**śuci-bhyām**	**śuci-bhyām**	**śuci-bhyām**	**mṛdu-bhyām**	**mṛdu-bhyām**	**mṛdu-bhyām**
G. L.	**śucyoḥ**	**śucinoḥ**	**śucyoḥ**	**mṛdvoḥ**	**mṛdunoḥ**	**mṛdvoḥ**
N. V. pl.	**śucayaḥ**	**śucīni**	**śucayaḥ**	**mṛdavaḥ**	**mṛdūni**	**mṛdavaḥ**
A.	**śucīn**	**śucīni**	**śucīḥ**	**mṛdūn**	**mṛdūni**	**mṛdūḥ**
I.	**śucibhiḥ**	**śucibhiḥ**	**śucibhiḥ**	**mṛdubhiḥ**	**mṛdubhiḥ**	**mṛdubhiḥ**
D. Ab.	**śuci-bhyaḥ**	**śuci-bhyaḥ**	**śuci-bhyaḥ**	**mṛdu-bhyaḥ**	**mṛdu-bhyaḥ**	**mṛdu-bhyaḥ**
G.	**śucīnām**	**śucīnām**	**śucīnām**	**mṛdūnām**	**mṛdūnām**	**mṛdūnām**
L.	**śuciṣu**	**śuciṣu**	**śuciṣu**	**mṛduṣu**	**mṛduṣu**	**mṛduṣu**

Stems in **ṛ**: **kartṛ** m. 'maker', **pitṛ** m. 'father', **svasṛ** f. 'sister', **mātṛ** f. 'mother'

	Masculine		*Feminine*	
N. sg.	**kartā**	**pitā**	**svasā**	**mātā**
A.	**kartāram**	**pitaram**	**svasāram**	**mātaram**
I.	**kartrā**	**pitrā**	**svasrā**	**mātrā**
D.	**kartre**	**pitre**	**svasre**	**mātre**
Ab. G.	**kartuḥ**	**pituḥ**	**svasuḥ**	**mātuḥ**
L.	**kartari**	**pitari**	**svasari**	**mātari**
V.	**kartar**	**pitar**	**svasar**	**mātar**
N. V. A. du.	**kartārau**	**pitarau**	**svasārau**	**mātarau**
I. D. Ab.	**kartṛbhyām**	**pitṛbhyām**	**svasṛbhyām**	**mātṛbhyām**
G. L.	**kartroḥ**	**pitroḥ**	**svasroḥ**	**mātroḥ**
N. V. pl.	**kartāraḥ**	**pitaraḥ**	**svasāraḥ**	**mātaraḥ**
A.	**kartṝn**	**pitṝn**	**svasṝḥ**	**mātṝḥ**
I.	**kartṛbhiḥ**	**pitṛbhiḥ**	**svasṛbhiḥ**	**mātṛbhiḥ**
D. Ab.	**kartṛbhyaḥ**	**pitṛbhyaḥ**	**svasṛbhyaḥ**	**mātṛbhyaḥ**
G.	**kartṝṇām**	**pitṝṇām**	**svasṝṇām**	**mātṝṇām**
L.	**kartṛṣu**	**pitṛṣu**	**svasṛṣu**	**mātṛṣu**

Note: The feminine of **kartṛ** is **kartrī**.

2 Consonant stems

Unchangeable stems: **suhṛd** m. 'friend', **go-duh** m. f. 'cow-milker', **manas** n. 'mind', **sumanas** m. f. 'benevolent'

N. sg.	**suhṛt**	**godhuk**	**manaḥ**	**sumanāḥ**
A.	**suhṛdam**	**goduham**	**manaḥ**	**sumanasam**
I.	**suhṛdā**	**goduhā**	**manasā**	**sumanasā**
D.	**suhṛde**	**goduhe**	**manase**	**sumanase**
Ab. G.	**suhṛdaḥ**	**goduhaḥ**	**manasaḥ**	**sumanasaḥ**
L.	**suhṛdi**	**goduhi**	**manasi**	**sumanasi**
V.	**suhṛt**	**godhuk**	**manaḥ**	**sumanaḥ**
N. V. A. du.	**suhṛdau**	**goduhau**	**manasī**	**sumanasau**
I. D. Ab.	**suhṛdbhyām**	**godhugbhyām**	**manobhyām**	**sumanobhyām**
G. L.	**suhṛdoḥ**	**goduhoḥ**	**manasoḥ**	**sumanasoḥ**

N. V. A. pl.	**suhṛdaḥ**	**goduhaḥ**	**manāṃsi**	**sumanasaḥ**
I.	**suhṛdbhiḥ**	**godhugbhiḥ**	**manobhiḥ**	**sumanobhiḥ**
D. Ab.	**suhṛdbhyaḥ**	**godhugbhyaḥ**	**manobhyaḥ**	**sumanobhyaḥ**
G.	**suhṛdām**	**goduhām**	**manasām**	**sumanasām**
L.	**suhṛtsu**	**godhukṣu**	**manaḥsu**	**sumanaḥsu**

The neuter of **sumanas** is inflected like **manas**. The following are examples of stems ending in other consonants:

Stem	*N. sg.*	*N. pl.*	*I. pl.*	*L. pl.*
suyudh *m.* good fighter	**suyut**	**suyudhaḥ**	**suyudbhiḥ**	**suyutsu**
kakubh *f.* region	**kakup**	**kakubhaḥ**	**kakubbhiḥ**	**kakupsu**
vāc *f.* speech	**vāk**	**vācaḥ**	**vāgbhiḥ**	**vākṣu**
vaṇij *m.* business-man	**vaṇik**	**vaṇijaḥ**	**vaṇigbhiḥ**	**vaṇikṣu**
parivrāj *m.* medicant	**parivrāṭ**	**parivrājaḥ**	**parivrāḍbhiḥ**	**parivrāṭsu**
diś *f.* direction	**dik**	**diśaḥ**	**digbhiḥ**	**dikṣu**
viś *m.* settler	**viṭ**	**viśaḥ**	**viḍbhiḥ**	**viṭsu**
dviṣ *m.* enemy	**dviṭ**	**dviṣaḥ**	**dviḍbhiḥ**	**dviṭsu**
madhulih *m.* bee	**madhuliṭ**	**madhulihaḥ**	**madhuliḍbhiḥ**	**madhuliṭsu**

Stems in **ir**/**ur** (both rare) lengthen to **īr**/**ūr** before consonants and in the nominative singular. Stems in **is**/**us** become **iṣ**/**uṣ** or **ir**/**ur** according to sandhi, and also lengthen the vowel in the nominative, vocative and accusative neuter plural.

gir *f.* speech	**gīḥ**	**giraḥ**	**gīrbhiḥ**	**gīrṣu**
dhur *f.* yoke	**dhūḥ**	**dhuraḥ**	**dhūrbhiḥ**	**dhūrṣu**
barhis *n.* sacred grass	**barhiḥ**	**barhīṃṣi**	**barhirbhiḥ**	**barhiḥṣu**
cakṣus *n.* eye	**cakṣuḥ**	**cakṣūṃṣi**	**cakṣurbhiḥ**	**cakṣuḥṣu**
āśis[1] *f.* benediction	**āśīḥ**	**āśiṣaḥ**	**āśīrbhiḥ**	**āśīḥṣu**

Stems in **in**: **dhanin** m. n. (**dhaninī** f.) 'rich'

	SINGULAR		DUAL		PLURAL	
	m.	*n.*	*m.*	*n.*	*m.*	*n.*
N.	**dhanī**	**dhani**	**dhaninau**	**dhaninī**	**dhaninaḥ**	**dhanīni**
A.	**dhaninam**	**dhani**	,,	,,	**dhaninaḥ**	**dhanīni**
I.	**dhaninā**		**dhanibhyām**		**dhanibhiḥ**	
D.	**dhanine**		,,		**dhanibhyaḥ**	
Ab.	**dhaninaḥ**		,,		,,	
G.	**dhaninaḥ**		**dhaninoḥ**		**dhaninām**	
L.	**dhanini**		,,		**dhaniṣu**	
V.	**dhanin**	**dhani/dhanin**	(*as N.*)		(*as N.*)	

[1] Although an **is** stem, this noun lengthens its **i** in the same circumstances as a stem in **ir**.

Stems in **an**: **rājan** m. 'king', **ātman** m. 'self', **nāman** n. 'name', **panthan** m. 'road' (irreg.) **ahan** n. 'day' (irreg.)

N. Sg.	**rājā**	**ātmā**	**nāma**	**panthāḥ**	**ahar**
A.	**rājānam**	**ātmānam**	**nāma**	**panthānam**	**ahar**
I.	**rājñā**	**ātmanā**	**nāmnā**	**pathā**	**ahnā**
D.	**rājñe**	**ātmane**	**nāmne**	**pathe**	**ahne**
Ab. G.	**rājñaḥ**	**ātmanaḥ**	**nāmnaḥ**	**pathaḥ**	**ahnaḥ**
L.	**rājñi/ rājani**	**ātmani**	**nāmni/ nāmani**	**pathi**	**ahni/ ahani**
V.	**rājan**	**ātman**	**nāma/ nāman**	**panthāḥ**	**ahar**
N. V. A. du.	**rājānau**	**ātmānau**	**nāmnī/ nāmanī**	**panthānau**	**ahnī/ahanī**
I. D. Ab.	**rājabhyām**	**ātmabhyām**	**nāmabhyām**	**pathibhyām**	**ahobhyām**
G. L.	**rājñoḥ**	**ātmanoḥ**	**nāmnoḥ**	**pathoḥ**	**ahnoḥ**
N. V. pl.	**rājānaḥ**	**ātmānaḥ**	**nāmāni**	**panthānaḥ**	**ahāni**
A.	**rājñaḥ**	**ātmanaḥ**	**nāmāni**	**pathaḥ**	**ahāni**
I.	**rājabhiḥ**	**ātmabhiḥ**	**nāmabhiḥ**	**pathibhiḥ**	**ahobhiḥ**
D. Ab.	**rājabhyaḥ**	**ātmabhyaḥ**	**nāmabhyaḥ**	**pathibhyaḥ**	**ahobhyaḥ**
G.	**rājñām**	**ātmanām**	**nāmnām**	**pathām**	**ahnām**
L.	**rājasu**	**ātmasu**	**nāmasu**	**pathiṣu**	**ahaḥsu**

Stems in **ant** *and* **at**: **dhanavant** 'rich', **nayant** 'leading', **dadhat** 'putting'

	m.	*n.*	*m.*	*n.*	*m.*	*n.*
N. Sg.	**dhanavān**	**dhanavat**	**nayan**	**nayat**	**dadhat**	**dadhat**
A.	**dhanavantam**	,,	**nayantam**	,,	**dadhatam**	,,
I.	**dhanavatā**		**nayatā**		**dadhatā**	
D.	**dhanavate**		**nayate**		**dadhate**	
Ab. G.	**dhanavataḥ**		**nayataḥ**		**dadhataḥ**	
L.	**dhanavati**		**nayati**		**dadhati**	
V.	**dhanavan**	**dhanavat**	**nayan**	**nayat**	**dadhat**	**dadhat**
N. V. A. du.	**dhanavantau**	**dhanavatī**	**nayantau**	**nayantī**	**dadhatau**	**dadhatī**
I. D. Ab.	**dhanavadbhyām**		**nayadbhyām**		**dadhadbhyām**	
G. L.	**dhanavatoḥ**		**nayatoḥ**		**dadhatoḥ**	
N. V. pl.	**dhanavantaḥ**	**dhanavanti**	**nayantaḥ**	**nayanti**	**dadhataḥ**	**dadhanti**
A.	**dhanavataḥ**	,,	**nayataḥ**	,,	**dadhataḥ**	,,
I.	**dhanavadbhiḥ**		**nayadbhiḥ**		**dadhadbhiḥ**	
D. Ab.	**dhanavadbhyaḥ**		**nayadbhyaḥ**		**dadhadbhyaḥ**	
G.	**dhanavatām**		**nayatām**		**dadhatām**	
L.	**dhanavatsu**		**nayatsu**		**dadhatsu**	

Stems in **yāṃs**: **śreyāṃs** m. n. (**śreyasī** f.) 'better'

	SINGULAR *m.*	SINGULAR *n.*	DUAL *m.*	DUAL *n.*	PLURAL *m.*	PLURAL *n.*
N.	śreyān	śreyaḥ	śreyāṃsau	śreyasī	śreyāṃsaḥ	śreyāṃsi
A.	śreyāṃsam	śreyaḥ	,,	,,	śreyasaḥ	śreyāṃsi
I.	śreyasā		śreyobhyām		śreyobhiḥ	
D.	śreyase		,,		śreyobhyaḥ	
Ab.	śreyasaḥ		,,		,,	
G.	śreyasaḥ		śreyasoḥ		śreyasām	
L.	śreyasi		,,		śreyaḥsu	
V.	śreyan	śreyaḥ	as *N.*)		(*as N.*)	

Stems in **vāṃs**: **vidvāṃs** m. n. (**viduṣī** f.) 'learned'

	SINGULAR *m.*	SINGULAR *n.*	DUAL *m.*	DUAL *n.*	PLURAL *m.*	PLURAL *n.*
N.	vidvān	vidvat	vidvāṃsau	viduṣī	vidvāṃsaḥ	vidvāṃsi
A.	vidvāṃsam	vidvat	,,	,,	viduṣaḥ	vidvāṃsi
I.	viduṣā		vidvadbhyām		vidvadbhiḥ	
D.	viduṣe		,,		vidvadbhyaḥ	
Ab.	viduṣaḥ		,,		,,	
G.	viduṣaḥ		viduṣoḥ		viduṣām	
L.	viduṣi		,,		vidvatsu	
V.	vidvan	vidvat	(*as N.*)		(*as N.*)	

Stems in **añc**: **pratyañc** m. n. (**pratīcī** f.) 'western'

	SINGULAR *m.*	SINGULAR *n.*	DUAL *m.*	DUAL *n.*	PLURAL *m.*	PLURAL *n.*
N. V.	pratyaṅ	pratyak	pratyañcau	pratīcī	pratyañcaḥ	pratyañci
A.	pratyañ-cam	pratyak	,,	,,	pratīcaḥ	pratyañci
I.	pratīcā		pratyagbhyām		pratyagbhiḥ	
D.	pratīce		,,		pratyagbhyaḥ	
Ab.	pratīcaḥ		,,		,,	
G.	pratīcaḥ		pratīcoḥ		pratīcām	
L.	pratīci		,,		pratyakṣu	

In words such as **prāñc** 'eastern', where two **a**'s (**pra**+**añc**) coalesce, the middle and weak stems are identical: **prāc**. Thus ablative, genitive and locative plural **prāgbhyaḥ**, **prācām**, **prākṣu**.

PRONOUNS

1ST PERSON:		2ND PERSON	3RD PERSON		
	aham 'I'	**tvam** 'you'	**saḥ** 'he, that'		
(Enclitic forms in brackets.)					
			m.	*n.*	*f.*
N. Sg.	**aham**	**tvam**	**saḥ**	**tat**	**sā**
A.	**mām (mā)**	**tvām (tvā)**	**tam**	**tat**	**tām**
I.	**mayā**	**tvayā**	**tena**		**tayā**
D.	**mahyam (me)**	**tubhyam (te)**	**tasmai**		**tasyai**
Ab.	**mat** *or* **mattaḥ**	**tvat** *or* **tvattaḥ**	**tasmāt**		**tasyāḥ**
G.	**mama (me)**	**tava (te)**	**tasya**		**tasyāḥ**
L.	**mayi**	**tvayi**	**tasmin**		**tasyām**
N. A. du.	**āvām**	**yuvām**	**tau**	**te**	**te**
I. D. Ab.	**āvābhyām**	**yuvābhyām**	**tābhyām**		
G. L.	**āvayoḥ** (A. D. G. **nau**)	**yuvayoḥ** (A. D. G. **vām**)	**tayoḥ**		
N. pl.	**vayam**	**yūyam**	**te**	**tāni**	**tāḥ**
A.	**asmān (naḥ)**	**yuṣmān (vaḥ)**	**tān**	**tāni**	**tāḥ**
I.	**asmābhiḥ**	**yuṣmābhiḥ**	**taiḥ**		**tābhiḥ**
D.	**asmabhyam (naḥ)**	**yuṣmabhyam (vaḥ)**	**tebhyaḥ**		**tābhyaḥ**
Ab.	**asmat** *or* **asmattaḥ**	**yuṣmat** *or* **yuṣmattaḥ**	**tebhyaḥ**		**tābhyaḥ**
G.	**asmākam (naḥ)**	**yuṣmākam (vaḥ)**	**teṣām**		**tāsām**
L.	**asmāsu**	**yuṣmāsu**	**teṣu**		**tāsu**

The accusative singular enclitic forms **mā** and **tvā** are seldom used in the Classical language.

The following pronouns follow the inflexion of **saḥ, tat, sā** in any forms not quoted here.

(*a*) **eṣaḥ, etat, eṣā** this
(*b*) **yaḥ, yat, yā** who *relative pronoun*
(*c*) **anyaḥ, anyat, anyā** other
(*d*) **kaḥ, kim, kā** who? *interrogative pronoun*
(*e*) **sarvaḥ, sarvam, sarvā** all
(*f*) **ekaḥ, ekam, ekā** one
(*g*) **svaḥ, svam, svā** own

	ayam 'this'			**asau** 'that'		
	m.	*n.*	*f.*	*m.*	*n.*	*f.*
N. sg.	**ayam**	**idam**	**iyam**	**asau**	**adaḥ**	**asau**
A.	**imam**	**idam**	**imām**	**amum**	**adaḥ**	**amūm**
I.	**anena**		**anayā**	**amunā**		**amuyā**
D.	**asmai**		**asyai**	**amuṣmai**		**amuṣyai**

Ab.	asmāt	asyāḥ	amuṣmāt	amuṣyāḥ
G.	asya	asyāḥ	amuṣya	amuṣyāḥ
L.	asmin	asyām	amuṣmin	amuṣyām

N. A. du.	imau	ime	ime		amū	
I. D. Ab.		ābhyām			amūbhyām	
G. L.		anayoḥ			amuyoḥ	
N. pl.	ime	imāni	imāḥ	amī	amūni	amūḥ
A.	imān	imāni	imāḥ	amūn	amūni	amūḥ
I.	ebhiḥ		ābhiḥ	amībhiḥ		amūbhiḥ
D. Ab.	ebhyaḥ		ābhyaḥ	amībhyaḥ		amūbhyaḥ
G.	eṣām		āsām	amīṣām		amūṣām
L.	eṣu		āsu	amīṣu		amūṣu

For the pronoun **enam** 'him' see Chapter 10, p. 151.

NUMERALS

Cardinals				*Ordinals*	
1	**eka**	41	**eka;catvāriṃśat**	1st	**prathama**
2	**dvi**	42	**dvā;catvāriṃśat**	2nd	**dvitīya**
3	**tri**	43	**tri;catvāriṃśat**	3rd	**tṛtīya**
4	**catur**	44	**catuś;catvāriṃśat**	4th	**caturtha, turīya, turya**
5	**pañca**	45	**pañca;catvāriṃśat**	5th	**pañcama**
6	**ṣaṣ**	46	**ṣaṭ;catvāriṃśat**	6th	**ṣaṣṭha**
7	**sapta**	47	**sapta;catvāriṃśat**	7th	**saptama**
8	**aṣṭa**	48	**aṣṭā;catvāriṃśat**	8th	**aṣṭama**
9	**nava**	49	**nava;catvāriṃśat** / **ūna:pañcāśat**	9th	**navama**
10	**daśa**			10th	**daśama**
11	**ekādaśa**	50	**pañcāśat**	11th–18th	*as cardinals*
12	**dvādaśa**	60	**ṣaṣṭi**	19th	**navadaśa, ūnaviṃśa**
13	**trayodaśa**	70	**saptati**	20th	**viṃśa, viṃśatitama**
14	**caturdaśa**	80	**aśīti**	30th	**triṃśa, triṃśattama**
15	**pañcadaśa**	82	**dvy:aśīti**	40th	**catvāriṃśa, catvāriṃśattama**
16	**ṣoḍaśa**	90	**navati**	50th	**pañcāśa, pañcāśattama**
17	**saptadaśa**	96	**ṣaṇ;ṇavati**	60th	**ṣaṣṭitama**
18	**aṣṭādaśa**	100	**śataṃ**	61st	**ekaṣaṣṭa**
19	**navadaśa** / **ūna:viṃśati**	102	**dvy-adhikaṃ śataṃ** / **dvi;śataṃ**	70th	**saptatitama**
				71st	**ekasaptata**
20	**viṃśati**	200	**dve śate** / **dvi:śataṃ**	80th	**aśītitama**
23	**trayo;viṃśati**			81st	**ekāśīta**
30	**triṃśat**	1000	**sahasraṃ**	90th	**navatitama**
33	**trayas;triṃśat**	100 000	**lakṣaṃ**	91st	**ekanavata**
40	**catvāriṃśat**	10 000 000	**koṭi**	100th	**śatatama**

To form the cardinal numbers not included in the list, the

analogy of 41 to 49 may be followed, though some alternative forms are possible.

For the ordinals 60th, 70th, 80th, 90th by themselves only the forms in **-tama** are allowed. But wherever short forms are permitted, the forms in **-tama** are always a possible alternative: thus 61st **ekaṣaṣṭa** *or* **ekaṣaṣṭitama.**

The sandhi of **ṣaṣ** is as if it were **ṣaṭ**, except that **ṣaṣ+d** = **ṣoḍ** and **ṣaṣ+n** = **ṣaṇṇ.**

The ordinals are all inflected like **kānta.** Their feminine is always in **-ī**, except for **prathamā, dvitīyā, tṛtiyā, turīyā** and **turyā.**

Inflexion of cardinals

The cardinal numbers below 100 are all quoted above in stem form. **viṃśati** and higher numbers ending in **-i** are feminine **i** stems; those ending in **-t** are feminine consonant stems.

The inflexion of **eka** is mentioned under the pronouns. **dvi** inflects like the dual of **kānta: dvau, dve, dve; dvābhyām; dvayoḥ.**

	tri three			**catur** four		
N. V.	**trayaḥ**	**trīṇi**	**tisraḥ**	**catvāraḥ**	**catvāri**	**catasraḥ**
A.	**trīn**	**trīṇi**	**tisraḥ**	**caturaḥ**	**catvāri**	**catasraḥ**
I.	**tribhiḥ**		**tisṛbhiḥ**	**caturbhiḥ**		**catasṛbhiḥ**
D. Ab.	**tribhyaḥ**		**tisṛbhyaḥ**	**caturbhyaḥ**		**catasṛbhyaḥ**
G.	**trayāṇām**		**tisṛṇām**	**caturṇām**		**catasṛṇām**
L.	**triṣu**		**tisṛṣu**	**caturṣu**		**catasṛṣu**

	pañca five	**ṣaṣ** six	**aṣṭa** eight
N. V. A.	**pañca**	**ṣaṭ**	**aṣṭa/aṣṭau**
I.	**pañcabhiḥ**	**ṣaḍbhiḥ**	**aṣṭabhiḥ/aṣṭābhiḥ**
D. Ab.	**pañcabhyaḥ**	**saḍbhyaḥ**	**aṣṭabhyaḥ/aṣṭābhyaḥ**
G.	**pañcānām**	**ṣaṇṇām**	**aṣṭānām**
L.	**pañcasu**	**ṣaṭsu**	**aṣṭasu/aṣṭāsu**

The numbers 7 and 9 to 19 inflect like **pañca.**

VERBS

General view of the Sanskrit verb

The following scheme (which is not exhaustive) will give some idea of the range of possible formations from the verbal root.

The second column adds parallel formations from the most highly developed secondary stem, the causative. For the particular verb quoted, some forms are theoretical rather than actually found.

1 Finite formations

From the root **nī** 'lead'	From the stem **nāy(aya)** 'cause to lead'
Primary verb	*Secondary verb*
PRESENT	PRESENT CAUSATIVE
nayati 'he leads' (Included in the present system: *Imperfect* **anayat** 'he led' *Imperative* **nayatu** 'let him lead' *Optative* **nayet** 'he may lead')	**nāyayati** 'he causes to lead' (*Imperfect* **anāyayat** 'he caused to lead' *Imperative* **nāyayatu** 'let him cause to lead' *Optative* **nāyayet** 'he may cause to lead')
PERFECT	PERIPHRASTIC PERFECT
ninãya 'he led'	**nāyayām āsa** 'he caused to lead'
AORIST	REDUPLICATED AORIST (an independent formation)
anaiṣīt 'he led'	**anīnayat** 'he caused to lead'
FUTURE	FUTURE CAUSATIVE
neṣyati 'he will lead'	**nāyayiṣyati** 'he will cause to lead'
(*Conditional* **aneṣyat** 'he would have led')	(**anāyayiṣyat** 'he would have caused to lead')
PASSIVE	CAUSATIVE PASSIVE
nīyate 'he is led'	**nāyyate** 'he is caused to lead'
Secondary verbs	*Tertiary verb*
CAUSATIVE (see above, second column)	DESIDERATIVE CAUSATIVE
nāyayati 'he causes to lead'	**ninãyayiṣati** 'he wants to cause to lead'

DESIDERATIVE

ninīṣati 'he wants to lead'
(*Adjective* **ninīṣu** 'wanting to lead'
Substantive **ninīṣā** 'the wish to lead')

nināyayiṣu 'wanting to cause to lead'
nināyayiṣā 'the wish to cause to lead')

INTENSIVE

nenīyate 'he leads forcibly'

Two further independent formations from the root are the AORIST PASSIVE (third person singular only) **anāyi** 'he was led' and the PRECATIVE, or benedictive, an aorist optative, **nīyāt** 'may he lead!'

Parasmaipada or ātmanepada participles, as appropriate, may be formed from the present, the future and all other formations in **-ati**/**-ate**. The aorist has no participle, and of the perfect participles the parasmaipada is infrequent and the ātmanepada hardly found.

2 *Nominal formations*

With weak grade

PAST PARTICIPLE

nīta 'led'

nāyita 'caused to lead'

PAST ACTIVE PARTICIPLE

nītavant 'having led'

nāyitavant 'having caused to lead'

ABSOLUTIVE

(uncompounded) **nītvā** 'after leading'
(after prefix) **-nīya** ,,

nāyayitvā / **-nāyya** 'after causing to lead'

With strong grade

INFINITIVE

netum 'to lead'

nāyayitum 'to cause to lead'

AGENT NOUN

netṛ 'leader'

nāyayitṛ 'causer of leading'

GERUNDIVES

(*a*) **neya** '(requiring) to be led'		**nāyya** '(requiring) to be caused to lead'
(*b*) **netavya**	,,	**nāyayitavya** ,,
(*c*) **nayanīya**	,,	**nāyanīya** ,,

3 *Remoter nominal formations*

Formations of the following types may be regarded as less integrated into the verbal structure. Often they are lacking in particular roots or have developed some independent meaning. They fall into two broad categories:

(a) Action nouns ('leading, guidance'): **nayanaṃ**; **nayaḥ** 'prudent conduct'; **nīti** f. 'prudent conduct'

(b) Agentives ('that lead'): **-nī**; **-nāyin**; **nāyakaḥ** 'leading actor'; **netraṃ** '[instrument of guidance:] eye' (**nayanaṃ** may also have this sense).

Present paradigms

Thematic paradigm

The inflexions of the present system of class I verbs, as illustrated by **nī**, are shared by classes IV, VI and X, the future, the passive and all derivative verbs in **ati**/**ate** (which means all derivative verbs except one type of intensive).

nī 'lead'

	PRESENT	IMPERFECT	IMPERATIVE	OPTATIVE
		parasmaipada		
1st sg.	**nayāmi**	**anayam**	**nayāni**	**nayeyam**
2nd	**nayasi**	**anayaḥ**	**naya**	**nayeḥ**
3rd	**nayati**	**anayat**	**nayatu**	**nayet**
1st du.	**nayāvaḥ**	**anayāva**	**nayāva**	**nayeva**
2nd	**nayathaḥ**	**anayatam**	**nayatam**	**nayetam**
3rd	**nayataḥ**	**anayatām**	**nayatām**	**nayetām**
1st pl.	**nayāmaḥ**	**anayāma**	**nayāma**	**nayema**
2nd	**nayatha**	**anayata**	**nayata**	**nayeta**
3rd	**nayanti**	**anayan**	**nayantu**	**nayeyuḥ**
Part.	**nayant**			

ātmanepada

1st sg.	naye	anaye	nayai	nayeya
2nd	nayase	anayathāḥ	nayasva	nayethāḥ
3rd	nayate	anayata	nayatām	nayeta
1st du.	nayāvahe	anayāvahi	nayāvahai	nayevahi
2nd	nayethe	anayethām	nayethām	nayeyāthām
3rd	nayete	anayetām	nayetām	nayeyātām
1st pl.	nayāmahe	anayāmahi	nayāmahai	nayemahi
2nd	nayadhve	anayadhvam	nayadhvam	nayedhvam
3rd	nayante	anayanta	nayantām	nayeran
Part.	nayamāna			

Class II (root class)

dviṣ 'hate'

	PRESENT	IMPERFECT	IMPERATIVE	OPTATIVE
		parasmaipada		
1st sg.	dveṣmi	adveṣam	dveṣāṇi	dviṣyām
2nd	dvekṣi	adveṭ	dviḍḍhi	dviṣyāḥ
3rd	dveṣṭi	adveṭ	dveṣṭu	dviṣyāt
1st du.	dviṣvaḥ	adviṣva	dveṣāva	dviṣyāva
2nd	dviṣṭhaḥ	adviṣṭam	dviṣṭam	dviṣyātam
3rd	dviṣṭaḥ	adviṣṭām	dviṣṭām	dviṣyātām
1st pl.	dviṣmaḥ	adviṣma	dveṣāma	dviṣyāma
2nd	dviṣṭha	adviṣṭa	dviṣṭa	dviṣyāta
3rd	dviṣanti	adviṣan	dviṣantu	dviṣyuḥ
Part.	dviṣant			

ātmanepada

1st sg.	dviṣe	adviṣi	dveṣai	dviṣīya
2nd	dvikṣe	adviṣṭhāḥ	dvikṣva	dviṣīthāḥ
3rd	dviṣṭe	adviṣṭa	dviṣṭām	dviṣīta
1st du.	dviṣvahe	adviṣvahi	dveṣāvahai	dviṣīvahi
2nd	dviṣāthe	adviṣāthām	dviṣāthām	dviṣīyāthām
3rd	dviṣāte	adviṣātām	dviṣātām	dviṣīyātām
1st pl.	dviṣmahe	adviṣmahi	dveṣāmahai	dviṣīmahi
2nd	dviḍḍhve	adviḍḍhvam	dviḍḍhvam	dviṣīdhvam
3rd	dviṣate	adviṣata	dviṣatām	dviṣīran
Part.	dviṣāṇa			

as 'be'

	PRESENT	IMPERFECT	IMPERATIVE
		parasmaipada	
1st sg.	**asmi**	**āsam**	**asāni**
2nd	**asi**	**āsīḥ**	**edhi**
3rd	**asti**	**āsīt**	**astu**
1st du.	**svaḥ**	**āsva**	**asāva**
2nd	**sthaḥ**	**āstam**	**stam**
3rd	**staḥ**	**āstām**	**stām**
1st pl.	**smaḥ**	**āsma**	**asāma**
2nd	**stha**	**āsta**	**sta**
3rd	**santi**	**āsan**	**santu**
Opt.	**syām, syāḥ** *etc.*		
Part.	**sant**		

ās 'sit, stay'

	PRESENT	IMPERFECT	IMPERATIVE
		ātmanepada	
1st sg.	**āse**	**āsi**	**āsai**
2nd	**āsse**	**āsthāḥ**	**āssva**
3rd	**āste**	**āsta**	**āstām**
1st du.	**āsvahe**	**āsvahi**	**āsāvahai**
2nd	**āsāthe**	**āsāthām**	**āsāthām**
3rd	**āsāte**	**āsātām**	**āsātām**
1st pl.	**āsmahe**	**āsmahi**	**āsāmahai**
2nd	**āddhve**	**āddhvam**	**āddhvam**
3rd	**āsate**	**āsata**	**āsatām**
Opt.	**āsīya, āsīthāḥ,** *etc.*		
Part.	**āsīna** (*irreg.*)		

i 'go'

	PRESENT	IMPERFECT	IMPERATIVE
		parasmaipada	
1st sg.	**emi**	**āyam**	**ayāni**
2nd	**eṣi**	**aiḥ**	**ihi**
3rd	**eti**	**ait**	**etu**
1st du.	**ivaḥ**	**aiva**	**ayāva**
2nd	**ithaḥ**	**aitam**	**itam**
3rd	**itaḥ**	**aitām**	**itām**
1st pl.	**imaḥ**	**aima**	**ayāma**
2nd	**itha**	**aita**	**ita**
3rd	**yanti**	**āyan**	**yantu**
Opt.	**iyām, iyāḥ,** *etc.*		
Part.	**yant**		

i 'go' (in **adhi+i** 'study')

	PRESENT	IMPERFECT	IMPERATIVE
		ātmanepada	
1st sg.	**iye**	**aiyi**	**ayai**
2nd	**iṣe**	**aithāḥ**	**iṣva**
3rd	**ite**	**aita**	**itām**
1st du.	**ivahe**	**aivahi**	**ayāvahai**
2nd	**iyāthe**	**aiyāthām**	**iyāthām**
3rd	**iyāte**	**aiyātām**	**iyātām**
1st pl.	**imahe**	**aimahi**	**ayāmahai**
2nd	**idhve**	**aidhvam**	**idhvam**
3rd	**iyate**	**aiyata**	**iyatām**
Opt.	**iyīya, iyīthāḥ,** *etc.*		
Part.	**iyāna**		

Class III (*reduplicated class*)

hu 'sacrifice'

	PRESENT	IMPERFECT	IMPERATIVE	OPTATIVE
			parasmaipada	
1st sg.	**juhomi**	**ajuhavam**	**juhavāni**	**juhuyām**
2nd	**juhoṣi**	**ajuhoḥ**	**juhudhi**	**juhuyāḥ**
3rd	**juhoti**	**ajuhot**	**juhotu**	**juhuyāt**
1st du.	**juhuvaḥ**	**ajuhuva**	**juhavāva**	**juhuyāva**
2nd	**juhuthaḥ**	**ajuhutam**	**juhutam**	**juhuyātam**
3rd	**juhutaḥ**	**ajuhutām**	**juhutām**	**juhuyātām**
1st pl.	**juhumaḥ**	**ajuhuma**	**juhavāma**	**juhuyāma**
2nd	**juhutha**	**ajuhuta**	**juhuta**	**juhuyāta**
3rd	**juhvati**	**ajuhavuḥ**	**juhvatu**	**juhuyuḥ**
Part.	**juhvat**			

The second person singular imperative **juhudhi** (instead of **juhuhi*) is anomalous.

			ātmanepada	
1st sg.	**juhve**	**ajuhvi**	**juhavai**	**juhvīya**
2nd	**juhuṣe**	**ajuhuthāḥ**	**juhuṣva**	**juhvīthāḥ**
3rd	**juhute**	**ajuhuta**	**juhutām**	**juhvīta**
1st du.	**juhuvahe**	**ajuhuvahi**	**juhavāvahai**	**juhvīvahi**
2nd	**juhvāthe**	**ajuhvāthām**	**juhvāthām**	**juhvīyāthām**
3rd	**juhvāte**	**ajuhvātām**	**juhvātām**	**juhvīyātām**
1st pl.	**juhumahe**	**ajuhumahi**	**juhavāmahai**	**juhvīmahi**
2nd	**juhudhve**	**ajuhudhvam**	**juhudhvam**	**juhvīdhvam**
3rd	**juhvate**	**ajuhvata**	**juhvatām**	**juhvīran**
Part.	**juhvāna**			

Class V (ṇu *class*)

su 'press'

	PRESENT	IMPERFECT	IMPERATIVE
		parasmaipada	
1st sg.	**sunomi**	**asunavam**	**sunavāni**
2nd	**sunoṣi**	**asunoḥ**	**sunu**
3rd	**sunoti**	**asunot**	**sunotu**
1st du.	**sunuvaḥ/sunvaḥ**	**asunuva/asunva**	**sunavāva**
2nd	**sunuthaḥ**	**asunutam**	**sunutam**
3rd	**sunutaḥ**	**asunutām**	**sunutām**
1st pl.	**sunumaḥ/sunmaḥ**	**asunuma/asunma**	**sunavāma**
2nd	**sunutha**	**asunuta**	**sunuta**
3rd	**sunvanti**	**asunvan**	**sunvantu**
Opt.	**sunuyām**, *etc.*		
Part.	**sunvant**		
		ātmanepada	
1st sg.	**sunve**	**asunvi**	**sunavai**
2nd	**sunuṣe**	**asunuthāḥ**	**sunuṣva**
3rd	**sunute**	**asunuta**	**sunutām**
1st du.	**sunuvahe/ sunvahe**	**asunuvahi/ asunvahi**	**sunavāvahai**
2nd	**sunvāthe**	**asunvāthām**	**sunvāthām**
3rd	**sunvāte**	**asunvātām**	**sunvātām**
1st pl.	**sunumahe/ sunmahe**	**asunumahi/ asunmahi**	**sunavāmahai**
2nd	**sunudhve**	**asunudhvam**	**sunudhvam**
3rd	**sunvate**	**asunvata**	**sunvatām**
Opt.	**sunvīya**, *etc.*		
Part.	**sunvāna**		

Class VII (*infix nasal class*)

rudh 'obstruct'

	PRESENT	IMPERFECT	IMPERATIVE	OPTATIVE
		parasmaipada		
1st sg.	**ruṇadhmi**	**aruṇadham**	**ruṇadhāni**	**rundhyām**
2nd	**ruṇatsi**	**aruṇat**	**runddhi**	**rundhyāḥ**
3rd	**ruṇaddhi**	**aruṇat**	**ruṇaddhu**	**rundhyāt**
1st du.	**rundhvaḥ**	**arundhva**	**ruṇadhāva**	**rundhyāva**
2nd	**runddhaḥ**	**arunddham**	**runddham**	**rundhyātam**
3rd	**runddhaḥ**	**arunddhām**	**runddhām**	**rundhyātām**
1st pl.	**rundhmaḥ**	**arundhma**	**ruṇadhāma**	**rundhyāma**
2nd	**runddha**	**arunddha**	**runddha**	**rundhyāta**
3rd	**rundhanti**	**arundhan**	**rundhantu**	**rundhyuḥ**
Part.	**rundhant**			

	PRESENT	IMPERFECT	IMPERATIVE	OPTATIVE
		ātmanepada		
1st sg.	**rundhe**	**arundhi**	**ruṇadhai**	**rundhīya**
2nd	**runtse**	**arunddhāḥ**	**runtsva**	**rundhīthāḥ**
3rd	**runddhe**	**arunddha**	**runddhām**	**rundhīta**
1st du.	**rundhvahe**	**arundhvahi**	**ruṇadhāvahai**	**rundhīvahi**
2nd	**rundhāthe**	**arundhāthām**	**rundhāthām**	**rundhīyāthām**
3rd	**rundhāte**	**arundhātām**	**rundhātām**	**rundhīyātām**
1st pl.	**rundhmahe**	**arundhmahi**	**ruṇadhāmahai**	**rundhīmahi**
2nd	**runddhve**	**arunddhvam**	**runddhvam**	**rundhīdhvam**
3rd	**rundhate**	**arundhata**	**rundhatām**	**rundhīran**
Part.	**rundhāna**			

Class VIII (u *class*)

kṛ 'do'

	PRESENT	IMPERFECT	IMPERATIVE	OPTATIVE
		parasmaipada		
1st sg.	**karomi**	**akaravam**	**karavāṇi**	**kuryām**
2nd	**karoṣi**	**akaroḥ**	**kuru**	**kuryāḥ**
3rd	**karoti**	**akarot**	**karotu**	**kuryāt**
1st du.	**kurvaḥ**	**akurva**	**karavāva**	**kuryāva**
2nd	**kuruthaḥ**	**akurutam**	**kurutam**	**kuryātam**
3rd	**kurutaḥ**	**akurutām**	**kurutām**	**kuryātām**
1st pl.	**kurmaḥ**	**akurma**	**karavāma**	**kuryāma**
2nd	**kurutha**	**akuruta**	**kuruta**	**kuryāta**
3rd	**kurvanti**	**akurvan**	**kurvantu**	**kuryuḥ**
Part.	**kurvant**			
		ātmanepada		
1st sg.	**kurve**	**akurvi**	**karavai**	**kurvīya**
2nd	**kuruṣe**	**akuruthāḥ**	**kuruṣva**	**kurvīthāḥ**
3rd	**kurute**	**akuruta**	**kurutām**	**kurvīta**
1st du.	**kurvahe**	**akurvahi**	**karavāvahai**	**kurvīvahi**
2nd	**kurvāthe**	**akurvāthām**	**kurvāthām**	**kurvīyāthām**
3rd	**kurvāte**	**akurvātām**	**kurvātām**	**kurvīyātām**
1st pl.	**kurmahe**	**akurmahi**	**karavāmahai**	**kurvīmahi**
2nd	**kurudhve**	**akurudhvam**	**kurudhvam**	**kurvīdhvam**
3rd	**kurvate**	**akurvata**	**kurvatām**	**kurvīran**
Part.	**kurvāṇa**			

The other seven verbs of this class inflect like **su**.

Class IX (nā *class*)

krī 'buy'

	PRESENT	IMPERFECT	IMPERATIVE	OPTATIVE
		parasmaipada		
1st sg.	**krīṇāmi**	**akrīṇām**	**krīṇāni**	**krīṇīyām**
2nd	**krīṇāsi**	**akrīṇāḥ**	**krīṇīhi**	**krīṇīyāḥ**

3rd	**krīṇāti**	**akrīṇāt**	**krīṇātu**	**krīṇīyāt**
1st du.	**krīṇīvaḥ**	**akrīṇīva**	**krīṇāva**	**krīṇīyāva**
2nd	**krīṇīthaḥ**	**akrīṇītam**	**krīṇītam**	**krīṇīyātam**
3rd	**krīṇītaḥ**	**akrīṇītām**	**krīṇītām**	**krīṇīyātām**
1st pl.	**krīṇīmaḥ**	**akrīṇīma**	**krīṇāma**	**krīṇīyāma**
2nd	**krīṇītha**	**akrīṇīta**	**krīṇīta**	**krīṇīyāta**
3rd	**krīṇanti**	**akrīṇan**	**krīṇantu**	**krīṇīyuḥ**
Part.	**krīṇant**			
			ātmanepada	
1st. sg.	**krīṇe**	**akrīṇi**	**krīṇai**	**krīṇīya**
2nd	**krīṇīṣe**	**akrīṇīthāḥ**	**krīṇīṣva**	**krīṇīthāḥ**
3rd	**krīṇīte**	**akrīṇīta**	**krīṇītām**	**krīṇīta**
1st du.	**krīṇīvahe**	**akrīṇīvahi**	**krīṇāvahai**	**krīṇīvahi**
2nd	**krīṇāthe**	**akrīṇāthām**	**krīṇāthām**	**krīṇīyāthām**
3rd	**krīṇāte**	**akrīṇātām**	**krīṇātām**	**krīṇīyātām**
1st pl.	**krīṇīmahe**	**akrīṇīmahi**	**krīṇāmahai**	**krīṇīmahi**
2nd	**krīṇīdhve**	**akrīṇīdhvam**	**krīṇīdhvam**	**krīṇīdhvam**
3rd	**krīṇate**	**akrīṇata**	**krīṇatām**	**krīṇīran**
Part.	**krīṇāna**			

Perfect paradigms

	dṛś 'see'	**kṛ** 'do'	**vac** 'speak'	**pac** 'cook'	**dhā** 'put'
			parasmaipada		
1st sg.	**dadarśa**	**cakara/ cakāra**	**uvaca/ uvāca**	**papaca/ papāca**	**dadhau**
2nd	**dadarśitha**	**cakartha**	**uvaktha/ uvacitha**	**papaktha/ pecitha**	**dadhātha/ dadhitha**
3rd	**dadarśa**	**cakāra**	**uvāca**	**papāca**	**dadhau**
1st du.	**dadṛśiva**	**cakṛva**	**ūciva**	**peciva**	**dadhiva**
2nd	**dadṛśathuḥ**	**cakrathuḥ**	**ūcathuḥ**	**pecathuḥ**	**dadhathuḥ**
3rd	**dadṛśatuḥ**	**cakratuḥ**	**ūcatuḥ**	**pecatuḥ**	**dadhatuḥ**
1st pl.	**dadṛśima**	**cakṛma**	**ūcima**	**pecima**	**dadhima**
2nd	**dadṛśa**	**cakra**	**ūca**	**peca**	**dadha**
3rd	**dadṛśuḥ**	**cakruḥ**	**ūcuḥ**	**pecuḥ**	**dadhuḥ**
Part.	**dadṛśivāṃs**	**cakṛvāṃs**	**ūcivāṃs**	**pecivāṃs**	**dadhivāṃs**
			ātmanepada		
1st sg.	**dadṛśe**	**cakre**	**ūce**	**pece**	**dadhe**
2nd	**dadṛśiṣe**	**cakṛṣe**	**ūciṣe**	**peciṣe**	**dadhiṣe**
3rd	**dadṛśe**	**cakre**	**ūce**	**pece**	**dadhe**
1st du.	**dadṛśivahe**	**cakṛvahe**	**ūcivahe**	**pecivahe**	**dadhivahe**
2nd	**dadṛśāthe**	**cakrāthe**	**ūcāthe**	**pecāthe**	**dadhāthe**
3rd	**dadṛśāte**	**cakrāte**	**ūcāte**	**pecāte**	**dadhāte**
1st pl.	**dadṛśimahe**	**cakṛmahe**	**ūcimahe**	**pecimahe**	**dadhimahe**
2nd	**dadṛśidhve**	**cakṛdhve**	**ūcidhve**	**pecidhve**	**dadhidhve**
3rd	**dadṛśire**	**cakrire**	**ūcire**	**pecire**	**dadhire**
Part.	**dadṛśāna**	**cakrāṇa**	**ūcāna**	**pecāna**	**dadhāna**

as 'be' (parasmaipada): āsa āsitha āsa; āsiva āsathuḥ āsatuḥ; āsima āsa āsuḥ—no participle.

Aorist paradigms

Non-sigmatic aorists

	ROOT AORIST		a-AORIST	REDUPLICATED AORIST
	dhā 'put'	**bhū** 'be'	**sic** 'moisten'	**nī** (cause to) 'lead'
			parasmaipada	
1st sg.	**adhām**	**abhūvam**	**asicam**	**anīnayam**
2nd	**adhāḥ**	**abhūḥ**	**asicaḥ**	**anīnayaḥ**
3rd	**adhāt**	**abhūt**	**asicat**	**anīnayat**
1st du.	**adhāva**	**abhūva**	**asicāva**	**anīnayāva**
2nd	**adhātam**	**abhūtam**	**asicatam**	**anīnayatam**
3rd	**adhātām**	**abhūtām**	**asicatām**	**anīnayatām**
1st pl.	**adhāma**	**abhūma**	**asicāma**	**anīnayāma**
2nd	**adhāta**	**abhūta**	**asicata**	**anīnayata**
3rd	**adhuḥ**	**abhūvan**	**asican**	**anīnayan**
			ātmanepada	
1st sg.			**asice**	**anīnaye**
2nd			**asicathāḥ**	**anīnayathāḥ**
3rd			**asicata**	**anīnayata**
1st du.			**asicāvahi**	**anīnayāvahi**
2nd			**asicethām**	**anīnayethām**
3rd			**asicetām**	**anīnayetām**
1st pl.			**asicāmahi**	**anīnayāmahi**
2nd			**asicadhvam**	**anīnayadhvam**
3rd			**asicanta**	**anīnayanta**

Sigmatic aorists

	s-AORIST		iṣ-AORIST	siṣ-AORIST	sa-AORIST
	After vowel	*After consonant*			
	nī 'lead'	**dah** 'burn'	**pū** 'purify'	**yā** 'go'	**diś** 'point'
			parasmaipada		
1st sg.	**anaiṣam**	**adhākṣam**	**apāviṣam**	**ayāsiṣam**	**adikṣam**
2nd	**anaiṣīḥ**	**adhākṣīḥ**	**apāvīḥ**	**ayāsīḥ**	**adikṣaḥ**
3rd	**anaiṣīt**	**adhākṣīt**	**apāvīt**	**ayāsīt**	**adikṣat**
1st du.	**anaiṣva**	**adhākṣva**	**apāviṣva**	**ayāsiṣva**	**adikṣāva**
2nd	**anaiṣṭam**	**adāgdham**	**apāviṣṭam**	**ayāsiṣṭam**	**adikṣatam**
3rd	**anaiṣṭām**	**adāgdhām**	**apāviṣṭām**	**ayāsiṣṭām**	**adikṣatām**

	S-AORIST		IṢ-AORIST	SIṢ-AORIST	SA-AORIST
			parasmaipada		
1st pl.	**anaiṣma**	**adhākṣma**	**apāviṣma**	**ayāsiṣma**	**adikṣāma**
2nd	**anaiṣṭa**	**adāgdha**	**apāviṣṭa**	**ayāsiṣṭa**	**adikṣata**
3rd	**anaiṣuḥ**	**adhākṣuḥ**	**apāviṣuḥ**	**ayāsiṣuḥ**	**adikṣan**
			ātmanepada		
1st sg.	**aneṣi**	**adhakṣi**	**apaviṣi**		**adikṣi**
2nd	**aneṣṭhāḥ**	**adagdhāḥ**	**apaviṣṭhāḥ**		**adikṣathāḥ**
3rd	**aneṣṭa**	**adagdha**	**apaviṣṭa**		**adikṣata**
1st du.	**aneṣvahi**	**adhakṣvahi**	**apaviṣvahi**		**adikṣāvahi**
2nd	**aneṣāthām**	**adhakṣāthām**	**apaviṣāthām**		**adikṣāthām**
3rd	**aneṣātām**	**adhakṣātām**	**apaviṣātām**		**adikṣātām**
1st pl.	**aneṣmahi**	**adhakṣmahi**	**apaviṣmahi**		**adikṣāmahi**
2nd	**aneḍhvam**	**adhagdhvam**	**apaviḍhvam**		**adikṣadhvam**
3rd	**aneṣata**	**adhakṣata**	**apaviṣata**		**adikṣanta**

Precative

bhū 'be' (parasmaipada): **bhūyāsam bhūyāḥ bhūyāt**; **bhūyāsva bhūyāstam bhūyāstām**; **bhūyāsma bhūyāsta bhūyāsuḥ**.

Principal parts of verbs

The following list of verbs (arranged in Sanskrit alphabetical order) shows the main formations from each root. The less important verbs and those, such as class X verbs, whose derivative forms are obvious are omitted. The past participle is to be taken as a guide to the formation of the PAST ACTIVE PARTICIPLE and of the uncompounded ABSOLUTIVE in **-tvā**; the infinitive to the formation of the AGENT NOUN and of the GERUNDIVE in **tavya**. Similarly, the GERUNDIVE in **anīya**, when it is found, is based on the verbal noun in **ana** (here normally given as **anaṃ** since it is most often a neuter substantive). Where parasmaipada and ātmanepada forms both exist, only the former are mentioned. A blank indicates that the part of the verb in question is not known to appear in Classical Sanskrit; and even of those forms given some are rare or dubious.

ROOT	ad 'eat'	as 'be'	āp 'obtain'	ās 'sit'	i 'go'	iṣ 'want'
PRESENT	II atti	II asti	V āpnoti	II āste	II eti	VI icchati
PERFECT		āsa	āpa	āsāṃ cakre	iyāya	iyeṣa
AORIST			āpat			aiṣīt
FUTURE	atsyati		āpsyati	āsiṣyate	eṣyati	eṣiṣyati
PASSIVE	adyate		āpyate	āsyate	īyate	iṣyate
CAUSATIVE	ādayati		āpayati		āyayati	eṣayati
PAST PARTICIPLE	jagdha		āpta	āsita	ita	iṣṭa
ABSOLUTIVE in yạ			-āpya	-āsya	-itya	-iṣya
INFINITIVE	attum		āptum	āsitum	etum	eṣṭum
GERUNDIVE in ya	adya		āpya			eṣya
NOMINAL in ana	adanaṃ		āpanaṃ	āsanaṃ	ayanaṃ	eṣaṇaṃ
,, in in	ādin		āpin		āyin	eṣin

ROOT	īkṣ 'see'	kṛ 'do'	kṛṣ 'drag'	kḷp 'be fit'	kram 'stride'	krī 'buy'
PRESENT	I īkṣate	VIII karoti	I karṣati	I kalpate	I krāmati	IX krīṇāti
PERFECT	īkṣāṃ cakre	cakāra	cakarṣa	cakḷpe	cakrāma	
AORIST	aikṣīt	akārṣīt	akārkṣīt	(acīkḷpat)		
FUTURE	īkṣiṣyate	kariṣyati		kalpiṣyate	kramiṣyati	
PASSIVE	īkṣyate	kriyate	kṛṣyate		kramyate	krīyate
CAUSATIVE	īkṣayati	kārayati	karṣayati	kalpayati	kramayati	
PAST PARTICIPLE	īkṣita	kṛta	kṛṣṭa	kḷpta	krānta	krīta
ABSOLUTIVE in ya	-īkṣya	-kṛtya	-kṛṣya		-kramya	-krīya
INFINITIVE	īkṣitum	kartum	kraṣṭum		krāntum	kretum
GERUNDIVE in ya		kārya	kṛṣya		kramya	kreya
NOMINAL in ana	īkṣaṇaṃ	karaṇaṃ	karṣaṇaṃ	kalpanaṃ	kramaṇaṃ	krayaṇaṃ
,, in in	īkṣin	kārin	karṣin			-krayin

ROOT	kṣip 'throw'	(ā)khyā 'tell'	gam 'go'	gai 'sing'	grah 'seize'	car 'move'
PRESENT	VI kṣipati	II khyāti	I gacchati	I gāyati	IX gṛhṇāti	I carati
PERFECT	cikṣepa	cakhyau	jagāma	jagau	jagrāha	cacāra
AORIST			agamat		ajigrahat	acīcarat
FUTURE	kṣepsyati	khyāsyati	gamiṣyati	gāsyati	grahīṣyati	cariṣyati
PASSIVE	kṣipyate	khyāyate	gamyate	gīyate	gṛhyate	caryate
CAUSATIVE	kṣepayati	khyāpayati	gamayati	gāpayati	grāhayati	cārayati
PAST PARTICIPLE	kṣipta	khyāta	gata	gīta	gṛhīta	carita
ABSOLUTIVE in ya	-kṣipya	-khyāya	-gatya/ -gamya	-gīya	-gṛhya	-carya
INFINITVE	kṣeptum	khyātum	gantum	gātum	grahītum	caritum
GERUNDIVE in ya	kṣepya	-khyeya	gamya	geya	grāhya	
NOMINAL in ana	kṣepaṇaṃ		gamanaṃ		grahaṇaṃ	caraṇaṃ
,, in in	-kṣepin		gāmin	gāyin	grāhin	cārin

ROOT	ci 'collect'	chid 'cut'	jan 'be born'	ji 'win'	jīv 'live'	jñā 'know'
PRESENT	V cinoti	VII chinatti	IV jāyate	I jayati	I jīvati	IX jānāti
PERFECT	cikāya	cicheda	jajñe	jigāya	jijīva	jajñau
AORIST		achidat/ achaitsīt	ajaniṣṭa	ajaiṣīt		ajñāsīt
FUTURE	ceṣyati	chetsyati	janiṣyati	jeṣyati	jīviṣyati	jñāsyati
PASSIVE	cīyate	chidyate		jīyate	jīvyate	jñāyate
CAUSATIVE	cāyayate	chedayati	janayati		jīvayati	jñāpayati
PAST PARTICIPLE	cita	chinna	jāta	jita	jīvita	jñāta
ABSOLUTIVE in ya	-citya	-chidya		-jitya	-jīvya	-jñāya
INFINITIVE	cetum	chettum		jetum	jīvitum	jñātum
GERUNDIVE in ya	ceya	chedya		jeya		jñeya

NOMINAL in **ana**	**cayanaṃ**	**chedanaṃ**			**jīvanaṃ**	**jñānaṃ**
,, in **in**	**-cāyin**	**-chedin**		**-jāyin**	**-jīvin**	
ROOT	**tan** 'stretch'	**tud** 'strike'	**tuṣ** 'be content'	**tṝ** 'cross'	**tyaj** 'forsake'	**tvar** 'hurry'
PRESENT	VIII **tanoti**	VI **tudati**	IV **tuṣyati**	I **tarati**	I **tyajati**	I **tvarate**
PERFECT	**tatāna**	**tutoda**	**tutoṣa**	**tatāra**	**tatyāja**	**tatvare**
AORIST				**atārṣīt**	**atyākṣīt**	
FUTURE				**tariṣyati**	**tyakṣyati/ tyajiṣyati**	
PASSIVE	**tanyate**	**tudyate**		**tīryate**	**tyajyate**	**tvaryate**
CAUSATIVE	**tānayati**	**todayati**	**toṣayati**	**tārayati**	**tyājayati**	**tvarayati**
PAST PARTICIPLE	**tata**	**tunna**	**tuṣṭa**	**tīrṇa**	**tyakta**	**tvarita**
ABSOLUTIVE in **ya**	**-tatya/-tāya**	**-tudya**	**-tuṣya**	**-tīrya**	**-tyajya**	
INFINITIVE				**taritum**	**tyaktum**	
GERUNDIVE in **ya**				**tārya**	**tyajya**	
NOMINAL in **ana**			**toṣaṇaṃ**	**taraṇaṃ**		
,, in **in**			**toṣin**		**tyāgin**	
ROOT	**dah** 'burn'	**dā** 'give'	**diś** 'point'	**duṣ** 'spoil'	**dṛś** 'see'	**dru** 'run'
PRESENT	I **dahati**	III **dadāti**	VI **diśati**	IV **duṣyati**	I **paśyati**	I **dravati**
PERFECT	**dadāha**	**dadau**	**dideśa**		**dadarśa**	**dudrāva**
AORIST	**adhākṣīt**	**adāt**	**adikṣat**		**adrākṣīt/ adarśat**	
FUTURE	**dhakṣyati**	**dāsyati**	**dekṣyati**		**drakṣyati**	
PASSIVE	**dahyate**	**dīyate**	**diśyate**		**dṛśyate**	
CAUSATIVE	**dāhayati**	**dāpayati**	**deśayati**	**dūṣayati**	**darśayati**	**drāvayati**

PAST PARTICIPLE	**dagdha**	**datta**	**diṣṭa**	**duṣṭa**	**dṛṣṭa**	**druta**
ABSOLUTIVE	**-dahya**	**-dāya**	**-diśya**		**-dṛśya**	**-drutya**
INFINITIVE	**dagdhum**	**dātum**	**deṣṭum**		**draṣṭum**	**drotum**
GERUNDIVE in ya	**dāhya**	**deya**	**deśya**	**dūṣya**	**dṛśya**	
NOMINAL in ana	**dahanaṃ**	**dānaṃ**		**dūṣaṇaṃ**	**darśanaṃ**	
,, in in	**dāhin**	**dāyin**	**deśin**	**-dūṣin**	**-darśin**	**dravaṇaṃ**
ROOT	**druh** 'hurt'	**dhā** 'put'	**dhṛ** 'hold'	**nand** 'be glad'	**nam** 'bow'	**naś** 'perish'
PRESENT	IV **druhyati**	III **dadhāti**	(I **dharati**)	I **nandati**	I **namati**	IV **naśyati**
PERFECT	**dudruhe**	**dadhau**	**dadhāra**	**nanauda**	**nanāma**	**nanāśa**
AORIST	**adruhat**	**adhāt**			**anaṃsīt**	**anaśat**
FUTURE		**dhāsyati**	**dhariṣyati**		**naṃsyati**	**naśiṣyati/ naṅkṣyati**
PASSIVE		**dhīyate**	**dhriyate**	**nandyate**	**namyate**	
CAUSATIVE		**dhāpayati**	**dhārayati**	**nandayati**	**namayati**	**nāśayati**
PAST PARTICIPLE	**drugdha**	**hita**	**dhṛta**	**nandita**	**nata**	**naṣṭa**
ABSOLUTIVE in ya	**-druhya**	**-dhāya**	**-dhṛtya**	**-nandya**	**-namya**	
INFINITVE	**drogdhum**	**dhātum**	**dhartum**		**namitum/ nantum**	
GERUNDIVE in ya		**dheya**	**dhārya**	**-nandya**		
NOMINAL in ana		**-dhānaṃ**	**dhāraṇaṃ**	**nandana**	**namanaṃ**	**naśanaṃ**
,, in in	**drohin**	**-dhāyin**	**dhārin**	**nandin**		
ROOT	**nī** 'lead'	**nṛt** 'dance'	**pac** 'cook'	**pat** 'fall'	**pad** 'go'	**pā** 'drink'
PRESENT	I **nayati**	IV **nṛtyati**	I **pacati**	I **patati**	IV **padyate**	I **pibati**
PERFECT	**nināya**	**nanarta**	**papāca**	**papāta**	**papāda**	**papau**
AORIST	**anaiṣīt**			**apaptat**	**apādi**	**apāt**

FUTURE	neṣyati	nartiṣyati	pakṣyati	patiṣyati	patsyate	pāsyati
PASSIVE	nīyate	nṛtyate	pacyate			pīyate
CAUSATIVE	nāyayati	nartayati	pācayati	pātayati	pādayati	pāyayati
PAST PARTICIPLE	nīta	nṛtta	(pakva)	patita	panna	pīta
ABSOLUTIVE in ya	-nīya			-patya	-padya	-pāya
INFINITIVE	netum	nartitum		patitum	pattum	pātuṃ
GERUNDIVE in ya	neya					peya
NOMINAL in ana	nayanaṃ	nartanaṃ	pacanaṃ	patanaṃ		pānaṃ
,, in in	-nāyin	nartin		pātin	-pādin	-pāyin
ROOT	pṝ 'fill'	prach 'ask'	bandh 'bind'	budh 'wake'	brū 'say'	bhaj 'divide
PRESENT	III piparti	VI pṛcchati	IX badhnāti	I bodhati/ IV budhyate	II bravīti	I bhajati
PERFECT	pupūre	papraccha	babandha	bubudhe		babhāja
AORIST		aprākṣīt		abuddha		abhākṣīt
FUTURE		prakṣyati	bhantsyati	bhotsyate		bhajiṣyati
PASSIVE	pūryate	pṛchyate	badhyate	budhyate		bhajyate
CAUSATIVE	pūrayati		bandhayati	bodhayati		bhājayati
PAST PARTICIPLE	pūrṇa/pūrta	pṛṣṭa	baddha	buddha		bhakta
ABSOLUTIVE in ya	-pūrya	-pṛchya	-badhya	-budhya		-bhajya
INFINITIVE		praṣṭum	banddhum	boddhum		bhaktum
GERUNDIVE in ya		-pṛchya	bandhya	bodhya		
NOMINAL in ana	pūraṇaṃ		bandhanaṃ	bodhanaṃ		bhajanaṃ
,, in in			bandhin	bodhin		bhājin
ROOT	bhañj 'break'	bhid 'split'	bhī 'fear'	bhuj 'enjoy'	bhū 'be'	bhṛ 'carry'
PRESENT	VII bhanakti	VII bhinatti	III bibheti	VII bhunakti	I bhavati	III bibharti

PERFECT	babhañja	bibheda	bibhāya	bubhuje	babhūva	babhāra
AORIST	abhāṅkṣīt		abhaiṣīt	abhaukṣīt	abhūt	
FUTURE	bhaṅkṣyati	bhetsyati		bhokṣyati	bhaviṣyati	bhariṣyati
PASSIVE	bhajyate	bhidyate	bhīyate	bhujyate	bhūyate	bhriyate
CAUSATIVE	(bhañjayati)	bhedayati	bhāyayati/ bhīṣayate	bhojayati	bhāvayati	bhārayati
PAST PARTICIPLE	bhagna	bhinna	bhīta	bhukta	bhūta	bhṛta
ABSOLUTIVE in ya	-bhajya	-bhidya	-bhīya		-bhūya	-bhṛtya
INFINITIVE		bhettum	bhetum	bhoktum	bhavitum	bhartum
GERUNDIVE in ya		bhedya		bhojya	bhā̆vya	bhārya
NOMINAL in ana	bhañjanaṃ	bhedanam		bhojanaṃ	bhavanaṃ	bharaṇaṃ
,, in in		bhedin		bhojin	bhāvin	bhārin
ROOT	bhram 'wander'	mad 'rejoice'	man 'think'	muc 'let go'	mṛ 'die'	yaj 'sacrifice'
PRESENT	I bhramati/ IV bhrā-myati	IV mādyati	IV manyate	VI muñcati	IV mriyate	I yajati
PERFECT	babhrāma		mene	mumoca	mamāra	iyāja
AORIST		amādīt	amaṃsta	amucat		ayākṣīt
FUTURE	bhramiṣyati		maṃsyate	mokṣyati	mariṣyati	yakṣyati
PASSIVE			manyate	mucyate	(mriyate)	ijyate
CAUSATIVE	bhrā̆mayati	mā̆dayati	mānayati	mocayati	mārayati	yājayati
PAST PARTICIPLE	bhrānta	matta	mata	mukta	mṛta	iṣṭa
ABSOLUTIVE in ya	-bhramya		-manya/ -matya	-mucya		
INFINITIVE	bhrāntum		mantum	moktum	martum	yaṣṭum

GERUNDIVE in ya				mocya		ijya
NOMINAL in ana	bhramaṇaṃ	madana	mananaṃ	mocanaṃ	maraṇaṃ	yajanaṃ
,, in in			mānin	-mocin	-mārin	yājin
ROOT	yat 'strive'	yam 'reach'	yā 'go'	yuj 'join'	yudh 'fight'	rakṣ 'guard'
PRESENT	I yatate	I yacchati	II yāti	VII yunakti	IV yudhyate	I rakṣati
PERFECT		yayāma	yayau	yuyoja	yuyodha	rarakṣa
AORIST			ayāsīt	ayujat	ayuddha	arakṣīt
FUTURE	yatiṣyate	yamiṣyati	yāsyati	yokṣyati	yotsyati	rakṣiṣyati
PASSIVE	yatyate	yamyate		yujyate	yudhyate	rakṣyate
CAUSATIVE	yātayati	yāmayati	yāpayati	yojayati	yodhayati	rakṣayati
PAST PARTICIPLE	yatta	yata	yāta	yukta	yuddha	rakṣita
ABSOLUTIVE in ya		-yamya	-yāya	-yujya	-yudhya	-rakṣya
INFINITIVE		yantum/ yamitum	yātum	yoktum	yoddhum	rakṣitum
GERUNDIVE in ya				yojya	yodhya	rakṣya
NOMINAL in ana	-yatanaṃ	yamanaṃ	yānaṃ	yojanaṃ	yodhanaṃ	rakṣaṇaṃ
,, in in		yamin	yāyin		yodhin	rakṣin

ROOT	rabh 'grasp'	ram 'be pleased'	rudh 'obstruct'	ruh 'ascend'	labh 'grasp'	lamb 'hang'	likh 'write'
PRESENT	I rabhate	I ramate	VII ruṇad-dhi	I rohati	I labhate	I lambate	VI likhati
PERFECT	rebhe	reme	rurodha	ruroha	lebhe	lalambe	lilekha
AORIST		araṃsīt	arudhat/ arautsīt	aruhat/ arukṣat			
FUTURE	rapsyate	raṃsyate	rotsyati	rokṣyati	lapsyate	lambiṣyate	likhiṣyati
PASSIVE	rabhyate	ramyate	rudhyate	ruhyate	labhyate	lambyate	likhyate

CAUSATIVE	rambhayati	ramayati	rodhayati	rohayati/ ropayati	lambhayati	lambayati	lekhayati
PAST PARTICIPLE	rabdha	rata	ruddha	rūḍha	labdha	lambita	likhita
ABSOLUTIVE in ya	-rabhya	-ramya	-rudhya	-ruhya	-labhya	-lambya	-likhya
INFINITIVE	rabdhum	rantum	roddhum	roḍhum	labdhum	lambitum	likhitum
GERUNDIVE in ya		ramya	-rodhya		labhya		lekhya
NOMINAL in ana	-rambhaṇaṃ	ramaṇa	rodhanaṃ	rohaṇaṃ	lambhanaṃ	-lambanaṃ	lekhanaṃ
,, in in		rāmin	rodhin	rohin	lābhin	-lambin	lekhin

ROOT	vac 'speak'	vad 'speak'	vas 'dwell'	vah 'carry'	vid 'know'	viś 'enter'
PRESENT	II vakti	I vadati	I vasati	I vahati	II vetti (*pres. perf.* veda)	VI viśati
PERFECT	uvāca		uvāsa	uvāha	viveda	viveśa
AORIST	avocat	avādīt	avātsīt	avākṣīt	avedīt	avikṣat
FUTURE	vakṣyati	vadiṣyati	vatsyati	vakṣyati	vetsyati	vekṣyati
PASSIVE	ucyate	udyate	uṣyate	uhyate	vidyate	viśyate
CAUSATIVE	vācayati	vādayati	vāsayati	vāhayati	vedayati	veśayati
PAST PARTICIPLE	ukta	udita	uṣita	ūḍha	vidita	viṣṭa
ABSOLUTIVE in ya	-ucya	-udya	-uṣya	-uhya		-viśya
INFINITIVE	vaktum	vaditum	vastum/ vasitum	voḍhum	veditum	veṣṭum
GERUNDIVE in ya	vācya	vadya		vāhya	vedya	veśya
NOMINAL in ana	vacanaṃ	vadanaṃ	vasanaṃ	vahanaṃ	vedanaṃ	
,, in in	vācin	vādin	vāsin	vāhin	vedin	
ROOT	vṛt 'turn'	vṛdh 'increase'	śak 'be able'	śī 'lie'	śuc 'grieve'	śram 'be tired'

PRESENT	I vartate	I vardhate	V śaknoti	II śete	I śocati	IV śrāmyati
PERFECT	vavarta	vavardha	śaśāka	śiśye	śuśoca	śaśrāma
AORIST	avṛtat	avṛdhat/ avardhiṣṭa	aśakat	aśayiṣṭa	aśucat	
FUTURE	vartsyate/ vartiṣyate	vartsyati	śakṣyati	śayiṣyate	śociṣyati	
PASSIVE			śakyate			śramyate
CAUSATIVE	vartayati	vardhayati		śāyayati	śocayati	śrāmayati
PAST PARTICIPLE	vṛtta	vṛddha	śakta	śayita		śrānta
ABSOLUTIVE in ya	-vṛtya			-śayya		-śramya
INFINITIVE	vartitum	vardhitum		śayitum	śocitum	
GERUNDIVE in ya			śakya		śocya	
NOMINAL in ana	vartanaṃ	vardhanaṃ		śayanaṃ	-śocanaṃ	śramaṇa
,, in in	vartin	vardhin		śāyin	-śocin	

ROOT	śri 'resort'	śru 'hear'	śvas 'breathe'	sañj 'adhere'	sad 'sit'	sah 'endure'	sṛj 'emit'
PRESENT	I śrayati	V śṛṇoti	II śvasiti	I sajati	I sīdati	I sahate	VI sṛjati
PERFECT	śiśrāya	śuśrāva	śaśvāsa	sasañja	sasāda		sasarja
AORIST	aśiśriyat	aśrauṣīt	aśvasīt	asāṅkṣīt	asadat		asrākṣīt
FUTURE	śrayiṣyati	śroṣyati	śvasiṣyati		satsyati/ sīdiṣyati	sahiṣyate	srakṣyati
PASSIVE	śrīyate	śrūyate	śvasyate	sajyate	sadyate	sahyate	sṛjyate
CAUSATIVE		śrāvayati	śvāsayati	sañjayati	sādayati	sāhayati	sarjayati
PAST PARTICIPLE	śrita	śruta	śvasita/śvasta	sakta	sanna	soḍha	sṛṣṭa
ABSOLUTIVE in ya	-śritya	-śrutya	-śvasya	-sajya	-sadya	-sahya	-sṛjya
INFINITIVE	śrayitum	śrotum	śvasitum	saktum	sattum	soḍhum	sraṣṭum
GERUNDIVE in ya		śrāvya				sahya	
NOMINAL in ana	-śrayaṇaṃ	śravaṇaṃ	śvasana	sañjanaṃ	sadanaṃ	sahanaṃ	sarjanaṃ
,, in in	-śrayin	śrāvin	śvāsin	saṅgin	sādin	-sāhin	-sargin

ROOT	stu 'praise'	sthā 'stand'	spṛś 'touch'	smṛ 'remember'	svap 'sleep'	han 'strike'
PRESENT	II stauti	I tiṣṭhati	VI spṛśati	I smarati	II svapiti	II hanti
PERFECT	tuṣṭāva	tasthau	pasparśa	sasmāra	suṣvāpa	jaghāna
AORIST	astāvīt/ astauṣīt	asthāt	asprākṣīt		asvāpsīt	(avadhīt)
FUTURE	stoṣyati	sthāsyati	sprakṣyati	smariṣyati	svapsyati	haniṣyati
PASSIVE	stūyate	sthīyate	spṛśyate	smaryate	supyate	hanyate
CAUSATIVE	stāvayati	sthāpayati	sparśayati	smārayati	svāpayati	ghātayati
PAST PARTICIPLE	stuta	sthita	spṛṣṭa	smṛta	supta	hata
ABSOLUTIVE	-stutya	-sthāya	-spṛśya	-smṛtya		-hatya
INFINITIVE	stotum	sthātum	spraṣṭum	smartum	svaptum	hantum
GERUNDIVE in ya	stutya/ stavya	stheya	spṛśya	smarya		(vadhya)
NOMINAL in ana	stavanaṃ	sthānaṃ	sparśanaṃ	smaraṇaṃ	svapanaṃ	hananaṃ
,, in in		sthāyin	sparśin	smārin		ghātin

ROOT	hā 'leave'	hṛ 'take'	hve 'call'
PRESENT	III jahāti	I harati	I hvayati
PERFECT	jahau	jahāra	juhāva
AORIST	ahāt/ ahāsīt	ahārṣīt	
FUTURE	hāsyati	hariṣyati	
PASSIVE	hīyate	hriyate	hūyate
CAUSATIVE	hāpayati	hārayati	hvāyayati
PAST PARTICIPLE	hīna	hṛta	hūta
ABSOLUTIVE in ya	-hāya	-hṛtya	-hūya

INFINITIVE	**hātum**	**hartum**	**hvātum**
GERUNDIVE in ya	**heya**	**hārya**	
NOMINAL in ana	**hānaṃ**	**haraṇaṃ**	**hvānaṃ**
,, in in	**hāyin**	**hārin**	

Appendix 3

Classical Metres

1 Anuṣṭubh

Normal form:

o o o o ⏑ – – o / o o o o ⏑ – ⏑ o (half-verse)
(i) The second or third syllable of each pāda must be heavy.
(ii) The half-verse must not end ⏑ – ⏑ – ⏑ o.

Permitted variant forms of the first or third pāda:

(*a*) o o – } – ⏑ ⏑ ⏑ o (i.e. the fourth syllable as well as the
o – ⏑ } second or third must be heavy)
(*b*) o – ⏑ – – ⏑ ⏑ o
(*c*) o – ⏑ – – / – – o (caesura after fifth syllable)
(*d*) o o o – / – ⏑ – o (caesura after fourth syllable)

2 Samacatuṣpadī metres (in order of length)

(Name; analysis, including caesura; definition, normally taken from Kedāra's *Vṛttaratnākara.*)

Indravajrā – – ⏑ – – ⏑ ⏑ – ⏑ – – (**t t j g g**)

syād Indravajrā yadi tau ja;gau gaḥ

Upendravajrā ⏑ – ⏑ – – ⏑ ⏑ – ⏑ – – (**j t j g g**)

Upendravajrā ja;ta;jās tato gau

Upajāti Any mixture of Indravajrā and Upendravajrā pādas (i.e. first syllable light or heavy at will)

Rathoddhatā – ᴗ – ᴗ ᴗ ᴗ – ᴗ – ᴗ – (r n r l g)

rān na ;rāv iha Rathoddhatā la ;gau

Vaṃśastha ᴗ – ᴗ – – ᴗ ᴗ – ᴗ – ᴗ – (j t j r)

ja ;tau tu Vaṃśastham udīritaṃ ja ;rau

Indravaṃśā – – ᴗ – – ᴗ ᴗ – ᴗ – ᴗ – (t t j r)

syād Indravaṃśā ta ;ta ;jai ra-saṃyutaiḥ

Vaṃśamālā Any mixture of Vaṃśastha and Indravaṃśā pādas (i.e. first syllable light or heavy at will)

Vasantatilakā – – ᴗ – ᴗ ᴗ ᴗ – ᴗ ᴗ – ᴗ – – (t bh j j g g)

uktā Vasantatilakā ta ;bha ;jā ja ;gau gaḥ

Mālinī ᴗ ᴗ ᴗ ᴗ ᴗ ᴗ – – / – ᴗ – – ᴗ – – (n n m y y 8+7)

na ;na ;ma ;ya ;ya-yut» êyaṃ / Mālinī bhogi ;lokaiḥ

Śikhariṇī ᴗ – – – – – / ᴗ ᴗ ᴗ ᴗ ᴗ – – ᴗ ᴗ ᴗ – (y m n s bh l g 6+11)

rasai rudraiś chinnā / ya ;ma ;na ;sa ;bha ;lā gaḥ Śikhariṇī

Hariṇī ᴗ ᴗ ᴗ ᴗ ᴗ – / – – – – / ᴗ – ᴗ ᴗ – ᴗ – (n s m r s l g 6+4+7)

rasa ;yuga ;hayair / n ;sau m ;rau s ;lau go / yadā Hariṇī tadā

Mandākrāntā – – – – / ᴗ ᴗ ᴗ ᴗ ᴗ – / – ᴗ – – ᴗ – – (m bh n t t g g 4+6+7)

Mandākrāntā / jaladhi ;ṣaḍ ;agair / m ;bhau na ;tau tād gurū cet

Śārdūlavikrīḍitam – – – ᴗ ᴗ – ᴗ – ᴗ ᴗ ᴗ – / – – ᴗ – – ᴗ – (m s j s t t g 12+7)

sūry› ;âśvair yadi māt sa ;jau sa ;ta ;ta ;gāḥ / Śārdūlavikrīḍitam

Sragdharā – – – – ᴗ – – / ᴗ ᴗ ᴗ ᴗ ᴗ ᴗ – / – ᴗ – – ᴗ – – (m r bh n y y y 7+7+7)

m ;ra ;bh ;nair yānāṃ trayeṇa / tri:muni:yati-yutā / Sragdharā kīrtit» êyam

y ⏑ – –	bh – ⏑ ⏑	*Symbolic numbers*	
r – ⏑ –	j ⏑ – ⏑	4	**yuga** (age of world); **jaladhi** (ocean)
t – – ⏑	s ⏑ ⏑ –	6	**rasa** (flavour)
m – – –	n ⏑ ⏑ ⏑	7	**loka** (world); **aśva, haya** (horse); **aga** (mountain); **muni** (star of Great Bear)
g –	l ⏑	8	**bhogin** (serpent-demon)
		11	**rudra** (god)
		12	**sūrya** (sun)

3 Ardhasamacatuṣpadī metres

(The bracketed syllable occurs only in the second and fourth pādas.)

Viyoginī ⏑ ⏑ – (–) ⏑ ⏑ – ⏑ – ⏑ – **(s s j g+s bh r l g)**

viṣame sa;sa;jā guruḥ, same
sa;bha;rā lo ›tha gurur Viyoginī

Mālabhāriṇī ⏑ ⏑ – (–) ⏑ ⏑ – ⏑ – ⏑ – – **(s s j g g+s bh r y)**

sa;sa;jāḥ prathame pade gurū cet
sa;bha;rā yena ca Mālabhāriṇī syāt

Aparavaktra ⏑ ⏑ ⏑ ⏑ (–) ⏑ ⏑ – ⏑ – ⏑ – **(n n r l g+n j j r)**

a:yuji na;na;ra;lā guruḥ, same
tad Aparavaktram idaṃ na;jau ja;rau

Puṣpitāgrā ⏑ ⏑ ⏑ ⏑ (–) ⏑ ⏑ – ⏑ – ⏑ – – **(n n r y+n j j r g)**

a:yuji na-yuga;repha˘to yakāro
yuji ca na;jau ja;ra;gāś ca Puṣpitāgrā

(*Note*: Both the first two metres are known by a number of other names.)

4 Āryā

1	2	3		4	5	6
	⏑ – ⏑		/	⏑ – ⏑		⏑ – ⏑
⏑ ⏑ ⏑ ⏑	⏑ ⏑ ⏑ ⏑	⏑ ⏑ ⏑ ⏑	/	⏑ ⏑ ⏑ ⏑	⏑ ⏑ ⏑ ⏑	⏑/⏑ ⏑ ⏑
– –	– –	– –	/	– –	– –	

7 8

⏑ ⏑ ⏑ ⏑

– – – (half-verse)

In the usual form of the second half-verse a light syllable replaces the whole of the sixth foot. Such a stanza, made up of 30+27 mātras, constitutes the Āryā proper.

Āryā 30+27
Udgīti 27+30
Upagīti 27+27
Gīti 30+30
Āryāgīti or **Skandhaka** 32+32 (i.e. the eighth foot is extended to – – or ⏑ ⏑ –)

Sanskrit–English Exercises: Transcription

Exercise 2b

1 gacchāmi 2 atra na praviśāmaḥ 3 punar api likhati 4 adhunā kva vasatha? 5 evam icchasi? 6 kva punas tiṣṭhanti? 7 katham, ita āgacchati? 8 atra kim ānayataḥ? 9 paśyāmi likhāmi ca 10 bhramat› îva 11 nṛtyatho gāyathaś ca 12 smaranti ca śocanti ca 13 'atra praviśāva' iti vadataḥ 14 adhunā ›pi kathaṃ n› āgacchati? 15 jayām› îti mādyāmi 16 na jīvant› îti śocāmaḥ

Exercise 3a

1 ācāryaṃ śiṣyā ānayanti 2 apy aśvān icchasi? 3 ahaṃ sūrya;candrau paśyāmi 4 sukhaṃ ko n› êcchati? 5 svalpaṃ bhojanam 6 jalam aśvān naro nayati 7 'kas tvam?' iti māṃ pṛcchataḥ 8 kaṃ parvataṃ paṇḍito gacchati? 9 atra krodho na vasat› îti vanaṃ praviśataḥ 10 śīghraṃ vacanaṃ n› âvagacchāmaḥ 11 ācārya, parvata iva sa gajaḥ 12 kaṃ punaḥ pṛcchāmi? 13 kiṃ śiṣyā yūyam? 14 jalaṃ nara;bālāḥ praviśanti 15 'ramaṇīyam adhunā tat phalam' iti vismitā vadanti 16 katham, atr› âpi bālāḥ? 17 duḥkhāny api phalam ānayanti 18 'bālā, atra kiṃ sukhaṃ paśyath›?' êti śiṣyān ācāryo vadati

Exercise 4a

1 putraiḥ saha gṛhaṃ tyajati 2 etad udyānam—praviśāmaḥ 3 ācāryeṇa ca śiṣyaiś c› âdbhutaḥ prayatnaḥ kṛtaḥ 4 priyo madīyo vayasya iti jīvitam etena tyaktam 5 ka eṣa gṛham āgacchati? 6 ramaṇīyena darśanena kiṃ na mādyasi? 7 dṛṣṭam avagataṃ ca 8 'atr› aîte narāḥ kim icchant›?' îti kutūhalena gṛhaṃ praviśati 9 dūram eva nagaraṃ, vayaṃ ca pariśrāntā bhramāmaḥ 10 icchath› aîv› aîtan, na vā? 11 'kṛtaṃ vacanair, gato ›vasara' iti viṣādena vadataḥ 12 putrāḥ, sa ev› aîṣo ›vasaraḥ 13 ete vayaṃ nagaram āgatāḥ 14 vismṛto vayasyābhyāṃ prathamo viṣādaḥ 15 'he paṇḍita, tvam aśvaṃ kva nayas›?' îti pṛṣṭo ›pi vacanaṃ na vadati 16 kiṃ prayatnena?—n› aîva tvāṃ paśyati devaḥ

Exercise 5a

1 imau svaḥ 2 prativacanaṃ me śrutvā kim anyad icchanti? 3 n› âsty eva te pustakam 4 vayasya, hṛdayam iv› âsi mama 5 asminn udyāne muhūrtam upaviśāvaḥ 6 kṣetreṣu sarve bhramanti 7 deva, anyasmān nagarād brāhmaṇaḥ kaścid āgataḥ 8 kam upāyaṃ paśyasi mama putrāṇāṃ darśanāya? 9 krodham asya dṛṣṭv» āvega iva no hṛdaye 10 ayaṃ kumāras tiṣṭhati 11 kathaṃ, kṣaṇam ev› ôpaviśya dṛṣṭe mayā punar api mitre 12 anyaḥ ko ›pi mārgo na bhavati 13 duḥkhāy› aîva mitrāṇām idānīṃ Rāmasya darśanam 14 anyebhyo ›pi deven› aîtac chrutam 15 gṛhaṃ praviśya 'kva kv› êdānīm sa pāpa?' iti sarvān pṛcchati 16 andhānāṃ deśe kāṇa eva prabhavati 17 Kalahaṃsaka, ken› aîtan Mādhavasya praticchandakam abhilikhitam?

Exercise 6a

1 Śoṇottare, kim āgamana-prayojanam? 2 kaṣṭam, anartha-dvayam āpatitam 3 mahārāja, api kuśalaṃ kumāra:Lakṣmaṇasya? 4 kutaḥ punar iyaṃ vārttā? 5 satyam itthaṃ:bhūta ev› âsmi 6 amātya, vistīrṇaḥ Kusumapura-vṛttāntaḥ 7 tvam āryābhiḥ putra iva gṛhītaḥ 8 katamasmin pradeśe Mārīc›-āśramaḥ? 9 amba, kā ›si? kim-artham ahaṃ tvayā pratiṣiddhaḥ? 10 nanv anuśaya-sthānam etat 11 s» aîv› êyam 12 ubhābhyām api vāṃ Vāsava-niyojyo Duḥṣantaḥ praṇamati 13 kaṣṭā khalu sevā 14 na khalu Vṛṣalasya śravaṇa-patham upagato ›yaṃ mayā kṛtaḥ Kaumudī-mahotsava-pratiṣedhaḥ? 15 kiṃ tav› ânayā cintayā? 16 Mādhavya, apy asti te Śakuntalā-darśanaṃ prati kutūhalam? 17 śrotriya-likhitāny akṣarāṇi prayatna-likhitāny api niyatam asphuṭāni bhavanti

Exercise 7a

1 aye, iyaṃ devī 2 pratibodhita ev› âsmi ken› âpi 3 idam amātya:Rākṣasa-gṛham 4 aho vatsalena su-hṛdā viyuktāḥ smaḥ 5 su:vicintitaṃ bhagavatyā 6 ārya, api sahyā śiro-vedanā? 7 lajjayati mām atyanta: saujanyam eṣām 8 tena h› îmāṃ kṣīra-vṛkṣa-cchāyām āśrayāmaḥ 9 ciram adarśanen› āryasya vayam udvignāḥ 10 svāgataṃ devyai 11 alam asmad-avinay›-āśaṅkayā 12 amātya, kalpitam anena yoga-cūrṇa-miśram auṣadhaṃ Candraguptāya 13 aye, Urvaśī-gātra-sparśād iva nirvṛtaṃ me śarīram 14 ārye, kim atyāhitaṃ Sītā:devyāḥ? 15 yāvad imān vedi-saṃstaraṇ›-ârthaṃ darbhān ṛtvigbhya upaharāmi 16 kathitam Avalokitayā 'Madan›-ôdyānaṃ gato Mādhava' iti 17 kaṣṭam, ubhayor apy asthāne yatnaḥ 18 n› âyaṃ kathā-vibhāgo ›smābhir anyena vā śruta: pūrvaḥ 19 vayam api tāvad bhavatyau sakhī-gataṃ kiṃcit pṛcchāmaḥ 20 amātya, idam ābharaṇaṃ kumāreṇa sva:śarīrād avatārya preṣitam

Exercise 8a

1 hanta, siddh›:ârthau svaḥ 2 kṛtaṃ Rāma-sadṛśaṃ karma 3 asti dakṣiṇāpathe Padmapuraṃ nāma nagaram 4 vayasya, itaḥ stambh›-âpavārita:śarīrau tiṣṭhāvaḥ 5 ramaṇīyaḥ khalu divas›-âvasāna-vṛttānto rāja-veśmani 6 kim-artham a:gṛhīta:mudraḥ kaṭakān niṣkrāmasi? 7 vatsa, alam ātm›-âparādha-śaṅkayā 8 bho bhoḥ, kiṃ:prayojano ›yam aśvaḥ parivṛtaḥ paryaṭati? 9 kāṃ punar atrabhavatīm avagacchāmi? 10 kumāra, n› âyam atyanta:durbodho ›rthaḥ 11 kiṃ tv amātya:Rākṣasaś Cāṇakye baddha:vairo, na Candragupte 12 tad eṣa svayaṃ parīkṣita:guṇān brāhmaṇān preṣayāmi 13 hā kaṣṭam, atibībhatsa:karmā nṛśaṃso ›smi saṃvṛttaḥ 14 katham, kṛta:mahā›parādho ›pi bhagavatībhyām anukampito Rāmaḥ 15 yāvad idānīm avasita:saṃdhyā-jāpyaṃ mahārājaṃ paśyāmi 16 sa tad» aîva devyāḥ Sītāyās tādṛśaṃ daiva-durvipākam upaśrutya vaikhānasaḥ saṃvṛttaḥ 17 a:phalam an:iṣṭa:phalaṃ vā Dāruvarmaṇaḥ prayatnam adhigacchāmi 18 sundari, a:parinirvāṇo divasaḥ 19 Śakuntalā-darśanād eva mand›:autsukyo ›smi nagara-gamanaṃ prati

Exercise 9a

1 kim uktavān asi? 2 samprati nivartāmahe vayam 3 kṛt›:âñjaliḥ praṇamati 4 sarvān abhivādaye vaḥ 5 sakhe Puṇḍarīka, n› aîtad anurūpaṃ bhavataḥ 6 yāvad upasthitāṃ homa-velāṃ gurave nivedayāmi 7 kaccid aham iva vismṛtavāṃs tvam api? 8 paravanto vayaṃ vismayena 9 ārya, api śatror vyasanam upalabdham? 10 tat kim ity āśaṅkase? 11 aham adhunā yath»_ādiṣṭam anutiṣṭhāmi 12 bhagavan, na khalu kaścid a:viṣayo nāma dhīmatām 13 Śakuntalā sakhīm aṅgulyā tarjayati 14 sādhu sakhe Bhūrivaso sādhu 15 kim ayaṃ pratibuddho ›bhihitavān? 16 atha sā tatrabhavatī kiṃ:ākhyasya rāja:rṣeḥ patnī? 17 bhad-

ra, ath› âgni-praveśe suhṛdas te ko hetuḥ? 18 paravatī khalu tatrabhavatī, na ca saṃnihita:guruˇjanā 19 diṣṭyā dharma-patnī-samāgamena putra-mukha-saṃdarśanena c› āyuṣmān vardhate 20 tat kim ayam āryeṇa sa_lekhaḥ puruṣaḥ Kusumapuraṃ prasthāpitaḥ? 21 tatrabhavān Kaṇvaḥ śāśvate brahmaṇi vartate, iyaṃ ca vaḥ sakhī tasy› ātmaj» êti katham etat? 22 mam› âpi Kaṇva-sutām anusmṛtya mṛgayāṃ prati nir_utsukaṃ cetaḥ 23 api Candragupta-doṣā atikrānta:pārthiva-guṇān smārayanti prakṛtīḥ? 24 etām a:saṃbhāvyāṃ brāhmaṇasya pratijñāṃ śrutvā sa_sacivo rājā prahṛṣṭa:manā vismay›-ânvitaḥ sa_bahumānaṃ tasmai Viṣṇuśarmaṇe kumārān samarpitavān

Exercise 10a

1 paśya Mādhavasy› âvasthām 2 mahati viṣāde vartate te sakhī:janaḥ 3 idaṃ tat pratyutpanna:mati˜tvaṃ strīṇām 4 aho darśanīyāny akṣarāṇi 5 muhūrtam upaviśata 6 bhoḥ śreṣṭhin Candanadāsa, evam apathya-kāriṣu tīkṣṇa:daṇḍo rājā 7 anubhavatu rāj›-âpathya-kāri˜tvasya phalam 8 pratyāsannaḥ kila mṛgayā-vihārī pārthivo Duḥṣantaḥ 9 gacchatāṃ bhavantau 10 bhos tapasvin, cintayann api na khalu svīkaraṇam atrabhavatyāḥ smarāmi 11 sakhe Mādhavya, dṛḍha:pratijño bhava 12 aho nir_daya˜tā dur:ātmanāṃ paurāṇām—aho Rāmasya rājñaḥ kṣipra:kāri˜tā 13 bhagavan Manmatha, kutas te kusum›:āyudhasya satas taikṣṇyam etat? 14 nanu bhavatyaḥ paṭ›-âñcalair vatsau vījayadhvam 15 bhagn›:ôtsāhaḥ kṛto ›smi mṛgayā-›pavādinā Mādhavyena 16 aho bata, kīdṛśīṃ vayo-›vasthām āpanno ›smi 17 adya śiṣṭ›-ânadhyayanam iti khelatāṃ baṭūnām ayaṃ kalakalaḥ 18 svairaṃ svairaṃ gacchantu bhavatyaḥ 19 paritrāyatāṃ suhṛdaṃ Mahārājaḥ 20 tatrabhavataḥ kulapater asāṃnidhyād rakṣāṃsi nas tapo-vighnam utpādayanti 21 bhadra, anayā mudrayā mudray› aînam 22 śatru-prayuktānāṃ ca tīkṣṇa:rasa-dāyināṃ prati-

vidhānaṃ praty apramādinaḥ parīkṣita:bhaktayaḥ kṣitipati-pratyāsannā niyuktāḥ puruṣāḥ 23 samprati Madayantikā-saṃbandhena Nandan›-ôpagrahāt pratyasta:śaṅkāḥ khalu vayam 24 bhāvinam enaṃ cakravartinam avagacchatu bhavān 25 mayā tāvat suhṛttamasya Candanadāsasya gṛhe gṛha-janaṃ nikṣipya nagarān nirgacchatā nyāyyam anuṣṭhitam 26 devi, saṃstabhy› ātmānam anurudhyasva bhagavato Vasiṣṭhasy› ādeśam iti vijñāpayāmi

Exercise 11a

1 katham, iyaṃ sā Kaṇva-duhitā Śakuntalā? 2 vatse, yad aham īhe tad astu te 3 he dhūrta, lekho nīyate, na ca jñāyate 'kasy›?' êti? 4 priye Mālati, iyaṃ vīkṣyase 5 viśramyatāṃ parijanena 6 Mandārike, yad atra vastuny eṣa te vallabhaḥ kathayati, api tathā tat? 7 deven› aîvaṃ niṣiddhe ›pi Madh›-ûtsave, cūtakalikā-bhaṅgam ārabhase? 8 parirakṣyantām asya prāṇāḥ 9 bho rājan, kim idaṃ joṣam āsyate? 10 tad anuṣṭhīyatām ātmano ›bhiprāyaḥ 11 kiṃ c› âtisṛṣṭaḥ Parvateśvara-bhrātre Vairodhakāya pūrva:pratiśruto rājy›-ârdhaḥ 12 kathaṃ, 'Śakuntal»' êty asya mātur ākhyā? 13 kaḥ sa mahā:puruṣo yen› aîtan mānuṣa:mātra-duṣkaraṃ mahat karm› ânuṣṭhitam? 14 Priyaṃvadaka, jñāyatāṃ 'kā velā vartata?' iti 15 ārya Vaihīnare, dīyatām ābhyāṃ vaitālikābhyāṃ suvarṇa-śata-sahasram 16 Vṛṣala kim ayam asthāna eva mahān arth›-ôtsargaḥ kriyate? 17 bhoḥ śreṣṭhin, api pracīyante saṃvyavahārāṇāṃ lābhāḥ? 18 bhagavati Vasuṃdhare, ślāghyāṃ duhitaram avekṣasva Jānakīm 19 kathaṃ, nivāryamāṇo ›pi sthita eva? 20 bhagavan Vālmīke, upanīyetām imau Sītā-garbha-saṃbhavau Rāma:bhadrasya Kuśa;Lavau 21 yādṛśo ›yaṃ, tādṛśau tāv api 22 visṛṣṭaś ca Vāmadev›-ânumantrito medhyo ›śvaḥ. upakalpitāśca yathā_śāstraṃ tasya rakṣitāraḥ. teṣām adhiṣṭhātā Lakṣmaṇ›-ātmajaś Candraketur avāpta:divy›'âstra-saṃpradāyaś catur:aṅga:sādhan›-

ânvito ›nuprahitaḥ 23 hanta, hanta, sarvathā nṛśaṃso ›smi, yaś cirasya dṛṣṭān priya:suhṛdaḥ priyān dārān na snigdhaṃ paśyāmi 24 atha tasmād araṇyāt parityajya nivṛtte Lakṣmaṇe Sītāyāḥ kiṃ vṛttam? iti kācid asti pravṛttiḥ? 25 asti tāvad ekadā prasaṅgataḥ kathita eva mayā Mādhav›:âbhidhānaḥ kumāro, yas tvam iva māmakīnasya manaso dvitīyaṃ nibandhanam

Exercise 12a

1 bhadra, bhadra, na praveṣṭavyam 2 bhavatu, śṛṇomi tāvad āsāṃ viśrambha-kathitāni 3 tūṣṇīṃ bhava, yāvad ākarṇayāmi 4 amātya, tathā ›pi prārabdham a:parityājyam eva 5 tad atra śāla-pracchāye muhūrtam āsana-parigrahaṃ karotu tātaḥ 6 samupadiśa tam uddeśaṃ yatr› āste sa piṇḍapātī 7 hṛdaya sthirī˜bhava. kim api te kaṣṭataram ākarṇanīyam 8 kim anyad bravītu? 9 iyaṃ c› Ôrvaśī yāvad_āyus tava sahadharmacāriṇī bhavatu 10 tad yāvac Chrīparvatam upanīya lavaśo lavaśa enāṃ nikṛtya duḥkha:maraṇāṃ karomi 11 asti naḥ sucarita-śravaṇa-lobhād anyad api praṣṭavyam 12 tat kim ity udāsate bharatāḥ? 13 tatra c› aîvam anuṣṭheyaṃ yathā vadāmi 14 nanu bhavatībhyām eva Śakuntalā sthirīkartavyā 15 gṛhīta:gṛha-sāram enaṃ sa_putra˜kalatraṃ saṃyamya rakṣa tāvad yāvan mayā Vṛṣalāya kathyate 16 saṃpraty Agasty›-āśramasya panthānaṃ brūhi 17 vinīta:veṣa-praveśyāni tapo-vanāni 18 maru-sthalyāṃ yathā vṛṣṭiḥ, kṣudh» ārte bhojanaṃ tathā 19 udghātinī bhūmir iti raśmi-saṃyamanād rathasya mandībhūto vegaḥ 20 cakravartinaṃ putram āpnuhi 21 tat kiyantaṃ kālam asmābhir evaṃ saṃbhṛta:balair api śatru-vyasanam avekṣamāṇair udāsitavyam? 22 yad» aîv› âṅgurīyaka-darśanād anusmṛtaṃ devena 'satyam ūḍha:pūrvā rahasi mayā tatrabhavatī Śakuntalā mohāt pratyādiṣṭ»' êti, tad» aîva paścāttāpam upagato devaḥ 23 mahā:dhana˜tvād bahu:patnī˜ken› ânena bhavitavyam 24 amātya, īdṛśasy› ābha-

raṇa-viśeṣasya viśeṣataḥ kumāreṇa sva:gātrād avatārya prasādīkṛtasya kim ayaṃ parityāga-bhūmiḥ? 25 yāvac ca saṃbandhino na parāpatanti, tāvad vatsayā Mālatyā nagara-devatā-gṛham avighna:maṅgalāya gantavyam

Exercise 13a

1 dehi me prativacanam 2 tvayā saha Gautamī gamiṣyati 3 kathaṃ, śūnyā iv› âmī pradeśāḥ 4 eṣa tam iṣuṃ saṃdadhe 5 yadi rahasyaṃ, tadā tiṣṭhatu—yadi na rahasyaṃ, tarhi kathyatām 6 aham apy amuṃ vṛttāntaṃ bhagavatyai Lopāmudrāyai nivedayāmi 7 sa khalu mūrkhas taṃ yuṣmābhir atisṛṣṭaṃ prabhūtam artha-rāśim avāpya, mahatā vyayen› ôpabhoktum ārabdhavān 8 diṣṭyā su:prabhātam adya, yad ayaṃ devo dṛṣṭaḥ 9 kiṃ cid ākhyātu-kāmā ›smi 10 upālapsye tāvad enam 11 bhadra Siddhārthaka, kāmam a:paryāptam idam asya priyasya, tathā ›pi gṛhyatām 12 ayam asau rāj›-ājñayā rāj›-âpathya-kārī kāyasthaḥ Śakaṭadāsaḥ śūlam āropayituṃ nīyate 13 jñāsyathaḥ khalv etat 14 puṇy›:āśrama-darśanen› ātmānaṃ punīmahe tāvat 15 bhadre, na tat parihāryaṃ, yato vivakṣitam an:uktam anutāpaṃ janayati 16 n› âyam avasaro mama Śatakratuṃ draṣṭum 17 sakhe, na tāvad enāṃ paśyasi, yena tvam evaṃ:vādī 18 aye, etās tapasvi-kanyakāḥ sva:pramāṇ›-ânurūpaiḥ secana-ghaṭair bāla:pādapebhyaḥ payo dātum ita ev› âbhivartante 19 na cen muni-kumārako ›yaṃ, tat ko ›sya vyapadeśaḥ? 20 matimāṃś Cāṇakyas tucche prayojane kim iti Candraguptaṃ kopayiṣyati? na ca kṛtavedī Candragupta etāvatā gauravam ullaṅghayiṣyati 21 tena hi vijñāpyatāṃ mad-vacanād upādhyāyaḥ Somarātaḥ—'amūn āśrama-vāsinaḥ śrautena vidhinā satkṛtya svayam eva praveśayitum arhas›' iti 22 smartavyaṃ tu saujanyam asya nṛpater, yad aparādhinor apy an:aparāddhayor iva nau kṛta:prasādaṃ ceṣṭitavān 23 he vyasana-sabrahmacārin, yadi na

guhyaṃ n› âtibhārikaṃ vā, tataḥ śrotum icchāmi te prāṇa-parityāga-kāraṇam 24 ārya Vaihīnare, 'adya prabhṛty an:ādṛtya Cāṇakyaṃ Candraguptaḥ svayam eva rāja-kāryāṇi kariṣyat›' îti gṛhīt›:ârthāḥ kriyantāṃ prakṛtayaḥ 25 vayam apy āśrama-bādhā yathā na bhavati, tathā prayatiṣyāmahe 26 kim idānīṃ Candraguptaḥ sva:rājya-kārya:dhurām anyatra mantriṇy ātmani vā samāsajya svayaṃ pratividhātum a:samarthaḥ? 27 yat satyaṃ, kāvya-viśeṣa-vedinyāṃ pariṣadi prayuñjānasya mam› âpi su:mahān paritoṣaḥ prādur-bhavati 28 'Candragupta-śarīram abhidrogdhum anena vyāpāritā Dāruvarm›:ādaya' iti nagare prakhyāpya Śakaṭadāsaḥ śūlam āropitaḥ 29 sa khalu kasmiṃś cid api jīvati Nand›-ânvay›-âvayave Vṛṣalasya sācivyaṃ grāhayituṃ na śakyate 30 idam atra rāmaṇīyakaṃ, yad amātya:Bhūrivasu;Devarātayoś cirāt pūrṇo ›yam itaretar›-âpatya-saṃbandh›:âmṛta-manorathaḥ

Exercise 14a

1 Priyaṃvadaka, jñāyatāṃ ko ›smad-darśan›-ârthī dvāri tiṣṭhati 2 kva nu khalu gatā syāt? 3 āsīt tādṛśo munir asminn āśrame 4 āyuṣman, śrūyatāṃ yadartham asmi Hariṇā tvat-sakāśaṃ preṣitaḥ 5 evam ukto ›py aham enaṃ prābodhayaṃ punaḥ punaḥ 6 cirāt prabhṛty āryaḥ parityakt›:ôcita;śarīra-saṃskāra iti pīḍyate me hṛdayam 7 vismaya;harṣa:mūlaś ca kolāhalo lokasy› ôdajihīta 8 tad ucyatāṃ pātravargaḥ 'sveṣu sveṣu pāṭheṣv asaṃmūḍhair bhavitavyam' iti 9 sakhe, cintaya tāvat ken› âpadeśena punar āśrama-padaṃ gacchāmaḥ 10 api nāma dur:ātmanaś Cāṇakyāc Candragupto bhidyeta 11 ayam asau mama jyāyān āryaḥ Kuśo nāma Bharat›-āśramāt pratinivṛttaḥ 12 surata-kheda-prasuptayos tu tayoḥ svapne bisa-guṇa-nigaḍita:pādo jaraṭhaḥ kaś cij jālapādaḥ pratyadṛśyata. pratyabudhyetāṃ c› ôbhau 13 tad anviṣyatāṃ yadi kā cid āpanna:sattvā

tasya bhāryā syāt 14 āryaputra, n› âyaṃ viśrambha-
kathāyā avasaras, tato laghutaram ev› âbhidhīyase
15 katham īdṛśena saha vatsasya Candraketor dvanda-
saṃprahāram anujānīyām? 16 ity avadhāry› âpasar-
paṇ›-âbhilāsiṇy aham abhavam 17 kasmin prayojane
mam› âyaṃ praṇidhiḥ prahita iti prabhūtaˇtvāt
prayojanānāṃ na khalv avadhārayāmi 18 yadi kaś cid
asty upāyāḥ pati-droha-pratikriyāyai, darśay› âmum—
matir hi te paṭīyasī 19 anay» aîva ca kathayā tayā saha
tasminn eva prāsāde tath» aîva pratiṣiddh›:âśeṣaˇpari-
janaˇpraveśā divasam atyavāhayam 20 tad upāyaś
cintyatāṃ yathā saphala:prārthano bhaveyam 21
śrutvā c› aîtat tam eva matta:hastinam udast›:ādho-
raṇo rāja-putro ›dhiruhya raṃhas» ôttamena rāja-
bhavanam abhyavartata 22 upalabdhavān asmi pra-
ṇidhibhyo yathā tasya mleccha-rāja-balasya madhyāt
pradhānatamāḥ pañca rājānaḥ parayā suhṛtˇtayā Rāk-
ṣasam anuvartanta iti 23 yadi punar iyaṃ kiṃvadantī
mahārājaṃ prati syandeta, tat kaṣṭaṃ syāt 24 ity
avadhāry› ânveṣṭum ādaram akaravam. anveṣamāṇaś
ca yathā yathā n› âpaśyaṃ taṃ, tathā tathā suhṛt-
sneha-kātareṇa manasā tat tad aśobhanam āśaṅka-
mānas taru-gahanāni candana-vīthikā latā-maṇḍa-
pān saraḥ-kūlāni ca vīkṣamāṇo nipuṇam itas tato
datta:dṛṣṭiḥ su:ciraṃ vyacaram 25 ekasmiṃś ca
pradeśe jhaṭiti van›-ânilen› ôpanītaṃ nirbhara:vikasite
›pi kānane ›bhibhūt›:ânyaˇkusumaˇparimalaṃ visar-
pantam ati:surabhiˇtayā ›nulimpantam iva tarpayan-
tam iva pūrayantam iva ghrāṇ›-êndriyam, ahamaha-
mikayā madhukara-kulair anubadhyamānam an:āgh-
rāta:pūrvam a:mānuṣaˇlok›ˇôcitaṃ kusuma-gandham
abhyajighram

Exercise 15

evaṃ:vādini deva:rṣau pārśve pitur adhomukhī |
līlā-kamala-pattrāṇi gaṇayām āsa Pārvatī ||84||

evam iti || *deva:ṛṣau* (: Aṅgirasi) *evaṃ:vādini* sati *Pārvatī pituḥ pārśve adhomukhī* satī | lajjay» êti śeṣaḥ | *līlā-kamala-pattrāṇi gaṇayām āsa* (: saṃcakhyau) | lajjā-vaśāt kamala-dala-gaṇanā:vyājena harṣaṃ jugop› êty arthaḥ | anen› âvahitth»:̲ākhyaḥ saṃcārī bhāva uktaḥ | tad uktam—

'avahitthā tu lajj»:̲āder harṣ›:̲ādy-ākāra-gopanam'

iti ||

Śailaḥ saṃpūrṇa:̲kāmo ›pi Menā-mukham udaikṣata |

prāyeṇa gṛhiṇī:̲netrāḥ kanyā-›rtheṣu kuṭumbinaḥ ||85||

Śaila iti || *Śailaḥ* (: Himavān) *saṃpūrṇa:̲kāmo ›pi* | dātuṃ kṛta:̲niścayo ›p› îty arthaḥ | *Menā-mukham udaikṣata* | ucit›:ôttara-jijñāsay» êti bhāvaḥ | tathā hi | *prāyeṇa kuṭumbinaḥ* (: gṛhasthāḥ) *kanyā-›rtheṣu* (: kanyā-prayojaneṣu) *gṛhiṇy* eva *netraṃ* (: kārya-jñāna-kāraṇaṃ) yeṣāṃ te tath» ôktāḥ | kalatra:̲pradhāna:̲vṛttaya ity arthaḥ ||

mene Menā ›pi tat sarvaṃ patyuḥ kāryam abhīpsitam |

bhavanty avyabhicāriṇyo bhartur iṣṭe pati:̲vratāḥ ||86||

mena iti || *Menā ›pi patyuḥ* (: Himālayasya) *tat sarvam abhīpsitaṃ kāryaṃ mene* (: aṅgī˜cakāra) | tathā hi *patir* eva *vrataṃ* yāsāṃ tāḥ *bhartur iṣṭe* (: abhīpsite) (na vidyate vyabhicāro yāsāṃ tāḥ:) *avyabhicāriṇyo bhavanti* | bhartṛ-citt›-âbhiprāya-jñā bhavant› îti bhāvaḥ ||

'idam atr› ôttaraṃ nyāyyam' iti buddhyā vimṛśya saḥ |

ādade vacasām ante maṅgal›-âlaṃkṛtāṃ sutām ||87||

idam iti || *saḥ* (: Himavān) *vacasām ante* (: munivāky›-âvasāne) *atra* (: muni-vakye) *idam* (: uttara:śloke vakṣyamāṇaṃ dānam eva) *nyāyyam* (: nyāyād an:apetam) *uttaram iti buddhyā* (: cittena) *vimṛśya* (: vicintya) (maṅgalaṃ yathā tathā ›laṃkṛtāṃ :) *maṅgal›-âlaṃkṛtāṃ sutām ādade* (: hastābhyāṃ jagrāha) ||

'ehi, Viśvātmane, vatse, bhikṣā ›si parikalpitā |
arthino munayaḥ—prāptaṃ gṛhamedhi-phalaṃ mayā' ||88||

eh› îti || he *vatse* (: putri) *ehi* (: āgaccha) | tvaṃ *Viśvātmane* (: Śivāya) *bhikṣā parikalpitā ›si* (: niścitā ›si) |
'ratn›:ādi stamba:paryantaṃ sarvaṃ bhikṣā tapasvinaḥ'
iti vacanād iti bhāvaḥ | *arthinaḥ* (: yācitāraḥ) *munayaḥ* | *mayā gṛhamedhinaḥ* (: gṛhasthasya) *phalaṃ prāptam* | iha paratra ca tāraka˜tvāt pātre kanyādānaṃ gārhasthyasya phalam ity arthaḥ ||

etāvad uktvā tanayām ṛṣīn āha mahīdharaḥ |
'iyaṃ namati vaḥ sarvāṃs Trilocana-vadhūr' iti ||89||

etāvad iti|| *mahīdharaḥ* (: Himavān) *tanayām etāvat* (: pūrv›:ôktam) *uktvā ṛṣīn āha* | kim iti? | *'iyaṃ Trilocana-vadhūḥ* (: Tryambaka-patnī) *vaḥ sarvān namati'* iti | 'Trilocana-vadhūr' iti siddha˜vad abhidhānen› 'â:vipratipannaṃ dānam' iti sūcayati ||

īpsit›:ârtha-kriy»-ôdāraṃ te ›bhinandya girer vacaḥ
āśīrbhir edhayām āsuḥ puraḥ:pākābhir Ambikām ||90||

īpsit›:ârth› êti || *te* (: munayaḥ) *īpsit›:ârtha-kriyayā* (: iṣṭ›:ârtha-karaṇena) *udāraṃ* (: mahat) | 'udāro dātṛ;mahatoḥ' ity Amaraḥ | *gireḥ* (: Himavataḥ) *vacaḥ* (: vacanam) *abhinandya* (: 'sādhv' iti saṃstutya) | *Ambikām* (: Ambām) | 'pacyata' iti *pākaḥ* (: phalam) | *puraḥ:pākābhiḥ* (: purəskṛta:phalābhiḥ) *āśīrbhiḥ* (: āśīrvādaiḥ) *edhayām āsuḥ* (: saṃvardhayām āsuḥ) ||

tāṃ praṇām›-ādara-srasta꞉jāmbūnada˘vataṃsa-kam |
aṅkam āropayām āsa lajjamānām Arundhatī ||91||

tām iti || *praṇām›-ādareṇa* (: namaskār›-āsaktyā) *sraste jāmbūnade* (: suvarṇa-vikāre) *vataṃsake* (: kanaka-kuṇḍale) yasyās tāṃ *lajjamānāṃ tām* (: Ambikām) *Arundhatī aṅkam āropayām āsa* | 'ruhaḥ po ›nyatarasyām' iti pakāraḥ ||

tan-mātaraṃ c› âśru-mukhīṃ duhitṛ-sneha-vikla-vām |
varasy› ân:anya˘pūrvasya vi꞉śokām akarod guṇaiḥ ||92||

tad iti || *duhitṛ-snehena* (: putrikā-premṇā) *viklavāṃ* (: 'viyokṣyata' iti bhītām) | ata ev› (âśrūṇi mukhe yasyās tām :) *aśrumukhīm* (tasyāḥ (: Ambikāyāḥ) mātaram :) *tan-mātaram* (: Menām) *ca* | (anyā pūrvaṃ yasy› âsti so :) ›nya꞉pūrvaḥ | 'sarvanāmno vṛtti-viṣaye puṃvad-bhāvaḥ' iti pūrva:padasya puṃvad-bhāvaḥ | ('sa na bhavat›' îty an:anya꞉pūrvas, tasya:) *an:anya꞉pūrvasya* | sāpatnya-duḥkham a:kurvata ity arthaḥ | *varasya* (: voḍhuḥ) *guṇaiḥ* (: mṛtyuṃjaya˜tv›꞉ādibhiḥ) *vi꞉śokām* (: nir_duḥkhām) *akarot* ||

vaivāhikīṃ tithiṃ pṛṣṭās tatkṣaṇaṃ Hara-ban-dhunā |
te tryahād ūrdhvam ākhyāya ċeruś cīra꞉parigrahāḥ ||93||

vaivāhikīṃ iti || *cīra꞉parigrahāḥ* (: valkala-mātra꞉vasanāḥ) *te* (: tapasvinaḥ) *tatkṣaṇam* (: tasminn eva kṣaṇe) *Hara-bandhunā* (: Himavatā) *vaivāhikīm* (: vivāha-yogyāṃ) *tithiṃ pṛṣṭāḥ* (: 'k»?' êty anuyuktāḥ) santaḥ | trayāṇām ahnāṃ samāhāras try꞉ahaḥ | 'taddhit›꞉ârth›;ôttarapada;samāhāre ca' iti samāsaḥ | 'rāj›;âhaḥ;sakhibhyaṣ ṭac' iti ṭac:pratyayaḥ | dvigu˜tvād ekavacanam | 'rātr›;âhn›;âhāḥ puṃsi' iti puṃ꞉

liṅga˘tā | (tasmāt :) *try:ahāt ūrdhvam* (: upari) *ākhyāya* (: 'caturthe ›hani vivāhaḥ' ity uktvā) *ceruḥ* (: calitāḥ) ||

te Himālayam āmantrya punaḥ prāpya ca Śūlinam |
siddhaṃ c› âsmai nivedy› ârthaṃ tad-visṛṣṭāḥ kham udyayuḥ ||94||

ta iti || *te* (: munayaḥ) *Himālayam āmantrya* (: 'sādhu, yāma' ity āpṛcchya) *punaḥ Śūlinam* (: Haraṃ) saṃketa-sthāna-sthaṃ *prāpya ca* | *siddham* (: niṣpannam) *artham* (: prayojanam) *asmai nivedya* (: jñāpayitvā) *ca* | *tad-visṛṣṭāḥ* (: tena (: Śūlinā) visṛṣṭāḥ) *kham* (: ākāśaṃ) prati *udyayuḥ* (: utpetuḥ) | atra saṃkṣipt›:ârth›-âbhidhānāt 'saṃkṣepo' nāma guṇa uktaḥ | tad uktam—
'saṃkṣipt›:ârth›-âbhidhānaṃ yat, saṃkṣepaḥ parikīrtitaḥ' iti ||

bhagavān Paśupatis tryaha:mātra:vilambam api soḍhuṃ na śaśāka tad-autsukyād ity āha—

Paśupatir api tāny ahāni kṛcchrād
agamayad adri-sutā-samāgam›-ôtkaḥ |
kam aparam avaśaṃ na viprakuryur
vibhum api taṃ yad amī spṛśanti bhāvāḥ? ||95||

Paśupatir iti || (utkaṃ mano yasya saḥ :) utkaḥ | 'utka unmanāḥ' iti nipātaḥ | *adri-sutā-samāgam›-ôtkaḥ* (: Pārvatī-pariṇay›-ôtsukaḥ) *Paśupatir api tāni* | trīṇ› îti śeṣaḥ | *ahāni kṛcchrād agamayat* (: ayāpayat) | kavir āha—*amī bhāvāḥ* (: autsuky›:ādayaḥ saṃcāriṇaḥ) *avaśam* (: indriya-paratantram) *aparam* (: pṛthag:janaṃ) *kaṃ na viprakuryuḥ* (: na vikāraṃ nayeyuḥ) *yat* (: yasmāt) *vibhum* (: samartham) | jit›:êndriyam iti yāvat | *tam* (: Smaraharam) *api spṛśanti* | vikurvant› îty arthaḥ | atra vibhu-vikāra-samarthanād arthād itara:jana-vikāraḥ kaimutika:nyāyād āpatat› îty arth›-āpattir alaṃkāraḥ | tathā ca sūtram—'daṇḍāpūpikayā

›rth›-ântar›-āpatanam arth›-āpattiḥ' iti | arthāntara-nyāsa iti ke cit, tad upeksaṇīyam | yuktis tu vistara-bhayān n› ôcyate | puṣpitāgrā vṛttam—

'a:yuji na-yuga;repha˜to yakāro
yuji ca na;jau ja;ra;gāś ca puṣpitāgrā'

iti lakṣaṇāt ||

Sanskrit–English Exercises: Key

Exercise 2b

1 I am going. 2 We aren't going [/Let us not go] in here. 3 He writes yet again. 4 Where are you [*pl.*] living now? 5 Do you so wish? 6 But where are they standing? 7 What, is he coming this way? 8 What are the two of them bringing here? 9 I see and write. 10 He seems to be wandering [/to be confused]. 11 The two of you dance and sing. 12 They both remember and grieve. 13 'We are coming in here,' the two of them say. 14 How (is it that) he is not coming even now. 15 I rejoice that I am winning. 16 We grieve that they are not [living:] alive.

Exercise 3a

1 The pupils are bringing the teacher. 2 Do you want horses [/the horses]? 3 I see the sun and moon. 4 Who does not want happiness? 5 The food is scant. 6 The man takes the horses to the water. 7 'Who are you?' the two of them ask me. 8 To what mountain is the scholar going? 9 The two of them enter the forest because anger does not dwell there [here *of direct speech often becomes* there *of indirect*]. 10 We do not understand swift speech. 11 Teacher, that elephant is like a mountain. 12 But whom shall I ask? 13 Are you pupils? 14 Men and children are entering the water. 15 'That fruit is now pleasant' they say astonished. 16 What, children here too? 17 Even sorrows bring reward. 18 'Children, what pleasure do you see in this?' the teacher says to the pupils.

Exercise 4a

1 He quits the house with his sons. 2 Here is a garden: let us go in. 3 Both teacher and pupils made an extraordinary effort. 4 This man gave up life because his friend was dear [*or possibly* because my friend was dear (to him)]. 5 Who (is) this (who) is coming to the house? 6 Why do you not rejoice at the pleasant sight? 7 (I have) seen and understood. 8 In curiosity as to what these [/the] men want here [/there], he goes into the house. 9 The city is far, and we are wandering exhausted. 10 Do you *want* this or not? 11 'Have done with words, the opportunity is gone' the two of them say in despair (/dejectedly). 12 Sons, this is the very opportunity. 13 See, we have come to the city. 14 The two friends have forgotten (their) first despair. 15 Though asked, 'O paṇḍit, where are you taking the horse?' he speaks not a word. 16 What point in effort? His Majesty is not looking at you.

Exercise 5a

1 Here we (both) are. 2 [After hearing:] They have heard my answer—what else do they want? 3 You do not [/do you not] in fact have a book.[/?] 4 Friend, you are like my (own) heart. 5 Let the two of us sit for a while in this garden. 6 They are all wandering in the fields. 7 Your Majesty, a [certain] brahmin has come from another city. 8 What means (can) you see for seeing my sons? 9 When we see his anger, we feel alarm in our heart (/our heart feels alarm). 10 Here stands His Highness. 11 Why, after sitting for just a moment I have seen my two friends once more. 12 There is no other road. 13 The sight of Rāma now actually [is for sorrow:] causes sorrow to his friends. 14 Your Majesty has heard this from others too. 15 He goes into the house and asks everyone 'Where, where is the villain now?' [*The repetition of* **kva** *is for emphasis.*] 16 In the country of the blind it is the one-eyed man who has power. 17 Kalahamsaka, who drew this picture of Mādhava?

Exercise 6a

1 Śoṇottarā, what is (your) purpose in coming? 2 Alas, two disasters have befallen (me). 3 Great king, [is there welfare of:] is it well with Prince Lakṣmaṇa? 4 But where is this news from? 5 Truly I am exactly so. 6 Minister, the news from Kusumapura is extensive. 7 You are accepted as a son by the noble ladies [*in fact an honorific plural* = the Queen]. 8 In which place is Mārīca's hermitage? 9 Mother, who are you? Why did you restrain me? 10 Surely this is an occasion for regret. 11 This is the same (woman). 12 To both of you alike Indra's servant Duḥṣanta makes obeisance. 13 Servitude is indeed harsh. 14 Has this cancellation [made] by me of the Full Moon festival not indeed reached Vṛṣala's [path of hearing:] ears? 15 What have you (to do) with this worry? 16 Mādhavya, do you feel curiosity [with regard to seeing:] to see Śakuntalā? 17 [The characters written by a scholar, though written with care, are necessarily illegible:] However painstakingly a scholar writes, he is bound to be illegible.

Exercise 7a

1 Ah, here is Her Majesty. 2 Someone [/something] has woken me. 3 Here is Minister Rākṣasa's house. 4 Oh, we have been deprived of a loving friend. 5 (That was) well thought of by Her Reverence. 6 Sir, is (your) head-ache bearable? 7 Their excessive kindness embarrasses me. 8 Therefore let us [resort to:] shelter in this fig-tree's shade. [*Note that* this *more conveniently qualifies* tree *in English,* shade *in Sanskrit.*] 9 We have been distressed at not seeing Your Honour for a long time. 10 Welcome to Her [/Your] Majesty. 11 Do not fear discourtesy from us. 12 Minister, he prepared a medicine mixed with a magic powder for Candragupta. 13 Ah, my body is (as) happy as if [from the touch of Urvaśī's limbs:] it had been touched by Urvaśī. 14 Noble lady, [is there calamity of:] has some calamity happened to Queen Sītā? 15 I will just offer the priests this

grass for strewing on the altar. 16 Avalokitā has told (me) that Mādhava is gone to the park of (the) Love (temple). 17 Alas, the effort of both alike (was) misplaced. 18 This portion of the story has not been heard before by us or (anyone) else. 19 We for our part will just ask you [two ladies] something concerning your friend. 20 Minister, here is an ornament which His Highness has removed from his own person and sent (you).

Exercise 8a

1 Ah, we [two] have achieved our object. 2 A deed worthy of Rāma has been done. 3 There is in the Deccan a city called Padmapura. 4 Friend, let us stand over here [with our bodies] hidden by the pillar. 5 Pleasant indeed is the scene at the end of the day in the king's palace. 6 Why are you going out of the camp [with seal unreceived:] without getting a pass? 7 Dear child, do not fear [offence by (your)self:] that you have offended. 8 Ho there, for what purpose does this horse wander around with a retinue? 9 But whom (am) I (to) understand this lady (to be)? 10 Your Highness, this matter is not terribly difficult to understand. 11 But Minister Rākṣasa's hostility is fixed on Cāṇakya, not on Candragupta. 12 So I personally send (you) herewith [**eṣa**] brahmins of proven worth. [*Or* **svayaṃ** *may be taken with* **parīkṣita**: whose worth has been examined by myself.] 13 Alas, I am become a man of foul deeds, a monster. 14 What, though he has committed great offence, have the two blessed (goddesses) taken pity on Rāma? 15 I will just (go and) see the king, now that his evening prayers are over. 16 He at that very time, hearing of such a cruel turn of fortune for Queen Sītā, became an anchorite. 17 I perceive that Dāruvarman's efforts (were) fruitless or had an unwished-for fruit. 18 Beautiful one, the day is not completely over. 19 From meeting Śakuntalā, my eagerness to go (back) to the city has slackened.

Exercise 9a

1 What did you say? 2 Now we are going back. 3 He salutes [having made an añjali:] with joined hands. 4 I greet you all. 5 Friend Puṇḍarīka, this is [not proper for:] wrong of you. 6 I will just inform my teacher that the time of sacrifice is at hand. 7 Did you too perhaps forget like me? 8 We are overwhelmed with astonishment. 9 Have (you) discovered a weakness of the enemy, sir? 10 Why then are you afraid? 11 I shall now act as ordered. 12 Reverend sir, there is indeed no matter beyond the scope of the wise. 13. Śakuntalā threatens (/scolds) her friend with (a shaking of) her finger. 14 Bravo, friend Bhūrivasu, bravo! 15 What did he say on waking? 16 Now [that good lady is the wife of a royal seer called what?:] what is the name of the royal seer whose wife that lady is? 17 Now what (was) your friend's motive, good fellow, in entering the fire [*i.e.* committing suicide]? 18 The lady is of course under another's control, and her guardian is not present. 19 Congratulations to you, sire, on your (re)union with your lawful wife and on beholding the face of your son. 20 Then why did Your Honour despatch this man to Kusumapura with a letter? 21 How is it that His Honour Kaṇva lives in perpetual chastity and (yet) this friend of yours is his daughter? [*Note: The answer is that she is an adopted child.*] 22 For my part too, when I remember Kaṇva's daughter, my heart is without eagerness for the chase. 23 Do Candragupta's faults cause his subjects to remember the merits of bygone rulers? 24 Hearing this incredible promise by the brahmin, the king in company with his ministers, with delighted mind (and) full of astonishment, respectfully handed his royal sons over to that (same) Viṣṇuśarman.

Exercise 10a

1 See Mādhava's condition. 2 Your friends are in great distress. 3 This is women's well-known [**tat**] readiness of wit. 4 What attractive [characters:] handwriting! 5 Sit down [*pl.*] for a minute. 6 Oh merchant Candanadāsa, you see

how [**evam**] severe in punishment towards traitors is the king. 7 Let him [experience:] reap the reward of being a traitor to the king. 8 It seems that King Duḥṣanta is at hand, roaming in the hunt. 9 Go (both of) you. 10 Oh ascetic! Even when I think it over, I certainly do not remember marrying this lady. 11 Mādhavya my friend, be firm in your assertions. 12 How pítiless (were) the vile citizens! How precípitate King Rāma! 13 Blessed god of Love, from where do you, who are armed with flowers, get this sharpness? 14 Well (all of), you [*f.*] fan the two dear children with the borders of your robes. 15 In decrying hunting Mādhavya has made me [of shattered enthusiasm:] lose my enthusiasm. 16 Oh alas! to what a state of (old) age am I come! 17 This noise is (the sound) of young brahmins playing because today is a holiday in honour of learned (guests). 18 Go very gently, ladies. 19 Save (your) friend, sire. 20 Because the revered lord of our house is not present, devils are causing hindrance to our austerities. 21 Seal it, my dear fellow, with this ring. 22 Men of proven loyalty have been appointed about the king, vigilant in countermeasures against poisoners engaged by the enemy. 23 Now that Nandana is won over by Madayantikā's union, we have indeed cast aside our cares. 24 [You must understand him to be a future emperor:] know that in time to come he will be emperor. 25 Well, I did right to deposit my family in the house of my close friend Candanadāsa [and retire:] before retiring from the city. 26 Your Majesty [*f.*], I beg you to compose yourself and comply with the revered Vasiṣṭha's command.

Exercise 11a

1 What, is this Kaṇva's daughter Śakuntalā? 2 Dear child, may you have what I desire (for you). 3 You rogue. You are taking a letter and you don't known for whom? 4 Dear Mālatī, see you are spied [*or* See, I am searching you out]. 5 Let the servants take a rest. 6 Mandārikā, what your sweetheart here says on this matter—is it so? 7 Though the

Spring Festival has been thus cancelled by His Majesty, do you begin plucking the mango buds? 8 Spare his life. 9 Ho sire! Why do you remain silent like this? 10 Do, then, [your own inclination:] as you will. 11 Moreover (he) bestowed on Parvateśvara's brother Vairodhaka the half of the kingdom previously promised (to Parvateśvara). 12 What, is his mother's name 'Śakuntalā'? 13 Who is the great man who has performed this great deed, difficult for a mere mortal? 14 Priyaṃvadaka, find out what time it is. 15 Noble Vaihīnari, give these two bards a hundred thousand gold pieces. 16 Vṛṣala, why are you quite inappropriately making this vast expenditure? 17 Ho merchant! Are the profits of your transactions accumulating? 18 Blessed Vasuṃdharā, watch over your virtuous daughter Jānakī. 19 What, does he just stay, though driven off? 20 Reverend Vālmīki, bring these two offspring of Sītā's womb, Kuśa and Lava, to dear Rāma [*or* (who are) dear Rāma's (sons)]. 21 Just as he is, so also are the two of them. 22 And a sacrificial horse blessed by Vāmadeva has been released, and (men) assigned in conformity with the law-books to guard it. At their head, Lakṣmaṇa's son Candraketu, who has acquired the tradition of the celestial missiles, has been despatched, attended by a [four-limbed:] full army. 23 Alas, alas, I am a total monster not to look affectionately on the dear wife of a dear friend, seen after (so) long. 24 Is there any news as to [**iti**] what then happened to (/became of) Sītā when Lakṣmaṇa had returned from that forest after abandoning (her there)? 25 There is then a young man called Mādhava [actually spoken of by me:] whom I did mention once in passing, someone who is another bond such as you (yourself are) to my heart. [*The unusual possessive adjective* **māmakīna** *avoids the ugly sound of* **mama manaso** *or* **man-manaso**. *The speaker is a Buddhist nun who ought to shun all ties of affection.*]

Exercise 12a

1 My good fellow, my good fellow, you mustn't come in. 2 Right—I'll just listen to the confidential talk of these

(girls). 3 Be quiet while I listen. 4 Even so, minister, (you) should certainly not give up the enterprise [*or* one should not give up something one has undertaken]. 5 So [let father make an occupying of a seat:] take a seat, father, for a while in the shade of this sal tree. [**atra** *for* **asmin**; *cf. also note on Exercise* 8*a*, *no*. 8.] 6 Show (me) the place where that mendicant stays. 7 Be firm, my heart. You have something more grievous to listen to. 8 What else is she [/he] to say? 9 And let Urvaśī here be your [throughout life:] lifelong lawful spouse. 10 So I'll just take her to Śrīparvata, shred her piece by piece and make her have a painful death. 11 In our greed to hear of good deeds, we have (something) else to ask as well. 12 So why do the players sit idle? 13 And there you must do as I tell you. 14 It is rather *you* two (girls) who must sustain Śakuntalā. 15 Seize his household property, arrest him and his son and wife, and hold him while I tell Vṛṣala. 16 Now tell the way to Agastya's hermitage. 17 One should enter ascetic groves in modest attire. 18 Like rain on desert land is food to one oppressed by hunger. [*This is a line of verse—hence the unusual position of* **tathā**.] 19 From (my) tightening the reins because the ground was bumpy, the speed of the chariot has slackened. 20 May you get a son (to be) Emperor. 21 How long, then, must we sit idle like this, though with our forces assembled, watching for a weakness in the enemy? 22 As soon as His Majesty, from seeing the ring, remembered that he really had previously married in secret the Lady Śakuntalā (and) from delusion rejected her, His Majesty became remorseful. 23 Since he has great wealth, he must have many wives. 24 Minister, is this man a suitable recipient for such a special decoration, particularly one that His Highness removed from his own person and bestowed (upon you)? 25 And before the (bridegroom's) relatives arrive, dear Mālatī must go to the city temple (to make an offering) for unhindered good luck.

Exercise 13a

1 Give me an answer. 2 Gautamī will go with you. 3 Why, those places seem deserted! 4 See, I am aiming that arrow.

5 If (it is) a secret, let it be—if it is not a secret, then tell (me). 6 And I for my part will announce that news to the reverend Lopāmudrā. 7 That fool, of course, on obtaining that large pile of money that you lavished (on him), began to spend it with great extravagance. 8 Thank heaven, it has dawned fair today, in that I see His Majesty here. 9 I [*f.*] want to tell (you) something. 10 I will just rebuke him. 11 Good Siddhārthaka, admittedly this is (an) inadequate (reward) for this service, but take it! 12 There is that letter-writer Śakaṭadāsa, a traitor to the king, being taken by the king's order to be impaled. 13 You [*du.*] will certainly learn this. 14 Let us just purify ourselves by seeing a holy hermitage. 15 Dear (young) lady, do not omit it—since what is meant but unsaid causes remorse. 16 This is not the right moment for me to see Indra. 17 Well, friend, you [are not a seer of:] have not seen her, for you to talk in that way. 18 Oh! here are ascetics' girls making this way, to [give water to:] water the young trees with watering-pots appropriate to their own (small) size. 19 If he is not the son of a sage, what is his name? 20 Why should Cāṇakya, being sensible, anger [/have angered] Candragupta over a trifling cause? And Candragupta, conscious of his debt, would not violate [/have violated] his duty of respect (just) for this much. 21 In that case beg to tell (my) preceptor Somarāta in my name that he should entertain those hermitage dwellers [by the scriptural injunctions to ritual:] with scriptural rite and personally show them in (to me). 22 But we must remember the kindness of this king, in treating us though guilty as graciously as if (we had been) innocent. 23 Ah fellow-student in misery! if (it is) not secret, nor too burdensome, I should like to hear your reason for (your intention of) sacrificing your life. 24 Noble Vaihīnari, let the people be [made aware:] given to understand that from today onward Candragupta shall conduct state affairs in person, without reference to Cāṇakya. 25 We for our part will exert ourselves (to see) that there is no damage to the hermitage. 26 Is Candragupta now incapable of imposing the yoke of his state administration upon another [**anyatra** = **anyasmin**] minister or upon himself and (thus)

taking precautions for himself? 27 In truth, the greatest satisfaction arises for myself, performing (as I am) before an audience that appreciates especial(ly good) literature. 28 Śakaṭadāsa was impaled after proclamation in the city that he had employed Dāruvarman and others to do violence to Candragupta's person. 29 He of course while any member at all of Nanda's family is (still) alive [**jīvati** *loc. sg. pres. part.*] cannot be brought to accept the post of Vṛṣala's minister. 30 The delightful thing in this is that Ministers Bhūrivasu and Devarāta's desire for the ambrosia of a union of each other's offspring is at long last hereby fulfilled.

Exercise 14a

1 Priyaṃvadaka, find out who is standing at the door wanting to see us. 2 Now where, I wonder, can she have gone? 3 There was (once) such a sage in this hermitage. 4 Sire, hear for what purpose Hari has sent me to you. 5 Though addressed in these terms, I admonished him again and again. 6 My heart is grieved that Your Excellency has for (so) long given up proper adornment of your person. 7 And a clamour of [which the basis was] astonishment and delight rose up from the people. 8 So tell the cast to be [not confused:] well rehearsed in their various parts. 9 Just think, friend, on what pretext we can go to the hermitage again. 10 If only Candragupta can be separated from the vile Cāṇakya. 11 There is my noble elder (brother), named Kuśa, returned from Bharata's hermitage. 12 But when the two of them had fallen asleep from the exhaustion of lovemaking, they saw in a dream an old goose, its feet bound with strands of lotus fibre; and they both woke up. 13 So enquire whether he may have any wife who is pregnant. 14 Noble sir, this is no time for intimate conversation—and so I (will) speak to you quite briefly. 15 How can I allow dear Candraketu (to engage in) single combat with such a one? 16 So determining, I [*f*.] became anxious to get away. 17 [From the numerousness of concerns:] My concerns are so numerous that I cannot at all determine which concern it was that (I) sent this agent of

mine on. 18 If there exists any means of remedying (your) husband's hostility, reveal it—for you have the sharper mind [*or* a particularly sharp mind]. 19 And I spent the day with her in just such conversation—in just that room and in just that way, forbidding entry to all my servants. 20 Think of some means, then, whereby my desires may be fulfilled. 21 And hearing this, the prince mounted that same rutting elephant after pushing out the driver, and made for the palace at top speed. 22 I have learnt from my agents that out of the forces of the barbarian kings the five most important kings attend upon Rākṣasa with particular affection. 23 But if this rumour should reach the king, it would be disastrous. 24 So determining, I took care to search (for him). And, with my mind (made) nervous by my fondness for my friend, fearing some awful thing or other the more I failed to see him in my search, I roamed a good long time, directing my gaze sharply here and there, scrutinizing the woods, the groves of sandalwood trees, the bowers of vine and the banks of the lakes. 25 And in one place, borne suddenly on the jungle breeze, spreading so as to overpower the perfume of other flowers even in a forest fully in bloom, seeming with its extreme fragrance to anoint and satisfy and enrich the sense of smell, pursued by swarms of bees in rivalry (with each other), I smelt a scent of blossom, such as I had never smelt before, one [not appropriate:] alien to the human world.

Exercise 15

84 The divine sage so speaking, Pārvatī at her father's side, with face bent down, counted the petals on the [play lotus:] lotus she was playing with.

Stanza 84: *The divine sage* (Aṅgiras) *so speaking*, *Pārvatī at her father's side*, being *with face bent down* (understand 'because of shyness') *counted* (reckoned up) *the petals on her play-lotus*. In other words, out of shyness she hid her delight under the pretence of counting the petals on the lotus. This describes the Subsidiary State (of mind) known as 'Dissimulation': to quote—

'Now Dissimulation is the hiding of the expression of anything such as delight from (a motive) such as shyness'.

85 The Mountain(-god), though with his desires fulfilled, looked at Menā['s face]. Usually in matters (concerning) their daughters, family-men make their wives their eyes.

Stanza 85: *The Mountain* (Himālaya) *though with his desires fulfilled* (in other words, though resolved to bestow (her)) *looked at Menā's face* (i.e. in his wish to determine the right answer). The reason being: *usually family-men* (householders) *in matters concerning their daughters* (in their daughters' concerns) are described as ones whose *eye* (means of perceiving matters) is their *wife*. In other words, their conduct is submitted to the authority of their spouse.

86 And Menā approved the whole matter desired by her husband. [Those devoted to their husband:] Devoted wives are unswerving [in respect of their husband's wish:] in following their husband's wishes.

Stanza 86: *And Menā approved* (accepted) *the whole matter desired by her husband* (Himālaya). The reason being: those women whose *vow* is simply their *husband are unswerving* (ones in whom there exists no swerving) *in respect of their husband's wish* (desire): that is, are aware of the inclination of their husband's mind.

87 He, having deliberated in his mind ['this is the proper answer to this':] what would be the proper answer to this, at the end of the speech took hold of his auspiciously adorned daughter.

Stanza 87: *He* (Himālaya) *at the end of the speech* (at the conclusion of the sage's utterance) *having deliberated* (having reflected) *in his mind* (in his thoughts) *that this* (the bestowal about to be declared in the following stanza) *would be the proper* (not lacking in propriety) *answer to this* (to the sage's utterance), *took hold of* (grasped in his arms) *his auspiciously adorned* (adorned so that there was auspiciousness) *daughter*.

88 'Come, dear child, you are destined as alms for the Supreme Godhead; the Sages are the petitioners—I have won the reward of (being) a householder.'

Stanza 88: O *dear child* (daughter) *come* (approach). *You are destined* (fixed upon) *as alms for the Supreme Godhead* (for Śiva)—i.e. because of the saying that 'the alms given to an ascetic may be anything at all from a gem to a clump of grass'. *The Sages are the petitioners* (are (hẹre) to sue). *I have won the reward of a householder* (of one in (charge of) a house). In other words, because it is liberating in this world and the next, the bestowing of a daughter upon a worthy recipient is the reward of being a householder.

89 Having said this much to his daughter, the Mountain spoke to the Sages, 'Herewith the bride of the Three-Eyed God salutes you all!'.

Stanza 89: *The Mountain* (Himālaya) *having said this much* (the foregoing words) *to his daughter*, *spoke to the Sages*. In what terms?— '*Herewith the bride of the Three-Eyed God* (the wife of Tryambaka) salutes you all'. By saying 'the bride of the Three-Eyed God' as if it were an accomplished fact, he indicates that the bestowal is immutably determined.

90 They, applauding the Mountain's words, [generous in effecting the wished-for object:] which generously granted their wishes, blessed Ambikā with benedictions whose fulfilment would be immediate.

Stanza 90: *They* (the Sages), *applauding* (praising with 'bravo!') *the Mountain's* (Himālaya's) *words* (statement), *generous* (noble) *in effecting the wished-for object* (because of performing the desired object). According to Amara '**udāra** is used in the sense of **dātṛ** granting or **mahānt** great, noble'. [*Despite Mallinātha, the former sense is obviously not irrelevant* *here.*] **pākaḥ** *fulfilment* means that which is ripened, i.e. fruit, reward. *With benedictions* (benisons) *whose fulfilment would be immediate* (whose fruit was before the eyes) *they blessed* (congratulated) *Ambikā* (Ambā).

91 Her, when her golden earrings slipped in her anxiety to salute them, as she showed confusion, Arundhatī took upon her lap.

Stanza 91: *Her* (Ambikā), whose *golden* (made out of gold) *earrings* (gold ear-ornaments) *slipped in her anxiety to salute them* (because of intentness upon making obeisance), *as she showed confusion Arundhatī took upon her lap.* The **p** (in **āropayām āsa**) occurs by the rule '(before the causative suffix) for (the final **h** of) **ruh,** there occurs optionally **p**'.

92 And her mother, tearful-faced (and made) distressed by love for her daughter, she set at ease by (describing) the qualities of the suitor who had no other (with) prior (claim on him).

Stanza 92: *And her mother* (the mother (Menā) of her (Ambikā)) because of her *love for her daughter* (affection for her child) *distressed* (afraid that she would be separated), and therefore *tearful-faced* (one on whose face there were tears). **anyapūrva** means 'having another woman as a prior (claim)'. The masculine gender of the prior member of the compound occurs by the rule that 'a pronoun takes the masculine gender [in the sphere of synthetic expression:] when forming part of a compound'. **ananyapūrva** means not being this, and is here used in the genitive. *She set at ease* (without distress) *by the qualities* (such as being the Conqueror of Death) of the suitor (bridegroom) *who had no other with prior claim on him*—in other words, who did not occasion the distress caused by sharing a husband.

93 Being asked the date for the wedding thereupon by Hara's (new) kinsman, they the bark-garmented ones declared (it to be) after three days, and departed.

Stanza 93: *They* (the ascetics) *bark-garmented* (dressed only in bark) *thereupon* (at that very instant) *by Hara's kinsman* (Himālaya) being *asked* (questioned as to what was) *the date for the wedding* (suitable for the wedding). **tryahaḥ** means a group of three days. The compound occurs by the rule that '(words denoting a region or number compound with another word having the same case-relationship) also (*a*) to express the sense that would be expressed by a secondary suffix, (*b*) where there is a further member (added to the compound), (*c*) to express collective sense'. The suffix *ṭac* occurs by the rule that '(the compound-final suffix) *ṭac* occurs after the words **rājan, ahan** and **sakhi**'. The singular is because it is a **dvigu** compound. It is masculine in gender by the rule that '(when at the end of a co-ordinative or determinative compound) the words **rātra, ahna** and **aha** occur in the masculine'. Here the word is used in the ablative. *They declared it after* (subsequent to) *three days* (said 'the wedding (shall be) on the fourth day') *and departed* (went away).

94 They, after taking leave of Himālaya and going back to the Trident-bearer and reporting to him that their business was accomplished, dismissed by him rose up to heaven.

Stanza 94: *They* (the Sages) *taking leave* (saying goodbye with the words 'good, let us go') *of Himālaya, and going back to the Trident-bearer* (Hara), who was at the appointed place [*mentioned in fact in stanza 33*], and reporting (announcing) *to him that their business* (mission) *was accomplished* (completed), *dismissed by him* (by the Trident-bearer) *rose up* (flew up) towards *heaven* (the sky). In this (stanza), since there is a stating of matters in a concise form, the quality known as 'Conciseness' is expressed: to quote—

'Conciseness is declared to be [that which is] the stating of matters in a concise form'.

(The poet now) states that the blessed Paśupati could not bear even a delay of merely three days, because of his longing for her:

95 And Paśupati passed those days with difficulty, longing for union with the Mountain's daughter. What other helpless (person) would such emotions not torment, in that they affect even him who is (so) powerful?

Stanza 95: **utka** means 'of whom the mind is **utka** [raised up, i.e.] eager'. The form is given ready-made by the rule that '**utka** occurs (in the sense of) one who is **un_manas** longing'. *And longing for union with the Mountain's daughter* (eager for marriage with Pārvatī) *Paśupati passed* (spent) *those* (understand 'three') *days with difficulty*. The poet comments: *such emotions* (the Subsidiary (States) such as longing) *what other* (ordinary person) *helpless* (not in control of his senses) *would they not torment* (cause mental disturbance to), *in that* (since) *even him* (the Destroyer of Love) *who is powerful* (is capable—has conquered his senses, in fact) *they affect* (in other words, mentally disturb)?

The embellishment here is Strong Presumption, since from (one) matter, the confirmation of mental disturbance in the All-powerful one, (another matter) the mental disturbance of other people [presents itself:] is inferred on the *a fortiori* principle. As the sūtra states, 'Strong Presumption is the arising (through inference) of another matter by the stick-and-cake rule'. Some consider it Substantiation, but this should be disregarded, though the arguments (for rejection) are not stated for fear of going on too long.

The metre is Puṣpitāgrā, since this is defined as follows:

'In the odd (lines), after two **ns** and an **r**, a **y**,

And in the even (lines), **n** and **j**, **j**, **r** and **g**—(make) a Puṣpitāgrā.'

English–Sanskrit Exercises: Roman Key

Exercise 1b

mahāyāna, yoga, Mahābhārata, Rāmāyaṇa, purāṇa, jāti, Bhīma, Pāṇini, sādhu, Kāśī, Kailāsa, vihāra, mīmāṃsā, agni, ātman, paṇḍita, kṣatriya, vaiśya, śūdra, caṇḍāla, ṛgveda, mudrā, karma, Jagannātha, Gaṅgā, saṃskṛta, prākṛta, ardhamāgadhī, sandhi, aśvamedha, bodhisattva, avagraha, Indra, Kṛṣṇa, Arjuna, Bhagavadgītā, Pañcatantra

In the following sentences words have been separated where appropriate, but the student is of course not expected to have been able to do this for himself:

1 sakhy Anusūye na kevalaṃ tātasya niyogo, mamāpi sahodarasneha eteṣu 2 udakaṃ lambhitā ete grīṣmakālakusumadāyina āśramavṛkṣakāḥ 3 idānīm atikrāntakusumasamayān api vṛkṣakān siñcāmaḥ 4 atipinaddhenaitena valkalena Priyaṃvadayā dṛḍhaṃ pīḍitāsmi 5 tac chithilaya tāvad enat 6 atra tāvat payodharavistārayitāram ātmano yauvanārambham upālabhasva 7 sakhyāv eṣa vāteritapallavāṅgulībhiḥ kim api vyāharatīva māṃ cūtavṛkṣakaḥ

Exercise 2a

1 svairaṃ taması īśvarasyı āśvau durjanāḥ śastraiś

cirān muñcanti raśmibhya eva 2 aśvāv īśvarasy› aîva svairaṃ śastrai raśmibhyo muñcanti cirād durjanās tamasi 3 svairam ev› ēśvarasya muñcanty aśvau śastrair durjanāś cirāt tamasi raśmibhyaḥ 4 muñcanty eva tamasy aśvau śastrair īśvarasya cirād raśmibhyo durjanāḥ svairam 5 raśmibhyas tamasi śastrair muñcanti cirād eva svairam īśvarasy› âśvau durjanāḥ 6 śastrais tamasi raśmibhyaḥ svairaṃ durjanā īśvarasya cirād aśvau muñcanty eva 7 tamasi durjanā raśmibhyaś cirād īśvarasy› âśvau svairaṃ muñcanti śastrair eva 8 muñcanti durjanā eva raśmibhyo ›śvāv īśvarasya cirāt svairaṃ śastrais tamasi

Exercise 2c

1 bhramasi 2 adhunā ›vagacchāmaḥ 3 tatr› āpi nṛtyati 4 atra vasathaḥ? 5 kathaṃ, jayanti? 6 upaviśāvaḥ 7 evaṃ na vadataḥ 8 kiṃ punar api pṛcchasi? 9 atra kiṃ likhāmi? 10 kiṃ na paśyasi? 11 gāyath› êva 12 gacchanty āgacchanti ca (Note the usual order of this pair in Sanskrit.) 13 adhunā jīvati ca śocati ca 14 paśyati vadat› îva ca 15 'kim icchath›?' êti pṛcchanti 16 āgacchant› îti gacchāmaḥ 17 na punar mādyāmaḥ 18 evam api smarāvaḥ—kiṃ smarathaḥ?—'adya n› āgacchat›' îti (Note that the context shows 'you' to be dual.)

Exercise 3b

1 jala;bhojane icchāmaḥ [Note the absence of sandhi.] 2 śīghram aśvaṃ paśyataḥ 3 paṇḍitāḥ kim icchatha? 4 tvāṃ bālam iva krodho jayati 5 kāv ācāryau paśyasi? 6 sūrya iv› âdya candraḥ śobhanaḥ 7 api ramaṇīyaḥ saḥ? 8 ācārya, ko brāhmaṇa ita āgacchati? 9 atra kiṃ phalam? 10 bālāḥ, kva sa ācāryaḥ? 11 kiṃ ramaṇīyāny api vacanāni na smaratha? 12 svalpaṃ phalaṃ paśyāmaḥ 13 api vismitā ācāryāḥ? 14 kṣetra;parvata;vanāni bālau paśyataḥ 15 'sukham sa n›

êcchat›' îti kiṃ vadatha? 16 kṣetraṃ gajaṃ nayanti 17 kva punar bhojanam iti māṃ na vadasi 18 vismitaṃ janaṃ brāhmaṇa iva sa naro vadati

Exercise 4b

1 pariśrānto devaḥ—atr› ôpaviśāvaḥ 2 na vismṛtāni janen› aîtāni vacanāni 3 śobhanam ev› aîtat 4 vanaṃ gato ›pi [*or* gatam api] putraṃ smarati 5 ady› aîv› āgatā vayam 6 deva, adhunā ›py etābhyāṃ bālābhyām udyānaṃ na tyaktam 7 eṣa vayasyaiḥ saha tiṣṭhati 8 atra kim adbhutam?—prathamam eva dṛṣṭo may» aîṣa naraḥ 9 eṣa āgata eva devaś Candraguptaḥ 10 dṛṣṭaṃ kutūhalen› âsmābhir udyānam 11 vanaṃ v» ôdyānaṃ vā gataḥ 12 vayasyāḥ, dūram eten› âśvena vayam ānītāḥ 13 kṛtaṃ saṃdehena—etau jīvitāv āgacchataḥ śiṣyau 14 ady› âpi sukhen› aîva tad adbhutaṃ darśanaṃ smarāmaḥ 15 jitās te viṣādena 16 vismitā apy etena darśanena, prayatnaṃ na tyajanti

Exercise 5b

1 andhaḥ khalv asi 2 asmād gṛhād vanāni sa nītaḥ 3 tair apy udyānaṃ gatvā pāpā gṛhītāḥ 4 adbhuto ›nayoḥ krodhaḥ 5 putrāḥ, dṛṣṭāḥ stha 6 santi tv asmākaṃ Candanadāsasya gṛhe mitrāṇi 7 pariśrānto ›sm› îti pṛcchāmi 8 sarveṣu deśasya mārgeṣu dṛṣṭam idam asmābhiḥ 9 deva, sa ev› âsmi kumāraḥ 10 andhasya pādayoḥ patati 11 sarve mayā ken› âpy upāyena dṛṣṭāḥ 12 krodhāy› aîtat kumārasya prativacanam 13 śrutvā tv etan mārga upaviśanti 14 Kalahaṃsaka, na naḥ kutūhalaṃ pustakeṣu 15 ekasminn ev› ôdyāne puṣpāṇi kānicid bhavanti 16 dṛṣṭvā ›pi sarvaṃ n› aîva kiṃcid vadati kumāraḥ 17 kathaṃ saṃdeha ev› âtra te? 18 hā Makaranda, hā Kalahaṃsaka, gato vāṃ vayasyaḥ [Note that 'your' must be dual.] 19 kumāreṇa tv anyasmin deśe sthitvā sarvaṃ pāpasya prativacanaṃ śrutam 20 krodhe kiṃ phalam eṣa paśyati?

Exercise 6b

1 āśrama-mṛgo ›yam 2 kṛtaḥ kāry›-ārambhaḥ 3 ayam amātya:Rākṣasas tiṣṭhati 4 mūḍha, n› âyaṃ parihāsa-kālaḥ 5 iyaṃ tarhi kasya mudrā? 6 abhijñaḥ khalv asi loka-vyavahārāṇām 7 tat kiṃ na parigṛhītam asmad-vacanaṃ paura:janena? 8 aho, pravāta-subhago ›yaṃ van›-ôddeśaḥ 9 alam āśaṅkayā 10 labdhaṃ netra-nirvāṇam 11 kathaṃ na paśyasi Rāmasy› âvasthām? 12 Śārṅgarava, sthāne khalu pura-praveśāt tav› ēdṛśaḥ saṃvegaḥ 13 asty etat kula-vrataṃ Pauravāṇām 14 bhadre, prathitaṃ Duḥṣanta-caritaṃ prajāsu 15 tat kṛtam idānīm āśā:vyasanena 16 na khalu satyam eva tāpasa-kanyāyām abhilāṣo me 17 candr›-ôparāgaṃ prati tu, ken› âpi vipralabdhā ›si 18 ih› aîva priyā-paribhukte latā-maṇḍape muhūrtaṃ tiṣṭhāmi

Exercise 7b

1 Ātreyy asmi 2 vardhayasi me kutūhalam 3 tad idaṃ sarasī-tīram 4 yāvad etāś chāyām āśritaḥ pratipālayāmi 5 kṣudra:jana-kṣuṇṇa eṣa mārgaḥ 6 vyaktam etāny api Cāṇakya-prayuktena vaṇijā ›smāsu vikrītāni 7 aho, darśito mitra-snehaḥ 8 śirasi bhayaṃ dūre tat-pratīkāraḥ 9 sakhi Madayantike, svāgatam. anugṛhītam asmad-gṛhaṃ bhavatyā 10 eṣa vivāda eva māṃ pratyāyayati 11 samid-āharaṇāya prasthitāv āvām [āharaṇ›-ârtham would also do. Note samid from samidh by external sandhi.] 12 kimarthaṃ bhavatībhyāṃ pratiṣiddho ›smi? 13 Kalahaṃsaka;Makaranda-praveś›-âvasare tat su:vihitam 14 katham, tātena dhṛta:pūrvam idam ābharaṇam? 15 niyukt» aîva mayā tatra tat-priya:sakhī Buddharakṣitā 16 etāv eva Rāmāyaṇa-kathā-puruṣau? 17 anena priya:suhṛdā Siddhārthakena ghātakān vidrāvya vadhya-sthānād apahṛto ›smi 18 anya ev› âyam a:kṣuṇṇaḥ kathā-prakāro bhagavatyāḥ 19 kumāra:

Lava-prayukta:Vāruṇ›ˇâstra-prabhāvaḥ khalv eṣaḥ 20 sa khalu vaidyas tad ev› auṣadhaṃ pāyitaś c› ôparataś ca

Exercise 8b

1 rājñaḥ pratigraho ›yam 2 gato ›ham Avalokitā-janita:kautukaḥ Kāmadev›-āyatanam 3 amātya-nām›-âṅkit» êyaṃ mudrā 4 pariṣan-nirdiṣṭa:guṇaṃ prabandhaṃ n› âdhigacchāmaḥ 5 nanu yūyam apy anena dharma-karmaṇā pariśrāntāḥ 6 eṣo ›smi Kāmandakī saṃvṛttaḥ. aham apy Avalokitā 7 Vṛṣala, svayam an:abhiyuktānāṃ rājñām ete doṣā bhavanti 8 tat kim avanata:mukhaˇpuṇḍarīkaḥ sthito ›si? 9 tatra hi me priya:suhṛd vaitālika-vyañjanaḥ Stanakalaśo nāma prativasati 10 api vayasyena vidite tad-anvayaˇ nāmanī? 11 priye, krauryam api me tvayi prayuktam anukūla:pariṇāmaṃ saṃvṛttam. tad aham idānīṃ tvayā pratyabhijñātam ātmānam icchāmi 12 Urvaśī-gata:manaso ›pi me sa eva devyāṃ bahumānaḥ 13 kiṃ tv araṇya-sado vayam an:abhyasta:ratha-caryāḥ 14 tad asy› aîva tāvad ucchvasita:kusuma-kesara-kaṣāyaˇśītal›ˇāmoda-vāsit›: ôdyānasya kāñcanāra:pādapasy› âdhastād upaviśāvaḥ 15 vidita:Sītā-vṛttānt» êyam 16 aye, any›-āsakta:citto devaḥ 17 kiṃ:nāmadheyam etad devyā vratam? 18 sa c› âṅgurīyaka-darśan›:âvasānaḥ śāpaḥ 19 vaimanasya-parīto ›pi priya:darśano devaḥ

Exercise 9b

1 api nir_vighnaṃ tapaḥ? 2 vayasya Makaranda, api bhavān utkaṇṭhate Madayantikāyāḥ? 3 kva punar Mālatī Mādhavaṃ prāg dṛṣṭavatī? 4 ārye, eṣa nir_lajjo Lakṣmaṇaḥ praṇamati 5 kiṃ kathayanti bhavantaḥ? 6 atyudāra:prakṛtir Mālatī 7 ramaṇīyāḥ khalv amātya:Bhūrivasor vibhūtayaḥ 8 atidāruṇo jana-saṃmardo vartate 9 Śakuntalāyāḥ prathama:

darśana-vṛttāntaṃ kathitavān asmi bhavate 10 bhagavaty Arundhati, Vaidehaḥ Sīradhvajo ›bhivādaye 11 api kṣamante ›smad-upajāpaṃ Candragupta-prakṛtayaḥ? 12 a:saṃnihitam eva māṃ manyate 13 apūrvaḥ ko ›pi bahumāna-hetur guruṣu, Saudhātake 14 eṣa Rākṣasa-prayukto viṣa-kanyayā Parvateśvaraṃ ghātitavān 15 Mādhavasy› âñjalau bakula-mālāṃ nikṣipati 16 diṣṭyā Mahendr›-ôpakāra-paryāptena vikrama-mahimnā vardhate bhavān 17 tataḥ praviśati yath»_ôkta:vyāpārā saha sakhībhyāṃ Śakuntalā 18 vayasya, nanv amātya-bhavan›-āsanna: rathyay» aîva bahuśaḥ saṃcarāvahe—tad upapannam etat 19 Candragupta-prakṛtīnāṃ hi Cāṇakya-doṣā ev› âparāga-hetavaḥ 20 vayasya, nir_avagrahaṃ dahati daivam iva dāruṇo vivasvān 21 sādhu Vṛṣala sādhu—mam› aîva hṛdayena saha saṃmantrya saṃdiṣṭavān asi 22 aye, 'Kusumapura-vṛttānta-jño ›haṃ, bhavat-praṇidhiś c›' êti gāthā-›rthaḥ 23 etāv Aditi-parivardhita:mandāra˘vṛkṣakaṃ Prajāpater āśrama-padaṃ praviṣṭau svaḥ 24 imām ugr›:ātapāṃ velāṃ prāyeṇa latā-valaya˜vatsu Mālinī-tīreṣu sa_sakhī˘janā tatrabhavatī gamayati

Exercise 10b

1 āryāḥ paśyata 2 aho mahārghyāṇy ābharaṇāni 3 paśyantī tiṣṭhati 4 tvaratām atrabhavatī 5 trikāla-darśibhir munibhir ādiṣṭaḥ sur›;âsura-vimardo bhāvī 6 bahu:pratyavāyaṃ nṛpatvam 7 ata eva bhavad-vidhā mahāntaḥ 8 astu te kārya-siddhiḥ 9 mudrāṃ paripālayann udveṣṭya darśaya 10 aho viveka-śūnya˜tā mlecchasya 11 nigṛhya śok›-āveśaṃ mām anugacchatam 12 vatsa, kāry›-âbhiyoga ev› âsmān ākulayati, na punar upādhyāya-sahabhūḥ śiṣya:jane duḥśīlatā 13 pariharantam api māṃ Pañcavaṭī-sneho balād ākarṣat› îva 14 aho madhuram āsāṃ darśanam 15 Citralekhe, tvaray› Ôrvaśīm 16 asty etad anya-samādhi-bhīru˜tvaṃ devānām 17 utsarpiṇī khalu

mahatāṃ prārthanā 18 sāṃpratam eva Kusumapur›-ôparodhanāya pratiṣṭhantām asmad-balāni 19 vismṛtā bhavad-guṇa-pakṣapātinā mayā svāmi-guṇāḥ 20 Priyaṃvadaka, na naḥ kutūhalaṃ sarpeṣu—tat paritoṣya visarjay› aînam 21 Śacī-tīrthe salilaṃ vandamānāyās tava sakhyāḥ paribhraṣṭam 22 vatsa, sāvadhāno bhava 23 kārya-vyagra˜tvān manasaḥ prabhūtatvāc ca praṇidhīnāṃ vismṛtam 24 ārya Jājale, tvam api sa_parijano nivartasva—Bhāgurāyaṇa ev› aîko mām anugacchatu 25 aho śarat: samaya-saṃbhṛta:śobhā˜vibhūtīnāṃ diśām atiśaya:ramaṇīya˜tā 26 tata ekasmād bhitti-cchidrād gṛhīta:bhakt›˜âvayavānāṃ pipīlikānāṃ niṣkrāmantīnāṃ paṅktim avalokya, 'puruṣa:garbham etad gṛham' iti gṛhīt›:ârthena dāhitaṃ tad eva śayana-gṛham

Exercise 11b

1 dīyatām asmai prativacanam 2 bhrātarāv āvāṃ yamajau 3 na niṣ_prayojanam adhikāra˜vantaḥ prabhubhir āhūyante 4 atr› aîva sthīyatām 5 yat tad alaṃkaraṇa-trayaṃ krītaṃ, tan-madhyād ekaṃ dīyatām 6 vimucyantām abhīśavaḥ 7 kim ucyate 'dhairyam' iti? 8 bhadrās tvaryatāṃ tvaryatām 9 abhivyaktāyāṃ candrikāyāṃ kiṃ dīpikā-paunaruktena? 10 Lātavya, āhūyatām Urvaśī 11 aye, tad idam ābharaṇaṃ yan mayā sva:śarīrād avatārya Rākṣasāya preṣitam 12 ayi vatse, evam ātmā stūyate 13 paritoṣya vikretāraṃ gṛhyatām 14 ārya, asti kaścid yaḥ Kusumapuraṃ gacchati, tata āgacchati vā? 15 praveśyatām 16 kiṃ mṛṣā tarkeṇ› ânviṣyate? 17 'amātya' iti lajjā-karam idānīṃ viśeṣaṇa:padam 18 hanta, mūḍha ev› āsmi, yo ›smin vanecare vayasya:Makarand›-ôcitaṃ vyavaharāmi 19 samarpyatāṃ Rākṣasasya gṛha-janaḥ. anubhūyatāṃ ciraṃ vicitra:phalo rāja-prasādaḥ 20 rakṣyatāṃ para-kalatreṇ› ātmanaḥ kalatraṃ jīvitaṃ ca 21 sa eṣa Kāmandakī-suhṛt-putro mahā:māṃsasya paṇāyitā Mādhavaḥ 22 yeṣāṃ

antevāsināṃ hastena tat pustakaṃ Bharat›-āśramaṃ preṣitaṃ, teṣām ānuyātrikaś cāpa꞉pāṇiḥ pramād›-âpanodan›-ârtham asmad-bhrātā preṣitaḥ 23 anantaraṃ ca yātrā-bhaṅga-pracalitasya mahataḥ paura꞉janasya saṃkulena vighaṭitāyāṃ tasyām āgato ›smi 24 mūrkha, anyam eva bhāgam ete tapasvino nirvapanti, yo ratna-rāśīn api vihāy› âbhinandyate 25 evam ātm›-âbhiprāya-saṃbhāvit꞉êṣṭa꞉jana꞉cittavṛttiḥ prārthayitā vipralabhyate

Exercise 12b

1 kiṃ bravīṣi? 2 anena lekhena Rākṣaso jetavyaḥ 3 tatr› aîva Makaranda;Madayantik»-āgamanaṃ yāvat sthātavyam 4 śṛṇuvas tāvat 5 hanta, hṛdayam api me ripubhiḥ svīkṛtam 6 asyām aśoka-cchāyāyām āstām āyuṣmān, yāvat tvām aham Indra-gurave nivedayāmi 7 rakṣaṇīyā Rākṣasasya prāṇā ity āry›-ādeśaḥ 8 tad yathā bhavitavyaṃ tathā bhavatu 9 sarvam eva tantram ākulībhūtam 10 kiṃ bhavāṃs tūṣṇīm āste? 11 tad atra vastuny an꞉upālabhyo Rākṣasaḥ 12 bhadra Bhāsvaraka, bahir nītvā tāvat tāḍyatāṃ yāvat kathyate ›nena 13 śṛṇu vicitram idam 14 asminn eva vetasa;latā-maṇḍape bhavitavyaṃ Śakuntalayā 15 tad idānīṃ sahadharmacāriṇaṃ prati na tvayā manyuḥ karaṇīyaḥ 16 tam ev› ôddeśaṃ gacchāmi yatra me nayanayoḥ sā su꞉nayanā tiro꞉bhūtā 17 āviṣkṛtaṃ kathā-prāvīṇyaṃ vatsena 18 tena hi tat-prayogād ev› âtrabhavataḥ sāmājikān upāsmahe 19 kumāra iv› ân꞉atikramaṇīya꞉vacano bhavān api 20 a꞉samyak ceṣṭitaṃ priyāṃ samāsādya kāla-haraṇaṃ kurvatā mayā 21 kaṣṭam, ete suhṛd-vyasaneṣu para꞉vad udāsīnāḥ pratyādiśyāmahe vayam anena 22 bhoḥ śreṣṭhin, sa c› âparikleśaḥ katham āvirbhavat› îti nanu praṣṭavyā vayam eva bhavatā 23 yāvad ete Mānas›-ôtsukāḥ patatriṇaḥ saraso n› ôtpatanti, tāvad etebhyaḥ priyā-pravṛttir avagamayitavyā 24 tatas teṣu gṛhīta꞉saṃjñeṣu bhay›-

âpadeśād itas tataḥ pradruteṣu Śakaṭadāso vadhya-sthānād apanīya Rākṣasaṃ prāpayitavyaḥ 25 yad» aîv› âpsaras-tīrthāt pratyākhyāna-viklavāṃ Śakuntalām ādāya Dākṣāyaṇīm upagatā Menakā, tad» aîva dhyānād avagata:vṛttānto ›smi 'Durvāsasaḥ śāpād iyaṃ tapasvinī sahadharmacāriṇā pratyādiṣṭ»' êti

Exercise 13b

1 Vijaye, pratyabhijānāti bhavatī bhūṣaṇam idam? 2 śaṭhaḥ khalv asau baṭuḥ 3 su:vihitaṃ Lavaṅgikayā, yato Mādhav›-ânucaraḥ Kalahaṃsakas tāṃ vihāra-dāsīṃ Mandārikāṃ kāmayate 4 kva punar māṃ bhavatyaḥ pratipālayiṣyanti? 5 katham, a:dattv» aîva prativacanaṃ nartitum ārabdhaḥ 6 kathaṃ, mad-anveṣiṇaḥ sainikās tapo-vanam uparundhanti? 7 kāmam etad abhinandanīyaṃ, tathā ›pi vayam atra madhyasthāḥ 8 n› âticirād amātyo ›smān purātanīm avasthām āropayiṣyati 9 na yuktaṃ prākṛtam api puruṣam avajñātum 10 rājan Candragupta, viditam eva te yathā vayaṃ Malayaketau kiṃ cit kāl›-ântaram uṣitāḥ 11 bho Viṣṇugupta, na māṃ śvapāka-sparśa-dūṣitaṃ spraṣṭum arhasi 12 vatsa, kaccid abhinanditas tvayā vidhivad asmābhir anuṣṭhita:jāta˘karm›: ādi˘kriyaḥ putra eṣa Śākuntaleyaḥ? 13 tad anujānīhi māṃ gamanāya 14 na śaknumo vayam āryasya vācā vācam atiśayitum 15 yady evam abhiyoga-kālam āryaḥ paśyati, tat kim āsyate? 16 bhadra, praviśa—lapsyase śrotāraṃ jñātāraṃ ca 17 'idānīm eva duhitaram atithi-satkārāy› ādiśya, daivam asyāḥ pratikūlaṃ śamayituṃ Somatīrthaṃ gataḥ'—'yady evaṃ, tām eva drakṣyāmi' 18 sakhe, kim a:śraddadhānaḥ pṛcchasi? 19 kim a:kṣatriyā pṛthivī, yad evam udghuṣyate? 20 bhadra, kasmiṃś cid āpta:jan›-ânuṣṭheye karmaṇi tvāṃ vyāpārayitum icchāmi 21 sa cen muni-dauhitras tal:lakṣaṇ›-ôpapanno bhavati tataḥ pratinandya śuddhāntam enāṃ praveśayiṣyasi 22 tat kim ujjihāna:jīvitāṃ varākīṃ n› ânukampase? 23 na

niṣ_parigraham sthāna-bhraṃśaḥ pīḍayiṣyati 24 Candragupta-śarīram abhidrogdhum asmat-prayuktānāṃ tīkṣṇa:rasa-d›:ādīnām upasaṃgrah›-ârthaṃ prakṛty-upajāp›-ârthaṃ ca mahatā koṣa-saṃcayena sthāpitaḥ Śakaṭadāsaḥ 25 sakhe Mādhavya, an:avāpta:cakṣuḥ-phalo ›si, yena tvayā draṣṭavyānāṃ paraṃ na dṛṣṭam 26 bhoḥ śreṣṭhin Candanadāsa, evaṃ rāj›-âpathya-kāriṣu tīkṣṇa:daṇḍo rājā na marṣayiṣyati Rākṣasa-kalatra-pracchādanaṃ bhavataḥ 27 yato ›mī vyāghr›:ādayo varṇa-mātra-vipralabdhāḥ śṛgālam a:jñātvā rājānam amuṃ manyante, tad yathā ›yaṃ paricīyate tathā kuruta 28 deva, jīvitu-kāmaḥ ko ›nyo devasya śāsanam ullaṅghayiṣyati? 29 yady api svāmi-guṇā na śakyante vismartuṃ, tathā ›pi mad-vijñāpanāṃ mānayitum arhaty āryaḥ

Exercise 14b

1 Lāṭavya, api jānīte bhavān kasy› âyaṃ bāṇa iti? 2 aye mūrkha, kiṃ bhavān asmākam upādhyāyād dharma-vit-taraḥ? 3 nyaśāmayaṃ ca tasminn āśrame kasya cic cūta-potakasya cchāyāyāṃ kam apy udvigna:varṇaṃ tāpasam 4 vayasya, aṅgulī-svedena dūṣyerann akṣarāṇi 5 tat ko ›yaṃ pade pade mahān an:adhyavasāyaḥ? 6 ity uktvā ca sā tāmbūla-bhājanād ākṛṣya tām adarśayat 7 avasare khalv anurāg›:ôpakārayor garīyasor upanyāsaḥ 8 Raivataka, ucyatām asmat-sārathiḥ sa_bāṇa:kārmukaṃ ratham upasthāpay› êti 9 sa kadācid dhairya-skhalana-vilakṣaḥ kiṃ cid aniṣṭam api samācaret 10 yāvad aśṛṇavaṃ Mālaty ev› âsya manmath›-ônmātha-hetur iti 11 nikhil›:ântaḥpura-svāminī ca tasy› âbhavat 12 ucyatāṃ kiṃ te bhūyaḥ priyam upakaromi 13 ity abhidhāya kim iyaṃ vakṣyat› îti man-mukh›-āsakta:dṛṣṭis tūṣṇīm āsīt 14 tat kuto ›smin vipine priyā-pravṛttim āgamayeyam? 15 sa kila kṛpālus taṃ janam ārdrayā gir» āśvāsy› ārti-kāraṇaṃ tāṃ gaṇikām apṛcchat 16 kumāra, na kadācid api Śakaṭadāso ›mātya:Rākṣasasy›

âgrato 'mayā likhitam' iti pratipatsyate 17 sakhe Bhāgurāyaṇa, nanv asmākam amātya:Rākṣasaḥ priyatamo hitatamaś ca 18 apayātāyāṃ bhavatyāṃ muhūrtam iva sthitv» aîkākī 'kim ayam idānīm ācarat›?' îti saṃjāta:vitarkaḥ pratinivṛtya viṭap›-ântarita:vigrahas taṃ pradeśaṃ vyalokayam 19 api nāma mṛgatṛṣṇik» êva n› âyam ante prastāvo viṣādāya kalpeta 20 sūry›-ôpasthānāt pratinivṛttaṃ Purūravasaṃ mām upetya kathyatāṃ kuto bhavatyaḥ paritrātavyā iti 21 ity abhidadhānā madana-mūrchā-kheda-vihvalair aṅgaiḥ kathaṃ cid avalambya tām ev› ôdatiṣṭham. uccalitāyāś ca me durnimitta-nivedakam aspandata dakṣiṇaṃ locanam. upajāta:śaṅkā c› âcintayam 'idam aparaṃ kim apy upakṣiptaṃ daiven›' êti 22 yady asmatto garīyān Rākṣaso ›vagamyate, tadā ›smākam idaṃ śastraṃ tasmai dīyatām 23 sakhe, Candraguptasy› aîva tāvan nagara-praveśāt prabhṛti mat-prayuktais tīkṣṇa:rasa-d›:ādibhiḥ kim anuṣṭhitam iti śrotum icchāmi 24 yadi punar īdṛśaṃ tvām Aikṣvāko rājā Rāmaḥ paśyet tadā ›sya snehena hṛdayam abhiṣyandeta 25 iti vicārayantīm eva mām a:vicārita:guṇa˘doṣa-viśeṣo rūp›-aîka˘pakṣapātī nava:yauvana-sulabhaḥ kusum›-āyudhaḥ kusuma-samaya-mada iva madhukarīṃ paravaśām akarot

English–Sanskrit Exercises: Nāgarī Key

Exercise 1a

महाराज । सीता । रावण । मैथुन । देवनागरी । हिमालय । शिव । कालिदास । गुरु । अशोक । संसार । उपनिषद् । शकुन्तला । चैत्य । पिण्ड । मनुस्मृति । विष्णु । कौटिल्य । संस्कार । अनुस्वार । शक्ति । अश्वघोष । वात्स्यायन । वेदान्त । ब्रह्मन् । चक्र । चन्द्रगुप्त । कामसूत्र । मन्त्र । विसर्गः । निर्वाण । धर्मशास्त्र । भारतवर्ष । यक्ष । विज्ञानवादिन् ॥

को नियोगो ऽनुष्ठीयताम् । १ । एवं न्वेतत् । २ । अनन्तरकरणीयमिदानीमाज्ञापयत्वार्यः । ३ । अथ कतरं पुनर्ऋतुं समाश्रित्य गास्यामि । ४ । ननु प्रथममेवार्येणाज्ञप्तमभिज्ञानशकुन्तलं नामापूर्वं नाटकमभिनीयतामिति । ५ । इत इतः प्रियसख्यौ । ६ । सखि शकुन्तले त्वत्तो ऽपि तातकण्वस्याश्रमवृक्षकाः प्रिया इति तर्कयामि येन नवमालिकाकुसुमपरिपेलवापि त्वमेतेष्वालवालपूरणेषु नियुक्ता । ७ ।

Exercise 2a

स्वैरं तमसीश्वरस्याश्वौ दुर्जनाः शस्त्रैश्चिरान्मुञ्चन्ति रश्मिभ्य एव । १ । अश्वावीश्वरस्यैव स्वैरं शस्त्रै रश्मिभ्यो मुञ्चन्ति चिराद्दुर्जनास्तमसि । २ । स्वैरमेवेश्वरस्य मुञ्चन्त्यश्वौ शस्त्रैर्दुर्जनाश्चिरात्तमसि

रश्मिभ्यः । ३ । मुञ्चन्त्येव तमस्यश्वौ शस्त्रैरीश्वरस्य चिराद्रश्मिभ्यो दुर्जनाः स्वैरम् । ४ । रश्मिभ्यस्तमसि शस्त्रैर्मुञ्चन्ति चिरादेव स्वैरमीश्वरस्याश्वौ दुर्जनाः । ५ । शस्त्रैस्तमसि रश्मिभ्यः स्वैरं दुर्जना ईश्वरस्य चिरादश्वौ मुञ्चन्त्येव । ६ । तमसि दुर्जना रश्मिभ्यश्चिरादीश्वरस्याश्वौ स्वैरं मुञ्चन्ति शस्त्रैरेव । ७ । मुञ्चन्ति दुर्जना एव रश्मिभ्यो ऽश्वावीश्वरस्य चिरात्स्वैरं शस्त्रैस्तमसि ॥ ८ ॥

Exercise 2c

भ्रमसि । १ । अधुनावगच्छामः । २ । तत्रापि नृत्यति । ३ । अत्र वसथः । ४ । कथं जयन्ति । ५ । उपविशावः । ६ । एवं न वदतः । ७ । किं पुनरपि पृच्छसि । ८ । अत्र किं लिखामि । ७ । किं न पश्यसि । १० । गायथेव । ११ । गच्छन्त्यागच्छन्ति च । १२ । अधुना जीवति च शोचति च । १३ । पश्यति वदतीव च । १४ । किमिच्छथेति पृच्छन्ति । १५ । आगच्छन्तीति गच्छामः । १६ । न पुनर्माद्यामः । १७ । एवमपि स्मरावः । किं स्मरथः । अद्य नागच्छतीति ॥ १८ ॥

Exercise 3b

जलभोजने इच्छामः । १ । शीघ्रमश्वं पश्यतः । २ । पण्डिताः किमिच्छथ । ३ । त्वां बालमिव क्रोधो जयति । ४ । कावाचार्यौ पश्यसि । ५ । सूर्य इवाद्य चन्द्रः शोभनः । ६ । अपि रमणीयः सः । ७ । आचार्य को ब्राह्मण इत आगच्छति । ८ । अत्र किं फलम् । ९ । बालाः क्व स आचार्यः । १० । किं रमणीयान्यपि वचनानि न स्मरथ । ११ । स्वल्पं फलं पश्यामः । १२ । अपि विस्मिता आचार्याः । १३ । क्षेत्रपर्वतवनानि बालौ पश्यतः । १४ । सुखं स नेच्छतीति किं वदथ । १५ । क्षेत्रं गजं नयन्ति । १६ । क्व पुनर्भोजनमिति मां न वदसि । १७ । विस्मितं जनं ब्राह्मण इव स नरो वदति ॥ १८ ॥

Exercise 4b

परिश्रान्तो देवः — अत्रोपविशावः ।१। न विस्मृतानि जनेनै-तानि वचनानि ।२। शोभनमेवैतत् ।३। वनं गतो ऽपि (गतमपि) पुत्रं स्मरति ।४। अद्यैवागता वयम् ।५। देव अधुनाप्येताभ्यां बालाभ्यामुद्यानं न त्यक्तम् ।६। एष वयस्यैः सह तिष्ठति ।७। अत्र किमद्भुतम् — प्रथममेव दृष्टो मयैष नरः ।८। एष आगत एव देवश्चन्द्रगुप्तः ।९। दृष्टं कुतूहलेनास्माभिरुद्यानम् ।१०। वनं वोद्यानं वा गतः ।११। वयस्याः दूरमेतेनाश्वेन वयमानीताः ।१२। हतं संदेहेन — एतौ जीवितावागच्छतः शिष्यौ ।१३। अद्यापि सुखेनैव तदद्भुतं दर्शनं स्मरामः ।१४। जितास्ते विषादेन ।१५। विस्मिता अप्येतेन दर्शनेन प्रयत्नं न त्यजन्ति ॥१६॥

Exercise 5b

अन्धः खल्वसि ।१। अस्माद्गृहाद्वनानि स नीतः ।२। तैरप्युद्यानं गत्वा पापा गृहीताः ।३। अद्भुतो ऽनयोः क्रोधः ।४। पुत्राः दृष्टाः स्थ ।५। सन्ति त्वस्माकं चन्दनदासस्य गृहे मित्राणि ।६। परिश्रान्तो ऽस्मीति पृच्छामि ।७। सर्वेषु देशस्य मार्गेषु दृष्टमि-दमस्माभिः ।८। देव स एवास्मि कुमारः ।९। अन्धस्य पादयोः पतति ।१०। सर्वे मया केनाप्युपायेन दृष्टाः ।११। क्रोधायैत-त्कुमारस्य प्रतिवचनम् ।१२। श्रुत्वा त्वेतन्मार्ग उपविशन्ति ।१३। कलहंसक न नः कुतूहलं पुस्तकेषु ।१४। एकस्मिन्नेवोद्याने पुष्पाणि कानिचिद्भवन्ति ।१५। दृष्ट्वापि सर्वं नैव किंचिद्वदति कुमारः ।१६। कथं संदेह एवात्र ते ।१७। हा मकरन्द हा कलहंसक गतो वां वयस्यः ।१८। कुमारेण त्वन्यस्मिन्देशे स्थित्वा सर्वं पापस्य प्रतिवचनं श्रुतम् ।१९। क्रोधे किं फलमेष पश्यति ॥२०॥

Exercise 6b

आश्रममृगो ऽयम् । १ । छतः कार्यारम्भः । २ । अयममात्यराक्षसस्तिष्ठति । ३ । मूढ नायं परिहासकालः । ४ । इयं तर्हि कस्य मुद्रा । ५ । अभिज्ञः खल्वसि लोकव्यवहाराणाम् । ६ । तत्किं न परिगृहीतमस्मद्वचनं पौरजनेन । ७ । अहो प्रवातसुभगो ऽयं वनोद्देशः । ८ । अलमाशङ्कया । ९ । लब्धं नेत्रनिर्वाणम् । १० । कथं न पश्यसि रामस्यावस्थाम् । ११ । शार्ङ्गरव स्थाने खलु पुरप्रवेशात्तवेदृशः संवेगः । १२ । अस्त्येतत्कुलव्रतं पौरवाणाम् । १३ । भद्रे प्रथितं दुःषन्तचरितं प्रजासु । १४ । तत्कृतमिदानीमाशाव्यसनेन । १५ । न खलु सत्यमेव तापसकन्यायामभिलाषो मे । १६ । चन्द्रोपरागं प्रति तु केनापि विप्रलब्धासि । १७ । इहैव प्रियापरिभुक्ते लतामण्डपे मुहूर्तं तिष्ठामि ॥ १८ ॥

Exercise 7b

आत्रेय्यस्मि । १ । वर्धयसि मे कुतूहलम् । २ । तदिदं सरसीतीरम् । ३ । यावदेतांश्छायामाश्रितः प्रतिपालयामि । ४ । क्षुद्रजनक्षुण्ण एष मार्गः । ५ । व्यक्तमेतान्यपि चाणक्यप्रयुक्तेन वणिजास्मासु विक्रीतानि । ६ । अहो दर्शितो मित्रस्नेहः । ७ । शिरसि भयं दूरे तत्प्रतीकारः । ८ । सखि मदयन्तिके स्वागतम् । अनुगृहीतमस्म्यहं भवत्या । ९ । एष विवाद एव मां प्रत्याययति । १० । समिदाहरणाय प्रस्थितावावाम् । ११ । किमर्थं भवतीभ्यां प्रतिषिद्धो ऽस्मि । १२ । कलहंसकमकरन्दप्रवेशावसरे तत्सुविहितम् । १३ । कथम् तातेन धृतपूर्वमिदमाभरणम् । १४ । नियुक्तैव मया तत्र तत्प्रियसखी बुद्धरक्षिता । १५ । एतावेव रामायणकथापुरुषौ । १६ । अनेन प्रियसुहृदा सिद्धार्थकेन घातकान्विद्राव्य वध्यस्थानादपहृतो ऽस्मि । १७ । अन्य एवायमक्षुण्णः कथाप्रकारो भगवत्याः । १८ । कुमारलवप्रयुक्तवारुणास्त्रप्रभावः खल्वेषः । १९ । स खलु वैद्यस्तदेवौषधं पायितस्योपरतस्य ॥ २० ॥

Exercise 8b

राज्ञः प्रतिग्रहो ऽयम् ।१। गतो ऽहमवलोकिताजनितकौतुकः कामदेवायतनम् ।२। अमात्यनामाङ्कितेयं मुद्रा ।३। परिषन्निर्दिष्टगुणं प्रबन्धं नाधिगच्छामः ।४। ननु यूयमप्यनेन धर्मकर्मणा परिश्रान्ताः ।५। एषो ऽस्मि कामन्दकी संवृत्तः । अहमप्यवलोकिता ।६। वृषल स्वयमनभियुक्तानां राज्ञामेते दोषा भवन्ति ।७। तत्किमवनतमुखपुण्डरीकः स्थितो ऽसि ।८। तत्र हि मे प्रियसुहृद्वैतालिकव्यञ्जनः स्तनकलशो नाम प्रतिवसति ।९। अपि वयस्येन विदिते तदन्वयनामनी ।१०। प्रिये क्रौर्यमपि मे त्वयि प्रयुक्तमनुकूलपरिणामं संवृत्तम् । तदहमिदानीं त्वया प्रत्यभिज्ञातमात्मानमिच्छामि ।११। उर्वशीगतमनसो ऽपि मे स एव देव्यां बहुमानः ।१२। किंत्वरण्यसदो वयमनभ्यस्तरथचर्याः ।१३। तदस्यैव तावदुच्छ्रसितकुसुमकेसरकषायशीतलामोदवासितोद्यानस्य काञ्चनारपादपस्याधस्तादुपविशावः ।१४। विदितसीतावृत्तान्तेयम् ।१५। अये अन्यासक्तचित्तो देवः ।१६। किंनामधेयमेतद्देव्या व्रतम् ।१७। स चाङ्गुरीयकदर्शनावसानः शापः ।१८। वैमनस्यपरीतो ऽपि प्रियदर्शनो देवः ॥ १९ ॥

Exercise 9b

अपि निर्विघ्नं तपः ।१। वयस्य मकरन्द अपि भवानुत्कण्ठते मदयन्तिकायाः ।२। क्व पुनर्मालती माधवं प्राग्दृष्टवती ।३। आर्ये एष निर्लज्जो लक्ष्मणः प्रणमति ।४। किं कथयन्ति भवन्तः ।५। अत्युदारप्रकृतिर्मालती ।६। रमणीयाः खल्वमात्यभूरिवसोर्विभूतयः ।७। अतिदारुणो जनसंमर्दो वर्तते ।८। शकुन्तलायाः प्रथमदर्शनवृत्तान्तं कथितवानस्मि भवते ।९। भगवत्यरुन्धति वैदेहः सीरध्वजो ऽभिवादये ।१०। अपि क्षमन्ते ऽस्मदुपजापं चन्द्रगुप्तप्रकृतयः ।११। असंनिहितमेव मां मन्यते ।१२।

अपूर्वः को ऽपि बहुमानहेतुर्गुरुषु सौधातकेः । १३ । एष राक्षस-प्रयुक्तो विषकन्यया पर्वतेश्वरं घातितवान् । १४ । माधवस्याञ्जलौ बकुलमालां निक्षिपति । १५ । दिष्ट्या महेन्द्रोपकारपर्याप्तेन विक्रम-महिम्ना वर्धते भवान् । १६ । ततः प्रविशति यथोक्तव्यापारा सह सखीभ्यां शकुन्तला । १७ । वयस्य नन्वमात्यभवनासन्नरथ्ययैव बहुशः संचरावहे । तदुपपन्नमेतत् । १८ । चन्द्रगुप्तप्रकृतीनां हि चाणक्यदोषा एवापरागहेतवः । १९ । वयस्य निरवग्रहं दहति दैवमिव दारुणो विवस्वान् । २० । साधु वृषल साधु । ममैव हृदयेन सह संमन्त्र्य संदिष्टवानसि । २१ । अये कुसुमपुरवृत्तान्तज्ञो ऽहं भवत्प्रणिधिश्चेति गाथार्थः । २२ । एतावदितिपरिवर्धितमन्दा-रवृक्षकं प्रजापतेराश्रमपदं प्रविष्टौ स्वः । २३ । इमामुग्रातपां वेलां प्रायेण लतावलयवत्सु मालिनीतीरेषु ससखीजना तत्रभवती गमयति ॥ २४ ॥

Exercise 10b

आर्याः पश्यत । १ । अहो महार्घ्याण्याभरणानि । २ । पश्यन्ती तिष्ठति । ३ । त्वरतामत्रभवती । ४ । त्रिकालदर्शिभिर्मुनिभिरादिष्टः सुरासुरविमर्दो भावी । ५ । बहुप्रत्यवायं नृपत्वम् । ६ । अत एव भवद्विधा महान्तः । ७ । अस्तु ते कार्यसिद्धिः । ८ । मुद्रां परि-पालयन्नुद्वेष्ट्य दर्शय । ९ । अहो विवेकशून्यता म्लेच्छस्य । १० । निगृह्य शोकाविष्टं मामनुगच्छतम् । ११ । वत्स कार्याभियोग एवास्मानाकुलयति न पुनरुपाध्यायसहभूः शिष्यजने दुःशीलता । १२ । परिहरन्तमपि मां पञ्चवटीस्नेहो बलादाकर्षतीव । १३ । अहो मधुरमासां दर्शनम् । १४ । चित्रलेखे त्वरयोर्वशीम् । १५ । अस्त्येतदन्यसमाधिभीरुत्वं देवानाम् । १६ । उत्सर्पिणी खलु महतां प्रार्थना । १७ । सांप्रतमेव कुसुमपुरोपरोधनाय प्रतिष्ठन्तामस्मद्ब-लानि । १८ । विस्मृता भवद्गुणपक्षपातिना मया स्वामिगुणाः । १९ । प्रियंवदक न नः कुतूहलं सर्पेषु । तत्परितोष्य विसर्जयैनम्

।२०। शचीतीर्थे सलिलं वन्दमानायास्तव सख्याः परिभ्रष्टम्
।२१। वत्स सावधानो भव ।२२। कार्यव्यग्रत्वान्मनसः प्रभूतत्वाच्च
प्रणिधीनां विस्मृतम् ।२३। आर्य जाजले त्वमपि सपरिजनो
निवर्तस्व । भागुरायण एवैको मामनुगच्छतु ।२४। अहो शरत्स-
मयसंभृतशोभाविभूतीनां दिशामतिशयरमणीयता ।२५। तत
एकस्माद्भित्तिच्छिद्राद्गृहीतभक्तावयवानां पिपीलिकानां निष्क्राम-
न्तीनां पङ्क्तिमवलोक्य पुरुषगर्भमेतद्गृहमिति गृहीतार्थेन दाहितं
तदेव शयनगृहम् ॥२६॥

Exercise 11b

दीयतामस्मै प्रतिवचनम् ।१। भ्रातरावावां यमजौ ।२। न
निष्प्रयोजनमधिकारवन्तः प्रभुभिराहूयन्ते ।३। अत्रैव स्थीयताम्
।४। यत्तदलंकरणत्रयं क्रीतं तन्मध्यादेकं दीयताम् ।५। विमु-
च्यन्तामभीशवः ।६। किमुच्यते धैर्यमिति ।७। भद्रास्त्वर्यतां
त्वर्यताम् ।८। अभिव्यक्तायां चन्द्रिकायां किं दीपिकापौनरुक्त्येन
।९। लातव्य आहूयतामुर्वशी ।१०। अये तदिदमाभरणं यन्मया
स्वशरीरादवतार्य राक्षसाय प्रेषितम् ।११। अयि वत्से एवमात्मा
स्तूयते ।१२। परितोष्य विक्रेतारं गृह्यताम् ।१३। आर्य अस्ति
कश्चिद्यः कुसुमपुरं गच्छति तत आगच्छति वा ।१४। प्रवेश्यताम्
।१५। किं मृषा तर्केणान्विष्यते ।१६। अमात्य इति लज्जाकर-
मिदानीं विशेषणपदम् ।१७। हन्त मूढ एवास्मि योऽस्मिन्वनेचरे
वयस्यमकरन्दोचितं व्यवहरामि ।१८। समर्प्यतां राक्षसस्य गृह-
जनः। अनुभूयतां चिरं विचित्रफलो राजप्रसादः ।१९। रक्ष्यतां
परकलत्रेणात्मनः कलत्रं जीवितं च ।२०। स एष कामन्दकीसु-
हृत्पुत्रो महामांसस्य पणायिता माधवः ।२१। येषामन्तेवासिनां
हस्तेन तत्पुस्तकं भरताश्रमं प्रेषितं तेषामानुयात्रिकश्चापपाणिः
प्रमादापनोदनार्थमस्मद्भ्राता प्रेषितः ।२२। अनन्तरं च यात्रा-
भङ्गप्रचलितस्य महतः पौरजनस्य संकुलेन विघटितायां तस्यामा-

गतो ऽस्मि ।२३। मूर्ख अन्यमेव भागमेते तपस्विनो निर्वपन्ति यो रत्नराशीनपि विहायाभिनन्द्यते ।२४। एवमात्माभिप्रायसंभावितेष्टजनचित्तवृत्तिः प्रार्थयिता विप्रलभ्यते ॥ २५ ॥

Exercise 12b

किं ब्रवीषि ।१। अनेन लेखेन राक्षसो जेतव्यः ।२। तत्रैव मकरन्दमदयन्तिकागमनं यावत्स्थातव्यम् ।३। शृणुवस्तावत् ।४। हन्त हृदयमपि मे रिपुभिः स्वीकृतम् ।५। अस्यामशोकच्छायायामास्तामायुष्मान्यावत्त्वामहमिन्द्रगुरवे निवेदयामि ।६। रक्षणीया राक्षसस्य प्राणा इत्यार्यादेशः ।७। तद्यथा भवितव्यं तथा भवतु ।८। सर्वमेव तन्त्रमाकुलीभूतम् ।९। किं भवांस्तूष्णीमास्ते ।१०। तदत्र वस्तुन्यनुपालभ्यो राक्षसः ।११। भद्र भास्वरक बहिर्नीत्वा तावत्ताड्यतां यावत्कथ्यते ऽनेन ।१२। शृणु विचित्रमिदम् ।१३। अस्मिन्नेव वेतसलतामण्डपे भवितव्यं शकुन्तलया ।१४। तदिदानीं सहधर्मचारिणं प्रति न त्वया मन्युः करणीयः ।१५। तमेवोद्देशं गच्छामि यत्र मे नयनयोः सा सुनयना तिरोभूता ।१६। आविष्कृतं कथाप्रावीण्यं वत्सेन ।१७। तेन हि तत्प्रयोगादेवात्रभवतः सामाजिकानुपास्महे ।१८। कुमार इवानतिक्रमणीयवचनो भवानपि ।१९। असम्यक्चेष्टितं प्रियां समासाद्य कालहरणं कुर्वता मया ।२०। कष्टम् एते सुहृद्व्यसनेषु परवदुदासीनाः प्रत्यादिश्यामहे वयमनेन ।२१। भोः श्रेष्ठिन् स चापरिक्लेशः कथमाविर्भवतीति ननु प्रष्टव्या वयमेव भवता ।२२। यावदेते मानसोत्सुकाः पतत्रिणः सरसो नोत्पतन्ति तावदेतेभ्यः प्रियाप्रवृत्तिरवगमयितव्या ।२३। ततस्तेषु गृहीतसंज्ञेषु भयापदेशादितस्ततः प्रद्रुतेषु शकटदासो वध्यस्थानादपनीय राक्षसं प्रापयितव्यः ।२४। यदैवाप्सरस्तीर्थात्प्रत्याख्यानविक्लवां शकुन्तलामादाय दाक्षायणीमुपगता मेनका तदैव ध्यानादवगत-

वृत्तान्तो ऽस्मि दुर्वाससः शापादियं तपस्विनी सहधर्मचारिणा प्रत्यादिष्टेति ॥ २५ ॥

Exercise 13b

विजये प्रत्यभिजानाति भवती भूषणमिदम् । १ । शठः खल्वसौ बटुः । २ । सुविहितं लवङ्गिकया यतो माधवानुचरः कलहंसकस्तां विहारदासीं मन्दारिकां कामयते । ३ । क्व पुनर्मां भवत्यः प्रतिपालयिष्यन्ति । ४ । कथम् अदत्त्वैव प्रतिवचनं नर्तितुमारब्धः । ५ । कथं मदन्वेषिणः सैनिकास्तपोवनमुपरुन्धन्ति । ६ । काममेतदभिनन्दनीयं तथापि वयमत्र मध्यस्थाः । ७ । नातिचिरादमात्यो ऽस्मान्पुरातनीमवस्थामारोपयिष्यति । ८ । न युक्तं प्राकृतमपि पुरुषमवज्ञातुम् । ९ । राजन् चन्द्रगुप्त विदितमेव ते यथा वयं मलयकेतौ किंचित्कालान्तरमुषिताः । १० । भो विष्णुगुप्त न मां श्वपाकस्पर्शदूषितं स्प्रष्टुमर्हसि । ११ । वत्स कच्चिदभिनन्दितस्त्वया विधिवदस्माभिरनुष्ठितजातकर्मादिक्रियः पुत्र एष शाकुन्तलेयः । १२ । तदनुजानीहि मां गमनाय । १३ । न शक्नुमो वयमार्यस्य वाचा वाचमतिशयितुम् । १४ । यद्येवमभियोगकालमार्यः पश्यति तत्किमास्यते । १५ । भद्र प्रविश । लप्स्यसे श्रोतारं ज्ञातारं च । १६ । इदानीमेव दुहितरमतिथिसत्कारायादिश्य दैवमस्याः प्रतिकूलं शमयितुं सोमतीर्थं गतः । यद्येवं तामेव द्रक्ष्यामि । १७ । सखे किमश्रद्दधानः पृच्छसि । १८ । किमक्षत्रिया पृथिवी यदेवमुद्घुष्यते । १९ । भद्र कस्मिंश्चिदाप्तजनानुष्ठेये कर्मणि त्वां व्यापारयितुमिच्छामि । २० । स चेन्मुनिदौहित्रस्तल्लक्षणोपपन्नो भवति ततः प्रतिनन्द्य शुद्धान्तमेनां प्रवेशयिष्यसि । २१ । तत्किमुज्जिहानजीवितां वराकीं नानुकम्पसे । २२ । न निष्परिग्रहं स्थानभ्रंशः पीडयिष्यति । २३ । चन्द्रगुप्तशरीरमभिद्रोग्धुमस्मत्प्रयुक्तानां तीक्ष्णरसदादीनामुपसंग्रहार्थं प्रकृत्युपजापार्थं च महता कोषसंचयेन स्थापितः शकटदासः । २४ । सखे माधव्य अनवाप्तचक्षुःफलो ऽसि

येन त्वया द्रष्टव्यानां परं न दृष्टम् । २५। भोः श्रेष्ठिन् चन्दन-दास एवं राजापथ्यकारिषु तीक्ष्णदण्डो राजा न मर्षयिष्यति राक्षसकलत्रप्रच्छादनं भवतः । २६। यतो ऽमी व्याघ्रादयो वर्ण-मात्रविप्रलब्धाः शृगालमज्ञात्वा राजानममुं मन्यन्ते तद्यथायं परिचीयते तथा कुरुत । २७। देव जीवितुकामः को ऽन्यो देवस्य शासनमुल्लङ्घयिष्यति । २८। यद्यपि स्वामिगुणा न शक्यन्ते विस्मर्तुं तथापि मद्विज्ञापनां मानयितुमर्हत्यार्यः ॥ २९ ॥

Exercise 14b

तातव्य अपि जानीते भवान्कस्यायं बाण इति । १। अये मूर्ख किं भवानस्माकमुपाध्यायाद्धर्मवित्तरः । २। न्यग्रामयं च तस्मि-न्नाश्रमे कस्य चिच्चूतपोतकस्य च्छायायां कमप्युद्विग्नवर्णं तापसम् । ३। वयस्य अङ्गुलीस्वेदेन दूष्येरन्नक्षराणि । ४। तत्को ऽयं पदे पदे महाननध्यवसायः । ५। इत्युक्त्वा च सा ताम्बूलभाजनादाकृष्य तामदर्शयत् । ६। अवसरे खल्वनुरागोपकारयोर्गरीयसोरुपन्यासः । ७। रैवतक उच्यतामस्मत्सारथिः सबाणकार्मुकं रथमुपस्थापयेति । ८। स कदाचिद्धैर्यस्खलनविलक्षः किंचिदनिष्टमपि समाचरेत । ९। यावदशृणवं मालत्येवास्य मन्मथोन्माथहेतुरिति । १०। निखिलान्तःपुरस्वामिनी च तस्याभवत् । ११। उच्यतां किं ते भूयः प्रियमुपकरोमि । १२। इत्यभिधाय किमियं वक्ष्यतीति मन्मुखासक्तदृष्टिस्तूष्णीमासीत् । १३। तत्कुतो ऽस्मिन्विपिने प्रिया-प्रवृत्तिमागमयेयम् । १४। स किल कृपालुस्तं जनमार्द्रया गिरा-श्वास्यार्तिकारणं तां गणिकामपृच्छत । १५। कुमार न कदाचिदपि शकटदासो ऽमात्यराक्षसस्याग्रतो मया लिखितमिति प्रतिपत्स्यते । १६। सखे भागुरायण नन्वस्माकममात्यराक्षसः प्रियतमो हित-तमश्च । १७। अपयातायां भवत्यां मुहूर्तमिव स्थित्वैकाकी किम-यमिदानीमाचरतीति संजातवितर्कः प्रतिनिवृत्य विटपान्तरितवि-ग्रहस्तं प्रदेशं व्यलोकयम् । १८। अपि नाम मृगतृष्णिकेव नायमन्ते

प्रस्तावो विषादाय कल्पेत । १९। सूर्योपस्थानात्प्रतिनिवृत्तं पुरूरवसं मामुपेत्य कथ्यतां कुतो भवत्यः परित्रातव्या इति । २०। इत्यभिदधाना मदनमूर्छाखेदविह्वलैरङ्गैः कथंचिदवलम्ब्य तामेवोदतिष्ठम् । उच्चलितायाश्च मे दुर्निमित्तनिवेदकमस्पन्दत दक्षिणं लोचनम् । उपजातशङ्का चाचिन्तयम् इदमपरं किमप्युपक्षिप्तं दैवेनेति । २१। यद्यस्मत्तो गरीयान्राक्षसो ऽवगम्यते तदास्माकमिदं शस्त्रं तस्मै दीयताम् । २२। सखे चन्द्रगुप्तस्यैव तावन्नगरप्रवेशात्प्रभृति मत्प्रयुक्तैस्तीक्ष्णरसदादिभिः किमनुष्ठितमिति श्रोतुमिच्छामि । २३। यदि पुनरीदृशं त्वामैक्ष्वाको राजा रामः पश्येत्तदास्य स्नेहेन हृदयमभिष्यन्देत । २४। इति विचारयन्तीमेव मामविचारितगुणदोषविशेषो रूपैकपक्षपाती नवयौवनसुलभः कुसुमायुधः कुसुमसमयमद इव मधुकरीं परवशामकरोत ॥ २५॥

Vocabulary

1 Sanskrit–English

Alphabetical order

The order of the Sanskrit alphabet is **a, ā, i, ī, u, ū, ṛ, ṝ, ḷ, e, ai, o, au, ṃ, ḥ, k, kh, g, gh, ṅ, c, ch, j, jh, ñ, ṭ, ṭh, ḍ, ḍh, ṇ, t, th, d, dh, n, p, ph, b, bh, m, y, r, l, v, ś, ṣ, s, h.**

The position of anusvāra (**ṃ**) given above applies where the anusvāra is followed by **y, r, l, v, ś, ṣ, s** or **h**. But in accordance with the usual practice of Sanskrit dictionaries, anusvāra before a stop or nasal is given the alphabetical place of the appropriate class nasal. Thus the word **saṃtoṣaḥ** is treated as if it were **santoṣaḥ.** (The latter spelling, which better represents the pronunciation of the word, is in fact possible, though hardly ever found nowadays in printed texts.) In looking up a word containing anusvāra, therefore, the anusvāra should be converted mentally into a nasal consonant wherever this is possible.

A similar principle applies in the case of visarga (**ḥ**): **ḥś, ḥṣ** and **ḥs** occupy the position of **śś, ṣṣ** and **ss** respectively. In practice, however, this will cause comparatively little difficulty.

Gender

Substantives ending in **a** are given as ending in **aḥ** if masculine and **aṃ** if neuter. Substantives ending in **ā** or **ī** should be assumed to be feminine. The gender of nouns ending in **-in** and **-tṛ** is not normally specified, since these may, if appropriate, be treated as adjectival (with feminines in **-inī** and **-trī**).

Verbs

While a point has been made of quoting the present tense of all verbs listed, it should be mentioned that present stem formations may sometimes be far less common than the particular form, such as past participle or absolutive, which has led to the inclusion of the verb in the Vocabulary.

अ **a** *negative prefix* not, no, un- *etc.*

अंशुकं **aṃśukaṃ** cloth, garment

अकथयत् **akathayat** *3rd sg. imperf. para. of* **kath**

अकृतार्थ **a:kṛt›‿ârtha** [whose aim is unachieved:] unsuccessful

अक्षमाला **akṣa-mālā** [garland of Eleocarpus seeds:] rosary

अक्षरं **akṣaraṃ** syllable, written character

अगः **agaḥ** [not moving:] mountain

अगस्त्यः **Agastyaḥ** *pr. n.*

अग्नि **agni** *m.* fire

अग्रं **agraṃ** front, top, tip

अग्रतः **agrataḥ** in front of (*gen.*)

अघं **aghaṃ** evil, impurity

अङ्क् **aṅk** (X **aṅkayati**) brand, stamp

अङ्कः **aṅkaḥ** hook; curve of body, lap

अङ्गं **aṅgaṃ** limb, division

अङ्गीकृ **aṅgī˜kṛ** make a part, subordinate; adopt, accept, promise

अङ्गुरीयक **aṅgurīyaka** *m./n.* ring (for finger)

अङ्गुलि **aṅguli** *f. or* **aṅgulī** finger, toe

अङ्गुष्ठः **aṅguṣṭhaḥ** thumb, big toe

अचिर **a:cira** [not long:] soon

अचिरात् **acirāt** after a short while

अचिरेण **acireṇa** within a short while

अञ्चलः **añcalaḥ** border (of dress)

अञ्जलि **añjali** *m.* joined hands

अतः **ataḥ** from this, hence, for this reason; **ata eva** [precisely from this:] that is why

अति **ati** *prefix* excessive(ly), extreme(ly), too, very *etc.*

अतिक्रम् **ati+kram** (I **atikrāmati**) go beyond; transgress, go against

अतिक्रान्त **atikrānta** past, bygone

अतिचिर **ati:cira** very long

अतिथि **atithi** *m.* guest; **atithi-satkāraḥ** honouring of guests, hospitality

अतिदारुण **ati:dāruṇa** [very] dreadful

अतिदीप्त **ati:dīpta** exceptionally brilliant

अतिदुःखसंवेगः **ati:duḥkha˘saṃvegaḥ** extreme pangs of pain

अतिपातः **atipātaḥ** lapse, neglect

अतिभूमि **atibhūmi** *f.* culmination, excess

अतिमात्र **ati_mātra** [beyond measure:] excessive

अतिवह् **ati+vah** *caus.* (**ativāhayati**) spend (time)

अतिशय **atiśaya** surpassing

अतिशी **ati+śī** (II **atiśete**) surpass, triumph over

अतिसृज् **ati+sṛj** (VI **atisṛjati**) bestow, lavish

अतीत **atīta** [**ati+ita** gone beyond:] past

अतीव **atīva** excessively, intensely

अत्यन्त **aty_anta** [beyond limit:] excessive, extreme, intensely, 'terribly'

अत्याहितं **atyāhitaṃ** calamity, disaster

अत्र **atra** here, in this, on this; on this matter, about this

अत्रभवन्त् **atrabhavant** His Honour here

अत्रभवती **atrabhavatī** Her Honour here, this Lady

अथ **atha** *introductory or connecting particle* now, next, then

अथवा **atha vā** or rather, but no, but

अदर्शनं **a:darśanaṃ** not seeing

अद्भुत **adbhuta** extraordinary

अद्य **adya** today, now

अद्य प्रभृति **adya prabhṛti** from today onward

अद्रि **adri** *m.* rock, mountain

अधस्तात् **adhastāt** beneath (*gen.*)

अधिक **adhika** additional, superior

अधिकरणं **adhikaraṇaṃ** grammatical relationship

अधिकारः **adhikāraḥ** authority, responsibility, office, job

अधिगम् **adhi+gam** (I **adhigacchati**) find, obtain, receive; realise, perceive

अधिपति **adhipati** *m.* overlord, ruler

अधिरुह् **adhi+ruh** (I **adhirohati**) ascend, mount

अधिष्ठातृ **adhiṣṭhātṛ** *m.* superintending, at the head of

अधी **adhī** (**adhi+i**) (II **adhīte**) study; *caus.* (**adhyāpayati**) teach

अधुना **adhunā** now

अधोमुख **adho:mukha** down-faced, with face bent down

अध्ययनं **adhyayanaṃ** studying, study

अध्यवसायः **adhyavasāyaḥ** resolution

अध्यवसित **adhyavasita** resolved, accomplished, completed

अध्यवसो **adhy+ava+so** (IV **adhyavasyati**) resolve, decide, accomplish

अध्युषित **adhyuṣita** (*p.p. of* **adhi+vas**) inhabited

अनध्ययनं **an:adhyayanaṃ** freedom from study, (academic) holiday

अनध्यवसाय: **an:adhyavasāyaḥ** irresolution, hesitation

अनन्तरम् **an:̲antaram** [without interval:] immediately

अनपराद्ध **an:aparāddha** unoffending, innocent

अनर्थ: **anarthaḥ** reverse, disaster

अनादृत्य **an:ādṛtya** *absolutive* not heeding, without reference to

अनायास **an:̲āyāsa** [in which there is no exertion:] not strenuous

अनिमित्त **a:̲nimitta** without cause

अनिल: **anilaḥ** wind, breeze

अनिष्ट **an:iṣṭa** undesired, unpleasant, dreadful

अनुकम्प् **anu+kamp** (I **anukampate**) sympathize with, pity

अनुकारिन् **anukārin** (**anu+kṛ** imitate) imitative

अनुकूल **anukūla** favourable

अनुगम् **anu+gam** (I **anugacchati**) follow, attend

अनुग्रह् **anu+grah** (IX **anugṛhṇāti**) favour

अनुग्रह: **anugrahaḥ** favour, kindness

अनुचर: **anucaraḥ** companion, attendant

अनुज: **anujaḥ** [born after:] younger brother

अनुज्ञा **anu+jñā** (IX **anujānāti**) allow, give leave, assent

अनुताप: **anutāpaḥ** remorse

अनुत्सेक: **an:utsekaḥ** [non-arrogance:] modesty

अनुप्रहि **anu+pra+hi** (V **anuprahiṇoti**) send (someone after something), despatch

अनुबन्ध् **anu+bandh (IX anubadhnāti)** pursue, importune

अनुभू **anu+bhū (I anubhavati)** experience, undergo, 'reap, enjoy'

अनुमन्त्र् **anu+mantr (X anumantrayate)** consecrate with mantras, bless

अनुयायिन् **anuyāyin (anu+yā** attend) attendant upon

अनुयुज् **anu+yuj** (VII **anuyuṅkte**) question, examine

अनुरागः **anurāgaḥ** passion, love

अनुरुध् **anu+rudh** (IV **anurudhyate**) adhere to, comply with (*acc.*)

अनुरूप **anu_rūpa** conformable, suitable, proper, appropriate

अनुलिप **anu+lip** (VI **anulimpati**) anoint

अनुलेपनं **anulepanaṃ** ointment

अनुवृत् **anu+vṛt** (I **anuvartate**) go after, attend upon

अनुशयः **anuśayaḥ** consequence, repentance, regret

अनुष्ठा **anuṣṭhā (anu+sthā)** (I **anutiṣṭhati**) carry out, perform, act, do

अनुष्ठानं **anuṣṭhānaṃ** carrying out, [performance of task:] 'duties'

अनुस्मृ **anu+smṛ** (I **anusmarati**) remember

अनेक **an:eka** [not one:] several

अन्तः **antaḥ** end, boundary, final (syllable of word)

अन्तःपुरं **antaḥpuraṃ** women's quarters (of palace), harem

अन्तरं **antaraṃ** interval, juncture, difference; **-antaraṃ** *ifc.* a different, another

अन्तरात्मन् **antar:ātman** *m.* soul within, internal feelings

अन्तरित **antarita** (*p.p. of* **antar+i** go between) hidden, concealed

अन्तेवासिन् **antevāsin** [resident] disciple

अन्ध **andha** blind

अन्य **anya** *pron.* other, another, else, different

अन्यतरस्याम् **anyatarasyām** (*gram.*) optionally

अन्यत्र **anyatra** elsewhere, on *etc.* another

अन्यथा **anyathā** otherwise, in other circumstances

अन्वमंस्त **anvamaṃsta** *3rd sg. ātm.* **s**-*aorist of* **anu+man** 'assent, permit'

अन्वयः **anvayaḥ** succession, lineage, family

अन्वित **anvita** attended by, full of

अन्विष् **anviṣ** (**anu+iṣ**) (I **anveṣate**) look for, search for, enquire

अन्वेषिन् **anveṣin** searching for

अपकारः **apakāraḥ** doing harm, injury, ruination

अपकारिन् **apakārin** (*from* **apa kṛ** 'do harm') harming, offending

अपक्रम् **apa+kram** (I **apakrāmati**) go away, withdraw

अपत्यं **apatyaṃ** offspring

अपथ्य **a:pathya** unwholesome

अपथ्यकारिन् **apathya-kārin** doing what is inimical (to king), traitor

अपदेशः **apadeśaḥ** pretence, pretext

अपनी **apa+nī** (I **apanayati**) remove, take away

अपनोदनं **apanodanaṃ** driving away

अपया **apa+yā** (II **apayāti**) go away, depart

अपर **apara** other, different

अपरक्त **aparakta** disaffected, disloyal

अपरागः aparāgaḥ disaffection, disloyalty

अपराद्ध aparāddha having offended, guilty

अपराधः aparādhaḥ offence, guilt

अपराधिन् aparādhin offending, guilty

अपरिक्लेशः a:parikleśaḥ lack of vexation

अपर्याप्त a:paryāpta inadequate

अपवादिन् apavādin decrying

अपवारित apavārita hidden

अपवाहित apavāhita *p.p. of caus. of* **apa+vah** 'carry off'

अपश्यत् apaśyat *3rd sg. imperf. para. of* **dṛś** 'see'

अपसर्पणं apasarpaṇaṃ getting away, escape

अपसृप् apa+sṛp (I apasarpati) get away, escape

अपहृ apa+hṛ (I apaharati) carry off

अपह्नु apa+hnu (II apahnute) conceal

अपाप a:pāpa without sin, guiltless

अपि api *enclitic* also, too, as well, alike, and; even, though, however; *gives indefinite sense to interrog. pronouns*; api *non-enclitic marks a question*

अपि नाम api nāma *with opt.* could it be that?, if only!

अपूपः apūpaḥ cake: *see* **daṇḍāpūpikā**

अपूर्व a:pūrva unprecedented, strange

अपेक्षा apekṣā consideration, regard

अपेत apeta (apa+ita) departed; free from (*abl.*), lacking

अप्रमादिन् a:pramādin [not negligent:] vigilant

अप्सरस apsaras *f.* nymph (of heaven)

अभिघ्रा abhi+ghrā (I abhijighrati) smell

अभिज्ञ abhijña knowing, conversant with (*gen.*)

अभिद्रुह् abhi+druh (IV abhidruhyate) do violence to

अभिधा abhi+dhā (III abhidadhāti/abhidhatte) tell, say, speak

अभिधानं **abhidhānaṃ** appellation, name; speaking, stating

अभिनन्द् **abhi+nand (I abhinandati)** rejoice in, greet with enthusiasm, prize

अभिनिविष्ट **abhinivișța** concentrated, intent

अभिप्रायः **abhiprāyaḥ** inclination, will, intention

अभिप्रेतं **abhipretaṃ** [thing willed:] wish

अभिभू **abhi+bhū (I abhibhavati)** overpower

अभिमत **abhimata** respected, honoured

अभियुक्त **abhiyukta** diligent

अभियोक्तृ **abhiyoktṛ** attacker

अभियोगः **abhiyogaḥ** intentness, preoccupation; assault, attack

अभिलष् **abhi+laṣ (I abhilaṣati)** wish for, crave, hanker after

अभिलाषः **abhilāṣaḥ** craving, passion for (*loc.*)

अभिलाषिन् **abhilāṣin** desirous, anxious

अभिलिख् **abhi+likh (VI abhilikhati)** draw (picture)

अभिवद् **abhi+vad** *caus.* **(abhivādayate)** greet

अभिवृत् **abhi+vṛt (I abhivartate)** approach, go towards, make for

अभिव्यक्त **abhivyakta** manifest, visible

अभिष्यन्द् **abhiṣyand (abhi+syand) (I abhiṣyandate)** flow

अभिसंधि **abhisaṃdhi** *m.* agreement, condition

अभिहित **abhihita** *p.p. of* **abhidhā**

अभीप्सित **abhīpsita** desired; **abhīpsitaṃ** [thing desired:] desire

अभीशु **abhīśu** *m.* rein, bridle

अभूत् **abhūt** *3rd sg. aorist of* **bhū**

अभ्यस्त **abhyasta** practised, familiar

अभ्रं **abhraṃ** cloud

अमरः **Amaraḥ** *author of the* **Amarakośaḥ**

अमात्यः **amātyaḥ** minister (of king)

अमी अमुम् अमुष्य **amī, amum, amuṣya** *forms of* **asau**

अमृतं **amṛtaṃ** nectar, ambrosia

अम्बा **ambā** mother

अम्बा अम्बिका **Ambā, Ambikā** *pr. n.*

अयम् **ayam** *pron.* this, this one, he; here (is), see, hereby

अयशस् **a:yaśas** *n.* [non-fame:] disgrace

अयि **ayi** ha!, ah!

अयुक्त **a:yukta** [not right:] wrong

अयुज् **a:yuj** uneven, odd

अयोध्या **Ayodhyā** *name of a city* (Oudh)

अये **aye** ah!, oh!

अरण्यं **araṇyaṃ** forest

अरि **ari** *m.* enemy

अरुन्धती **Arundhatī** *pr. n.*

अर्थः **arthaḥ** matter, business; object, purpose, point, aim, interests; meaning, sense; wealth, property

अर्थम् **-artham** *ifc.* for the sake of, in order to

अर्थान्तरन्यासः **arth›-ântara-nyāsaḥ** (*lit. crit.*) Substantiation

अर्थापत्ति **arth›-āpatti** *f.* (*lit. crit.*) Strong Presumption

अर्थिन् **arthin** having an object, wanting, petitioning

अर्थोत्सर्गः **arth›-ôtsargaḥ** expenditure of money

अर्धः **ardhaḥ** half (portion)

अर्धरात्रः **ardharātraḥ** midnight

अर्पयति **arpayati** *caus. of* **ṛ**

अर्ह् **arh** (I **arhati**) be worthy; be able, 'aspire to'; should, ought

अर्ह **arha** deserving, meriting; proper, deserved

अलंकरणं **alaṃkaraṇaṃ** ornament

अलंकारः **alaṃkāraḥ** ornament; (*lit. crit.*) embellishment, literary figure

अलंकृ **alam+kṛ** (VIII **alaṃkaroti**) adorn, embellish

अलम् **alam** enough; +*instr*. enough of, do not *etc.*; +*inf.* capable of

अल्प **alpa** small

अवकाशः **avakāśaḥ** space, scope

अवगम् **ava+gam** understand, learn, know; suppose, consider

अवगम् **ava+gam** *caus.* (**avagamayati**) procure

अवगाह् **ava+gāh** (I **avagāhate**) plunge into, bathe in (*acc.*)

अवग्रहः **avagrahaḥ** obstacle, restraint; separation (of words)

अवचयः **avacayaḥ** gathering, picking

अवज्ञा **ava+jñā** (IX **avajānāti**) despise

अवज्ञा **avajñā** contempt

अवतॄ **ava+tṝ** *caus.* (**avatārayati**) remove

अवधृ **ava+dhṛ** *caus.* (**avadhārayati**) determine, resolve

अवनत **avanata** (*p.p. of* **ava+nam**) bent down

अवयवः **avayavaḥ** portion, particle, member

अवरुह् **ava+ruh** *caus.* (**avaropayati**) cause to descend, dismiss from office

अवलम्ब् **ava+lamb** (I **avalambate**) cling to, hold on to; adopt (position)

अवलोक् **ava+lok** (X **avalokayati**) see, look at

अवलोकनं avalokanaṃ looking at, gazing on

अवलोकिता Avalokitā *pr. n.*

अवश a:vaśa powerless, helpless

अवश्यम् avaśyam necessarily

अवसरः avasaraḥ opportunity, occasion, right moment, time (for)

अवसरे avasare at the right moment, opportune

अवसानं avasānaṃ termination, end, conclusion

अवसित avasita (*p.p. of* ava+so) terminated, over, fulfilled

अवस्था ava+sthā stay (in a state), remain

अवस्था avasthā state, condition, period of life

अवहित्थं avahitthaṃ, avahitthā dissimulation

अवाप् avāp (ava+āp) (V avāpnoti) obtain, acquire

अविघ्न a:vighna unhindered

अविद्वान् a:vidvān ignorant

अविनयः a:vinayaḥ lack of breeding, discourtesy

अविप्रतिपन्न a:vipratipanna not uncertain, entirely fixed

अविषयः a:viṣayaḥ [non-sphere:] matter beyond the scope (of)

अवेक्ष् avekṣ (ava+īkṣ) (I avekṣate) watch, watch over

अव्यभिचारिन् a:vyabhicārin undeviating, unswerving

अशरण a:śaraṇa without refuge, helpless

अशरण्य a:śaraṇya without refuge, helpless

अशेष a:śeṣa [without remainder:] complete, whole, all

अशोकः aśokaḥ aśoka tree

अशोभन a:śobhana unpleasant, awful

अश्रु aśru *n.* tear

अश्रुमुख aśru:mukha tearful-faced

अश्वः aśvaḥ horse

अस् **as** (II **asti**) be, exist; *may express* 'have' *etc.*

असंतोषः **a:saṃtoṣaḥ** dissatisfaction

असमर्थ **a:samartha** incapable

असंभाव्य **a:saṃbhāvya** incredible

असम्यक् **a:samyak** wrongly

असु **asu** *m.* breath; *pl.* life

असुरः **asuraḥ** demon

असौ **asau** *pron.* that

अस्त्रं **astraṃ** missile, weapon

अस्थाः **asthāḥ** *2nd sg. aorist para. of* **sthā**

अस्थाने **a:sthāne** not in place, misplaced, inappropriately

अस्फुट **a:sphuṭa** unclear, illegible

अस्मत् **asmat** *stem of 1st pl. pron.* **vayam**

अस्वस्थशरीर **a:svastha-śarīra** [whose body is not well:] [physically] unwell

अस्वास्थ्यं **a:svāsthyaṃ** discomfort, illness

अह् **ah** *see* **āha**

अहन् **ahan** *n. irreg.* day

अहः अह्नः **-ahaḥ, -ahnaḥ** *ifc. for* **ahan**

अहमहमिका **ahamahamikā** rivalry

अहो **aho** oh!, what a—!; **aho bata** oh alas!

आ **ā**+*abl.* up to, until

आकर्णयति **ākarṇayati** (*denom.*) give ear, listen to

आकारः **ākāraḥ** form, appearance, (facial) expression

आकाशं **ākāśaṃ** ether, air, sky

आकुल **ākula** confused

आकुलयति **ākulayati** (*denom.*) confuse, disturb

आकुलीभू **ākulī¯bhū** grow confused

आकुलीभूत **ākulī¯bhūta** [being] in confusion

आकृति **ākṛti** *f.* appearance, figure

आकृष् **ā+kṛṣ** (I **ākarṣati**) drag, draw

आक्रन्द् **ā+krand** (I **ākrandati**) cry out, scream, lament

आख्या **ā+khyā** (II **ākhyāti**) declare, tell, announce

आख्या **ākhyā** appellation, name; **:ākhya** [having as a name:] called, known as

आगम् **ā+gam** (I **āgacchati**) come, approach, arrive

आगम् **ā+gam** *caus.* (**āgamayati**) acquire

आगमः **āgamaḥ** arrival, accession

आगमनं **āgamanaṃ** coming, arrival

आघ्रा **ā+ghrā** (I **ājighrati**) smell

आचक्रन्द **ācakranda** *3rd sg. para. perf. of* **ākrand**

आचर् **ā+car** (I **ācarati**) conduct oneself, act, do

आचार्यः **ācāryaḥ** teacher

आच्छद् **ā+chad** (X **ācchādayati**) hide, conceal

आज्ञा **ājñā** command, order

आज्ञा **ā+jñā** *caus.* (**ājñāpayati**) order, say (authoritatively)

आतपः **ātapaḥ** heat (*esp.* of sun)

आत्मजः **ātma-jaḥ** [born of oneself:] son

आत्मजा **ātma-jā** daughter

आत्मन् **ātman** *m.* self, myself *etc.*

आत्यन्तिक **ātyantika** (*cf.* **atyanta**) perpetual, lasting

आत्रेयी **Ātreyī** *pr. n.*

आदरः **ādaraḥ** care, respect, trouble, anxiety (to do something); **ādaraṃ kṛ** take care (to)

आदा **ā+dā** (III **ādatte**) take, take hold of, bring

आदि **ādi** *m.* beginning

आदि **:ādi** etc.

आदिश् **ā+diś** (VI **ādiśati**) order, proclaim, direct

आदृ **ā+dṛ** (IV **ādriyate**) heed, respect, defer to, refer to

आदेशः **ādeśaḥ** command, order, instruction

आद्य **ādya** initial, first, earliest

आधोरणः **ādhoraṇaḥ** elephant-driver

आनी **ā+nī (I ānayati)** bring

आनुयात्रिकः **ānuyātrikaḥ** escort

आप् **āp (V āpnoti)** obtain, get

आपत् **ā+pat (I āpatati)** occur, befall, appear suddenly, present oneself

आपतनं **āpatanaṃ** occurrence, (sudden) appearance, arising

आपत्ति **āpatti** *f.* (*from* **ā+pad**) happening, occurrence

आपद् **ā+pad (IV āpadyate)** attain, come to, happen, occur

आपन्नसत्त्व **āpanna꞉sattva** [to whom a living creature has occurred:] pregnant

आपीडः **āpīḍaḥ, āpīḍakaḥ** chaplet, crest

आप्त **āpta** trustworthy

आप्रछ् **ā+prach (VI āpṛcchati)** take leave of, say goodbye

आभरणं **ābharaṇaṃ** ornament, jewel, decoration, insignia

आमन्त्र् **ā+mantr (X āmantrayate)** salute; take leave of

आमोदः **āmodaḥ** scent

आयतनं **āyatanaṃ** abode, [abode of god:] temple

आया **ā+yā (II āyāti)** come

आयासः **āyāsaḥ** effort, exertion

आयुधं **āyudhaṃ** weapon

आयुस् **āyus** *n.* life

आयुष्मन्त **āyuṣmant** long-lived, (*title of respect*) sire *etc.*

आयोध्यक **Āyodhyaka** inhabiting Ayodhyā

आरभ **ā+rabh (I ārabhate)** undertake, begin, start

आरम्भः **ārambhaḥ** beginning, undertaking

आरामः **ārāmaḥ** pleasure; pleasure-grove, woodland

आरुह् **ā+ruh (I ārohati)** ascend, climb, mount, get in(to chariot)

आरुह् **ā+ruh** *caus.* **(āropayati)** cause to mount, raise on to; *with* **śūlam** impale

आर्त **ārta** afflicted, oppressed

आर्ति **ārti** *f.* affliction, distress

आर्द्र **ārdra** moist, tender

आर्य **ārya** noble, honourable

आर्यः **āryaḥ** Your/His Excellency/Honour, sir, *etc.*

आर्यपुत्रः **ārya-putraḥ** [son of] nobleman; *voc.* noble sir

आर्या **āryā** noble lady, Madam, *etc.*

आलक्ष्य **ālakṣya** discernible, just visible

आलिख् **ā+likh (VI ālikhati)** draw (picture)

आलिङ्ग् **ā+liṅg (I āliṅgati)** embrace

आलोक् **ā+lok (X ālokayati)** gaze, look at

आवासः **āvāsaḥ** dwelling, house

आविद् **ā+vid** *caus.* **(āvedayati)** make known, tell

आविर्भू **āvir˜bhū** become manifest, reveal oneself

आविष्कृ **āviṣ˜kṛ** make manifest, reveal

आवेगः **āvegaḥ** alarm, agitation

आवेशः **āveśaḥ** attack (of emotion)

आशङ्क् **ā+śaṅk (I āśaṅkate)** fear, doubt, suspect, be afraid

आशङ्का **āśaṅkā** apprehension, fear

आशा **āśā** hope

आशिस् **āśis** *f. irreg.* prayer, benediction

आशीर्वादः **āśīrvādaḥ** blessing, benison

आश्रमः **āśramaḥ** hermitage; *more widely* one of the four stages of life (of which entering a hermitage is the third)

आश्रमपदं **āśrama-padaṃ** [site of] hermitage

आश्रि **ā+śri** (I **āśrayati/āśrayate**) resort to, take shelter with (*acc.*)

आश्रित्य **āśritya** [having resorted to:] at, in, by

आश्वस् **ā+śvas** *caus.* (**āśvāsayati**) cause to breathe freely, comfort, console

आश्वासः **āśvāsaḥ** [breathing freely:] feeling of comfort, optimism

आश्वासनं **āśvāsanaṃ** comforting, consolation

आस् **ās** (II **āste**) sit, stay, remain

आसक्त **āsakta** fastened, fixed, occupied

आसक्ति **āsakti** *f.* adherence, intentness (on)

आसद् **ā+sad** *caus.* (**āsādayati**) reach, overtake; find, acquire

आसनं **āsanaṃ** seat, couch

आसन्न **āsanna** near; *ifc.* beside

आसीत् **āsīt** *3rd sg. imperf. of* **as** 'be'

आस्कन्द् **ā+skand** (I **āskandati**) leap upon, attack

आह **āha** (*3rd sg. para. perf. of* **ah** 'say') says, said

आहर **-āhara** *ifc.* bringer, carrier

आहरणं **āharaṇaṃ** bringing, fetching

आहारः **āhāraḥ** fodder

आहितुण्डिकः **āhituṇḍikaḥ** snake-charmer

आहूय **āhūya** *absolutive of* **āhve**

आहृ **ā+hṛ** (I **āharati**) bring, fetch

आह्वे **ā+hve** (I **āhvayati**) summon, call

इ **i (II eti)** go

इच्छा **icchā** wish, desire

इतः **itaḥ** from here, from this; in this direction, this way, over here; **itas tataḥ** hither and thither

इतर **itara** other

इतरेतर **itaretara** mutual, of/to *etc.* each other

इति **iti** [thus:] with these words, with this thought *etc.*; *see Chapters 2, 14 and 15*

इत्थम् **ittham** in this way, so

इत्थंभूत **ittham̩:bhūta** [being in this way:] such, so·

इदम् **idam** *n. sg. of* **ayam**

इदानीम् **idānīm** now

इन्दु **indu** *m.* moon

इन्द्रः **Indraḥ** the god Indra

इन्द्रायुधं **Indrɔ-āyudhaṃ** [Indra's weapon:] rainbow

इन्द्रियं **indriyaṃ** (organ or faculty of) sense

इव **iva** as it were, as if, like, as, such as, *etc.*

इष् **iṣ (VI icchati)** want, wish, desire, 'should like'

इषु **iṣu** *m.* arrow

इष्टं **iṣṭaṃ** thing wished, wish

इष्टजनः **iṣṭa:janaḥ** the loved one

इह **iha** here, in this; in this world

ईक्ष् **īkṣ** **(I īkṣate)** look upon, see

ईदृश **īdṛśa** (*f.* **ī**) of this kind, such

ईप्सित **īpsita** desired, wished for

ईषत् **īṣat** slightly

ईह् **īh (I īhate)** long for, desire

उक्त **ukta** *p.p. of* **vac**

उग्र **ugra** fierce, grim

उचित **ucita** suitable, appropriate, proper, right

उच्चल् **uccal (ut+cal) (I uccalati)** move away; rise

उच्छ्वस् **ucchvas (ut+śvas) (II ucchvasiti)** breathe, bloom, blossom

उच्छ्वासः **ucchvāsaḥ** breath

उत् **ut** *prefix* up *etc.*

उताहो **utāho** or? (*marking alternative question*)

उत्क **utka** eager, longing for

उत्कण्ठते **utkaṇṭhate** *denom.* long for, be in love with (*gen.*)

उत्क्षिप् **ut+kṣip (VI utkṣipati)** throw up, raise

उत्खात **utkhāta** (*p.p. of* **ut+khā**) dug up, uprooted

उत्तम **uttama** uppermost, supreme, top

उत्तमाङ्गं **uttama:aṅgaṃ** [highest limb:] head

उत्तर **uttara** following, subsequent, further; upper, superior to, above

उत्तरं **uttaraṃ** answer, reply; consequence, prevalent result

उत्पत् **ut+pat (I utpatati)** fly up

उत्पत्ति **utpatti** *f.* arising

उत्पद् **ut+pad (IV utpadyate)** arise

उत्पद् **ut+pad** *caus.* **(utpādayati)** cause to arise, cause

उत्पीडित **utpīḍita** squeezed

उत्सर्गः **utsargaḥ** pouring out, expenditure

उत्सर्पिन् **utsarpin** (*from* **ut+sṛp** 'soar up') high-soaring

उत्सवः **utsavaḥ** festival

उत्साहः **utsāhaḥ** enthusiasm

उत्सुक **utsuka** eager

उत्सुकं **utsukaṃ** eagerness

उत्स्था **ut+sthā (I uttiṣṭhati)** get up

उदकं **udakaṃ** water

उदग्र **udagra** intense

उदपान **udapāna** *m./n.* well, water-tank

उदयः **udayaḥ** (*from* **ut+i**) rising

उदस **udas (ut+as) (IV. udasyati)** throw up, throw out, push out

उदार **udāra** noble, generous

उदास **udās (ut+ās) (II udāste)** sit idle

उदीक्ष **udīkṣ (ut+īkṣ) (I udīkṣate)** look at

उद्घातिन् **udghātin** having elevations, bumpy

उद्घुष् **udghuṣ (ut+ghuṣ) (I udghoṣati)** cry out

उद्देशः **uddeśaḥ** region, part, place, spot

उद्धरणं **uddharaṇaṃ** (*from* **ut+hṛ**) tearing out, destruction

उद्धा **uddhā (ut+hā) (III ujjihīte)** rise up, start up; depart

उद्या **udyā (ut+yā) (II udyāti)** rise up

उद्यानं **udyānaṃ** garden, park

उद्योगः **udyogaḥ** exertion

उद्विग्न **udvigna** distressed, love-sick, melancholy

उद्वेष्ट् **udveṣṭ (ut+veṣṭ)** *caus.* **(udveṣṭayati)** unwrap, open (letter)

उन्मत्त **unmatta** insane, crazed

उन्मनस् **un_manas** eager, longing

उन्माथः **unmāthaḥ** shaking up, pangs

उन्मादः **unmādaḥ** insanity

उन्मुखम् **un_mukham** [with the face] upwards

उपकारः **upakāraḥ** help, aiding (of), service

उपकारिन् **upakārin** helper, ally

उपकृ **upa+kṛ (VIII upakaroti)** furnish, provide, help

उपक्लृप् **upa+kḷp** *caus.* **(upakalpayati)** equip; assign

उपक्षिप् **upa+kṣip** (VI **upakṣipati**) hint at

उपगम् **upa+gam** (I **upagacchati**) go to, come to, reach, approach

उपग्रहः **upagrahaḥ** conciliation, winning over

उपजन् **upa+jan** (IV **upajāyate**) come into being, be roused

उपजापः **upajāpaḥ** (secret) instigation to rebellion, 'overtures'

उपत्यका **upatyakā** foothill

उपनयनं **upanayanaṃ** bringing, carrying

उपनी **upa+nī** (I **upanayati**) bring, take, carry, bear; initiate (into adulthood)

उपन्यासः **upanyāsaḥ** mention, allusion

उपपन्न **upapanna** suitable, possible; possessed of

उपप्लवः **upaplavaḥ** affliction, molestation

उपभुज् **upa+bhuj** (VII **upabhuṅkte**) enjoy, consume, spend

उपमा **upamā** simile

उपयेमे **upayeme** *3rd sg. ātm. perf. of* **upa+yam** 'marry'

उपयोगः **upayogaḥ** use, utility

उपरम् **upa+ram** (I **uparamate**) cease, die

उपरागः **uparāgaḥ** eclipse

उपरि **upari** above, on; about, concerning (*gen.*); after (*abl.*)

उपरुध् **upa+rudh** (VII **uparuṇaddhi**) besiege, invade, molest, hinder

उपरोधः **uparodhaḥ** obstruction, interruption

उपरोधनं **uparodhanaṃ** besieging

उपलभ् **upa+labh** (I **upalabhate**) acquire, ascertain, discover, learn

उपविश् **upa+viś** (VI **upaviśati**) sit down

उपश्रु **upa+śru** (V **upaśṛṇoti**) hear of, learn of

उपश्लिष **upa+śliṣ** *caus.* (**upaśleṣayati**) cause to come near, bring near

उपसंग्रहः **upasaṃgrahaḥ** embracing; collecting; looking after

उपसदनं **upasadanaṃ** respectful salutation

उपसृ **upa+sṛ** (I **upasarati**) go up to, approach

उपस्था **upa+sthā** (I **upatiṣṭhate**) stand near, be at hand; (**upatiṣṭhati**) attend

उपस्था **upa+sthā** *caus.* (**upasthāpayati**) cause to be at hand, bring near

उपस्थानं **upasthānaṃ** attendance

उपहत **upahata** struck, hurt, killed

उपहारः **upahāraḥ** offering up, sacrifice

उपहृ **upa+hṛ** (I **upaharati**) offer; offer up, sacrifice

उपाध्यायः **upādhyāyaḥ** teacher, preceptor

उपायः **upāyaḥ** means, way, expedient

उपारूढ **upārūḍha** *p.p. of* **upa+ā+ruh** 'mount'

उपालभ् **upa+ā+labh** (I **upālabhate**) reproach, rebuke, blame

उपास् **upās** (**upa+ās**) (II **upāste**) sit by, wait upon, honour

उपे **upe** (**upa+i**) (II **upaiti**) approach, come to

उपेक्ष् **upekṣ** (**upa+īkṣ**) (I **upekṣate**) overlook, disregard

उपोढ **upoḍha** (*p.p. of* **upa+ūh**) produced, increased

उभ **ubha** (*dual only*) both

उरस् **uras** *n.* chest, bosom, breast

उर्वशी **Urvaśī** *pr. n.*

उल्लङ्घ् **ullaṅgh (ut+laṅgh)** *caus.* **(ullaṅghayati)** transgress, violate

उशीर **uśīra** *m./n.* a fragrant root

उषित **uṣita** *p.p. of* **vas**

ऊढ **ūḍha** *p.p. of* **vah**

ऊर्ध्वम् **ūrdhvam** after (*abl.*)

ऋ **ṛ** *caus.* **(arpayati)** transfer, hand over

ऋणं **ṛṇaṃ** debt

ऋत्विज् **ṛtvij (ṛtvik)** *m.* priest

ऋषि **ṛṣi** *m.* seer, sage

एक **eka** *pron.* one, a, only, alone, single

एकदा **ekadā** at one time, once

एकवचनं **eka-vacanaṃ** (*gram.*) singular (number)

एकाकिन् **ekākin** alone

एकादश **ekādaśa** (*f.* **ī**) eleventh

एतत् **etat** *n. sg. and stem form of* **eṣaḥ**

एतावन्त् **etāvant** this much

एध् **edh** *caus.* **(edhayati)** cause to prosper, bless

एनम् **enam** *enclitic pron.* him, her, it, *etc.*

एव **eva** *enclitic particle of emphasis* in fact, really, actually, exactly, just, only, entirely, quite, (the) very, the same, it is . . . that, *etc.*

एवम् **evam** in this way, like this, thus, so, you see how

एषः **eṣaḥ** *pron.* this, this one, he; here (is), see, herewith

एहि **ehi** (*2nd sg. para. imperv. of* **ā+i**) come

ऐक्ष्वाक **Aikṣvāka** (*f.* **ī**) descended from King Ikṣvāku

ओकस **okas** *n.* home

औत्सुक्यं **autsukyaṃ** eagerness, longing

औरस **aurasa** (*f.* **ī**) produced from the breast (**uras**), belonging to oneself

औशनस **Auśanasa** (*f.* **ī**) originating from Uśanas

औषधं **auṣadhaṃ** medicine

क **ka** *suffix sometimes added to exocentric compounds*

कः **kaḥ** *interrog. pron.* who? what? which?; **kaḥ+api/cit** any(one), any(thing), some(one), some(thing), **a** (certain), a few

कच्चित् **kaccit** I hope that . . .?

कञ्चुकिन् **kañcukin** *m.* chamberlain

कटक **kaṭaka** *m./n.* (royal) camp

कठोर **kaṭhora** hard, full-grown

कठोरगर्भ **kaṭhora:garbha** [with foetus full-grown:] late in pregnancy

कण्ठः **kaṇṭhaḥ** neck, throat

कण्वः **Kaṇvaḥ** *pr. n.*

कतम **katama** *pron.* which?

कतर **katara** *pron.* which (of two)?

कतिपय **katipaya** a few

कथ् **kath (X kathayati)** tell, relate, say, mention, speak of

कथम् **katham** how? in what way? What, . . .? why, . . .!

कथंचित् **kathaṃ cit, katham api** somehow, only just

कथा **kathā** story, talk, speaking, conversation

कथितं **kathitaṃ** thing spoken, talk, conversation

कदा **kadā** when?

कदाचित् **kadācit** sometimes, perhaps

कनकं **kanakaṃ** gold

कन्यका **kanyakā, kanyā** girl, daughter

कम् **kam** *caus.* (**kāmayate**) desire, love, be in love with

कमल **kamala** *m./n.* lotus

कर **-kara** *ifc.* making, causing

करः **karaḥ** hand **kara-talaḥ** palm of the hand

करङ्कः **karaṅkaḥ** skull, vessel, box

करणं **karaṇaṃ** doing, performing; sense organ

कराला **Karālā** *name of a goddess*

कर्णः **karṇaḥ** ear

कर्तृ **kartṛ** *m.* doer, agent

कर्मन् **karman** *n.* deed, task, [the work of:] 'role'

कलकलः **kalakalaḥ** disturbance, noise

कलत्रं **kalatraṃ** wife, spouse

कलहंसकः **Kalahaṃsakaḥ** *pr. n.*

कलिका **kalikā** bud

कल्पः **kalpaḥ** sacred precept or practice, rite

कल्याण **kalyāṇa** (*f.* **ī**) fair, auspicious, beneficial

कवि **kavi** *m.* poet, (creative) writer

कश्चित् **kaś cit** *see* **kaḥ+cit**

कषाय **kaṣāya** astringent, sharp(-smelling)

कष्ट **kaṣṭa** grievous, harsh, disastrous, calamitous

कष्टम् **kaṣṭam** alas!

काकु **kāku** *f.* tone of voice

काञ्चनारः **kāñcanāraḥ** mountain ebony

काण **kāṇa** one-eyed

कातर **kātara** timid, nervous

कादम्बिनी **kādambinī** bank of clouds

काननं **kānanaṃ** forest

कान्त **kānta** (*p.p. of* **kam**) beloved

कापालिकः **kāpālikaḥ** (repulsive) Śaiva ascetic

कामः **kāmaḥ** wish, desire, love

कामः **Kāmaḥ, Kāma:devaḥ** the God of Love

कामम् **kāmam** at will, wilfully; admittedly, granted that, though

कामयिष्यते **kāmayiṣyate** *3rd sg. ātm. fut. of* **kam**

कामिन् **kāmin** loving, lover

कायस्थः **kāyasthaḥ** scribe, letter-writer

कारणं **kāraṇaṃ** reason, cause; instrument, means

कारिन् **kārin** doing, doer

कात्स्न्यं **kārtsnyaṃ** totality; **kārtsnyena** in full

कार्पण्यं kārpaṇyaṃ wretchedness

कार्मुकं **kārmukaṃ** bow

कार्यं **kāryaṃ** task, duty, affair, business, matter

कालः **kālaḥ** time, right time, occasion

कालक्षेपः **kāla-kṣepaḥ, kāla-haraṇaṃ** wasting of time, delay

काव्यं **kāvyaṃ** poetry, (creative) literature

काशी **Kāśī** *name of city* (Banaras)

किंवदन्ती **kiṃvadantī** rumour

किंच **kiṃ ca** moreover

किंचित् **kiṃ cit** something; somewhat, slightly

किंतु **kiṃ tu** but

किंनुखलु **kiṃ nu khalu** can it be that?

किम् **kim** (*n. sg. of* **kaḥ**) what?; why?; *may mark a question*; +*instr.* what is the point in? what business (have you *etc.*) with?

किमपि **kim api** something; somewhat, at all

किमिति **kim iti** in what terms?; with what in mind? why?

किमुत **kim uta, kiṃ punar** [what then of:] let alone

कियन्त् **kiyant** how much?

किल **kila** it seems that, apparently, I believe

कीदृश **kīdṛśa** (*f.* ī) of what kind? of what kind! what (a)!

कीर्त् **kīrt** (X **kīrtayati**) declare

कु **ku:** *pejorative prefix* ill

कुटुम्बं **kuṭumbaṃ** household, family

कुटुम्बिन् **kuṭumbin** *m.* householder, family-man

कुट्मल **kuṭmala** *m./n.* bud

कुण्डलं **kuṇḍalaṃ** earring, ear-ornament

कुतः **kutaḥ** from where? from what?; in what direction, whereabouts?

कुतूहलं **kutūhalaṃ** curiosity, interest

कुप् **kup** *caus.* **(kopayati)** make angry, anger

कुमति **ku:mati** *f.* ill thought, wrongheadedness

कुमारः **kumāraḥ** (well-born) young man, son; prince; Your/His Highness

कुमारः **Kumāraḥ** the Prince (*name of Skanda, god of war*)

कुमारकः **kumārakaḥ** young man, son

कुमारी **kumārī** girl, daughter, princess

कुम्भः **kumbhaḥ** pot

कुलं **kulaṃ** family, dynasty, house; herd, swarm (of bees)

कुलविद्या **kula-vidyā** learning that is [in a family:] hereditary

कुशः Kuśaḥ *pr. n.*

कुशलं **kuśalaṃ** welfare

कुसुमं **kusumaṃ** flower, blossom

कुसुमपुरं **Kusumapuraṃ** 'flower-city' *name of Pāṭaliputra*

कुसुमायुधः **kusum›-āyudhaḥ** [the flower-weaponed:] God of Love

कूलं **kūlaṃ** bank, shore

कृ **kṛ (VIII karoti)** do, act, see to, conduct (affairs); make, cause, contrive; *forms verbal periphrasis with abstract or action nouns, e.g.* **avajñāṃ kṛ** feel contempt, despise

कृच्छ्रं **kṛcchraṃ** hardship; **kṛcchrāt** with difficulty

कृतम् **kṛtam**+*instr.* have done with

कृतज्ञ **kṛta-jña, kṛta-vedin** conscious of [things done for one:] debt, grateful, obliged

कृतज्ञता **kṛtajña˜tā** gratitude

कृतपुण्य **kṛta꞉puṇya** [who has done meritorious things (in a previous life):] fortunate, lucky

कृतिन् **kṛtin** [having something done:] satisfied, fulfilled

कृपण **kṛpaṇa** niggardly, wretched

कृपाणः **kṛpāṇaḥ** sword, (sacrificial) knife; **kṛpāṇa꞉pāṇi** *cf. Chapter 15, p. 249*

कृपालु **kṛpālu** compassionate

कृष्ण **kṛṣṇa** black

कृष्णशकुनि **kṛṣṇa:śakuni** *m.* [black bird:] crow

कॢप् **kḷp (I kalpate)** be suitable, conduce to, turn to (*dat.*)

कॢप् **kḷp** *caus.* **(kalpayati)** arrange, prepare

केतु **ketu** *m.* flag, banner

केशवः **Keśavaḥ** *name of the god Kṛṣṇa*

केसरं **kesaraṃ** hair, filament

कैमुतिकन्यायात् **kaimutika:nyāyāt** [from the principle **kim uta** 'let alone':] *a fortiori*

कोपः **kopaḥ** anger

कोऽपि **ko ›pi** *see* **kaḥ+api**

कोमल **komala** tender

कोलाहलः **kolāhalaḥ** clamour

कोशः **kośaḥ, koṣaḥ** treasury, resources, wealth

कौतुकं **kautukaṃ** curiosity

कौमुदी **kaumudī** moonlight; day of full moon

क्रिया **kriyā** doing, performing, effecting, action; rite

क्री **krī (IX krīṇāti)** buy

क्रीड् **krīḍ (I krīḍati)** play

क्रोधः **krodhaḥ** anger

क्रौर्यं **krauryaṃ** cruelty

क्व **kva** where? in what?

क्वण् **kvaṇ** *caus.* **(kvā̆ṇayati)** [cause to] sound

क्षणः **kṣaṇaḥ** instant of time, second, moment

क्षत्रियः **kṣatriyaḥ** [member of] warrior [caste]

क्षम् **kṣam (I kṣamate)** be patient, endure, tolerate

क्षयः **kṣayaḥ** destruction, ruin

क्षात्त्र **ksātra** (*f*. ī) relating to the kṣatriya caste

क्षितिपति **kṣiti-pati** *m*. [lord of earth:] king

क्षिप् **kṣip (VI kṣipati)** throw; waste (time)

क्षिप्र **kṣipra** swift, quick

क्षिप्रकारिन् **kṣipra:kārin** [swift-acting:] precipitate

क्षीरवृक्षः **kṣīra-vṛkṣaḥ** fig-tree

क्षुद् **kṣud (I kṣodati)** trample, tread

क्षुद्र **kṣudra** mean, common, low

क्षुध् **kṣudh** *f*. hunger

क्षेत्त्रं **kṣetraṃ** field

क्षेपः **kṣepaḥ** (*from* **kṣip**) throwing, wasting

खं **khaṃ** hole; vacuum; sky, heaven

खद्योतः **khadyotaḥ** firefly

खलु **khalu** *confirmatory particle* indeed, of course, after all, certainly, don't forget; **na khalu** certainly not, not at all

खेदः **khedaḥ** exhaustion

खेल **khel (I khelati)** play

ग **-ga** *ifc.* going

गः **gaḥ** the lettter **g**; (*in prosody*) heavy syllable

गङ्गा **Gaṅgā** the Ganges

गजः **gajaḥ** elephant

गडु **gaḍu** *m.* goitre

गण् **gaṇ (X gaṇayati)** count

गणना **gaṇanā** counting

गणिका **gaṇikā** courtesan

गत **gata** (*p.p. of* **gam**) gone; *ifc.* gone to, [being] in, concerning, *etc.*

गन्धः **gandhaḥ** scent, smell, fragrance

गम् **gam (I gacchati)** go, attain

गम् **gam** *caus.* **(gamayati)** spend, pass (time)

गमनं **gamanaṃ** going

गरीयांस् **garīyāṃs** important, considerable; worthy/worthier of respect

गर्भः **garbhaḥ** womb, foetus; *ifc.* containing

गर्भिन् **garbhin** [having foetuses:] productive of offspring

गल् **gal (I galati)** drip, slip away

गहनं **gahanaṃ** dense place, thicket

गात्रं **gātraṃ** limb, body, 'person'

गाथा **gāthā** verse (*esp.* in the āryā metre)

गामिन् **gāmin** going

गार्हस्थ्यं **gārhasthyaṃ** being a householder

गिर् **gir** *f.* speech, voice, tone

गिरि **giri** *m.* mountain

गीत **gīta** *p.p. of* **gai**

गीता **gītā, gīti** *f.* song

गुणः **guṇaḥ** merit, quality, worth; strand, string; '-fold', *e.g.* **tri:guṇa** threefold

गुप् **gup** (*denom. pres.* **gopāyati**) guard; hide

गुरु **guru** heavy, important; *m.* teacher, elder, senior, guardian

गुह्य **guhya** [to be concealed:] secret

गृहं **gṛhaṃ** (*m. in pl.*) house, home, household; quarters, chamber

गृहजनः **gṛha-janaḥ** family (*more particularly* wife)

गृहमेधिन् **gṛhamedhin** *m.*, **gṛhasthaḥ** householder

गृहिणी **gṛhiṇī** housewife, wife

गृहीत **gṛhīta** *p.p. of* **grah**

गृहीतार्थ **gṛhīta̱ârtha** [by whom the fact has been grasped:] aware

गै **gai** (I **gāyati**) sing

गो **go** *m.* ox; *f.* cow; **go-kulaṃ** herd of cows, cattle

गोपः **gopaḥ** cowherd

गोपनं **gopanaṃ** concealment, hiding

गौतमी **Gautamī** *pr. n.*

गौरवं **gauravaṃ** high esteem, regard, duty of respect [towards an elder]

ग्रह् **grah** (IX **gṛhṇāti**) seize, grasp, take, receive, accept

ग्रहणं **grahaṇaṃ** seizing, taking

ग्रामः **grāmaḥ** village

घटः **ghaṭaḥ** pot

घातकः **ghātakaḥ** executioner

घातयति **ghātayati** *caus. of* **han** 'strike, kill'

घुष् **ghuṣ** (I **ghoṣati**) proclaim

घोषणा **ghoṣaṇā** proclamation

घ्राणं **ghrāṇaṃ** smelling, (sense of) smell

च **ca** *enclitic* and, in addition; **. . . ca . . . ca** both . . . and . . ., no sooner . . . than . . .

चक्रवर्तिन् **cakravartin** *m.* emperor

चक्षुस् **cakṣus** *n.* eye

चण्ड **caṇḍa** violent

चतुर् **catur** four

चतुर्थ **caturtha** (*f.* ī) fourth

चतुःषष्टि **catuḥ;ṣaṣṭi** *f.* sixty-four

चन्दन **candana** *m./n.* sandal, sandalwood tree

चन्दनदासः **Candanadāsaḥ** *pr. n.*

चन्द्रः **candraḥ** moon

चन्द्रकेतु **Candraketu** *m. pr. n.*

चन्द्रगुप्तः **Candraguptaḥ** *pr. n.*

चन्द्रिका **candrikā** moonlight

चर् **car (I carati)** move, go, depart; behave, act; do, effect

चरणं **caraṇaṃ** *m./n.* foot; **caraṇa-nikṣepaḥ** [putting down of feet:] tread

चरितं **caritaṃ** conduct, deeds, 'story'

चर्या **caryā** going about, riding (in vehicle)

चल् **cal** (I **calati**) stir, move, go away

चाणक्यः **Cāṇakyaḥ** *pr. n.*

चाप **cāpa** *m./n.* bow

चामुण्डा **Cāmuṇḍā** *name of the goddess Durgā*

चिकीर्षितं **cikīrṣitaṃ** [thing desired to be done:] inten-tion

चित् **cit** *enclitic, gives indefinite sense to interrogative pro-nouns*

चित्तं **cittaṃ** thought, mind

चित्तवृत्ति **citta-vṛtti** *f.* [activity of mind:] mental process, thought

चित्र **citra** variegated

चित्रं **citraṃ** picture

चित्रलेखा **Citralekhā** *pr. n.*

चिन्त् **cint** (X **cintayati**) reflect, think (things over), think of

चिन्ता **cintā** thought, worry

चिर **cira** long (*of time*)

चिरम् **ciram** for a long time

चिरस्य **cirasya, cirāt** after a long time

चीनांशुकं **cīna-âṃśukaṃ** [Chinese cloth:] silk

चीरं **cīraṃ** strip of bark (worn by ascetic)

चुर् **cur** (X **corayati**) steal

चूतः **cūtaḥ** mango tree

चूर्णं **cūrṇaṃ** powder

चेत् **cet** *enclitic* if

चेतना **cetanā** consciousness

चेतस् **cetas** *n.* mind, heart, intelligence, understanding

चेष्ट् **ceṣṭ** (I **ceṣṭati, ceṣṭate**) move, act, behave (towards), treat (*loc.*)

चेष्टा **ceṣṭā** conduct, action

चेष्टितं **ceṣṭitaṃ** action

चैत्ररथं Caitrarathaṃ **pr. n.**

छद्मन् **chadman** *n.* disguise

छलं **chalaṃ** fraud, fallacy, error

छाया **chāyā** shade

छिद् **chid** (II **chinatti**) cut, cut out

छिद्रं **chidraṃ** hole, chink

छिन्न **chinna** (*p.p. of* **chid**) cut, divided

छेदिन् **chedin** cutting out, removing

जः **jaḥ** the letter **j**; (*prosody*) the syllables ⏑ – ⏑

जटा **jaṭā** matted locks (of ascetic)

जन् **jan** (IV **jāyate**) be born, arise, become

जन् **jan** *caus.* (**janayati**) cause to arise, cause, beget, produce, rouse

जनः **janaḥ** person, people, folk; *ifc. gives plural or indefinite sense*

जननं **jananaṃ** thing producing, 'ground for'

जनयितृ **janayitṛ** *m.* begetter, father

जनार्दनः **Janārdanaḥ** *name of Kṛṣṇa*

जन्मन् **janman** *n.* birth; **janma-pratiṣṭhā** [birth-foundation:] mother

जयः **jayaḥ** conquest

जरठ **jaraṭha** old, decrepit

जलं **jalaṃ** water

जलधि **jaladhi** *m.* ocean; the number four

जागृ **jāgṛ** (II **jāgarti**) be awake, wake up

जाजलि **Jājali** *m.*, *pr. n.*

जात **jāta** (*p.p. of* **jan**) born, become; **jāta-karman** *n.* birth ceremony

जाति **jāti** *f.* birth

जानकी **Jānakī** *pr. n.*

जाप्यं **jāpyaṃ** (muttered) prayer

जाम्बूनद **jāmbūnada** (*f.* **ī**) golden

जालं **jālaṃ** net, lattice, window

जालपादः **jālapādaḥ** [web-footed:] goose

जि **ji** (I **jayati**) win, conquer, beat, defeat

जिज्ञासा **jijñāsā** desire to know, wish to determine

जितकाशिन् **jita-kāśin** flushed with victory, arrogant

जीव् **jīv** (I **jīvati**) live, be alive

जीवः **jīvaḥ** living creature, soul

जीवित **jīvita** alive

जीवितं **jīvitaṃ** life

जोषमास् **joṣam ās (II joṣam āste)** remain silent

ज्ञ **-jña** *ifc.* knowing, aware of, recognising

ज्ञा **jñā (IX jānāti)** know, learn, find out, recognise

ज्ञा **jñā** *caus.* **(jñāpayati)** make known, announce

ज्ञातृ **jñātṛ** knower, person to know/understand

ज्ञानं **jñānaṃ** knowledge, perceiving

ज्ञेय **jñeya** *ger. of* **jñā**

ज्यायांस् **jyāyāṃs** older, elder

ज्योतिस् **jyotis** *n.* light; heavenly body; **jyotiḥ-śāstraṃ** astronomy, astrology

ज्योत्स्ना **jyotsnā** moonlight

झटिति **jhaṭiti** suddenly, at once

टच् **ṭac** (*gram.*) the suffix **a**

तः **taḥ** *adverbial suffix* from, in respect of *etc.*

तटः **taṭaḥ** slope, bank

तड् **taḍ (X tāḍayati)** strike, beat

तत् **tat** *n. sg. and stem form of* **saḥ**

तत् **tat** *connecting particle* then, so

ततः **tataḥ** from there, from that, thereupon, then, and so, therefore

तत्क्षणम् **tat:kṣaṇam** at that moment, thereupon

तत्र **tatra** there, in/on *etc.* that, among them

तत्रभवन्त् **tatra:bhavant** His Honour [there], that (honourable) man, the revered

तत्रभवती **tatra:bhavatī** Her Honour [there], that (good) lady

तथा **tathā** thus, in such a way, so

तथापि **tathā ›pi** even so, nevertheless, but, yet

तदा **tadā** then, at that time

तदानीम् **tadānīm** (*cf.* **idānīm**) then, at that time; **tadā-nīṃ˜tana** belonging to that time, of that period

तद्धितः **taddhitaḥ** (*gram.*) ['suitable for that':] secondary suffix

तन् **tan** (VIII **tanoti**) extend, stretch

तन **tana** *suffix added to words denoting time*

तनया **tanayā** daughter

तन्त्रं **tantraṃ** framework; administration; chapter of a text-book

तपस् **tapas** *n.* (religious) austerity

तपस्विन् **tapasvin** practiser of austerities, ascetic; wretched, 'poor'

तपोवनं **tapo-vanaṃ** ascetics' grove

तम **tama** *superlative suffix* most, pre-eminently, very

तमस् **tamas** *n.* darkness

तर **tara** *comparative suffix* more, notably, particularly

तरु **taru** *m.* tree; **taru-gahanaṃ** thicket of trees, wood

तर्कः **tarkaḥ** conjecture

तर्ज **tarj** *caus.* (**tarjayati**) threaten, scold

तर्हि **tarhi** in that case, then

तल **tala** *m./n.* palm (of the hand)

तव **tava** of you, your, of yours

ता **tā** *abstract noun suffix* -ness *etc.*

तातः **tātaḥ** (one's own) father

तादृश **tādṛśa** (*f.* **ī**) (of) such (a kind), so

तापसः **tāpasaḥ** ascetic

ताम्बूलं **tāmbūlaṃ** betel

तारक **tāraka** causing to cross over, rescuing, liberating

तारका **tārakā** star; pupil of eye

तावत् **tāvat** (*n. sg. of* **tāvant**) during that time, for so long, meanwhile

तावत् **tāvat** *enclitic* well now, (now) then, to start with, now as for—; + *pres. or imperv.* (I'll) just, (would you) just *etc.*

तावन्त् **tāvant** that much, so much

तिथि **tithi** *m. f.* lunar day (*esp. as auspicious date for ceremony*)

तिमिरं **timiraṃ** darkness

तिरोभू **tiro˘bhū (I tirobhavati)** become hidden, vanish

तीक्ष्ण **tīkṣṇa** sharp, severe

तीक्ष्णरसः **tīkṣṇa:rasaḥ** [sharp liquid:] poison

तीरं **tīraṃ** bank

तीर्थं **tīrthaṃ** ford, sacred bathing-place, pool

तु **tu** *enclitic* but, yet, now

तुच्छ **tuccha** trifling

तूष्णीमस् **tūṣṇīm as, tūṣṇīṃ bhū** fall silent

तूष्णीमास् **tūṣṇīm ās** remain silent

तृतीय **tṛtīya** third

तृप् **tṛp** *caus.* **(tarpayati)** satisfy

ते **te** (i) *nom. pl. m. etc. of* **saḥ**, (ii) *enclitic dat./gen. sg. of* **tvam**

तेन **tena** therefore, in that case

तैक्ष्ण्यं **taikṣṇyaṃ** sharpness

त्यज् **tyaj (I tyajati)** abandon, quit, leave, give up, sacrifice

त्रयं **trayaṃ** triad; *ifc.* three

त्रयी **trayī** triad, the Three (Vedas)

त्रस् **tras** *caus.* (**trāsayati**) make afraid, frighten

त्रि **tri** three

त्रिकालं **tri꞉kālaṃ** (*dvigu cpd.*) [the three times:] past, present and future

त्रियामा **tri꞉yāmā** [containing three watches:] night

त्रिलोचनः **tri꞉locanaḥ** the three-eyed (god), Śiva

त्र्यम्बकः **Tryambakaḥ** *name of Śiva*

त्र्यहः **try꞉ahaḥ** [period of] three days

त्वं **tvaṃ** *abstract noun suffix* -ness *etc.*

त्वम् **tvam** (*stem forms* **tvat** *and* **yuṣmat**) you

त्वर् **tvar** (**I tvarate**) hurry; *caus.* **tvarayati**

त्वरितम् **tvaritam** hurriedly, quickly, at once

त्वादृश **tvādṛśa** (*f.* **ī**) like you

द **-da** *ifc.* giving, administering

दक्षिण **dakṣiṇa** right, on the right hand; **dakṣiṇena** on the right, to the right

दक्षिणापथः **dakṣiṇāpathaḥ** southern region (of India), the Deccan

दण्डः **daṇḍaḥ** stick; punishment; vertical stroke (as punctuation mark)

दण्डनीति **daṇḍa-nīti** *f.* administration of justice, political science

दण्डापूपिका **daṇḍāpūpikā** [the 'stick-and-cake' principle:] reasoning *a fortiori*

दत्त **datta** *p.p. of* **dā**

दधत् **dadhat** *nom. sg. m. pres. part. para. of* **dhā**

दन्तः **dantaḥ** tooth

दम्पति **dam-pati** *m.* (*Vedic*) lord of the house; *du.* husband and wife

दया **dayā** pity, compassion

दर्भः **darbhaḥ** *sg. and pl.* *a type of* (sacrificial) grass

दर्शनं **darśanaṃ** (act of) seeing, meeting, sight, appearance; sight (of king or god), audience

दर्शनीय **darśanīya** worth seeing, attractive

दर्शयति **darśayati** *caus. of* **dṛś**

दर्शिन् **darśin** seeing

दलं **dalaṃ** petal, leaf

दश **daśa** ten

दह् **dah (I dahati)** burn

दह् **dah** *caus.* **(dāhayati)** cause to burn

दा **dā (III dadāti)** give, bestow, direct (gaze)

दाक्षायणी **Dākṣāyaṇī** [daughter of Dakṣa:] Aditi

दातृ **dātṛ** giver, granting

दानं **dānaṃ** gift, bestowal, provision (of)

दायिन् **dāyin** giving, administering

दाराः **dārāḥ** *m. pl.* (*NB number and gender*) wife

दारुण **dāruṇa** cruel

दारुवर्मन् **Dāruvarman** *m., pr. n.*

दासः **dāsaḥ** slave, servant

दासी **dāsī** slave girl, servant girl

दिनं **dinaṃ** day

दिवसः **divasaḥ** day

दिव्य **divya** celestial

दिश् **diś (dik)** *f.* direction, cardinal point, region; *pl.* sky, skies

दिष्ट्या **diṣṭyā** [by good luck:] thank heaven that; +**vṛdh** congratulations!

दीपिका dīpikā lamp

दीप्त dīpta (dīp 'blaze, shine') brilliant

दुःखं duḥkham sorrow, unhappiness, pain, distress

दुरात्मन् dur:ātman evil-natured, evil, vile

दुर्गं durgam [hard to get at:] stronghold, citadel; durga-saṃskārah preparation of stronghold, fortification

दुर्निमित्तं dur:nimittam ill omen

दुर्बोध dur:bodha difficult to understand

दुर्मनस् dur:manas in bad spirits, miserable

दुर्मनायते durmanāyate *denom.* be miserable

दुर्लभ dur:labha hard to obtain, inaccessible

दुर्वासस् Durvāsas *m., pr. n.*

दुर्विपाकः dur:vipākaḥ cruel turn (of fortune)

दुश्चेष्टितं duś:ceṣṭitam mischievous action

दुःशील duḥ:śīla bad-tempered, irritable

दुष् duṣ *caus.* (dūṣayati) spoil, defile

दुष्कर duṣ:kara difficult [to do]

दुःषन्तः Duḥṣantaḥ *pr. n.*

दुस् dus *pejorative prefix* ill, bad, evil, mis- *etc.*; difficult to

दुह् duh (II dogdhi) milk; (dugdhe) yield milk

दुहितृ duhitṛ *f.* daughter

दूर dūra far (off), remote; dūram (for) a long way; dūrāt from afar; dūre at a distance, far away

दूरीभवन्तम् dūrī˜bhavantam *acc. sg. m. pres. part. of* dūrī˜bhū 'be far away'

दृढ dṛḍha firm

दृश् dṛś (I paśyati) see, look/gaze at/on, watch

दृश् dṛś *caus.* (darśayati) show, reveal

दृश् dṛś *f.* look, glance

दृष्ट dṛṣṭa *p.p. of* dṛś

दृष्टि **dṛṣṭi** *f.* look, gaze

देवः **devaḥ** god; His/Your Majesty

देवता **devatā** divinity, god

देवतागृहं **devatā-gṛhaṃ** [house of god:] temple

देवपादाः **deva-pādāḥ** the feet (*NB pl.*) of Your Majesty, *honorific for* Your Majesty

देवरातः **Devarātaḥ** *pr. n.*

देवी **devī** goddess; (the) Queen, Her/Your Majesty

देशः **deśaḥ** place, country

दैवं **daivaṃ** fate, chance, fortune

दोग्ध्री **dogdhrī** *f.* of **dogdhṛ** (**doh**+**tṛ**), *agent noun of* **duh**

दोषः **doṣaḥ** fault, demerit, blemish, sin, offence, harm

दोहदः **dohadaḥ** (pregnant) longing

दौहित्रः **dauhitraḥ** daughter's son, grandson

द्रविणं **draviṇaṃ** wealth

द्रष्टव्य **draṣṭavya** *ger. of* **dṛś**

द्रोहः **drohaḥ** injury, hostility

द्वन्द्वं **dvandvaṃ** pair; **dvandva-saṃprahāraḥ** single combat, duel

द्वयं **dvayaṃ** couple, pair; *ifc.* two

द्वार् **dvār** *f.*, **dvāraṃ** door; **dvāra-prakoṣṭhaḥ** fore-court

द्वि **dvi** two

द्विगु **dvigu** *m.* (*gram.*) numerical compound

द्वितीय **dvitīya** second, another, a further

द्विष् **dviṣ** (II **dveṣṭi**) hate

द्विष् **dviṣ** (**dviṭ**) *m.* enemy

धनं **dhanaṃ** wealth, money

धनुस् **dhanus** *n.* bow

धन्य **dhanya** lucky

धर्मः **dharmaḥ** religious law, duty, piety

धर्मपत्नी **dharma-patnī** lawful wife

धा **dhā** (III **dadhāti**) put, hold, wear

धातु **dhātu** *m.* (primary) element; (*gram.*) root

धातृ **dhātṛ** creator, supporter

धात्री **dhātrī** nurse, fostermother

धारणं **dhāraṇaṃ (dhṛ)** holding, wearing

धाव् **dhāv** (I **dhāvati**) run

धी **dhī** *f.* intelligence

धीमन्त् **dhī˜mant** intelligent, wise

धीर **dhīra** steady, firm, resolute, strong

धुरा **dhurā** pole, yoke, burden

धूम्र **dhūmra** smoke-coloured, grey

धूर्तः **dhūrtaḥ** rogue

धूलि **dhūli** *f.* dust

धृ **dhṛ** *caus.* (**dhārayati,** *p.p.* **dhārita/dhṛta**) hold, carry, wear

धैर्यं **dhairyaṃ** steadiness, firmness, self-control

ध्यानं **dhyānaṃ** meditation, meditating

ध्वनि **dhvani** *m.* sound; (*lit. crit.*) 'Suggestion'

न **na** not, no, 'fail to'; (*in comparisons*) rather than, than; **na kaś cit, na ko ›pi** [not anyone]: no one, nobody

नः **naḥ** the letter **n**; (*prosody*) the syllables ⏑ ⏑ ⏑

नगरं **nagaraṃ, nagarī** city, town

नदी **nadī** river

ननु **nanu** why! well!; (*in objection or qualification*) surely, rather

नन्दः Nandaḥ *pr. n.*

नन्दनः Nandanaḥ *pr. n.*

नम् **nam** (I **namati**) bow, salute

नमस् **namas** *n.* homage

नमस्कारः **namaskāraḥ** making obeisance

नयनं **nayanaṃ** eye

नरः **naraḥ** man

नरपति **narapati** *m.* king

नलिनी **nalinī** lotus

नव **nava** new, fresh

नवयौवनं **nava:yauvanaṃ** [fresh] youth

नाट्यं **nāṭyaṃ** acting, drama

नाम **nāma** *enclitic* by name; indeed

नामधेयं **nāmadheyaṃ** appellation, name

नामन् **nāman** *n.* name; *ifc.* named, called

नारी **nārī** woman

निकृत् **ni+kṛt** (VI **nikṛntati**) cut up, shred

निक्षिप् **ni+kṣip** (VI **nikṣipati**) throw, cast into (*loc.*); place, deposit

निक्षेपः **nikṣepaḥ** (act of) putting down

निखिल **nikhila** entire

निगडयति **nigaḍayati** *denom.* fetter, bind

निग्रह् **ni+grah** (IX **nigṛhṇāti**) repress, restrain

निघ्नती **nighnatī** *nom. sg. f. pres. part. para. of* **ni+han** 'strike'

निज **nija** one's own

निपातः **nipātaḥ** (*gram.*) ready-made form, particle

निपुण **nipuṇa** clever, sharp

निबन्धनं **nibandhanaṃ** bond

निभृत **nibhṛta** secret, quiet

निमित्तं **nimittaṃ** sign, omen; cause, motive

नियत **niyata** constrained; **niyatam** necessarily, assuredly

नियुज् **ni+yuj** (VII **niyuṅkte**) engage (someone) upon (*loc.*), appoint, set to (doing)

नियोगः **niyogaḥ** employment, entrusting

नियोज्यः **niyojyaḥ** servant

निरुणध्मि **niruṇadhmi** *1st sg. pres. para. of* **ni+rudh** 'confine, restrain'

निरुत्सुक **nir_utsuka** without eagerness

निर्गम् **nirgam (nis+gam)** (I **nirgacchati**) go away, retire from (*abl.*)

निर्दय **nir_daya** pitiless, fierce

निर्दिश् **nirdiś (nis+diś)** (VI **nirdiśati**) designate, specify

निर्भर **nirbhara** excessive, full

निर्भिन्न **nirbhinna** blossomed forth, found out, betrayed

निर्मा **nirmā (nis+mā)** (II **nirmāti**) create, compose

निर्माणं **nirmāṇaṃ** creation

निर्मित **nirmita** created

निर्वप् **nirvap (nis+vap)** (I **nirvapati**) sprinkle, offer, donate

निर्वर्ण् **nirvarṇ (nis+varṇ)** (X **nirvarṇayati**) gaze upon

निर्वाणं **nirvāṇaṃ** bliss

निर्वृत **nirvṛta** content, happy, satisfied

निवासिन् **nivāsin** living (in), inhabitant

निविद् **ni+vid** *caus.* (**nivedayati**) report, announce, inform someone (*dat./gen.*) of (*acc.*), present someone (*acc.*)

निविश् **ni+viś** *caus.* (**niveśayati**) cause to settle, put in place

निवृ **ni+vṛ** *caus.* (**nivārayati**) ward off, drive off; check, restrain

निवृत् **ni+vṛt** (I **nivartate**) go back, turn back, return

निवृत् **ni+vṛt** *caus.* (**nivartayati**) turn back (*trans.*)

निवेदक **nivedaka** announcing, indicating

निशम् **ni+śam** *caus.* (**niśāmayati**) perceive, observe

निशा **niśā** night

निश्चयः **niścayaḥ** determination, resolve, certainty

निश्चि **niści** (**nis+ci**) (V **niścinoti**) ascertain, settle, fix upon

निषिध् **niṣidh** (**ni+sidh**) (I **niṣedhati**) prohibit, cancel, prevent, check

निष्क्रम् **niṣkram** (**nis+kram**) (I **niṣkrāmati**) go out of (*abl.*), emerge

निष्पण्ण **niṣpaṇṇa** (*p.p. of* **nis+pad** 'be brought about') completed

निस् **nis** *prefix* without, -less, *etc.*

निःसह **niḥsaha** weak, exhausted

निहित **nihita** *p.p. of* **ni+dhā** 'place'

नी **nī** (I **nayati**) lead, guide, take, carry; +*abstract noun* cause a condition in someone

नीति **nīti** *f.* conduct, policy, political science

नु खलु **nu khalu** *enclitic, stressing interrogative* now (who *etc.*) I wonder?

नूपुर **nūpura** *m./n.* (ornamental) anklet

नृत् **nṛt** (IV **nṛtyati**) dance

नृपः **nṛpaḥ** king

नृपति **nṛpati** *m.* king

नृशंस **nṛśaṃsa** injurious; *m.* monster

नेतृ **netṛ** leader

नेत्रं **netraṃ** eye

नेपथ्यं **nepathyaṃ** area behind stage

न्याय: **nyāyaḥ** rule, principle; propriety

न्याय्य **nyāyya** regular, right, proper

न्यास: **nyāsaḥ** deposit, pledge

न्यासीकृ **nyāsī˜kṛ** deposit, entrust

प: **paḥ, pakāraḥ** the letter **p**

पक्व **pakva** cooked, ripe

पक्ष: **pakṣaḥ** wing, 'flank', side

पक्षपातिन् **pakṣa-pātin** on the side of, partial to

पङ्कजं **paṅkajaṃ** [mud-born:] lotus

पङ्क्ति **paṅkti** *f.* row, line

पच् **pac (I pacati)** cook, ripen (*trans.*); *pass.* be cooked, ripen (*intrans.*)

पञ्च **pañca** five

पञ्चम **pañcama** (*f.* **ī**) fifth

पञ्चवटी **Pañcavaṭī** *name of a place*

पट: **paṭaḥ** cloth, robe

पटु **paṭu** sharp; **paṭīyāṃs** sharper

पठ् **paṭh (I paṭhati)** read (aloud), study; cite, mention

पणायितृ **paṇāyitṛ** hawker

पण्डित **paṇḍita** clever, learned; *m.* scholar, paṇḍit

पत् **pat (I patati)** fall, fly

पत् **pat** *caus.* (**pātayati**) cause to fall, drop

पतत्रिन् **patatrin** bird

पति **pati**, *m.* lord, king; (*irreg.*) husband

पत्त्रं **pattraṃ** feather; leaf, petal; leaf for writing, 'paper'

पत्नी **patnī** wife

पथ: **-pathaḥ** (*usually ifc.*) path (*cf.* **panthan**)

पथ्य **pathya** suitable, salutary, regular

पदं **padaṃ** step, footstep, foot; position, site; word, member of nominal compound

पद्मं **padmaṃ** lotus

पद्मपुरं **Padma-puraṃ** *name of city*

पन्थन् **panthan** *m.* (*irreg.*) road, path, way

पयस् **payas** *n.* water, juice

पर **para** *pron. adj.* other, another; *m.* stranger; far, ultimate, supreme, great, particularly marked, (+**na**) greater than

परम् **param** beyond, further than (*abl.*)

परतन्त्र **para-tantra** under another's control, not in control (of)

परत्र **paratra** elsewhere, in the next world

परवन्त् **paravant** under another's control; beside oneself, overwhelmed

परवश **paravaśa** in another's power, helpless

परस्पर **paraspara** mutual; **parasparam** one another, each other

पराञ्च् **parāñc** turned the other way

परापत् **parā+pat** (I **parāpatati**) approach, arrive

परिकर्मन् **parikarman** *n.* preparation

परिकीर्त् **pari+kīrt** (X **parikīrtayati**) proclaim, declare

परिकॢप् **pari+kḷp** *caus.* (**parikalpayati**) fix, destine for (*dat.*)

परिक्लेशः **parikleśaḥ** vexation

परिक्षिप् **pari+kṣip** (VI **parikṣipati**) encircle, encompass

परिगम् **pari+gam** (I **parigacchati**) surround, encircle

परिग्रह् **pari+grah** (IX **parigṛhṇāti**) accept, adopt, possess, occupy

परिग्रहः **parigrahaḥ** acceptance, welcome; possession, wrapping round, dress

परिचि **pari+ci** (V **paricinoti**) become acquainted with, recognise

परिजनः **parijanaḥ** attendant, servant

परिज्ञानं **parijñānaṃ** realisation

परिणम् **pariṇam (pari+nam)** (I **pariṇamati**) develop, turn out (to be)

परिणयः **pariṇayaḥ** marriage

परिणामः **pariṇāmaḥ** development, outcome

परिणी **pariṇī (pari+nī)** (I **pariṇayati**) marry

परितुष् **pari+tuṣ** *caus.* (**paritoṣayati**) make satisfied, reward, tip

परितोषः **paritoṣaḥ** satisfaction

परित्यज् **pari+tyaj** (I **parityajati**) give up, abandon

परित्यागः **parityāgaḥ** giving up, sacrificing; liberality

परित्रस्त **paritrasta** frightened

परित्रै **pari+trai** (I **paritrāyate**) rescue, save, protect

परिनिर्वाणं **parinirvāṇaṃ** complete extinction

परिपाल् **pari+pāl** (X **paripālayati**) guard, preserve, keep intact

परिप्लु **pari+plu** (I **pariplavate**) float, move restlessly, tremble

परिभुज् **pari+bhuj** (VII **paribhunakti**) enjoy

परिभूति **paribhūti** *f.* humiliation, defeat

परिभ्रंश् **pari+bhraṃś** (IV **paribhraśyate**) fall, drop, slip

परिभ्रम् **pari+bhram** (I **paribhramati**) wander around

परिमलः **parimalaḥ** perfume

परिमेय **parimeya** measurable, limited

परिरक्ष् **pari+rakṣ** (I **parirakṣati**) protect, look after, save, spare

परिवाहिन् **parivāhin** overflowing

परिवृत **parivṛta** surrounded, having a retinue

परिवृध् **pari+vṛdh** *caus.* **(parivardhayati)** cause to grow, tend (plants)

परिश्रमः **pariśramaḥ** fatigue, exertion

परिश्रान्त **pariśrānta** exhausted, tired

परिषद् **pariṣad** *f.* assembly, audience

परिस्फुट **parisphuṭa** clear, distinct

परिहा **pari+hā** *passive* **(parihīyate)** be deficient, be inferior to (*abl.*)

परिहासः **parihāsaḥ** joke, laughter

परिहृ **pari+hṛ (I pariharati)** avoid, shun, omit (to do), resist

परीक्ष् **parīkṣ (pari+īkṣ) (I parīkṣate)** examine, scrutinise; *p.p.* **parīkṣita** examined, proven

परीत **parīta** encompassed, overcome

पर्यट् **paryaṭ (pari+aṭ) (I paryaṭati)** wander about

पर्यन्तः **paryantaḥ** limit, end; *ifc.* [having as an end:] ending with, up to

पर्याप्त **paryāpta** sufficient, adequate

पर्वतः **parvataḥ** mountain

पर्वतेश्वरः **Parvateśvaraḥ** *pr. n.*

पशु **paśu** *m.* animal, sacrificial animal

पशुपति **Paśupati** *m.* [lord of beasts:] *name of Śiva*

पश्चात् **paścāt** behind, backward; after, afterwards

पश्चात्तापः **paścāt:tāpaḥ** [after-pain:] remorse

पश्यति **paśyati** *present of* **dṛś** 'see'

पा **pā (I pibati)** drink; *caus.* **(pāyayati)** make to drink

पाकः **pākaḥ** cooking; ripeness, fulfilment

पाठः **pāṭhaḥ** recitation, reading; part (in play)

पाणि **pāṇi** *m.* hand

पाण्डित्यं **pāṇḍityaṃ** learning, scholarship

पातकं **pātakaṃ** [causing to fall:] sin, crime

पातिन् **pātin** falling, flying

पात्रं **pātraṃ** vessel, receptacle; worthy recipient; actor;
pātra-vargaḥ cast (of play)

पादः **pādaḥ** foot

पादपः **pādapaḥ** [drinking by the foot:] tree

पादमूलं **pāda-mūlaṃ** [foot-root:] feet (*in deferential reference to person*)

पाप **pāpa** evil, bad, wicked; *m.* villain; *n.* wickedness

पारावतः **pārāvataḥ** pigeon

पाराशरिन् **pārāśarin** wandering mendicant

पार्थिवः **pārthivaḥ** king, ruler

पार्वती **Pārvatī** *pr. n., wife of Śiva*

पार्श्वं **pārśvaṃ** flank, side

पाल् **pāl (X pālayati)** protect

पिण्डः **piṇḍaḥ** ball of rice, ritual offering to ancestors

पिण्डपातिन् **piṇḍapātin** *m.* mendicant

पितृ **pitṛ** *m.* father; *du.* parents

पिपीलिका **pipīlikā** ant

पीड् **pīḍ (X pīḍayati)** squeeze, oppress, torture, grieve

पीडा **pīḍā** oppression, affliction

पीत **pīta** *p.p. of* **pā** 'drink'

पुंलिङ्ग **puṃ:liṅga** having masculine gender

पुंवन्त् **puṃvant** (*gram.*) masculine

पुंस् **puṃs** *m.* (*irreg.*) man, male, masculine

पुंगवः **puṃgavaḥ** bull

पुण्डरीकं **puṇḍarīkaṃ** lotus

पुण्डरीकः **Puṇḍarīkaḥ** *pr. n.*

पुण्य **puṇya** auspicious, virtuous, holy; *n.* religious merit

पुत्रः **putraḥ** son

पुत्रिका **putrikā, putrī** daughter

पुनर् **punar** again, back (again); *enclitic* however, but, even so, yet, nevertheless

पुनरपि **punar api** yet again, once more

पुनरुक्त **punar:ukta** repeated, redundant

पुर् **pur** *f.* rampart, city

पुरं **puraṃ** city

पुरः **puraḥ** forward, in front, immediate, in the east

पुरस्कृत **puraskṛta** placed in front, before the eyes; honoured

पुरस्तात् **purastāt** forward, from there on

पुरःसरः **puraḥsaraḥ** forerunner, attendant; *pl.* entourage

पुरा **purā** formerly, previously, once

पुरातन **purā˜tana** (*f.* ī) former

पुरुषः **puruṣaḥ** man

पुरूरवस् **Purūravas** *m. pr. n.*

पुष् **puṣ** *caus.* (**poṣayati**) cause to thrive, rear

पुष्कल **puṣkala** abundant, strong

पुष्पं **puṣpaṃ** flower

पुष्पिताग्रा **puṣpitāgrā** (*prosody*) *name of a metre*

पुस्तकं **pustakaṃ** book

पू **pū** (**IX punāti/punīte**) purify

पूरयति **pūrayati** *caus. of* **pṝ**

पूर्ण **pūrṇa** full (*p.p. of* **pṝ**)

पूर्व **pūrva** *pron. adj.* previous, earlier, first, prior, foregoing

पूर्वम् **pūrvam** previously, earlier; before (*abl.*)

पृथक् **pṛthak** separately

पृथग्जनः **pṛthag:janaḥ** separate person, ordinary person

पृथिवी **pṛthivī, pṛthvī** earth

पृष्ट **pṛṣṭa** *p.p. of* **prach**

पॄ **pṝ** *caus.* (**pūrayati**) fill, fulfil, 'enrich'

पोतकः **potakaḥ** young animal/plant

पौनरुक्तं **paunaruktaṃ** redundancy

पौर **paura** urban; *m.* citizen; **paura:janaḥ** townsfolk

पौरव **Paurava** (*f.* **ī**) descended from Puru

प्रकारः **prakāraḥ** manner, way, type, kind

प्रकाशनं **prakāśanaṃ** displaying

प्रकृति **prakṛti** *f.* nature, disposition; *pl.* subjects (of king), people

प्रकोष्ठः **prakoṣṭhaḥ** courtyard

प्रख्या **pra+khyā** *caus.* (**prakhyāpayati**) publish, proclaim

प्रचलित **pracalita** in motion

प्रचारः **pracāraḥ** roaming, movement

प्रचि **pra+ci** (V **pracinoti**) accumulate (*trans.*); *pass.* **pracīyate** accumulate (*intrans.*)

प्रच्छन्नम् **pracchannam** secretly, stealthily

प्रच्छादनं **pracchādanaṃ** concealment

प्रच्छायं **pracchāyaṃ** shade

प्रछ् **prach** (VI **pṛcchati**) ask, question

प्रजा **prajā** subject (of king)

प्रजापति **Prajāpati** *m., pr. n.*

प्रज्ञा **prajñā** intelligence, understanding, guile

प्रणम् **praṇam** (**pra+nam**) (I **praṇamati**) make obeisance to, salute

प्रणयः **praṇayaḥ** affection, entreaty

प्रणयिन् **praṇayin** entreating, suppliant, petitioner; **praṇayi-kriyā** acting for a petitioner, carrying out a request

प्रणामः **praṇāmaḥ** salutation

प्रणिधि **praṇidhi** *m.* (secret) agent

प्रति **prati** +*acc.* towards, against, with regard to, about

प्रतिकूल **prati_kūla** [against the bank:] contrary, hostile

प्रतिक्रिया **pratikriyā** [action against:] remedy, remedying

प्रतिग्रहः **pratigrahaḥ** present (*to a brahmin from a king*)

प्रतिच्छन्दकं **praticchandakaṃ** portrait, picture

प्रतिज्ञा **pratijñā** promise, assertion

प्रतिदृश् **prati+dṛś** (I **pratipaśyati**) see

प्रतिनन्द् **prati+nand** (I **pratinandati**) receive gladly, welcome

प्रतिनिवृत् **prati+ni+vṛt** (I **pratinivartate**) return

प्रतिपक्षः **pratipakṣaḥ** opposite side, enemy

प्रतिपद् **prati+pad** (IV **pratipadyate**) assent, admit

प्रतिपाल् **prati+pāl** (X **pratipālayati**) wait for

प्रतिबुध् **prati+budh** (IV **pratibudhyate**) wake up (*intrans.*)

प्रतिबुध् **prati+budh** *caus.* (**pratibodhayati**) wake up (*trans.*)

प्रतिरूपक **pratirūpaka** (*f.* **ikā**) corresponding in form, like

प्रतिवचनं **prativacanaṃ** answer, reply

प्रतिवस् **prati+vas** (I **prativasati**) dwell, live (in)

प्रतिवातम् **prati_vātam** against the wind, into the wind

प्रतिविधा **prati+vi+dhā** (III **pratividadhāti**) prepare against, take precautions

प्रतिविधानं **pratividhānaṃ** countermeasure

प्रतिश्रु **prati+śru** (V **pratiśṛṇoti**) promise

प्रतिषिध् **pratiṣidh (prati+sidh) (I pratiṣedhati)**, restrain, forbid

प्रतिषेधः **pratiṣedhaḥ** prohibition, cancellation

प्रतिष्ठा **pratiṣṭhā** foundation

प्रती **pratī (prati+i)** *caus.* **(pratyāyayati)** make confident

प्रतीकारः **pratīkāraḥ** remedy

प्रतीक्ष् **pratīkṣ (prati+īkṣ) (I pratīkṣate)** wait (for)

प्रतीहारः **pratīhāraḥ** door-keeper, porter

प्रत्यग्र **pratyagra** fresh, recent

प्रत्यभिज्ञा **pratyabhi+jñā (IX pratyabhijānāti)** recognise

प्रत्ययः **pratyayaḥ** (*gram.*) suffix

प्रत्यर्थिन् **pratyarthin** hostile

प्रत्यर्पयति **pratyarpayati** (*caus. of* **prati+ṛ**) hand over, give back

प्रत्यवायः **pratyavāyaḥ** reverse, annoyance

प्रत्यस् **pratyas (prati+as) (IV pratyasyati)** cast aside

प्रत्याख्यानं **pratyākhyānaṃ** rejection

प्रत्यादिश् **pratyā+diś (VI pratyādiśati)** reject; put to shame (by example)

प्रत्यापन्न **pratyāpanna** returned

प्रत्यासन्न **pratyāsanna** near, at hand, about

प्रत्युत्पन्न **pratyutpanna** prompt, ready

प्रथम **prathama** first, previously; **prathamam** already

प्रथित **prathita** widely known

प्रदृश् **pra+dṛś (I prapaśyati)** see

प्रदेशः **pradeśaḥ** place, area

प्रद्रु **pra+dru (I pradravati)** run (*p.p. intrans.*)

प्रधान **pradhāna** principal, important, (person) in authority; *ifc.* having as one's authority

प्रबन्धः **prabandhaḥ** (literary) work

प्रबुध् **pra+budh** *caus.* (**prabodhayati**) wake up; inform, admonish

प्रभा **pra+bhā** (II **prabhāti**) shine forth, dawn

प्रभावः **prabhāvaḥ** power

प्रभु **prabhu** *m.* master

प्रभू **pra+bhū** (I **prabhavati**) arise; prevail, have power over, govern (*gen.*)

प्रभूत **prabhūta** numerous, abundant, large

प्रभृति **prabhṛti** *f.* beginning; *ifc.* etc. *etc.*

प्रभृति **prabhṛti** +*abl. or ifc.* (ever) since; **cirāt prabhṛti** [since a long time:] for (so) long

प्रमत्त **pramatta** negligent, inattentive

प्रमाणं **pramāṇaṃ** measure, size; standard of authority, 'judge'

प्रमादः **pramādaḥ** negligence, mishap

प्रमुग्ध **pramugdha** (*p.p. of* **pra+muh**) in a swoon, faint

प्रयत् **pra+yat** (I **prayatate**) strive, exert oneself

प्रयत्नः **prayatnaḥ** effort, attempt

प्रयुज् **pra+yuj** (VII **prayuṅkte**) employ; put into practice; perform (on stage)

प्रयोगः **prayogaḥ** performance (of play)

प्रयोजनं **prayojanaṃ** purpose, motive, need, mission, matter, concern

प्रलप् **pra+lap** (I **pralapati**) talk idly, babble

प्रवातं **pravātaṃ** breeze

प्रवादः **pravādaḥ** talk, report

प्रवासः **pravāsaḥ** travel abroad, journey

प्रवाहः **pravāhaḥ** stream, current

प्रविश् **pra+viś** (VI **praviśati**) enter, go/come in(to)

प्रविश् **pra+viś** *caus.* (**praveśayati**) cause to come in, show in, introduce into

प्रवृत्त **pravṛtta** commenced, under way, in operation, current

प्रवृत्ति **pravṛtti** *f.* news, events, what has been happening

प्रवेशः **praveśaḥ** entry, entering

प्रशंस् **pra+śaṃs (I praśaṃsati)** praise, extol

प्रशस्य **praśasya** praiseworthy, to be admired

प्रशान्त **praśānta** calm

प्रसङ्गः **prasaṅgaḥ** contingency, occasion: **prasaṅga˜taḥ** in passing

प्रसद् **pra+sad (I prasīdati)** become tranquil, be at peace

प्रसन्न **prasanna** tranquil

प्रसवः **prasavaḥ** parturition, childbirth

प्रसादः **prasādaḥ** favour, grace, graciousness; free gift

प्रसादीकृ **prasādī˜kṛ** bestow (as free gift)

प्रसिद्ध **prasiddha** established, recognised

प्रसुप्त **prasupta** *p.p. of* **pra+svap**

प्रसृ **pra+sṛ (I prasarati)** move forward, extend, stretch

प्रस्तावः **prastāvaḥ** prelude

प्रस्था **pra+sthā (I pratiṣṭhate)** set out/off/forth

प्रस्था **pra+sthā** *caus.* **(prasthāpayati)** send off, despatch

प्रस्थानं **prasthānaṃ** departure; system, way

प्रस्वप् **pra+svap (II prasvapiti)** fall asleep

प्रहि **pra+hi (V prahiṇoti)** despatch, send

प्रहृष्ट **prahṛṣṭa** delighted

प्राक् **prāk** previously, before, first(ly); +*abl.* before

प्राकारः **prākāraḥ** rampart, wall

प्राकृत **prākṛta** (*f.* **ā/ī**) of the people, vulgar, common

प्राण् **prāṇ (pra+an) (II prāṇiti)** breathe

प्राणः prāṇaḥ breath; *pl.* life

प्रातराशः prātar:āśaḥ [morning eating:] breakfast

प्रादुर्भू prādur+bhū (prādurbhavati) become manifest, arise

प्राप् prāp (pra+āp) (V prāpnoti) reach, arrive, go to; obtain, win

प्राप् pra+āp *caus.* **(prāpayati)** cause to reach, convey

प्राप्त prāpta obtained, arrived, upon one

प्रायशः prāyaśaḥ, prāyeṇa generally, usually

प्रारब्धं prārabdhaṃ [thing undertaken:] enterprise

प्रार्थ् prārth (pra+arth) (X prārthayate) long for, seek, sue for

प्रार्थना prārthanā longing, desire

प्रार्थयितृ prārthayitṛ suitor

प्रावीण्यं prāvīṇyaṃ proficiency

प्रासादः prāsādaḥ mansion, palace, pavilion; terrace; [upstairs-]room

प्रिय priya dear, dearest, beloved, welcome; *ibc. or ifc.* fond of; *m./f.* sweetheart, loved one

प्रियं priyaṃ benefit, service, blessing

प्रियंवदकः Priyaṃvadakaḥ *pr. n.*

प्रियङ्गु priyaṅgu *m./f. a type of creeper*

प्रियसखी priya:sakhī [dear] friend

प्रीतिमन्त् prīti˜mant full of joy or affection, glad

प्रेक्ष् prekṣ (pra+īkṣ) (I prekṣate) see, discern

प्रेमन् preman *m./n.* affection

प्रेयांस् preyāṃs dearer; *m.* loved one, lover

प्रेर् prer (pra+īr) *caus.* **(prerayati)** drive on, impel, stir

प्रेष् preṣ (pra+iṣ) *caus.* **(preṣayati)** despatch, send

प्रेषणं preṣaṇaṃ sending

प्रौढ **prauḍha** full-grown

फलं **phalaṃ** fruit, reward, recompense, advantage

फलकं **phalakaṃ** board, bench, table

बकुलः **bakulaḥ** *a type of tree*; **bakulaṃ** bakula-tree blossom

बटु **baṭu** *m.* young brahmin (student); fellow (*contemptuously*)

बत **bata** *enclitic* alas!

बन्ध् **bandh** (IX **badhnāti**) tie, bind, fix; enter into (friendship or hate)

बन्धु **bandhu** *m.* kinsman

बर्ह **barha** *m./n.* (peacock's) tail-feather

बलं **balaṃ** force, strength; *sg./pl.* (military) forces; **balāt** forcibly

बलवन्त् **bala˜vant** possessing strength, strong; **balavat** strongly, extremely

बलिन् **balin** possessing strength, strong

बहिः **bahiḥ** outside

बहु **bahu** much, many; +**man (bahu manyate)** think much of, esteem highly

बहुमानः **bahu:mānaḥ** high esteem, respect

बहुवचनं **bahu-vacanaṃ** (*gram.*) plural (number)

बहुशः **bahu˜śaḥ** many times, often

बाणः **bāṇaḥ** arrow

बाधा **bādhā** molestation, damage

बाल **bāla** young; *m.* boy, child; *f.* girl, child

बाहुल्यं **bāhulyaṃ** abundance, multitude

बाह्य **bāhya** external

बिसं **bisaṃ** lotus fibre

बीभत्स **bībhatsa** repulsive, foul; *n.* repulsiveness

बुद्धरक्षिता **Buddharakṣitā** *pr. n.*

बुद्धि **buddhi** *f.* intelligence, mind

बुद्धिमन्त् **buddhi˘mant** possessing intelligence, sentient

बुध् **budh** (I **bodhati/bodhate**, IV **budhyate**) awake, perceive, learn

बोधिसत्त्वः **bodhi:sattvaḥ** [whose essence is enlightenment:] Buddhist saint in the final stage of enlightenment

ब्रह्मचारिन् **brahmacārin** student

ब्रह्मन् **brahman** *n.* spirituality, (religious) chastity

ब्राह्मणः **brāhmaṇaḥ** brahmin

ब्रू **brū** (II **bravīti**) say, tell, speak

भक्तं **bhaktaṃ** food

भक्ति **bhakti** *f.* devotion, loyalty

भगवन्त् **bhagavant** reverend, revered, venerable, blessed; *m.* His Reverence, Reverend Sir, *f.* (**bhagavatī**) Her Reverence

भग्न **bhagna** *p.p. of* **bhañj**

भङ्गः **bhaṅgaḥ** breaking; plucking (of buds); dispersal (of crowds)

भञ्ज् **bhañj** (VII **bhanakti**) break, shatter

भञ्जनं **bhañjanaṃ** breaking

भट्टः **bhaṭṭaḥ** lord, master, learned man

भद्र **bhadra** good, dear; *voc.* **bhadra** my good man, **bhadre** dear lady, madam

भयं **bhayaṃ** fear, danger

भरतः **bharataḥ** actor, player

भरतः **Bharataḥ** *pr. n.*

भर्तृ **bhartṛ** *m.* [supporter:] master; husband

भर्तृदारिका **bhartṛ-dārikā** [daughter of (my) master:] mistress

भवती **bhavatī** *f. of* **bhavant**

भवतु **bhavatu** [let it be:] right then!

भवनं **bhavanaṃ** house, home; [house (of king):] palace

भवन्त् **bhavant** *pres. part. of* **bhū**

भवन्त् **bhavant** *m.*, **bhavatī** *f.* you (*politely*), you sir *etc.*

भवेत **bhavet** (*3rd sg. para. opt. of* **bhū**) might be

भागः **bhāgaḥ** division, portion, allotment, tithe

भागुरायणः **Bhāgurāyaṇaḥ** *pr. n.*

भाजनं **bhājanaṃ** receptacle, box

भाण्डं **bhāṇḍaṃ** box

भारः **bhāraḥ** burden, load, luggage

भारिक **bhārika** burdensome

भार्या **bhāryā** wife

भावः **bhāvaḥ** state of being; essence, meaning, implication; emotional state, emotion

भाविन **bhāvin** future, imminent

भास्वरकः **Bhāsvarakaḥ** *pr. n.*

भिक्षा **bhikṣā** alms

भित्ति **bhitti** *f.* wall

भिद् **bhid** (VII **bhinatti**) split, separate

भिन्न **bhinna** split, open, different; **bhinn›:ârtha** with open meaning, plain

भीत **bhīta** afraid

भीरु **bhīru** fearful

भू **bhū** (I **bhavati**) become, be; arise, happen; *expresses* 'have, get' *etc.*

भू **bhū** *f.* earth

भूत् **bhūt** *3rd sg. injunctive of* **bhū**

भूत **bhūta** having become, being

भूमि **bhūmi** *f.* ground; fit object (for); **parityāga-bhūmi** suitable recipient (of)

भूमिपालः **bhūmi-pālaḥ** king, ruler

भूयांस् **bhūyāṃs** more, further

भूरिवसु **Bhūrivasu** *m., pr. n.*

भूषणं **bhūṣaṇaṃ** ornament

भृ **bhṛ** (I **bharati**, III **bibharti**) bear, support

भृत्यः **bhṛtyaḥ** servant

भेदः **bhedaḥ** division, separation, variety

भैष्ट **bhaiṣṭa** *2nd pl. para. injunctive of* **bhī** 'fear'

भोः **bhoḥ** oh! ho!; **bho bhoḥ** ho there!

भोगः **bhogaḥ** enjoyment

भोगिन् **bhogin** serpent; the number eight

भोजनं **bhojanaṃ** food

भ्रंशः **bhraṃśaḥ** fall, decline

भ्रम् **bhram** (I **bhramati**) wander, be confused

भ्रातृ **bhrātṛ** *m.* brother

मंस्थाः **maṃsthāḥ** *2nd sg. ātm. injunctive of* **man**

मकरन्दः **Makarandaḥ** *pr. n.*

मघवन्त् **Maghavant** *m. irreg.* (*gen. sg.* **Maghonaḥ**) *name of Indra*

मङ्गलं **maṅgalaṃ** welfare, good luck, auspicious omen, auspiciousness

मणि **maṇi** *m.* jewel

मण्डप **maṇḍapa** *m./n.* pavilion, bower

मत् **mat** *stem form and abl. sg. of* **aham**

मति **mati** *f.* thought, wit, mind, opinion, notion

मतिमन्त् **mati˜mant** possessing wit, sensible

मत्त **matta** in rut, rutting

मत्तः **mat˜taḥ** from me

मद् **mad (IV mādyati)** rejoice, be intoxicated

मदः **madaḥ** intoxication

मदनः **madanaḥ** love, passion; god of love

मदयन्तिका **Madayantikā** *pr. n.*

मदीय **madīya** my, mine

मधु **madhu** *m.* (season or first month of) spring

मधुकरः **madhukaraḥ, madhukarī** [honey-maker:] bee, honey-bee

मधुर **madhura** sweet

मध्य **madhya** middle; **madhyāt** from the middle of, from among; **madhye** in the middle of, among

मध्यस्थ **madhya-stha** [mid-standing:] neutral

मन् **man (IV manyate)** think, suppose, regard (as), esteem, approve

मन् **man** *caus.* **(mānayati)** esteem, honour

मनस् **manas** *n.* mind, heart, intelligence

मनोरथः **manorathaḥ** desire, fancy

मनोवृत्ति **mano-vṛtti** *f.* process of mind, fancy, imagination

मन्त् **˜mant** *possessive suffix*

मन्त्रिन् **mantrin** minister

मन्द **manda** slow, slack, gentle; **mand〈a〉:ādara** careless

मन्दारः **mandāraḥ, mandāra:vṛkṣakaḥ** coral tree

मन्दारिका **Mandārikā** *pr. n.*

मन्दीभू **mandī˜bhū** become slack, slacken

मन्मथः **manmathaḥ** love, god of love

मन्यु **manyu** *m.* passion, anger

मरणं **maraṇaṃ** death, dying

मरीचि **Marīci** *m. name of a sage*

मरु **maru** *m.* desert

मर्त्य **martya** mortal, human

मलयकेतु **Malayaketu** *m., pr. n.*

मषी **maṣī, masī** black powder, ink; **masī-bhājanaṃ** receptacle for ink, ink-pot

महा **mahā** *descriptive stem form of* **mahānt**

महादेवी **mahā:devī** chief queen

महान्त् **mahānt** great, noble, vast, numerous

महामांसं **mahā:māṃsaṃ** [great flesh:] human flesh

महाराजः **mahā:rājaḥ** great king, king

महार्घ्य **mahārghya** valuable

महिमन् **mahiman** *m.* greatness

मही **mahī** earth

महीधरः **mahī-dharaḥ** [earth-supporter:] mountain

महीपति **mahī-pati** *m.* [lord of earth:] king

महेन्द्रः **Mah»:êndraḥ** [great] Indra

महोत्सवः **mah»:ôtsavaḥ** [great] festival, holiday

मा **mā** *prohibitive particle* (do) not *etc.*

मांसं **māṃsaṃ** flesh, meat

मातृ **mātṛ** *f.* mother

मात्रा **mātrā** measure, size; **-mātra** having the size of, mere, only *etc.*

माधवः **Mādhavaḥ** *pr. n.*

माधव्यः **Mādhavyaḥ** *pr. n.*

मानयितव्य **mānayitavya** (*ger. of caus. of* **man**) requiring to be honoured

मानसं **mānasaṃ** [that which is mental:] mind

मानसं **Mānasaṃ** *name of a lake*

मानुषः **mānuṣaḥ** human being, mortal
मामकीन **māmakīna** my, mine
मारीचः **Mārīcaḥ** (Kaśyapa) son of Marīci
मार्गः **mārgaḥ** road, path, way
मालती **Mālatī** *pr. n.*
माला **mālā** garland
मालिनी **Mālinī** *name of river*
माहात्म्यं **māhātmyaṃ** greatness of spirit, generosity
मित्रं **mitraṃ** friend
मिथः **mithaḥ** together, mutually
मिथुनं **mithunaṃ** pair
मिथ्या **mithyā** wrong(ly), improper(ly)
मिश्र **miśra** mixed
मुकुलं **mukulaṃ** bud
मुखं **mukhaṃ** (*f.* ī *when ifc.*) face, mouth, front, forepart
मुखर **mukhara** talkative
मुखरयति **mukharayati** *denom.* make talkative
मुखोच्छ्वासः **mukh›-ôcchvāsaḥ** breath [of the mouth]
मुग्ध **mugdha** naïve, simple
मुद्रयति **mudrayati** *denom.* stamp, seal
मुद्रा **mudrā** seal, stamp, (signet-)ring, [authorising seal:] 'pass'
मुनि **muni** *m.* sage
मुहूर्त **muhūrta** *m./n.* (short) while, 'minute', moment
मूक **mūka** dumb, silent
मूढ **mūḍha** deluded, idiotic; *m.* idiot
मूर्ख **mūrkha** foolish; *m.* fool
मूर्छा **mūrchā** faint, swoon
मूलं **mūlaṃ** root, basis, foundation
मृगः **mṛgaḥ** deer

मृगतृष्णिका mṛgatṛṣṇikā [deer-thirst:] mirage

मृगया mṛgayā hunting, the chase

मृणालवन्त् mṛṇāla˜vant possessing lotus-fibres

मृत mṛta (*p.p. of* mṛ 'die') dead

मृत्युंजयः mṛtyuṃ-jayaḥ Conqueror of Death

मृदु mṛdu soft

मृष् mṛṣ *caus.* (**marṣayati**) overlook, excuse

मृषा mṛṣā vainly

मेधा **medhā** mental power, intellect

मेध्य **medhya** fit for sacrifice, sacrificial

मेनका **Menakā** *pr. n.*

मेना **Menā** *pr. n.*

मेने **mene** *3rd sg. ātm. perf. of* **man**

मैथिल **Maithila** belonging to Mithilā; *m.* king of Mithilā

मोहः **mohaḥ** delusion

म्लेच्छः **mlecchaḥ** barbarian

म्लै **mlai** (**I mlāyati**) fade, wither

यः **yaḥ, ya-kāraḥ** the letter **y**; (*prosody*) the syllables ⏑ – –

यः **yaḥ** *rel. pron.* who, which, that; *n. sg.* **yat** that, in that, inasmuch as *etc.* (*Chapters 11 to 13*)

यः कश्चित् **yaḥ kaś cit** whoever

यतः **yataḥ** *rel. adv.* from which, since *etc.*

यति **yati** *f.* (*prosody*) caesura

यत्नः **yatnaḥ** effort

यत्र **yatra** *rel. adv.* in which, where

यत्सत्यम् **yat satyam** [what is true:] truth to tell, in truth

यथा **yathā** *rel. adv.* in the way that, as; so that *etc.*; **yathā yathā . . . tathā tathā** in proportion as, the more that

यथा yathā *ibc.* as, according to, in conformity with

यथावत् **yathāvat** exactly, properly

यदा yadā *rel. adv.* when; **yad» aîva** as soon as

यदि yadi *rel. adv.* if, whether; **yady api** even if, though

यमः yamaḥ twin

यमज yamaja twin[-born]

या yā (II yāti) go

या yā *caus.* (yāpayati) spend (time)

याचितृ yācitṛ (*from* yāc 'solicit') suer, petitioner

यात्रा yātrā procession

यादृश yādṛśa (*f.* ī) *rel. adj.* of which kind, such as, just as

यामः yāmaḥ night watch (of three hours)

यावत् yāvat *connective particle* [during which time:] (I'll) just

यावत् yāvat +*acc.* until, up to; *ibc.* throughout

यावत् yāvat *rel. adv.* for as long as, while, until; **yāvat+na** before

यावन्त् yāvant *rel. adj.* as much as

युक्त yukta proper, right

युक्ति yukti *f.* argument

युगं yugaṃ pair; *ifc.* two

युज् yuj joined, even (in number); **a:yuj** uneven, odd

युत yuta united, equipped with

युष्मत् yuṣmat *pl. stem form and abl. pl. of* tvam

युष्मदीय yuṣmadīya belonging to you (*pl.*)

युष्माकम् yuṣmākam of you (*pl.*), your, of yours

योगः yogaḥ use, application, managing; magical art; system of meditation

योग्य yogya suitable

र: रेफः **raḥ, rephaḥ** the letter **r**; (*prosody*) the syllables – ᴗ –

रंहस् **raṃhas** *n.* speed

रक्ष् **rakṣ (I rakṣati)** protect, save, guard, hold

रक्षणं **rakṣaṇam** protection, defending

रक्षस **rakṣas** *n.* devil

रक्षितृ **rakṣitṛ** protector, guard

रचित **racita** placed

रति **rati** *f.* pleasure, lovemaking, love

रत्नं **ratnaṃ** jewel, gem

रथ्या **rathyā (rathaḥ** carriage) [carriage-]road, street

रमणीय **ramaṇīya** pleasant, attractive, lovely, delightful

रम्य **ramya** attractive

रश्मि **raśmi** *m.* rein, bridle

रसः **rasaḥ** juice, liquid; flavour, taste

रहस् **rahas** *n.* solitude, secrecy; **rahasi** in secret, secretly

रहस्य **rahasya** secret

राक्षसः **Rākṣasaḥ** *pr. n.*

रागः **rāgaḥ** passion; redness; musical mood

राजकन्या **rāja-kanyā** princess

राजकार्यं **rāja-kāryaṃ** [king's business:] state administration

राजन् **rājan** *m.* king, prince, chieftain; *voc.* sire

राजपुत्रः **rāja-putraḥ** king's son, prince

राजभवनं **rāja-bhavanaṃ** palace

राजलोकः **rāja-lokaḥ** [company of] kings or princes

राज्यं **rājyaṃ** kingdom, state; kingship, reign

रात्रः **rātraḥ** *at end of cpd. for* **rātri** *f.* night

रामः **Rāmaḥ** *pr. n.*

रामणीयकं **rāmaṇīyakaṃ** loveliness, delightful aspect

रामायणं **Rāmāyaṇam** *name of an epic poem*

राशि **rāśi** *m.* heap

रिपु **ripu** *m.* enemy

रुध् **rudh** (VII **ruṇaddhi**) obstruct

रुह् **ruh** (I **rohati**) rise, grow

रुह् **ruh** *caus.* (**rohayati/ropayati**) raise, grow

रूपं **rūpam** form; beauty, looks

रूपकं **rūpakam** (*lit. crit.*) metaphor

रेफः **rephaḥ** *see* **raḥ**

रैवतकः **Raivatakaḥ** *pr. n.*

लक्ष् **lakṣ** (X **lakṣayati**) notice

लक्षणं **lakṣaṇam** characteristic, (auspicious) mark; definition

लक्ष्मणः **Lakṣmaṇaḥ** *pr. n.*

लघु **laghu** light; brief

लज्ज् **lajj** (VI **lajjate**) be embarrassed, blush, show confusion

लज्ज् **lajj** *caus.* (**lajjayati**) embarrass

लज्जा **lajjā** shame, embarrassment, shyness

लज्जाकर **lajjā-kara** (*f.* **ī**) embarrassing

लण्ड्र **Laṇḍra** London

लता **latā** creeper, vine

लभ् **labh** (I **labhate**) take, gain, win, get, obtain, find

लभ् **labh** *caus.* (**lambhayati**) cause to take, give

लवः **lavaḥ** fragment; **lavaśo lavaśaḥ** piece by piece

लवः **Lavaḥ** *pr. n.*

लवङ्गिका **Lavaṅgikā** *pr. n.*

लाघवं **lāghavam** lightness, levity, [light treatment of a guru:] disrespect

लातव्यः **Lātavyaḥ** *pr. n.*

लाभः **lābhaḥ** getting, winning, acquisition; profit

लिख् **likh (VI likhati)** write

लिङ्गं **liṅgaṃ** mark, sign; phallus; (*gram.*) gender

लीला **līlā** play, sport

लेखः **lekhaḥ** letter, document

लोकः **lokaḥ** world, people

लोचनं **locanaṃ** eye

लोपामुद्रा **Lopāmudrā** *pr. n.*

लोभः **lobhaḥ** greed

लोमन् **loman** *n.* hair (on body)

वंशः **vaṃśaḥ** lineage, dynasty, race

वच् **vac (II vakti)** tell, say, state, express, declare, speak of, describe, speak to, address

वचनं **vacanaṃ** saying, statement, speech, word; **-vacanāt** [from the statement of:] in the name of

वचस् **vacas** *n.* word, words, speech

वज्र **vajra** *m./n.* thunderbolt, diamond, hard substance

वञ्चना **vañcanā** cheating, trick

वणिज् **vaṇij (vaṇik)** *m.* businessman, trader

वत् **˜vat (*n. sg. of* vant)** like, as, in accordance with

वतंसः **vataṃsaḥ, vataṃsakaḥ** ornament, *esp.* earring

वत्सः **vatsaḥ** calf; dear child

वत्सल **vatsala** affectionate, loving

वद् **vad (I vadati)** say, speak, tell

वदनं **vadanaṃ** mouth, face

वधः **vadhaḥ** killing, death

वधू **vadhū** *f.* woman, bride

वध्य **vadhya** [due to be executed:] condemned to death

वनं **vanaṃ** forest, jungle, wood, grove; **vana-mālā** [jungle-garland:] garland of wild flowers

वनस्पति **vanaspati** *m.* [lord of the jungle:] (forest) tree

वनेचरः **vanecaraḥ** forest-dweller

वन्त् **˜vant** *possessive suffix*

वन्द् **vand (I vandate)** venerate, worship

वन्ध्य **vandhya** barren

वयम् **vayam** (*nom. pl. of* **aham**) we *etc.*

वयस् **vayas** *n.* vigour, youth; age (in general)

वयस्यः **vayasyaḥ** [one of same age:] friend

वरं **varaṃ** a preferable thing, better

वरः **varaḥ** suitor

वराक **varāka** (*f.* **ī**) wretched, pitiable, 'poor'

वर्गः **vargaḥ** group

वर्ण् **varṇ (X varṇayati)** depict, describe

वर्णः **varṇaḥ** colour, appearance; social class

वर्त्मन् **vartman** *n.* track, path, way

वर्षः **varṣaḥ** rain; year

वलय **valaya** *m./n.* bracelet; circle, enclosure

वल्कल **valkala** *m./n.* bark (of tree), bark-dress (worn by ascetic)

वल्लभ **vallabha** beloved; *m.* sweetheart

वशः **vaśaḥ** power; **-vaśāt** from the power of, because of

वस् **vas (I vasati)** dwell, live (in)

वसनं **vasanaṃ** dress

वसिष्ठः **Vasiṣṭhaḥ** *pr. n.*

वसुंधरा **Vasuṃdharā** *pr. n.*

वस्तु **vastu** *n.* thing, matter, substance; **vastu-vṛttam** [what has happened in substance:] the facts

वह् **vah (I vahati)** carry, take, marry

वा vā *enclitic* or; . . . vā . . . vā either . . . or . . .; **na vā** or not; **na . . . na vā** not . . . nor

वाक्यं **vākyaṃ** statement, utterance, sentence

वाच् **vāc** *f.* speech, words

वातः **vātaḥ** wind

वादिन् **vādin** speaking, talking

वामदेवः **Vāmadevaḥ** *pr. n.*

वायु **vāyu** *m.* wind

वारि **vāri** *n.* water

वारुण **Vāruṇa** (*f.* ī) deriving from the god Varuṇa

वार्त्ता **vārttā** news

वाल्मीकि **Vālmīki** *m.*, *pr. n.*

वास् **vās (X vāsayati)** perfume

वासः **vāsaḥ** dwelling, living

वासवः **Vāsavaḥ** (Indra) chief of the Vasus

वासिन् **vāsin** living in, dweller

वाहिन् **vāhin** carrier

विकस् **vi+kas (I vikasati)** burst, blossom, bloom

विकारः **vikāraḥ** transformation; mental disturbance; *ifc.* made out of

विकृ **vi+kṛ (VIII vikaroti)** alter, change, distort, mentally disturb

विक्रमः **vikramaḥ** valour

विक्रम्य **vikramya** (*absol. of* **vi+kram**) after attacking, by force

विक्री **vi+krī (IX vikrīṇīte)** sell to (*loc.*)

विक्रेतृ **vikretṛ** vendor

विक्लव: **viklava** bewildered, distressed

विग्रहः **vigrahaḥ** separation; body

विघट् **vi+ghaṭ (I vighaṭate)** become separated

विघातः vighātaḥ destruction, elimination

विघ्नः vighnaḥ obstacle, hindrance

विचर् vi+car (I **vicarati**) move about, roam

विचर् vi+car *caus.* (**vicārayati**) deliberate, ponder

विचारः vicāraḥ pondering, thought

विचित्र **vicitra** variegated, various, wonderful

विचिन्त् **vi+cint** (X **vicintayati**) consider, think of, reflect

विजया **Vijayā** *pr. n.*

विज्ञा **vi+jñā** (IX **vijānāti**) find out, discern, understand, know

विज्ञा **vi+jñā** *caus.* (**vijñāpayati**) say politely, request, beg, beg to say/tell

विज्ञापना **vijñāpanā** request

विटप **viṭapa** *m./n.* branch, bush, thicket

वितर्कः **vitarkaḥ** conjecture, doubt

वितॄ **vi+tṝ** (I **vitarati**) grant, bestow

विद् **vid** (II **vetti**) know, learn, discover

विद् **vid** (VI **vindati**) find, acquire, possess; *pass.* **vidyate** is found, exists

विद् **-vid** *ifc.* knowing, learned in

विदग्ध **vidagdha** skilful, clever

विद्या **vidyā** learning, science

विद्रु **vi+dru** *caus.* (**vidrāvayati**) chase away, disperse

विद्वांस् **vidvāṃs** (*perf. part. of* **vid**) learned, wise

विधा **vi+dhā** (III **vidadhāti**) arrange, manage, provide for (something)

विधा **vidhā** kind, sort; *ifc.* of the same sort as, such as

विधानं **vidhānaṃ** arrangement

विधि **vidhi** *m.* injunction (*esp. of ritual*); **vidhi˜vat** according to [the injunction of] ritual

विध्वंस् **vi+dhvaṃs** (I **vidhvaṃsate**) fall to pieces, shatter

विनयः **vinayaḥ** discipline, good breeding

विनश् **vi+naś** (IV **vinaśyati**) perish, die; *caus.* (**vināś-ayati**) destroy

विनष्ट **vinaṣṭa** *p.p. of* **vi+naś**

विना **vinā** *+instr.* without

विनाशः **vināśaḥ** destruction

विनीत **vinīta** disciplined, well bred, modest

विनुद् **vi+nud** *caus.* (**vinodayati**) divert, distract

विपरीत **viparīta** inverted, reverse, opposite

विपिनं **vipinaṃ** forest

विप्रकृ **vi+pra+kṛ** (VIII **viprakaroti**) injure, torment

विप्रतिपन्न **vipratipanna** perplexed, uncertain

विप्रलभ् **vi+pra+labh** (I **vipralabhate**) mislead, deceive

विभागः **vibhāgaḥ** part, portion

विभु **vibhu** powerful *esp. as epithet of Śiva*

विभू **vi+bhū** *caus.* (**vibhāvayati**) make manifest; perceive distinctly, detect

विभूति **vibhūti** *f.* splendour, wealth; *pl.* riches

विमनस् **vi:manas** despondent

विमर्दः **vimardaḥ** conflict

विमर्शः **vimarśaḥ** deliberation, doubt

विमुच् **vi+muc** (VI **vimuñcati**) release, loose

विमृश् **vi+mṛś** (VI **vimṛśati**) perceive, reflect, deliberate

वियुज् **vi+yuj** (VII **viyuṅkte**) disjoin, separate, deprive of (*instr.*)

विरच् **vi+rac** (X **viracayati**) construct, fashion, work

विरहित **virahita** separated, bereft

विराज् vi+rāj (I **virājati**) gleam, shine out; **virājant** *pres. part.* gleaming out

विलक्ष **vilakṣa** disconcerted, ashamed

विलम्बः **vilambaḥ** delay

विलासः **vilāsaḥ** coquetry, playful movement

विलोक् vi+lok *caus.* (**vilokayati**) look at, watch

विलोल **vilola** unsteady, tremulous

विवक्षित **vivakṣita** (*p.p. of desiderative* **vivakṣati**) wished to be said, meant

विवस्वन्त् **vivasvant** *m.* [the Shining One:] sun

विवादः **vivādaḥ** disagreement, dispute

विवाहः **vivāhaḥ** wedding

विविध **vi:vidha** of various kinds

विवेकः **vivekaḥ** discrimination

विशेषः **viśeṣaḥ** distinction; *ifc.* a particular —, a special —; **viśeṣa˜taḥ** in particular

विशेषणपदं **viśeṣaṇa:padaṃ** [distinguishing word:] epithet

विशोक **vi:śoka** free from sorrow, at ease

विश्रम् vi+śram (IV **viśrāmyati**) rest, cease, take a rest

विश्रम्भः **viśrambhaḥ** confidence; **viśrambha-kathā/kathitaṃ** confidential or intimate conversation

विश्रान्त **viśrānta** *p.p. of* vi+śram

विश्रामः **viśrāmaḥ** rest, respite

विश्रुत **viśruta** widely heard of, known, famous

विश्लेषः **viśleṣaḥ** separation, estrangement

विश्वं **viśvaṃ** the whole world, universe

विश्वात्मन् **viśv›-ātman** *m.* Soul of the Universe, Supreme Godhead

विषं **viṣaṃ** poison

विषम **viṣama** uneven

विषयः **viṣayaḥ** dominion, sphere, field of action

विषादः **viṣādaḥ** despair, dejection, disappointment, distress

विष्णुगुप्तः **Viṣṇuguptaḥ** *pr. n.*

विष्णुशर्मन् **Viṣṇuśarman** *m., pr. n.*

विसृज् **vi+sṛj** (VI **visṛjati**) discharge, release, dismiss

विसृज् **vi+sṛj** *caus.* (**visarjayati**) release, dismiss, bid farewell to

विसृप् **vi+sṛp** (I **visarpati**) be diffused, spread, glide

विस्तरः **vistaraḥ** expansion, prolixity; **vistara˜taḥ** at length, in detail

विस्तीर्ण **vistīrṇa** extensive

विस्मयः **vismayaḥ** astonishment

विस्मित **vismita** astonished

विस्मृ **vi+smṛ** (I **vismarati**) forget

विहगः **vihagaḥ** bird

विहत **vihata** (*p.p. of* **vi+han**) struck, broken

विहस्त **vi⁚hasta** [with hands awry:] clumsy

विहाय **vihāya** [having left behind:] beyond (*acc.*)

विहारः **vihāraḥ** (Buddhist) monastery/convent

विहारिन् **vihārin** roaming

विहित **vihita** *p.p. of* **vi+dhā**

विह्वल **vihvala** tottering, unsteady

वीक्ष् **vīkṣ** (**vi+īkṣ**) (I **vīkṣate**) discern, spy, scrutinize

वीज् **vīj** (X **vījayate**) fan

वीथिका **vīthikā** row, grove

वृक्षः वृक्षकः **vṛkṣaḥ, vṛkṣakaḥ** tree

वृत् **vṛt (I vartate)** proceed, currently exist, abide, happen; (*of promises etc.*) be entered upon

वृत **vṛta** (*p.p. of* **vṛ**) chosen, preferred, asked in marriage

वृत्त **vṛtta** (*p.p. of* **vṛt**) happened *etc.*

वृत्तं **vṛttaṃ** metre; **vṛtta-ratnākaraḥ** 'Treasury of Metres'

वृत्तान्तः **vṛttāntaḥ** news, what has happened, 'scene', 'story'

वृत्ति **vṛtti** *f.* behaviour, conduct; (*gram.*) synthetic expression (*i.e. by cpds.*)

वृध् **vṛdh (I vardhate)** grow; + **diṣṭyā** be congratulated

वृध् **vṛdh** *caus.* **(vardhayati)** increase (*trans.*); +**diṣṭyā** congratulate

वृषलः **Vṛṣalaḥ** *pr. n.*

वृष्टि **vṛṣṭi** *f.* rain

वेगः **vegaḥ** haste, speed

वेणु **veṇu** *m.* bamboo, reed; flute

वेतसः वेत्र **vetasaḥ, vetra** *m./n.* reed, cane

वेदः **vedaḥ** (*from* **vid**) knowledge, sacred knowledge, scripture

वेदना **vedanā** ache, pain, pang

वेदिका **vedikā** balcony

वेदिन् **vedin** knowing, conscious (of), appreciative

वेदी **vedī** (sacrificial) altar

वेला **velā** boundary; shore; time (of day)

वेश्मन् **veśman** *n.* residence, house, *etc.*

वेषः **veṣaḥ** dress, attire

वैक्लव्यं **vaiklavyaṃ** **(viklava)** bewilderment, despondency

वैखानसः **vaikhānasaḥ** hermit, anchorite

वैतालिकः **vaitālikaḥ** (royal) bard

वैदग्ध्यं **vaidagdhyaṃ (vidagdha)** cleverness (*esp.* verbal dexterity)

वैदेह **Vaideha** (*f.* **ī**) belonging to (the country of) Videha; *m.* King of Videha; *f.* Queen/Princess of Videha

वैद्य **vaidya** learned; *m.* physician, doctor

वैधेय **vaidheya** foolish; *m.* fool

वैनतेयः **Vaiṇateyaḥ** [Vinatā's son:] Garuḍa (King of the Birds)

वैमनस्यं **vaimanasyaṃ** despondency

वैरं **vairaṃ** hostility

वैरोधकः **Vairodhakaḥ** *pr. n.*

वैवाहिक **vaivāhika** (*f.* **ī**) (suitable) for a wedding

वैहीनरि **Vaihīnari** *m., pr. n.*

वोढृ **voḍhṛ** *m.* bridegroom

व्यक्त **vyakta** clear, obvious

व्यग्र **vyagra** engrossed, intent

व्यञ्जनं **vyañjanaṃ** sign, indication; insignia, disguise

व्यतिकरः **vyatikaraḥ (kṝ** 'mix') blending together, confluence, 'expanse'

व्यतिरेकिन् **vyatirekin** differing, distinct

व्यपदेशः **vyapadeśaḥ** designation, name

व्यभिचारः **vyabhicāraḥ** deviation, swerving

व्यभिचारिन् **vyabhicārin** liable to deviate, swerving

व्यभ्र **vy-abhra** cloudless

व्ययः **vyayaḥ** loss; expense, extravagance

व्यवसो **vyavaso (vi+ava+so)** (IV **vyavasyati** *p.p.* **vyavasita**) decide, resolve

व्यवहारः **vyavahāraḥ** dealings, usage; litigation

व्यवहृ **vyavahṛ (vi+ava+hṛ) (I vyavaharati)** act, deal with, behave towards (*loc.*)

व्यसनं **vyasanaṃ** vice, vicious failing, weakness, deficiency; misfortune, misery

व्याघ्रः **vyāghraḥ** tiger

व्याजः **vyājaḥ** fraud, pretence

व्यापद् **vyā+pad** *caus.* **(vyāpādāyati)** [cause to perish:] kill, slay

व्यापारः **vyāpāraḥ** occupation

व्यापॄ **vyā+pṝ** *caus.* **(vyāpārayati)** set to work, employ

व्यावृत् **vyā+vṛt** *caus.* **(vyāvartayati)** cause to turn back, drive back

व्रतं **vrataṃ** vow; *ifc.* [having as one's vow:] devoted to

व्रीहि **vrīhi** *m.* rice

शः **˜śaḥ** *distributive suffix*: **eka˜śaḥ** in ones, singly; **lava˜śaḥ** in pieces

शंस् **śaṃs (I śaṃsati)** praise, proclaim

शंसिन् **śaṃsin** proclaiming

शक् **śak (V śaknoti)** be able, 'can'

शकटदासः **Śakaṭadāsaḥ** *pr. n.*

शकुनि **śakuni** *m.* bird

शकुन्तला **Śakuntalā** *pr. n.*

शक्ति **śakti** *f.* ability, power

शक्य **śakya** possible, able to be

शङ्का **śaṅkā** suspicion, fear, anxiety, care

शची **Śacī** *name of Indra's wife*

शठ **śaṭha** cunning

शतं **śataṃ** a hundred

शतक्रतु **Śatakratu** *m. name of Indra*

शतगुण **śata-guṇa** hundredfold; **śataguṇayati** *denom.* multiply by a hundred

शत्रु **śatru** *m.* enemy

शनैः **śanaiḥ** quietly, gently; **śanaiḥ śanaiḥ** very gently

शब्दः **śabdaḥ** sound, noise; word

शम् **śam** *caus.* (**śamayati**) quieten, appease

शयनं **śayanaṃ** (**śī** 'lie') repose, sleeping; **śayana-gṛhaṃ** sleeping-quarters, bedchamber

शरः **śaraḥ** arrow

शरणं **śaraṇaṃ** shelter, refuge

शरद् **śarad** *f.* autumn

शरीरं **śarīraṃ** body, 'person'

शशिन् **śaśin** *m.* moon

शस्त्रं **śastraṃ** knife, sword, weapon

शाकुन्तलेय **Śākuntaleya** born of Śakuntalā

शाखा **śākhā** branch

शापः **śāpaḥ** curse

शार्ङ्गरवः **Śārṅgaravaḥ** *pr. n.*

शार्दूलः **śārdūlaḥ** tiger

शालः **śālaḥ** sal tree

शाला **śālā** hall, apartment

शाश्वत **śāśvata** (*f.* **ī**) perpetual

शास् **śās** (II **śāsti**) govern, teach

शासनं **śāsanaṃ** command

शास्त्रं **śāstraṃ** (technical) treatise, law-book

शिखर **śikhara** *m./n.* point, tip

शिखा **śikhā** crest

शिथिल **śithila** loose, slack

शिरस् **śiras** *n.* head

शिवः **Śivaḥ** *name of a god*

शिशिर **śiśira** cold

शिशु **śiśu** *m.* child

शिष्ट **śiṣṭa** (*p.p. of* **śās**) learned; **śiṣṭ-ânadhyayanaṃ** holiday in honour of learned (guests)

शिष्यः **śiṣyaḥ** [one requiring to be taught:] pupil

शीघ्र **śīghra** swift, fast

शीतल **śītala** cool

शीर्षं **śīrṣaṃ** head

शुच् **śuc** (I **śocati**) grieve, mourn

शुचि **śuci** pure, clean

शुद्धान्तः **śuddhāntaḥ** women's apartments, household

शुभ **śubha** auspicious

शुश्रूषा **śuśrūṣā** (*desiderative of* **śru**) desire to hear/learn

शून्य **śūnya** empty, devoid (of), deserted, desolate

शूल **śūla** *m./n.* stake, spit, lance, trident (*of Śiva*); **śūlam āruh** *caus.* [cause to mount the stake:] impale

शूलिन् **śūlin** Trident-bearer (*epithet of Śiva*)

शृगालः **śṛgālaḥ** jackal

शेषः **śeṣaḥ** remainder, portion to be supplied

शैलः **śailaḥ** mountain

शोकः **śokaḥ** grief, sadness

शोचनीय **śocanīya, śocya** (*ger. of* **śuc**) to be mourned for, pitiable, lamentable

शोणोत्तरा **Śoṇottarā** *pr. n.*

शोभन **śobhana** shining, bright, beautiful

शोभा **śobhā** brilliance, beauty

श्मशानं **śmaśānaṃ** burning ground, cemetery

श्याम **śyāma, śyāmala** dark

श्रद्धा **śrad+dhā** (III **śraddhatte**) put trust in, believe

श्रमः **śramaḥ** exertion

श्रवणं **śravaṇaṃ** hearing

श्रवणः **śravaṇaḥ** ear

श्रान्त **śrānta** (*p.p. of* **śram** 'tire') tired

श्रावकः **śrāvakaḥ** Buddhist disciple, student

श्रीपर्वतः **Śrīparvataḥ** *name of a mountain*

श्रु **śru** (V **śṛṇoti**) hear, listen to

श्रेयांस **śreyāṃs** better; *n. sg.* **śreyas** welfare, blessing

श्रेष्ठ **śreṣṭha** best, supreme

श्रेष्ठिन् **śreṣṭhin** *m.* eminent businessman, merchant

श्रोतृ **śrotṛ** listener, someone to listen

श्रोत्रं **śrotraṃ** (organ *or* act of) hearing

श्रोत्रियः **śrotriyaḥ** learned (brahmin), scholar

श्रौत **śrauta** (*f.* **ī/ā**) deriving from scripture, scriptural

श्लाघ्य **ślāghya** praiseworthy, virtuous

श्लोकः **ślokaḥ** stanza

श्वः **śvaḥ** *adv.* tomorrow

श्वपाकः **śvapākaḥ** outcaste

श्वापद **śvāpada** *m./n.* beast of prey, 'big game'

षष **ṣaṣ** (**ṣaṭ**) six

षोडश **ṣoḍaśa(n)** sixteen

स **sa** *prefix* co-, fellow-; having (with one), accompanied by, possessing, sharing *etc.*

सः **saḥ** *pron.* that, the, that one, he *etc.*; **saḥ+eva** just that, that very, the same

सं सम् **saṃ, sam**[1] *verbal prefix* together *etc.*

संयम् **saṃ+yam** (I **saṃyacchati**) restrain, arrest

[1] **sam** is the basic form, but for brevity in the following entries **saṃ+yam** is written instead of **saṃyam** (**sam+yam**) and so forth.

संयमनं **saṃyamanaṃ** restraint, tightening

संयुत **saṃyuta** joined

संवद् **saṃ+vad (I saṃvadati)** accord, fit

संवरणं **saṃvaraṇaṃ** covering up, duplicity

संविग्न **saṃvigna** agitated, overwhelmed

संवृत्त **saṃvṛtta** (*p.p. of* **sam+vṛt**) become, turned into *etc.*

संवृध् **saṃ+vṛdh** *caus.* **(saṃvardhayati)** congratulate

संवेगः **saṃvegaḥ** agitation

संव्यवहारः **saṃvyavahāraḥ** transaction

संस्कारः **saṃskāraḥ** preparation, adornment

संस्तम्भ् **saṃ+stambh (IX saṃstabhnāti)** make firm, sustain, compose

संस्तरणं **saṃstaraṇaṃ** strewing

संस्तु **saṃ+stu (II saṃstauti)** praise

संस्थित **saṃsthita** standing, remaining, steady

सकल **sakala** whole

सकाशम् **sakāśam** [to the presence of:] to

सखि **sakhi** *m.* (*irreg.*) comrade, friend; *voc.* **sakhe** (my) friend, my dear—*etc.*

सखी **sakhī** (female) friend, wife of friend; *voc.* **sakhi** my dear *etc.*

संकल्पनिर्मित **saṃkalpa-nirmita** [created by conception:] imagined

संकुल **saṃkula** crowded, thronged; *n.* throng

संकेतः **saṃketaḥ** agreement, assignation; **saṃketa-sthānaṃ** place of assignation

संक्षिप्त **saṃkṣipta** abbreviated, in concise form

संक्षेपः **saṃkṣepaḥ** abridgement, conciseness

संख्या **saṃ+khyā (II saṃkhyāti)** count, reckon up

संख्या **saṃkhyā** number, numeral

संगम् **saṃ+gam (I saṃgacchate)** come together, agree, fit

सचिवः **sacivaḥ** counsellor, minister

सज्ज **sajja** prepared, equipped

सज्जीभू **sajjī˘bhū (I sajjībhavati)** become prepared, prepare

संचयः **saṃcayaḥ** collection, quantity

संचर् **saṃ+car (I saṃcarate)** walk, stroll

संचारः **saṃcāraḥ** movement

संचारिन् **saṃcārin** going together, transitory; **saṃcārī bhāvaḥ** (*lit. crit.*) Subsidiary Emotional State

संजन् **saṃ+jan (IV saṃjāyate)** come into being, be aroused

संज्ञा **saṃjñā** signal

सत्कारः **satkāraḥ** honouring, hospitality, entertainment

सत्कृ **sat˘kṛ (VIII satkaroti)** honour; receive with hospitality, entertain

सत्त्वं **sattvaṃ** being, essence; creature

सत्य **satya** true, real; **satyam** truly, really; **satyaṃ** truth

सत्यसंध **satya‿saṃdha** [whose compact is true:] true to one's word

सत्वर **sa_tvara** full of haste, busy

सद् **sad (I sīdati)** sit, abide

सद् **-sad** *ifc.* dweller (in)

सदृश **sadṛśa** (*f.* **ī**) similar, like, suitable, in keeping with, worthy

सन्त् **sant** *pres. part. of* **as**; true, virtuous

संतापः **saṃtāpaḥ** burning, torment

संतोषः **saṃtoṣaḥ** satisfaction

संदर्शनं **saṃdarśanaṃ** sight, beholding

संदिश् **saṃ+diś** (VI **saṃdiśati**) command

संदेशः **saṃdeśaḥ** message

संदेहः **saṃdehaḥ** doubt, confusion

संधा **saṃ+dhā** (III **saṃdhatte**) bring together; agree, come to terms; aim (arrow)

संधा **saṃdhā** agreement, compact

संध्या **saṃdhyā** twilight, evening

संनिहित **saṃnihita** present, [in the area of:] about

सप्त **sapta(n)** seven

सप्तम **saptama** seventh

सफल **sa_phala** [having fruit:] fulfilled

सम **sama** even, equal

समक्षम् **samakṣam** visibly, in front of

समनन्तरम् **samanantaram** immediately after, thereupon

समयः **samayaḥ** occasion, season, time

समर्थ **samartha** capable, able

समर्थनं **samarthanaṃ** establishment, confirmation

समर्पयति **samarpayati** (*caus. of* **sam+ṛ**) hand over

समवायः **samavāyaḥ** coming together, union

समस्त **samasta** combined, all

समागमः **samāgamaḥ** meeting with, union

समाचर् **sam+ā+car** (I **samācarati**) conduct oneself, act, do

समाचारः **samācāraḥ** conduct, behaviour

समाधि **samādhi** *m.* concentration, (religious) meditation

समान **samāna** similar, same

समाम्नायः **samāmnāyaḥ** traditional enumeration, list

समारुह् **sam+ā+ruh (I samārohati)** ascend, attain

समासः **samāsaḥ** (*gram.*) compound

समासञ्ज् **sam+ā+sañj (I samāsajati)** attach to (*loc.*), impose upon

समासद् **sam+ā+sad** *caus.* **(samāsādayati)** approach, attain, meet

समाहारः **samāhāraḥ** group, collection

समिध् **samidh** *f.* firewood

समुचित **samucita** suitable, in accord with

समुत्था **samutthā (sam+ut+sthā) (I samuttiṣṭhati)** rise up

समुद्रः **samudraḥ** ocean

समुपदिश् **sam+upa+diś (VI samupadiśati)** point out, show

संपद् **saṃ+pad** *caus.* **(saṃpādayati)** bring about

संपूर्ण **saṃpūrṇa** fulfilled

संप्रति **saṃprati** now

संप्रदायः **saṃpradāyaḥ** tradition

संप्रधृ **saṃ+pra+dhṛ** *caus.* **(saṃpradhārayati)** deliberate, wonder

सम्प्रहारः **saṃprahāraḥ** fighting, combat

संप्राप् **saṃprāp (sam+pra+āp) (V saṃprāpnoti)** arrive, come to

संप्लुत **saṃpluta** flowed together, flooding

संबन्धः **saṃbandhaḥ** union

संबन्धिन् **saṃbandhin** relative (by marriage)

संबुद्धि **saṃbuddhi** *f.* calling out; (*gram.*) vocative

संभव **-saṃbhava** *ifc.* arising from, offspring of

संभवः **saṃbhavaḥ** birth, origin

संभावना **saṃbhāvanā** supposing

संभाव्य **saṃbhāvya** credible, conceivable, adequate

संभू **saṃ+bhū (I saṃbhavati)** arise, be born

संभू **saṃ+bhū** *caus.* **(saṃbhāvayati)** conceive, imagine; meet with, find

संभृत **saṃbhṛta** assembled, concentrated, augmented

संभेदः **saṃbhedaḥ** union, confluence

संमन्त्र् **saṃ+mantr (X saṃmantrayati)** take counsel, consult

संमर्दः **saṃmardaḥ** crush, encounter, throng

संमूढ **saṃmūḍha** (*p.p. of* **sam+muh**) bewildered, confused, deluded

संमोहः **saṃmohaḥ** bewilderment, delusion

सरस् **saras** *n.*, **sarasī** lake

सरित् **sarit** *f.* river

सर्पः **sarpaḥ** snake

सर्व **sarva** *pron.* all, whole, every; *n. sg.* everything, anything (at all); *m. sg.* everyone (in general)

सर्वतः **sarvataḥ** on all sides, in all directions; totally, in full detail

सर्वथा **sarvathā** in every way, totally, at all events, [in all circumstances:] always

सर्वदा **sarvadā** always, ever

सर्वनामन् **sarva-nāman** *n.* (*gram.*) [name for anything:] pronoun

सलिलं **salilaṃ** water

सविशेषम् **sa_viśeṣam** [with particulars:] particularly, completely

सह् **sah (I sahate)** withstand, endure, bear

सह **saha** + *instr.* together with, with

सहचारिन् **sahacārin** accompanying, companion

सहधर्मचारिन् **sahadharmacārin** *m.* lawful husband; **sahadharmacāriṇī** lawful wife

सहभू **sahabhū** inherent, natural

सहसा **sahasā** vehemently, suddenly

सहस्रं **sahasraṃ** a thousand

सहाध्ययनं **sah›:âdhyayanaṃ** studying together, common lessons

सहायः **sahāyaḥ** companion

सह्य **sahya** (*ger. of* **sah**) bearable

सांग्रामिक **sāṃgrāmika** (*f.* **ī**) relating to war (**saṃgrāmaḥ**), military

साचिव्यं **sācivyaṃ** being minister, post of minister

साधनं **sādhanaṃ** army

साधु **sādhu** good, virtuous, right; *adv.* **sādhu** bravo!; **sādhu˜tara** better

सांनिध्यं **sāṃnidhyaṃ** presence

सापत्न्यं **sāpatnyaṃ** the state of being the sharer of a husband (**sapatnī**)

सामाजिकः **sāmājikaḥ** spectator

सामान्य **sāmānya** common, general

सांप्रत **sāṃprata** [relating to now (**saṃprati**):] timely, proper; *adv.* **sāṃpratam** now, at once

सायम् **sāyam** at evening; **sāyaṃ˜tana** (*f.* **ī**) [relating to] evening

सार **sāra** *m./n.* substance; property

सारथि **sārathi** *m.* driver of chariot

सावधान **s›_âvadhāna** careful, watchful

साहस **sāhasa** rash, reckless

साहसिक **sāhasika** (*f.* **ī**) reckless, adventurous

सिच् **sic** (VI **siñcati**) sprinkle, moisten

सित **sita** white

सिद्ध **siddha** (*p.p. of* **sidh**) achieved, accomplished

सिद्धार्थकः **Siddhārthakaḥ** *pr. n.*

सिद्धि **siddhi** *f.* achievement, success, fulfilment

सीता **Sītā** *pr. n.*

सीरध्वजः **Sīradhvajaḥ** *pr. n.*

सु **su** *laudatory prefix* well, fair, good, very *etc.*; easily, easy

सुकुमार **su:kumāra** (*f.* **ī**) delicate

सुखं **sukhaṃ** pleasure, happiness; *adv.* **sukham** comfortably, at one's ease

सुचरितं **su:caritaṃ** good deed

सुतः **sutaḥ** son

सुता **sutā** daughter

सुन्दर **sundara** (*f.* **ī**) beautiful

सुप्त **supta** (*p.p. of* **svap**) asleep

सुभग **subhaga** fortunate, lovely, delightful

सुभ्रू **su:bhrū** fair-browed, fair

सुरः **suraḥ** god

सुरतं **su:rataṃ** lovemaking

सुरभि **surabhi** fragrant

सुलभ **su:labha** easily got, natural

सुवर्णं **suvarṇaṃ** gold; **suvarṇaḥ** gold piece

सुहृत्तमः **suhṛt˜tamaḥ** close friend

सुहृत्ता **suhṛt˜tā** being friendly, affection

सुहृद् **suhṛd** *m.* friend

सूच् **sūc** (X **sūcayati**) point out, indicate

सूतः **sūtaḥ** driver of chariot

सूत्रं **sūtraṃ** thread; aphorism, aphoristic rule

सूर्यः **sūryaḥ** sun

सेचनं **secanaṃ** (act of) sprinkling, watering

सेना **senā** army

सेनापति **senā-pati** *m.* [lord of army:] general

सेवा **sevā** attendance (upon someone), servitude

सैनिकः **sainikaḥ** [belonging to army:] soldier

सोढुम् **soḍhum** *inf. of* **sah**

सोदरः **sodaraḥ, sodaryaḥ** [one born of same womb:] brother [of same mother]

सोमतीर्थं **Somatīrthaṃ** *name of pilgrimage place*

सोमरातः **Somarātaḥ** *pr. n.*

सौजन्यं **saujanyaṃ** kindness

सौधातकि **Saudhātaki** *m., pr. n.*

सौहार्दं **sauhārdam** friendship, fondness

स्खलनं **skhalanaṃ** failure, lapse

स्तनकलशः **Stanakalaśaḥ** *pr. n.*

स्तम्बः **stambaḥ** clump of grass

स्तम्भः **stambhaḥ** pillar

स्तु **stu (II stauti)** praise

स्त्री **strī** *irreg.* woman

स्थ **-stha** standing, being at/in, *etc.*

स्थली **sthalī** dry land

स्था **sthā (I tiṣṭhati)** stand, stay, remain, abide, stop, halt

स्था **sthā** *caus.* **(sthāpayati)** cause to stand, establish

स्थानं **sthānaṃ** place, occasion; **sthāne** in place, appropriate(ly)

स्थानभ्रंशः **sthāna-bhraṃśaḥ** fall from position, loss of place

स्थायिन् **sthāyin** lasting, stable

स्थास्यति **sthāsyati** *3rd sg. fut. para. of* **sthā**

स्थित **sthita** (*p.p. of* **sthā**) standing *etc.*

स्थिर **sthira** firm; **sthirī˜kṛ** make firm, sustain; **sthirī˜bhū** be[come] firm

स्नानं **snānam** bathing, bathe

स्निग्ध **snigdha** affectionate

स्निह् **snih (IV snihyati)** feel affection for (*loc.*)

स्नेहः **snehaḥ** affection, fondness, tenderness, love

स्पन्द् **spand (I spandate)** quiver

स्पर्शः **sparśaḥ** touch

स्पृश् **spṛś (VI spṛśati)** touch, affect

स्प्रष्टुम् **sprașțum** *inf. of* **spṛś**

स्फुट **sphuṭa** clear, distinct

स्मरहरः **Smara-haraḥ** Destroyer of Love (*epithet of Śiva*)

स्मि **smi (I smayate)** smile

स्मितं **smitam** smile

स्मृ **smṛ (I smarati)** remember (*acc. or gen.*)

स्मृ **smṛ** *caus.* **(smārayati)** cause to remember, remind

स्यन्द् **syand (I syandate)** flow, move rapidly

स्यात् **syāt** *3rd sg. opt. of* **as**

स्रंस् **sraṃs (I sraṃsate)** drop, slip

स्रज् **sraj** f. garland

स्रु **sru (I sravati)** flow

स्व **sva** *pron. adj.* (one's) own

स्वच्छन्दम् **svacchandam** at one's will, as one would wish

स्वनः **svanaḥ** sound

स्वप् **svap (II svapiti)** sleep

स्वप्नः **svapnaḥ** sleep; dream

स्वयम् **svayam** *emphatic pron.* myself *etc.*, by/for myself *etc.*, personally, of one's own accord

स्वरः **svaraḥ** sound, tone, syllable

स्वल्प **sv:alpa** small, scant

स्वसृ **svasṛ** *f.* sister

स्वागतम् **sv:āgatam** welcome to (*dat.*)

स्वामिन् **svāmin** owner, master; **svāminī** mistress

स्वास्थ्यं **svāsthyaṃ** comfort, ease

स्वीकरणं **svī˘karaṇaṃ** [making one's own:] marrying

स्वीकृ **svī˘kṛ** make one's own, appropriate

स्वेदः **svedaḥ** sweat

स्वैरम् **svairam** gently

हत **hata** *p.p. of* **han**

हतक **hataka** *ifc.* accursed

हन् **han** (II **hanti**) kill, slay, murder

हन् **han** *caus.* (**ghātayati**) get killed, have killed, put to death

हन्त **hanta** ah! alas!

हयः **hayaḥ** horse

हरः **Haraḥ** *name of Śiva*

हरणं **haraṇaṃ** (*from* **hṛ**) taking

हरि **Hari** *m. name of Viṣṇu or Indra*

हर्षः **harṣaḥ** joy, delight

हस् **has** (I **hasati**) laugh

हस्तः **hastaḥ** hand, arm, trunk (of elephant)

हस्तिन् **hastin** elephant

हा **hā** ah! oh!

हानि **hāni** *f.* abandonment

हारिन् **hārin** taking, bringing

हार्य **hārya** *ger. of* **hṛ**

हासः **hāsaḥ** laugh, chuckle

हि **hi** *enclitic particle* for; assuredly, certainly, *etc.*

हित **hita** (*p.p. of* **dhā**) put; beneficial, well-disposed, good (friend)

हिमं **himaṃ** frost, snow, ice

हिमवन्त् **Himavant** *m.*, **Himālayaḥ** the mountain (range) Himālaya

हु **hu** (III **juhoti**) sacrifice

हृ **hṛ** (I **harati**) take, carry, carry off, take away

हृ **hṛ** *caus.* (**hārayati**) cause to carry

हृदयं **hṛdayaṃ** heart, mind

हे **he** (*before vocatives*) O, ah

हेतु **hetu** *m.* motive, ground for (*loc.*), cause; **hetoḥ** for the sake of, for

होमः **homaḥ** oblation, sacrifice

2 English–Sanskrit

THIS is solely a vocabulary to the English–Sanskrit exercises: words which occur only in the Sanskrit–English sections or in the body of the chapters are not included. No exhaustive attempt has been made to indicate the limits within which the Sanskrit word is equivalent to the English. It must be gathered from the context of the sentences themselves that, for instance, **prati+pad** corresponds to 'admit' in its sense of 'confess' and that **smārayati** means 'recall' in the sense of 'bring to another's mind'. Where distinctions are made, the colon is used to mean 'in the sense of'—e.g. 'call (:summon)', 'call in the sense of summon'.

Where an English word (e.g. 'wish') occurs as more than one part of speech, its verbal usage is normally listed first; but the Sanskrit equivalent should at any rate indicate which part of speech is in question. The same applies to forms in -ing such as 'seeing': **darśanaṃ** is the substantive (action noun), **darśin** the adjective (agent noun).

Morphological indications such as verb class are not usually given where these may be found in the special vocabularies or in the verb list.

a/an *usually omit*, **kaś cit, ko ›pi, ekaḥ**
abandon **hā, vi+hā**; abandoned **ujjhita** (*p.p. of* **ujjh**)
abide **ās**
able, be — (to) **śak**
about (:concerning) **prati**; about this (:on this matter) **atra**
absent-minded **śūnya-hṛdaya**
abundance **bāhulyaṃ**
accept **grah, pari+grah, prati+grah, aṅgī˜kṛ**
acceptance **parigrahaḥ**
acclamation **praśaṃs›-ālāpaḥ**
accompany **anu+vṛt**
accomplished **siddha**
accomplishment (:act of achieving) **siddhi** *f.*; (:technical ability) **śilpaṃ**
accord, of one's own — **svayam**
according to **˜vat**
accursed **hatakaḥ** *ifc.*
acknowledge **abhi+upa+i**
acquire **ā+gam** *caus.*
act (:do) **anu+sthā**
act (a play) **naṭ** *caus.*
acting (:doing) **kārin**
acting (in play) **nṛttaṃ**; science of acting **nāṭya-śāstraṃ**
activity **kriyā**
actual *use* **eva**
actually **eva**
address **abhi+dhā**
administration **tantraṃ**
admit **prati+pad**
adored one **priyatamā**
advantage **phalaṃ**
advice **upadeśaḥ**
affair **kāryaṃ**
affection **praṇayaḥ**
after **pareṇa**+*abl.*; *use absol.*; after very long **aticirāt**
after all **khalu**
afterwards **paścāt**
again **punar**; yet again **punar api**
agent **praṇidhi** *m.*
agitation **saṃvegaḥ**
ah! **aye**
aiding **upakāraḥ**
alas! **hanta, kaṣṭam**
alight, set — **ut+dīp** *caus.* (**uddīpayati**)
alive **jīvita**
all **sarva** *pron.*; on all sides **sarvataḥ**; at all **eva**; after all **khalu**
allusion **upanyāsaḥ**
alone **eka**; (:solitary) **ekākin**
already **prathamam, pūrva** *in cpd. with p.p., sometimes just* **eva**
also **api** *enclitic*
altercation **saṃgharṣaḥ**
although **api**
among, from — **madhyāt**+*gen. or ifc.*
amorous swoon **madana-mūrchā**
and **ca** *enclitic*, **ca . . . ca**; *connecting two verbs, usually expressed by absol.*; *connecting sentences, often expressed by* **api** *after new subject*
anger **krodhaḥ, kopaḥ, manyu** *m.*
announce **ni+vid** *caus.*
announcing **nivedanaṃ**
annoyance **pratyavāyaḥ**
another **anya, para**

answer **prativacanaṃ**
ant **pipīlikā**
anxiety **śaṅkā**
anxious to **-kāma**
any **kaś cit, ko ›pi**
anyone **kaś cit, ko ›pi**; (:no matter who) **sarvaḥ**
apart from **antareṇa**+*acc.*
appearance **varṇaḥ**
appease (:quieten) **śam** *cause.*; (curry favour with) **ā+rādh** *caus.*
appeasement **anunayaḥ**
appointment **saṃketaḥ**
apprehension **āśaṅkā**
appropriate, to — **svī˜kṛ**
appropriate **ucita**; appropriate(ly) **sthāne**
approve **abhi+nand**
army (:forces) **balaṃ**
arouse (:bring about) **jan** *caus.*; aroused **janita, saṃjāta**
arrival **āgamanaṃ**
arrive **ā+gam, pra+āp**
arrow **bāṇaḥ, śaraḥ**
as (:like) **iva**; *introducing subordinate clause* **yathā . . . tathā**; *in cpd.* **yathā**
as if *use* **iva**
as soon as **yad» aiva . . . tad» aiva**
as well (:also) **api**
ascetic **tāpasaḥ, tapasvin**
ascetic grove **tapo-vanaṃ**
ashamed **vilakṣa**
ask (about) **prach** (+ *acc.*)
asleep **supta**
assistant in gambling-house **sabhyaḥ**
assume (role) **grah**
assuredly **hi**
astonished **vismita**
astonishment **vismayaḥ**
at *use loc.*
at all **eva**
at once **sāṃpratam**
attachment **prasakti** *f.*
attack (of emotion) **āveśaḥ**; (on enemy) **abhiyogaḥ**
attempt **prayatnaḥ**
attend **anu+gam**
attendance **upasthānaṃ**
attendant **anucaraḥ**
attentive **avahita**
attractive **ramaṇīya**
audience **pariṣad** *f.*
augmented **saṃbhṛta**
aunt (maternal) **mātṛ-ṣvasṛ**
austerity (religious-) **tapas** *n.*
autumn **śarad** *f.*
avoid **pari+hṛ**

bad news **a:priyaṃ**
bakula (blossom) **bakulaṃ**
banish **nis+vas** *caus.*
bank **tīraṃ**
barb **śalya** *m./n.*
barbarian **mlecchaḥ**
bard (royal —) **vaitālikaḥ**
battle **samaraḥ**
be **as, bhū**; (be currently) **vṛt**
bearing **dhārin**
beat **taḍ**
beat off **apa+han**
beating **tāḍaḥ**
beautiful **śobhana**
beauty **śobhā, rūpaṃ**
because *use instr. or abl. of abstract noun*; (:with the thought that) **iti**
become **bhū** (*in past* **saṃvṛtta**), *or use verb of motion with abstract noun*
become an object **viṣayī˜bhū**
bedchamber **śayana-gṛhaṃ**
before (:previously) **prāk**; *in cpd. with p.p.* **pūrva**
before (*conj.*) **yāvat na . . . tāvat**
begin (:undertake) **sam+ā+rabh**, (:make a start) **upa+kram**

beginning **ārambhaḥ**
behalf, on — of **-artham**
behave **ceṣṭ, ā+ceṣṭ**; (:deal with) **vi+ava+hṛ**
belief **pratyayaḥ**
believe **śrad+dhā**
beloved **priya, vallabha**; beloved wife **praṇayinī**
bend down **ava+nam**
beneath **adhastāt**+*gen.*
benefit **priyaṃ**
besieging **uparodhanaṃ**
beside **āsanna, -samīpe**
bestow **pra+dā** (+*dat.*)
betel **tāmbūlaṃ**; betel-box **tāmbūla-bhājanaṃ**
beyond **vihāya**
bird **patatrin, pakṣin**
birth **janman** *n.*; birth-ceremony **jāta-karman** *n.*
bit **chedaḥ**
blame **upa+ā+labh**
blessing **maṅgalaṃ**
blind **andha**
bliss **nirvāṇaṃ**
blossom **ut+śvas**
blossom **kusumaṃ**
boast **ślāgh (I ślāghate)**
body **śarīraṃ, vigrahaḥ, gātraṃ**
bodyguard, provide a — for **pari+vṛ** (V **parivṛṇoti**)+*acc.*
bondage **bandhanaṃ**
book **pustakaṃ**
born of Śakuntalā **Śākuntaleya**
both (*adj.*) **ubha**; both . . . and . . . **ca . . . ca**
bow **cāpa** *m./n.*, **kārmukaṃ**
bower **maṇḍapa** *m./n.*
box **bhāṇḍaṃ**
boy **bālaḥ**
brahmin **brāhmaṇaḥ**
bravo! **sādhu**
breast **uras** *n.*

breeze **pravātaṃ**
bride **vadhū**
bridegroom **varaḥ**; bride and groom **vara;vadhū**
bright **śobhana**
bring **ā+nī, ā+dā**; bring to a pass **avasthām gam** *caus.*
bring up (chariot) **upa+sthā** *caus.*
broken **bhagna**
brother **bhrātṛ**
brother-in-law **śyālaḥ**
burn **dah**
busy **vyagra**
busy oneself on **abhi+yuj** *pass.*+*loc.*
but **punar** *enclitic*, **tu** *enclitic*, **kiṃ tu**; but then **athavā**
buy **krī**
by *normally use instr.*; by (virtue of doing something) *use pres. part.*

call (:summon) **ā+hve**
called (:named) *use* **nāma** 'by name' *or* **;nāman**
camp **ni+viś**
can *use* **śak**; *sometimes not necessary to translate*
cancellation **pratiṣedhaḥ**
capture **grah**
careful **s›_âvadhāna**
carriage **pravahaṇaṃ**
carry off **apa+hṛ**
case, in that — **tarhi, tena hi, yady evam**
cast **ni+kṣip**
cause (to) *use caus.*
cause **hetu** *m.*
ceremony **saṃskāraḥ**
certain, a — **kaścit, ko ›pi**
certainly **khalu**
change **pariṇāmaḥ**
character **śīlaṃ**
chariot **rathaḥ**
chase away **vi+dru** *caus.*

check **prati+sidh**
chieftain **rājan** *m.*
child **bālaḥ**; dear child **vatsaḥ**
childless **an꞉apatya**
circumstances **daśā**
citizen **pauraḥ**
city **nagaraṃ, puraṃ**
clamour **kolāhalaḥ**
clean **śuci**
clearly **vyaktam**
clever **nipuṇa**
clod of earth **loṣṭa** *m./n.*
come **ā+gam, upa+gam, upa+i, ā+yā, sam+ā+gam**
come! (*imperv.*) **ehi**
come in **pra+viś**
comfort **ā+śvas** *caus.*
command **sam+diś**
command **śāsanaṃ, saṃdeśaḥ, ājñā**
common **prākṛta**
company, in the — of **-sameta**
compassion, feel — **day** (I **dayate**)
compassionate **kṛpālu**
complacent **subhagaṃmanya**
complete **sam+āp**
complete with **sa_**
conceal **ā+chad** (X **ācchādayati**)
concealed **antarita**
concealment **pracchādanaṃ**
conceive **pari+kḷp** *caus.*
concern **cintā**
conclusion **avasānaṃ**
condemned **vadhya**
condition (:state) **avasthā**
conduct **caritaṃ**
confer (on) **prati+pad** *caus.* + *dat.*
confidence, inspiring of — **viśvasanīya**
confident, make — **prati+i** *caus.*
confirmation **pratipatti** *f.*
conflict **vimardaḥ**
confused **ākula**
confusion, in — **ākulī˜bhūta**
congratulate *use* **diṣṭyā vṛdh** *or its caus.* (*see Chapter* 9)
conjecture **tarkaḥ**
connive at (:overlook) **upa+īkṣ**
conquer **ji**
conscious of **-vedin**
consciousness **saṃjñā**
consecrated **abhimantrita**
consider **ava+gam, cint** (X **cintayati**)
considerable **garīyāṃs**
contemporary **vartamāna**
contemptuous **avamānin**
contrive [:bring about] **ut+pad** *caus.*
control, under one's own — **svādhīna**
convent **vihāraḥ**
conversant with **abhijña**+*gen.*
conversation **saṃlāpaḥ**
convey **pra+āp** *caus.*
cool **śītala**
coral-tree **mandāraḥ**
correctly **samyak**
council **pariṣad** *f.*
counsellor **sacivaḥ**
countermeasures, take — **prati+vi+dhā**
country **deśaḥ**
course **gati** *f.*
course, of — **khalu** *enclitic*
court **rāja-kulaṃ**
courtesan **gaṇikā**
crag **śilā-cayaḥ**
creak **vi+ru** (II **virauti**)
create **nis+mā** (*p.p.* **nirmita**)
creeper **latā**
crime **doṣaḥ**
crowd of people **janapada-samavāyaḥ**
cruel **dāruṇa**
cruelty **krauryaṃ**

cry **ā+krand (I ākrandati)**
cry out **ut+ghuṣ**
cunning **śaṭha**
curiosity **kutūhalaṃ, kautukaṃ**
curlew **krauñcaḥ**
curse **śāpaḥ**

dance **nṛt**
danger **bhayaṃ**
dare **ut+sah**
darkness **tamas** *n.*
daughter **kanyā, sutā, duhitṛ**
day **divasaḥ**; by day **divā**
dead **mṛta**
dear **priya, vallabha**; dear child **vatsaḥ/vatsā**; my dear X (*voc.*) *use* **sakhe** *m.*/**sakhi** *f.*; my dear fellow **bhadra**; dear Rāma **Rāma:bhadraḥ**
death **mṛtyu** *m.*
debtless **an:ṛṇa**
decayed **jīrṇa**
deceive **vi+pra+labh**
declare **ā+cakṣ (II ācaṣṭe),** *but normally* **ā+khyā** *outside pres. stem*
decoration **bhūṣaṇaṃ**
decrepit **jīrṇa**
deed **karman** *n.*
deer **mṛgaḥ**
defeat **ji**
defeat **parājayaḥ**
defile **duṣ** *caus.*
deity **devatā**
delay **kāla-haraṇaṃ kṛ, ās**
delight **harṣaḥ**; (:delightful event) **utsavaḥ**
delighted **prahṛṣṭa**
delightful **subhaga**
deluded **mūḍha**
demerit **doṣaḥ**
demon **asuraḥ**
denounce **apa+diś**
depart **ut+hā, apa+yā**
departure **prasthānaṃ**
depict **abhi+likh**
depressed, feel — **durmanāyate**
descendant of *use vṛddhi derivative*
describe **varṇayati**; as described **yath»_ôkta**
desert **pari+tyaj**
desirable **kānta**
desire **prārthitaṃ, prārthanā**
despatch **pra+hi** (*p.p.* **prahita**)
despise **ava+jñā**
despondency **vaimanasyaṃ**
destiny **vidhi** *m.*
destroying **vadhaḥ**
destruction **vināśaḥ**
determination **niścayaḥ**
devoid **śūnya**
die **upa+ram**
different **anya** *pron.*
difficult **dus:kara**; difficult (to achieve) **dur:labha**
diligence **abhiyogaḥ**
diligent **abhiyukta**
direct **ā+diś**
direction **diś** *f.*; in one — ... in another **anyataḥ ... anyataḥ**
disaffection **aparāgaḥ**
disappointment **viṣādaḥ**
discern **sam+vi+jñā, upa+lakṣ (X upalakṣayati)**
disciple **antevāsin**
discover **vid, pari+jñā**
discrimination **vivekaḥ**
disgrace, in — **sa_nikāram**
disguise **vyañjanaṃ**
disinclined **parāṅmukha**
disloyalty **aparāgaḥ**
dismiss **vi+sṛj** *caus.*
dispersal (of crowd) **bhaṅgaḥ**
dispute **vivādaḥ**
distance, at a good — from **atidūre**+*gen.*
distinction **viśeṣaḥ**

distract (pleasurably) **vi+nud** *caus.*
distracted (:crazed) **unmatta**
distress **ārti** *f.*; distress of mind **citta-khedaḥ**
distress, be in — **duḥkhaṃ sthā, duḥkham ās**
distressed **viklava**
disturb **ākulayati**
do **kṛ, anu+sthā, ā+car; sam+ā+car**
do violence to **abhi+druh**
doctor **vaidyaḥ**
don **pari+dhā** *ātm.*
donate **nis+vap**
done, have — with **kṛtam+** *instr.*
don't *use* **alam,** *or* **na+***ger.*
door **dvāraṃ, kapāṭaṃ**
doubt **saṃdehaḥ, vitarkaḥ**
draw **ā+kṛṣ**
draw near **prati+ā+sad**
dreadful **atidāruṇa, aniṣṭa**
drink **pā**
drink **pānaṃ**
drinking **-pa** *ifc.*
drive *use* **nī** *with abstract noun*
driver **sārathi** *m.*
driving away **apanodanaṃ**
dweller **-sad**
dynasty **vaṃśaḥ**

each other **anyonya**
eager **utsuka**
ear **karṇaḥ**
earlier **pūrva** *pronom.*
earth **pṛthivī, bhū** *f.*
easy **sulabha**
eclipse **uparāgaḥ**
effect **kṛ**
either . . . or **. . . vā . . . vā**
elder **jyāyāṃs**; elder (person) **guru** *m.*
elder brother **jyāyāṃs bhrātṛ, agrajaḥ**
elephant **gajaḥ**
else **anya** *pron.*; somewhere else **anyatra kv› âpi**
embarrassing **lajjā-kara**
embrace **pari+svaj** (I **pariṣvajate**)
emerge **nis+kram**
employ **pra+yuj, vi+ā+pṝ** *caus.*
enclosure **valaya** *m./n.*, **vāṭikā**
end **antaḥ**; to what end? **kim:nimittam**; an end of **kṛtam+***instr.*
enemy **ripu** *m.*
engage **ni+yuj**
engrossed **vyagra**
enjoin **vi+dhā**
enjoy **pari+bhuj,** (:experience) **anu+bhū**
enough **alam**
enrage **caṇḍī˜kṛ**
enter **pra+viś**
enter upon (vow) **sam+ā+ruh**
entering **praveśaḥ**
enterprise **ārambhaḥ**
entire **nikhila**
entirely **eva**
entry **praveśaḥ**
epithet **viśeṣaṇa:padaṃ**
escape **apakramaṇaṃ**
escort **ānuyātrikaḥ**
especially **˜tara**
establish **sthā** *caus.*
even **api** *enclitic*
ever **kadācit**
every **sarva** *pron.*
everyone (of a number) **sarve** (*pl.*); (in general) **sarvaḥ** (*sg.*)
everything **sarvaṃ**
evil **pāpa**
evil-natured **dur:ātman**
Excellency, His/Your **āryaḥ**
excessively **ati** *prefix*
execution-ground **vadhya-sthānaṃ**
executioner **ghātakaḥ**

exertion **pariśramaḥ**
exhausted **pariśrānta**
exploits **caritaṃ**
extermination **unmūlanaṃ**
extraordinary **adbhuta**
extremely **ati** *prefix*
eye **netraṃ, nayanaṃ, cakṣus** *n.*, **locanaṃ**

face **mukhaṃ, vaktraṃ**
fact, in — **eva**; from the fact that **yathā . . . tathā**
faint **moham upa+gam**
fair-eyed **su꞉nayana**
fall **pat, ni+pat**; (to one's lot) **upa+nam**
fall silent **tūṣṇīm as**
falling **nipātaḥ**
fame **yaśas** *n.*
familiar **abhyasta**
family **kulaṃ, anvayaḥ, kuṭumbaṃ**; (:members of immediate household) **gṛha-janaḥ**
far away **dūre**
fast to death **an꞉aśanena sam+sthā** *ātm.*
fate **daivaṃ**
father **pitṛ**; (one's own) **tātaḥ**
father-in-law **śvaśuraḥ**
fault **doṣaḥ**
favour **anu+grah**
favour **prasādaḥ**
favourable **anukūla**
fearful **trasta**
fearfulness **bhīru˜tvaṃ**
fearing **śaṅkin**
fellow **baṭu** *m.*; good fellow, dear fellow **bhadraḥ**
festival **mahotsavaḥ**
fetch down (from carriage) **ava+tṝ** *caus.*
fetching **āharaṇaṃ**
few, a — *use* **kaścit**
field **kṣetraṃ**
fierce **ugra**
filament **kesaraṃ**
find **adhi+gam**
find out **upa+labh**
finger **aṅguli/aṅgulī** *f.*
fire **agni** *m.*, **analaḥ, vahni** *m.*
fired, cause to be — **dah** *caus.*
firewood **samidh** *f.*
firmness **dhairyaṃ**
first **prathama**
fixed (on) **-āsakta**
flame **jvālā**
flesh **māṃsaṃ**
flow **abhi+syand**
flower **puṣpaṃ, kusumaṃ**
fly up **ut+pat, ut+ḍī (uḍḍī)**
folk **janaḥ**
follow **anu+gam**
follower **anuyātrikaḥ**
fondness **prīti** *f.*
food **bhojanaṃ, bhaktaṃ**
fool **mūrkhaḥ**
foot **pādaḥ**
for (*prep.*) *use gen.*; for (a period of time) *use acc.*; for (the sake of) **-artham** *or use dat.*
for (*conj.*) **hi** *enclitic*
for oneself (:of one's own accord) **svayam**
forcibly **balāt**
ford **tīrthaṃ**
forest **vanaṃ, araṇyaṃ, vipinaṃ**
forest-dweller **vanecaraḥ**
forget **vi+smṛ**
forgive **kṣam** (*pass.* **kṣamyate**)
form **vapus** *n.*
former **purātana** (*f.* **ī**)
forsooth **kila**
forth, and so — **꞉ādi**
fortune **bhāgyaṃ**
forward **anu+pra+iṣ** *caus.* **anupreṣayati**)
four **catur**
free **muc**
free from **nis** *prefix*
freedom (:scope) **prasaraḥ**

friend **vayasyaḥ, mitram, suhṛd** *m.*, **sakhi** *m.* (*voc.* **sakhe**); (female) friend **sakhī**, (= *pl.*) **sakhī:janaḥ**
friend's wife **sakhī**
friendship **sakhyam**
frivolous **cañcala**
from *use abl.*; from what/where? **kutaḥ**; from someone **kutaś cit**
front, in — of **agrataḥ**+*gen.*, **-samakṣam**
fruit **phalam**
fruitful **sa_phala**
fruitless, make — **viphalī˜kṛ**
fulfil **pṝ** *caus.*
full of **-pūrṇa**
Full Moon Festival **Kaumudī-mahotsavaḥ**
further **bhūyāṃs**

gain **labh**
gale **nabhasvant** *m.*
gallery **vīthikā, śālā**
game **krīḍā**
gaming master **sabhikaḥ**
Gandharva **Gandharvaḥ**; Gandharva rite **Gāndharva vidhi** m.
garden **udyānam**
garland **mālā**
garment **vāsas** *n.*
gaze **dṛś**
gaze **dṛṣṭi** *f.*
gem **ratnam**
generally **prāyeṇa**
get **labh**; get (done) *use caus.*
get up **ut+sthā** (**s** *lost between the* **t** *and* **th** — *e.g. p.p.* **utthita**)
girl **kanyā, kanyakā**
give **dā**
give up **tyaj**
giving **dānam**
glory **śrī**
go **gam, yā**
go against **ati+kram**
go back **ni+vṛt**
go in(to) **pra+viś**
god **suraḥ, devaḥ**
God of Love **Manmathaḥ, Kusumāyudhaḥ**
goddess **devī**
going **gamanam**
gold **suvarṇam, heman** *n.*
good **sādhu**, (friend) **hita**, (*in voc.*) **bhadra**; (:prosperity) **śreyas** *n.*
good fellow **bhadraḥ**
good man **su:janaḥ**
good woman (*voc.*) **bhadre**
gotra **gotram**
grandson **dauhitraḥ**
grant **pra+yam**
granted that **kāmam**
grasp **grah**
great **mahānt**
greatness **mahiman** *m.*
greet (person) **abhi+vad** *caus. ātm.*; (thing) **abhi+nand**
grief **śokaḥ**
grieve **śuc**
groom *see* bridegroom
ground **bhūmi** *f.*; (:cause) **hetu** *m.*
guard **rakṣ**
guest **atithi** *m.* **abhyāgataḥ**
guide, someone to — **netṛ**

ha! **ayi, hanta, āḥ**
half (portion) **ardhaḥ**
hand, hand over **sam+ṛ** *caus.*, **ṛ** *caus.*
hand **hastaḥ, pāṇi** *m.*
hand, at — **āsanna**
handmaid **ājñākarī**
happen: what happens/has happened *etc.* **vṛttāntaḥ**
happiness **sukham**
hard to attain **dur:adhigama**
hard to win **dur:labha**
harem **antaḥpuram**
harlot **veśyā**
harsh **viṣama**

hate **dviṣ**
have *use gen. with verb meaning 'be'* — *usually* **as**, *sometimes* **bhū** *or* **vṛt**; have (something done) *use caus.*
having *use bahuvrīhi, suffixes* **vant/mant, sa,** *etc.*
hawker **paṇāyitṛ**
he, him *etc.* **saḥ, ayam, enam, eṣaḥ, asau** *or omit*
head **śiras** *n.*
heap **rāśi** *m.*
hear **śru**
heart **hṛdayaṃ, cittaṃ**
heat **ātapaḥ**
heavens, thank — **diṣṭyā**
hell **naraka** *m./n.*
helpful **upakārin**
helpless **paravaśa**
here **atra, iha,** *or use* **eṣaḥ, ayam**; over here **itaḥ**
hereditary **pitṛ-paryāy›-āgata**
herewith *use* **eṣaḥ**
hermitage **āśramaḥ, āśrama-padaṃ**
hero **vīraḥ**
hesitation **an:adhyavasāyaḥ**
high-soaring **utsarpin**
highest (:most excellent) **parārdhya**
Highness, Your/His — **kumāraḥ**
hindrance **vighnaḥ, antarāyaḥ**
hint at **upa+kṣip**
his **tasya** *etc.*; his (own) **sva**
hither and thither **itas tataḥ**
ho, ho there! **bhoḥ**
hold on to **ava+lamb**
hole **chidraṃ**
homage **namas** *n.*
home **gṛhaṃ, āvasathaḥ**
honey-bee (female) **madhukarī**
honour (request *etc.*) **man** *caus.*; (:do honour to) **puras+kṛ, pūj** (X **pūjayati** *ger.* **pūjya**)
Honour, His/Your — **āryaḥ**; His Honour here **atrabhavant**
honourable **ārya**
hope **ā+śaṃs** (I **āśaṃsate**); I hope **kaccid** (*particle*)
hope **āśā**
horse **aśvaḥ**
hospitality **satkāraḥ**
hostile (:adverse) **pratikūla**
house **gṛhaṃ, gehaṃ**
household **śuddhāntaḥ, gaṇaḥ**
how? **katham**; *in exclamations use* **aho**
however **punar** *enclitic*
human flesh **mahā:māṃsaṃ**
huntsman **vyādhaḥ**
hurry **tvar** *ātm.*
husband, lawful — **sahadharmacārin**
husband and wife **dampatī** (*du.*)

I **aham**
idiot **mūḍhaḥ**
idle, sit — **ut+ās**
if **yadi, cet** *enclitic*; if only! **api nāma**
ignoble **an:ārya**
ignorant **an:abhijña**
ill-disposed to **vimukha**+*gen.*
ill omen **dur:nimittaṃ**
imagine **sam+bhū** *caus.*
immediately **an:antaram, sadya eva**; immediately upon **-anantaram eva**
imminent **bhāvin**
impairment **śaithilyaṃ**
important thing **pradhānaṃ**
in *use loc., sometimes adverb in* **-tra**; (being) in **-gata**; having (with)in **:garbha**; in . . . ing *often use pres. part.*
inclination **abhiprāyaḥ**
incline **pra+vṛt**

including **urīkṛtya**+*acc.*
inconvenience *use* **doṣaḥ**
increase **vṛdh** *caus.*
indeed **khalu** *enclitic*
indicate **upa+diś**
indicating **nivedaka**
inevitably **niyatam**
inferiority **lāghavam**
inflammatory **saṃdīpana**
inform **ni+vid** *caus.*+*dat.*/*gen.*
ingratitude **kṛtaghna˜tā**
inscrutable **acintya**
instigation to rebellion **upajāpaḥ**
instructed **śikṣita**
instructions **ādeśaḥ**
intact, keep — **pari+pāl**
intelligence **buddhi** *f.*
intention **abhiprāyaḥ**
interest **kutūhalam**
interval **antaram**
intimacy **viśrambhaḥ**
intoxication **madaḥ**
introduce (into) **pra+viś** *caus.*, **upa+nī**+*acc.*
invade **upa+rudh**
invite **upa+ni+mantr** (X **upanimantrayati**)
irritability **duḥśīla˜tā**
it **saḥ, ayam, enam, eṣaḥ, asau** (*usually in n.*)
its **tasya** *etc.*

jackal **śṛgālaḥ**
jewel **ābharaṇam**
join **ghaṭ** *caus.* (**ghaṭayati**)
joined hands **añjali** *m.*
joke **parihāsaḥ**
juncture **antaram**; at this juncture **atr› ântare**
just **eva** *enclitic* (:merely) **-mātra**; (I'll) just . . . **tāvat** *enclitic*, **yāvat**

kill **vi+ā+pad** *caus.*; have (:cause to be) killed **ghātayati**
killing **vināśaḥ**
king **rājan** *m.* (*ifc.* **-rājaḥ**), **nṛpaḥ**
king of Videha **Vaidehaḥ**
kingdom **rājyam**
kinsman **bandhu** *m.*
know **jñā, vid, ava+gam**; know how to **jñā**

lack of *use* **a:/an:**
lady, noble lady **āryā**; this lady **atrabhavatī**; that lady **tatrabhavatī**
lake **sarasī**
lamp **dīpikā**
lapse **skhalanam**
later, some time — **kasya cit kālasya**
laugh **has (I hasati)**
Lāvāṇaka, (being) at — **Lāvāṇaka** *adj.*
law, sacred — **dharmaḥ**
lay **ā+ruh** *caus.*
lead **nī**
learn **vid, ava+gam**
learned in the sacred law **dharma-vit**
leave **tyaj, pari+tyaj**
leave, give — **anu+jñā**
-less **nis_, a:/an:**
let *use imperv., sometimes indicative*
let alone **kim punar**
let go **muc**
letter **lekhaḥ, pattrikā, pattram**
licked **avalīḍha**
life **jīvitam, prāṇa** *m. pl.*
like, I should — to **icchāmi**
like *use* **iva, ˜vat, sadṛśa** (*f.* **ī**) +*instr.*
limb **aṅgam**
line **paṅkti** *f.*
listen (to) **śru**
listen, someone to — **śrotṛ**
little while **muhūrta** *m./n.*

live (:be alive) **jīv**; (:dwell) **vas, prati+vas, ni+vas**
long **dūra**; (for) a long way **dūram**; for a long time **ciram**
long, after very — **aticirāt**
long, at — last **cirāt**
long-lived **āyuṣmant**
look (at) **dṛś**; look upon **īkṣ**
looking after **upasaṃgrahaḥ**
loose **vi+muc**
lord **pati** *m.*, **adhipati** *m.*
loss of place **sthāna-bhraṃśaḥ**
lotus **puṇḍarīkaṃ**
loudly **uccaiḥ**
love (:fondness) **snehaḥ**, (:devotion) **anurāgaḥ**, (:passion) **manmathaḥ**
Love (god of-) **Manmathaḥ, Kusumāyudhaḥ, Makaradhvajaḥ**
love, be in — with **utkaṇṭhate, kam** *caus.*
loved one **iṣṭa:janaḥ**
lovely **ramaṇīya, manohara**
low (:mean) **kṣudra**

Madam (*voc.*) **bhadre**
magnanimous **mah»:ātman**
maidservant **paricārikā**
maintain (fire) **ā+dhā**
Majesty, Her/Your — **devī**
Majesty, His/Your — **devaḥ, āyuṣmant**
make **kṛ, ut+pad** *caus.*
maker **kartṛ**
man **naraḥ, puruṣaḥ**; (:person) **janaḥ**
manage **vi+dhā**; manage to *use* **kathaṃ cit**
mango tree **cūtaḥ**
manœuvre **ceṣṭā**
many **bahu**
mark **lakṣaṇaṃ**
marriage **dāra-karman** *n.*
marry **vah**
mass **saṃghātaḥ**
master **svāmin** *m.*
matching **saṃvādaḥ**
mating **yugma-cārin** ('going in a pair')
matter **vastu** *n.*
me **māṃ** *etc.*
meaning **arthaḥ**
means **upāyaḥ**
measure **mā** (*caus.* **māpayati**)
measure **pramāṇaṃ**
medicine **auṣadhaṃ**
meditating **dhyānaṃ**
meditation **samādhi** *m.*
meet **sam+ā+sad** *caus.*; (:receive) **prati+ut+gam**
meeting **samāgamaḥ**
melancholy **udvigna**
memory **smṛti** *f.*
mendicant **kṣapaṇakaḥ**
mental turmoil **vikāraḥ**
merchant **śreṣṭhin** *m.*
mere **-mātra, eva**
merit **guṇaḥ**; of merit **guṇa˜vant**
milk **kṣīraṃ**
mind **manas** *n.*, **cittaṃ, cetas** *n.*, **hṛdayaṃ**
mine, of mine *say* 'of me, my'
minister **amātyaḥ**
mirage **mṛgatṛṣṇikā**
misconduct **apacāraḥ**
misdeed **akāryaṃ**
misfortune **vyasanaṃ**
mishap **pramādaḥ**
mislead **vi+pra+labh**
mission **prayojanaṃ**
mistress **svāminī, īśvarī**
moment **muhūrta** *m./n.*
money **dhanaṃ**
monster **nṛśaṃsaḥ**
moon **candraḥ**
moonlight **candrikā**
morning (:of the —) *adj.* **pragetana** (*f.* **ī**)

mother **jananī, ambā** (*voc.* **amba**), **mātṛ**
motion, in — **pracalita**
mountain **parvataḥ, śailaḥ, acalaḥ**
mouth **vadanaṃ**
murder **vi+ā+pad** *caus.*
must *use ger. in* **tavya**
mutual (:of *etc.* each other) **itaretara-**
my **madīya,** *or say* 'of me', *or omit*
my own **sva**; of my own accord **svayam**
myself *reflexive* **ātman**; (:me) *use* **aham**

name **nāman** *n.*, **nāmadheyaṃ**
natural **sulabha,** (:innate) **sahabhū**
nature **prakṛti** *f.*, **ātman** *m.*
necklace **mālā**
negligent **pramatta**
neutral **madhyastha**
never **na kadācit**
news **vṛttāntaḥ, pravṛtti** *f.*
night, by — **rātrau**
no *use* **na** *or* **a:**
noble **ārya, atyudāra**
noise **śabdaḥ**
normal **ucita**
not **na, a:**; A not B **A na tu B**
nothing **na kiṃ cit**
notice **lakṣ** (X **lakṣayati**)
now (:at the present time) **adhunā, idānīm, saṃprati**; (*connective*) **atha, yāvat, tāvat**
numerous **prabhūta, mahānt**
nymph **apsaras** *f.*

object (:province) **viṣayaḥ**
observe **ni+śam** *caus.*
obstacle **vighnaḥ**
obstruct **ni+rudh**
obtain **ava+āp**
obviously **nūnam**
occasion **avasaraḥ, sthānaṃ**
occupation **vyāpāraḥ**
occupy **adhi+ās**
occur **jan**
ocean **sāgaraḥ**
of *use gen., vṛddhi derivative, bahuvrīhi cpd. etc.*
offend against **apa+rādh** + *gen.* (*p.p.* **aparāddha**)
office **adhikāraḥ**
often **bahuśaḥ**
oh! **hā, aye, bhoḥ, ayi**
on *use loc.*; on . . . ing *use absol. or loc. of verbal noun*
once *use* **pūrva**; once more **punar api**
one **eka** *pron.*; (:a person) *use impersonal construction*
only **eva, -mātra**
open (letter) **ut+veṣṭ** *caus.*
opportune **avasare**
opportunity **avasaraḥ**
oppress **pīḍ**
or **vā** *enclitic*; (:nor) **vā na**
ornament **ābharaṇaṃ, alaṃkaraṇaṃ, bhūṣaṇaṃ**
other **anya, para**; and other(s) **:ādi**
otherwise **anyathā**
our, of ours *say* 'of us'
out of *use abl.*
outcaste **śvapākaḥ**
outcome **pariṇāmaḥ, vijṛmbhitaṃ**
outside **bahiḥ**
over here **itaḥ**
overcome **parīta**
overlook **mṛṣ** *caus.*
overtures (:instigation to rebellion) **upajāpaḥ**
own, my/your *etc.* — **sva, ātmanaḥ**; make one's own **svī˜kṛ**

paint **ā+likh**
painter **citrakaraḥ**
pair **yugalaṃ**
palace **rāja-kulaṃ**; Sugāṅga Palace **Sugāṅga:prāsādaḥ**
pang **vedanā**; pangs of love **manmath›-ônmāthaḥ**
pardon **mṛṣ** (IV **mṛṣyati**)
parents **pitṛ** *du.*
park **udyānaṃ**
part **uddeśaḥ**; for (someone's) part *use* **api**
partial **pakṣapātin**
particle **avayavaḥ**
partisan **pakṣapātin**
pass **avasthā, daśā**
pass over **ati+kram**
passion **abhilāṣaḥ**
past **atīta**
past, present and future **trikālaṃ**
path **-pathaḥ**
peak **sānu** *m.*
people **janaḥ**
perceive **ava+lok** (X **avalokayati**)
perform (:do) **anu+sthā**; (a play) **pra+yuj**
performance **prayogaḥ**
perfume **vas**
persistence (:adherence) **anubandhaḥ**
person **janaḥ**; (:body) **śarīraṃ, deha** *m./n.*
personally **svayam eva**
petition **pra+arth** (X **prārthayate**)
picking **avacayaḥ**
picture **citraṃ**
piety **dharmaḥ**
pity **anu+kamp**
place **ni+kṣip**
place **deśaḥ, sthānaṃ, pradeśaḥ**
place of sacrifice **agnihotraśaraṇaṃ**
plan **saṃkalpaḥ**
play a role **bhūmikāṃ kṛ** *ātm.*
pleasant **ramaṇīya, priya**
pleasure **sukhaṃ**
pluck out **ut+hṛ**
poet **kavi** *m.*
point, what — in? **kim**+*instr.*
poison **viṣaṃ**
poisoner **tīkṣṇa:rasa-daḥ**
ponder **vi+car** *caus.*
pool **tīrthaṃ**
poor, poor fellow (*pityingly*) **tapasvin**; poor girl **varākī**
poor material **adravyaṃ**
portrait **ālekhyaṃ**
possessed of **-upapanna**
possessions **parigrahaḥ**
possessor of **˜mant**
possible **upapanna**
power **prabhāvaḥ**; have power over **pra+bhū**+*gen.*
practise (cruelty) **pra+yuj**, (austerities) **car**
praise **stu**
prayer **japaḥ**
preceptor **upādhyāyaḥ**
prelude **prastāvaḥ**
presence, to the — of **-sakāśam**; in the — of **pratyakṣam**+*gen.*
present **saṃnihita**
present **pratigrahaḥ**
present with **prati+pad** *caus.* +*double acc.*
pretence **apadeśaḥ**
previously **pūrva** *ifc.*
prince **kumāraḥ**
princess **rāja-putrī**
prisoner **bandhana-sthaḥ**
prize (:value highly) **abhi+nand**
proceed **ut+cal**
procession **yātrā**
proclaim **ut+ghuṣ** *caus.*; (:declare authoritatively) **ā+diś**

proclamation, after — **prakhyāpya** (*lit.* 'having proclaimed')
procure **ava+gam** *caus.*
proficiency **prāvīṇyaṃ**
promised **pratiśruta**
proper **yukta**
protect **rakṣ, pari+trai, pari+pāl**; (someone) to protect (one) **trātṛ**
provide **upa+kṛ**
punishment **daṇḍaḥ**
pupil **śiṣyaḥ, śiṣyā**
purse-proud **artha-matta**
pursue **anu+sṛ**
put to shame **prati+ā+diś**

quality **guṇaḥ**
quantity **saṃcayaḥ**
queen **rājñī**, (*as title*) **devī**
quickly **āśu**
quiet **nibhṛta**
quite **eva** *enclitic*
quiver **spand**

rag **paṭaccaraṃ**
rather **nanu**
reach **anu+pra+āp**
ready **udyata**
realize **ava+gam**
really **satyam**
reason **kāraṇaṃ**
rebuke **upa+ā+labh**
rebuking **upālambhaḥ**
recall **smṛ** *caus.*
receive **grah**
recklessness **asamīkṣya:kāri˜tā**
recognise **prati+abhi+jñā, pari+ci**
reconciled **prasanna**
redundancy **paunaruktaṃ**
reed **vetasaḥ**
refuse to *use* **na**
regain (consciousness) **upa+labh**
regard (:think) **man**
regard for **-anurodhaḥ**; with regard to **prati**+*acc.*
rein **abhīśu** *m.*
reject **prati+ā+diś**
rejection **pratyākhyānaṃ, pratyādeśaḥ**
rejoice **mad**
release **vi+sṛj**
relent **prasādaṃ kṛ**
religious power **siddhi** *f.*
remain **sthā**
remaining part **śeṣaḥ**
remark **vacanaṃ**
remedy **pratīkāraḥ**
remember **smṛ**
remnant **śeṣaḥ**
remove **apa+nī**; (ornaments etc.) **ava+tṝ** *caus.*
reply **prativacanaṃ**
report **prasiddhi** *f.*
request **vijñāpanā**
rescue **abhi+upa+pad**
rescue **prāṇa-rakṣā**
residence **bhavanaṃ**
resist **pari+hṛ**
resolve **niścayaḥ**
resort to **ā+śri**
respect for **bahumānaḥ**+*loc.*
respect, worthier of — **garīyāṃs**
respectfully **sa_gauravam**
resplendent **dīpti˜mant**
restrain **ni+grah, upa+saṃ+hṛ**
restraint **avagrahaḥ**
return **prati+ni+vṛt**
reveal **āviṣ˜kṛ, pra+kāś** *caus.*
reveal oneself **āvir˜bhū**
revered **tatrabhavant**; my revered father **tāta-pādāḥ**
Reverence, Her/Your — **bhagavatī**
reverend **bhagavant** (*f.* **bhagavatī**)
reward **pari+tuṣ** *caus.*

reward **phalaṃ**
rewarding **paritoṣaḥ**
riches **vibhūti** *f. pl.*
riding **caryā**
right *adv.* **eva**
right (:proper) **yukta**; rightly **yuktam**
right (*opp.* left) **dakṣiṇa**; to the right of **dakṣiṇena**+*acc.*
ring **aṅgurīyaka** *m./n.*
rise **ut+cal, ut+sthā**
rite **kriyā, vidhi** *m.*, **maṅgalaṃ**
river **nadī**
road, roadway **mārgaḥ**
rock **śilā**
role **bhūmikā**
rosary **akṣamālā**
roused **upajāta**
royal bard **vaitālikaḥ**
royal seer **rāja:rṣi** *m.*
ruined, be — **ava+sad**
ruler **īśvaraḥ**
run **pra+dru**

sacred law **dharmaḥ**
sacrifice **hu**
sacrifice, place of — **agnihotraśaraṇaṃ**
sacrificial **medhya**
sacrilege **abrahmaṇyaṃ**
safeguard **rakṣ**
sage **muni** *m.*
sake, for the — of **-artham**
salute **pra+nam, vand** (*ger.* **vandya**)
same, the/that — **saḥ+eva**; this same **ayam** *etc.*+**eva**
say **vad, vac, kath, brū, abhi+dhā**
scandal **kaulīnaṃ**
scant **svalpa**
scare **ut+tras** *caus.* (**uttrāsayati**)
scent **āmodaḥ**
scholar **paṇḍitaḥ**
science **śāstraṃ**
scold **upa+ā+labh**
seal **mudrā**
search **anu+iṣ**
search, in — of **anveṣin**
season **samayaḥ**
seated, be — **ni+sad**
second **dvitīya**
secret **rahasyaṃ**
seduce **ā+vṛj** *caus.*
see **dṛś, ava+lok, ā+lok**; see to it that **kṛ+yathā**
see, see how *use* **eṣaḥ** *or* **ayam**
seeing **darśanaṃ**
seeing **darśin**
seem *use* **iva**
seer **ṛṣi** *m.*, great seer **maha:rṣi** *m.*
seize **grah**
self, myself *etc.* (*reflexive*) **ātman** *m. sg.*; (*emphatic*)/for oneself *etc.* **svayam**
self-control **dhairyaṃ**
selfsame **eva**
sell **vi+krī**
send **pra+iṣ** *caus.* (**preṣayati**)
senior to **guru**+*gen.*
separated, having become — **vighaṭita**
serpent **viṣadharaḥ, nāgaḥ, phaṇabhṛt** *m.*
servant **parijanaḥ, dāsī**; servant girl **dāsī**
service **upakāraḥ, priyaṃ**
set **sthā** *caus.*
set forth, set out **pra+sthā**
severe (punishment) **tīkṣṇa**; (austerity) **kaṣṭa**
shade **chāyā**
shake **cal** *caus.* (**calayati**)
shame **lajjā**; shame (on) **dhik** (+*acc.*)
shame, put to — **prati+ā+diś**
sharp **niśita**; (:astringent) **kaṣāya**
shoot **vyadh** (*pass.* **vidhyate**)

should *use* **arh** *or ger. in* **ya/anīya**
show **dṛś** *caus.*
show **prekṣaṇīyakaṃ**
shower **abhi+vṛṣ** (I **abhivarṣati**)
shower (:multitude) **nikaraḥ**
shut **āvṛta**
side **pakṣaḥ**
sides, on all — **sarvataḥ**
sight **darśanaṃ**
sign **liṅgaṃ, cihnaṃ**
signal **saṃjñā**
signature **svahastaḥ**
silent, stay — **tūṣṇīm ās**; fall silent **tūṣṇīm as** (*in imperf.*)
sin **pāpman** *m.*
since (*prep.*) **prabhṛti**+*abl.*; (:because) *use abl./instr. of abstract noun, or* **yena, yataḥ, yat, iti**
sing **gai**
sir **ārya**
sire **rājan**
sister **bhaginī, svasṛ**
sit (down) **upa+viś**
skill **kauśalaṃ**
sky **gaganaṃ**; skies **diś** *f. pl.*
slab **talaṃ**
slender *use* **yaṣṭi** *f.*
slip **pari+bhraṃś**
slow, by — stages **śanaiḥ śanaiḥ**
snake **sarpaḥ**
snatch **hṛ**
so (*simple connective*) **tat**, (:I infer that) **tarhi**; (:thus) **evam**, (:to such an extent) **evam**
sobriquet **prasiddhi** *f.*
soft **mṛdu**
sojourn **sahavāsaḥ**
soldier **sainikaḥ**
solely **kevalam**; solely partial **eka:pakṣapātin**
solitary **ekākin**
some, someone **kaś cit, ko ›pi**; someone (to do something) *agent noun*
son **putraḥ, dārakaḥ, sutaḥ, putrakaḥ**
sorrow **viṣādaḥ**
sovereignty **rājyaṃ**
speak **vad, vac, abhi+dhā**
speaking **kathā**
specify **nis+diś**
spectator **sāmājikaḥ**
speech **vāc** *f.*
spend (time) **gam** *caus.*, **yā** *caus.* (**yāpayati**)
spoil **duṣ** *caus.*
spot (:place) **uddeśaḥ**
stages, by slow — **śanaiḥ śanaiḥ**
stamp **aṅk**
stand **sthā**
standing **-stha** *ifc.*
start **ā+rabh**
state **avasthā**
stay **sthā, ās**
step **padaṃ**
still **idānīm api**
stone **śilā**
stop **sthā**
story **vṛttāntaḥ**
strange (:unprecedented) **apūrva**; (:marvellous) **citra**
stranger **paraḥ**
strategy **nīti** *f.*
street **rathyā**
stroll through **anu+vi+car**+*acc.*
student **baṭu**
stupid **bāliśa**
subject **prajā, prakṛti** *f.*
success **siddhi** *f.*
such **īdṛśa, evaṃ:vidha, īdṛś** (**īdṛk**)
such as **:vidha, :ādi**
suddenly **sahasā**
śūdra **śūdraḥ**
suffering **vyathā**

sufficient **paryāpta**
suicide **ātma-tyāgaḥ**
suited **anurūpa**
suitor **prārthayitṛ**
summon **ā+hve, sam+ā+hve**
sun **sūryaḥ, vivasvant** *m.*
support **nibandhanaṃ**
suppress **ni+grah**
suppressing **nigrahaḥ**
surely **khalu**
surmise **tark (X tarkayati)**
surpassing (:extreme) **atiśaya**; (:going beyond) **-atirikta**
surround **pari+vṛ**
sweat **svedaḥ**
sweet **madhura**
swift **śīghra, kṣipra**
swoon **mūrchā**
sword **śastraṃ**
syllable **akṣaraṃ**

take (:convey) **nī**; (aocept, understand) **grah**
take away **apa+nī**
talk **kath**
talking **ālāpaḥ**
task **kāryam, karman** *n.*
taunt **adhi+kṣip**
teacher **ācāryaḥ, upādhyāyaḥ**
tell **vad, vac, kath**
temple **āyatanaṃ**
tend (plants) **pari+vṛdh** *caus.*
tender **ārdra**; make tender **vatsalayati**
tenderness **snehaḥ**
that (*demon.*) **saḥ, asau**; (*conj.*) **iti, yat, yathā**
the *usually omit,* **saḥ, asau**
then **tadā, tataḥ**; (:so) **tat**; but then **atha vā**
there **tatra**; from there **tataḥ**
there is **asti**; thére is **ayam asau**
therefore **ataḥ**
thereupon **tataḥ**
thicket **viṭapa** *m./n.*
think **man, cint**
this **eṣaḥ, ayam, enam**; in/on/about this **atra**; from this **ataḥ**
though **api, yady api**
thoughts **citta-vṛtti** *f.*
thread **sūtraṃ**
three **-trayaṃ**; three or four **tricatura**
threshold **dvār** *f.*
throne **siṃhāsanaṃ**
throng **saṃmardaḥ, saṃkulaṃ**
thus **evam**
tiger **vyāghraḥ**
time **kālaḥ, velā, avasaraḥ**; some time later **kasya cit kālasya**
tip **pari+tuṣ** *caus.*
tired **pariśrānta**
tithe **bhāgaḥ**
title **śabdaḥ**
to *use gen., dat., inf. etc.*; (:in the direction of) *use acc.*, **prati, -antikam**; (:in order to) *use dat. or* **-artham**
today **adya**
together with **saha+***instr.*
tone **gir** *f.*
too **api**
top **śikharaṃ**
touch **spṛś**
touch **sparśaḥ**
towards **prati+***acc.*; (— an object of feeling) **prati** *or use loc.*
town **puraṃ**
townsfolk **paura:janaḥ**
trader **vaṇij** *m.*
trainer **vinetṛ**
traitor **rājı-âpathya-kārin**
tread **kṣud**
tree **pādapaḥ, vṛkṣakaḥ, vṛkṣaḥ**; young tree **potakaḥ**

tremble **kamp (I kampate)**
triumph over **ati+śī**
trouble **bādh (I bādhate)**
true **satya**
truly **satyam, nanu**
trust **vi+śvas (I visvasati)+** *loc.*
trustworthy **āpta**
try **yat**
turmoil, in a — **tumula**
turn (to) **kḷp+***dat.*
turn away **parā+vṛt** *caus.*
turn back **prati+ni+vṛt**
turn into (:become) *use* **saṃvṛtta**; (:convert into) *use* **kṛ** *in compound*
turn round **pari+vṛt** *caus.*
twin **yamaja**
two *use du. or* **-dvayam**
twofold **dvaya** (*f.* **dvayī**)

ugliness **vairūpyaṃ**
ultimate **para**
un- **a:/an:**
uncalled for **a:kāraṇa**
uncertainty **vikalpaḥ**
understand **ava+gam, grah**
understand, someone to— **jñātṛ**
underway **pravṛtta**
unite **yuj** *caus.*
unshakeable (resolve) **ahārya**
unsteady **vihvala**
until **yāvat**
untoward **apara**
upon *use loc.*
us **asmān** *etc.*
usher in **pra+viś** *caus.*
utterance **bhāratī**

vain **vitatha**
vainly **mṛṣā**
valour **vikramaḥ**
valuable **mahārghya**
vanish **tiras+bhū**
vapour **dhūmaḥ**
various **vicitra**; various-ness **vaicitryaṃ**
vendor **vikretṛ**
verse **gāthā**
very (*adj.*) *use* **eva**
vexation **parikleśaḥ**
victorious, be — **vi+ji** *ātm.*
victory **vijayaḥ**
Videha, of — **Vaideha** (*f.* **ī**)
vile **dur:ātman**
villain **pāpaḥ**
vine **latā**
violate **ut+laṅgh** *caus.*
violence, do — to **abhi+druh**
violent **pracaṇḍa**
virtuous **sādhu** (*f.* **sādhvī**)
visible **abhivyakta**
voice **vāc** *f.*
void **śūnya**
vow **vrataṃ, pratijñā**

wait for **prati+pāl**
wait upon **upa+ās**
walk **sam+car** *ātm.*
wall **bhitti** *f.*
wander **bhram**
want **iṣ**
warrior **kṣatriyaḥ**
washed **dhauta**
watch **vi+lok** *caus.*, **dṛś**
water **jalaṃ, salilaṃ**
way **prakāraḥ**; in this way **evam**; this way (:in this direction) **itaḥ**; on the way **antarā**
wayward **dur:vinīta**
wealth **vibhūti** *f.*, **koṣaḥ, dyumnaṃ**
weaning **stanya-tyāgaḥ** ('leaving the breast')
weapon **astraṃ**
wear **dhṛ**
wed **upa+yam**
weep **rud**
welcome **prati+nand**; welcome! **svāgatam**

welfare **kuśalaṃ**
well **su** *prefix*
well, as — **api**
wet **klinna**
what? **kaḥ (kim)**; what, . . . ? **katham**; what (a)! *use* **aho**; what (:that which) **yat**; from what? **kutaḥ**; what of it? **tataḥ kim**
when **yadā, yāvat**
where? **kva**; where (*conj.*) **yatra**; where from? **kutaḥ**
whereabouts? **kutaḥ**
which? **kaḥ**; which (*rel. pron.*) **yaḥ**
while (:short time) **muhūrta** *m./n.*; for a little while **muhūrtam iva**
while (*conj.*) **yāvat**
who/whom? **kaḥ**; who/whom (*rel. pron.*) **yaḥ**; it is . . . who *use* **eva**
whole **sarva, sakala, aśeṣa**
whore **puṃścalī**
whose **kasya** *etc.*, **yasya** *etc.*
why? **kim**, (:for what purpose?) **kim-artham**, (:from what cause?) **kasmāt**; why! (*in surprise*) **katham**, (*in mild admonition*) **nanu**
wicked **dur;ātman**
widespread **prathita**
wife **kalatraṃ, dārāḥ** *m. pl.*; friend's wife **sakhī**
win **ji**
wine **madhu** *n.*
wish **iṣ**
wish **manorathaḥ**
with *use instr.*; (:together with) **saha+***instr.*, **sa** *in cpd.*; (:possessing) **˜vant** *or bahuvrīhi*
withdraw **sam+hṛ**
without *use prefixes* **nis** *or* **a**; without (doing) **a+***absol.*
witness **pratyakṣī˜kṛ**
witness (to) **-sākṣin**
woman **strī, nārī, yoṣit** *f.*
wonder, I — (*after interrog.*) **nu khalu**
wonderful **vicitra**
woo **pra+arth** (X **prārthayate**)
wood **vanaṃ, kānanaṃ**
word **vacanaṃ**
work **karman** *n.*; (:literary work) **prabandhaḥ, prayoga-bandhaḥ, kṛti** *f.*
working **vyāpāraḥ**
world **lokaḥ**
worried, be — **śaṅk** (I **śaṅkate**)
worship **vand**
worthier of respect **garīyāṃs**
worthy **ārya**
worthy holder **bhājanaṃ**
wounded **vraṇita**
wretch **varākaḥ**
write **likh, abhi+likh**
writer **kavi** *m.*

yet **tathā›pi, punar** *enclitic*
you **tvam (tvat/yuṣmat)** *etc.*; *you (*polite form*) **bhavant** (*f.* **bhavatī**)
young tree **potakaḥ**
younger **kanīyāṃs**
your/yours/of yours *say* 'of you'
youth **nava:yauvanaṃ**

Supplementary English–Sanskrit Exercises

FOR fuller practice in the material covered in each chapter, students are strongly advised at least to read through the exercises, with keys, provided in the body of the book—particularly from Chapter 6 onwards, where all sentences are taken directly from Sanskrit literature.

Up to Exercise 5 the special vocabulary of the corresponding chapter will be found adequate. Thereafter words required will not necessarily be found anywhere except in the general English–Sanskrit vocabulary.

A short drill in grammatical forms is provided from Exercise 6 onwards: much of the point of this will, of course, be lost unless the grammatical paradigms prescribed for each chapter are previously committed to memory. The English equivalents given for the forms are purely conventional—'from the two clean (men)' is merely a more convenient and less abstract way of saying 'give the ablative dual masculine of the adjective **śuci**'. The cases are represented by 'with' (instrumental), 'to' (dative), 'from' (ablative), 'of' (genitive) 'at/in' (locative), 'O' (vocative). The use of 'stay' (**tiṣṭhati** etc.) and 'he sees' (**paśyati**)—'the girls stay, he sees the girls'—is an adaptation of a device used by Sanskrit grammatical commentators to distinguish nominative and accusative case respectively. It need hardly be said that where synonyms exist the grammatically relevant one should be chosen (e.g. in Exercise 7 for 'friend' use **suhṛd**).

Exercise 1

Transcribe into the nāgarī script the following words, some of which may be familiar to you already:

jātaka, hīnayāna, pūjā, gopī, rāga, guṇa, jaina, Gaṇeśa, kaliyuga, Kālī, hitopadeśa, ahiṃsā, ṛṣi, tapas, mahātmā, stūpa, maṇḍala, apsaras, Avalokiteśvara, Cāṇakya, advaita, āraṇyaka, bhakti, śāntiḥ, buddha, brahmacārin, Vikramāditya, apabhraṃśa, āśrama, Pāṭaliputra, tantrá, Durgā, arthaśāstra, maurya, Harṣa, Takṣaśilā, prajñāpāramitā

Transcribe the following sentences, remembering that in the nāgarī script a word ending in a consonant (ḥ and ṃ apart) will be joined with the next word:

1 **sakhi Śakuntale ihaiva muhūrtaṃ tiṣṭha** 2 **tvayā samīpasthitayā latāsanātha ivāyaṃ cūtavṛkṣakaḥ pratibhāti** 3 **ata eva Priyaṃvadeti tvam ucyase** 4 **iyaṃ svayaṃvaravadhūḥ sahakārasya tvayā kṛtanāmadheyā vanajyautsnīti navamālikā** 5 **sakhy Anasūye ramaṇīyaḥ khalv asya pādapamithunasya vyatikaraḥ saṃvṛttaḥ** 6 **iyaṃ navakusumayauvanā navamālikā, ayam api baddhaphalatayopabhogakṣamaḥ sahakāraḥ** 7 **jānāsi kiṃnimittaṃ Śakuntalā vanajyautsnīm atimātraṃ prekṣata iti** 8 **yathā vanajyautsnī sadṛśena pādapena saṃgatā tathāpi nāmāham apy ātmano ›nurūpaṃ varaṃ labheyeti** 9 **eṣa ātmanas te cittagato manorathaḥ**

Exercise 2

(*a*) With the help of the sandhi grid arrange the following sequences of separate words into continuous utterances (in the order of sentence 1, the words mean 'the-women; indeed; in(to)-this; garden; by-the-ascetics; angrily; from-the-house; (were) brought.'):

1 **nāryaḥ. khalu. asmin. udyāne. tapasvibhiḥ. sakopam.**

gṛhāt. ānītāḥ 2 asmin. khalu. udyāne. nāryaḥ. tapasvibhiḥ. gṛhāt. sakopam. ānītāḥ 3 ānītāḥ. sakopam. khalu. nāryaḥ. gṛhāt. udyāne. asmin. tapasvibhiḥ 4 ānītāḥ. asmin. nāryaḥ. udyāne. sakopam. khalu. tapasvibhiḥ. gṛhāt 5 tapasvibhiḥ. khalu. sakopam. gṛhāt. nāryaḥ. asmin. udyāne. ānītāḥ 6 sakopam. khalu. gṛhāt. tapasvibhiḥ. asmin. nāryaḥ. ānītāḥ. udyāne 7 asmin. ānītāḥ. gṛhāt. khalu. udyāne. nāryaḥ. sakopam. tapasvibhiḥ 8 udyāne. gṛhāt. asmin. sakopam. khalu. ānītāḥ. tapasvibhiḥ. nāryaḥ

(*b*) Translate into Sanskrit:

1 So they are saying 2 The two of them sing. 3 Do you remember? 4 Why are you [*pl.*] asking now? 5 Let us see. 6 I won't write. 7 What, is she going? 8 I understand that they are dancing. 9 Where are the two of you wandering? 10 They are now winning. 11 The two of them are coming this way. 12 Here the two of us stand. 13 You both see and understand. 14 'Where are you going?' they seem to ask. 15 But you [*pl.*] do not understand. 16 We won't sit down now. 17 What do the two of you want here today? 18 We don't go in, because they are living there once more. 19 Now the two of them seem to be grieving again. 20 So, however, do we wish. 21 I ask because I do not remember.

Exercise 3

1 Pupils, where are you taking me? 2 'Does the brahmin live?' they again ask the two men. 3 The sun and moon are beautiful. 4 Who wants water? 5 The children do not see the sun today. 6 Let us two go into the forest. 7 Let us too go to the mountains. 8 Children, the teacher is writing. 9 What, do you ask me, a brahmin? 10 Those two children want food. 11 Teacher and pupils stand astonished. 12 Teacher, that field is small. 13 'Where are those scholars going?' he asks us. 14 Even the brahmins do not remember it. 15 That too we do not understand. 16 Anger leads men

to unhappiness. 17 Who now remembers those scholars? 18 Like a child, he does not see (any) advantage in this. 19 Are you Makaranda? 20 Child, why do you speak to me so?

Exercise 4

1 This is a pleasant town. 2 Shall I go *there*? 3 Look, he is coming into the house with (his) friends. 4 The children are gone: I will go too. 5 (They) have brought the two scholars, alive. 6 I ask this, dear friend: what have my sons done? 7 You have forgotten the *previous* words. 8 What, are you asking *me*? 9 No more despair. 10 They want either a swift horse or a beautiful (one). 11 But Your Majesty has not seen *my* two sons. 12 Though he has come to the forest, he does not see the pupils. 13 Your Majesty, these (men) are exhausted by the attempt. 14 My friends brought a quite extraordinary person to the house. 15 It was he who made this garden. 16 I did not write this, Your Majesty. 17 Your Majesty, although we had already come here, we did not in fact look at it because (our) friends were tired.

Exercise 5

1 Your Majesty, we are beaten. 2 You [*pl.*] have occasion for anger. 3 We have brought this (man) from the fields. 4 Leaving his home he wanders with his sons in the woods. 5 Dear friend, where are you? 6 We'll go to another house and ask. 7 Your Highness is indeed exhausted. 8 What is this extraordinary alarm of everyone? 9 Nothing (makes) for happiness in this world. 10 Did you see Stanakalaśa in Kusumapura? 11 After being [**bhū**] blind for a while, they now see all. 12 'There is in another country a certain blind prince,' he says to the children. 13 We feel exhausted. 14 Mārīca wants [a sight of you:] to see you. 15 Has His Highness too just one son? 16 From the alarm of (my) two friends I apprehend [**avagam**] something evil. 17 Whose book is this? 18 Oh, (there is) no one here. 19 'Here is the villain,' (he) said, and seized the one-eyed (man). 20 A tree

[**pādapaḥ**] has fallen right on the road. 21 The very letter [**lekhaḥ**] is not mine. 22 What is this? Where has your extraordinary love [**anurāgaḥ**] for me gone? 23 What, even after seeing me have you deserted (me) and gone? 24 This is the determination [**niścayaḥ**] of us *all*.

Exercise 6

Grammatical practice (*first memorise prescribed paradigms*): 1 from the girls 2 of Ūrmilā 3 with the two noble (ladies) 4 O Sītā 5 in the seals 6 he sees the girl 7 to those *f.* 8 with this seal 9 these two *f.* stay 10 at that *f.*

(Words joined together by points (·) should be translated by a single compound.)

1 Your Majesty, where is this girl from? 2 The noble lady is asking about Ūrmilā. 3 Here is the honourable·Cāṇakya's house. 4 I've forgotten my [thread·of·measure:] tape measure. 5 Vṛṣala, why have (you) summoned us? 6 Ha, he has flown up from the mountain-top to the sky and is showering me with arrows. 7 I have bestowed her upon you. 8 The time·for·advice is of course long·past. 9 It is by my·father's·command that I have come here to·your·presence. 10 (I) have seen this decayed·garden. 11 And I for my part will not grant (you) the seal. 12 Oh, two·men asleep. 13 Madam, is this really the same gold·box? 14 She has defeated me [*f.*], Your Majesty. 15 And I gave this to Siddhārthaka on some occasion·for·rewarding (him). 16 It is still you who have power over this (girl). 17 And the sacrificial horse has been released, consecrated·by·Vāmadeva. 18 The painter has depicted in this gallery Your Honour's exploits (as) indicated·by·us. 19 Good fellow, is it this cancellation·of·the·Full·Moon·festival alone that is Candragupta's reason·for·anger towards Cāṇakya, or [**uta**] is there another (reason) as well? 20 What, have I brought the two of them to this pass through (*abl.*) announcing·bad·news? But then [**athavā**] what else, apart from poison, emerges from a serpent's·mouth?

Exercise 7

Grammatical practice: 1 in a friend 2 with minds 3 of two rivers 4 to Her Majesty 5 the direction stays 6 from friends 7 he sees rivers 8 minds stay 9 to the direction 10 in rivers

1 This is well·known to me. 2 Vetravatī, did you not indeed see Queen Vasumatī on your way [**antarā**]? 3 Vasantasenā's [two] garments are wet. 4 What, did Rākṣasa have my father killed—not Cāṇakya? 5 The time·for·going·home is drawing near. 6 Bābhravya, this (girl) is like [**sadṛśa**] the princess. 7 Your Majesty, I will so announce to the council·of·ministers. 8 You are telling an excessively·confused (story). 9 Pṛthvī·and·Bhāgīrathī have rescued the noble lady. 10 She did not go surely in [*instr.*] that direction? 11 Concerning·oneself·[**vyavahāraḥ**]·with·another's·wife is ig·noble. 12 Now where, I wonder, with a mind disinclined·for·normal·occupation shall I spend this remaining·part·of·the·day? 13 The mere sight of these ladies has honoured me. 14 Sir, is this cancellation·of·the·Full·Moon·Festival actually un·known to His Majesty Candragupta? 15 The word·'abandoned' has aroused our curiosity. 16 You have beaten me (while I am) actually in·the·roadway. 17 What, has Her Majesty gone without at all relenting? 18 I'll just get my followers to camp at a good distance from the ascetic·grove. 19 Has the scandal·of·Śakuntalā's·rejection not come to the [path·of·the·ears:] hearing of these two ladies? 20 By this diligence·in·service·to·me you recall my earlier·pupil Saudāmanī. 21 So I'll just sit for a moment on this broken·stone·slab, natural·in·the·harsh·change·in·(my)·circumstances. 22 (You) whore! My friends have been [*use pres.*] describing your [**tvad-gata**] misconduct. 23 For this is some girl (whom I) conceived [with:] in my own·mind and painted, not one seen·before. 24 Let us [two] go to the bower·of·mādhavī·vines and wait for the time·of·appointment·with·(my)·adored·one.

Exercise 8

Grammatical practice: 1 O king 2 from names 3 the king

stays 4 to the self 5 to the king 6 to two names 7 he sees two kings 8 of selves 9 in kings 10 the two names stay

1 Homage to this (man) whose·austerities·are·severe. 2 See, immediately·upon·the·command of Your Highness, all the chieftains have turned back. 3 Here comes Candrikā, maid-servant to your friend's wife, her·hands·busy·with·picking·flowers. 4 I'll just conceal myself and remain. 5 This is not the remedy for this sin. 6 A vapour·drinking śūdra called Śambūka is practising austerities in this same Janasthāna. 7 So I'll just send Śatrughṇa [for the extermination of:] to exterminate this evil·natured son·of·Kumbhīnasī. 8 I can see (that) appeasement (is) difficult·to·achieve here. 9 When·I·have·plucked·out·the·barb·of·sorrow, I will tell. 10 Why, this show has turned into (something) quite different. 11 The highest blessing in marriage is assuredly mutual·love. 12 Why do you ask me, though you·know·what·has·happened? 13 And it was he who created this extremely·lovely wood called Caitraratha. 14 Everyone of course sees himself (as) desirable. 15 I seem to be entering a darkness where·support·for·(my)·steps·is·not·discerned. 16 From·[**gata**]·the·Sugāṅga·palace His Majesty perceived entirely for himself that Kusuma-pura [did·not·have·underway:] was·not·celebrating·the·Full·Moon·Festival. 17 Ha! Who (is) this villain (who) has [become a hindrance to:] intruded upon us? 18 With·my·freedom·of·manœuvre·obstructed so on all sides by Your Excellency, [sovereignty is like bondage to me, not like sovereignty:] I feel more like a prisoner than a king.

Translate the following as nominal sentences with bahuvrīhis for predicate:

19 I have completed·my·prayers. 20 Your intention·has·been·grasped by Vasantaka. 21 What·is·the·name·of her [male] friend? 22 Your Majesty, in the science·of·acting assuredly the important·thing·is·performance. 23 Now my exertions·have become·fruitful.

Exercise 9

Use the past active participle where indicated. 'You' when preceded by an asterisk is to be translated by **bhavant**.

Grammatical practice: 1 You two hurry 2 to the fire 3 by *you 4 of the two clean (women) 5 of the two clean (things) 6 they hurry 7 of the soft ones 8 he sees *you *pl.* 9 the clean (things) stay 10 *you two hurry

1 Welcome Mitrāvasu! 2 *You are clever. 3 See, we are hurrying. 4 Then what did she say? [*use past active part.*] 5 But the audience has often seen the work of earlier poets. 6 I greet *you [two]. 7 And the king's·daughter is (at present) with [*loc.*] her father-in-law's·family. 8 Bravo, lord·of·Kosala, bravo! 9 Who are *you two [*f.*], and who is this (girl)? 10 With regard to (my) beloved Mālatī, I am become without·hope. 11 Such persistence·in·anger towards one's friends [*f.*] is certainly not right. 12 You have understood correctly, my friend. [*p.a.p.*] 13 Did *you [*pl.*] hear? 14 Here is the house of some good (person), with·its·side·door·un·shut. 15 Friend, (they) seem to be having a conversation. 16 Thank heavens my uncertainty about Śakaṭadāsa is removed. 17 Sire, possessors·of·religious·power of course have·their·welfare·under·their·own·control. 18 But to·what·end have these mass·deaths occurred? 19 Is he (still) living right there?—he didn't go to an ascetic·grove, or again enter upon [**samāruh** *p.a.p.*] a vow? 20 I'll get (it) measured and begin the work. 21 How [**aho**] fraught·with·[**vant**]·obstacles is success·[*pl.*]·in·one's·desires. 22 Bravo, friend—cleverly begun! Now we (can feel) hope in this enterprise, though success·in·it·is·hard·to·attain. 23 Susaṃgatā, how did *you know me (to be) [standing·] here? 24 (I) congratulate husband and wife on (their) son's·victory. 25 Your Reverence [*f.*], here (is) a letter (which) the King, the ruler·of·Padmāvatī, approved·by·a·delighted·Nandana, has written in the presence of Bhūrivasu and sent [*use absol. plus p.p.*] to the long-lived Mādhava. 26 But for one·who·maintains·the·(sacred)·fire [**āhita:âgni**] the ceremony (of cremation) is enjoined (to be)

by no other fire. Therefore let us bring fires from the place·of·sacrifice and set ourselves alight. 27 And after (their) weaning, the Goddess·Gaṅgā herself handed the two·sons of that (queen) to the great-seer Prācetasa.[*p.a.p.*] 28 At this juncture a brahmin laid [**āruh** *caus.*] his dead son at the king's·threshold and with·a·beating·of·his·breast proclaimed (an act of) sacrilege.

Exercise 10

Clauses marked as compounds (as in sentence 14) should be translated by means of abstract nouns.

Grammatical practice: 1 go *pl.* 2 in ascetics 3 from a bride 4 of the two leading 5 see the women 6 to an ascetic (while) leading. 7 let great (men) stay 8 hurry, ascetics 9 in the earth 10 singing, the two should go

1 Welcome! Be seated (both of you) over here. 2 Obviously being·childless makes me tender. 3 What, have I offended against the ascetics? 4 So call her and come. 5 All this is the outcome of my recklessness, monster (that I am). 6 May Your [two] Highnesses be victorious. 7 And this (tree) in falling has killed a woman. 8 Oh magnanimous one, I am in distress, thinking myself to be as it were licked·by·the·flames of·the·fires·of·hell. 9 Mother, you too go back now. 10 What inflammatory sýllables. 11 Her Majesty and I [*reverse order*] are partisans of the two of them. 12 Vardhamānaka, turn the carriage round. Maitreya my friend, fetch Vasantasenā down. 13 Dear child, may this utterance of yours be not·vain. 14 Since·gems·are·abundant in a great palace, a matching of ornaments is not improbable [**durlabha**]. 15 Do not think of [**alam alam**] rebuking (her). She is helpful to you. 16 *You should consider yourself similarly [**api**] a worthy·holder·of·the·title·'queen'. 17 Other women too have been driven distracted by the wayward god of love. 18 How várious is the noble·Cāṇakya's·strategy. 19 Let my revered father pardon [Lava's being:] Lava for being·stupid. 20 Shame on me [contemptuous·of:] in·my·contempt·for·the·

good·(that·had)·fallen (to me). 21 Thereupon fearing·the destruction·of·the·whole·serpent·world, the king·of·the·serpents Vāsuki addressed Garutmant. 22 Know Sumati, Mādhavasena's·counsellor, to be my elder brother. 23 Jayasenā, when·the·task·is·accomplished bring confirmation (of the fact) quickly. 24 The accursed·Cāṇakya surely did not discover them to be living there? 25 And I for my part acted quite rightly in placing her respectfully in·Her·Majesty's·hand(s). 26 But my father because·he·was·childless greeted my·birth with a festival surpassing·the·birth·of·a·son. 27 [At the end of me too:] And when I myself die, this (will be) what happens [**vṛttāntaḥ**] to the glory·of·the·dynasty·of·Puru. 28 Reverend (sir), I have offended against the revered Kaṇva (who is) of·your·gotra, in (first) wedding [*absol.*] this your handmaid by the Gandharva rite, (then, when she had been) brought by her kinsmen some time later, rejecting (her) because·my·memory·was·impaired. Afterwards, from seeing·the·ring, I realized her (to have been) previously·married (to me). [*The p.p. of* **avagam** *may have an active sense.*] 29 And (I) introduced him into Kusumapura [bearing·the·signs·of:] disguised·as·a·mendicant immediately upon (my) vow·of·destroying·the·dynasty·of·Nanda, and had him make friends with all·the·Nanda·ministers. [make friends **sakhyaṃ grah**]

Exercise 11

Translate all present actives (except in 8, 13, 16 and 30) and all imperatives by means of the passive.

Grammatical practice: 1 with two makers 2 he sees the sisters 3 of fathers 4 we two are led 5 he sees the mother 6 the sisters stay 7 from a maker 8 let the two mothers be led 9 O sister 10 to the father

1 So give (me) this seal. 2 That royal·seer is [heard:] reputed to be a good man. 3 Homage to Yogācārya, whose first pupil I am. 4 Lava dear child, withdraw your weapon. 5 What, have (my) parents left me and gone to an ascetic·

grove? 6 But *you, where are you going? 7 Why, this is the one in whose [hand:] care your aunt forwarded the letter. 8 With Her Majesty now reconciled, it is solely concern·for·Sāgarikā that troubles me. 9 Who (is) to protect you, (my) son? 10 Swiftly pursue and seize the vile Śakaṭadāsa. 11 Ah, to the right of the enclosure·of·trees (I) seem to hear talking. 12 Susaṃgatā, this is actually just·a·game. 13 Kāṇelīmātṛ, is there any sign you (can) discern? 14 Vasantaka, meet [**pratyudgam**] Vasubhūti and usher him in. 15 With the Minister to guide, this is easy for His Highness. 16 It is a trainer's acceptance·of·poor·material which reveals the inferiority·of·(his)·intelligence. 17 This is the same necklace·of·jewels His Majesty gave to the princess at the time·of·(her)·departure. 18 Remember your own remark to [**prati**] me on seeing·the·portrait. 19 He gave his·own·daughter to Vatsarāja though (she was) being·wooed·by·me. 20 Free all prisoners including Yajñasena's·brother-in-law. 21 Forgive (me) what I did without·informing Your Majesty. 22 We too are busying ourselves upon our·own·work. 23 Go into the picture·gallery quiet(ly) with Manoramā and stay watching our·acting. 24 Oh (you [*f.*] who are) conscious·only·of·the pangs·of·your·own·heart (while) ignorant·of·another's·suffering—see, (I) scold you. 25 Well, say what [**kim**] is to be done with [*gen.*] this villain. 26 This mendicant Jīvasiddhi who, employed·by·Rākṣasa, had Parvateśvara killed by a poison·girl shall after proclamation of this same crime be banished in disgrace from the city. 27 When (you had) thus discovered·the·grounds·for·the·disloyalty·of these (people) [*use loc. abs. with predicative bahuvrīhi*], why did Your Excellency not swiftly take countermeasures? 28 Gautama, who is so ill-disposed to us [who has:] as to have enraged Her Majesty? 29 Worthy Cārudatta, do *you have in relation to [**saha**] the daughter of this worthy (lady) (any) attachment, affection or fondness? 30 Reverend (sir), in (the course of) some altercation [of:] between that (woman) who today at Court acknowledged defeat at my hands [**mattaḥ**] and myself, she taunted me [*f.*] ['you are boasting . . .':] with boasting as if I had [*past. act. part.*] seduced Marīci.

Exercise 12

For convenience, 'must' represents a gerundive in **tavya**, 'should' one in **ya** or **anīya**.

Grammatical practice: 1 they are doing 2 he hates 3 the two go 4 let him do 5 you two abide 6 are you listening? 7 they abide 8 we do 9 listen 10 hating, the two abide

1 Ah, Vṛṣala occupies the throne! 2 One·should·not·go· against Divaspati's command, friend. 3 You too [make your own office not·void:] be about your affairs. 4 He must be here, where (there is) this crowd·of·people. 5 Because° the house °is·decrepit, the door creaks. 6 Have *you two (ladies) ever witnessed this? 7 And the gold·box here you must guard by night, and Vardhamānaka by day. 8 I won't let go before you look at my heart's·beloved [*f.*] painted on the rock. 9 One should of course salute (all) deities. 10 Let the two of us just listen attentive(ly). 11 Here is that hero, [become·an object·of·speech for you:] (now) within range of your voice. 12 So I'll [make her debtless:] discharge her debt. 13 And now, in returning, dear·Rāma must inévitably see in the Pañcavaṭī·forest the places (that were) witness·to·the·intimacies·of·his·sojourn·with·his·bride. 14 As my heart declares, Gautama is free·from·the·poison. 15 Frivolous (girl), (you) must not go a single step further [**padāt padam api**] from this place without·giving (me) this rosary. 16 [Let there abide:] Never mind this un·instructed wretch. 17 What, has Śaṅkhacūḍa (by) coming (here) made·fruitless my wish? 18 How am I indeed to distract myself, whose·desires·are·(so)·hard·to·win? 19 Then [while I [*f.*] having fainted was regaining consciousness (*present tense*), she became one·whose·sight·was·hard·to·win:] when I came round after my swoon, she had vanished from sight. 20 Rather, since [**iti**] a guest is senior to anyone, it is *you who should be honoured by us. 21 Ho there students! Turn this horse away (by) surrounding it and beating (it) off with clods of earth. 22 Worthy lady, with the Nāgānanda to be acted, why these quite uncalled for tears? [*use impersonal passive of* **rud**] 23 And from the fact

that (there is) this violent gale which·has·shaken·the·crags·of·the·Malaya·mountain, I surmise that the king·of·the·birds is at hand [**āsannī˜bhūta**]. 24 And complacent (as I was), I made that same (woman) mistress of my·[own]·money, my·house, my·household [**gaṇaḥ**], my·person and my·life. 25 Then, when the ruler·of·Siṃhala, though often petitioned by us on·(our)·master's·behalf because of (our) belief·in·that·(prophecy), in his avoidance of [*pres. part. of* **parihṛ**] distress·of·mind to Queen Vāsavadattā refused to give her (i.e. the girl, in marriage), (we) contrived a report that Her Majesty had been burnt [by:] in the fire at Lāvāṇaka, and despatched Bābhravya to him. 26 How inspiring of cónfidence [**viśvasanīya**] is (his) form, though resplendent. 27 And this (man), obviously, must be her son, for·whose·sake she is crying. 28 So (by) coming and personally playing [his own role:] the part of himself, let him enjoy the delight·of·a·meeting. 29 But the decorations previously·worn·by·Parvateśvara (being) of·merit should be conferred only on brahmins of·merit. 30 Until I come (back) after going to the city and having [**kṛ**] a drink·of·wine in·the·company·of·my·friends, you [*f.*] should [be not·negligent upon:] look after the house.

Exercise 13

Grammatical practice: 1 of that (man) 2 sacrifice 3 he obstructs 4 they two buy 5 let them know 6 in those (men) 7 give that [*n.*] 8 we two obstruct 9 those (women) sacrifice 10 buy those two

1 Take this box. 2 Where, I wonder, will there be water? 3 If (it is) not a secret, I should like to hear the cause·of·(your)·grief 4 Why, you will be [**vṛt**] right beside·me. 5 Oh, thére is the woman. 6 Manoramā, is it true what Vasantaka says? 7 You know, dear child, how to distract Her Majesty (when she is) feeling depressed. 8 People are taking (it) in this way. 9 Then what is that man going to say to (his) friends, poor fellow? 10 If you are *really* going back, you should [**arh**] take me too to the hermitage. 11 The workings of men's·fortunes are indeed inscrutable, since I have reached such a pass.

12 So, Vṛṣala, we have been summoned to be rebuked? 13 Reverend sir, why do you say [**abhidhā**] so? 14 Poison is difficult to turn·into·medicine. 15 Highness, if Śakaṭadāsa wrote it [the letter *m.*], then *I* wrote it. 16 Give me leave (to go), dear child [*f.*]. 17 So I will go in here and find out news·of·Candanadāsa from someone. 18 And it is strange that, although understanding (this to be) so, I [*f.*] cannot restrain my own mental turmoil. 19 Highness, those are *not* the peaks·of·the·Malaya·mountain. 20 How is this proper for *you even to consider [with:] in your mind, let alone declare or look upon? 21 I will try (to see to it) that that selfsame harlot [will unite you with your own wealth:] restores your wealth to you. 22 So let Your Highness don this. 23 What, are the very ones who are ready to appease Candragupta by killing·me providing my bodyguard? 24 That man is the noble·Cārudatta after all—how could he have done this misdeed? 25 Lakṣmaṇa dear child, the reverend Vālmīki has invited us to see his·own·work [being] performed by the nymphs. 26 Shame (on you, you) fool! Why did you scare her by laughing (so) loudly that she flew up and went somewhere else? 27 But a heart (that has) inclined in one direction cannot be made to incline in another. Therefore I dare not accept her. 28 Are you worried that Mataṅga is going to snatch the kingdom? If so, what of it? Why, it is for·the·sake·of·others that I protect everything, starting with my·own·person [**sva:śarīra˜taḥ prabhṛti**]. But that (I) don't give it (to him) of my own accord is out of regard·for·my·father. 29 How [does:] can an audience pass over the works of those·whose·fame·is·widespread such·as·Bhāsa·Saumilla·and·Kaviputra, and have respect for the activity of Kālidāsa, a contemporary·writer? 30 If this same girl [**sā iyam**] [is of·unshakeable·resolve:] continues to be stubborn, all these people will [having·no·other·course:] have no choice but to fast to death right here.

Exercise 14

Use the imperfect tense where possible, except in 28 and the first part of 15.

Grammatical practice: 1 we two led 2 they may lead 3 of two better (things) 4 you *pl.* hurried 5 I obstructed 6 they may hate 7 you two abided 8 we may see the two elder (men) 9 you were elder 10 they would be better

1 In falling to [*loc.*] the ground it might make a noise. 2 So I should like to hear who you are. 3 There he saw one of the two mating curlews being shot by a huntsman. 4 Here is my younger brother actually arrived, having·assumed·the·role·of·Yaugandharāyaṇa. 5 Destiny would at long last indeed be acting·rightly, if it should join this pair suited·to·each·other. 6 As if fearful·of·the·falling·of·a·shower·of·Love's·sharp·arrows, the slender·body [**gātra:yaṣṭi** *f.*] trembled. 7 Now is Mālatī especially·attractive. 8 If only the vile Rākṣasa may be captured. 9 But because of my ugliness I had the sobriquet 'Virūpaka'. 10 She was immediately summoned together with her mother by the king. 11 Why, your elder sister here is in distress—so embrace her. 12 But with you denounced, all our·family would be ruined. 13 And Haṃsa, Lord·of·the second·Gandharva·family. made her his beloved wife as (did) the Ocean·of·Milk Mandākinī. 14 What may (a man who is) being beaten not say? 15 But what she did on coming there, what she said, how [*use* **kim**] she behaved [everything (being) absent·minded I [*f.*] did not notice:] I was so absent-minded that I did not notice at all. 16 No other (thing) is more·wholly·evil [**pāpiṣṭha˜tama**] than suicide. 17 Your Majesty, we had great hope(s) that your·servant Rāgamañjarī, whose·character·accomplishments·and·skill·are·suited·to·her·beauty, would fulfil (our) wishes. 18 The purse·proud Arthapati, [having·bits·of·rag·as·remnants:] reduced to rags, was banished in·front·of·all·the·townsfolk. 19 And feeling compassion I said, 'Come virtuous lady, let me [*opt.*] take you to the home·of·your·beloved,' and proceeded three·or·four steps. 20 Say now what is in your mind, Gautama. 21 Otherwise, perhaps, on suddenly seeing me in·such·a·condition my parents might abandon life. 22 And Rumaṇvant, having set my ˆelder ˆbrother Jayavarman over [*loc.*] the Kosalas, is in fact coming by slow stages accompanying his whole·army (which has been)

wounded·in·battle. 23 If only I were able to effect the rescue of even one serpent by [*abl.*] giving·my·own·body. 24 So thus with·my·plans·accomplished I made Rāgamañjarī's· house full·of·gold·and·jewels. 25 Where are (you) going, abandoning a person dearer even than life? 26 And Candragupta might accept (him) because he is in fact an hereditary (servant). In which case [**evaṃ sati**] His Highness would not trust us [too:] either. 27 I gave half·of·it to the gaming-master and his assistants, appropriated half, and rose; and there rose (with me) the delighted [**harṣa‿garbha**] acclamations of those·who·were·there. 28 (I) did not say (anything) because I was going to congratulate Her Majesty when this mission was actually accomplished [*loc. abs.*]. 29 Vṛṣala, if Malayaketu's escape·had·not·been·connived·at [*loc. abs. with bahuvrīhi*], (we) should have had [a twofold course:] two courses: he might have been either suppressed or presented with the half·of·the·kingdom already·promised. Now [**tāvat**] in suppressing him, (our) signature would have been given [*p.p. with* **as**] [to the ingratitude that [**iti**] Parvataka was murdered by us:] to a confession of having treacherously murdered Parvataka. 30 And we [two] got up and with·washed·faces performed the morning rites, and (as we were) strolling through the town (which was) in·a·turmoil·at·our·deeds, we heard a clamour in the houses·of·the·bride·and·groom.

Supplementary Exercises: Key

Exercise 2a

1 nāryaḥ khalv asminn udyāne tapasvibhiḥ sakopaṃ gṛhād ānītāḥ 2 asmin khal’ ûdyāne nāryas tapasvibhir gṛhāt sakopam ānītāḥ 3 ānītāḥ sakopaṃ khalu nāryo gṛhād udyāne ’smiṃs tapasvibhiḥ 4 ānītā asmin nārya udyāne sakopaṃ khalu tapasvibhir gṛhāt 5 tapasvibhiḥ khalu sakopaṃ gṛhān nāryo ’sminn udyāna ānītāḥ 6 sakopaṃ khalu gṛhāt tapasvibhir asmin nārya ānītā udyāne 7 asminn ānītā gṛhāt khal’ ûdyāne nāryaḥ sakopaṃ tapasvibhiḥ 8 udyāne gṛhād asmin sakopaṃ khalv ānītās tapasvibhir nāryaḥ

Exercise 2b

1 evaṃ vadanti 2 gāyataḥ 3 api/kiṃ smarasi? 4 adhunā kiṃ pṛcchatha? 5 paśyāmaḥ 6 na likhāmi 7 kathaṃ, gacchati? 8 ‘nṛtyant’’ îty avagacchāmi 9 kva bhramathaḥ? 10 adhunā jayanti 11 ita āgacchataḥ 12 atra tiṣṭhāvaḥ 13 paśyasi c’ âvagacchasi ca 14 ‘kva gacchas’?’ îti pṛcchant’ îva 15 na punar avagacchatha 16 adhunā n’ ôpaviśāmaḥ 17 adya kim atr’ êcchathaḥ? 18 tatra punar api vasant’ îti na praviśāmaḥ 19 punar adhunā śocata iva 20 evaṃ punar icchāmaḥ 21 na smarām’ îti pṛcchāmi

Exercise 3

1 śiṣyāḥ, māṃ kva nayatha? 2 ‘api jīvati sa brāhmaṇa?’ iti punar api narau pṛcchanti 3 śobhanau sūrya;candrau 4

jalaṃ ka icchati? 5 sūryam adya bālā na paśyanti 6 vanam (āvāṃ) praviśāvaḥ 7 vayam api parvatān gacchāmaḥ 8 bālāḥ, likhaty ācāryaḥ 9 kathaṃ, brāhmaṇaṃ māṃ pṛcchasi? 10 bhojanaṃ tau bālāv icchataḥ 11 ācārya;śiṣyā vismitās tiṣṭhanti 12 ācārya, svalpaṃ tat kṣetram 13 'te kva gacchanti paṇḍitā?' ity asmān pṛcchati 14 brāhmaṇā api tan na smaranti 15 tad api n' âvagacchāmaḥ 16 duḥkhaṃ nayati narān krodhaḥ 17 tān paṇḍitān adhunā kaḥ smarati? 18 bāla iva phalam atra na paśyati 19 kiṃ tvaṃ Makarandaḥ? 20 bāla, kim evaṃ māṃ vadasi?

Exercise 4

1 ramaṇīyam etan nagaram 2 kiṃ tatr' aîva gacchāmi? 3 eṣa vayasyaiḥ saha gṛhaṃ praviśati 4 gatā bālāḥ—aham api gacchāmi 5 ānītau jīvitāv eva paṇḍitau 6 priya vayasya, etat pṛcchāmi—kiṃ madīyaiḥ putraiḥ kṛtam (iti)? 7 vismṛtāni tvayā prathamāny eva vacanāni 8 kathaṃ, mām eva pṛcchasi? 9 alaṃ viṣādena 10 śīghraṃ vā 'śvaṃ śobhanaṃ v' êcchanti 11 na punar dṛṣṭau devena madīyāv eva putrau 12 vanam āgato 'pi śiṣyān na paśyati 13 deva, pariśrāntā ete prayatnena 14 adbhuta eva jano madīyair vayasyair gṛham ānītaḥ 15 ten' aîv' aîtad udyānaṃ kṛtam 16 deva, n' aîtan mayā likhitam 17 deva, prathamam atr' āgatair apy asmābhiḥ pariśrāntā vayasyā iti n' aîva dṛṣṭam

Exercise 5

1 deva, jitāḥ smaḥ 2 asti vaḥ krodhasy' âvasaraḥ 3 kṣetrebhyo 'yam asmābhir ānītaḥ 4 gṛhaṃ tyaktvā vaneṣu putraiḥ saha bhramati 5 priya vayasya kv' âsi? 6 gṛham anyad gatvā pṛcchāmaḥ 7 pariśrāntaḥ khalu kumāraḥ 8 adbhutaḥ ko 'yaṃ sarveṣām āvegaḥ? 9 iha na kiṃcit sukhāy' aîva 10 api dṛṣṭas tvayā Kusumapure Stanakalaśaḥ? 11 andhā muhūrtaṃ bhūtvā sarvam idānīṃ paśyanti 12 'asty anyasmin deśe 'ndhaḥ kaścit kumāra' iti bālān vadati 13 pariśrāntā iva smaḥ 14 Mārīcas te darśanam icchati 15 kiṃ kumārasy' âpy eka eva putraḥ? 16 mitrayor āvegāt pāpaṃ kiṃcid

avagacchāmi 17 kasy) êdaṃ pustakam? 18 hā na kaścid atra 19 'ayam eva sa pāpa' ity uktvā kāṇo gṛhītaḥ 20 mārga eva pādapo nipatitaḥ 21 lekha eva madīyo na bhavati 22 kim etat? kva gatas tava mayy adbhuto)nurāgaḥ? 23 katham, māṃ dṛṣṭvā)pi parityajya gato)si? 24 sarveṣām ev) âsmākam ayaṃ niścayaḥ

Exercise 6

1 deva, kuta iyaṃ kanyakā? 2 Ūrmilāṃ pṛcchaty āryā 3 idam ārya:Cāṇakyasya gṛham 4 pramāṇa-sūtraṃ me vismṛtam 5 Vṛṣala, kim-arthaṃ vayam āhūtāḥ? 6 hanta, śaila-śikharād gaganam utpatya bāṇair māṃ abhivarṣati 7 sā mayā tubhyaṃ pradattā 8 dūr):âtītaḥ khal) ûpadeśa-kālaḥ 9 tāta-saṃdeśen) aîv) âsmi tvat-sakāśam ih) āgataḥ 10 dṛṣṭam etaj jīrṇ):ôdyānam 11 aham api mudrāṃ na prayacchāmi 12 aye, puruṣa-dvayaṃ suptam 13 bhadre, satyaṃ tad ev) êdaṃ suvarṇa-bhāṇḍam? 14 deva, jitā)mayā)ham 15 mayā)py etat kasmiṃścit paritoṣa-sthāne Siddhārthakāya dattam 16 idānīm api tvam ev) âsyāḥ prabhavasi 17 visṛṣṭaś ca Vāmadev)-âbhimantrito medh-yo)śvaḥ 18 tena citrakareṇ) âsmad-upadiṣṭam āryasya caritam asyāṃ vīthikāyām abhilikhitam 19 bhadra, kim ayam ev) aîkaḥ Kaumudī-mahotsava-pratiṣedhaś Candraguptasya Cāṇakyaṃ prati kopa-kāraṇam, ut) ânyad apy asti? 20 katham, apriya-nivedanān may) aîtām avasthāṃ gamitau [*or* nītau]? athavā viṣadhara-vadanād viṣam antareṇa kim anyan niṣkrāmati?

Exercise 7

1 su:viditam etan mama 2 Vetravati, na khalv antarā dṛṣṭā tvayā devī Vasumatī? 3 klinne vāsasī Vasantase-nāyāḥ 4 katham, Rākṣasena ghātitas tāto, na Cāṇakyena? 5 pratyāsīdati gṛha-gamana-kālaḥ 6 Bābhravya, sadṛś) îyaṃ rāja-putryā 7 deva, evam amātya-pariṣade nive-dayāmi 8 aty: ākulaṃ kathayasi 9 Pṛthvī;Bhāgīrathī-bhyām abhyupapann) āryā 10 na gatā khalu sā tayā diśā? 11 an:āryaḥ para-dāra-vyavahāraḥ 12 ath) êmaṃ divasa-śeṣam ucita:vyāpāra-parāṅmukhena cetasā kva nu khalu yāpayāmi? 13 darśanen) aîv) âtrabhavatīnāṃ

puraskṛto 'smi 14 ārya, kim a:vidita ev' âyaṃ devasya Candraguptasya Kaumudī-mahotsava-pratiṣedhaḥ? 15 'ujjhita':śabdena janitaṃ naḥ kutūhalam 16 ahaṃ tvayā mārga-gata eva tāḍitaḥ 17 katham, akṛtv' aîva prasādaṃ gatā devī? 18 yāvad anuyātrikān atidūre tapo-vanasya niveśayāmi 19 kim atrabhavatyoḥ karṇa-pathaṃ n' āyātaṃ Śakuntalā-pratyādeśa-kaulīnam? 20 anena mat-priy'-âbhiyogena smārayasi me pūrva: śiṣyāṃ Saudāmanīm 21 tad yāvad asmin viṣama: daśā˘pariṇāma-sulabhe bhagna:śilā˘tale muhūrtam upaviśāmi 22 puṃścali, tvad-gatam apacāraṃ suhṛdo me varṇayanti 23 iyaṃ hi kā 'pi kanyakā sva:cetas' aîva parikalpy' ālikhitā, na tu dṛṣṭa:pūrvā 24 mādhavī-latā-maṇḍapam gatvā priyatamā-saṃket'-âvasaraṃ pratipālayāvaḥ

Exercise 8

1 namo 'smai kaṣṭa:tapase 2 ete kumārasy' ājñā-'nantaram eva pratinivṛttāḥ sarve rājānaḥ 3 eṣā kusum'-âvacaya-vyagra:hastā sakhyās te paricārikā Candrikā samāgacchati 4 yāvad ātmānam ācchādya tiṣṭhāmi 5 n' âyaṃ pratīkāro 'sya pāpmanaḥ 6 Śambūko nāma dhūma-paḥ śūdro 'sminn eva Janasthāne tapaś carati 7 tad yāvad asya dur:ātmanaḥ Kumbhīnasī-putrasy' ônmūlanāya Śatrughnaṃ preṣayāmi 8 dur:labham atr' ânunayaṃ paśyāmi 9 uddhṛta:viṣāda˘śalyaḥ kathayāmi 10 katham, anyad ev' êdaṃ prekṣaṇīyakaṃ saṃvṛttam 11 itaretar'-ânurāgo hi dāra-karmaṇi parārdhyaṃ maṅgalam 12 vidita:vṛttānto 'pi kiṃ māṃ pṛcchasi? 13 ten' aîva c' êdaṃ Caitrarathaṃ nām' âti:manoharaṃ kānanaṃ nirmitam 14 sarvaḥ khalu kāntam ātmānaṃ paśyati 15 a:saṃvijñāta:pada˘nibandhanaṃ tama iva praviśāmi 16 svayam eva Sugāṅga:prāsāda-gatena deven' âvalokitam a:pravṛtta:Kaumudī-mahotsavaṃ Kusumapuram 17 āḥ, ka eṣa pāpo 'smākam antarāyaḥ saṃvṛttaḥ? 18 āryeṇ' aîvaṃ sarvato niruddha:ceṣṭā˘prasarasya mama bandhanam iva rājyaṃ, na rājyam iva 19 samāpta:japo 'smi 20 gṛhīt':âbhiprāyo 'si Vasantakena 21 kiṃ:nāmadheyaṃ tasyā mitram? 22 deva, prayoga:pradhānaṃ hi nāṭya-śāstram 23 idānīṃ saphala:pariśramo 'smi saṃvṛttaḥ

Exercise 9

1 Mitrāvaso, svāgatam 2 nipuṇo bhavān 3 ete tvarāmahe 4 tataḥ kim uktavatī 5 bahuśas tu pariṣadā pūrveṣāṃ kavīnāṃ dṛṣṭaḥ prayogabandhaḥ 6 abhivādaye bhavantau 7 rāja-sutā ca śvaśura-kule vartate 8 sādhu, Kosala-pate, sādhu 9 ke bhavatyau, kā cı êyam? 10 priyāṃ Mālatīṃ prati nir_āśaḥ saṃvṛtto ›smi 11 na khalu yuktaḥ sakhī:jana evaṃvidhaḥ kop›-ânubandhaḥ 12 sakhe, samyag gṛhītavān asi 13 śrutaṃ bhavadbhiḥ? 14 idaṃ kasyı âpi sādhor an:āvṛta:pakṣa-dvāraṃ geham 15 vayasya, saṃlāpa iva vartate 16 diṣṭyā Śakaṭadāsaṃ praty apanīto me vikalpaḥ 17 rājan, svādhīna:kuśalāḥ khalu siddhi˜mantaḥ 18 kiṃ:nimittaṃ punar ime saṃghāta-mṛtyavo jātāḥ? 19 kiṃ tatrı aîva prativasati? na tapo-vanaṃ gataḥ, pratijñāṃ vā na punaḥ samārūḍhavān? 20 māpayitvā karma samārabhe 21 aho vighnavatyaḥ prārthita-siddhayaḥ 22 sādhu, vayasya—nipuṇam upakrāntam. idānīṃ dur:adhigama:siddhāv apy asminn ārambhe vayam āśaṃsāmahe 23 Susaṃgate, katham aham iha:stho bhavatyā jñātaḥ? 24 diṣṭyā putra-vijayena dampatī vardhete 25 Bhagavati, etat prahṛṣṭa:Nandan›-âbhinanditena rājñā Padmāvat›-īśvareṇa Bhūrivasoḥ pratyakṣam abhilikhya pattram āyuṣmato Mādhavasya preṣitam 26 kiṃ tv āhit:âgner n› ânyen› âgninā saṃskāro vihitaḥ. ato ›gnihotra-śaraṇād agnīn ādāyı ātmānam uddīpayāmaḥ 27 stanya-tyāgāt pareṇa dāraka-dvayaṃ ca tasyāḥ Prācetasasya maharṣer Gaṅgā: devī svayam arpitavatī 28 atrı ântare brāhmaṇena mṛtaṃ putram āropya rāja-dvāri sı_ôras-tāḍam abrahmaṇyam udghoṣitam

Exercise 10

1 svāgatam. ito niṣīdatam 2 nūnam an:apatya˜tā māṃ vatsalayati 3 katham, aparāddhas tapasvināṃ asmi? 4 tad enām āhūyı āgaccha 5 sarvam idaṃ mama nṛśaṃsasyı âsamīkṣya:kāri˜tāyā vijṛmbhitam 6 vijayetāṃ kumārau 7 anena ca patatā strī vyāpāditā 8 bho mah›:ātman, narak›-ânala-jvālā-›valīḍham ivı ātmānaṃ manyamāno duḥkhaṃ tiṣṭhāmi 9 amba, tvam api nivartasvı êdānīm 10 aho saṃdīpanāny akṣarāṇi 11 pakṣapātināv

anayor ahaṃ devī ca 12 Vardhamānaka, parivartaya pravahaṇam—sakhe Maitreya, avatāraya Vasantasenām 13 vatsa, a:vitatho aîṣā bhāratī te bhavatu 14 mahati rāja-kule ratna-bāhulyān na durlabho bhūṣaṇānāṃ saṃvādaḥ 15 alam alam upālambhena. upakāriṇī tavo êyam 16 'rājñī':śabda-bhājanam ātmānam api cintayatu bhavatī 17 anyā api durvinītena Manmatheno ônmatta˘tāṃ nītā nāryaḥ 18 aho vaicitryam ārya:Cāṇakya-nīteḥ 19 mṛṣyantv idānīṃ Lavasya bāliśa˘tāṃ tāta-pādāḥ 20 dhiṅ mām upanata:śreyo-vamāninam 21 tataḥ sakala:nāga-loka-vināśa-śaṅkinā nāga-rājena Vāsukinā Garutmān abhihitaḥ 22 Mādhavasena-sacivaṃ Sumatiṃ mamo âgrajam avagaccha 23 Jayasene, karma-siddhāv āśu pratipattim ānaya 24 na khalu viditās te tatra nivasantaś Cāṇakya:hatakena? 25 mayā 'pi co aînāṃ devī-haste sa_gauravaṃ nikṣipatā yuktam evo ânuṣṭhitam 26 tātas tv an:_apatya˘tayā suta-janmo-âtiriktena mahotsavena majjanmo âbhinanditavān 27 mamo âpy ante Puru-vaṃśa-śriya eṣa vṛttāntaḥ 28 bhagavan, imām ājñākarīṃ vo Gāndharveṇa vidhino ôpayamya kasya cit kālasya bandhubhir ānītāṃ smṛti-śaithilyāt pratyādiśann, aparāddho 'smi tatrabhavato yuṣmad_gotrasya Kaṇvasya. paścād enām aṅgurīyaka-darśanād ūḍha:pūrvām avagato 'smi 29 sa ca kṣapaṇaka-liṅga-dhārī Nanda-vaṃśa-vadha-pratijñā-'nantaram eva Kusumapuram upanīya sarva: Nanda-âmātyaiḥ saha sakhyaṃ grāhitaḥ

Exercise 11

1 tad dīyatām eṣā mudrā 2 su:janaḥ sa rāja:rṣiḥ śrūyate 3 namo Yogācāryāya, yasyo âhaṃ prathamaḥ śiṣyaḥ 4 vatsa Lava, saṃhriyatām astram 5 katham, māṃ parityajya tapo-vanaṃ yātau pitarau? 6 bhavatā punaḥ kva gamyate? 7 nanu sa eṣa yasya haste mātṛ-ṣvasā te pattrikām anupreṣitavatī 8 idānīṃ devyāṃ prasannāyāṃ Sāgarikā-cinto aîva kevalaṃ māṃ bādhate 9 kas trātā tava putraka? 10 śīghram anusṛtya gṛhyatāṃ dur:_ātmā Śakaṭadāsaḥ 11 aye, dakṣiṇena vṛkṣa-vāṭikām, ālāpa iva śrūyate 12 Susaṃgate, krīḍā_mātram evo aîtat 13 Kāṇelīmātaḥ, asti kiṃ cic cihnaṃ yad upalakṣayasi? 14 Vasantaka, pratyudgamya praveśyatāṃ Vasubhūtiḥ 15 amātye

netari, sulabham etat kumārasya 16 vinetur adravya-parigraha eva buddhi-lāghavaṃ prakāśayati 17 sa aiva êyaṃ ratna-mālā yā devena rāja-putryai prasthāna-kāle dattā 18 smaryatām ālekhya-darśane māṃ praty ātmano vacanam 19 mat-prārthyamānā apy anena sva:duhitā Vatsarājāya dattā 20 Yajñasena-śyālam urīkṛtya mucyantāṃ sarve bandhana-sthāḥ 21 kṣamyatāṃ yan mayā devasya â:nivedya kṛtam 22 vayam api sva: karmaṇy abhiyujyāmahe 23 nibhṛtena citra-śālāṃ praviśya Manoramayā saha âsman-nṛttaṃ paśyatā sthīyatām 24 ayi sva:citta-vedanā-mātra-vedini para-vyathā-anabhijñe, iyam upālabhyase 25 nanu ûcyatāṃ kim asya pāpasya ânuṣṭhīyatām 26 ya eṣa kṣapaṇako Jīvasiddhī Rākṣasa-prayukto viṣa-kanyayā Parvateśvaraṃ ghātita-vān, sa enam eva doṣaṃ prakhyāpya sa_nikāraṃ nagarān nirvāsyatām 27 evam eteṣu parijñāto:âparāga-hetuṣu, kṣipram eva kasmān na prativihitam āryeṇa? 28 Gautama, ka evaṃ vimukho asmākaṃ yena caṇḍī-kṛtā devī? 29 ārya Cārudatta, asti bhavato asyā āryāyā duhitrā saha prasaktiḥ praṇayaḥ prītir vā? 30 bhagavan, yayā adya rāja-kule mattaḥ parājayo abhyupetas, tasyāś ca mama ca kasmiṃś cit saṃgharṣe 'Marīcim āvarjitavati îva ślāghasa' iti tayā asmy aham adhikṣiptā

Exercise 12

1 aye, siṃhāsanam adhyāste Vṛṣalaḥ 2 vayasya, an: atikramaṇīyā Divaspater ājñā 3 tvam api svam adhi-kāram a:śūnyaṃ kuru 4 atra tena bhavitavyaṃ, yatra âyaṃ janapada-samavāyaḥ 5 jīrṇa-tvād gṛhasya virauti kapāṭam 6 bhavatībhyāṃ kadācid etat pratyakṣī-kṛtam? 7 idaṃ ca suvarṇa-bhāṇḍaṃ rakṣitavyaṃ tvayā rātrau, Vardhamānakena âpi divā 8 na tāvan muñcāmi yāvan mama hṛdaya-vallabhāṃ śilāyām ālikhitāṃ na paśyasi 9 vandyāḥ khalu devatāḥ 10 avahitau śṛṇuvas tāvat 11 eṣa te vāg-viṣayī-bhūtaḥ sa vīraḥ 12 tad aham enām an:ṛṇāṃ karomi 13 adhunā ca pratinivartamānena Rāma:bhadreṇa niyatam eva Pañcavaṭī-vane vadhū-sahavāsa-viśrambha-sākṣiṇaḥ pradeśā draṣṭavyāḥ 14 yathā me hṛdayam ācaṣṭe, tathā nir_viṣo Gautamaḥ 15 cañcale, pradeśād asmād imām akṣamālām a:dattvā padāt padam api na gantavyam 16 āstām ayam a:śikṣito

varākaḥ 17 katham, viphalī~kṛto me manorathaḥ Śaṅkhacūḍen' āgacchatā? 18 mayā khalu durlabha:prārthanaḥ katham ātmā vinodayitavyaḥ 19 tato 'haṃ moham upagatā yāvat saṃjñām upalabhe, tāvad iyaṃ durlabha:darśanā saṃvṛttā 20 nanu sarvasy' âbhyāgato gurur iti bhavān ev' âsmākaṃ pūjyaḥ 21 bho baṭavaḥ, parivṛtya loṣṭair apaghnantaḥ parāvartayat' aīnam aśvam 22 ārye, Nāgānande nāṭayitavye kim idam a:kāraṇam eva rudyate? 23 yathā c' âyaṃ calita:Malay':âcala-śilā-cayaḥ pracaṇḍo nabhasvāṃs, tathā tarkayāmy 'āsannī~bhūtaḥ pakṣi-rāja' iti 24 subhagaṃmanyena ca mayā sva:dhanasya sva:gṛhasya sva:gaṇasya sva:dehasya sva:jīvitasya ca s' âiv' ēśvarī kṛtā 25 tatas tat-pratyayād asmābhiḥ svāmy-arthaṃ bahuśaḥ prārthyamānen' âpi Siṃhal'-ēśvareṇa devyā Vāsavadattāyāś citta-khedaṃ pariharatā yadā na dattā, tadā Lāvāṇakena vahninā devī dagdh' êti prasiddhim utpādya tad-antikaṃ Bābhravyaḥ prahitaḥ 26 aho dīptimato 'pi viśvasanīya~tā vapuṣaḥ. 27 nūnam anen' âpy asyāḥ sutena bhavitavyaṃ, yad-artham ākrandati 28 tad āgatya svayam eva svāṃ bhūmikāṃ kurvāṇaḥ samāgam': ôtsavam anubhavatu 29 kiṃ tu Parvateśvara-dhṛta:pūrvāṇi bhūṣaṇāni guṇavanti guṇavadbhya eva brāhmaṇebhyaḥ pratipādanīyāni 30 yāvad ahaṃ nagaraṃ gatvā suhṛt-sameto madhu-pānaṃ kṛtv' āgacchāmi tāvad a:pramattayā gṛhe tvayā bhāvyam

Exercise 13

1 gṛhāṇ' âitad bhāṇḍam 2 kva nu khalu salilaṃ bhaviṣyati? 3 na ced rahasyam, icchāmi śrotuṃ śoka-hetum 4 nanu mat-samīpa eva vartiṣyase 5 aye, iyam asau yoṣit 6 Manorame, satyam idaṃ yad Vasantako 'bhidhatte? 7 jānāsi vatsa durmanāyamānāṃ devīṃ vinodayitum 8 evaṃ jano gṛhṇāti 9 tataḥ suhṛdbhyaḥ kim asau kathayiṣyati tapasvī? 10 yadi satyam eva nivartase, mām apy āśramaṃ netum arhasi 11 puruṣa-bhāgyānām acintyāḥ khalu vyāpārā yad aham īdṛśīṃ daśām anuprāptaḥ 12 Vṛṣala, upālabdhuṃ tarhi vayam āhūtāḥ? 13 bhagavan, kasmād evam abhidhatse? 14 duṣkaraṃ viṣam auṣadhī~kartum 15 kumāra, yadi Śakaṭadāsena likhitas tadā may' âiva likhitaḥ 16 vatse, anujānīhi mām 17 tad atra praviśya kutaś cic Candanadāsa-vṛttāntam upalapsye 18

citraṃ cı êdaṃ yad aham evam avagacchanty api na śaknomy ātmano vikāram upasaṃhartum 19 kumāra, nı aîvı âmī Malayı:âcala-sānavaḥ 20 katham etad yuktaṃ bhavato manasā ıpi cintayituṃ, kiṃ punar ākhyātum īkṣituṃ vā? 21 nijena dyumnenı āsāv veśyā yathā tvāṃ yojayiṣyati, tathā yatiṣye 22 tad etat paridhattāṃ kumāraḥ 23 kathaṃ, ya eva mad-vināśena Candraguptam ārādhayitum udyatās, ta eva māṃ parivṛṇvanti? 24 ārya: Cārudattaḥ khalv asau—katham idam akāryaṃ kariṣyati? 25 vatsa Lakṣmaṇa, bhagavatā Vālmīkinā sva:kṛtim apsarobhiḥ prayujyamānāṃ draṣṭum upanimantritāḥ smaḥ 26 dhiṅ mūrkha, kim uccair hasatā tvayı êyam uttrāsitā yenı ôḍḍīyı ânyatra kvı âpi gatā 27 kiṃ tu na śakyate cittam anyataḥ pravṛttam anyataḥ pravartayitum. ato nı âham enāṃ pratigrahītum utsahe 28 kiṃ Mataṅgo rājyaṃ hariṣyatı îti śaṅkase? yady evaṃ, tataḥ kim? nanu sva:śarīra˜taḥ prabhṛti parı-ârtham eva sarvaṃ mayā paripālyate. yat tu svayaṃ na dīyate, tat tātı-ânurodhāt 29 prathita:̱yaśasāṃ Bhāsa;Saumilla;Kaviputrı:̱ādīnāṃ prabandhān atikramya vartamāna:kaveḥ Kālidāsasya kriyāyāṃ kathaṃ pariṣado bahumānaḥ? 30 sā ced iyam ahārya:̱niścayā, sarva eṣa jano ıtrı aîvı ân:anya:̱gatir an:aśanena saṃsthāsyate

Exercise 14

1 bhūmau patac chabdam utpādayet 2 tat kas tvam iti śrotum icchāmi 3 tatra yugma-cāriṇoḥ krauñcayor ekaṃ vyādhena vidhyamānam apaśyat 4 eṣa mama kanīyān bhrātā gṛhīta:̱Yaugandharāyaṇa˜bhūmikaḥ prāpta eva 5 cirāt khalu yukta-kārī vidhiḥ syād, yadi yugalam etad anyonyı-ânurūpaṃ ghaṭayet 6 Makaradhvaja-niśita˜śara-nikara-nipāta-trastı êvı âkampata gātra:yaṣṭiḥ 7 saṃprati ramaṇīya˜tarā Mālatī 8 api nāma dur:̱ātmā Rākṣaso gṛhyeta 9 vairūpyāt tu mama 'Virūpaka' iti prasiddhir āsīt 10 sā sadya eva rājñā saha jananyā samāhūyata 11 nanv iyaṃ jyāyasī te bhaginī duḥkham āste—tat pariṣvajasvı aînām 12 tvayi tv apadiṣṭe sarvam asmat-kuṭumbam avasīdet 13 tāṃ ca dvitīya: Gandharva˜kulı-âdhipatir Haṃso Mandākinīm iva kṣīra-sāgaraḥ praṇayinīm akarot 14 tāḍyamānaḥ kiṃ na brūyāt? 15 tayā tu tatrı āgatya kiṃ kṛtaṃ, kim abhihitaṃ, kim

āceṣṭitam iti śūnya:hṛdayā sarvaṃ n' âlakṣayam 16 n' ânyat pāpiṣṭha˜tamam ātma-tyāgāt 17 deva, yuṣmad-dāsī Rāgamañjarī rūp'-ânurūpa:śīla;śilpa;kauśalā pūrayiṣyati manorathān ity āsīd asmākam mahaty āśā 18 paṭaccara-ccheda:śeṣo 'rthapatir artha-mattaḥ sarva:paurajana-samakṣaṃ niravāsyata 19 dayamānaś c' âham abravam, 'ehi sādhvi, tvāṃ nayeyaṃ tvat-priy'-āvasatham' iti tri; caturāṇi padāny udacalam 20 Gautama, vad' êdānīṃ yat te manasi vartate 21 anyathā kadācid īdṛg:avasthaṃ māṃ sahas" aîv' ālokya pitarau jīvitaṃ jahyātām 22 Rumaṇvān api Kosaleṣu mad-bhrātaraṃ jyāyāṃsaṃ Jayavarmāṇaṃ sthāpayitvā samara-vraṇitam aśeṣa: balam anuvartamānaḥ śanaiḥ śanair āgacchaty eva 23 api nāma śaknuyām ahaṃ sva:śarīra-dānād ekasy' âpi phaṇabhṛtaḥ prāṇa-rakṣāṃ kartum 24 tad evaṃ siddha: saṃkalpo Rāgamañjarī-gṛhaṃ hema;ratna-pūrṇam akaravam 25 kva prāṇebhyo 'pi vallabha˜taraṃ janaṃ vihāya gamyate? 26 Candragupto 'pi 'pitṛ-paryāy'-āgata ev' âyam' ity aṅgīkuryāt. evaṃ saty asmāsv api kumāro na viśvaset 27 tad-ardhaṃ sabhikāya sabhyebhyaś ca dattvā 'rdhaṃ svīkṛty' ôdatiṣṭham. udatiṣṭhaṃś ca tatra: gatānāṃ harṣa:garbhāḥ praśaṃs'-ālāpāḥ 28 siddha ev' âsmin prayojane devīṃ diṣṭyā vardhayiṣyām' îti n' ôktam 29 Vṛṣala, Malayaketāv an:upekṣit:âpakramaṇe dvayī gatiḥ syāt—nigṛhyeta vā pūrva: pratiśrutaṃ rājy'-ârdhaṃ vā pratipādyeta. nigrahe tāvad asya, Parvatako 'smābhir vyāpādita iti kṛtaghnatāyāḥ svahasto dattaḥ syāt 30 utthāya ca dhauta:vaktrau pragetanāni maṅgalāny anuṣṭhāy' âsmat-karma-tumulaṃ puram anuvicarantāv aśṛṇuva vara;vadhū-gṛheṣu kolāhalam

Grammatical Practice: Keys

6 1 **kanyābhyaḥ** 2 **Ūrmilāyāḥ** 3 **āryābhyām** 4 **Sīte** 5 **mudrāsu** 6 **kanyāṃ paśyati** 7 **tābhyaḥ** 8 **anayā/ etayā mudrayā** 9 **ime/ete tiṣṭhataḥ** 10 **tasyām**

7 1 **suhṛdi** 2 **manobhiḥ** 3 **nadyoḥ** 4 **devyai** 5 **dik tiṣṭhati** 6 **suhṛdbhyaḥ** 7 **nadīḥ paśyati** 8 **manāṃsi tiṣṭhanti** 9 **diśe** 10 **nadīṣu**

8 1 **rājan** 2 **nāmabhyaḥ** 3 **rājā tiṣṭhati** 4 **ātmane**

5 rājñe 6 nāmabhyām 7 rājānau paśyati 8 ātmanām 9 rājasu 10 nāmnī/nāmanī tiṣṭhataḥ

9 1 tvarethe 2 agnaye 3 bhavatā 4 śucyoḥ 5 śucinoḥ 6 tvarante 7 mṛdūnām 8 bhavataḥ paśyati 9 śucīni tiṣṭhanti 10 tvarete bhavantau

10 1 gacchata 2 tapasviṣu 3 vadhvāḥ 4 nayatoḥ 5 strīḥ/strīyaḥ paśya 6 nayate tapasvine 7 mahāntas tiṣṭhantu 8 tapasvinaḥ, tvaradhvam 9 bhuvi 10 gāyantau gacchatām

11 1 kartṛbhyām 2 svasṝḥ paśyati 3 pitṝṇām 4 nīyāvahe 5 mātaraṃ paśyati 6 svasāras tiṣṭhanti 7 kartuḥ 8 mātarau nīyetām 9 svasaḥ 10 pitre

12 1 kurvanti 2 dveṣṭi 3 itaḥ 4 karotu 5 āsāthe 6 śṛṇoṣi 7 āsate 8 kurmaḥ 9 śṛṇu 10 dviṣantāv āsāte

13 1 amuṣya 2 juhudhi 3 ruṇaddhi 4 krīṇītaḥ 5 jānantu 6 amīṣu 7 ado dehi 8 rundhvaḥ 9 amūr juhvati 10 amū krīṇīhi

14 1 anayāva 2 nayeyuḥ 3 śreyasoḥ 4 atvaradhvam 5 aruṇadham 6 dviṣyuḥ 7 āsāthām 8 jyāyāṃsau paśyema 9 jyāyān āsīḥ 10 śreyāṃsaḥ syuḥ

English Index

Abbreviations used in this index are as follows: abl. = ablative; acc. = accusative; adj. = adjective; caus. = causative; fem. = feminine; gen. = genitive; indef. = indefinite; inf. = infinite; intrans. = intransitive; irreg. = irregular; masc. = masculine; neut. = neuter; part. = participle; pass. = passive; poss. = possessive; prep. = preposition; pres. = present; sg. = singular; trans. = transitive.

Sanskrit Index